New Social Policy Agendas for Europe and Asia

Challenges, Experience, and Lessons

New Social Policy Agendas for Europe and Asia

Challenges, Experience, and Lessons

Edited by
Katherine Marshall
Olivier Butzbach

THE WORLD BANK

ISBN 0-8213-5201-6

Library of Congress Cataloging-in-Publication Data

New social policy agendas for Europe and Asia: challenges, experience, and lessons/ edited by Katherine Marshall, Olivier Butzbach.
    p. cm.
  Includes bibliographical references.
  ISBN 0-8213-5201-6
    1. Europe—Social policy. 2. East Asia—Social policy. 3. Public welfare—Europe. 4. Public welfare—East Asia. 5. Welfare state—Europe. 6. Welfare state—East Asia. I. Marshall, Katherine, 1947- II. Butzbach, Olivier.

HN373.5 .N496 2002
361.6'1'094—dc21

2002034340

Contents

Foreword

The human toll of abrupt macroeconomic setbacks is high. It can be measured in specific facts and statistics—people who suddenly lose their jobs, who cannot buy food, who cannot afford to seek medical help, and whose children drop out of school. We know that there are a host of other effects, swirling in concentric circles, that tear the social fabric. Times of trouble sometimes can bolster community ties and leadership, but these heartening examples are not the norm. Suffering and erosion of communities are the rule. Some harm is short-lived, forgotten quickly once good times return, but most human shocks leave painful legacies and can set back years of progress.

The international community today is fully forewarned about these social effects of crisis. The issues and calls for action to remedy social problems come quickly to the agendas of national and international institutions, and of civil society organizations, in times of crisis. Some lessons and attendant remedies are very clear—above all, keep social issues at the fore, work to maintain momentum, and do not allow economic setbacks to deflect focus from the challenge of reducing poverty. There is now a body of lessons that are part of a clear international consensus: fight the tendency to cut social expenditures, work to keep children in school, beware the impact of spiraling food and medicine prices, and keep the spotlight on vulnerable groups, especially children. Examples abound of policies and programs—successful and unsuccessful—to address social fallout of crises. Nonetheless, much more work and reflection are still needed to understand fully what happens to people and communities affected by the specific phenomena of today's sweeping economic ups and downs and, above all, what can be done to cushion their inevitable impact.

The Asia-Europe Meeting (ASEM) Trust Fund has offered a special opportunity to build on and add to this body of international experience. Its combination of practical, timely support for policy design and implementation has been juxtaposed with reflections on "lessons learned" and on implications for future medium-term strategies.

This book is designed to make more widely available the products of the special ASEM Trust Fund Project that aimed to draw upon and explore European social policy experience and make it available for Asia's decisionmakers and analysts. It is framed above all to inform the reflections and actions of East Asian policymakers as they grapple with issues for social policy in the new millennium, though evidently the experience and the approach have a global application.

Europe is, of course, both a continent of great diversity and a continent engaged in unprecedented integration and unification. Although there is a distinctive European flavor to policies and institutions, notably the strong public sector and the explicit social contract, the challenges facing the European public and the range of solutions aimed to address them vary widely. A large part of Europe's recent history can be seen in terms of a social agenda—how governments, the European Union, and communities have responded to social forces and challenges. This evolution has produced a rich array of policies, experience, and institutions. It is both a tale of history, as Europe has contended with so many social issues over the decades, and of current challenge, as the Europe of today addresses employment creation, social exclusion, empowerment of communities, the changing role of the family, immigration, and new trends in work and private life. Europe's experience is neither unique nor always exemplary, but the social policy choices in recent European history demonstrate that equity and efficiency need not be enemies of each other, and that a vibrant economy will support and, critically, be supported by strong commitments to social welfare and protection of the vulnerable.

The premises for the European Social Policy Lessons Project are four—first, that the common elements in challenges facing European and Asian countries are useful to explore and highlight (for example, with respect to urbanization, aging, and migration); second, that differences, for example, in employment practices and the dynamics of the family unit, also bear rigorous reflection as they can inform policy choices; third, that the common human challenges ahead for Europe and Asia have more similarities than differences, so networks for policy reflection offer scope for mutual learning; and fourth, that Europe's intensive investment in regional policies, standards, and programs offers a mine of information to other regions, including East Asia.

The material in the book reflects a means not an end, a process not a product. The project's goal has been to explore how to build networks designed to support policy reform and implementation, across classic discipline lines and geographic regions, and to explore also what kinds of experience and what manner of presentation of such experience could be most useful to the policymakers who seek ideas, sobering lessons, options, and inspiration. The interesting material distilled here is designed in the first instance to be useful and relevant to policymakers. It is designed even more to encourage continuing networks and continuing reflection on cross-regional sharing of experience that is inspired and driven by a concern with the centrality of a broad social agenda.

Mats Karlsson
Vice President
External Affairs and UN Affairs

Acknowledgments

This book is a product of many partnerships, in the very best sense, and we can acknowledge only a small portion of them here. The entire effort owes a special tribute to those who designed and conceived the Asia-Europe Meeting (ASEM) Trust Fund and its European focus, including, among many others, Geoffrey Lamb, David Peretz, Paul Ackroyd, and Alistair MacDonald. Jean-Michel Séverino, then vice president of the World Bank for East Asia and now director general of the Agence Française de Développement, was an inspiration from start to finish. Many others played important roles in the Trust Fund and project, including Keiko Sato, Paula Donovan, and Jannes Hutagalung. Warm thanks go to Louis-Charles Viossat, who was critical to the design and launch of the project. In the final stages, Tara Karacan played a pivotal role in organizing the diverse group of actors to move toward production and ensure high-quality results. We acknowledge the major role of our superb editor, Sandra Hackman, and support also from Min Gyo Koo, Manuel Rossini, Kathrin Plangemann, Sonya Woo, Julianne Turner, Rebecca Ling, Mary Imamura, and Monika Ploch at different project stages.

Among the dedicated partners who should receive special tribute are Hélène de Largentaye and the team of the Conseil d'Analyse Économique in Paris, as well as Jean-Christophe Bas and the organizing teams for the ABCDE (Annual Bank Conference on Development Economics) conferences in Paris and Oslo; Jacques van der Gaag, Wim Driehuis, and the Amsterdam Institute of International Development; Mitsuko Horiuchi, Moazam Mahmood, and the Asia Pacific Office of the International Labor Organization in Bangkok; Hyekyung Lee and the Korea Social Security Association in Seoul; Sven Hort and Stein Kuhnle in Bergen; Anita Kelles-Viitanen, Isabel Ortiz, and the Asian Development

Bank in Manila; Willem van der Geest and the European Institute for Asian Studies in Brussels; and Giuseppe Pennisi and Italy's National Institute for Public Administration in Rome and Caserta.

We also thank several individuals who have taken a special interest in this effort from beginning to end. They include Nicholas Barr and Howard Glennerster (London School of Economics), Amar Siamwalla (Thailand Development Research Institute), Keith Bezanson (Institute of Development Studies, University of Sussex), Patrick Guillamont (Centre d'Etudes et de Recherches sur le Développement International), Alice Sindzingre (Centre National de la Recherche Scientifique), Manfred Bardeleben and Roland Feicht (Friedrich Ebert Stiftung), and Peter Scherer and Peter Whiteford (Organization for Economic Cooperation and Development).

Abbreviations and Glossary

ADB—Asian Development Bank
AF—Arbejdsformidlingen
AIID—Amsterdam Institute for International Development
AIS—information system of the Swedish Labor Market Administration
APEC—Asia Pacific Economic Cooperation organization
APIS—Annual Poverty Indicators Survey
ASABRI—Indonesian Armed Forces Social Insurance Plan
ASEAN—Association of Southeast Asian Nations
ASEF—Asia Europe Foundation
ASEM—Asia-Europe Meeting
ASKES—Asuransi Kesehatan Pegawai Negeri (means-tested free public health
    center service for civil servants and military)
BA—Bundesanstalt für Arbeit
CAP—Common Agricultural Policy
CEREQ—French Research Center on Employment and Qualifications
CGIL—Confederazione Generale Italiana dei Lavatori
CHWE—Council on Health and Welfare for the Elderly
CWA—Civil Works Administration
DAC—Development Assistance Committee
DB—defined-benefit
DC—defined-contribution
DPJ—Democratic Party of Japan
DREAM—Danish Rational Economic Agents Model
EC—European Commission

EEA—European Economic Area
EPF—Employee Provident Fund
ES—employment services
ESCAP—Economic and Social Commission for Asia and the Pacific
ESF—European Social Fund
EU—European Union
FDI—foreign direct investment
FERA—Federal Emergency Relief Administration
FIES—Family Income and Expenditure Survey
GDI—Gender-Related Development Index
GDP—gross domestic product
GDR—former German Democratic Republic
GNP—gross national product
HDI—Human Development Index
HPI—Human Poverty Index
ICESCR—International Covenant on Economic, Social and Cultural Rights
IEFP—Instituto do Empreso e Formaçao Profissional
IFLS—Indonesia Family Life Survey
IFS—International Financial Statistics
ILO—International Labor Organization
IMF—International Monetary Fund
JAMSOSTEK—Jaminan Sosial Tenaga Kerja (means-tested free public health
    center service for private sector)
JMA—Japan Medical Association
JSP—Japan Socialist Party
KLI—Korean Labor Institute
LDP—Liberal Democratic Party
LES—Local Employment Service
LO—Norwegian Confederation of Trade Unions
MERCOSUR—Latin America Common Market
MISEP—Mutual Information System on Employment Policies
MSE—micro- and small enterprises
MVO—market value of the output
NAFTA—North American Free Trade Agreement
NDYP—New Deal for Young People
NGO—nongovernmental organization
NHI—national health insurance
NHS—national health services

NPS—national pension scheme
OAED—Labor Force Employment Organization
ODA—official development assistance
OECD—Organization for Economic Cooperation and Development
ONEM—Office National de l'Emploi
OPK—Operasi Pasar Khosus (Indonesian rice subsidy program)
PES—public employment services
RESEARCH— European Employment Observatory advisory group
SADC—Southern Africa Development Community
Schengen Treaty—Signed at Schengen, Luxembourg, March 1995, to end
     internal border checkpoints and controls, together with enhanced visa
     controls at the external borders through a common approach to visas and
     asylum requests. There are 15 signatory countries at present.
SCI—Sezione Circoscrizionale per l'Impiego
SEU—Social Exclusion Unit
SMERU—Social Monitoring and Emergency Response Unit
SUSENAS—Social and Economic Survey of Indonesian Households
SYSDEM—System of Documentation, Evaluation, and Monitoring of
     Employment Policies
TASPEN—Tabungan dan Asuransi Pegawi Negeri (Government Civilian
     Employees' Savings and Insurance Scheme)
TLM—transitional labor market
TUC—French public temporary employment scheme
UDHR—Universal Declaration of Human Rights
UGT—General Worker's Union
UN—United Nations
UNDP—United Nations Development Programme
UNEDIC—French unemployment insurance, run by social partners
VTML—Valtion Työmarkkinalaitos
WCIAS—Women's Committee for the Improvement of the Aging Society
WPA—Works Progress Administration
WTO—World Trade Organization
ZUS—Polish state-owned Social Security Office

European Social Policy Lessons: Reflections for East Asia

East Asia is at a crucial stage in its development. Its impressive and rapid economic and social achievements are unparalleled elsewhere in the world. No other region can boast comparable performance in fostering economic growth; reducing poverty; and improving education, health, and nutrition. East Asian countries have, with few exceptions, shared the fruits of 30 years of economic growth equitably within their societies, leading to steadily lower levels of absolute poverty.

Partly because of this success, the severity of the economic turmoil that spread after 1997 stunned governments throughout the region. The crisis revealed the devastating vulnerability of many households—especially poor households—to a sudden downturn in macroeconomic fortunes.

During the early months of the crisis, the attention inevitably focused on resolving critical problems such as rising unemployment and poverty, mass bankruptcies, and breakdowns in the financial system. However, the need to formulate sustainable policy responses soon forced East Asian countries to reflect on longer-term lessons from the crisis, as it shook important assumptions regarding development for both individual countries and the region. This challenge was particularly strong in the field of social policy, as East Asian countries had long essentially relied on economic growth to provide social safety nets, which proved frail and patchy.

The crisis prompted a recognition that, with rapid modernization, demographic change, and exposure to global economic and social pressures, the region needed new models for social policy. Governments, trade unions, civil society organizations, and international partners alike embarked on a dynamic process of reflection on the future social agenda and the institutions that would move it forward.

This book is a product of that process of reflection. It is the culmination of an endeavor supported by European and East Asian nations to encourage new thinking about social policy for East Asia in the shadow of the 1997–98 socioeconomic crisis. The book reflects the guiding objectives of the Asia-Europe Meeting (ASEM) Trust Fund, an informal process of cooperation and dialogue (see Box I and <http://europa.eu.int/comm/external_relations/asem/intro>), and also a specific ASEM-supported project to explore European experience in social policy that might prove useful for postcrisis East Asian countries.

ASEM and the ASEM Trust Fund

The ASEM process itself has deep roots and an evolving role as a Europe–Asia governmental initiative. Launched in the mid-1990s,[1] its central aim has been to strengthen ties between East Asia and Europe as global pressures highlighted the need for both policy exchange and concerted action to address human needs. Heads of state and ministers from both regions have been meeting periodically (with a summit every 2 years) to discuss political, economic, and cultural issues of mutual interest. The process has expanded to encompass a civil society forum and ongoing institutions, prominent among them being the Asia Europe Foundation (ASEF) in Singapore.

A special context surrounded the second formal meeting of ASEM heads of state in London in April 1998. East Asia's financial and economic crisis was reaching a peak, and the region's governments faced new issues, new demands, and new pressures. Leaders at the London meeting decided to respond by creating the ASEM Crisis Response Trust Fund with contributions of about US$45 million, which would finance a series of projects in three priority areas: social policy, financial restructuring, and corporate restructuring. The ASEM Trust Fund directed the projects to support not only overall reform in the seven most critically affected countries but also analytical and policy work to encourage continued rebuilding.

The ASEM Trust Fund represents a remarkable story in development assistance; it has supported the launch and completion of more than 80 separate initiatives. Nearly half addressed issues of social policy, generally taking the form of technical assistance projects targeted at specific country challenges and populations. A recent independent evaluation highlights the fact that the ASEM-financed projects played a catalytic role in the postcrisis period for East Asia.

The specific project that is the genesis of this book—Beyond the East Asian Socio-Economic Crisis: Lessons Towards the New Social Policy Agenda—was designed, approved, and implemented within the ASEM Trust Fund context. The project focused on the countries most affected by the crisis: Indonesia, the Republic of Korea, Malaysia, the Philippines, and Thailand, or the "East Asia five." It was approved in mid-1999 and executed from 2000 to 2002 under the direction of Katherine Marshall. The project sought to cull and disseminate meaningful social policy lessons from East Asia and from Europe, where the welfare state is over a century old.

A secondary goal was to establish intellectual networks and a closer dialogue between European and East Asian experts and policymakers on social policy issues arising from the crisis. Vehicles for achieving these goals included a series of seminars among European and East Asian policymakers and specialists on specific social policy issues, and some 30 papers to bolster that discussion and explore issues in greater depth. Participants at the seminars discussed most of these papers. A project Web site acted as a resource reaching far beyond the network of experts and policymakers directly involved in the project. The site includes the papers generated through the project, summary notes from the seminars, a calendar of events within the project, and links to related sites and items of interest to the Social Lessons network (see <http://www.worldbank.org/eapsocial/asemsocial>).

Although the project produced tangible outputs, the less tangible outputs were perhaps the most important. Those included personal contacts and friendships between European and East Asian participants and a host of informal networks, with countless examples of follow-up collaboration.

The ASEM partnership entrusted the management of the ASEM Trust Fund to the World Bank, to ensure that the activities under the partnership would link tightly to the overall international effort to support East Asia's recovery, in which the World Bank played a leadership role. Some participants expressed doubt as to whether the Bank would fully embrace the spirit of the ASEM Trust Fund, so it was incumbent on the Bank to preserve this spirit. The European Social Policy Lessons Project was a principal vehicle toward that end.

The Social Agenda

It is worth emphasizing that no government organizes social policy as a single institution or program: it is simply much too broad. Social policy encompasses labor, welfare, health, and education policy; support for older people; gender relations; social exclusion; and the welfare of the poorest communities. The point of departure for this book was, nonetheless, the concept of a "social agenda"—essentially the full range of issues that focus on the human dimensions of public policy. A central reason for this focus is the strength of the links between these issues.

This social agenda extends beyond common notions of poverty alleviation, social protection, and social development, which are important organizational concepts within the World Bank, for example. The concept of a social agenda is well understood in Europe. As East Asia moves beyond the urgent imperative of raising the standard of living for large masses of people in dire poverty, it confronts the familiar challenges of maintaining a broad focus and stimulating dynamic and creative thinking on social policy issues that affect virtually every resident.

Neither the project nor the book purports to cover this agenda comprehensively. Some issues are almost entirely absent—most prominently, education and health policy. Indeed, throughout the course of the project, ideas for exploratory work abounded that available time and resources could not address. Examples include training social policy analysts and leaders, and rethinking drug policies.

The East Asian Focus

This book is *for* East Asia but not essentially *about* that region. East Asia enters the discussion at many junctures as the authors apply their analysis to that region, but the book does not purport to analyze exactly where East Asia stands or, more important, exactly what it should do next.

Why Europe?

A frequent and logical question is, Why European lessons? ASEM leaders and those involved in the ASEM Trust Fund perceived European experience in the social policy realm as deserving special exploration. The welfare state is one of the core characteristics of modern European history and of Europe's current political economies, and European policymakers and institutions have engaged in precisely the kind of building and reforming of welfare systems that East Asian countries are now pursuing.

Europe is far from homogeneous, of course, which makes for diverse social policy lessons. Indeed, Europe offers a natural and well-studied laboratory for varying social policy responses to broadly similar social problems, and it includes several distinct "welfare regimes."[2]

Yet despite the vital differences within Europe, the European Union is distinct from other OECD regions, notably the United States, as the role of the state in social welfare is notably greater and its form qualitatively different. The European model of welfare is characterized by high levels of spending, insurance-based social programs, marked intergenerational solidarity, and modest-to-high redistribution of resources. In a majority of states, a "breadwinner" model provides considerable employment protection and benefits for the core work force, and substantial investment in human and social infrastructure has achieved moderate to low levels of poverty and inequality.[3]

ASEM participants built on several hypotheses about this experience.[4]

First, Europe differs in important respects from other regions. As a very broad approximation, the Americas (North and South) tend to put more weight on individualism (including voluntary charity), whereas Europe emphasizes social solidarity.

Second, Europe offers a host of examples. There is no "European model" but many different examples of what might loosely be termed a European approach.

Third, European experience makes a critical distinction between structure and scale. "Structure" refers to whether activities designed to enhance human well-being are publicly funded or produced, or largely or wholly private. "Scale" refers to the level of public spending on the welfare state.

Fourth, the European welfare state has not failed. Despite its mixed reputation, it is alive and vibrant and engaged in a dynamic process of adapting to new realities. Some countries may have made promises that now seem too generous given demographic trends, but some policymakers have responded by making social guarantees less generous—the reform of the Swedish pension system being an important example.[5]

Our hope is that the chapters in this book will provide the basis for learning and comparing without conveying linear "lessons" from Europe. There are not any—far from it. Europe's welfare states were created over several decades and have gone through several stages. Countries that face challenges today will need to reflect on both the systems and the dynamics that have shaped them.

What is more, despite the deliberate, pointed effort to focus this work on Europe, the project was multidirectional in practice, as the process of reflection led us to far-flung regions of the world. Chapter 5, in fact, shows how an idea and experience can take root in different societies at different times and in different forms (the example is the evolution of Japanese health systems).

A key maxim was that the inquiry would offer a balanced exploration across nations and disciplines into experiences often known only secondhand and in a fragmentary, even distorted fashion. Delving into these rich experiences opened doors for all participants, from whatever sector, country, or continent, to question, learn, explore, and venture into new ideas. The most remarkable feature of the process was the dynamic interchange it spawned on the issues that confront all societies at the start of the 21st century.

The Seminar Program

A major feature of the European Social Policy Lessons Project was the series of eight formal seminars and several less formal meetings. Half were set in East Asia and half in Europe, with participants also roughly 50–50 from the two regions. The seminars constituted the heart of the project, allowing participants to pursue new insights and to build partnerships whose scope extended well beyond the project agenda itself. Many participants contributed fresh perspectives reaching beyond their traditional fields of expertise. The seminars are summarized in short boxes for this volume.

Analysts often reveal marked tendencies to separate thinking from action, decisionmaking from implementation, and basic research from policy studies. These divides exist at the international level and within countries. Projects such as this one that aim to amass and refine knowledge run the risk of worsening such segmentation. Thus the project made an explicit effort to encourage and bring together academics and policymakers, unionists and government officials, representatives of businesses and the media, and people working in the field. Every meeting was designed to blend policymaking and expertise, different points of view, and different experiences. In most cases this produced challenging discussions.

We identified partners and participants progressively over the life of the project, allowing us to tap different policy arenas and institutions. Some participants were present at several meetings, others at only one; the group changed at each encounter. Partners included the Asian Development Bank, the International Labor Organization (ILO), the Amsterdam Institute for International Development, the Economic Analysis Council in France, the Korean Social Security Association, the University of Bergen in Norway, the European Institute for

Asian Studies in Belgium, and Italy's Public Administration Institute. Each meeting was organized with a different partner.

Participants often referred to strong crosscutting themes.

One such theme was *the need to strike the right balance and coordination between macroeconomic and social policy.* Participants from developing and industrial countries alike expressed frustration that countries tend to put macroeconomic policy at the top of the policy hierarchy. Social policy ministers must too often work with choices already determined by their colleagues in charge of finance. Integrating the two arenas is essential to good policy, especially good development policy, as macroeconomic and fiscal policy strongly affect social welfare, whereas social policy exerts a considerable impact—positive and negative—on public finances and overall economic performance. However, some participants argued that the gap within their countries between finance and economics, and health, education, and social protection is more significant than the supposed gap that separates European and East Asian social policy.

Only in times of crisis do the urgency, the breadth, and the links between social and economic issues force policymakers to try to keep all elements in balance. It is not by chance that European welfare states took their modern shapes in such a context, after World War II. The crisis that hit East Asia 5 years ago represented a similar window of opportunity. Many perceive a risk that with a return to more normal growth patterns and less urgency, the traditional divides between macroeconomic policy and all other policy fields could return, and momentum could be lost.

Participants also pointed to hopeful exceptions to this rule. Some stressed the traditional importance of social policy and welfare in European government agendas, not least because of the strong political weight of unions and social-democratic and agrarian parties. Some critics have questioned the welfare state as a pillar of the post–World War II social compact, especially in the 1970s and 1980s, when they blamed Keynesian policies—characterized by high levels of public investment, redistribution, and social protection—for stagnation and unemployment. But since the mid-1990s Europe has seen a revival of the welfare state, reflecting the central position of social issues on the political agenda, including at the level of the European Union (witness the focus on employment and social protection in the proceedings of the most recent European Councils of Ministers).

Participants also saw hopeful signs that social issues would emerge from their traditional political marginalization in East Asia. In many countries an active public debate on social policy challenges and options has continued since the crisis, although some participants doubted that the window of opportunity will remain open. There was clear consensus about the urgent need to improve social protection to avoid similar disasters in future crises.

A related issue was the *need to integrate social policy with other policy instruments*. Several seminars (at Brussels and Bangkok) stressed the positive links between social policy and economic growth (the former supports demand and ensures the transferability of skills, for instance). Participants also highlighted links between social policy and poverty (the Amsterdam meeting) and social policy and industrial policy (Bangkok). Participants in the Seoul seminar focused on the need for complementarity within the social policy realm, such as among employment policies, pension reform, and social security.

A third crosscutting issue was the *regional dimension of social policy*. European experience highlights a gradual intensification of regional coordination in several policy fields, including immigration policy, labor standards, and employment strategies. Participants in several meetings cited regional trading blocks as the natural place to build regional frameworks for social policy. But how to start? Several participants emphasized the rights-based approach as embraced by the ILO and the Council of Europe. This is still controversial, however, and the Rome/Caserta seminar shed light on an alternative and innovative way to coordinate regional social policy: through peer review and spreading of best practice exemplified by the "open method of coordination" launched by the European Union.[6]

The role of social capital as both a goal and an instrument of social policy was the specific focus of the Manila meeting. One of the key objectives of social policy is to empower citizens and social groups rather than simply treating them as "objects of care." This approach underpins many of the recent welfare reforms in Europe, which put more emphasis on individual responsibility and initiative. However, fostering social capital as a force for change presents complex challenges and may exacerbate social tensions if it accentuates divisions within societies and shifts the balance of power among groups.

The *political nature of social policy* is also important. Participants often stressed social policy as the outcome of political struggle, underscoring the importance of social dialogue and the core need to provide a "level playing field." Social dialogue requires the presence of strong actors such as trade unions, the state, business, and political parties. A vital new issue, addressed in several seminars, notably Bangkok and Rome/Caserta, is the role of public information and the media in creating social policies. This issue merits much more detailed exploration.

The importance of *gender* in policymaking (hearteningly) recurred often during the seminars. Gender relations have emerged as a vital engine of social change—witness the impact of growing female participation in the labor force in most countries in Europe and East Asia. Gender is also one of the most problematic areas of social policy, given the heavier burden that women bear during crises and given the "social risks" of maternity, unemployment, and disease. Virtually every discussion, from Paris to Bangkok and Manila, raised the point that policymaking forums too seldom include women's voices, with the result that social policies do not fully take into account gender relations. For example, because policymakers have often designed welfare schemes, especially in Europe, during times when the sole-breadwinner household prevails, changes in gender relations can mean that this traditional design runs the risk of perpetuating existing inequalities instead of correcting them.

Social Policy Lessons?

Against the backdrop of a project that focused on process more than on specific recipes—that eschewed formulas for successful social policy and celebrated the diversity and dynamism of experience—some core ideas nonetheless emerged time and time again. They form the structure and argument of the book.

A first lesson is the need to find effective ways to link social and economic practices. Successful country examples from Europe offer insight into the political drive and specific mechanisms (such as social pacts) that encourage effective integration of social and macroeconomic policies.

A second insight is the need to incorporate exceptional dynamism into social policy. A corollary is that decisions that affect the welfare of millions prove exceptionally difficult to change. Social policy decisions and designs often have very long lead times and application periods. The experience of many countries shows that designs well suited to certain socioeconomic and political configurations may well no longer work as social demands, individual behavior, and demographics change. In Europe, for instance, unemployment insurance designed for a period of high employment and short length of joblessness spells cannot cope with high unemployment levels and joblessness that lasts more than a year. Another classic example is the fate of pension systems conceived in the baby-boom era, which face fundamental problems as societies struggle to cope with aging populations. These outcomes call for building "permanent learning" mechanisms into social security systems at the design stage. Such flexibility can take the shape, for instance, of mechanisms to evaluate the employability of individuals and provide further training, which some European countries are beginning to include in their mechanisms to address unemployment.

A final insight turns on the complexity and interrelationships within social policy. Examples abound of unexpected consequences of social policy. Many case studies that emerged from the project highlighted the links between pensions and health issues, and between social policies and gender relations.

Box II reflects a set of hypotheses, articulated by Ian Gough, about social policy issues and lessons as they emerge from the juxtaposed analysis of European and East Asian experience.

The Content and Structure of the Book

This book includes many but not all papers discussed at the project seminars. The papers are abridged to make them more accessible; full versions remain on the project Web site, together with full proceedings of seminars and some papers that could not be included in this volume.

The book's coverage is exploratory and illustrative, and it does not aspire to investigate fully the rich array of European experience or its possible implications for East Asia. The book is designed to whet the appetite but not to satisfy it. Each section and chapter aims to highlight references and experiences for further exploration.

The book's structure follows the basic narrative of the project's trajectory. Part I provides a framework for the analysis in the rest of the book, offering background on how Europe defines welfare regimes, juxtaposed with an illustration of how reality may differ from image in the classic issue of the family as a core element of social policy. Two chapters provide background on the East Asia crisis to ground further discussion. The final chapter describes the evolution of Japan's health insurance system, with its complex origin, borrowing, adapting, and ultimately succeeding.

Part II tackles links between macroeconomic and social policies through case studies of Ireland and Norway and a Danish planning tool. The book does not delve into history and debate on macroeconomic policy, often deeply influenced by the East Asia crisis, but project participants do summarize arguments about the implications of that crisis for future policy, especially in the social arena.

Part III turns to the complex issue of social exclusion, a topic woven throughout the book from start to finish. Poverty is clearly one form of social exclusion, but the challenges are much deeper and wider, and present themselves differently in different societies. The chapters cover a range (though far from comprehensive) of current issues, such as gender relations, migration, and policies toward poor citizens in contemporary Europe.

Part IV focuses on a central challenge facing Europe today (as well as many East Asian countries): the phenomenon of aging societies and welfare systems. Strong patterns and challenges emerge in countries as diverse as Italy and Scandinavia; also at the heart of the discussion is the vital role of political economy in addressing them.

Part V highlights the wealth of experience on what many consider the "end and the beginning" of social policy—labor policies. The chapters include case studies from different countries on topics ranging from worker participation to public employment services. The section also addresses the important role of the European Union from different angles.

Part VI follows up this orientation with chapters on the complex topic of setting international standards for social policy. The most concrete example is the Council of Europe, which stands out in monitoring and moving toward enforcing social standards. This section also treats the broader issue of human rights, now very much at center stage in global debates on labor standards, the role of children, and the right to minimum health care and education. The discussion is set against the background of the growing international consensus about the urgency of fighting poverty reflected in the Millennium Development Goals that were the focus, for example, of the March 2002 United Nations Summit on Financing Development held in Monterrey, Mexico.

This book represents both a record and stock-taking. Its central purpose is to encourage continued exploration and even stronger networks.

Notes

1. See <http://asem.inter.net.th/ASEM> for the ASEM homepage of the opening event in Bangkok, Thailand.
2. See Chapter 1 for further details on the different regimes.
3. Ian Gough, "Social Aspects of the European Model and Its Social Consequences," in *The Social Quality of Europe*, ed. Wolfgang Beck (The Hague: Kluwer, 1997).
4. This framework owes a particular debt to Nicholas Barr, professor at the London School of Economics, who in discussions and notes helped participants explore these hypotheses.
5. A more sophisticated set of arguments can be found in A. B. Atkinson, *The Economic Consequences of Rolling Back the Welfare State* (Cambridge, Mass.: MIT Press, 1999).
6. See Box 6.2.

The ASEM Trust Fund

by Katherine Marshall

The ASEM Trust Fund for the Asian Financial Crisis was created at the initiative of leaders of the Asia-Europe Meeting (ASEM) at the ASEM summit in London in April 1998. The fund was launched in June 1998 with the signing of the first letter of agreement between the United Kingdom and the World Bank. Ten partners contributed a total US$45 million. The fund's purpose was to facilitate recovery in countries affected by the Asian economic crisis and to support reform programs by providing technical assistance and advice to address immediate policy issues in the financial, corporate, and social sectors.

East Asian countries participating in the ASEM process could draw on the fund if they were eligible to borrow from the World Bank or the International Development Association and they were in crisis or vulnerable to financial or economic shocks or contagion; thus China, Indonesia, the Republic of Korea, Malaysia, the Philippines, Thailand, and Vietnam were eligible. The fund was not viewed as an injection of capital but rather as a vehicle to provide expertise, especially from Europe. It formed part of the broader ASEM effort to enhance relations between Europe and East Asia.

As the fund administrator, the World Bank established a special governing structure to ensure that all activities and programs met high standards commensurate with agreed country and sector strategies, following the World Bank's operating procedures. An ASEM committee within the World Bank oversaw its administration. The ASEM Trust Fund agreements provided that ASEM members meet with the World Bank every 6 months to review country strategies and progress reports, and that the ASEM donors approve specific project proposals over US$1 million.

The letters of agreement between the World Bank and donors provided that:

continued on next page

BOX I, continued

- Activities supported by the ASEM Trust Fund were to address two key priorities, with roughly 50 percent of funding for each:
  - Technical assistance and training to governments for policy and institutional reform in the financial and corporate sectors
  - Technical assistance and training to governments to design interventions to mitigate adverse social effects of the crisis and reorient poverty reduction efforts to meet the new social agenda
- ASEM Trust Fund was to fund consultants and experts engaged by the World Bank, and grants to host governments, nongovernmental organizations, educational entities, and other entities to finance technical assistance, training, and related costs, for activities supported by the fund.
- At least 50 percent of ASEM Trust Fund allocations were to go toward activities in lower-income and lower-middle-income countries.
- The Trust Fund closed on December 31, 2002.

In March 2002, an independent evaluation of ASEM was conducted by European Commission consultants; their findings and recommendations were discussed in a workshop in Bangkok in March 2002.

An ASEM II Trust Fund was launched at the ASEM leaders' Third Summit in October 2000 and endorsed at the Third ASEM Finance Ministers' Meeting in Kobe in January 2001. Activities supported by the ASEM II Trust Fund will address two key priorities: (a) providing technical assistance and training to governments for sustainable reform of their financial and corporate sector policies and institutions, and (b) providing technical assistance and training to governments to design and implement interventions to reorient sustainable poverty reduction efforts to meet evolving country requirements. Total contributions amount to about US$30 million; the expected closing date is December 31, 2005.

Further information about ASEM Trust Fund may be found at <http://www.worldbank.org/rmc/asem/asem.htm>. See also the European Union Web site on ASEM at <http://europa.eu.int/comm/external_relations/asem/intro/index.htm>.

BOX II

European Social Policy Lessons: 12 Theses
by Ian Gough

Europe's modern welfare state, at least the "social insurance state," is well over a century old, if the introduction of Bismarck's sickness funds in 1883 is treated as its foundation. What lessons might this experience offer for the developing world?

Social welfare policies must be seen in context, taking careful account of existing patterns of social provision, institutional responsibilities, and the interests that these express and perpetuate. Policy learning, transfer, and change can occur, and universal principles should apply to policy goals. However, universal policy designs should not be sought and any social policy idea must account for political economies and inherited institutions. In that spirit, I offer 12 lessons, with both negative warnings and positive role models.[1]

The 12 Theses

1. *From "strong" to "weak."* Social insurance was the dominant form of social protection in all European countries from the start (even in the United Kingdom after 1925). It began by covering state workers and manual workers in large industrial firms, gradually rippling out to include employees in medium and small enterprises; agricultural, white-collar, and service workers; the self-employed; and later, in some countries, the unemployed and homemakers. Thus the social insurance state proceeded "from the strong to the weak"[2] or, more accurately, from groups central to an industrial economy to those nearer the periphery. Social insurance offers a transitional strategy to universal coverage that starts with those employed in the formal economy. It is the opposite of today's dominant "target the poor" approach.

2. *Industrialization.* Social policies in Europe developed in societies that were industrializing rapidly and came to fruition during the mass rural exodus following World War II (except in the United Kingdom,

continued on next page

BOX II, continued

where the shift from agriculture to industry took place a century earlier). These countries initially followed an "extensive" rather than an "intensive" growth path; they grew through expansion of capital and the labor force rather than through increasing productivity.[3] Labor accepted a capitalist economy in exchange for capital's tolerance of collective representation and bargaining, social services, and social protection. This welfare system was ill suited to deindustrialization and postindustrial capitalism from the 1970s onward.

3. *Civil society and labor movements.* Proletarian struggles, trade unions, and socialist parties formed a backdrop to the emerging welfare state throughout Europe. In many northern European countries, these developments were linked to a range of other class mobilizations, notably by agricultural workers and later the "service class"; other social movements, such as the temperance movement in Scandinavia; and self-help institutions, such as Friendly Societies in the United Kingdom. The imprint of these movements on social policies differed according to dominant class coalitions, the orientation of business and the propertied classes, and the form of the national state. Thus there have been "etatist" (France) and "corporatist" (Germany and Italy) routes to social policy. Fears of social unrest and breakdown provided a constant backdrop.

4. *Crowding out versus crowding in.* The growing state role crowded out some prior forms of social provision and protection, such as friendly societies and private hospitals, but "crowding in" has also occurred. This is evident in the state role as a supplier of resources for the third, or nonprofit, sector in every modern European country.[4] Civil society social movements have served to strengthen the voice and claims of the poor.

5. *The productive welfare state.* Originally introduced in Sweden in the 1930s, this term recognizes the contribution to modernization and prosperity of high-quality and equitable education, health care, family planning, and other family strengthening policies. This notion has undergone a recent resurgence as human capital assumes even greater importance in the postindustrial economy. Thus social policies have a "public goods" role; they were never solely about redistribution. Innovation in social policy often reflects "reforms from above" by progressive elites who recognize the collective benefits of managed capitalism.

BOX II, continued

6. *Open economies and social protection.* The inverse statistical relationship between extent of trade and levels of spending on social protection in Organization for Economic Cooperation and Development (OECD) countries amounts almost to a law. A stark argument holds that social protection is the only alternative to trade protection if societies are to avoid social disintegration, implying that a globalized world "requires" more social protection.[5] For such systems to develop in practice, though, preconditions need to be in place: pressure from below and reforms from above.

7. *The family and the household economy.* The family and household still play a critical role in providing care and managing security, even in Nordic countries, whose governments have developed the most deliberate strategies to cope with modern changes in household structure. In Japan and southern Europe, the extended family and cohabitation across generations are declining much more slowly. In these countries—and in countries such as the Republic of Korea and Taiwan, China—"grandmother welfare" may have bought respite for one generation from the contradictions between women working and providing childcare. Even in such countries, the capacity of the family to provide protection against insecurity and invest in human capital is limited unless income distribution is equitable or labor and social mobility ensure that most families have at least one member in the protected formal sector (the *garantismo*).

8. *Labor markets and welfare states.* Postwar Keynesian welfare states were founded on extensive employment opportunities and complementarity between labor markets and welfare systems. Employment systems supplied incomes and taxes, whereas welfare systems moderated the effects of the trade cycle and employed men and growing numbers of women in public services. Many now see contradictions between the two. Greater mobility and structural power of capital forces greater flexibility and insecurity on the labor market, whereas high taxes and labor market regulation impede employment. This is most evident in the conservative regimes of continental Europe. Some countries with social democratic welfare regimes, such as Denmark and the Netherlands, appear to be

continued on next page

BOX II, continued

overcoming these challenges through a combination of social bargaining, mild labor market regulation, and generous universal support services, a "win-win" scenario dubbed "flexicurity." (The United Kingdom and Ireland have had recent success in overcoming mass unemployment but poverty and insecurity remain high.) The lesson is to favor education, health, and family services above cash transfers.

9. *Pensions.* Classic social insurance, pay-as-you-go pensions, face a crisis of unsustainability. Reasons include falling contributor-pensioner ratios stemming from demographic change, high nonwage labor costs, early retirement, and the shift from an extensive to an intensive growth path, coupled with a rising profit share that limits wage growth. The hardening of political support for the "breadwinner" model of social insurance, which impedes pension reform, is another critical factor, though Europe also offers examples of successful incremental pension reforms.

10. *From safety nets to activation policies.* Europe's extensive means-tested social assistance has been attacked for creating disincentives and moral hazards. Countries across Europe now generally complement such assistance with a variety of policies designed to activate the labor force. These policies, which differ from U.S.-style "workfare," offer several policy lessons: successful activation efforts are expensive, they require substantial administrative capacity, and they may redistribute employment opportunities more than they create new jobs.[6]

11. *Health care.* European countries have all developed universal, publicly guaranteed rights to health care, largely because health care consumers organized before private health care providers did.[7] Countries broadly divide into those with national health insurance (NHI) and those with national health services (NHS). Beginning in the 1970s several southern European countries switched from NHI to NHS, partly in recognition of the macro-inefficiency of NHI. Public insurance schemes, when coupled with fee-for-service payment to providers, generate moral hazard and cost inflation. Compared with NHI and private medical insurance, tax-financed national health services are superior in delivering standardized medical treatments within fixed budgets.

BOX II, continued

12. *Universal citizenship-based services.* Universal citizenship-based services and benefits offer several advantages over both social insurance and social assistance. They are administratively simple: a child benefit and an elder pension require only a birth certificate or other proof of identity and age. They are "minimally presumptuous,"[8] making the fewest assumptions about people's income, pattern of activities, living arrangements, and livelihood strategies. And they are thus well adapted to postindustrial breakdowns in families and labor markets. Such systems appear to be one basis for the Nordic countries' economic revival, and the United Kingdom's decision to raise universal child benefits substantially follows such reasoning. These arguments apply still more in developing countries with large informal sectors and complex livelihood strategies.

A general and obvious overall conclusion is that all this costs money. The weight of the public sector must and should grow as economies modernize, so fiscal reform moves to center stage. This seems to swim against strong tides in East Asia, but universal education, health care, and citizenship transfers could in time rebuild middle-class support for new taxes.

Implications for East Asia

There are new threats to the revenue base of all states, especially in East Asia,[9] including growing competition for taxes with the mobility of capital and skilled labor; for fees imposed on off-revenue services such as airports; for middle-class spending; and for more opportunities to evade taxes through e-commerce. Downward pressure on import duties from the Association of Southeast Asian Nations (ASEAN) Free Trade Area and weakening of pro-tax, pro-spending political coalitions through middle-class exit also undercut government revenue. Meanwhile, other factors are boosting demand for public spending, notably

continued on next page

BOX II, continued

Asia's high postcrisis debt burden, and rising insecurity and aging. Helpful European experience includes the importance of value added, consumption, income, and capital gains taxes; an emphasis on social security contributions to fund transfer expenditures; and the benefits of harmonizing regional taxes.

These experiences show that welfare states *can* be competitive if they invest in people and communities and avoid large-scale, unproductive transfers.[10] Productive social policies form the foundation for high-quality, intensive economic development. East Asia's welfare regimes embody some of these attributes, notably substantial public investment in basic education and health; they can and should build on this legacy.

An important avenue could be to extend universal citizenship benefits to secondary education and curative health. East Asian countries would be wise to avoid committing totally to social insurance, though it may prove useful in specific circumstances. Given constrained resources, priority should go to health, education, family services, and housing, though cash transfers will need to expand with urbanization and the growth of nuclear families. In-kind services are likely to contribute in the medium term to economic competitiveness and social justice.

1. See also Anthony B. Atkinson and John Hills, "Social Security in Developed Countries: Are There Lessons for Developing Countries?" in *Social Security in Developing Countries,* ed. Ehtisham Ahmad et al. (Oxford, England: Clarendon Press, 1991).

2. Bob Deacon, Michelle Hulse, and Paul Stubbs, *Global Social Policy: International Organisations and the Future of Welfare* (London: Sage, 1997).

3. Paul Krugman, "The Myth of Asia's Miracle," *Foreign Affairs* 73 (1994): 62–78.

4. This also appears to be the case in Asia. Even *zakat* (the Islamic wealth tax earmarked for the poor, the indigent, and others in need) raises significant sums of money only if it has strong government backing. See Mohamed Ariff, "Resource Mobilization through the Islamic Voluntary Sector in Southeast Asia," in *The Islamic Voluntary Sector in Southeast Asia,* ed. Mohamed Ariff (Singapore: Institute of Southeast Asian Studies, 1991).

5. Elmer Rieger and Stephan Leibfried, "Welfare State Limits to Globalization," *Politics and Society* 26, no. 3 (1998): 363–90.

6. Fresh experience in southern European countries in developing activation policies in a context of extensive informal labor markets and continued familial employment deserves careful study.

7. In the United States, the medical profession, private insurers, and private hospitals organized first a century ago and have managed to block proposals for national health insurance ever since.

BOX II, continued

8. Robert Goodin, "Towards a Minimally Presumptuous Welfare Policy," in *Arguing for Basic Income*, ed. Philippe van Parijs (London: Verso, 1992).

9. Mishra Ramesh with Mukul Asher, *Welfare Capitalism in Southeast Asia: Social Security, Health, and Education Policies* (New York, St. Martin's Press, 2000).

10. Ian Gough, *Global Capital, Human Needs, and Social Policies: Selected Essays 1994–99* (Basingstoke, England: Macmillan, 2000).

Frameworks and Models: European and Asian Approaches to Welfare and Social Policy

Introduction

Part I offers a comparative overview of European and East Asian social policy and provides background on the social consequences of the 1997–98 financial crisis in East Asia, as well as lessons learned from the crisis.

Chapter 1 offers a theoretical and practical framework for the book's discussion of social policy experiences in Europe and East Asia. Ian Gough categorizes "welfare regimes" in Europe into four broad types that place varying emphasis on social assistance versus social insurance and on private versus public providers of social services. Social systems in East Asia, in turn, reveal common aspects such as low levels of government expenditure, but as in Europe they more often mask wide differences, some linked to varying levels of economic development. (For more detailed information on social policy patterns in Europe and East Asia, see Appendixes A and B.)

Chapter 2 questions the commonly held view that Asian and European social systems differ greatly because they place different weight on family obligations. Peter Scherer argues that, contrary to conventional wisdom, family obligations are still very important in Europe and are usually legally enforceable. European welfare history shows that formal social insurance did not develop as a substitute for family obligations but rather as a reaction to the burden such obligations impose. The chapter holds that better understanding of the true basis for social systems in Europe and Asia will shed light on alternative approaches, and on how countries that are suspicious of legal obligations can best cope with weakening family and community ties as they unfold.

Chapter 3 shifts to the aftermath of the 1997–98 East Asian crisis and its role in revealing serious weaknesses in the social safety nets in countries that had been part of the East Asian "miracle." Tamar Manuelyan Atinc highlights major household responses to the crisis as well as two central findings: the wide differences in the effects by country, region, and social group (including severe effects on women), and the remarkable coping strategies that many families exhibited in the face of unprecedented economic challenges. The chapter holds that growing urbanization and an aging population will make further strengthening of social safety nets in the region essential.

In Chapter 4 Katherine Marshall builds on the previous analyses to encapsulate lessons that East Asian countries and their international partners have learned from the 1997–98 crisis. The lessons highlight the strong interaction between macroeconomic and social policy and suggest a continuing need to learn from this experience to prepare for future shocks.

In Chapter 5 Christian Oberländer offers a case study of a conscious effort to adapt a European welfare model to an Asian situation: Japan's National Health Insurance. The Japanese experience is notable because the country quickly achieved universal health coverage with more reach than even European insurance schemes. At the design stage, policymakers skillfully relied on research of international as well as domestic experience in providing health insurance. The Japanese experience is an example to its neighbors and one worth referring to in Japan's own development plans.

The crisis period generated a remarkable series of reflections and analysis that continues to this day. One institution taking an active part in the reflections is the Association of Southeast Asian Nations (ASEAN) (see Box 1.1). Throughout the crisis years and since, ASEAN has worked to move regional social policy issues to the fore, devoting considerable effort to framing lessons from the crisis and to understanding the role of social safety nets in ensuring a healthy economy. This is one illustration of the extensive international reflection on crisis lessons that has also marked much work by the multilateral development institutions, the United Nations (Economic and Social Commission for Asia and the Pacific), and the Asia Pacific Economic Cooperation Forum.

Box 1.2 discusses some of the political aspects of the challenges posed by the legacy of decades of economic growth and then the financial crisis on the traditional social contract in Asia. Although each country must clearly develop solutions to social and economic challenges that reflect its culture and history, Box 1.3 offers key principles that can inform effective programs and improve the overall efficacy of government spending in East Asia. Box 1.4 offers a summary of the Paris seminar on European Social Policy and the Asian Crisis. This seminar set out to frame the analytic work of the ASEM European Social Lessons Project, first, by providing background on the East Asian crisis and, second, by exploring possible theoretical frameworks for future discussion of social policy issues.

CHAPTER 1

Welfare Regimes in East Asia and Europe Compared

by Ian Gough

ABSTRACT: This chapter uses the concept of "welfare regimes" to compare the social policy systems of East Asian countries—including Indonesia, the Republic of Korea, Malaysia, Thailand, and the Philippines—with those of European countries. European welfare regimes include a large, active public sector and high state expenditures with small market and declining family provision of social services. East Asian welfare regimes, in contrast, rely on substantial family provisioning and a very small public sector, with the private sector providing a growing share of social services. The two regions' welfare regimes also differ in outcomes: European regimes provide much more security and equality than do those in East Asia. The chapter focuses on policy areas where East Asian countries might benefit from exploring the experience of European welfare regimes.

"An integrated approach of social policies and poverty reduction in the region has been lacking so far. Today Asia deeply needs a framework which brings synergy between the different social policy instruments." (Jean-Michel Severino, Vice President, East Asia and Pacific Region, World Bank; Philippines, November 9, 1999)

The Asian financial crisis of 1997–98 called into question a core principle of East Asian welfare regimes: that economic growth obviates the need for an elaborate system of social protection.[1] This chapter aims to bridge the gap highlighted in Jean-Michel Severino's statement by comparing social policy in Europe[2] to that in East Asia. Overall, European social welfare regimes provide much more security and equality than do East Asian regimes.

The chapter first recaps the concept of welfare regimes[3] and then analyzes them in four countries of Southeast Asia (Indonesia, Malaysia, the Philippines, and Thailand) and one in Northeast Asia (the Republic of Korea).[4] The second section analyzes welfare regimes in Europe, and the third section compares East Asian welfare regimes with those in Europe, where policies and outcomes often represent opposite ends of the welfare spectrum. The chapter concludes by examining policy areas where East Asian countries might benefit from the experience of European welfare regimes.

Welfare Regimes in East Asia

A welfare regime extends well beyond social safety net programs such as cash income supports, unemployment insurance, and old-age pensions, to encompass health and education. The concept also embraces the interdependent way states, markets, and households produce and allocate social welfare. Analysts have derived this definition of the welfare state from European experience, but several factors distinguish East Asia from the European experience.[5] First, the role of the state in ensuring social welfare in East Asia is tiny, even by the standards of the developing world. Second, East Asian societies retain significant agricultural populations, a fact that implies a lesser role for formal social welfare institutions in shaping economic stratification and interest groups. Finally, the effect of external factors—the global economy and supranational institutions—is larger than in the world of the Organization for Economic Cooperation and Development (OECD).

Thus the welfare mix in East Asia entails relatively low public responsibility for welfare expenditure, provision, and regulation; instead it is characterized by reliance on the family and community to provide services and redistribute wealth and by growing involvement of both private markets and community-based organizations in providing social services. In East Asian countries the public sector gives priority to social investment in basic health care and primary education, paying little attention to social safety nets that aim to maintain minimum levels of income. Until the 1997–98 financial crisis, East Asian countries had been curtailing their dependence on foreign aid but increasing their openness to commercial penetration from abroad in providing social services. In all countries in the region, government personnel receive the most generous state support.

In terms of welfare outcomes, the region achieves high scores in public health, education, and poverty reduction. However, persistent gaps and inequalities remain, especially in less well-monitored areas such as morbidity, school dropout rates, working conditions, and patterns of exclusion from society of specific social groups (social exclusion).

Variations do occur within this common pattern. Korea, by far the richest economy in the region, enjoys higher standards of education and other social outcomes and is embarking on a rapid expansion of social insurance in areas such as unemployment benefits. The Philippines exhibits much lower growth; a long-established, segmented, and partial social insurance tradition; and high levels of unemployment, poverty, and inequality, yet good access to education. The result has been labor emigration and high remittances from workers abroad that augment the role of the family. Malaysia maintains a different policy profile, with its provident fund,[6] alongside a U.K.-influenced national health system, and relatively low levels of private finance for health care. Welfare regimes in Indonesia and Thailand are less institutionally developed and differentiated. (For more information on all these regimes, see Appendix A.)

Welfare Regimes in Europe

Europe encompasses several distinct welfare regimes; there is considerable consensus on this typology, which is described, for example, by Gosta Esping-Andersen.[7] They include different welfare mixes and outcomes as well as varying development paths and degrees of economic stratification. Many scholars now delineate four regime types in Europe (see Table 1.1):[8]

- Liberal: Ireland and the United Kingdom
- Social democratic: the Nordic countries (excluding Norway)
- Continental: Austria, the Benelux countries, France, and Germany
- Southern: Italy, Greece, Portugal, and Spain

Table 1.1 Dominant Elements in the Social Regimes of the European Union and East Asia

	State	*Market*	*Community*	*Family*
Education	EU,[a] EA[a]	EA		
Health	EU,[a] EA	EA	EU	EA[a]
Pensions	EU[a]	EU, EA		EA,[a] EU
Safety net	EU[a]			EA,[a] EU

EU = European Union; EA = East Asia.

a. Dominant institutional responsibility.

The classic continental model is characterized by high levels of spending on income transfers (notably pensions), highly regulated labor markets, and relatively good outcomes in terms of poverty and inequality, but poor labor market performance. In the southern European variant, inequality and poverty are more pronounced, but the role of the family is greater.

Both these systems generate high old-age dependency through two mechanisms. First, work force participation rates are low, especially among women and middle-aged men, owing to weak demand for labor. This low demand, some argue, stems from the high contributions that the labor force and employers must make to fund social insurance.[9] Second, fertility rates are very low, possibly owing to late household formation and the difficulties that mainly women face in combining work and family roles. The result is an unsustainable ratio of contributors to welfare recipients—1:1 in Italy at present. Yet short of an external crisis, political support for the continental and southern European regimes is self-sustaining; as long as every family has one member in the protected labor market, it can benefit from his or her entitlement to a social safety net. The results are a lack of employment opportunities for women and young people and concerns about social exclusion.

However, this situation does not occur in the other two "social Europes," which offer a market and state solution to the contradictions of the continental social model. In the liberal regime of the United Kingdom, employment growth has been high, owing partly to labor market deregulation and low benefit levels. But like other liberal regimes, this one generates poverty and low wages, a problem that the U.K. Labour government is now beginning to tackle.

The social democratic regimes in the Nordic countries (excluding Norway) have managed to avoid the continental trap through a different mechanism: substantial public investment in childcare and other forms of family care. This investment permits women and men to combine employment and child raising and, incidentally, provides a growing number of service sector jobs. In these countries, employment and fertility are higher, so dependency ratios are lower (with a ratio of 2.4 workers to 1 dependent in Sweden). The essence of the Nordic social model is relatively high spending on state services coupled with surprisingly unregulated labor markets, at least in Denmark. Social programs are typically universal rather than based on social insurance or targeted, though this is changing. Universal benefits do not discourage or distort labor market activity and do not make presumptions about people's behavior and preferences, and thus universal benefits are better adapted to a world of rapidly changing work, family, and life-cycle patterns.[10] (For a more detailed account of education, health, pensions, and safety nets in Europe, see Appendix B.)[11]

Comparing Welfare Regimes

Overall, Western Europe retains the classic welfare state form: a large, active public sector; high state expenditures (particularly on income transfers); declining family social provision (*if,* a crucial assumption, we ignore unpaid domestic labor); and small but growing private sector involvement. Southeast Asia is almost the opposite: substantial family provision, a small public sector, and a growing market share of social welfare. Differences between the two regions are less pronounced in terms of program outcomes, especially in education, although European superiority in health provision and life expectancy is still marked (see Table 1.2).

In terms of equity and security, European welfare regimes are far superior to their East Asian counterparts, notwithstanding strong families in the latter. Europe does better on measures of poverty, decommodification (that is, the extent to which social goods and services are protected from market transactions), inequality, the real income of the poorest, female employment, and other measures. Europe also compares well with the "liberal" U.S. welfare regime in terms of poverty and inequality. Recent research has shown that the poor in the United States are more deeply poor, more frequently poor, and remain poor longer.[12] The last finding is especially important: once poor, people in the United States have less chance of escaping poverty. One commentator notes, "Whatever it is we want from welfare regimes—whether it is income stability, income equality, low poverty, or high economic prosperity—the social democratic welfare regime seems the best on offer. . . . Conversely, the liberal welfare regime is unambiguously the worst on offer."[13] Apart from income growth, the same verdict would hold true for comparisons with East Asian regimes.

Annual growth of the gross domestic product (GDP) in the 15 countries of the European Union from 1994 to 1998 averaged 3.2 percent, the same as in the United States. However, the employment effect of growth in Europe is notably lower than in the United States, achieved through productivity growth stemming from falling average hours of work and falling employment levels. The desirability of this is difficult to evaluate. On the one hand, intensive growth of this sort can maximize leisure and choice between consumption and leisure. On the other hand, it creates social exclusion—a divide between those inside and outside the labor force in countries that lack income supports (such as those of southern Europe). However, families in southern Europe can redistribute the benefits from insiders to outsiders.

Overall, the European social model must continue to explore ways of combining wage moderation and labor market flexibility with social security and public

Table 1.2   Social Expenditure and Outcomes: Europe and East Asia Compared

	EU 15[a]	East Asia	Nordic Europe	Continental Europe	Southern Europe	United Kingdom and Ireland
Income per head (US$ thousand)	22.3	3.1				
Income per head, purchasing power parity (US$ thousand)	21.3	6.2				
Public social expenditure (% of GDP)	34.1	7.0				
Public social expenditure (% of total government expenditure)	85	39				
Education (% of GDP)	5.0	3.4	5.7	5.0	4.7	4.6
Health (% of GDP)	6.8	1.2	6.5	7.7	5.5	5.8
Social security (% of GDP)	22.3	2.2				
Education						
Secondary enrollment (% of eligible population)	90	66				
Tertiary enrollment (% of eligible population)	44	24				
Average years of study	14.6	10.4				
Health						
Under 5 mortality rate (% of children under 5)	6.6	32				
Life expectancy (years)	77.4	69.2				
Doctors per 1,000 population (%)	2.8	0.4				
Hospital beds per 1,000 population (%)	7.2	2.0				
Private health expenditure (% of total health expenditure)	23	59				
Elderly living with children (% of elderly population)	17	80	7	14	38	16

GDP = gross domestic product.

a. Averages weighted by population or total GDP.

services. A recent study suggests that Denmark and the Netherlands (as well as Ireland and Portugal) offer practical models for adapting to new external and internal pressures (see Table 1.3 for information on those pressures).[14]

European Social Policy Lessons for East Asia

A basic premise of the welfare regime paradigm is that policy proposals must take into account existing patterns of social provision, the distribution of institutional responsibility, and the interests that these express and perpetuate. That does not mean that policy learning, transfer, and change cannot occur, nor does it necessarily reject applying universal principles to policy goals.[15] But it does caution against recommending universal policy designs and instead favors context-specific proposals that consider political economies and inherited institutions. These "lessons from Europe" are framed in that light.[16]

Health

Notwithstanding their generally good record,[17] East Asian health systems are unable to address several emerging problems. These include a falling share of GDP devoted to public expenditures; low pay, training, and incentives for

Table 1.3　Pressures Affecting Welfare Systems

Source	Pressure	Sample consequences for advanced countries
External (globalization)	Trade competition	Deindustrialization, loss of unskilled jobs
	Capital mobility and integrated production	Tax competition, "social dumping," reduced bargaining power for states and labor
	Internationalized financial markets	Decline of states' autonomy in setting macroeconomic policy
Internal (postindustrialization)	Low service sector productivity	Slow growth in service sector productivity; "trilemma" of employment, equity, and budget stability
	Aging	Growing pension and health expenditures
	Household transformation	Smaller household sizes, more single-parent households, more women working
	Maturing of social entitlements	Automatic growth of social expenditures

doctors and nurses; a multi-tiered division of responsibility among public agencies; low government capacity for regulating, coordinating, and implementing health care; and weak regulation of the growing private sector involvement.

A 1999 World Bank report presents a convincing analysis of these problems and offers options for reform.[18] These include raising health expenditures, empowering consumers through health promotion campaigns, strengthening the regulatory and administrative capacities of health ministries, improving providers' pay and incentives, changing price structures to favor primary care, extending social insurance (beginning with catastrophic health insurance), requiring higher co-payments, and mobilizing the resources of the private sector.

Some of those options may be contradictory. European experience suggests that public insurance schemes, when coupled with fee-for-service payment of providers, the usual approach in Southeast Asia, generate cost inflation. Tax-financed national health services (NHS) are better at delivering standardized medical treatments within fixed budgets. When NHS-type systems are in place, "there is little insurance gain from switching to social health insurance."[19]

For example, the commendable Malaysian health system continues to be threatened with corporatization, privatization, and integration with the medical accounts of the Employee Provident Fund (EPF). Further inefficiencies stem from growing private provision alongside an underfunded public sector (for example, maldistribution of doctors results in high workloads and low incentive to work in the public sector).[20] Moreover, health insurance typically excludes more costly treatments, which providers offer privately for higher remuneration. This gives providers a political incentive to keep such treatments out of the health insurance fee schedule. More generally, the gradual move of the middle classes into the private health care sector undermines political support for the public system.[21] Countries can reduce the major drawback of NHS systems—inefficiency in public provision—through a clearer purchaser-provider split and managed competition, as the United Kingdom, Sweden, and other European countries have done.

East Asian health systems should aim to move from (mainly) private financing and mixed provision toward (mainly) public financing and mixed provision. This unusual prescription may be complicated by recent reports that foreign multinationals are purchasing indigenous health care providers. For example, AIA United Healthcare bought the oldest managed care business in the Philippines in 1999.[22] Forthcoming liberalization under the Association of Southeast Asian Nations (ASEAN) Free Trade Area, which will allow unrestricted foreign investment in hospitals, clinics, and laboratories by 2003, will only reinforce this trend. Foreign investment may well bring improved practices, but it could inhibit national health care planning and coordination. The comparative history of public health care suggests that to avoid the domination of providers over consumers, the latter need powerful independent financial bodies, whether state run or owned or nonprofit, to protect their interests. The dangers of admitting powerful international health care providers into developing markets is that they, rather than health care consumers, may dominate the agenda.

Pensions

To draw lessons we must consider the emerging environment for pension systems in East Asia and Europe, including demographic trends (see Table 1.4).

In East Asia over the last 30 years, falling fertility rates and rising life expectancies have cut the share of children and raised the share of working-age adults in the population. The share of aged people rose slightly. The result has

Table 1.4 Demographic Trends in East Asia

	Korea (%)	Malaysia (%)	Thailand (%)	Philippines (%)	Indonesia (%)	Average (%)
65+ dependency ratio,[a] 2000	9.3	6.8	8.4	6.1	7.2	7.56
65+ dependency ratio,[a] 2030	25.8	14.5	19.6	12.2	14.2	17.26
Change in 65+ dependency ratio, 2000–30	16.5	7.7	11.2	6.1	7.0	9.7
Change in total dependency ratio,[b] 2000–30	15.1	−16.0	3.1	−19.8	−8.2	−5.16
Change in weighted dependency ratio,[c] 1995–2030	16.7	−2.5	8.3	−4.0	0.7	3.84

a. The 65+ dependency ratio = the number of persons over age 65, expressed as a percentage of persons aged 15–64 years.

b. The total dependency ratio = the number of persons over age 65, plus children under 15 years, expressed as a percentage of persons aged 15–64 years.

c. The weighted dependency ratio = the number of persons over age 65, plus one-third of children under 15 years, expressed as a percentage of persons aged 15–64 years.

Source: David I. Stanton and Peter Whiteford, *Pension Systems and Policy in the APEC Economies* (Manila: Asian Development Bank, 1998).

been a sharp fall in the overall dependency ratio. The prospects for the next three decades are very different, as the larger working-age cohorts enter old age and the smaller child cohorts enter working age. The share of those 65 years and over is projected to double in East Asia and to grow by two and one-half times in Korea alone. Thus the demographic profile of East Asia will mature in the coming period.

The pattern of employment growth is important in determining whether these potential dependency ratios translate into actual dependency ratios. I am unaware of any projections of future work force participation rates, but the region's economies will probably shift gradually from high employment and wage growth to slower, more labor-intensive growth. This will disadvantage pay-as-you-go schemes for financing old-age pensions.

The role of the family both in effecting transfers of wealth and in providing shared housing and other services will probably diminish, but at a slow rate typical today of Japan and southern Europe. In any case, the high levels of income inequality in East Asia (except in Korea) undermine the ability of household savings and transfers of wealth to act as a source of old-age security.[23]

Thus, in comparison with Europe, East Asia faces a rapid demographic transition, plus a gradual shift from extensive to intensive growth, in a context of extensive household transfers plus weak public pension schemes. The possibilities for learning from Europe appear weak. Nevertheless, the retirement age in East Asia is low in relation to life expectancy, and raising it offers a potential source of improvement. Europe offers practical examples of how to raise the retirement age within existing schemes (as discussed later).

A strong case can be made for establishing universal first-tier pension systems in East Asia. Such systems can take one of two main forms: an unconditional grant or a means-tested, income-tested, or pension-tested allowance.[24] In countries such as Thailand, where formal pension provision is weak, a universal citizenship pension has much to recommend it. Such a system would offer administrative simplicity, equity (for women and workers in the informal sector), adaptability to less-patterned work lives owing to global economic change, national solidarity, and political support. Scandinavian countries introduced citizenship pensions when a large proportion of the population was employed in the informal agricultural sector.[25] For example, Finland introduced a flat-rate pension for all in 1956 when its GDP per capita (at purchasing power parity) was US$4,600, a level that is below that in Malaysia and Thailand today and only slightly above that in the Philippines. On the other hand, in countries such as the Philippines and Malaysia, where pension entitlements are accruing, a pension-tested supplement available to all over the retirement age, as can be found in Korea, makes sense.

When we turn to potential second-tier pensions, clear differences emerge between the social insurance schemes in the Philippines, Korea, and Thailand and the provident funds in Malaysia and, to a more limited extent, Indonesia. The Malaysian EPF was the world's first mandatory provident fund. It remains one of the most significant and has many unique features. It is therefore worth noting its institutional strengths as well as its weaknesses:

- *Adequacy of benefits.* The fund posted an annual real rate of return of more than 4.7 percent from 1987 to 1996, enabling millions of workers to share in the returns to capital. Administrative costs are only 2 percent,[26] and most members are happy with the proposed benefits. However, the scheme is costly, with a combined contribution rate of 23 percent (11 percent from employees and 12 percent from employers). The ability of members to withdraw 30 percent of their entitlement for house purchases or improvement and another 30 percent at age 50 before retirement undermines the fund's role as an old-age pension.
- *Equity.* The system offers weak protection against poverty in old age, given the unequal distribution of work incomes and the lack of any provision for redistributing benefits. Furthermore, extensive tax exemptions favor higher-income groups, and the system excludes casual workers and those in the informal sector.
- *Security.* Capitalized defined-contribution schemes are at risk from falling share prices, as demonstrated during the East Asian financial crisis. The result is that payouts can fluctuate substantially among cohorts of retirees and that guaranteeing payments against inflation (let alone keeping pace with rising living standards) can be difficult. Recipients can also spend their lump-sum payments unwisely, although housing purchased with EPF withdrawals may offer an important alternative to social security.[27]

Raising the pension age and introducing a citizenship pension would overcome some of these drawbacks. But more specific reforms, such as removing tax exemptions, introducing annuities as the normal form of payment, and improving the rate-of-return guarantee, are also necessary.

The fundamental case for social insurance–based, defined-benefit, pay-as-you-go pensions is that they replace the traditional intergenerational solidarity of the household and extended family with a more formal and wider-based solidarity in tune with modernized societies. They also permit and usually undertake intragenerational redistribution. The result is a lower rate of poverty among the aged.

Critics claim that an aging population creates a fundamental problem for these programs, because the programs must demand higher contributions from the working population, lower pensions, or both, producing intergenerational conflict. However, this analysis is almost always premised on a two-generational model. With a more realistic three-generational model, the nature and degree of intergenerational conflict change.[28] A falling birthrate leads at first to a rise in the working population and a fall in the total dependency ratio. The key measure is the total dependency ratio over a cohort's lifetime. In Southeast Asia falling numbers of children will continue to offset the aging process, except in Korea and Thailand (see Table 1.4). This suggests that countries can finance pensions and health care by transferring resources from education.[29]

Nevertheless, reforms in addition to raising the retirement age will be needed to ensure that the implicit pension debt does not grow out of hand. Here European experience has much to offer. Pension reform in Europe has entailed higher contributions and new sources of financing, shifts toward defined-contribution benefits, discouragement of early retirement, and the incremental introduction of a capitalized element into the total pension package. Economists have debated the negative effects of higher contributions on the labor market supply. However, the alternative—means-tested pensions—may dissuade work and savings. The fears of an adverse effect on labor supply may well be exaggerated.[30]

The final lesson to be learned from Europe is political. Proposed pension reform in France in 1995 brought millions out on strike and into the streets, suggesting that any attempt to challenge rights in a mature pay-as-you-go pension regime is doomed to failure. However, France did successfully retrench excessive pension entitlements in 1993, as did Italy in 1995 and 1997.[31] The difference was the active involvement of trade unions and other parties in these reform exercises. Pension reform requires open democratic government to succeed. The attempted French pension reform in 1995 was the first to tackle excessive public sector pensions—a warning about the potential difficulties that East Asian countries will likely face in equalizing public and private pension entitlements.

Safety Nets

Safety nets can operate at three levels: employment, income, and consumption. At the first level, government offers destitute people work programs, usually at wages so low that they automatically exclude those who are not poor. At the second level, government gives needs-based cash transfers or unemployment insurance to supplement income. At the third stage, government provides direct services to satisfy the needs of poor families, such as food programs, "stay in school" programs (which include specific measures to prevent dropouts from school), emergency health cards, and housing assistance. A World Bank review[32] highlights how, in the wake of the East Asian crisis, many countries in East Asia employed all three strategies, as do European welfare states.[33]

In assessing lessons, we must consider how these efforts interact with other components of the welfare regime. Asian families are a far more important source of assistance (in the form of work, cash, and kind) than European families—with the partial exception of those in southern European countries, which also have weak formal safety nets. In Greece, Italy, Portugal, and Spain, family members employ around three-fifths of young people. Those countries rely on political organizations and faith-based organizations (for example, Catholic charities) to provide for the elderly and people with disabilities. Except for Portugal, they exhibit low rates of female employment. This cluster of factors explains the absence of national safety nets in those countries.[34] For this reason, recent experiments in Italy and elsewhere to adjust assistance programs to situations involving strong families, weak compliance with regulations, and the participation of nonstate institutions such as political parties are of obvious relevance to East Asia. Yet, despite their common elements, southern Europe and Southeast Asia differ in their degree of labor market regulation and flexibility. The recent East Asian crisis resulted in lower wages rather than lower employment, an outcome that undermines the effectiveness of work programs and enhances the effectiveness of cash and in-kind benefits.[35]

Future Priorities for Welfare Regimes in Southeast Asia

Productive social policies form the foundation for a high-quality, intensive path of economic development.[36] The welfare regimes of East Asia embody some of these attributes, notably substantial public investment in basic education and health. East Asian countries need to build on this legacy, extending citizenship benefits to include universal secondary education and curative health, as well as giving priority to services such as health, education, and housing rather than to cash transfers. Experience shows that welfare states can remain competitive by investing in people and communities rather than by relying on unproductive, large-scale cash benefits.[37] Urbanization and family nucleation will steadily undermine the capacity of households to protect their members against economic risks and insecurities; hence it is likely that East Asian countries will need to augment their social protection systems. However, social services are more likely to contribute to economic competitiveness while satisfying people's needs and promoting social justice.

Notes

1. World Bank, *Towards an East Asian Social Protection Strategy* (draft, Human Development Unit, East Asia and Pacific Region, September 1999).

2. By "Europe," I mean the 15 member states of the European Union. This definition excludes, among other countries, Norway, Switzerland, and all the countries of Central and Eastern Europe.

3. There remains a problem of terminology. The term "welfare" in the Asian context frequently denotes state handouts or charity. It is often contrasted with "development," as in human resource development or social development, concerned with investing in people and productivity-enhancing social institutions. Thus the term "welfare regime" is likely to be seriously misunderstood. Perhaps "social policy regime" or "human development regime" would be a preferable term. In this chapter, I use the term "welfare regime," with the understanding that it refers to a wide definition of social programs encompassing broad social and developmental goals.

4. In places in this chapter, the countries are ordered in terms of their present income per head: Korea, Malaysia, Thailand, the Philippines, and Indonesia.

5. For a more detailed argument see Ian Gough, "Welfare Regimes: On Adapting the Framework to Developing Countries," SPDC Paper No. 1, University of Bath, 1999.

6. Provident funds are private savings funds for pension purposes.

7. See especially Gøsta Esping-Andersen, *The Three Worlds of Welfare Capitalism* (Princeton, N.J.: Princeton University Press, 1990).

8. See, for example, Maurizio Ferrera with A. Hemerijck and M. Rhodes, *The Future of Social Europe: Recasting Work and Welfare in the New Economy* (Oeiras, Portugal: Celta Editora, 2000).

9. Gøsta Esping-Andersen rejects this argument on the grounds that the alternative—high direct and indirect taxes—will fall on employees, who will in return demand higher wages and thus push up wage costs through another route. See Gøsta Esping-Andersen, "Do Spending and Finance Structures Matter," in *The Social Quality of Europe*, eds. Wolfgang Beck, Laurent van der Maesen, and Alan Walker (The Hague, Netherlands: Kluwer, 1997), p. 122. In my view, the likelihood of this scenario will depend on the balance of advantage in the labor market: if labor is weaker owing to high unemployment, it may be unable to recoup its losses. In this scenario, the form of taxation may have an effect independent of its level.

10. Robert Goodin, "Towards a Minimally Presumptuous Welfare Policy," in *Arguing for Basic Income*, ed. Philippe van Parijs (London: Verso, 1992).

11. For further comparative and prospective works on European welfare states, see Gosta Esping-Andersen, ed., *Welfare States in Transition: National Adaptations in Global Economies* (London: Sage, 1996); Beck, van der Maesen, and Walker, op. cit.; Martin Rhodes and Yves Mény, eds., *The Future of European Welfare: A New Social Contract?* (New York: Macmillan, 1998); Gosta Esping-Andersen, ed., *The Social Foundations of Post-Industrial Economies* (Oxford, England: Oxford University Press, 1999); Giuliano Bonoli, Vic George, and Peter Taylor-Gooby, eds., *European Welfare Futures: Towards a Theory of Retrenchment* (London: Polity Press, 2000); Stein Kuhnle,

ed., *Survival of the European Welfare State* (London: Routledge, 2000); and Ferrera, Hemerijck, and Rhodes, eds., op. cit.

12. Robert E. Goodin et al., *The Real Worlds of Welfare Capitalism* (Cambridge, England: Cambridge University Press, 1999), and Chris Pierson and Francis Castles, eds., *The Welfare State Reader* (Cambridge, England: Polity Press, 2000).

13. Goodin, p. 184.

14. See Ferrera et al., op. cit.

15. See Len Doyal and Ian Gough, *A Theory of Human Need* (Basingstoke, England: Macmillan, 1991).

16. Owing to lack of space and knowledge, I omit discussion of education policy here.

17. According to Mishra Ramesh, "Most sick people have some access to health care." Mishra Ramesh with Mukul Asher, *Welfare Capitalism in Southeast Asia* (New York: St. Martin's, 2000), p. 113.

18. World Bank, *East Asia Health, Nutrition and Population Strategy* (Human Development Sector Unit, East Asia and Pacific Region, October 1999).

19. Paul Gertler, "On the Road to Health Insurance: The Asian Experience," *World Development* 26, no. 4 (1998): 725.

20. Ramesh, op. cit.

21. Gertler, op. cit.

22. J. Haresnape, ed., *Health Care Global Outlook 2000* (London: Economic Intelligence Unit, 1999), p. 148.

23. Ramesh, op. cit, pp. 73–74.

24. Pension-testing raises existing pension income to a minimum level, income-testing takes into account all other income, and means-testing takes into account income and capital assets.

25. See Evelyne Huber and John Stephens, "The Political Economy of Pension Reform: Latin America in Comparative Perspective," UNRISD Occasional Paper no. 7, May 2000.

26. The lessons from Europe here are the mis-selling and excessive administrative costs experienced in the decentralized, individually managed personal pensions accounts introduced in the United Kingdom, where various fees and costs consume 40–45 percent of the value of individual accounts. See Peter Orszag and Joseph Stiglitz, "Rethinking Pension Reform: Ten Myths about Social Security Systems" (paper presented at the World Bank Conference, Washington, D.C., 14–15 September 1999), p. 31.

27. See Frank Castles, "The Really Big Tradeoff: Home Ownership and the Welfare State in the New World and the Old," *Acta Politica* 33, no. 1 (1998).

28. David Collard, "Generational Transfers and the Generational Bargain," *Journal of International Development* 12, no. 4 (2000): 453–62.

29. The World Bank argues that the costs of aging will exceed the savings on education by a substantial amount. One attempt to take this into account is to calculate a weighted dependency ratio, as shown in Table 1.4, which weights the costs of a child at one-third that of an elderly person. This suggests small changes, except in Korea and Thailand, which still show a growing burden of dependency. But given high education spending and low pension spending in East Asia, this overstates the problem. See World Bank, *Averting the Old Age Crisis* (Oxford, England; New York: Oxford University Press, 1994), pp. 34–36.

30. See Orszag and Stiglitz, op. cit.

31. See Giuliano Bonoli, "Pension Politics in France: Patterns of Co-operation and Conflict in Two Recent Reforms," *West European Politics* 20, no. 4 (1997): 160–81.

32. World Bank, *Towards an East Asian Social Protection Strategy*, op. cit., Table 3.

33. Unlike in the United States, where Medicaid and food stamps are important, in-kind assistance in Europe is limited mostly to housing. According to Atinc and Walton, estimates of the cost of restoring the consumption of poor households in Indonesia following the crisis to 1996 levels are 1 percent of 1998/99 budgetary revenues for full targeted benefits, 3.5–5 percent for public works programs, and 6.5 percent for untargeted cash transfers. These are all relatively small amounts. See Tamar Manuelyan Atinc and Michael Walton, "The Social Consequences of the East Asian Crisis," Background paper prepared for *Responding to the Global Financial Crisis* (Washington, D.C.: World Bank, 1998), p. 22.

34. Ian Gough, "Social Assistance in Southern Europe," *South European Society and Politics* 1, no.1 (1996): 1–23, and Ian Gough, *Global Capital, Human Needs, and Social Policies: Selected Essays, 1994–99* (Macmillan, 2000).

35. World Bank, *Towards an East Asian Social Protection Strategy*, op. cit., p. 25.

36. Bowles also arrives at this result, using an economic model that assumes completely unimpeded mobility of capital among countries. He concludes, "Globalization does not rule out all egalitarian interventions. There remain a large class of governmental and other collective interventions leading to substantial improvements in the wages, employment prospects, and economic security of the less well off. Included are redistribution of assets which are productivity-enhancing, namely those that provide efficient solutions to incentive problems arising in principal agent relationships such as wage employment, farm and residential tenancy, and the provision of environmental and social public goods in local commons situations." Sam Bowles, "Globalization and Economic Justice," Benjamin H. Hibbard Lecture, University of Wisconsin, March 2000, p. 5.

37. Ian Gough, "Social Welfare and Competitiveness," *New Political Economy* 1, no. 2 (1996): 210–32, and Ian Gough (2000), op. cit.

BOX 1.1

Social Policy Priorities in Asia:
ASEAN Consultations in 2002
by Tara Karacan

Indonesia, Malaysia, the Philippines, Singapore, and Thailand established the Association of Southeast Asian Nations (ASEAN) in 1967 in Bangkok to represent "the collective will of the nations of Southeast Asia to bind themselves together in friendship and cooperation and, through joint efforts and sacrifices, secure for their peoples and for posterity the blessings of peace, freedom and prosperity."[1] Brunei Darussalam, Cambodia, the Lao People's Democratic Republic, Myanmar, and Vietnam later became members. Today the 10-nation bloc represents 500 million people and a combined GDP of US$737 billion. Its secretary-general, Rodolfo C. Severino Jr., has observed that "closer integration among the economies of Southeast Asia in ASEAN has made them more competitive than they would otherwise have been."[2]

ASEAN has moved cautiously on the social policy front, focusing more on learning lessons than on defining common standards or approaches. Each of the 10 member countries has different concerns and priorities, generally reflecting its income and level of social development. For example, Singapore, the richest, is focusing on issues comparable to those confronting Western Europe—such as subsidies and welfare, universal health insurance schemes, upgrading its citizens' skills, and fostering lifelong learning. On the other end of the scale, Cambodia is contending with large numbers of orphans, elderly people, people with disabilities, and demobilized military personnel from its civil war; low rates of participation in education; growing levels of HIV/AIDS; and human trafficking.

Nonetheless, ASEAN countries share many challenges, and an analysis of best practices among their social programs can allow them to develop regional programs. Thus, since the East Asian crisis began in 1997, ASEAN has organized efforts to reflect on the future policy agenda. It was in this spirit that the Secretariat convened in January 2002 a conference in Jakarta that focused specifically on social policy

continued on next page

BOX 1.1, continued

challenges. Participants in "Social Development in the National Development Agenda" included senior officials responsible for key social sectors, representatives of nongovernmental organizations (NGOs) and international organizations, and academics and specialists.

Country papers for the conference reflected common concerns such as containing the HIV/AIDS epidemic, reducing poverty, creating employment and income-generating activities, bringing basic health and sanitation services to the poor and rural areas, and assisting people with disabilities, children, and the elderly. Other common concerns included fostering participation by governments, NGOs, private businesses, community-based organizations, mass organizations, and international organizations in delivering social services; promoting more involvement by women; and building local technical and financial capabilities.

Participants' central conclusion was that the challenge is less to integrate social sectors into countries' national agendas—practically all have done so—but rather to determine how governments can reach social development goals in a context of globalization and market liberalization, economic cycles and financial crises, and demographic transitions. A related need is to ensure that economic planning encompasses social development, especially by allocating adequate resources.

Overall the region is rich in innovative poverty alleviation programs, including those mobilizing and devolving responsibilities to local governments and community organizations. Regional action should aim at linking these practices and practitioners in a continuous learning process. As President Gloria Macapagal Arroyo of the Philippines has observed, "One of the ways to make ASEAN continue to be relevant is to make agreements binding. But another way . . . is to make sure that when there is a new cataclysmic development in the world, ASEAN knows how to respond, taking into account our cultural diversities, the different social organizations, and the different historical antecedents." What will count most in establishing a regional action plan will be actual practices and a clear learning curve rather than any well-concocted blueprint.

1. <http://www.aseansec.org/64.htm>.

2. Julia Clerk, *International Herald Tribune* online, <http://www.IHT.com>, January 21, 2002.

CHAPTER 2

The Role of Family Obligations in Developed Economies

by Peter Scherer

ABSTRACT: Analysts often portray a formal European system of social insurance that gradually crowds out family-based assistance, while maintaining that in East Asia family welfare systems dominate. However, family obligations in Europe are still a reality. In fact, formal social insurance is much less a substitute for family obligations than a reaction to the financial impact of those obligations. That is why, for instance, public-funded pension schemes are still very popular in Europe and their reform meets such resistance. Family obligations, in sum, are much less culture specific than is often assumed. They are common to all welfare systems. The issue today is how Asian countries can move toward law-based welfare schemes as families gradually disengage from assistance in the context of economic development.

Discussions of social security in Asian countries have been strongly influenced by "positive orientalism"—the tendency to associate rapid economic growth and social progress in Asia with the absence of the dependency culture that has supposedly developed in the West.[1] This chapter examines the role of family obligations in Western social security systems. It argues that the perception that such systems have displaced family obligations is inaccurate. Furthermore, this perception has tended to divert debate over changing Asian social security systems away from key questions.

The views in this chapter are those of the author and do not necessarily represent those of the OECD or its member countries.

Obligations for Social Support under European Civil Law

In 1996 Singapore passed the Maintenance of Parents Act, which introduced a legal obligation for children to support their elderly parents and established the Tribunal for the Maintenance of Parents to mediate and, if necessary, adjudicate such claims. A Singapore minister summarized the need for such a measure by contrasting it with the "negative experiences" of other countries:

> The key question behind the proposed Parents Maintenance Bill is who should support vulnerable old people who cannot maintain themselves adequately. Over the last four decades, the people in Europe, North America, and Australia have chosen the welfare state with high taxes and high social security transfers.[2]

The World Bank draws the same contrast between the "family solidarity–based" systems of Asia and the social protection systems found in member countries of the Organization for Economic Cooperation and Development (OECD). For example, a 1994 World Bank report on pension system reform makes a clear distinction between informal systems based on intrafamily obligations and formal systems based on wealth-transfer entitlements.[3] A recent World Bank strategy paper also implies that these approaches are distinct:

> The dramatic negative effects of global financial crisis revealed the importance of having well-designed formal SP [social protection] systems in place, which were lacking due to governments' resistance to the adoption of OECD-type SP programs and reliance on a different tradition of family-based support.[4]

Such analyses imply that formal social protection systems "crowd out" informal ones. However, despite this conventional wisdom, civil law in most continental European countries does require family members to support one another when in need. This requirement is not confined to underage children living in the parental home: parents must support adult children and grandchildren who are still engaged in full-time education or unable to support themselves, and children and grandchildren must support elderly parents and grandparents.

Under French law, these provisions appear today in almost the same form as the *Code Napoléon*, the 1804 codification of civil law. Although many elements of the code (such as the requirement that a wife obey her husband and the stipulation that a husband has authority over the couple's common property) have been abandoned, the family obligations remain. These requirements entail far more than a bare minimum of support. French civil tribunals have stated that family support must extend beyond basic needs to allow the beneficiaries to "live in a decent manner and even to enjoy a certain level of comfort, a function evidently of the resources of the payer."[5] Civil tribunals can enforce these obligations, and over the past two centuries an extensive jurisprudence has interpreted how they apply in particular circumstances.

Social insurance as it has developed in Europe and Japan is thus partly a response to family obligations rather than a substitute for them.[6] Such systems also provide a powerful incentive for popular support of public pension and health care systems, and for opposition to their reform. This is because in the absence of such social insurance provisions, citizens would be legally liable for providing for extended family members who were in need. One consequence has been a growing tolerance of subsidies from the general budget to social insurance systems. For example, in Germany this subsidy has grown from 4.1 percent of pension payouts in 1960 to more than 25 percent in 1998.[7]

The impact of these provisions varies greatly from country to country, and often within each country. In most cases the requirement to contribute is means tested: a poor family does not have to contribute to its relatives' upkeep. However, the requirement to provide support is not necessarily confined to cases of dire poverty: within each family, members are required to support each other in line with their established standard of living. The concept in this respect is similar to alimony between divorced partners, but extends further than the nuclear family.

These provisions characterize the European countries that have now developed comprehensive social insurance systems. But under the common law that originated in England and that has been adopted as the basis of civil law in English-speaking immigrant countries (including the United States), support of one family member by another is not enforceable in law, with the exception of underage children.[8] The laws governing public assistance, the "poor laws," did stipulate that family could be required to pay for the upkeep of someone who would otherwise have been reliant on social assistance. But in contrast to European civil law, this provision was purely ancillary to the assistance law: its purpose was to minimize calls on public expenditure.[9] No right to support existed for those who had not applied for public assistance.[10] These provisions have now disappeared from public policy in these countries: legal liability for the upkeep of adult family members no longer exists in the English-speaking world (except in Singapore). In those countries social insurance institutions are found, but the level of coverage is in general more modest than in continental Europe or in Japan.

It would, however, be an exaggeration to suggest that family responsibility laws are the sole reason for the growth of European social insurance systems. In particular, the European countries with the highest rates of social transfers, the Nordic countries, have long abolished such laws.[11] In those countries, community rather than family responsibilities are emphasized.

Family Responsibility and Assistance Arrangements

In Italy and Spain residents can request municipal assistance only if no family member can afford to provide enough support. In Austria, Germany, Luxembourg, and Switzerland—and generally in France—a person in need has a right to have local authorities meet those needs. However, parents or children of the recipients can be required to compensate authorities for the portion they can afford. In France the legal duty to provide support extends to daughters and to sons-in-law (though not to grandchildren-in-law), and in Italy, Portugal, and Spain it extends to siblings and half-siblings.[12]

In all these countries social restraints discourage potential applicants from exploiting the system. In any country where governments can, in principle, recover social assistance costs from relatives, the shame of having to nominate relatives means that the number of applicants and recipients is always far lower than the number who are eligible. In Switzerland, for example, only one-fifth of eligible applicants apply in rural areas, and only about one-half in urban areas,[13] even though benefit rates are high compared with average incomes.[14] In most countries local discretion also determines whether family members eligible to contribute must do so. For example, in Germany, local governments under social democratic administration tend not to enforce the rules.

Another indirect but important factor also keeps the take-up rate low. Local municipalities usually administer social assistance, and in most countries the expenditures are charged to local budgets. (Exceptions include Australia and New Zealand, and to some extent Ireland and the United Kingdom.) This often means that local councillors make final decisions on assistance, even if they usually act on the advice of social workers who have reviewed applicants' needs. In Switzerland, this usually occurs at the level of the commune. Although Zurich consists of one commune of 450,000 inhabitants, the typical rural commune has 200 inhabitants, so councillors know applicants personally and understand the impact of granting assistance on local taxes. This type of pressure operates even in Finland, Norway, and Sweden, which do not require relatives to contribute. A social worker must still thoroughly examine each applicant's personal circumstances and often report the results to the local committee, which decides, for example, whether a homeowner must sell his or her property if rental accommodations are available.

Relying on municipalities makes sense because people may need assistance for reasons that go beyond low earnings. In most countries municipalities assess an applicant's other assets and determine whether the income shortfall results from problems within the household. National administrations are not well suited to undertake these detailed investigations.

Overall, these provisions do not greatly affect affluent families, as few members are likely to have incomes low enough to apply for assistance. However, the more general requirements of the civil law still apply, and these can result in claims for support by families that would not be eligible for social assistance. Certainly, for middle-class families with modest incomes, the impact of supporting indigent relatives can be considerable. This obligation also imposes the risk that a nuclear family cannot control its own affairs, because no matter how well a couple manages its finances it may still be liable for destitute parents.

Defining Minimum Living Standards

In Europe, Norway and the Mediterranean countries—notably Italy and Spain—allow regional governments to set their own standards for social assistance. However, most other OECD countries establish national standards, although even these countries, which have fully monetarized economies and almost universal tax and administrative systems, can find it difficult to agree on such standards. Until the early 1990s Canada and the United States addressed the issue by offering matching grants to provinces or states, with the result that provinces and states with high rates of assistance received higher federal subsidies. However, in the mid-1990s these countries began providing block grants to provinces and states that no longer depend on actual assistance rates, although past rates of assistance do influence the grant levels. Provinces and states have been left free to set their own standards.

In the Czech Republic and the Netherlands local authorities claim that some 90 percent of their expenditures are financed by national authorities. This means that localities have no incentive to control expenditures (and might, in the course of seeking local influence, exaggerate their constituents' needs). To avoid this form of political "moral hazard," municipalities more commonly finance assistance out of their own tax revenues but receive additional grants according to their socioeconomic characteristics, such as the local unemployment rate.

Safety Nets, Family Obligations, and Poverty Alleviation

Those examples show that drawing a line between informal systems based on family solidarity and formal systems based on social insurance is difficult. Formal systems based on family solidarity are common and form an essential part of today's safety nets.

The introduction of social insurance systems that originate from such European sources into societies with a large informal sector can have perverse effects. By definition, only those in the formal sector—that is, in general, those with higher incomes and better social connections—will be covered. Experience has shown that it is very difficult to run such systems without incurring a deficit. As incomes are generally higher in the formal sector than in the informal sector, the subsidy itself will be regressive in its overall impact[15]—and may still not address the most urgent needs.[16]

But this does not mean that families alone can provide a safety net, formally or informally. The informal networks that tie families together are, of course, the basis for both economic development and mutual protection—economists know well that economic development does not result from the actions of disconnected individuals. Business networks and arrangements, within both families and communities, are essential for a successful economy; understanding their contributions propels current interest in "social capital" as a component of economic growth.

Social networks can block change as well as promote it. Families work together to build up businesses and pool investment funds, but they can also work together to exclude outsiders and protect established ways. Ethnic groups draw on common understandings to launch new ventures, but they sometimes close ranks to exclude outsiders and prevent competition.

The sense of obligation and gratitude toward parents by children, an underlying feature of the family relations in many societies, can have perverted consequences, particularly when fast economic development is driving aspirations to rapid increases in wealth. In Thailand, for example, concepts of obligation and gratitude toward parents can lead young people to leave school and their home villages in order to provide remittances to their parents—sometimes by entering harmful occupations, including prostitution.[17]

Such defensive uses of family and community ties are particularly likely to occur during times of crisis. Competition that was tolerated, if resented, during periods of economic growth can be feared and attacked when times are hard. When there is no safety net to limit social distress resulting from failure, such tensions can become violent and destructive. These tensions were a major cause of the rise of fascist regimes in Europe, and the generalization of social insurance after World War II was largely a response to this tragedy.

For countries with very low per capita income, policies that promote economic growth are clearly essential to reduce durably the rate of absolute poverty. Any safety net program that impedes growth is, therefore, likely to be potentially counterproductive, because it risks, at best, protecting part of the population from sharing endemic poverty. Safety nets in countries with a large formal sector can easily fall into this defensive role.

Economic growth that leaves significant portions of the population feeling insecure, with only community and family resources to rely on in times of crisis, is vulnerable to social unrest. Such unrest will pose a continuing threat even if the disposable income of the majority of the population continues to grow. The growth process is particularly vulnerable to the withdrawal of investor capital that can quickly follow the first sign of unrest—a process that, in inducing a decline in capital values, can become self-perpetuating.

Supplementing Family Support in Asia

The continued importance of family obligations in most developed Western economies shows that such obligations occur in all types of societies—there is nothing particularly "Asian" or "non-Western" about them. Even in countries that confine formal family obligations to underage children, families provide mutual support to their members throughout the life cycle. For example, relatives provide most care of the frail elderly in all countries.[18]

Countries with a strong Confucian influence on public affairs will be uncomfortable with the emphasis on formal legal processes found in Romano-Germanic law and English common law. For example, the Republic of Korea is now revising its social assistance legislation to make aid an entitlement in cases of established need. While Korea's Confucian tradition establishes a strong moral expectation that family members will care for each other, the law has no role in enforcing this. However, the newly defined entitlements are conditional on an assessment of the capacity of family members to assist. Authorities can refuse to provide public assistance if an able-bodied relative should provide assistance, even if that relative does not have the resources to do so.[19]

Countries with a colonial past, such as Indonesia, tend to mistrust formal law as a foreign imposition. Customary and religious laws have standing in formal courts, but community leaders rather than courts generally enforce the law. As internal migration increases, other mechanisms will have to supplement these traditional means of ensuring social support, particularly in urban areas, but it is not clear what form these should best take.

Families remain a significant focus of social obligations and support in almost all societies. The question is how systems that are suspicious of legal obligations can best cope with the attenuation of family and community ties that accompany economic development. Must these societies invent formal obligations, as Singapore has done? Can the expansion of social insurance, as in Japan, Korea, and Taiwan, China, fill the gaps? The answers await further research and experience.

Notes

1. Roger Goodman and Gordon White, "Welfare Orientalism and the Search for an East Asian Welfare Model," in *The East Asian Welfare Model: Welfare Orientalism and the State*, eds. Roger Goodman, Gordon White, and Huck-Ju Kwon (London: Routledge, 1998), 3–24.

2. Boon Heng Lim, "Family Values" (speech at the opening of the Singapore National Trade Union Congress Seminar on Family Values, Singapore), available at <http://www.gov.sg/mita/speech/speeches/v18n60ll.htr.1994>. An account of the origins and functioning of the Singapore tribunal can be found in Peter Scherer, "Formalizing the Informal: Family Obligations in Modern Asia," in *Children and Social Security: International Studies in Social Security*, ed. Jonathan Bradshaw (Aldershot, England: Ashgate, 2002).

3. World Bank, "Averting the Old Age Crisis: Policies to Protect the Old and Promote Growth" (policy research paper, Oxford, England: Oxford University Press, 1994).

4. R. Holtzmann and S. Jorgensen, *Social Risk Management: A New Conceptual Framework for Social Protection, and Beyond*, World Bank Social Protection Discussion Paper No. 0006, 2000.

5. Léopold Peyrefitte, "Considérations sur la Règle 'Aliments N' Arréragent Pas," *Revue Trimestrielle de Droit Civile* 67, no. 3 (1968): 286–308.

6. My full paper prepared for the ASEM Project, available on the ASEM Web site, lays out this argument in more detail. See <http://www.worldbank.org/eapsocial/asemsocial>.

7. A. Börsch-Supan, "A Model Under Siege: A Case Study of the German Retirement Insurance System," *Economic Journal* 110, no. 461 (2000): F24–F44.

8. These countries began to formalize and enforce child-support obligations of absent parents only in the 1980s. Public officials used rhetoric about family obligations to justify this change, but it was largely inspired by the desire to reduce the budgetary burden of public support for single parents.

9. Alvin L. Schorr, *Filial Responsibility in the Modern American Family* (Washington, D.C.: U.S. Department of Health, Education, and Welfare, Social Security Administration, Division of Program Research, 1960).

10. David Thompson, "I Am Not My Father's Keeper: Families and the Elderly in Nineteenth Century England," *Law and History Review* 2, no. 2 (1984): 265–86.

11. For example, these obligations were deleted from Finnish law in 1970, when Finland adopted the Nordic welfare ideology. See Marjatta Marin, "Generational Relations and the Law," in *The Myth of Generational Conflict*, ed. Sara Arder and Claudine Attias-Donfut (London: Routledge, 2000), p. 108.

12. The principle applies in all continental members of the European Union except the Netherlands (where, though still formally present in civil law, the provision has disappeared from the rules governing the provision of social assistance) and Denmark. See J. Millar and A. Warman, *Family Obligations in Europe* (London: Family Policy Studies Centre, 1996). The principle also survives in some former members of the Soviet bloc, such as Hungary. See OECD, *Social and Labour Market Policies in Hungary.* (Paris: OECD, 1995), p. 168.

13. OECD, *The Battle against Exclusion, Volume 3: Social Assistance in Canada and Switzerland* (Paris: OECD, 1999): p. 158.

14. Ibid., p. 87.

15. The overall regressive impact of the subsidy depends, of course, on the net incidence of the taxes through which revenue is raised. If consumption taxes and import levies are a significant revenue source, they will clearly have an impact, at least in part, on the informal sector.

16. For a discussion of how a system of income security for employees in the formal sector could be designed to avoid this problem, see. A. C. Edwards and C. Manning, "The Economics of Employment Protection, and Unemployment Insurance Schemes: Policy Options for Indonesia, Malaysia, the Philippines, and Thailand," in *East Asian Labour Markets and the Economic Crisis: Impacts, Responses and Lessons,* ed. Gordon Betcherman and Rizwanul Islam (Washington, D.C., and Geneva: World Bank and International Labor Organization, 2000), pp. 345–78.

17. I am grateful to Chongcharen Sornkaew (Country Director for Thailand, Global Alliance for Workers and Communities) for this observation in the course of the ASEM Social Lessons Bangkok seminar.

18. OECD, *Caring for Frail Elderly People: Policies in Evolution* (Paris: OECD, 1996). For a discussion of the relation of social protection to family living arrangements in Asian countries, see Peter Scherer, op. cit.

19. OECD, *Labour Market and Social Safety Net Policies in Korea* (Paris: OECD, 2000).

CHAPTER 3

How the East Asian Crisis Changed the Social Situation

by Tamar Manuelyan Atinc

ABSTRACT: This chapter reviews the effect of the 1997–98 East Asian crisis on households in the five most affected countries—Indonesia, the Republic of Korea, Malaysia, the Philippines, and Thailand—and their responses to the crisis. It focuses on what actually happened to poverty levels and inequality during the crisis years. It addresses the four major ways that the crisis affected households: through falling demand for labor associated with the economic contraction, relative price changes caused by massive devaluation of the region's currencies, a potential public spending squeeze in response to falling revenues, and possible erosion of the social fabric. It details what is known about how households in fact responded and how governments pursued measures in response. The main messages are that households and governments largely reacted to the crisis in sensible ways and that the impact on household welfare, though substantial, was less than originally feared. However, the crisis exposed important limitations in the ability of private and public safety nets to cope with a shock of this magnitude. The chapter ends by briefly outlining major social and demographic changes (aging, urbanization) that lie ahead.

In the wake of the Asian financial crisis of 1997–98, households and governments in East Asia had to adjust to the first serious economic contraction in a generation, and with it wild swings in the relative prices of food, manufactured products, and services (see Table 3.1). This chapter reviews the impact of the crisis on households in the five East Asian countries most affected by it—Indonesia, the Republic of Korea, Malaysia, the Philippines, and Thailand—and the responses, of both households and governments, to the crisis.

Table 3.1 Main Indicators of Economic Activity and Household Impact (%)

	Per capita GDP growth		Per capita private consumption growth		Inflation (Consumer Price Index)		Poverty incidence[a]		Unemployment rates[b]		Government spending[c]	
	1990–96	1998	1990–96	1998	1990–96	1998	1996	1998	1996	1998	Education	Health
Indonesia	5.7	–14.4	6.8	–4.7	8.8	57.6	11.3	16.7	4.9	5.5	72.3	87.8
Korea	6.3	–6.6	6.5	–10.2	6.0	7.5	9.6	19.2	2.0	6.8	94.2	96.8
Malaysia	7.0	–9.3	5.4	–12.6	4.2	5.3	8.2	n.a.	2.5	3.2	86.3	90.3
Philippines	0.4	–2.6	1.0	1.3	9.8	9.7	37.5	n.a.	8.6	10.1	103.8	92.2
Thailand	7.0	–10.8	6.4	–15.1	5.0	8.1	11.4	13.0	1.8	4.5	98.7	89.3

n.a. = not available.

a. The numbers for poverty incidence are derived using national poverty lines and are based on income for Malaysia, the Philippines, and Thailand, and on consumption expenditure for Indonesia and Korea. Poverty incidence numbers for Malaysia and the Philippines are for 1997; figures for Korea are for urban areas only.

b. Unemployment rates are annual averages.

c. In general, the figures show the ratio of government spending in 1998 to government spending in 1997. These figures are adjusted using the gross domestic product (GDP) deflator from International Financial Statistics (IFS) for Korea, the Philippines, and Thailand. The figures for Malaysia reflect the GDP deflator from the Malaysian Department of Statistics. For Indonesia, the figure for education spending is the ratio of spending for 1998 to spending for 1996, and the health spending was obtained from World Bank staff estimates.

Effects of the Crisis on Poverty, Inequality, and Households

Poverty

Poverty increased substantially in all countries hit by the crisis.[1] Korea experienced the sharpest rise, as the proportion of poor people in Korea's cities rose from 7.5 percent just before the crisis in the first quarter of 1997 to a peak of 22.9 percent in the third quarter of 1998. Poverty rates then declined rapidly to 15.7 percent in the last quarter of 1998.

Indonesia was hardest hit by the confluence of financial, political, and El Niño shocks, and saw the ranks of the poor swell dramatically. The percentage of households falling below the poverty line rose from 11.3 percent in 1996 to 16.7 percent in 1998; an additional 10 million to 12 million people were thus pushed into poverty.[2]

In Thailand the poverty head count grew from 11.4 percent in 1996 to almost 13 percent in 1998, as an additional 1.1 million people fell below the poverty line. In Malaysia simulations suggest a rise in poverty incidence from 8.2 percent in 1997 to 11.2 percent in 1998. In the Philippines more than 90 percent of families reported being adversely affected by higher prices of food and other commodities, whereas 17 percent reported a job loss within the country, and a further 5 percent reported a job loss from retrenchment of migrant workers.[3] Throughout the region, investment fell much more sharply than consumption—a typical pattern in systemic economic shocks.

Inequality

Concern about rising inequality in many East Asian economies was growing before the financial crisis. Inequality had been rising particularly sharply in China, Hong Kong (China), Malaysia, Thailand, and the Philippines, as indicated by Gini indexes (a measure of inequality) ranging from the mid- to high 40s, close to averages in Sub-Saharan Africa and Latin America, the two most notoriously unequal regions of the world. Strikingly, aggregate indexes for inequality in Indonesia, Korea, and Thailand, appear to have moved little during the crisis years. However, the crisis affected various social groups in quite different ways and degrees.

In Thailand the percentage of people living in poverty in urban areas changed little (1.6 percent in 1996 versus 1.5 percent in 1998) despite the clearly urban nature of the initial shock, whereas rural poverty rose from 15 percent to 17.2

percent. The drop in real incomes was most severe for those with education below elementary levels.

In Indonesia urban areas and Java were hit substantially harder than other parts of the country, and the percentage of people living in poverty in urban areas rose more sharply than in rural areas. However, because a majority of Indonesia's population lives in rural areas, more rural people became poor as a result of the crisis. While the nominal Gini coefficient changed very little over the crisis period, there were important differences in urban and rural areas. The nominal Gini does not account for price changes in measuring inequality, which is important in Indonesia because the poor have faced higher inflation than the rich (because of the increase in the relative price of food, which accounts for a larger share of the consumption basket of the poor). Calculating the Gini coefficient on the basis of appropriately deflated household incomes yields a slight drop in urban inequality (0.299 to 0.289) but an increase in rural inequality (0.265 to 0.289).

There was practically no change in the Gini coefficient for urban Korea calculated on the basis of household consumption levels, whereas the Gini coefficient that was based on income registered a significant rise from 0.271 to 0.301 between 1997 and 1998. This is caused, in part, by the differential savings behavior of households during the crisis. The data show very sharp increases in the ranks of the ultrapoor (from 1.2 million in 1996 to 3 million in 1998; see Table 3.2), consistent with the higher increases observed in the distributionally more sensitive poverty indicators. Between the first quarter of 1997 and the third quarter of 1998, the head–count index tripled, the poverty gap quadrupled (1.3 percent to 5.6 percent), and the severity of poverty quintupled (0.4 percent to 2.0 percent). Poverty incidence rose more for households headed by individuals with lower levels of education, although households headed by high school graduates and above accounted for a full two-thirds of the poor, reflecting Korea's high overall levels of educational attainment.

Despite the material effects of the crisis on the welfare of poor households throughout the region, increases in poverty and inequality were generally smaller than originally anticipated. Five main factors help explain this unexpected outcome. First, contraction of economic output was smaller and less protracted than expected. Second, labor mobility between the formal and informal and urban and rural sectors may have cushioned the impact of the crisis by distributing the burden more broadly. Third, the relative price changes induced by currency devaluations probably favored the rural poor engaged in producing marketable surpluses, especially for export. Fourth, poor households reduced savings and reallocated items within their budgets to protect their consumption of critical

Table 3.2 Changes in Korea's Poor Show the Vulnerability of the Poorest People

	1996	*1997*	*1998*
Ultrapoor:			
Number (millions)	1.2	1.1	3.0
Growth (%)	−27.7	−11.1	178.7
Marginal poor:			
Number (millions)	1.9	1.7	3.3
Growth (%)	−20.6	−8.4	90.0
Poor:			
Number (millions)	3.1	2.8	6.2
Growth (%)	−23.5	−9.5	123.8
Near-poor:			
Number (millions)	2.9	2.7	4.1
Growth (%)	−13.4	−6.5	50.6

Note: The ultrapoor are households with per capita consumption at less than 80 percent of the poverty line. The marginal poor and the near-poor have per capita consumption at 80–100 percent and 100–120 percent of the poverty line, respectively.

Source: Nonak Kakwani and Nicholas Prescott, "Impact of Economic Crisis on Poverty and Inequality in Korea," mimeo., World Bank, Washington, D.C., 1999.

items, such as staple foods. Finally, public transfers in the form of unemployment insurance and other safety nets may also have played a role.

Households

In the book *East Asia: The Road to Recovery*, I identified four main mechanisms through which the crisis affected household welfare: falling demand for labor associated with the economic contraction, relative price changes caused by the massive devaluation of the region's currencies, potential public spending squeezes in response to falling revenues, and possible erosion of the social fabric.[4] In the following sections I discuss the first two areas, for which reasonable data are available.

Labor Markets

A drop in demand for labor was the most important channel through which the crisis affected most households. High-income households also suffered substantial losses in property incomes (from dividends, capital gains, and rents). Shocks in labor demand hurt households through lower real wages, higher unemployment or underemployment (those working less than 20 hours), and reduced self-employment earnings. Whether the major impact stemmed from a change in the number of people working or a change in their income depends on the structure of the labor market, in which regulations make it more difficult or costly for employers to lay off workers, and collective bargaining arrangements, which affect the extent of downward wage flexibility. The prevalence of migrants, domestic or foreign, in urban areas also influences the outcome. Households, in turn, respond to shocks in various ways. Labor force participation (including child labor) and the number of hours worked may rise or decline to compensate for lower wages. Sectoral employment patterns can also change in response to the impact of currency devaluation (for example, away from construction and manu-facturing, initially, toward agriculture), and labor may move from the formal sec-tor, which sustains the initial impact, toward self-employment and informal activities. Those initial effects and responses can produce different outcomes with respect to gender, age, income level, and differentials between skilled and unskilled wages.

What does the evidence show for the impact of the crisis on labor markets in the five most affected countries? The largest shocks to the domestic labor force occurred in Indonesia, Korea, and Thailand. The Philippines had participated less in the recent economic boom (and hence suffered less from the crisis), and in Malaysia foreign labor bore the brunt of the adjustment burden. In all coun-tries, younger, less-skilled casual workers, as well as workers in the informal sec-tor, were particularly vulnerable. Much of the adjustment to the fall in labor demand occurred through a decline in real wages. However, substantial variation occurred across the five countries, depending on the importance of the formal sector and the rigidity of the labor market. Unemployment and underemploy-ment increased significantly in Korea and Thailand. Work force participation rates fell in Korea and Malaysia, stayed constant in Thailand, and rose in Indonesia, where women, especially those age 25 and older, scrambled to supple-ment household resources in the wake of huge income drops.[5] Work became much more informal, as labor shifted from the formal sector and employee sta-tus into self-employment, unpaid family work, and agriculture. In Indonesia and Thailand the relatively larger (smallholder) agriculture sector appears to have acted as a shock absorber, leading to smaller increases in open unemployment in those countries (especially Indonesia) than in Korea.

Korea experienced the sharpest rise in open unemployment, from 2.5 percent just before the crisis to a peak of 8.7 percent in February 1999, before it fell to 4.6 percent in October 1999. Many people gave up searching for another job when they became unemployed and thus became part of the inactive population; between the second quarter of 1997 and the fourth quarter of 1998, the econom-ically inactive population grew by 9 percent, or 1.2 million people. Most of the newly unemployed were low-paid workers—temporary and daily workers, self-employed workers, and unpaid family workers—and therefore could not benefit from unemployment insurance. Women were significantly affected, representing nearly three-quarters of those who became economically inactive. Female workers were laid off before their male counterparts, and many opted for voluntary retirement in anticipation of layoffs; some were subsequently rehired on short-term contracts with reduced benefits. From October 1997 to October 1998 the number of regular female employees dropped by nearly 20 percent, compared with a 7.4 percent fall for males, and the number of female workers with short-term contracts rose while the same figure fell for males. Real wages in Korea also saw a substantial decline of 12.5 percent from mid-1997 until the end of 1998 before recovering during 1999. A large part of this decline may represent changes in the composition of employment: if workers shifted from higher-wage, formal-sector jobs to lower-wage, informal jobs, the average wage level would decline.

Indonesia presents a marked contrast to Korea—not unexpectedly, because Korea is the wealthiest, most urbanized, and most industrialized country in the region, whereas Indonesia is still poor, rural, and largely agricultural. In Indonesia, the decline in real wages proved far more important than the rise in unemployment. Open unemployment rose by very little (4.7 percent in August 1997 to 5.5 percent in August 1998) despite massive contraction in economic output. Underemployment also rose: 3.7 million more people were working fewer than 35 hours per week in 1998 than in 1997.[6] Labor force participation rates, meanwhile, rose overall, remaining constant for men but increasing substantially for women (49.9 percent to 51.1 percent). Only 55 percent of women age 25 and older participated in the labor force in 1996, compared with 72 percent in 1998. Indonesia is the only country among the "crisis five" in which labor force participation rose, reflecting relatively low levels of initial income (and therefore heightened vulnerability of poorer households), the severity of the economic crisis, and the inability of formal and informal safety nets to cope with the shock. The main effect on family welfare occurred through a decline in real wages. Formal sector wages fell by 34 percent in real terms between 1997 and 1998, and agricultural wages also fell massively—by 40 percent in real terms. The period also saw a major shift from formal to informal sector employment and from modern to agricultural sector employment (a net 5 million workers increase in agriculture).

In Thailand open employment increased more than in Indonesia but less than in Korea; unemployment rose from 2.3 percent in February 1997 to 4.8 percent in February 1998 and to 5.4 percent in February 1999. Unlike in Korea, the pickup in Thai economic activity does not appear to have boosted labor demand, so unemployment remained stubbornly high. Underemployment also increased sharply during the crisis, and some cuts in working hours observed between 1997 and 1998 may have translated into open unemployment by 1999. But falling wages had the largest effect on household incomes. Between February 1997 and February 1998, wages fell by 6 percent in real terms; the decline was higher in urban areas (–8.3 percent) than in rural areas (–4.7 percent). Lower wages appear to explain two-thirds of the decline in real per capita incomes, with lower employment accounting for the remaining third.[7] Well-integrated rural and urban labor markets in Thailand explain the widely distributed drop in wages and the rise in rural poverty—many unemployed migrants sought work in rural areas. Changes in patterns of internal migration during the crisis were significant.

The effect of the economic crisis on domestic labor was less adverse in Malaysia and the Philippines. Malaysia's large number of foreign workers (20 percent of the labor force) provided an extensive cushion for Malaysian workers because foreign migrants bore the brunt of the adjustment burden. With a fall in participation rates, particularly for women, open unemployment was limited; the unemployment rate rose modestly, from 2.7 percent in 1997 to 3.2 percent in 1998. Unemployment rates in the Philippines tend to be high (8–9 percent) compared with those in Korea, Malaysia, and Thailand, and, like Indonesia, the Philippines is a net exporter of labor to the region and beyond. Unemployment rates rose throughout 1998 but fell thereafter, whereas real wages remained essentially constant throughout the period.

Price Changes

Massive depreciation of the region's currencies meant large changes in relative prices (see Figure 3.1). This raised incentives for the production of tradable goods and should therefore have benefited the agriculture sector in particular. These changes help the rural poor if they are net producers of food and if increases in consumer prices or in world prices in terms of domestic currency are passed down to producers. Regrettably, important unknowns remain here; detailed information on household expenditure patterns is available, but there is less information on the production side. Food prices rose relative to other commodities in all five crisis countries, but these changes were minor except in Indonesia, where food prices rose by 40 percent between mid-1997 and mid-1998. The sharp increase in relative prices of food was particularly hard on the urban poor and on rural workers who are net consumers, but most rural households benefited from the favorable shift in the terms of trade.

In Indonesia the direction of change in farmers' terms of trade varied by region, from +10 percent to –15 percent. Regions with substantial production of

Figure 3.1   Relative Food Prices

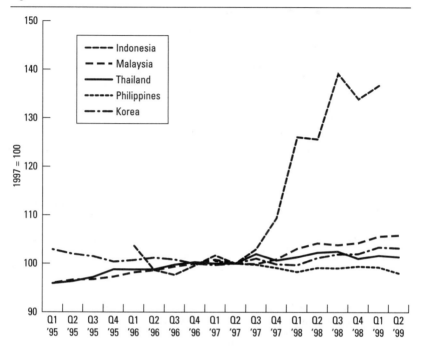

key export commodities, such as sea products, plywood, and rubber (Kalimatan, Sulawesi), experienced favorable changes in terms of trade, while rice-producing regions (Java) did not reap net benefits from the rise in rice prices.

Concern arose early in the crisis that prices for pharmaceuticals, essential drugs, and contraceptives would rise to unaffordable levels, sharply curtailing use, with adverse effect on morbidity, fertility, and HIV/AIDS rates, in particular. Higher medical costs did hit the poor and the elderly particularly hard in several countries, including Malaysia. In Korea, among all categories of household spending, prices of medical expenditures rose at the fastest rate, averaging 1.8 percent per quarter compared with an overall quarterly inflation rate of 1.4 percent.

Household Responses to the Crisis

Apart from experiencing changes in labor supply, households in the five crisis-affected countries reacted to the shock in a multitude of ways. Households reallocated expenditures to protect critical items in their budget. In Indonesia, per capita food expenditures declined in absolute terms for urban and rural households between 1997 and 1998, but the share of expenditures allocated to food rose.[8] Despite the overall decline in food expenditures, households raised per capita spending on staples by 5 percent in urban areas and by 11.5 percent in rural areas (see Table 3.3). Data for Indonesia and Korea suggest that households also reduced their expenditures on nonessential expenditures that could be delayed (clothing, recreation, household goods), so the share of these expenditures within household budgets fell.

The extent to which households protected their expenditures on education and health varied considerably across countries. In Indonesia, such expenditures fell in both absolute and relative terms. In Korea, in contrast, cuts in spending on education and health were smaller than overall reductions in household expenditures. Meanwhile, in Indonesia per capita expenditures on adult goods—alcohol and tobacco—declined only slightly (7 percent) in urban areas, while the share of these goods among total household expenditures

Table 3.3 Consumption Patterns for Households in Indonesia during the Crisis (thousand rupiahs per month, in 1997 prices)

	Urban			*Rural*		
	1997	*1998*	*% change*	*1997*	*1998*	*% change*
Household expenditure	319	211	−33.9	194	168	−13.4
Food[a]	188.1	134.9	−28.3	147.8	135.8	−8.1
Staples	41.4	43.5	4.9	59.3	66.2	11.5
Meat	40.5	21.9	−45.8	24.2	16.4	−32.3
Dairy	11.7	7.9	−32.4	5.2	4.4	−14.4
Oil	6.2	6.1	−1.0	5.2	4.2	−20.5
Vegetables	28.4	18.0	−36.8	22.3	21.7	−2.3
Nonfood[a]						
Alcohol/tobacco	13.0	12.1	−6.9	8.6	6.8	−21.0
Health	5.5	3.1	−43.0	2.3	1.2	−48.5
Education	15.7	9.5	−39.2	4.6	3.0	−34.1
Household goods	26.1	14.3	−44.9	7.0	5.3	−23.5
Transport	10.0	6.8	−32.8	3.5	2.5	−27.4
Clothing	9.4	5.2	−44.2	4.3	2.5	−41.0
Housing	34.4	19.3	−43.9	11.9	8.1	−32.0
Recreation	8.2	4.3	−47.4	3.6	2.9	−19.6

a. Per capita expenditures on different data.

Source: Indonesia Family Life Surveys (IFLS); IFLS2 and IFLS2+ data. E. Frankenberg, D. Thomas, and K. Beegle, "The Real Costs of Indonesia's Economic Crisis: Preliminary Findings from the Indonesia Family Life Surveys," Rand Labor and Population Program, Working Paper Series 99-04, Santa Monica, Calif., 1999.

actually rose. In rural areas, although the overall share of alcohol and tobacco declined slightly, the percentage decline was among the lowest among nonfood items.

It is somewhat surprising that households did not reduce savings by more to protect their overall consumption levels. Indeed, the data for Korea suggest that, in the aggregate, households *increased* savings in 1998 relative to previous years, although saving behavior varied significantly depending on household income.

Households unable to smooth consumption (by spending savings, borrowing, selling assets, and receiving public or private transfers) may take shorter-term coping measures, some of which have severe long-run implications. Reduced nutritional intake, a delay in seeking preventive health care, and shortened schooling may spell irreversible losses in human capital and related income-earning potential. Although family survival may depend on a child's income, such responses are costly: children are denied an opportunity to escape poverty and can face physical and mental harm. It is precisely the role of public policy to ensure that families do not have to resort to destructive coping mechanisms while taking care not to displace effective family and community responses to temporary income shocks.

In Thailand the use of public education and health services expanded during the crisis, including the use of basic services. By contrast preliminary data from Indonesia showed a large drop in health care utilization rates: whereas 53 percent of those reporting an illness sought modern medical care in 1997, only 41 percent sought care in 1998. Among people who sought care, fewer went to public facilities (27 percent in 1997 and 20 percent in 1998), perhaps reflecting a perceived drop in quality following budget cuts. But there is no evidence of an increase in the number of children with low weight for their height (wasting) or low height for their age (stunting). In Indonesia aggregate school enrollment rates did not change much during the crisis: primary enrollment rose slightly from 1997–98 to 1998–99, from 94 percent to 95 percent, whereas secondary enrollment dropped slightly, from 54.5 percent to 53.2 percent. However, whereas in 1997 there was no correlation between per capita expenditure and enrollment rates, in 1998 lower per capita expenditure was associated with a lower probability of enrollment, indicating that poorer families had more difficulty keeping their children in school.[9] There are also indications that some students elected to prolong tertiary studies until labor market opportunities improved. In Thailand evidence points to a limited or negligible impact of the crisis on school dropouts. A 1998 nationwide survey in the Philippines suggested that 7 percent of families included in the study pulled children out of school during the crisis period.

Government Responses to the Crisis

The onset of the financial crisis was sudden, and its social consequences caught policymakers off guard. Designing policies and interventions quickly in the context of severe information gaps, rapid change, declining revenues, weak institutional capacity, and a limited menu of pro-poor programs proved a considerable challenge. Citizens, meanwhile, did not place clear demands on governments for social programs, possibly because of an ethos of self-reliance or an absence of channels for citizens' voices. Even so, governments generally pursued sensible policies under the circumstances. Many East Asian countries made substantial efforts to collect more information on social conditions during the crisis, using rapid qualitative assessments to diagnose particular points of vulnerability and quantitative surveys to monitor more systematically the effect on households and benefits of government programs.

Korea went the furthest in expanding safety nets. This reflected greater demands for public action—possibly encouraged by democratic institutions—as well as a greater capacity of the government to respond and a more extensive network of precrisis pro-poor programs. All countries tried to restore health and education spending once fiscal targets were loosened, but they succeeded to varying degrees. Efforts were least successful in Indonesia, where total public sector health spending fell by 8 percent in 1997–98 and a further 12 percent in 1998–99, whereas total public expenditures on education collapsed by 41 percent between 1996–97 and 1997–98, but rebounded somewhat in 1998–99 to 72 percent of precrisis levels. Those dramatic reductions in real spending reflect significant inflation in Indonesia during the crisis period. The effect of real spending cuts on service delivery is difficult to determine, as the bulk would have translated into real wage declines for teachers and health workers. In Korea and Thailand social sector spending also declined in real terms between 1997 and 1998 but stayed constant as a share of gross domestic product (GDP). There is evidence that within the smaller envelope for health, countries protected spending on primary care.

Differences also appeared in the instruments that countries used to mitigate the effect of the crisis (see Table 3.4). In light of the considerable corruption problems associated with public service delivery, Indonesia stayed away from reliance on direct cash transfers. Indonesia pursued specific interventions to keep children in school, as did Thailand (with the highest ratio of youth in the labor force). Food security was a primary concern in Indonesia and the Philippines, where the impact of the drought was most severe. Social funds—special institutions and programs designed to support community and nongovernmental organization (NGO)–sponsored social programs—were introduced in countries with an active NGO community or where government institutions were failing, such as Indonesia. Finally, training programs, not particularly effective as a crisis response, were perhaps most suitable for Thailand, where a skills gap had emerged before the crisis.

Prior to the crisis, publicly provided safety nets tended to be limited in scale and coverage, reflecting reliance on rapid growth and full employment, strong family-level and community-level supports, and social stigmas associated with public transfers. In Thailand major safety net programs represented only 2 percent of the government budget in 1996; in Malaysia spending on social assistance amounted to 1.7 percent of the current budget in 1997. After the crisis began, social safety nets expanded in all countries. This was most evident in Korea—which made concerted policy decisions—where the share of GDP for social protection rose from 0.6 percent in 1997 to 1.26 percent in 1998, and to almost 2 percent in 1999. In Indonesia outlays for redefined "core" safety net programs rose from about 1 percent of GDP in 1998–99 to 1.25 percent in 1999–2000.

A dominant strategy across virtually all countries was the use of public works to generate employment. Indonesia substantially expanded its *padat karya* program in response to the crisis, creating an estimated 58 million days of labor that annually benefited more than 400,000 people. In Korea, since most of the jobless did not benefit from unemployment insurance despite expansion of the scheme, the government introduced a new public works program in May 1998. By January 1999 the program was providing 437,000 jobs and making a dent in the unemployment rate. However, the number of applicants was even higher at 650,000. Community-based investment funds, notably newly introduced programs in Indonesia and Thailand, were intended to generate both employment-driven and demand-driven infrastructure.

Among the five countries, only Korea had an expanded unemployment insurance scheme. The country expanded this relatively young program of mandated insurance in 1998 from firms with more than 30 employees to cover firms with at least 5 employees, as well as to cover temporary and daily workers. This meant a substantial increase in coverage, from 5.7 million people in January 1998 to 8.7 million people by the end of the year. The government also shortened the contribution period required to activate eligibility and extended the duration of benefit payments. As a result of these changes, the number of unemployment insurance beneficiaries rose but still stood at a low

Table 3.4. Upgraded Social Safety Net Programs in East Asia during the Crisis

	Food security	Cash transfers	Social funds	Health and education	Workfare programs	Unemployment assistance/ insurance/ severance pay	Active labor market policies
Indonesia	New program of targeted distribution of cheap rice (OPK).		Community-based programs.	New back-to-school program (provided scholarships for the poorest students and school grants for schools in the poorest communities). Subsidies to maintain prices of essential drugs.	Expanded and redesigned *padat karya* program.		
Korea		New temporary, noncontributory, means-tested livelihood protection program and social pension for the elderly.			New public workfare scheme.	Expanded unemployment insurance program.	Expanded active labor market programs (vocational training, wage subsidies, job placement).

Country						
Malaysia						Expanded training for unemployed workers.
Philippines						New computerized job assistance network and some expansion of training.
Thailand	Expanded social pension for the elderly and cash transfers to needy families.	New community-based programs.	Expanded programs to provide low-income health card for the poor and voluntary health insurance card for the near-poor. Expanded scholarships and educational loan programs. Provision for families to pay fees in installments, for fee waivers, and for free uniforms to students. Expanded school lunch program.	New public workfare scheme.	Higher severance payments. New Employee Welfare Fund to partially finance unpaid severance claims for workers from bankrupt firms.	Expanded training for unemployed workers. Self-employment loans.

10 percent of the unemployed labor force in March 1999, up from 1.9 percent initially.

Korea also implemented a large wage-subsidy program, which paid one-third to two-thirds of a worker's wage if the firm could demonstrate a need for economic adjustment.[10] In 1998 the program covered 800,000 workers, and in 1999 it was expanded and the duration of the subsidy increased from 6 to 8 months.[11] A survey of enterprises suggests that 22.3 percent of jobs would have been lost without the subsidy, confirming international experience that wage subsidies usually subsidize jobs that would have existed in any event. Korea, Malaysia, and Thailand modified their severance pay schemes. Thailand extended the maximum amount of severance pay to 10 months and set up a fund to pay legislated severance amounts to workers whose firms went bankrupt. Malaysia also extended its severance pay scheme, allowing workers who quit voluntarily to receive severance pay.

Other strategies for income maintenance included cash or in-kind transfers. In Korea, the government expanded the means-tested Livelihood Protection Program—which provided cash and in-kind aid to those unable to work—in terms of both the number of people covered and the budget (nearly a 40 percent increase in 1998). In drought-stricken Indonesia, the government increased the public provision of rice while introducing a targeted rice subsidy program (*Operasi Pasar Khosus*—OPK) in July 1998 to replace a general rice price subsidy. Education scholarships and block transfers through the Indonesian Stay in School campaign provided incentives to families to keep children enrolled in school. Thailand expanded the low-income health insurance card program.

How effective was the public response to the crisis? Full evaluations are not yet available for most programs in most countries.[12] However, although we do not yet know the full effect of these public programs, we do have important indicators (rates of enrollment, health care utilization, and child labor) that can change in the short term. We also know that severance pay, unemployment insurance, and wage subsidies largely benefit formal sector workers; there is evidence that the Indonesian *padat karya* program did not adequately reach women, among other specific findings.

In sum, the five governments implemented largely sensible policies in response to the economic crisis, expanding some safety net programs and attempting to protect expenditures in key sectors such as education and health (albeit with only partial success). But governments throughout the region were clearly hampered by their own lack of preparedness and menu of social programs to upgrade, by poor information, and by poor coordination.

Looking Ahead

This chapter highlights three main conclusions. First, the recent economic crisis in East Asia exerted a large, negative effect on household welfare. Poverty became more acute throughout the region, and other social indicators, such as school attendance, took a turn for the worse in some countries. However, the effect of the crisis on household welfare was less than had originally been feared. Second, households and governments reacted to the crisis largely in sensible ways. Households protected their consumption of critical items, such as staple foods, while the labor market reflected the impact of falling wages and the reduced availability of formal sector jobs. Governments beefed up safety net programs and worked hard to gather data that could be used to inform policies. Nonetheless, the crisis exposed important limitations in the ability of private and public safety nets to cope with a shock of this magnitude. This is a source of concern as the region's growing integration into the international economy may make incomes more volatile even as it heightens the need for institutions that can help households manage risk.

This is especially true because the faces and structures of East Asian societies are changing rapidly: they are becoming grayer, more urban, more formal, and more open economically and politically. These trends have important implications for social policies. Demographic changes will bring the issue of old-age security to the forefront and require changes in patterns of public spending. Economic changes, driven by shifts in employment, urbanization, and continued globalization, will be associated with greater labor mobility and more household insecurity. Expanded political participation will put social issues on the political agenda. These trends will exert pressure on informal, family-based mechanisms for household protection and expand demands for more formal, government-mandated schemes.

Demographic Trends

East Asia's population is aging rapidly, thanks to falling fertility and rising life expectancy at all ages; the region has one of the world's most pronounced aging patterns. The old-age dependency ratio is still relatively low, ranging mostly from 5 percent to 8 percent, but it is projected to double in 30 years, reaching the current old-age dependency ratio of Organization for Economic Cooperation and Development (OECD) economies.[13] The ratio is expected to triple to 27 percent by 2040—near projected levels in Europe and Central Asia and well above those of other developing regions. This aging is extremely rapid by historical comparisons: the elderly population doubled in France in 140 years and in Sweden in 86 years.

Changing demographics imply important consequences for public spending patterns and the design of social protection schemes. The changes suggest potentially greater vulnerability among the elderly population and the need to focus on old-age security programs, including pensions and health care. The youth dependency ratio is projected to fall from about the current 41 percent to 31 percent by 2040.[14] This, too, has important consequences for government spending, particularly in education.

Changes in fertility and life expectancy are closely related to income levels; Korea is furthest along in the demographic transition, with an old-age dependency ratio projected to reach 40 percent by 2040, whereas the corresponding figures for Lao People's Democratic Republic and Cambodia are 7.8 percent and 11.3 percent, respectively. There are exceptions: China's population is aging more rapidly than its income level would suggest, and the reverse seems true for Malaysia. Most East Asian countries will see fewer working-age people supporting a growing proportion of elderly people, with particularly significant implications for pension schemes.

Economic Trends

Urbanization and Services
In 1960 all East Asian countries were still largely agrarian, with less than one-third of their populations living in urban areas. Over the last 40 years the percentage of the urban population has grown, most dramatically in Korea, where the urban population rose from less than 30 percent in 1960 to over 80 percent in 1995. The urban share of the population is expected to top 50 percent in all but a few countries by 2030 and to reach more than 70 percent in Malaysia and the Philippines. Urbanization tends to go hand in hand with economic transformation. In 1996 the agriculture sector still accounted for a significant share of GDP and an even higher share of employment in many countries, reaching 70 percent and more in China and other transition economies. With continued industrialization and market liberalization, the share of agricultural employment is expected to drop quickly. Despite the recent crisis, more workers are projected to form part of the formal labor market in both market economies and those in transition.

Those trends are likely to weaken traditional social support systems and coping mechanisms. In predominantly agrarian societies with large families, informal arrangements, such as intergenerational income support for the elderly, have worked well. Cultural traditions in Asian societies, which emphasize strong family values, have helped preserve this system. However, the experience of Japan and Korea suggests that the forces of modernity are strong. More than two-thirds of parents age 60 and older still live with an adult child in Malaysia, the Philippines, Thailand, and Vietnam, but only 49 percent (1994) live with an adult child in Korea, down from 78 percent in 1984. In Japan, the proportion of people age 60 and above whose main source of income is the family was 5.7 percent in 1990, down from 15.6 percent in 1981 but still substantially higher than in Western countries (0.1 percent in the United Kingdom and 0.7 percent in the United States). Asian societies may exhibit great family solidarity, but the extent and coverage of private transfers is unlikely to be sufficient. Rapid urbanization, combined with falling fertility rates and overall increases in old-age dependency ratios, will place growing pressure on informal family- and community-based income support systems.

An increase in formal sector jobs generates a greater need for more formal mechanisms of social protection. Korea's recent experience illustrates the point: agriculture and the informal sector were unable to absorb the unemployed (unlike in Indonesia), spurring the largest increases in levels of open unemployment. Rising incomes, greater institutional capacity, and a more accessible tax base are all associated with growing formalization, making it more possible for countries to meet these demands.

The transition toward greater democracy and public participation is influencing the social agenda in much of East Asia. NGOs and civil society more broadly are demanding greater accountability in the use of public resources, most strikingly in Indonesia but also in Thailand. As political systems in the region mature, concerns articulated by civil society groups will put pressure on mainstream political institutions. New demands on governments will tend to push up government spending on social safety nets, as market economies respond to a more vocal middle class and transition economies ratchet down their support for state employees in favor of more affordable and equitable systems. Labor relations are an area in which such pressure seems particularly likely. Labor unions are seeking to redefine industrial relations, both to protect workers during hard times and to ensure that they share the benefits during good times. Striking a balance between the legitimate concerns of workers and the need to maintain flexible labor markets will be important. Mechanisms that mitigate the downside risks—unemployment insurance, for example—while retaining wage flexibility may offer a way forward.

An important risk is that political and social debate may revolve largely around the needs and aspirations of the new middle class, to the detriment of the needs of poor households and regions. A greater voice for the poor and for the champions of the poor is essential. The international community can play a part by keeping this issue squarely on the table.

Notes

1. Comparable pre- and postcrisis data are available for Indonesia, Korea, and Thailand. The 1999 round of the Malaysian Household Income Survey has not yet become publicly available. The Philippines conducted a new survey (Annual Poverty Indicators Survey—APIS) in 1998, but, unfortunately, consumption data are not comparable between the regular survey (Family Income and Expenditure Survey—FIES) conducted in 1997 and the APIS because the latter used a truncated consumption questionnaire. Income data are also not comparable because the APIS used a 6-month reference period, whereas the FIES used an annual reference period.

2. This estimate is based on the 1998 Social and Economic Survey of Indonesian Households (SUSENAS) subsample of 10,000 households; other sources suggest that poverty may have been higher at the peak of the crisis.

3. These results stem from the initial findings of the APIS survey.

4. World Bank, *East Asia: The Road to Recovery* (Washington, D.C.: World Bank, 1998).

5. Susan Horton and Dipak Mazumdar, "Vulnerable Groups and the Labor Market: The Aftermath of the Asian Financial Crisis" (paper presented at a meeting of the World Bank, International Labor Organization, Japan Ministry of Labor, and Japan Institute of Labor on "Economic Crisis, Employment, and Labor Markets in East and Southeast Asia," Tokyo, October 13–15, 1999.

6. Ibid.

7. Nanak Kakwani and J. Pothong, "Impact of Economic Crisis on the Standard of Living in Thailand" (Bangkok: National Economic and Social Development Board, Development Evaluation Division, 1999).

8. Data are from the Indonesia Family Life Survey (IFLS).

9. Data are from IFLS2+.

10. The firm could demonstrate need by shutting down 2 or more days a month, cutting hours by more than 10 percent, granting leave of a month or more to employees, transferring workers to affiliates, or switching to a new line of business while retaining at least 60 percent of existing employees. See Horton and Mazumdar, op cit.

11. See Horton and Mazumdar, op cit.

12. In 1999 Thailand conducted a special round of the regular household survey (Socioeconomic Survey) containing a crisis module, which included information on the assistance that each household member received from specific social safety net schemes.

13. The old-age dependency ratio is defined as the ratio of population age 65 and above to the population age 15–64.

14. The youth dependency ratio is defined as the ratio of population age 0–14 to the population age 15–64.

BOX 1.2

Models and Politics for Asian Social Policies
by François Godemont

Throughout the 1980s and early 1990s the European welfare state repelled Asians more than it attracted them.[1] It was seen as addressing issues specific to Europe (high social costs and unemployment, graying demographic forecasts, and conflictual labor relations), whereas the Western liberal market model seemed better suited to East Asia's needs. Traditional employment systems based on customary relationships and stratification were seen as ensuring equitable economic growth and social stability, making a redistributive welfare system such as Europe's irrelevant and unnecessary.

Two developments jolted this Asian social model out of its complacency. It was shaken first by a decade of accelerating growth that pushed several Asian countries into the ranks of developed or nearly developed economies, and second by the Asian financial crisis of 1997–98.

Challenge from Above: Impact of Economic Growth on Welfare Policies

As Asia's most advanced economies (after Japan)—Hong Kong (China), the Republic of Korea, Singapore, and Taiwan (China)—grew richer and began exhibiting characteristics inherent to the European welfare system, they created new social protection policies such as medical care, social or housing assistance, and minimum retirement levels. Japan itself was the precursor; Japan's social spending rose in the late 1980s to levels greater than those in the United States—social security disbursement was 10.9 percent of national income in 1987 (against 8.8 percent in the United States). Other examples of far-reaching social policy reforms include the national health system in Korea; the unified medical care system in Taiwan, China, which has mandatory pricing of doctor fees; the

This summary is based on a presentation at the June 2000 Paris Asia–Europe Meeting (ASEM) seminar.

continued on next page

BOX 1.2, continued

Provident Fund in Singapore, which in effect functions as a potential insurance scheme; the complex welfare systems in Hong Kong, China, which in effect guarantee minimum incomes to citizens; and generous public housing schemes in Hong Kong (China) and Singapore.

A striking political feature of these reforms is how they came about and who supported them. They have been promoted either directly by political forces that defend the status quo, or indirectly in response to new challenges from electoral competition. Increased social spending was often backed by established political forces. Because long-standing political majorities were traditionally associated with clientary relationships and promotion of Asian family values, their conversion to social spending was not viewed as a revolutionary development but as a traditional form of public action, countering market forces and forcing a collective approach to social problems.

Challenge from Below: Social Welfare after the Asian Financial Crisis

The financial crisis revealed the huge underlying inequality created by gains in capital stock. As asset values collapsed, so did the fortunes of the well-connected entrepreneurial class and the new urban class. Gross domestic product (GDP) decline and resulting business failures suddenly brought lower wages and high unemployment to both formal and informal sectors. The financial crisis had two contradictory results: reversing the trend to underlying property inequality that had been growing since the early 1980s,[2] and increasing absolute poverty. Urban middle classes were proportionally harder hit by a crisis that was financial in nature than lower-income groups. The trend toward poverty eradication by way of economic growth was reversed and East Asia faced increased unemployment and dislocation of many public services.

The crisis presented further challenges to the traditional social contract, and it accelerated the transition from "old" economies, based on labor costs and delocalization of mature and labor-intensive industries, to the "new" economy and technology-based enterprises, especially in

BOX 1.2, continued

the electronic and information sector. The shape of recovery in Asian economies dictated a shift to industries and activities based on knowledge and new skills. New directions of growth will surely accentuate education gaps, with an added twist. Asian economies have relied on Asian graduates and returnees from top Western universities to fill important technical and managerial positions. This educational flow slowed because of lower incomes and higher relative costs. In Malaysia, students going abroad dropped sharply, and in poorer countries, particularly Indonesia, enrollment at every level of education declined.

These fundamental changes will leave an imprint on future politics and necessitate changes in public policies. Public demand for accountability, repudiation of past corrupt practices, and a general move toward a more open democracy and social system are one feature. In Korea, unions formerly torn between recognized entities and extralegal organizations have acquired a new collective sense of legitimacy, and with it increased social bargaining power.

From the political point of view, it makes sense for Asian governments to pursue proactive social policies. These policies will almost always run the risk of being tainted with locally corrupt practices, but social subsidies are not the only or the most vulnerable areas of public policies for corruption; privatization policies in the Philippines, for example, have been described as a key area of public fraud.[3] An intermediate course can be to supplement market economics with social welfare actions managed, if not entirely financed, by nongovernmental organizations (NGOs) rather than by state bureaucracies. Charity and private welfare are a tradition in many Asian cultures, from Buddhism to the philanthropic actions of merchant classes and local organizations. NGO action complements state authority but does not necessarily compete with it. It may bypass corrupt practices in local bureaucracies. The concept of NGO action fits the image of a minimal safety net that would cost little, imply minimum overall administrative reform, and interfere little with what is seen as the only desirable course: a speedy transition to free market economics and open competition, including for social practices.

continued on next page

BOX 1.2, continued

Models

It is important to beware the temptation to characterize East Asia's social policies simplistically in terms of models. Japan, for example, suggests a zigzag course, from the rise of a public and corporatist welfare system along with economic growth to that model's present demise after a decade of economic and financial crisis. The more advanced emerging economies of Asia each created elements of a public welfare system. At the other end of the scale, China is an emerging economy that created very early on elements of a complex social security system, chiefly to deal with unemployment and retirement issues. The legacy of the socialist era "iron bowl" is compelling, but China's mixture of experimentation, pragmatism, and legal enactment is unique among developing economies. These reforms acted as an essential stabilizer during the Asian crisis.

East Asian governments have tinkered with social formulas that answer partial and temporary needs, but this has had much less impact than self-help on family and subsistence sectors. Korea is an exception, as the only country with a balance of active social forces, mirroring some European examples; it is also the only one that has implemented significant social reforms, a mix of liberal (or new "third way") approaches enhancing the back-to-work priority of more classic welfare policies. This is definitely not a safety net approach but a welfare system. Indonesia and Thailand have pursued much more limited social policies, in keeping with both their income levels and the safety net concept. The poorer of the two (Indonesia) has the most comprehensive and nonideological approach, mixing NGO, community, and local administration approaches in a state led (and internationally financed) approach. Civil servants, if not the state itself, are agents of these programs that hinge on community watchdogs. Thailand's *pro bono* approach is a gratifying story of community action and NGOs, though on a limited scale.

Reform and transition from a political or customary model to a market economy seem unavoidable. This political dynamic will increasingly dictate public social policies that would have seemed unimaginable before the Asian crisis. Democratic debate and voter preferences will certainly push in this direction.

BOX 1.2, continued

1. An exception is the Philippines, where after the fall of the Marcos regime in 1986, the Aquino and Ramos administrations called often for a more humane social model involving European features.

2. Except for those who kept hidden assets overseas invested in Western financial and real estate markets. A major problem today (for example, in Indonesia), is to persuade owners of this hidden capital to return it.

3. See Walden Bello, "Payoff Scandal Hits ADB-Backed Power Privatization in the Philippines," available at the Web site of the Asia-Europe Dialogue on Alternative Political Strategies, <http://www.ased.org/resources/global/articles/bello3.htm>.

CHAPTER 4

The East Asian Crisis: Lessons for the Social Policy Agenda

by Katherine Marshall

ABSTRACT: This chapter highlights key lessons from the East Asian economic crisis about the implications of economic swings and crises for the social agenda. The first and most obvious lesson is that countries and their partners need to better prepare for socioeconomic crises by developing more extensive safety net programs, as well as the information essential to designing, managing, and assessing them. The means by which countries transform social policy—especially how far they enhance transparency and accountability and involve civil society—emerges as critical.

Although the 1997–98 socioeconomic crisis in East Asia affected different countries differently, its rapid progression and the clear role of economic and social contagion jolted preconceptions of national and international policymakers about economic management, development, and social safety nets. The resulting rethinking of many assumptions has been perhaps most evident in the realm of social policy.

This policy rethinking focused on three major elements. The first entailed a quest for effective measures to address the immediate and visible consequences of the crisis. Countries launched programs to create jobs, created mechanisms to protect social expenditures during budget cuts, and sought to cushion the impact of increases in food and medical prices and the tendency of parents during hard times to take children out of school. Second, as it became apparent that "normal" times would not return for some time, if ever, leaders pursued a broader-based effort to redesign the social safety net to respond to both current and future crises. Finally, individual countries and the region as a whole began to reconsider the prevailing assumptions—that economic growth and job creation should constitute the core of social policy, and that the dangers of the "welfare state" (creating dependency on government and undermining family values) outweigh its social and economic benefits.

Civil society, including nongovernmental organizations and trade unions, drove this reflection and rethinking in the initial period. The process emerged most quickly and evidently in the Republic of Korea, but debates in Indonesia, the Philippines, and Thailand quickly became vocal and widespread, and other countries followed suit. Regional organizations, including the Association of Southeast Asian Nations (ASEAN) and the United Nations Economic and Social Commission for Asia and the Pacific (ESCAP), took an early role. At the international level, the Asia Pacific Economic Cooperation (APEC) organization focused sharply on the social implications of the crisis and launched task forces to explore lessons for social policy. The topic was the focus of various meetings at different levels, including meetings of heads of state and government ministers.

The region's major development partners, meanwhile—notably the World Bank and the Asian Development Bank—inspired by the unfortunate experience of the social costs of crises in other regions of the world, focused on social dimensions almost as soon as it was apparent that the crisis would not end quickly. They convened two international meetings—in Bangkok in January 1999[1] and in Manila in November 1999[2]—to build support for immediate assistance and reflect on future policy issues and changes. A ministerial meeting organized by the Australian government in Melbourne in March 1999 gave further impetus to rethinking and action within the broader international community; numerous other gatherings at national and international forums focused on specific topics such as pension reform, labor-intensive public works, and migration issues.

At the 1999 Bangkok meeting it was striking how far the national leaders expressed the widespread fear that the crisis was bringing severe and lasting social costs. They called then for urgent and ambitious new social programs requiring large-scale international assistance. A year later the social agenda was much less crisis driven and more hopeful and optimistic. However, policy responses across the board reflect, in retrospect, how far the crisis did change the social policy agenda in fundamental ways. As hope returned and allowed a longer-term vision of the future, the need to prepare for hard times and unexpected shocks, and to deepen efforts to combat poverty, emerged as new imperatives.

The lack of effective systems for gathering information on the results of social policies was and remains a critical concern. In January 1999 gaps in knowledge from all quarters and all actors—policymakers and researchers alike—stared forth. But by then, not far into the crisis, policymakers already had launched many remarkable information-gathering efforts and had begun to note their results. This information focus had a marked and growing impact on policy as time progressed.

The basic messages at the later conference in Manila (thus by November 1999) were threefold. First, the impact of the crisis was much more complex—more varied by place, time, and social group—than initial assumptions and reports had suggested. Second, the resilience of societies in the face of crisis offered an endless series of inspirational stories and underscored the realization that new social policies needed to take careful note of traditional coping mechanisms, tailoring programs to the cultural views and wishes of beneficiaries. Third, the enormous suffering of many groups brought home vividly the human face of globalization, the costs of economic swings, and the need to prepare much better for future uncertainties and troubles.

The Manila conference also focused on the many examples of successful partnerships among official agencies, members of the civil society, and private-sector institutions. It also, though, highlighted duplicated efforts and missed opportunities. Participants expressed a determination to build on the best experiences, improve communication and synergy, and ensure a broad understanding of the development partnership.

A consensus about key lessons for social policy began to emerge from these gatherings. This chapter summarizes those lessons.[3] They represent a distillation of thinking at the World Bank and other institutions, and reflect conscious efforts to mine "good practices" regarding the use of public policy to manage economic and social crises.

Seven Lessons from the Crisis

Lesson 1: The crisis was a wake-up call that countries could no longer take uninterrupted economic growth for granted. The price of deeper integration with the world economy is likely to be fluctuating levels of economic growth. This had significant implications for economies that had relied on growth and full employment to provide their social safety nets.

Lesson 2: Policymakers need to concentrate more of their analysis and response on the key factors that are critical to household welfare in times of crisis. In 1997–98, for example, the focus was too much on formal unemployment and too little on changes in wage levels and shifts to the informal sector. Changes in demand for labor exert the largest short-run impact on households. In East Asia, unemployment increased significantly during the crisis, but falling wages and the movement of workers into low-paying, low-productivity jobs in the informal sector were even more significant. Few policy measures addressed these issues with effect. Currency devaluation and price changes had harsh consequences for the poorest segments of society, because they have urgent daily needs and tend to hold a greater proportion of their wealth in cash. Price increases for food hurt households that are net consumers of food. In East Asia, these include the urban poor and poor farmers, whose food production and food stocks dropped sharply because of the El Niño drought. And across-the-board budget belt-tightening tends to harm those who rely on public services, especially the poor.

Overall, the social consequences of macroeconomic shocks can be large and unpredictable, undermining years of investment in education and other forms of human capital, notably health. Some households' rational short-term responses (like pulling children out of school to supplement household income or delaying medical treatment) have lasting adverse effects that are sometimes irreversible. Efforts by governments, the civil society, and their partners to keep children in school worked remarkably well in several countries. The public focus on "stay-in-school" programs linked to material financial support for parents, as well as practical solutions to specific problems that emerged, underscored for parents and communities alike the importance of education.

Lesson 3: Safety nets work much better if they are established before a crisis. Setting up effective safety nets, let alone social insurance mechanisms, during a crisis is particularly difficult: financial resources are severely curtailed and subject to numerous pressures, there are inevitable implementation lags for programs designed essentially from scratch, and challenges in managing programs and navigating political pressures generated by crisis circumstances are great. During the crisis of 1997–98, social assistance, despite ambitious goals and announcements, fell far short of demand, as existing safety nets were patchy and served a small minority of people. Poor communities were often unaware of programs designed to help them, and leakage of benefits to people for whom these programs were not designed was sometimes substantial.

When no crisis is in sight, effective safety nets help ensure that various economic shocks or other unexpected setbacks (such as droughts or other natural calamities) do not halt development, and that households continue to invest in health and education, thereby boosting productivity and spurring growth. Effective safety nets aimed at poor families and communities are thus a long-term investment. In economies in which the formal sector is dominant, unemployment insurance or savings plans are likely to be most appropriate.

During a major national crisis, safety net programs can provide a solid foundation for rapid expansion to meet crisis needs. Experience suggests that workfare programs are likely to be a key element that can help directly mitigate households' loss of income. Several countries in East Asia, along with Latin American countries, have developed effective programs. Targeted transfers of cash or food to specific subgroups of the poor, such as pregnant women, the elderly, and those who should not work, such as school-age children, can also play an important role.

Lesson 4: Mechanisms to monitor the impact of a crisis and evaluate policy responses are essential, not desirable. Timely and complete information on the effects of a crisis on various groups and areas helps policymakers design appropriate responses and allows for corrections if the desired improvements do not materialize. In retrospect, there are ample examples of misdirected policy initiatives in East Asia that can be traced to the door of poor information. In contrast, several examples of effective information systems were developed during the 1997–98 crisis, such as Indonesia's Social Monitoring and Emergency Response Unit (SMERU). Public information on the intended and actual results of social policies can also help reduce leakage and corruption.

Lesson 5: Enhanced social dialogue and participation by civil society are keys to effective crisis management. Social conflicts divert resources from economically productive activities. Dialogue among workers, employers, the government, and the civil society can limit such conflicts and generate cooperative solutions to serious problems. Empowering marginalized groups and actors not only enhances social cohesion but also improves decisionmaking about social services and economic development. East Asian governments face a particularly urgent need to explore better and more diverse mechanisms that allow the intended beneficiaries of social policies to participate in decisionmaking.

Lesson 6: The 1997–98 crisis highlighted a host of interconnected governance issues. Government accountability requires effective institutions, clear rules, and respect for individual rights. The two peak crisis years in East Asia focused sharp attention on weak regulatory systems and financial mechanisms, as well as on lack of coordination among social service agencies. Efforts to strengthen and reform the public sector will remain crucial if East Asian countries are to respond more effectively to future shocks. Policymakers also need to consider how attempts to decentralize and privatize social service functions affect accountability. An active press and civil society can prove crucial in ensuring accountability under these conditions.

Corruption thrives in the absence of transparency and accountability. Countries cannot afford, and donors cannot accept, social and developmental losses because of corruption. Anticorruption efforts are now a central focus of East Asian governments as well as of international donors and multilateral agencies.

Lesson 7: No group needs more focus than the very poor, yet they are easily left aside as middle classes and organized groups dominate the agenda. The weakness of institutions and programs directed to the poorest communities—whether government or nongovernmental organization—was apparent during the crisis. In many instances these communities had nowhere to turn, and despite goodwill, it took many months to identify their needs and gear up to respond to them.

Conclusion

Overall, the crisis revealed how far the social agenda encompasses but also extends well beyond strategies for reducing poverty. Policies directed to the very poor could not be isolated from the broader social issues for the population. The need to link social and economic policies stood out as an imperative. Policymakers still can learn much from the experience of how these two domains intersected and interacted during the crisis years.

The risk, of course, is that once the crisis has passed, all parties will return to the precrisis norm. It is worth recalling the maxim that those who forget history are condemned to repeat it; thus, we should focus on the urgent need to continue to mine the crisis experience to prepare for the future.

Notes

1. The background document prepared for the meeting by the World Bank is titled "Social Impact of the East Asia Crisis: A Work in Progress," January, 1999 <http://www.worldbank.org/eapsocial/library/socialimpact1.htm>.

2. The work of the Manila Conference is reflected in a joint Asian Development Bank and World Bank publication, *The New Social Policy Agenda in Asia: Proceedings of the Manila Social Forum* (Manila: Asian Development Bank, 2000).

3. The author presented this list at the November 1999 Social Policy meeting in Manila.

CHAPTER 5

Universal Health Insurance in Japan

by Christian Oberländer

ABSTRACT: This chapter gives a historical overview of the construction of a national health insurance system in Japan that is designed to illustrate the adaptation of models from one region (Europe) to another (Asia). Universal coverage through a multi-tiered insurance system and a uniform fee schedule have ensured the success of the Japanese health system. In the 1930s policymakers made extensive use of international research as well as local pilot projects to study possible schemes for national health insurance. The mixed nature of those schemes—half voluntary, half mandatory—built on a decentralized network of existing institutions such as cooperatives. When World War II broke out, coverage was almost universal. In the postwar period implementation and financial consolidation of national health insurance resumed through the granting of state subsidies and the creation of a specific tax. A nationwide drive to expand coverage again relied on a decentralized approach to win support from local politicians and stakeholders.

Japan recently achieved the world's lowest infant mortality rate and highest life expectancy. In 1996 infant mortality in Japan was 3.8 per 1,000 live births, whereas life expectancy at birth was 84 years for women and 77 years for men.[1] Long-time observers of the Japanese health care system Naoki Ikegami and John Creighton Campbell have concluded that "Japan's health care system . . . helps to keep its population healthy at an exceptionally low cost." They "rate the Japanese system as excellent in cost control and access and very good in equality."[2] Universal health insurance has been key in bringing about those results.

The Japanese health care experience, though not free of flaws—witness issues relating to long-term care, drug policy, and control of medical technology—is relevant to other nations for several reasons. Confronted with the Great Depression after 1929, Japanese policymakers recognized early the close connection between improving health and reducing poverty. They boldly aimed to ensure broad access to health care among workers in the large informal sector because they realized such availability was crucial to enable that population to weather economic crises. The search for relief for a distressed rural population led to expansion of health insurance with the ultimate aim of universal coverage. Japan took these key steps when it was still at an early stage of economic development, with average per capita income close to that of Latin America, and was still borrowing from the World Bank.[3] The nation's early drive to expand health insurance allowed Japan to achieve universal coverage in 1961, well before many other industrialized countries.

This chapter examines the Japanese drive for universal health insurance, highlighting innovations that met the particular needs of Japanese society as well as potential lessons for other nations. The next section introduces key features of Japanese health care financing that appear essential to its success. Then the chapter reviews the historical process that led to universal coverage from the initial planning stages by the Home Ministry during the Great Depression to the completion of universal health insurance in 1961. Next the chapter examines European influences and models in the Japanese planning and policy process. The final section discusses lessons that Japan's historical experience may hold for other nations.

Two Key Features of Japanese Health Care Financing

The multi-tiered Japanese health care system[4] offers varying degrees of subsidization according to people's economic vulnerability. In the 1920s, Japanese national health insurance focused on the formally employed, following the Bismarckian model.[5] National health insurance (*kokumin kenkô hoken*), organized by regions and covering the self-employed and pensioners, was the central innovation in the drive for universal insurance coverage.

On the payment side, the Japanese health care system reimburses providers according to a nationally uniform fee schedule, which the country introduced with the Bismarckian model. Because of this uniform schedule, people covered under any insurance scheme receive essentially the same set of treatments. Providers cannot offer health services outside the fee schedule or collect charges in addition to what insurance pays for the services. (Informal payments are so small that they do not jeopardize the principle.)[6] The fee schedule is subject to regular review and renegotiation.

These two key features—universal coverage through a multi-tiered insurance system combined with a uniform fee schedule—lie at the heart of Japan's successful health care system. Universal coverage allows the fee schedule to exert tremendous control over prices and provider behavior. Although the fee schedule was an element of Japanese health insurance from the beginning, the country achieved universal coverage in four stages: legislation in the aftermath of the Great Depression, implementation of the plan, forced expansion and consolidation during and after World War II, and subsidized expansion to achieve universal coverage.

The Great Depression and the Creation of National Health Insurance

Industrial and mining companies had formed mutual aid organizations by the 1880s, but Japan's first health insurance law was passed by the Diet in 1922. The country delayed enforcement until 1926 and began paying benefits in 1927. The early health insurance system, modeled after German sickness funds, covered disease and injury and provided some cash allowances but excluded dependents of the insured. The system provided compulsory coverage for employees whose annual wage was less than 1,200 yen and who worked more than 120 successive days at factories and mines covered by the Factory Act and the Mining Act. Employees at any workplace with fewer than five employees were voluntarily insured. Employees made a contribution proportional to their wage or salary, while their employers also picked up part of the contribution. Because of the restrictions on income and size of workplace, fewer than 2 million of some 4.7 million formally employed workers were subject to compulsory insurance.[7]

The Great Depression of 1929 hit farmers and others living in rural areas hardest. Urban workers who lost their jobs often returned to their villages, adding to overcrowding and poor living conditions. Doctors, in turn, were overburdened and often unpaid, and they began to move away from the villages into urban areas in great numbers.[8] Home Ministry officials who organized emergency assistance for the farming population recognized that sickness and death were among the leading factors in poverty. Medical spending was highest among urban dwellers, and higher among those living in villages with a resident physician than among those without direct access to a health care provider.

Policymakers concluded that ability to pay and physical access, not need, determined health care utilization. The rationale for expanding health insurance was thus twofold: to lower the effect of health care costs on agricultural households, and to expand the presence of physicians and medical facilities in rural villages, thereby improving access to medical care.

Japan expanded the health insurance system in 1934 but added only 370,000 participants to the 2 million members already covered. The Home Ministry began planning to introduce a second insurance scheme covering the rest of the 10 million people employed in the formal sector as well as many more people working in fisheries, as small shopkeepers, and in other informal sectors.

To prepare the ground, officials documented the health care situation in rural villages and the effect of health spending on agricultural households. They learned of local insurance cooperatives that had existed since the beginning of the 20th century in the north of the island of Kyushu, where villagers made regular payments to physicians to receive care in the event of injury and sickness. These arrangements often aimed at ensuring a living for doctors who would otherwise have left the community. Villagers calculated their contributions according to their ability to pay, making payments in cash or rice. Substantial co-payments lightened the burden and prevented moral hazard of unneeded access to health care. Some organizations even required members to make good any deficit in proportion to the medical treatment they had received.

A second type of precedent the Home Ministry studied was medical facilities established and owned by the rural population itself to reduce health care costs. Agricultural cooperatives were operating medical facilities by the second half of the 1920s, but many did not survive because the cooperatives lacked managerial know-how and had difficulty retaining doctors. In 1928, to overcome the challenges of small-scale provision of care dependent on private practitioners, a cooperative in Aomori in rural northeast Japan founded a full-scale hospital with 60 beds as well as specialty departments. Other cooperatives followed its example: by 1936, 738 cooperatives managed 2,791 beds, employing 461 physicians and providing medical services to 502,122 members.[9] The Home Ministry concluded that the approach developed by rural people might solve the problem of reducing the financial burden of medical care.

In July 1934 the ministry released an initial proposal for a health insurance system for the self-employed (mainly farmers and fishers) called National Health Insurance (NHI). The home minister noted that the plan was designed to eventually establish a health insurance system for *all* Japanese. The original plan called for local insurance societies with compulsory membership, but it met with massive political resistance, especially from physicians who feared the bargaining power of highly organized demand. Faced with a need for health insurance schemes with voluntary membership, the Home Ministry conducted a detailed assessment of the health insurance situation in 20 European countries. Among all the foreign insurance systems studied, the policymakers found Denmark, with its noncompulsory and mostly regional health insurance societies for the general population, most relevant to the Japanese situation.[10]

Despite domestic precedents, the Home Ministry expected further criticism of its plans because most regions of Japan lacked familiarity with a local insurance system. To demonstrate and evaluate the operation of the planned system under local circumstances, the ministry launched and studied 12 health insurance societies in different parts of the country as pilot projects. Those organizations later became formal National Health Insurance societies.

In 1936, the cabinet conference formally decided to introduce the National Health Insurance (NHI) Act in the Japanese Diet. During its 70th session, the Diet debated the act intensely, focusing on the position of private practitioners in relation to the new insurance societies. The law passed the lower house in 1937 after amendments opening the provision of medical care to all physicians subject to a group agreement. Because the upper house could not complete deliberations, supporters reintroduced the draft law in the legislature in 1938, where it passed after brief debate. Enforcement of NHI began on July 1, 1938.

Implementation of National Health Insurance

The enactment of NHI marked the first time the Japanese government extended health insurance to the general population. Under the NHI Act, municipalities and employers organized three types of societies to act as insurance carriers. "Ordinary societies" covered residents of a local administrative unit; members of the same trade or business, such as barbers or grocers, organized "special associations"; and existing cooperatives formed "substitute associations." Membership was voluntary but could be made compulsory when two-thirds of the population concerned had joined the local society. The NHI unit insured all members of a household.

The NHI Act of 1938 granted insurance carriers the freedom to set their own contribution rates and methods of collection. To encourage localities to implement the scheme, the government granted each insurance carrier subsidies for the first year at a fixed rate per insured person, which gradually decreased. Under this voluntary scheme, policymakers expected communities to found some 500 local insurance societies each year and hoped to achieve reasonable coverage and a nationwide network of insurance societies within 20 years. The initial increase in insurance societies to 2,025 during the first 4 years of operation seemed to confirm that estimate.[11]

Although the NHI Act of 1938 laid down a broad organizational framework, it contained few provisions regarding benefits. Each insurance carrier had to provide care for sickness and injury; maternal and funeral benefits were optional. In 1944–45, 73 percent of insurance carriers provided maternity benefits, and 3 percent paid funeral benefits. The act also left each carrier free to decide on the scope and duration of medical care.

Organizers expected health expenditures to drop significantly under NHI for two reasons. First, NHI introduced co-payments to Japanese health insurance on a national basis for the first time. Although the administration had recommended co-payments at 20 to 30 percent of the cost of care, by 1941 most carriers had set a level between 30 and 45 percent. Second, prices set earlier by doctors would fall because consumption would rise, payment rates would also increase, and a markup for unpaid services that had been part of the old pricing system would no longer be needed. For example, the Okayama prefecture estimated the rate of unpaid bills at 20 to 30 percent at the time (whereas the rate in the United States was 10 to 20 percent).[12] Although in theory insurance societies could enter freely into contracts with providers of medical care, actual negotiations nevertheless tended to gravitate toward the existing fee schedule because providers would not accept lower prices and insurance societies were not willing to pay more.

Insurance carriers were free to offer services and create facilities to maintain and improve health. The government actively encouraged the introduction of such services through technical and financial aid to insurance carriers. Public health nurses, for example, began to play an important role in rural areas after the introduction of the NHI scheme. According to a 1941 survey, 309 of 899 insurance carriers employed 344 public health nurses. Having their own medical facilities allowed carriers to combine insurance operations with preventive services and medical care that was largely free of the profit motive. In 1944 the government began granting subsidies to cover part of the cost of construction of new medical facilities. Ownership and direct management of medical facilities also helped correct geographical maldistribution in the rural sector. By 1948 NHI carriers owned and ran 83 hospitals and 1,093 clinics.[13]

Forced Expansion during World War II and Postwar Consolidation

Humanitarian concerns had driven the advent of NHI, but when the war in Asia expanded during the 1930s, so did military preoccupation with the farming village as a source of wartime labor. The government supported its extension of health insurance coverage first to farmers, then to the entire population, with the rationale "healthy people, healthy soldiers." In 1939 the Employees Health Insurance Law extended coverage to urban white-collar workers, while the Seaman's Insurance Law extended coverage to sailors. In 1940 the national convention of insurance carriers formally endorsed the goal of establishing an NHI society in each municipality, thus approving universal health insurance. In January 1941 the cabinet council adopted the Plan for the Establishment of Population Policy, which, among other things, underscored that the health insurance system must be strengthened and must cover the entire population.

A drastic increase in the number of insurance carriers and insured persons after 1941 stemmed from changes in the principles underlying the original scheme (see Table 5.1). In 1942 a prefectural governor's order made the scheme compulsory in areas not yet covered. The status of health care providers also

Table 5.1 Insurance Carriers and Insured Persons (1938–62)

Year	Number of insurance carriers	Number of insured persons	Average number of insured persons per carrier
1938	174	523,223	3,007
1940	937	3,045,046	3,250
1942	6,596	22,661,192	3,436
1944	10,474	41,161,301	3,930
1946	9,526	41,820,949	4,390
1948	5,446	25,826,890	4,742
1950	5,050	24,353,974	4,823
1952	5,008	23,088,674	4,610
1954	3,669	26,633,438	7,259
1956	2,870	30,582,065	10,656
1958	3,167	37,238,964	11,758
1960	3,599	46,171,092	12,829
1962	3,618	45,792,064	12,657

changed: they now had to serve as insurance doctors by government appointment. By 1943 NHI societies had been established in more than 95 percent of all municipalities in Japan. This period thus witnessed the creation of Japan's first "universal" insurance system, even though it did not quite cover the entire population. However, the question of universality soon became irrelevant because World War II destroyed most of Japan's health care delivery system.

Many insurance carriers created under the 1942 amendments were too weak to survive the disruption of economic and social life; of more than 10,000 NHI societies begun during the war, less than half were functioning by war's end. The number of insured persons dropped sharply in 1948, and remaining insurance carriers faced difficulties. The postwar withdrawal of medical providers previously ordered to serve under NHI during the war also posed a serious challenge to insurance carriers.

During this crisis, the government granted subsidies to cover carriers' expenditures for administrative personnel, public health nurses, and medical facilities. When fears of famine developed, these funds included grants to purchase cows to supply milk and to produce simple pharmaceuticals. However, public subsidies still played only a limited role in NHI. In 1949 state and prefectural subsidies totaled only 572 million yen, whereas income from contributions totaled 4,196 million yen.[14]

Policymakers took two steps to revitalize the NHI system after the war. The first was a 1948 amendment to the NHI law making each municipal government responsible for organizing and managing its own NHI society. The prestige of local mayors with a direct role in organizing the NHI restored physicians' confidence in the system. Ordinary insurance societies now required the consent of at least half the eligible residents, but after they were established all residents had to become members. Industrial associations—especially cooperative societies—that had helped develop the scheme no longer played any part. The organizing principle had become completely regional.

To stabilize the system financially, the government introduced the NHI tax in 1951. Before then, insurance carriers had individually prescribed contribution rates and methods of collection, but now the government assessed and collected uniform levies as taxes according to each municipality's number of households and insured persons. In 1952 the government introduced an incentive: reimbursements would depend on the rate of contribution individual carriers could collect during a given period. This scheme was replaced in 1953 by a general subsidy for NHI equal to 20 percent of the cost of medical care borne by the insurance carrier. However, this subsidy also depended on the financial situation of the local government, the level of protection it granted, and its performance in collecting contributions and controlling medical expenditures. The objective was to allow insurance carriers to overcome financial difficulties while providing an incentive for maintaining and upgrading their coverage to a reasonable level of protection.

Subsidized Expansion toward Universal Coverage

In 1955 the government introduced new subsidies covering 20 percent of the cost of medical care, one-third of the cost of public health nurses, and all NHI administrative costs. These subsidies departed from earlier predetermined budgetary limits and strengthened the financial basis of the scheme by establishing central government subsidies for all insurance carriers. This encouraged local governments that had not implemented NHI to do so, paving the way for compulsory application of the scheme throughout the country in the 1960s.[15]

The Advisory Council on Social Security, led by Hyoe Ôuchi, president of Tokyo University, had recommended the establishment of a universal health insurance system in 1950. In November 1955 the Ministry of Health and Welfare—successor to the Home Ministry—released its Five-Year Plan for Social Security, which proposed comprehensive medical care coverage by 1960. Although the plan was not official ministry policy, it attracted a great deal of media and popular attention and triggered a public debate on universal health insurance. In January 1956 Prime Minister Ichirô Hatoyama proposed his own plan to provide universal coverage by 1960. With 30 million Japanese still uninsured, universal coverage was high on the political agenda during the July 1956 election, and in January 1957 the cabinet council formally stated its intention to establish a universal health insurance system within 5 years.

Providers represented by the Japan Medical Association (JMA) opposed specifics in the proposed amendment, but they were not averse to the concept of universal coverage. The JMA reconciled itself to the plan because of the likelihood that eliminating bad debt would boost provider earnings. Also, the mass training of physicians during the war had created another problem for the JMA, because the nation saw a rapid rise in the number of physicians returning from military service. The number of doctors per 100,000 inhabitants rose by 19 percent from 1946 to 1955, from 89 to 106. Many physicians saw universal health insurance as a way to provide a continued livelihood for this growing group.

In December 1958 amendments to the NHI Act made health insurance coverage mandatory for all Japanese. Many saw the 1958 changes as an entirely new National Health Insurance law. Local authorities in all cities, towns, and villages had to establish health insurance funds by April 1961. To alleviate the financial burden of the NHI tax on lower-income groups, the government dropped uniform levies by 40 and 60 percent in 1963. The state's financial participation consisted of providing subsidies, fixing the contribution rate by law, and offering grants within the limits of the national budget. As a result, national subsidies to states and prefectures in 1966 totaled 156,815 million yen, compared with income from contributions of 106,612 million yen.[16] The 1958 act aimed to eliminate discrepancies by prescribing that co-payments could not exceed 50 percent. A June 1966 amendment reduced this limit to 30 percent.

The timing of those measures proved fortunate because Japan experienced rapid economic growth from 1955 to 1957 and from 1959 to 1961, so the country had enough fiscal strength to implement universal insurance rapidly. The effect of the 1958 legislation is evident in the remarkable rise in the number of insured persons in 1959 and thereafter. The Japanese universal health insurance system was fully enacted nationwide in 1961, and the system continues to operate today.

Japanese versus European Experience and Health Policies

When introducing NHI, Japanese bureaucrats, politicians, and other players were keenly aware of European health insurance systems. Officials took their estimate that leading foreign countries had achieved health insurance coverage for about 30 percent of their population as a strong indication that Japan needed to expand coverage beyond the 2 million initially insured under the 1922 Health Insurance Act.

In planning the prewar drive to expand health insurance, the Home Ministry noted that in Denmark private medical practitioners had cooperated in the drive to expand voluntary health insurance in order to secure their livelihood, and professionally oriented health insurance associations had turned mostly regional by 1892.[17] Aware of the much more critical attitude toward health insurance of Japanese doctors, the ministry initially took a careful approach to extending the new NHI scheme.

During the debate about the organizational structure of NHI, industrial cooperatives repeatedly invoked the cases of European countries to support their calls for a greater role for themselves. The cooperatives highlighted the successful contribution of different types of cooperatives as carriers of health insurance in France.[18] Criticizing the role of private physicians under NHI, cooperatives argued that it would only repeat in Japan the failure of the health insurance of Germany and the United Kingdom.

As Japan switched from a voluntary system to forced development of near-universal coverage during World War II, European policies again served as important guideposts for Japanese decisionmakers. Officials referred to the fact that England and Germany had strengthened their health care systems as part of their wartime policies with expanded insurance coverage playing a central part.

During the final drive for universal coverage, Japan appears to have acted largely without conscious reference to foreign models. The brief existence of near-universal coverage during the war gave Japan a structure for renewed postwar expansion, and an egalitarian public consensus allowed political actors to implement this expansion despite postwar chaos.

Japan set ambitious goals and achieved universal coverage quite early compared with many European countries. Germany has still not achieved 100 percent coverage.[19] France expanded its insured population significantly as late as the 1960s, when first farmers (1961) and later self-employed people outside agriculture (1966) became part of the system. France achieved near total coverage only during recent reforms. Only in the United Kingdom did the entire population gain access to all areas of medical services with the implementation of the National Health Service in 1948.

Lessons for Other Nations

The Japanese experience in introducing and expanding NHI offers many potential lessons for other countries. First, clearly defined values and objectives are important. Once officials at the Home Ministry had developed the vision of a relief program for the farming population that would ultimately lead to universal coverage, they could screen domestic and international precedents and norms effectively. Policymakers invested several years in implementing pilot projects that were financed largely by a nongovernmental third party. To gain public acceptance more quickly, officials drew preexisting organizations that expressed social solidarity into the new scheme. By referencing an international precedent (Denmark) that accommodated key political stakeholders (physicians) by making their participation voluntary, the officials preemptively weakened potential opposition to NHI.

The second lesson is that expanded coverage should not be rushed. NHI was initially meant to grow at a slow pace, with modest financial support leading to universal coverage. The introduction of coercive elements during World War II allowed sudden expansion to near-universal coverage, but it proved short-lived. The final push for universal coverage in a democratic environment after the war required general government subsidies for insurance carriers and specific support for low-income groups. Although officials used coercion and subsidies temporarily, they still took more than 20 years to cover the entire Japanese population. The initial estimate of NHI planners proved roughly correct.

Third, the stance taken by professional care providers as key stakeholders can profoundly influence the fate of a drive for universal coverage. When officials announced plans for NHI, powerful groups of physicians had already voiced opposition. Policymakers overcame this resistance only at the price of abandoning initial plans for compulsory health insurance. Local physicians' groups also opposed the creation of insurance societies in many places. The command economy of the war years briefly eliminated physicians' resistance, as NHI forced them to serve as providers. However, this led to massive defection of physicians from health insurance as soon as the country lifted the coercive measures. What finally led physicians to accept universal coverage through NHI was the prospect of income security at a time when the profession had grown strongly in numbers.

Fourth, a gradual approach combining different organizational principles and creating (temporarily) independent risk pools can draw in more social groups, finally leading to universal coverage. NHI was basically organized regionally like its Danish model, but it also initially left room for carriers organized along professional lines. After the war, risk pools gradually linked themselves into larger units, and government subsidies provided redistributive financing. The three tiers of the Japanese health insurance system therefore correspond today to three levels of subsidization by the central government. Health insurance managed by societies mostly for employees of large companies must cover benefits solely out of premium income, whereas government-managed insurance mostly for employees of small companies and NHI receive subsidies of 14 percent and 50 percent, respectively.

Fifth, growing coverage of underserved groups need not lead to massively rising costs. The initial introduction of NHI included cost-control measures in the form of substantial co-payments and elimination of markups for unpaid services. The Japanese experience after 1961 confirms observations from other countries that lower unit costs from co-payments and a steady income flow for medical practitioners help offset the cost of greater use of health services.[20] In the Japanese case universal coverage combined with strict enforcement of the uniform fee schedule has been critical in avoiding some of the cost inflation observed in other countries.[21] Overall, the Japanese experience suggests that policymakers can effectively manage the main risks of health insurance: incomplete coverage of the population and rising costs.[22]

Notes

1. Richard Cash, Christian Oberländer, and Akiko Matsumoto, "Lowering Infant Mortality in Japan (1915 to 1965): The Role of Government and Civil Society" (Cambridge, Mass., 2000, unpublished manuscript).

2. Naoki Ikegami and John Creighton Campbell, "Health Care Reform in Japan: The Virtues of Muddling Through," *Health Affairs* 18, no. 3 (1999): 56–75.

3. Angus Maddiso, *Monitoring the World Economy 1820–1992* (Paris: Organization for Economic Cooperation and Development, 1995), pp. 20, 196–97.

4. For a full discussion of the Japanese health system, see Ikegami and Campbell, op. cit.

5. For a detailed discussion of the Bismarckian insurance concept, see Frank A. G. den Butter and Udo Kock, "Social Security, Economic Growth, and Poverty: Theoretical Considerations and Guidelines for Institutional Arrangements," available at <http://www.worldbank.org/eapsocial/asemsocial/files/815_Asempap1.pdf>, last accessed September 30, 2002.

6. Naoki Ikegami and John Creighton Campbell, "Medical Care in Japan," *New England Journal of Medicine* 333, no. 19 (1995): 1295–99.

7. Margaret Powell and Masahira Anesaki, *Health Care in Japan* (London: Routledge, 1990).

8. Takashi Saguchi, *National Health Insurance. Foundation and Development* (Tokyo: Kôseikan, 1995).

9. T. Higuchi, "Medical Care through Social Insurance in the Japanese Rural Sector," *International Labour Review* 109, no. 3 (1974): 251–74.

10. Home Ministry, *Health Insurance Systems in Foreign Countries* (Tokyo: Social Affairs Department, 1937).

11. George F. Rohrlich and Margaret Jane Thompson Mettert, "National Health Insurance in Japan," *International Labour Review* 61, pp. 337–66.

12. Saguchi, op. cit.

13. Higuchi, op. cit.

14. Ibid., p. 271.

15. In 1953, legislation encouraging the merger of towns and villages to boost administrative efficiency expanded the average number of insured persons per insurance carrier and enlarged the risk pools.

16. Higuchi, op. cit.

17. Yoshifumi Itô, *The Development of Health Insurance Policy in Northern Europe—Denmark, Sweden* (1980), p. 21.

18. Toyohiko Kagawa, *Opinion Presented to the Social Insurance Investigations Committee,* 1935, pp. 118–20.

19. Jens Alber, *Western European Health Systems in Comparison: FR Germany, Switzerland, France, Italy, United Kingdom* (Frankfurt: Campus, 1992), pp. 68, 350, 540.

20. Marie Lassey, William Lassey, and Martin Jinks, *Health Care Systems around the World: Characteristics, Issues, Reforms* (Upper Saddle River, N.J.: Prentice Hall, 1998).

21. See, for example, Paul J. Gertler, "On the Road to Social Health Insurance: The Asian Experience," *World Development* 26, no. 4 (1998): 717–32.

22. Charles Normand, "Using Social Health Insurance to Meet Policy Goals," *Social Science and Medicine* 48 (1999): 865–69.

BOX 1.3

Ten Principles for Sound Social Policy
by Tamar Manuelyan Atinc

Each country in East Asia (as elsewhere) will strike its own social bargain, reflecting an agenda, constituency, and process unique to that country. Some broad principles for social policy nonetheless emerge from the region's history, international experience, and lessons from the 1997–98 financial crisis:

1. *Growth remains a poor man's (and woman's) best friend.* The 1997–98 crisis interrupted steady gains in reducing poverty and improving overall welfare, but this setback should not call into question the importance of sound macroeconomic and social policies. The crisis years only underscored the notion that growth is vital to reducing poverty—and that contractions in economic output can prove devastating for the poor.

2. *Quality of growth is as important as growth itself.* Growth has been the biggest factor in reducing Asia's overall poverty levels, but shifts in the distribution of that growth have had significant adverse effects, generally increasing inequality. In some countries during some periods, those effects have swamped the positive contributions of growth. Thailand's experience from 1975 to 1986 is most striking, but rural China from 1985 to 1990 and the Philippines from 1988 to 1991 saw similar outcomes. Policies that contribute to rural growth are especially important because East Asian poverty is overwhelmingly rural.

3. *Labor remains a poor man's (and woman's) most important asset, and policies that contribute to rising demand for labor and boost its quality are essential to broad-based growth.* Improvements in human capital have contributed importantly to Asia's growth record, and widespread provision of basic education and health services underpins poverty reduction in the "miracle" countries. In the region's more advanced countries, poverty is now concentrated among those with little or no education.

4. *Continued investments in human capital are arguably even more important today, because the premium for skills will grow as industries and economies become more reliant on human knowledge and information technology.* The

continued on next page

BOX 1.3, continued

central challenge is to broaden access to and improve the quality of secondary education. Improving access to public health services is also critical. Declining fertility should allow more spending per pupil and additional spending per patient on maternal and child health care. However, an aging population may strain budgets unless fiscally sustainable solutions can provide pensions and health care to the elderly.

5. *Governments need to be sensitive to the distributional implications of their policies.* The impact of tax and expenditure policies should ideally be pro-poor. Governments need better information about how spending, taxes, and other policies affect different income groups, and they need to build this information into the budgetary process so political leaders understand the trade-offs of policy decisions. Rising levels of public debt reflecting government assumption of bank recapitalization costs during the East Asian crisis make such efforts doubly important: the poor should not be left holding this bill.

6. *Countercyclical fiscal policies can cushion the impact of economic shocks.* Given East Asian traditions of prudent fiscal policy, social programs that expand automatically in times of crisis—that is, have a built-in stabilization function—can help sustain economic activity and support vulnerable groups without undermining fiscal sustainability and investors' confidence. The choice of instrument will vary by country and will normally reflect income level, institutional capacity, and cultural norms and values. East Asian governments have generally opted for programs that do not reduce the incentive to work and have therefore been reluctant to introduce unemployment insurance and expand income transfers.

7. *When countries introduce unemployment insurance, an effective administrative structure is crucial to prevent politically driven benefit levels and raiding of reserve funds in good times.* When countries rely on community-level information to identify those in need, local elites may capture the programs. A close administrative relationship between unemployment insurance and job-placement services can motivate unemployed workers to register and report regularly and ensure that benefits go only to people willing to work. A legal framework that penalizes fraudulent behavior is essential.

BOX 1.3, continued

8. *Targeted unemployment programs need special attention because few low-income countries are able to manage such demanding programs well.* Higher-income countries have the capacity to implement means-targeted safety-net programs but have rarely done so in East Asia. Ideal safety nets are those that not only provide a consumption floor but also encourage investment in the human capital and social and physical infrastructure of the poor. Public "workfare" is the best example of such programs designed to reach the able-bodied poor. Benefits are maximized if the projects create assets that the poor value, such as schools and rural roads, and provide income to maintain current consumption. Because unemployed workers must show up for work to receive the benefits, workfare programs solve the incentive problem. Such human development programs should appeal to the East Asian ethos of self-help.

9. *Stronger mechanisms to coordinate social policy are urgently needed.* The 1997–98 crisis brought home the critical need for a strategic and coordinated view of social policy and the importance of more transparent and accountable institutions. Some interministerial councils created during the crisis have proved durable in the wake of the crisis, whereas others have not. Countries need to lock in mechanisms for regional accountability in their social programs because decentralization can allow social services to deteriorate, especially during transition periods, and can worsen regional disparities and inequity.

10. *Probing evaluation of existing programs that focus on poor communities would arm governments much better to make critical decisions on public spending in times of severe budget constraints.* East Asian countries can greatly enhance survey instruments and information systems to foster political support for effective programs, enhance crisis-preparedness, and improve the overall effectiveness of government spending.

BOX 1.4

Seminar on European Social Policy and the Asia Crisis, Paris, June 27, 2000

The European Social Policy Lessons Project was formally launched with a seminar, held in conjunction with a large annual conference organized by the World Bank in Europe on leading development issues. Both were run in cooperation with the French Council for Economic Analysis and the French Ministry of Economy, Finance, and Industry.

The seminar framed the analytic work of the project, first by providing background on the East Asian crisis, and second by exploring theoretical frameworks for future discussion of social policy issues. It was organized around three successive roundtables, each chaired by leading social policy experts from East Asia (Amar Siamwalla from Thailand, Luis Corral from the Philippines, and Moon-Soo Kang from the Republic of Korea). Three papers were the focus of discussion (Chapters 1 and 3, by Ian Gough and Tamar Manuelyan Atinc, respectively, and Box 1.2 by François Godement). East Asian participants made a field visit to a local health insurance agency in Paris to examine the modernization and computerization program of the French health insurance system.

The first roundtable probed the complex challenges surrounding the social impact of the East Asian crisis—what was known, what was not known, and what it portended for the future. Relative merits of and needs for formal and integrated insurance schemes, the widely varying definitions of safety nets, the importance of flexible labor markets, the availability and reliability of data for monitoring the crisis, and the applicability of European social policy frameworks to East Asia in light of significant demographic differences (as well as similarities) were the focus.

The second roundtable focused on a theoretical framework for welfare regimes presented by Ian Gough (see Chapter 1). Discussions highlighted the important role of family obligations and family law in both Europe and East Asia. Given the path-dependent nature of social policy, the transferability of European welfare regimes to East Asia sparked intense debate.

continued on next page

BOX 1.4, continued

François Godement focused on changing social policies that accompanied rapid industrialization and economic growth in East Asia (see box 1.2). These policies were not, he argued, part of a reformist agenda but constituted a traditional form of public action promoted by defenders of the status quo, very much linked to Asian values and economic and social institutions. He underscored contradictory efforts both to establish safety nets and to adopt market-oriented models of economic policy during the crisis and the growing importance of local actors and nongovernmental organizations in the policymaking process and in promoting a reformist agenda. Discussion focused on public participation and management of risk as forces driving policies in both East Asia and Europe.

Social Policy and Macroeconomic Management: Challenges Following the East Asian Crisis

Introduction

All chapters in this book reflect—implicitly or explicitly—the premise that social policy is a critical part of solutions to broad socioeconomic problems such as unemployment, poverty, inequality, and even crime. However, although most senior political officials hold that social and macroeconomic policy are inextricably linked, and that social policy helps drive macroeconomic policy, in practice those tenets often prove difficult to apply. The Asia-Europe Meeting (ASEM) Social Policy Lessons Project made them a central focus of analysis, both at a theoretical level and in a series of case studies designed to learn from real-world experience.

In Part II, two case studies highlight the powerful links between social and macroeconomic policies in Europe and show how careful attention to those links has helped countries boost their economic performance. Chapter 6, by F. Desmond McCarthy, shows how Ireland grounded its remarkable economic turnaround on a strong social compact, including concerted efforts to address structural unemployment. This experience reveals not only how a consensus for reform can yield positive results, but also highlights current questions about Ireland's ability to sustain its success in the face of recent changes in the global economy.

In Chapter 7, Jonas Gahr Støre provides a fascinating account of the Solidarity Alternative, the story of Norway's success in transforming basic economic parameters by pursuing a comprehensive social pact. Although this record illustrates the positive synergies between social and macroeconomic policies, especially those that focus on the labor force, the policy's very success has raised new challenges to the social consensus on which it rests.

Chapter 8 is a brief discussion by Thørkil Casse of Danish experience in using computer models to monitor policy implementation and predict the social effects of changes in economic policy.

Although the ASEM Social Policy Lessons Project did not specifically analyze macroeconomic policies except as they relate to the social agenda, Part II includes three contrasting views of contemporary macroeconomic management challenges by project participants. Box 2.1 by K. S. Jomo focuses on the importance of investing in social needs such as education to counter the cyclical effects of the macroeconomy, particularly economic crises. Box 2.2 by Robert Wade maintains that although East Asian countries—like Western countries before them—have used protection to develop their economies, they will need to do a better job of fostering domestic demand by linking social policy to macroeconomic policy. Box 2.3 by Colin Moynihan highlights issues arising from debates about globalization and the shared challenges for all to benefit from the fruits of globalization and to address the revolutionary social changes it has unleashed.

Two short vignettes present summaries of contemporary issues and challenges for national social policy, the first for France (Box 2.4), the second, Italy (Box 2.5). Box 2.6 gives highlights of the October 2000 Amsterdam seminar, which linked several social policy frameworks, poverty reduction strategies, and issues for the life cycle. Box 2.7 outlines the program of a joint seminar in August 2001 organized with the University of Bergen.

BOX 2.1

Social Policy, Financial Crisis, and Macroeconomic Response

by K. S. Jomo

East Asian countries face two significant challenges:

- They need to take full advantage of the opportunity for policy change and fresh thinking resulting from the 1997–98 regional crisis and its aftermath.
- They need to better integrate social policy needs with macroeconomic and development policies.

The challenges of the post-1999 period call for a fresh view of macroeconomic policies that step back from the preconceptions of the standard formulas of the past. The pre-1999 consensus for more liberalization was exemplified by the policy prescriptions of most international financial institutions and agreements of the World Trade Organization.

Today the East Asian region broadly recognizes that financial liberalization has not brought the promised fruits. Net capital flows have shifted from poor to rich countries over the long term, the cost of funds has actually risen since the late 1970s, and new sources of volatility—rather than greater stability—have appeared.

Financial liberalization has encouraged macroeconomic policies that are procyclical rather than countercyclical, with a deflationary bias. Financial liberalization limits policymakers' room to maneuver in promoting economic development through both macroeconomic and industrial policy. The Republic of Korea and Malaysia successfully adopted countercyclical macroeconomic policies that contrasted with orthodox recommendations.

As part of this postcrisis search for new policies for renewed and more sustainable development, East Asia needs to restore social policy needs

This writeup is based on a presentation at the Brussels December 2001 ASEM seminar and on "Macroeconomic Policy Responses to the 1997–98 Crisis in Malaysia," a paper prepared for the International Labor Organization in 2001.

continued on next page

BOX 2.1, continued

to their rightful place. Economists have tended to view social policy as dealing only with externalities, but a much broader and deeper concept and vision are needed. Leaders must integrate social policy more creatively with all facets of macroeconomic policy, especially fiscal policy, while avoiding the fiscal crises of recent decades.

As in other regions, social policy should entail far more than social safety nets, which are important countercyclical instruments. During the 1998 crisis, Malaysia increased social spending, with positive economic and social effects. The post-1999 period has seen a sharper focus on the social dimensions of policy across the board in East Asia. A key example is education, which should be central to all policy planning and implementation. Southeast Asia's newly industrializing countries, including Malaysia, suffer from inadequate development of human resources. Although better social policy provisions may not fully address this challenge, Southeast Asia's inadequate past efforts—compared with those in China, Japan, and the first-tier newly industrialized East Asian economies—are a major cause for concern.

A national commitment to better single-session schools within 5 years, for example, would bring greater social benefits than major infrastructure investments. Schools are needed throughout Southeast Asian countries, with better facilities and more teachers to improve teacher–pupil ratios. Better-educated people would presumably be more productive, enabling Malaysia and other countries to escape their low-level technological and industrial trap. A low-cost housing initiative, meanwhile, would help offset gluts in upper-end residential and commercial property.

In sum, beware the recent tendency to limit social policy to providing safety nets in times of crisis, as important and desirable as such countercyclical emergency provisions may be.

"Globalization Plus": Fostering Truly Integrated Economies
by Robert Wade

The official view of the World Bank and the International Monetary Fund, echoed in much commentary in the *Financial Times* and the *Economist*, could be described as "globalization plus." The "globalization" part refers to the need for developing countries to integrate fully into the international economy by eliminating government-induced price differences between international and domestic prices and hence eliminating barriers to trade and foreign investment. The "plus" part, which has entered the integration agenda more recently, refers to the raft of domestic reforms required to make full integration viable. Those reforms include tighter bank supervision to prevent excessive foreign borrowing, legal reforms that protect foreign direct investment, enforcement of intellectual property rights for the same purpose, improvements in the tax-collecting bureaucracy so that domestic taxes can rise as tariffs fall, and social safety nets to buffer the population from the external shocks to which a fully integrated economy is more exposed. And how could one forget good governance, participation, transparency, democratization, environmental protection, and protection of cultural artifacts?

The remarkable thing about this agenda is how poorly it fits the historical experience of the successful developers. Almost all developed countries went through protectionist stages before their firms reached the point where a policy of (more-or-less) free trade was declared in the national interest. The United Kingdom was protectionist when it was trying to catch up with the Netherlands. Germany was protectionist when it was trying to catch up with the United Kingdom. The United States was protectionist when it was trying to catch up with Germany and the United Kingdom. Japan was protectionist for most of the 20th

This writeup is based on a presentation at the December 2001 Brussels ASEM seminar.

continued on next page

BOX 2.2, continued

century right up to the 1970s, and the Republic of Korea and Taiwan (China) were protectionist to the 1990s; none came close to matching today's criteria for "democracy" till the late stages of their catch-ups. Hong Kong (China) and Singapore are the great exceptions in that they did have free trade and they did catch up—but they are city-states dependent on entrepôt trade and are not to be treated as countries. In light of this historical experience, we should be skeptical of claims by representatives of developed countries that ever-freer trade benefits just about everybody.

Nineteenth-century economist Friedrich List laid out a strategy to enable Germany, then a relatively underdeveloped country, to catch up with its Western neighbors. Although more developed neighbors were advocating free trade, List argued that Germany had to use selective protection to help build up the manufacturing capacities of German firms. He generalized in the form of an observation and a prescription. The observation: "It is a very common clever device that when anyone has attained the summit of greatness, he kicks away the ladder by which he has climbed up, in order to deprive others of the means of climbing up after him. In this lies the secret of the cosmopolitan doctrine of Adam Smith." The prescription: "In order to allow freedom of trade to operate naturally, the less advanced nation must first be raised by artificial measures to that stage of cultivation to which the English nation has been artificially elevated."[1]

Yet it is clear from East Asian experience that in the post–World War II world protection alone is not enough and it can hinder more than it helps. Protection has to be part of a larger industrial strategy to nurture the capabilities of domestic firms and raise the rate of domestic investment, always in the context of a private enterprise, market-based economy. The problem in many developing countries—in Latin America and South Asia, for example—has been the absence of this larger industrial strategy, as well as the unwillingness of the "aid" community to help those countries develop sensible industrial strategies.

Today's fast growers—including China, India, and Vietnam—began their fast economic growth well before their fast trade growth, and even longer before their trade liberalizations. They have limited their trade

BOX 2.2, continued

liberalizations by considering the capacities of domestic firms to compete against imports. The World Bank would be the first to question their current trade policies—if they were not growing so fast. If nothing else, their experience shows how little we understand the root causes of economic growth.

In today's development discourse, "integration" refers exclusively to integration into the world economy. However, we need to distinguish between "external" and "internal" integration (or articulation) and to recognize that more external integration can undermine internal integration. So, too, can more internal integration undermine external integration. Development strategy has to operate in the zone where the two forms of integration reinforce rather than undermine each other.

An internally integrated economy has a dense set of input–output linkages between sectors (sectoral articulation), and wage growth is a source of rising demand for domestic production (social articulation). Export demand is not the main source of economic growth. Political coalitions between capitalists and employees become possible in this type of economy because capitalists, employees, and the government recognize that wages are a source of demand as well as a cost of production. This is the economy of Henry Ford, who raised the wages of Ford workers to well above the market rate on the grounds that he wanted his workers to be able to buy the cars they were producing.

In less-articulated economies, by contrast, wages are viewed simply as a cost, not as a source of demand (social disarticulation). Domestic production is not well connected to domestic consumption, leaving exports as the main stimulus to economic growth. Industrial and agricultural sectors producing for foreign markets remain or become enclaves (sectoral disarticulation). This disarticulated structure limits the creation of class alliances and encourages authoritarian political regimes.

How can developing countries create more articulated economies? The fact is that the issues of internal integration—including nuts-and-bolts issues such as how to nurture supply links between domestic firms and the subsidiaries of multinational corporations—have largely

continued on next page

BOX 2.2, continued

dropped out of the development agenda outlined by Western development organizations. This urgently needs remedying. Insofar as these issues are reintroduced, and insofar as developing countries do become internally more articulated over the next 10 to 50 years, the role of social policy in buffering against shocks can remain quite limited.

1. Friedrich List, *The National System of Political Economy* (New York: Kelley, 1966 [1885]), p. 368.

The Great Globalization Debate: Good versus Evil?
by Colin Moynihan

In the late 1990s globalization was hotly debated in international circles, polarizing participants across the black-and-white divide of good versus evil. Nongovernmental organizations (NGOs), the press, international institutions, and academics weighed in: What does globalization mean? Who benefits? What can we do to steer it?

The vociferous opponents of globalization identify capitalism, international institutions, and multinational corporations as root causes of world poverty and inequality. For them, globalization is a term of abuse, and they contend that growth through globalization serves the interests only of the rich and exacerbates inequalities: the rich get richer, but the poor stay poor. Proponents of globalization fight back, arguing that while globalization in all its forms is not perfect and may not be fair, it is the best hope for millions who live in the developing world, and that economic growth must be the point of departure for all improvements in living standards. The global market economy may have flaws, it may need better regulation, it may bring an inequity of rewards, but it is the best agent of social harmony we have. Furthermore, they argue, allowing globalization to become a universal scapegoat—a loose term misused and applied to all the ills afflicting humankind—can be disastrous.

Not surprisingly, truth is more complicated than this simple schism.

Economic integration is globalization in perhaps its most obvious guise. Broadly speaking, economic globalization is the process of creating a single global marketplace through liberalized trade and greater flows of capital across national borders, facilitated by advances in information technology and communications. Globalization, in the shape of rapidly shared expertise, may offer the best hope—not the worst fear—for a host of issues from the environment to local infrastructure and from the labor market to health care.

Based on a presentation at the November 2001 Manila Asia-Europe Meeting (ASEM) seminar.

continued on next page

BOX 2.3, continued

However, wider dissemination of ideas, cultures, and lifestyles has spawned visions of an Orwellian world of uniformity, where the young dress in Gap clothing, eat McDonald's food, drink Coca-Cola, buy coffee from Starbucks, listen to Eminem, and watch *Baywatch*. Is globalization simply a vehicle for Americanizing the world? Are the true colors of globalization standardization, a narrowing of choice, and the lowest common denominator? Or is the opposite more likely to be true? Proponents argue that globalization and the information technology revolution can enhance rather than undermine individual liberty and consumer choice.

The Internet essentially democratizes information and, as for other aspects of the globalization debate, has both its supporters and critics. Some argue that globalization expands people's freedom to make their own choices rather than having them proscribed by the accident of nationality and government. They conclude that such a resource enables democracy and the power and freedom of the individual to penetrate every corner of the globe at incredible speeds, bringing positive change. However, critics hold that the empowerment of the individual portends a crisis of democracy as individual will is pitted against the collective will in the form of democratically elected institutions.

Yet the Internet and e-mail have proved potent weapons in the hands of activists, enabling them to globalize faster than the firms and institutions they target. This has led to the "NGO swarm," where an unstructured grouping of NGOs, linked online, descend on a target, such as the World Trade Organization (WTO) in Seattle in 1999, and plague it with their protests. The result, in that case, was to rob the world's leaders of the political will to reach consensus on the difficult issues confronting them, derailing for a time negotiations to launch a new WTO trade round.

Not too far back in history we can find precedents for today's profound suspicions of the social consequences of rapid economic and technological change. "Luddism" entered our vocabulary nearly 200 years ago, when Ned Ludd's destruction of new textile machinery in factories in England sparked riots in 1812–18, sending shock waves throughout Europe. Richard McCormick, president of the International Chamber of Commerce, described protestors at the Davos World Economic Forum

BOX 2.3, continued

as "modern-day Luddites who want to make the world safe for stagnation."[1] Like Ned Ludd and his reaction to unfamiliar and swift forces out of his control, today's protesters are attempting to understand and influence the currents of change to avoid being swept under them.

The challenge before proponents and opponents alike is to determine how all can benefit from the bountiful fruits of globalization—the variety of goods and services, investment and employment opportunities, and added wealth—while addressing the revolutionary social changes it has unleashed in its wake.

1. World Economic Forum, Davos, Switzerland, January 25–30, 2001.

CHAPTER 6

Linking Macroeconomic and Social Policy: The Irish Experience

by F. Desmond McCarthy

ABSTRACT: Prominent among recent economic success stories is the remarkable achievement of the Irish economy. Within little more than a decade, unemployment fell from more than 17 percent to less than 4 percent, while the country's debt-to-gross domestic product ratio dropped from 117 percent to less than 50 percent. The country achieved this record by negotiating a social pact that cut overall government spending while retaining social welfare provisions. Broad political support combined with the institutional umbrella of the European Union lent credibility, while a strong global economy yielded dramatic results.

In the early 20th century, Irish living standards were comparable to those of northern European economies,[1] with per capita income levels greater than those of Greece, Italy, and Portugal and converging toward those of the United Kingdom and most of Western Europe.[2] However, Ireland's relative position began to slip following independence in the 1920s, especially when the Fianna Fáil Party, which came to power in 1932, emphasized import-substituting industrialization.[3]

The country's economic record remained dismal even into the late 1980s. Chronically high levels of unemployment led many people to emigrate and dampened entrepreneurial activity. The civil service offered one of the main possibilities of employment to those who could pass the extremely competitive exam.

Patrick Honohan provided assistance throughout this project and commented on an earlier draft. The chapter also benefited from discussions with François Bourguignon, Philip Lane, Ronald Long, Colm McCarthy, Dermot McAleese, Kenneth Meyers, Brian Nolan, Philip O'Connell, Rory O'Donnell, Cormac O'Grada, Kevin O'Rourke, John Edelman, and Holger Wolf. Hedy Sladovich provided excellent editorial advice and assistance. An earlier version of this chapter was published in 2001 as a World Bank working paper.

The resulting stable and technically competent cadre would later play an important role in implementing the reforms that revitalized the Irish economy.

Ireland's cultural ethos, which emphasized empathy toward the less fortunate, provided some cushion during difficult times, as did the country's willingness to provide modest social benefits. Stipends were available to the unemployed, and virtually all residents had access to minimum levels of health care. Education, at least through the primary level, was also available to all, with a network of schools within walking distance of most students.

The need for change, however, became apparent by the mid-1980s as the economic situation reached crisis proportions. The oil shocks of the 1970s, aggravated by high interest rates, propelled unemployment levels to 18 percent by 1987, and the ratio of the country's external debt to its gross domestic product (GDP) reached nearly 120 percent. Some analysts feared that the country would even default on its international loans. Awareness grew that the population could no longer tolerate deteriorating living standards, and a broad consensus emerged on the need to improve public finances.

In 1987 the new prime minister, C. Haughey, pushed through a set of dramatic reforms, and the opposition party, which had outlined a similar plan a few years earlier, showed political maturity by supporting the necessary cuts in government spending. A centerpiece of the reforms was the Program for National Recovery (1987–90), which maintained a strong social contract even while the government was curbing overall spending. These reforms occurred alongside the country's growing links to the European Union (EU), which invested in the country's infrastructure to enable it to boost its exports and thus create jobs.

The Program for National Recovery

The Program for National Recovery drew on analysis by the National Economic and Social Council,[4] an advisory body that includes representatives of employers, trade unions, the agriculture sector, and senior civil servants.[5] The social partnership those participants produced was less a bargaining solution than "a shared understanding of the problems facing the Irish economy and society and the main lines of policy required to address them."[6] The timing of the pact was particularly fortunate,[7] because the weak economy and growing role of forward-thinking union leaders facilitated a tripartite agreement between government, employers, and unions.[8] The fact that the previous government had been part of developing the strategy helped secure broad political support.

The social pact covered a wide array of issues, but a key formula provided for moderate wage agreements over 3 years, which helped ensure relatively peaceful labor relations. In return, the government agreed to reform income tax in favor of employees, with an eye toward boosting domestic demand. The agreement also ensured that social welfare programs would not have to bear the brunt of the fiscal retrenchment.[9] The Central Review Committee would monitor progress on the pact, with key questions subject to consultation among the partners.[10]

Fiscal policy included a hiring freeze, an early retirement scheme, and cutbacks in public infrastructure programs, including public housing. Instructions to all government departments to hold the line on expenditures benefited from the political climate and the relative strength of the civil service, because senior civil servants implemented these reforms. A tax amnesty in 1988 backed by credible threats boosted compliance with tax laws immediately and over several ensuing years.

Meanwhile, fiscal balance required an appropriate exchange rate. Ireland's real exchange rate (see Table 6.1) was appreciating by about 1 percent a year against other EU currencies, owing to higher wage and price inflation. This upward trend slowed in the late 1980s because of domestic wage restraint, and the real exchange rate remained competitive until 1992. However, when the Bank of England withdrew the pound sterling from the economic and monetary union and its value fell 15 percent on the foreign exchange market, Irish exports to the United Kingdom lost competitiveness because the Irish pound was overvalued. After expensive intervention, the Central Bank of Ireland devalued the Irish pound by 10 percent in early 1993, and for the rest of the 1990s Ireland was able to maintain its export competitiveness.

The confidence that ensued from these stabilization measures allowed favorable interest rates, though initially not quite as low as deutsche mark rates. All these factors allowed Finance Minister Ray MacSharry to restrain public spending, wiping out the fiscal deficit in 3 years. In 1986 the budget deficit totaled 7.9 percent of GDP, whereas public sector borrowing had reached 14.2 percent. By 1990 the corresponding figures had dropped to 0.6 and 2.8 percent, respectively.[11] During these years the government's share of total revenue went from 37.9 to 34.5 percent of gross national product (GNP), while spending fell dramatically from 45.8 to 35.1 percent of GNP.

The successful fiscal correction, a competitive real exchange rate, and the concomitant fall in interest rates provided the macroeconomic basis for growth, and by 1990 Ireland's growth rate had reached 8.5 percent. As confidence in the overall policy grew, participants in the tripartite agreement negotiated a series of ensuing 3-year agreements. These included the Program for Economic and

Table 6.1 Ireland: Selected Economic Indicators

Year	Growth of GDP (%)	Unemployment (% total labor force)	Gross general government debt/GDP (%)	Fiscal deficit (% of GDP)[a]	Current account (% of GDP)[b]	Inflation rate (CPI)	Real exchange rate (earnings)[c]	Current government expenditures (% of GNP)[d]		
								Education	Health	Social security
1981	3.33	9.9	78.0	-13.7	-14.6	20.3	91	6.0	7.3	10.4
1982	2.28	11.4	87.2	-13.3	-10.9	17.2	97	6.3	7.4	12.6
1983	-0.24	14.0	97.4	-10.9	-7.5	10.5	96	6.2	7.4	13.3
1984	4.35	15.6	102.5	-10.2	-6.6	8.6	96	6.2	7.1	13.6
1985	3.09	17.4	104.0	-10.3	-4.8	5.4	98	6.2	7.2	13.8
1986	-0.43	17.4	114.5	-10.3	-4.2	3.8	104	6.2	7.0	14.1
1987	4.66	16.9	116.8	-8.2	-1.3	3.2	102	6.3	6.6	13.6
1988	5.22	16.3	112.4	-4.3	-1.2	2.1	99	5.8	6.2	12.9
1989	5.81	15.0	101.8	-1.7	-2.9	4.0	96	5.6	6.0	11.9
1990	8.47	12.9	96.0	-2.2	-1.8	3.3	100	5.3	6.3	11.3

1991	1.93	14.7	95.3	-2.3	-0.4	3.2	98	5.4	6.7	12.0
1992	3.34	15.1	92.3	-2.4	0.4	3.0	100	5.8	7.0	12.6
1993	2.69	15.7	96.3	-2.3	3.7	1.4	94	5.9	7.1	12.2
1994	5.76	14.7	88.2	-1.7	2.9	2.4	92	5.9	7.0	11.7
1995	9.74	12.2	78.9	-2.2	2.8	2.5	93	5.5	6.8	11.7
1996	7.69	11.9	74.1	-0.6	3.3	1.7	95	5.3	6.5	10.7
1997	10.74	10.3	65.1	0.8	3.1	1.5	95	5.1	6.6	9.8
1998	8.56	7.8	55.0	2.1	0.9	2.4	92	4.9	6.5	9.0
1999	9.82	5.7	50.1	1.9	0.4	1.6	91	4.9	6.7	8.4
2000	11.00	4.3	39.1	4.7	-1.7	5.7	88	n.a.	n.a.	n.a.

n.a. = not available.

a. Before 1987, Exchequer borrowing requirement; from 1987, general government surplus (EU definition). (In 1987 the former was almost exactly the same as the latter, at 8.1.)
b. Based on Central Statistics Office, Ireland, *National Income and Expenditure 2000*.
c. Based on hourly earnings. Index 1992 = 100. *Sources*: Department of Finance (to 1990); Central Bank of Ireland.
d. Central Statistics Office, Dublin: *Social Protection Accounts, Expenditure of Central and Local Governments* (Stationery Office, various years).

Social Progress of 1990–93, the Program for Competitiveness and Work of 1994–96, the Partnership 2000 of 1997–2000, and the Program for Prosperity and Fairness. As economic gains continued through the 1990s, the agreements placed growing emphasis on fostering social cohesion and regional development and on reducing poverty.

The Opening to Europe

As stabilization measures progressed, Ireland needed to take additional action to stimulate economic growth. Given the country's large external debt, the export sector had to play a larger role. This, in turn, required a competitive economy supported by adequate foreign investment.

Ireland had become a member of the European Economic Community in 1973, which led to a broader free trade regime[12] and a new economic awakening. The United Kingdom and the United States had long tended to play a dominant role in the Irish economy. However, the growing importance of the European Union encouraged the younger generation to look to Europe, and this new attitude fostered a steady rise in entrepreneurial spirit. EU membership also imposed fiscal and macroeconomic constraints on policymakers while providing rewards for prudent action. Foreign business, in turn, saw the advantages of a well-educated, English-speaking populace with ready access to the large European market and the broad institutional stability provided by the European umbrella.

After years of indifferent performance, however, the domestic economy was ill prepared to face international competition; the country's communications, transport, and power infrastructure was weak. Ireland's Industrial Development Authority had focused its strategy on attracting dynamic U.S. firms by offering a well-educated work force, good labor relations, access to the large European market, and a low corporate income tax rate—10 percent after 1979.[13] Although some foreign firms took advantage of such enticements in the 1970s and early 1980s, links between foreign subsidiaries and the rest of the economy were weak, and many companies tended to gravitate toward more favorable offers in other countries.

In the late 1980s two fortuitous changes occurred. First, multinational entities moved from the mass-production model and reliance on relatively insulated subsidiaries toward the Japanese style of greater flexibility and investment in subsidiaries integrated with local economies.[14] New technology, meanwhile, reduced transport and communications costs, sharply offsetting Ireland's disadvantage as an island economy. The Industrial Development Authority perceived those trends and quickly attracted several flagship companies enjoying rapid global growth, such as Intel and Microsoft, as well as chemical and pharmaceutical multinationals.

Ireland benefited greatly from the European Union's Common Agricultural Policy (CAP), which maintained prices for agricultural goods above those of world markets. Consumers paid the cost, while Ireland, a net exporter of farm goods, was a major beneficiary. Estimates of the size of this economic transfer range from 2 to 6 percent of GNP annually.[15]

Ireland also received resources from three European Commission (EC) structural funds to develop its physical and social infrastructure to enable it to compete in the EU single market: the European Regional Development Fund, designed to assist development of poorer regions; the European Social Fund; and the guidance section of the European Agriculture Guidance and Guarantee Fund. The Maastricht Treaty of 1993 established a fourth fund, the Cohesion Fund, aimed at developing transport infrastructure. Net receipts from those sources totaled about 3 percent of Ireland's GNP, allowing the country to resume projects deferred during the fiscal crunch while at the same time easing the pressure on government expenditures.

Although this transfer of funds was important, the EU association also produced indirect benefits. The Maastricht Treaty, which provided a clear outline for achieving European economic and monetary union, helped curtail expansionary fiscal experiments among member governments.

By 1990 exports were growing by 8 percent annually,[16] expanding from 38 percent of GDP in 1973 to 62 percent by 1991 and to 86 percent by 1999. Exports also shifted from primary goods, mainly agricultural, to manufactured goods[17] (see Table 6.2). The North American share of those exports grew from 9.1 percent in 1987 to 17.9 percent in 2000, while the European share remained stable at close to 40 percent.

Table 6.2 Ireland: Destination of Exports by Area (%)

	United Kingdom	Other EU	NAFTA Countries	Rest of World	Total
1987	34.2	39.3	9.1	17.5	100
2000	22.2	39.8	17.9	20.1	100

NAFTA = North American Free Trade Agreement.

Source: Central Statistics Office, *Trade Statistics* (Dublin: Stationery Office, various years).

Addressing Unemployment

The strong increase in exports did not at first make significant inroads into the unemployment problem. In the 1970s and especially in the early 1980s, as the country removed protections from domestic industry and adjusted to the European market, many traditional Irish industries had declined precipitously, including the automobile, textile, and leather goods sectors. At first the stronger chemical, pharmaceutical, and electronic sectors, which tended to be more capital intensive, did not offset the earlier employment losses. Some critics commented that the multinationals were producing growth without employment; others argued that they were simply taking advantage of favorable corporate income tax rates. However, it soon became evident that these new companies were also building links with domestic suppliers, thereby strengthening the country's entrepreneurial skills.

The poor employment situation was further compounded in the 1980s by the sluggish economies in the United Kingdom and United States, the traditional destinations for Irish emigration. The result was a dramatic rise in unemployment to around 17.4 percent in 1986. By 1993 this level had changed little. Even more disconcerting, the share of the long-term unemployed (people who had remained jobless for more than 12 months) rose from one-third to one-half. By 1990 all groups agreed on the need to address unemployment, especially long-term joblessness. Toward that end, the state began to spend substantial amounts—which reached 1.75 percent of GDP in 1996—on active labor market policies. For example, public works programs provided an initial step toward better jobs for the long-term unemployed who lacked adequate education.

Ireland also sustained its spending on education, health, and income maintenance—what is broadly termed social security.[18] In Ireland, social security encompasses two main schemes: social insurance, which pays out contributions from employers, employees, and the state, and social assistance, which provides means-tested payments to older and unemployed workers. Ireland is a pay-related welfare state: it seeks to provide a basic level of security and service to virtually all residents while allowing them to supplement their social citizenship rights with their own resources.[19]

Under the terms of the social partnership accords, the government maintained and even raised the real value of unemployment and assistance payments and even increased some after 1987. However, the buoyant economy more than offset the steady rise in social security payments. Ireland spent about 13 percent of its GDP on social security in 1987, but by 1997 this number had dropped to 9 percent—lower than in most EU countries.

Expenditures on education followed a similar pattern. In 1967 secondary education became free, and in 1968 means-tested grants for higher education began to boost participation dramatically. Government spending on education was 50 percent higher in 1997 than in 1981, but had dropped from 6 percent to 5.1 percent of GDP. Those expenditures produced the highly skilled work force that helped propel the economic growth of the 1990s.

Expenditures on health similarly grew by 78 percent in real terms from 1987 to 1997, but because of spectacular economic growth rates, their share of GDP remained lower than in most Organization for Economic Cooperation and Development countries. About one-third of the population has access to free health care, and the remaining two-thirds to public hospitals at a modest fee, although many buy private health insurance.

By the end of 2000 the unemployment rate had dropped to 3.9 percent—even while the labor force was expanding from 1.3 million in 1987 to 1.8 million—and poverty levels also declined substantially. The dramatic turnaround reflected a rapid rise in participation rates, especially among females; the gradual spread of high economic growth to other parts of the Irish economy, especially the service sector; growth in government expenditures for health and education; and an active labor policy. Many Irish returned home, the government recruited new workers abroad, and autonomous flows of workers came from Eastern European and African countries. The returnees were generally better educated than those who had left Ireland, and their considerable technical and entrepreneurial skills enabled the country to respond to the demands of a dynamic economy.[20]

Lessons from the Irish Experience

Ireland's experience in the 1990s was remarkable: it went from a highly indebted, high-unemployment country to a low-debt, low-unemployment country in 10 years. Key factors underlying this record included facilitation of realistic discussion by institutions rather than clientism, a forward-looking trade union movement, and a realization among businesses that they could no longer count on direct and indirect protection.

Ireland solved its fiscal deficit by using forceful leadership to secure clear support from all major political parties, presenting objectives clearly to the public, and spreading the pain of stabilization across all groups while protecting social welfare. All key groups realized what they could gain by supporting reform measures.

Broad-based support for economic reform ensured moderate wage increases in exchange for tax concessions, together with a guaranteed social welfare package for all. The broad institutional umbrella of the European Union provided a combination of macroeconomic rules and an array of resource transfers. Growth resulted from innovative measures designed to attract foreign direct investment (FDI) and then reductions in the tax burden designed to buoy domestic demand. Analysis of the poverty situation identified unemployment as a major underlying problem, and an active labor policy then addressed it. Creation of locally based partnerships to address social exclusion and unemployment in a flexible, decentralized, and participatory way also played an important role.[21]

Although Ireland's approach would be difficult to replicate in its entirety, Ireland's experience may offer ideas for countries facing similar problems, including an untenable debt/GDP ratio, high unemployment, a large agricultural workforce, and a lack of confidence in institutions.[22] Ireland's response to those challenges needs to be viewed in the overall context of the global and domestic economy together with specifically Irish characteristics.

For example, considerable debate has ensued about why and how Ireland addressed unemployment so well. One argument stresses the country's improvements in competitiveness, noting the move to free trade, macroeconomic stability, acceptance of competition and the market system, and reductions in the fiscal deficit.[23] Other interpretations stress factors specific to Ireland, especially its emphasis on social inclusion. As incomes rose the government devised policies to address social exclusion and extended the concept of poverty to encompass noneconomic indicators. This created a virtuous cycle: raising real incomes reinforced economic growth and cut unemployment by expanding demand.

In 1981 agriculture accounted for about 14.7 percent of employment, but as the economy developed this share fell steadily to 9 percent in 2000. Many countries have seen agricultural employment decline—in fact, a structural shift from agriculture to the service sector seems to be an inevitable feature of development. The Irish experience is notable, however, because major social unrest did not accompany the sharp drop. In Ireland large transfers under the CAP scheme, together with a protective wall for European agriculture, cushioned the decline in employment and incomes in the agricultural sector, while a rapidly growing economy readily absorbed surplus labor. Many other countries have received similar transfers without achieving notable results, and more study of the efficient use of transfers might offer useful lessons.

Ireland's experience shows that success in attracting FDI requires strong administrative capacity, a good educational system, and stable public policies. A country may build foreign confidence in its institutions if it establishes clear accounting standards and a fair and equitable legal system. The EU's de facto supervision-cum-incentive structure helped support domestic politicians who sought greater accountability and transparency in the use of public funds. Although many countries cannot realistically aspire to EU membership, participation in another such umbrella group can provide important guidance and incentives.

A favorable corporate income tax regime, supported by taxation treaties with the United States and other FDI source countries, together with a well-educated, English-speaking labor force and the large European market, proved major attractions to foreign direct investment. The Industrial Development Authority's strategy of focusing initially on a few high-profile multinationals in the information technology and chemical sectors was fortuitous because their industrial structure allowed them the flexibility to invest while global demand was growing strongly. Underlying that strategy was rising confidence that Ireland would indeed be a reliable bridge to Europe, which led to a change in how companies saw Ireland. Rather than locating only branches there, companies began to establish European headquarters—a substantial change in multinationals' historic approach to FDI.

Sustaining Success

Is Ireland's approach sustainable? Much of its success relies on external factors. Risks include a likely decline in EU resources, a fall in global demand for exports, and a drop in investment by multinationals. In a favorable global climate, especially for the information technology sector, this FDI strategy has much to offer. In addition to its direct effect on exports and employment, it helped foster links to many domestic companies, thereby strengthening them. In a less favorable global climate, however, policymakers will face serious challenges in maintaining the flow of foreign investment because companies seek market advantages wherever they occur. Multinationals' links to the domestic economy may thus turn out to be a disadvantage in a dramatic economic downturn.

Policymakers will need to address downturns in the global economy while investing further in infrastructure needs such as roads, power, and housing. Environmental concerns are likely to move toward center stage. The present education system has served the country well, but the health care system needs upgrading, with long waiting lists for hospital services among the major concerns. Both areas will need continued investment to meet residents' expectations and ensure a healthy and highly skilled labor force.

Pervading all these policy choices is the issue of the appropriate roles for the public and private sectors. Ireland's approach has been pragmatic; it has moved to privatize some public entities while subjecting others to regulation. In a small domestic economy, it may be unrealistic to expect many firms to compete in certain sectors. These decisions will become more difficult as authorities face the need to ensure adequate incentives for investment while maintaining social cohesion.

Notes

1. Cormac O'Grada, "From 'Frugal Comfort' to Ten Thousand a Year: Trade and Growth in the Irish Economy" (University College Dublin, 2001).

2. J. J. Lee, *Ireland: 1912–1985: Politics and Society* (Cambridge, England: Cambridge University Press, 1989).

3. Cormac O'Grada and Kevin O'Rourke, "Irish Economic Growth 1950–1988," in *Economic Growth in Europe since 1945*, ed. N. F. R. Crafts and G. Toniolo (Cambridge, England: Cambridge University Press, 1995).

4. The Program for National Recovery was to be the first of five subsequent agreements. Each social partnership agreement was preceded by a National Economic and Social Council strategy report, which set out the parameters within which the social partners should negotiate a new program. Rory O'Donnell, "Towards Post-Corporatist Concertation in Europe" in *Interlocking Dimensions of European Integration*, ed. Wallace Hellen (London: Pinter, 2001).

5. O'Donnell (op. cit.) suggests that Ireland, together with some other small European member states, is inventing a new postcorporatist form of macroeconomic concertation and structural reform, which differs from the dominant continental European models—French, German, and Scandinavian.

6. Rory O'Donnell, "Ireland's Economic Transformation," Center for West European Studies, European Union Center, Working Paper No. 2, University of Pittsburgh, 1998.

7. Some argue that a consensus evolved only when the situation became truly desperate and, thus, was endogenous to the crisis.

8. Over time the partnership widened to include representatives of voluntary and community organizations. Partnership 2000 involved representatives of the unemployed, women's groups, and others addressing social exclusion.

9. The Irish social welfare system does not lend itself to easy categorization. Many features follow U.K. precedents and so may be loosely termed "liberal." In the mid-1990s, Ireland's expenditures on social insurance plus social assistance totaled about 10 percent of GDP, among the lowest in Europe. See Tim Callan and Brian Nolan, "Taxation and Social Welfare," in *Bust to Boom: The Irish Experience of Growth and Equality*, ed. Brian Nolan, Philip J. O'Connell, and Christopher T. Whelan (Dublin: Institute of Public Administration, Johnswood Press, 2000). Other major welfare expenditures for health and education typically added a further 10 percent (see Table 6.1 for yearly figures).

10. Patrick Honohan discusses the background and linkages in greater detail. See Patrick Honohan, "Fiscal Adjustment and Disinflation in Ireland Setting the Macro Basis of Economic Recovery

and Expansion," in *Understanding Ireland's Economic Growth,* ed. Frank Barry (New York: Palgrave Macmillan, 1999).

11. Ireland Department of Finance. The primary deficit is the exchequer borrowing requirement exclusive of interest payment.

12. Ireland had already established free trade with the United Kingdom beginning in the mid-1960s.

13. The European Commission viewed the special rate of taxation as a state subsidy. The government is now committed to having the standard rate of corporate income tax at 12.5 percent by 2003.

14. See Charles F. Sabel, *Local Development in Ireland: Partnership, Innovation and Social Justice,* (Paris, Organization for Economic Cooperation and Development, 1996).

15. A. Matthews, *Managing the Structural Funds in Ireland* (Cork, Ireland: Cork University Press, 1994).

16. The volume index would quadruple from 1990 to 2000, for an average annual growth rate of 15 percent.

17. In 1987 agricultural produce was 17.5 percent of exports. This share fell to 4.8 percent in 2000. Industrial produce rose from 80.2 percent to 92.8 percent over the same period.

18. See Sean O'Riain and Philip J. O'Connell, "The Role of the State in Growth and Welfare," in *Bust to Boom: The Irish Experience of Growth and Equality,* ed. Brian Nolan, Philip J. O'Connell, and Christopher T. Whelan (Dublin: Institute of Public Administration, Johnswood Press, 2000). Historically housing has been an important component of public expenditure. In Ireland the rate of house ownership has been one of the highest in the world, at around 80 percent. Since 1987 expenditures on housing have dropped from 5 percent of public expenditure in 1987 to 2.5 percent in 1990. For a discussion of this policy change, see Tony Fahey and James Williams, "The Spatial Distribution of Disadvantage in Ireland," in *Bust to Boom,* op. cit.

19. P. O'Connell and D. Rottman, "The Irish Welfare State in Comparative Perspective," in *The Development of Industrial Society in Ireland,* ed. J. Goldthorpe and C. Whelan (London: The British Academy and Oxford University Press, 1992).

20. Philip J. O'Connell, "Are They Working? Market Orientation and the Effectiveness of Active Labour Market Programmes in Ireland," Economic and Social Research Institute, *European Sociological Review,* 2000.

21. Sabel, op. cit.

22. Alan W. Gray, ed., *International Perspectives on the Irish Economy* (Dublin: Indecon Economic Consultants, 1997).

23. Dermot McAleese, "Economic Policy and Performance: The Irish Experience," *Journal of the Statistical and Social Inquiry Society of Ireland* 37, no. 5 (1997): 1–31.

CHAPTER 7

The Solidarity Alternative: Lessons from a Norwegian Experience

by Jonas Gahr Støre

ABSTRACT: This chapter examines the Norwegian initiative to address deep-seated unemployment that was introduced in the early 1990s by a multistakeholder coalition of government, trade unions, and business. The strong consensus for reform yielded important results, but the coalition may be fraying.

The Norwegian experience known today as the Solidarity Alternative aimed to address unemployment in the early 1990s that was unacceptably high by Norwegian standards. A national commission proposed an action plan that was also designed to improve public finances and industrial competitiveness.

The story of the Solidarity Alternative reflects what is often referred to as the Nordic social model: it was a comprehensive approach requiring the active participation of all stakeholders, including labor unions, employers, parliament, and the central government. The scheme was successful: unemployment dropped and industrial competitiveness improved beyond expectations and forecasts, illustrating the potential inherent in a comprehensive, multistakeholder approach.

Hindsight nonetheless suggests some lessons and shortcomings. Today, with the scourge of unemployment seemingly in the past, the collective wisdom that delivered the Solidarity Alternative may be vanishing.

The Starting Point

Postwar Norway secured full employment decade after decade. Indeed, Organization for Economic Cooperation and Development (OECD) experts observed in the 1950s that Norway's main challenge was a lack of labor and urged the government to encourage women to participate in the labor market.

Despite that plea, Norway had among the lowest work force participation rates among women in Europe until the late 1960s. However, the situation changed radically beginning in the early 1970s, when both women's enrollment in higher education and participation in the labor market grew rapidly, bringing their participation to near the top of Europe in only 10–15 years.

Since the 1970s Norwegian governments have faced the opportunities and challenges of rising revenues from the petroleum sector. With full employment, growing domestic demand, and the gradual phasing-in of oil revenues, governments saw their prime challenge as maintaining low inflation and industrial competitiveness. Income policies and wages were seen as key instruments toward that end. Norway had long pursued comprehensive wage settlements among a powerful labor union confederation speaking on behalf of many, a unified employer organization setting standards for sectors, and individual companies. Government facilitated mutually acceptable agreements by offering tax cuts to secure workers' purchasing power and providing legislation on social reforms.

But the system also had flaws. From the 1970s until 1986 the government was repeatedly obliged to devalue the country's currency to reduce pressure on the Norwegian economy and to safeguard industrial competitiveness. In the mid-1980s wage increases outpaced those in competing countries, and inflation rose well above 10 percent. Then, after the fall of oil prices in 1986, the economy went into recession. In response, Norway accepted an unprecedented measure in 1988: a law limiting increases in wages and prices.

Toward the end of the 1980s, unemployment rose to 6–7 percent—record levels by Norwegian standards. A broad understanding emerged among the social partners and political parties that they needed stronger collaboration on labor market policies.

A National Commission on Employment

In 1991 the government of Prime Minister Gro Harlem Brundtland established the National Commission on Employment, which included representatives of all parties in parliament as well as all unions and employer organizations. The commission worked for less than a year. The chair, former finance minister Per Kleppe, recounts how the commission leaned on the theories of U.K. economists Richard Layard, Stephen Nickell, and Richard Jackman, writing in *Unemployment: Macroeconomic Performance and the Labour Market*.[1] The authors analyzed modern unemployment largely from a structural and institutional point of view, whereas older studies had emphasized simple demand for labor.

The commission's mandate was ambitious. A key condition was to secure a stable currency: no more managed devaluations or revaluations. Norway had to accept the full consequences of living in an open world economy, in particular an open European economy. The country had to improve competitiveness through other means—namely, by controlling industrial costs and wages, because Norwegian costs were high compared with those of most other OECD countries.

The commission targeted a 10 percent improvement in cost competitiveness from 1993 to 1997 and set a goal of 3 percent annual wage increases, in contrast to expected increases in other countries of 4–5 percent. The commission also aimed to reduce joblessness from 6 percent in 1993 to the "nonaccelerating inflation rate of unemployment"—estimated to lie around 3 percent—by the end of the 1990s.

Solidarity Alternative became the name of the comprehensive policy as implemented by the government of Gro Harlem Brundtland in 1992. The political message was short and simple: We who have jobs must show solidarity toward those who do not. We need to lower the barriers to the labor market by showing restraint in individual demands. If we succeed, we all stand to gain: as more people work, industry's costs will be lower, and real purchasing power will benefit from falling interest rates. All major parties in the political spectrum bought into this approach and argued the case before their constituencies, pointing to the potential gains from acting collectively.

Five key consensus recommendations underlay the Solidarity Alternative:

- *Wage settlement.* Social partners pledged themselves to a binding scheme to moderate wage increases and to seek instead higher purchasing power through lower inflation and interest rates. Key to the wage settlement was the leading role of LO (Norwegian Confederation of Trade Unions), the main labor union, because LO could speak on behalf of many. A central feature of the wage provision was that parties representing industry exposed to foreign competition settle first, setting the standard for ensuing negotiations and thus ensuring that sectors more protected from outside competition did not override the needs of the competitive sector.
- *Financial policy as a stabilizing factor.* To a large extent, Norwegian unemployment resulted from declining economic activity, which the government addressed through a very active fiscal policy aimed at boosting domestic demand. Between 1989 and 1993 Norway's was the most expansive fiscal policy of all OECD countries. However, after 1993, as industrial activity increased and interest rates came down, the government pursued a

more contractive approach and reexamined public expenditures that did not support employment, in particular, transfers to individuals. This proved politically complex, but participants applied the commission's recommendations fully.

- *Active labor market policies.* As a distinctive feature of the Solidarity Alternative, participants agreed to keep unemployment benefits significantly lower than those in Denmark and Sweden and to maintain strict provisions on job alternatives: a decline of a job offer could lead to a loss of unemployment benefits. The government also allocated significant resources to providing jobs and training programs to the unemployed.
- *Education.* Although not initially a major feature, education turned out to be central to the pact. Unemployment was hitting young people with limited training, and Norway had a far less comprehensive trainee tradition than, for example, Germany. Thus, the pact emphasized creating more trainee posts as well as lifelong learning opportunities. The major change, however, was a set of educational reforms aimed at expanding the capacity of higher education. The number of Norwegian students in higher education doubled in a few years, changing the nature of higher education institutions and helping keep many young people off unemployment while offering them new skills and qualifications.
- *Social policy.* The number of people on public assistance and pensions had risen significantly in the 1980s. The commission aimed to focus attention and resources on leading people back into the labor market—a goal that rendered the target of full employment even harder. By implementing the "working line"—that is, by emphasizing the importance of work—the government now saves money on social expenditures but spends more on sick leave and rehabilitation as it brings more vulnerable people into the labor market.

How Did It Go?

The Solidarity Alternative must be judged as a whole, because its elements were meant to work in concert. Moderate wage settlements were to lead to low inflation, improved competitiveness, and more jobs, as well as to allow the state to shift its labor market focus. The government delivered a number of major social reforms to facilitate comprehensive settlements among the social partners, such as lowering the pension age (a paradox when the challenge switched from high unemployment to a labor shortage), ensuring a right to lifelong learning, and extending vacation time and a number of social family reforms (bringing paid maternity leave from 15 weeks to 52 weeks).

Toward the end of the 1990s these policies delivered a success story: Norway experienced strong growth in employment. The commission had expected the creation of 100,000 new jobs, but they totaled nearly 160,000. Unemployment fell sharply—more than the commission anticipated—to less than 3 percent. Despite moderate wage settlements, real purchasing power grew by 1.75 percent annually, securing legitimacy for the approach among labor unions. Private consumption and investment have also risen more than expected, leading to more employment in the private sector and more industrial exports.

The Limits to Solidarity

Two underlying conditions were essential to the Solidarity Alternative. The first was a clearly identified challenge inviting all stakeholders to unite, and the second was their acceptance of the need to share burdens and gains equitably. Those conditions were in place in 1991–92.

As the years went by, both conditions came under pressure. First, unemployment rates fell sharply, and by 1996–97 "Jobs for All" was a slogan with far less meaning than in 1990, when unemployment was high. The glue of the comprehensive approach was losing its strength.

Second, major stakeholders held different views on the sharing of burdens and gains. At the major wage settlement in 1998, raises were substantially higher than in competing countries. The LO leadership first recommended moderate wage increases, but LO members voted down the recommended settlement and a national strike followed. The same sequence of events occurred in 2000. A key component of the Solidarity Alternative had been shaken. A decade after the work of the National Employment Commission, Norway was returning to a familiar landscape. After a few years of discipline and moderation, the country again suffered significantly higher cost increases than competing countries, putting exposed industries in immediate danger of being priced out of business.

During the second half of the 1990s, the Norwegian public also saw record high wage increases for chief executive officers of Norwegian companies, as well as comfortable and even extravagant pension and option schemes for top management. The media gave such developments significant attention. Norwegian top managers are paid less than their counterparts in other OECD countries, and they argue that they are only catching up. But they overlooked a crucial point: the traditional Nordic model views relatively small wage differentials among employees as a virtue. In a setting where all pledged to support the cause of soli-darity and moderation, the meaning of such a pledge is severely damaged when one group defines a very different set of obligations.

Furthermore, after some years of expanding public budgets, the government shifted toward seeking to cool the economy through stricter budget discipline, but pressure gradually grew for larger public expenditures to meet a variety of needs. On top of this came a gradual transformation of Norway's macroeconomic setting. Since 1996 Norway has been accumulating budget surpluses because of higher revenues from the oil and gas sector. The government has transferred almost all these surpluses to the state-controlled Petroleum Fund, which the government invests outside Norway to help smooth growing pension costs and, eventually, falling revenues from the petroleum sector.

The budget surplus has rapidly changed expectations. Low unemployment, a rich state, and a number of remaining gaps in the welfare state have exerted pres-sure on both wage increases ("we want our share") and more expansive public expenditures ("how can we let hospitals run with old equipment when we have billions in the accounts?").

The social partners are also changing. LO is no longer as dominant a force on the union side, and alternative unions want their say. On the employer side, busi-nesses are calling for more diversified wage settlements that would allow each sector and each company to settle more freely.

Norway's challenge today resembles that of the 1950s in that it has a shortage of labor, but with one significant difference: Norway has already mobilized most of its labor reserves. Debate now focuses on getting people on short- and long-term sick leave back to work and on enacting rules and regulations to increase immigration, with all the sensitive political strings attached.

Goodbye Solidarity?

Was the Solidarity Alternative a last unified show of collective wisdom? Can Norwegian stakeholders reunite around a new set of shared objectives and shoul-der those burdens? In the late winter of 2002, as we headed toward a major new round of wage settlements, LO still pledged its support for the Solidarity Alternative, although some critics say that the confederation has lost its clout. On the employer side, many say that the Solidarity Alternative is dead.

The Solidarity Alternative reflects specific Norwegian features. Most impor-tant is the Nordic tradition of uniting stakeholders around common political and economic objectives when necessary. This requires a common reading of the challenges, as well as opportunities for all to reap benefits. The approach should inspire policymakers in other countries, even those with very different social structures. However, they should realize that a common challenge strong enough to require collective wisdom is essential to convincing stakeholders to sing the same tune.

Note

1. Richard Layard, Stephen Nickell, and Richard Jackman, *Unemployment: Macroeconomic Performance and the Labour Market* (Oxford, England: Oxford University Press, 1991).

BOX 2.4

A Social Agenda in Practice—France
by Jean-Michel Severino

The ideal of a comprehensive agenda driving social policy has been a reality for some decades now in France, not only because of political vision but also because of the play of political forces.

This agenda is dynamic and moving rapidly. Successive changes come in part as a result of popular and visionary "models," which have inspired the evolution of a wide range of economic and fiscal policies, social protection schemes, and institutions. However, the true engine of change lies with social forces and structural changes, which are putting fierce pressures on the models and the hypotheses behind them.

France today is a prime illustration. Demographic changes probably constitute the major force that challenges the status quo. Today, in France, a woman can expect to live to 81 years and a man to 74 years, and life expectancy rises by about 4 months each year. Despite a recent baby boom, an aging population is very much a reality and has wide-ranging repercussions. These changes have obvious effects on the economy and the society, but also on the way social policy is designed: for instance, more attention is now paid to in-kind services to the elderly, and infant care is a prime issue especially in large cities. Immigration is another source of pressure. Even though mass arrivals of young foreign workers have tapered off, migration flows have not stopped. Whether legal or illegal, such new arrivals exert pressure on the country's capacity to provide social services for all, and those issues are tightly linked to growing instances of social exclusion and social tension.

Parallel to demographic changes are changes in France's industrial structure and in the nature of work. Despite a recent decline, unemployment has remained high in the past 20 years for many reasons, including a macroeconomic policy that has put the reduction of inflation at its forefront. The reduction of working time to 35 hours a week has been seen as a solution, but only a partial one, because implementation problems have arisen and unemployment persists at high levels. Two decades of stubborn unemployment have created a whole range of new problems,

continued on next page

BOX 2.4, continued

such as juvenile delinquency, urban insecurity, and real urban misery, which burst out as issues at the core of the 2002 French presidential and legislative elections.

France, of course, benefits from very solid and well-performing social institutions, such as health care, where extraordinary achievements are reflected in the 2001 World Health Organization survey,[1] and the education system, which regularly stands out in cross-national reviews and surveys. French welfare as a whole offers many benefits, and French people today enjoy much more time for leisure and family than their ancestors. But important issues are looming, and the political leaders confront continuous questions about the nature of welfare benefits, appropriate and fair levels of financial contributions, and the organization of delivery. Those questions indicate the shape of the social agenda for the future. To meet those challenges successfully and preserve its welfare state at the same time, France will have to try to strike the right balance between competitiveness and high social taxes, between extensiveness of protection and fairness in its delivery as well as risk of fraud, and between generosity in access and concerns about illegal immigration.

1. *World Health Report 2001* (Geneva: World Health Organization, 2001).

BOX 2.5

The "Pact for Italy": An Integrated Strategy toward Growth and Employment
by Olivier Butzbach

In July 2002, the Italian government, together with its social partners (all but one of the major trade unions plus business organizations), signed a document called "*Patto per l'Italia*" (Pact for Italy), which outlines a set of objectives to attain higher growth, productivity, and employment.

The pact's main innovation is its comprehensiveness, especially the integration between macroeconomic and social objectives and between fiscal and labor market instruments. This integration is in line with the European summits of Lisbon and Barcelona, which also highlighted the interlocking of economic growth and social justice. The pact's philosophy is summarized in its introduction: "The organization of a transparent and efficient labor market, the formalization of informal work, education, and training policies, and the reduction of fiscal pressure on low-to-middle incomes constitute converging tools to promote a better translation of economic growth into more and better jobs."

The pact's three sections each cover a specific policy field. The first (titled "Revenue and Social Cohesion Policy") is fiscal reform aimed at reducing fiscal pressure on low and middle-income households (priority is given to those with incomes below 25,000 euros a year) and on firms; making the fiscal system simpler (especially for small and medium-size enterprises, with the introduction of simplified tax documents); and improving monitoring and control. The "theory of change" behind these measures aims to create a virtuous circle among economic growth, competitiveness, increased employment, and social cohesion. The fiscal reform aims to keep public spending and inflation rates low and give households more available revenue.

The second section addresses employment. Called "welfare to work," it is directly inspired by similar programs elsewhere in Europe. It touches on various broad areas of employment policies. The first is job-matching, one of the weaknesses of Italy's labor market (the pact notes that only 4 percent of working relationships go through formal

continued on next page

BOX 2.5, continued

job-matching mechanisms). It aims to create an efficient network of job services by reorganizing existing systems, expanding private schemes, and launching a permanent (and virtual) place of exchange between Ministry of Labor, social protection organizations, and service providers. Another action area is "education for employability" (*l'educazione per l'occupabilità*). Again in line with European strategy, the pact aims to "enrich human resources" through reforms in public education and support for permanent and professional training schemes. More courses are to be offered in basic skills (languages, mathematics, technology) for up to 700,000 people a year after 2003. "Support for job reinsertion" aims to reform the system of "active protection" (*tutele attive*) with support to the unemployed during a job search. The reform's objectives are to guarantee general and homogeneous coverage of the unemployed (equity), to ensure availability of supplementary schemes agreed upon by social partners, and to contain the cost of labor. Measures to meet these goals include increasing unemployment insurance benefits (up to 60 percent of previous work income for the first 6 months), tightening links between benefits and active job search (a ceiling of 24 months for benefits—30 months in the south—and frequent checking of the veracity of search), and providing mandatory training sessions for insurance beneficiaries.

The pact addresses "temporary and experimental measures" to encourage the transition from informal to formal work. This envisages suspension of the application of dispositions of article 18 of the Statute of Workers that guarantee equal social protection to all workers for all firms with more than 15 workers; existing provisions were seen as impeding firms from declaring all workers because such action would increase labor costs. This issue has been at the center of a tense struggle between the government and the CGIL (Confederazione Generale Italiana dei Lavatori), Italy's main trade union. Though the government modified its proposals, the union delayed signing the pact essentially because of this issue.

The pact's final section covers investment and employment in the *Mezzogiorno*, Italy's disadvantaged southern regions. It provides *inter alia* for investments in infrastructure, a tax credit (*credito d'imposta*) to

BOX 2.5, continued

attract private investment from the north, and a guarantee fund to ensure availability of credit for firms from the south.

The pact is conceived as a framework for action. It requires further negotiations between the government, social partners, and local governments on specific action plans. The insistence on concerted and negotiated action and on partnerships is noteworthy: it translates into differentiated partnerships at different levels of policymaking—between central and local administrations (for instance, for measures aimed at improving job-matching), between social partners and the state, and among social partners.

The "Pact for Italy" is an ambitious plan integrating social with macroeconomic goals to promote growth and employment, relying on commitments from all actors involved in the policy process.

CHAPTER 8

Measuring the Social Effects of Macroeconomic Policy in Denmark

by Thørkil Casse

ABSTRACT: During the economic crisis, Asian governments and international organizations alike found themselves hobbled by poor data in efforts to evaluate and anticipate social effects. This chapter describes two models developed in Denmark to predict the social effects of changes in economic policy, with a view to their possible adaptation for East Asian use.

Denmark is a small, open economy. Because of its extensive and highly specialized welfare system, politicians have been eager to measure the social effects of any changes in taxes, pensions, and unemployment benefits. This chapter outlines two basic models—the Danish Rational Economic Agents Model (DREAM) and the Law model—that Danish analysts use to quantify and anticipate the social effects of changes in the country's economic policies.

East Asian governments as well as international organizations might opt to modify these models to quantify the effects of an economic crisis or as continuing policy instruments. The crisis triggered dramatic increases in unemployment and poverty, but the absence of thorough social monitoring made the real impact of the crisis difficult to evaluate. Better data gathering will be essential if Asian governments are to apply models like those used in Denmark to measure social effects of macroeconomic changes.

In Denmark people 67 and older are entitled to an old-age pension if they possess Danish nationality and have maintained at least 3 years of permanent residence in the country between the ages of 15 and 67. The pension consists of a basic amount, a supplement, and a special supplement for single pensioners. People between the ages of 18 and 67 who lose at least half of their earning capacity owing to permanent physical or mental disability may retire early. For a given

Table 8.1   Size of the Government Sector in Denmark and the Republic of Korea

	Denmark	Korea
GDP per capita (US$, 1998)	33,000	8,600
Government consumption (as % of GDP, 1995–97)	25	11
Tax revenue (as % of GDP, 1998)	33	17
Public expenditures on health (as % of GDP, 1996–98)	6.7	2.5
Public expenditures on education (as % of GDP, 1995–97)	8.1	3.7
Population over age 65 (as % of total population, 1998)	15	6.2

Note: Korea data presented as an illustration for comparative purposes.

Source: UN Development Programme, *Human Development Report 2000* (New York: UNDP, 2001).

generation, overseers calculate actual pensions so that the discounted value of contributions equals the discounted value of payments. The pension fund contributes to the accumulated stock of Denmark's capital, on which private firms draw to fund their investments. (See Table 8.1 for data comparing Denmark and the Republic of Korea.)

The DREAM

The Danish government's statistics office (Statistics Denmark) develops and runs the DREAM, which is designed to assess the social effects of changes in welfare instruments such as pension rules and tax reforms. This behavioral model accounts for the responses of households, private firms, government producers, pension funds, the public sector, and the foreign sector. Despite this range of agents, the complexity of the household economy, which stems from the country's system of public transfers and large number of direct taxes, forced model builders to concentrate largely on the household sector at the expense of the corporate and foreign sectors.

To run the model, analysts construct a representative sample of households—accounting for 10 percent of the country's labor force—from national registers of people and workplaces. The model includes income from wages, unemployment benefits, pensions, and inheritances. Because Danish wealth data are incomplete, the model does not account for this major source of household income.

The model follows standard rules in specifying the behavior of firms. A two-factor production function includes labor and capital inputs. The value added plus materials yields the gross output. The model assumes that firms finance their investments through a combination of debt and retained profits. However, the equations somewhat arbitrarily assume that domestic bonds supply some 60 percent of firms' funding, and the calculations representing the behavior of private firms do not include risks.

The model's foreign sector is weak, and most of its foreign variables are exogenous, reflecting the fact that Denmark is a small, open economy. The model assumes that foreign capital is perfectly mobile, that the exchange rate is fixed (Danish kroner are pegged to the euro), and that domestic and foreign pretax earnings are identical. Only imports can change over time. In an Asian context, analysts would have to modify and extend this part of the model considerably to give a clear picture of the social effects of macroeconomic changes.

Denmark has used the DREAM on at least two occasions: to analyze the welfare effects of the tax reforms of 1993 and to analyze the effects of the aging of the Danish population from 2001 to 2075. The tax reforms cut the capital income tax and the average income tax, raised the capital gains tax, and initiated green taxes. The model showed that those changes would boost domestic consumption, but since the various provisions would tend to counteract one another, the overall effect on welfare would prove marginal.

The model assessed the net effect of the aging of the Danish population by weighing higher pension receipts from individuals, a rise in public expenditures owing to greater demand for health services, and an overall drop in contributions owing to fewer people in the work force. The model revealed that from 2010 to 2035 tax revenues would fall short of public expenditures.

The Law Model

Denmark uses the Law model to assess changes in income and consumption of resources such as electricity, water, and heating that would result from new laws passed by parliament. The model is not behavioral: it reveals the immediate effects of potential new laws, but it does not chart long-term, dynamic effects.

The model's database, updated each year, stems from a random sample of 3 percent of the Danish population—some 177,000 people. Each year the model merges information from various registers of income, taxes, public transfers, employment, pension contributions, use of daycare institutions, education, real estate, housing allowances, vehicles, and resource consumption. In some cases the data include more than 1,000 variables for each person in the sample.

The model can show the effects of new laws, such as changes in taxation, on all employees or on a typical Danish family, such as a couple with two incomes and one child who are tenants of a dwelling. Submodels can modify the latter assumption to reveal results for other types of families. A first run of the model shows the situation before any new law, and a second run calculates the outcome after modifying the variables that the new law would affect.

Although the Law model requires detailed and accurate household data, it yields very precise calculations. However, it can measure the direct effects of external shocks to the economy only by translating them into government laws.

Applying the Models in an Asian Context

To apply such models, East Asian policymakers would need to solve three problems. First, they would need better household data, regularly updated to include information on income, household size, income tax rates, unemployment, and frequency of illness by household type or income group. This information not only should come from surveys but also should show changes in household characteristics over time.

Second, as the East Asian economic crisis demonstrated, the corporate and foreign sectors are key in Asia. Modelers would thus have to account for corporate financing; international financial flows; and the often murky relationship among governments, financial institutions, and private companies in Asian countries.

Third, East Asian modelers might also need to take into account fundamental values common to Asian societies, such as loyalty to elderly people and to workplace supervisors. In the Republic of Korea, adults earmark a high percentage of their personal savings for tutorial expenditures for children, which is not the case in Denmark. Such cultural and religious values are difficult to translate into the mechanistic terms of model. Although modifying the models to account for these differences could prove challenging, the Danish experience suggests that such models might prove quite valuable in economic policymaking as Asian social security systems and tax structures become more complex.

BOX 2.6

Seminar on Social Policy, Poverty Reduction, and the Life Cycle, Amsterdam, October 5–6, 2000

This seminar, a joint endeavor with the Amsterdam Institute for International Development (AIID), followed a major conference on poverty and growth. It focused on two topics at the core of East Asia's social agenda: poverty reduction and the life cycle. The former touched on broad policy options and an immediate challenge: unequal access to health services, still a leading cause of poverty in East Asia. The second examined social policies through the lens of demography and the life cycle, with three roundtables and panels on the elderly, youth, and migrants.

The seminar included about 40 participants, among them a core group associated with the Asia-Europe Meeting project from the outset (most of whom are leading academic figures), several new partners from East Asia (including representatives from the International Labor Organization and the Asian Development Bank), and important actors from Europe (particularly the Netherlands). Participants notably included Ruud Lubbers, former Netherlands prime minister and now United Nations High Commissioner for Refugees, and representatives from the Organization for Economic Cooperation and Development, the Council of Europe, and the French Council for Economic Analysis. The seminar included discussions with Amsterdam city officials on their approach to social policy, including welfare management, drug policies, and excluded populations such as migrants.

The first seminar segment (led by Jacques Van der Gaag, director of AIID) built on issues emerging from the poverty and growth conference, notably trends for globalization and private sector roles in reducing poverty and overall social policy decisionmaking. Given the rising importance of business and the ratio of public aid to private capital flows (1:5), participants placed great importance on enhancing public-private partnerships for social policy.

continued on next page

BOX 2.6, continued

The next session focused more specifically on links among social security, growth, and sustainable reduction of poverty (with the paper by Frank A. G. den Butter and Udo Kock—Chapter 14 in this book—as the focal point). At issue was whether and how to balance the Beveridgian and Bismarckian models of social protection. For example, the social security system of the Republic of Korea is firmly grounded in social insurance, but the country also assists those whom unemployment insurance does not cover. Participants argued that the design of social security systems must take into account differences in culture and levels of development. In the Netherlands, high levels of solidarity correspond to a mature and prosperous economy. Psychological consequences of social security, specifically the tendency for social security systems to treat beneficiaries as objects of care instead of empowering them, have special importance.

A second roundtable, based in part on Christian Oberländer's paper on Japan's universal health insurance (see Chapter 5), focused on access to health care for the poor. The discussion underscored that efforts to achieve universal health coverage are usually long and complex. The possibility of combining two organizational principles in health insurance— coverage by profession and coverage by locality—received significant attention.

The third roundtable focused on social policy in aging societies, with a paper by Huck-Ju Kwon (Sung Kyun Kwan University, Republic of Korea) on income transfers to the elderly in Korea and Taiwan, China. A central issue was whether there is indeed an Asian model for social policy toward the elderly. In Korea and Taiwan, China, private transfers play an important role in maintaining the incomes of elderly households, whereas European countries accord a larger role to public transfers (pensions and allowances). That difference, argued Huck-Ju Kwon, aligns with differences in family structure. Participants emphasized the rapid changes in family structures and relations in East Asia, calling into question the notion of a specific Asian model. Neither private nor public transfers alone can maintain the income of households with elderly members, and discussion focused on the degree to which public transfers crowd out private ones, as well as the

BOX 2.6, continued

role of political factors, such as the voice of the elderly, in setting social policy.

The fourth roundtable focused on social policy and migration, based on the paper by Dieter Oberndörfer and Uwe Berndt (see Chapter 11). Discussion focused on contrasts and similarities between Europe and East Asia. Europe experiences weak internal migration, very little emigration, but significant immigration from the global South and East, whereas East Asia has seen strong internal migration, strong emigration, and very strong immigration.

Different patterns of industrialization and their implications for labor migration, and economic and social impacts of migration, were also at issue. Receiving countries may face difficulties in absorbing the new labor force, but immigrants are very often the most entrepreneurial part of a population, so the overall impact may be positive. Sending countries, meanwhile, benefit from migrant remittances. The politics of providing migrants with health, education, and social protection are a significant issue in most receiving countries. A third issue was regional cooperation—a necessary and desirable measure but dependent on whether the goal is to regulate migration flows or provide social protection. Who should take the lead in coordinating regional migration policy? The Schengen agreements in Europe offer a good example of a common immigration policy, but their relevance for East Asia is unclear because they are embedded in the process of European integration.

The final panel focused on unemployed youth, with a presentation by Ruperto Alonzo (National Economic Development Authority, the Philippines) focused on the Philippines.

The Amsterdam seminar highlighted many issues that gave direction to the project. Among these were the importance of pushing more aggressively the topic of private sector roles in social policy, responsibilities of transnational companies in implementing existing regulations, and the growing role of socially responsible investors such as Domini Investment Fund. Seminar participants underscored the need to better understand the size, role, and sustainability of informal arrangements for social welfare, from family ties to mutual aid organizations, in rapidly

continued on next page

BOX 2.6, continued

changing economies. They zeroed in on the urgent need for more accurate and up-to-date social monitoring and efficient systems to collect that information. The 1997–98 crisis brought home the serious costs of inadequate information for social policymakers and the international development community and how hard it was to improve data collection systems rapidly. New investments in this area are crucial.

BOX 2.7

Seminar on Asian Welfare Policy Responses to the Crash of 1997, Bergen, August 16–18, 2001

The Bergen seminar was a collaborative venture with the University of Bergen in Norway, financed by the European Science Foundation Asia Committee, with Asia-Europe Meeting (ASEM) project support. The seminar aimed to bring together scholars from different social science disciplines to assess policy responses by East and Southeast Asian countries to the financial crash of summer 1997. The hope was that a better understanding of relationships among economic development, modernization, demographic change, and social policy responses in different cultural and political contexts would result.

The workshop addressed three major subject areas. The first, welfare and social policy developments after 1997, focused on what happened after the crash in both social policy thought and actions taken in the fields of social security, protection, and welfare. The workshop drew on work by Mukul Asher ("The Impact of the 1997 Crisis on Social Security Reform in Southeast Asia"), Baladas Ghoshal ("Asian Welfare Policy Responses to the Economic Crisis: the Case of Indonesia"), Wang Zhikai ("Reconstructing the Chinese Social Security Net in a Market-Oriented Economy with Chinese Socialist Characteristics"), Titiporn Siriphant ("Collapsing and Emerging: Challenges in the State-of-the-Art Formulation of Social Welfare Policy in Thailand"), Huck-ju Kwon ("Unemployment and Social Policy Issues in Relation to the Crisis of 1997–98"), Rajah Rasiah ("Currency and Capital Market Liberalization and the Southeast Asian Financial Crisis"), and Mary Racelis ("The Asian Crisis of 1997: Poverty, Resilience, and Safety Nets").

The second topic turned around models of social protection and welfare policy and focused on agenda-setters in the field of social policy and the influence of American or European experience in building social protection systems in East Asia. It drew on presentations by Rei Shiratori, who focused on Japan and Asia at different development stages, Annette H. K. Soon ("Timing and Priorities—The Introduction of Social

continued on next page

BOX 2.7, continued

Insurance in Korea and Taiwan, 1945–1965"), Henry Mok ("Toward a Model of Retirement Protection with Real Chinese Characteristics: The Policy Experimentation in 2000"), Decha Sungakawan and Luckana Stienswasdi ("Revitalizing the Traditional Welfare Systems: A Trend Toward Welfare Society in Thailand"), Bernd Schramm ("Explaining Social Policy: An Analysis of the Social Security Scheme in Thailand"), M. Ramesh ("Social Security in the Asian NIEs"), and Stephan Leibfried and Elmar Rieger ("Welfare State and Social Policy in East Asia: The Impact of Religion in a Comparative Cultural Perspective").

The third topic dealt with responses to long-term challenges from demographic transitions and included presentations by Kuanjeng Chen and Chingli Yang ("Population Changes and the Development of Social Security in Taiwan"), Ito Peng ("Impacts of the Changing Demography and Gender Relations on the Welfare State Restructuring in Japan"), and Xizhe Peng and Liang Hong ("Population Aging and Its Impacts on Social Security in China, with Special Reference to Shanghai").

The seminar's two organizers, Sven E. O. Hort and Stein Kuhnle, summarized their ongoing research ("European-Asian Comparative Welfare State Research"). Most papers will be published in a forthcoming book in 2003.

Policies to Combat
Social Exclusion

Introduction

The chapters in Part III address social exclusion—the marginalization of social groups through such mechanisms as gender discrimination and limited access to social benefits. European analysts have conceptualized such notions only recently, although they have underpinned social policy for several decades. Both social exclusion generally and gender discrimination specifically challenge the well-established structure and functioning of European welfare states because they encompass numerous policy issues, elude traditional policy schemes, and demand the involvement of new actors, including "civil society" and regional and international organizations. Box 3.1 by Gareth Api Richards summarizes some of the concepts behind debates on social capital and social exclusion.

Even though urbanization in some East Asian countries is far lower than that in Western Europe, the rise of "megapoles" has accentuated patterns of urban poverty that bear considerable similarity to those in Europe. Changing migration patterns in East Asia tend to resemble European experience, for example, while gender discrimination is a universal problem. These overlays could make policy exchanges particularly fruitful, with particular reference to the major challenges of social integration.

The first two chapters focus on policies targeted toward the urban poor—groups marginalized because of poverty, unemployment, and ethnic origin and concentrated in specific urban areas.

In Chapter 9 Søren Villadsen examines a key policy used to address the needs of the urban poor: social housing. Such policies are an essential feature of European welfare states because they encompass public health, public order, and social equity, but they are as diverse as European welfare states themselves (see Part I). Despite this variation, experience shows that social housing tends to produce social exclusion. Housing policies also vary widely across East Asia, but countries in the region are urbanizing much more quickly than European states and thus confront even more pressing problems. Although a new concept of social citizenship that includes a right to housing has begun to emerge, especially in Scandinavia, the author argues that a more pressing and realistic need is to give marginalized tenants a greater voice.

In Chapter 10 Vincent Delbos traces the growth of new forms of urban poverty in Western Europe, exemplified by recent trends in migration, poverty, and crime, and he highlights the degree to which the urban poor are excluded from democratic participation. To address such challenges, the European Union Urban Initiative has mounted comprehensive efforts to attract public investment to hard-hit urban areas, with nongovernmental organizations (NGOs) and the private sector playing crucial roles.

In Chapter 11 Dieter Oberndörfer and Uwe Berndt show how immigration challenges the traditional structure of welfare states and calls for specific responses that foster integration and social protection. East Asia is just beginning to experience the large-scale labor migration that occurred in Western Europe 50 years ago, and the remittances of low-skilled and unskilled workers working abroad are financing home countries' economic development. Receiving and sending countries have relied on ad hoc, short-term policies to address the needs of such migrants, but the 1997–98 crisis highlighted the shortcomings of such policies. Future challenges for East Asian migration include attaining more active regional coordination, paying sharper attention to labor market demand, protecting female migrants, addressing the needs of returnees, and evaluating migration policies. Box 3.2 highlights the immediate and practical challenges facing East Asia from migration trends, including specific problems such as trafficking and the need for marginalized individuals such as women and the urban poor to gain greater access to social capital networks and the crucial role governments can play in making that possible.

The final two chapters examine gender discrimination, as fostered—and reversed—by welfare states in Scandinavia and Japan. In Chapter 12, Ann-Charlotte Ståhlberg argues that family models of social insurance and social welfare benefits based on income are detrimental to women because they perpetuate wage differentials between men and women. Such policies, common to European welfare states, underscore that even well-intentioned policy designs may not benefit women and men equally, and that poor women often benefit least. Gender discrimination is also widespread throughout East Asia, with discriminatory laws and poor working conditions common.

In Chapter 13, Ito Peng shows how—breaking with the traditional model of the male breadwinner and female housewife—successive Japanese governments introduced ambitious plans for public provision of social services for the elderly and children in the 1990s. This profound shift stems from women's political mobilization, as well as from low birthrates and an aging population, provoked partly by working women's reluctance to embrace married life in the light of prevailing policies and norms.

Boxes 3.3 and 3.4 round out the discussion of policies to combat social exclusion through an overview of specific government initiatives in the United Kingdom, through the Social Exclusion Unit attached to the prime minister's office, and in France, on continuing challenges for health policy. Box 3.5 gives highlights of the November 2001 Manila seminar, which focused on the issues of social exclusion, and which marked a special turning point in the project with its provocative discussion about what social exclusion meant and what it implied for future social policies for nations and internationally.

BOX 3.1

A Genealogy of Social Capital and New Policy Implications

by Gareth Api Richards

Most social capital researchers agree on a few basic tenets. One is that the higher a society's level of social capital, the more democratic it is likely to be. As with other forms of capital—including physical and human capital—the amount of social capital can expand or contract. However, social capital differs in that it grows with use and diminishes with disuse. Social capital, the thinking goes, also resides in groups rather than individuals and incorporates expectations of reciprocity.

The origins of the concept lie in classical 19th-century sociology, but Pierre Bourdieu, James Colman, and, above all, Robert Putnam have pushed the evolution of the idea significantly. Yet recent research, particularly by Michael Foley and Bob Edwards, has questioned some of these earlier tenets and suggested new social policy implications, particularly regarding social exclusion.

This "post-Putnam paradigm" shifts the focus partly back to individuals, raising a host of new issues, the most pressing being inequality and exclusion. Not everyone has equal access to stocks of social capital, because social capital is unequally distributed across classes. Put another way, as social capital is seen as residing in different "pockets" within society, social capital networks will produce "insiders" and "outsiders."

This new vision of social capital creates a crucial role for government. A style of governance or form of capitalism will partly determine individuals' access to resources and influence. This further suggests that political institutions, including the state, powerfully influence the networks, norms, and trust that govern relationships among individuals.

Inequitable distribution of social capital impedes development. To compensate, practitioners must focus on sharing information more widely, coordinating activities more broadly, and making decisions more collectively.

This discussion is based on a presentation at the Manila, November 2001, Asia-Europe Meeting (ASEM) seminar.

CHAPTER 9

Social Housing Policies in Europe and East Asia

by Søren Villadsen

ABSTRACT: Urbanization and demographic changes put the issue of social housing at the core of Europe's welfare states, but housing policies are as varied as the states themselves. East Asian countries, facing new and diverse housing challenges, might gain from exploration of these experiences.

In 19th- and 20th-century Europe industrialization and the demographic transition spurred rapid changes in the organization of cities, which in turn led to social unrest, concentration of poverty, and the spread of epidemic diseases. Social housing thus took on crucial importance in Europe's nascent welfare regimes.

Social housing is understood as a broad category of public interventions aimed at subsidizing housing for poor families and other less privileged groups. In its early days, social housing was more narrowly defined as the activities of nonprofit institutions dedicated to improving housing for working-class families.[1] While social housing in Europe is still sometimes associated with nonprofit groups and public arrangements, a wide variety of institutional and financial arrangements has emerged. For example, policymakers rely most heavily on market mechanisms to supply the housing stock but also regulate housing for groups with particular needs such as young people, elderly people, and people with disabilities. The concept of social housing therefore needs to be set in a broader context of social protection systems.

There is no common goal of social housing, and national practices reflect different political and social traditions. Still, common denominators in Europe include the regulatory role of the state and some guarantee of access to low-cost, good-quality housing for poor households. Social housing also invariably includes subsidies to either households or housing units through support for construction or maintenance.

Some analysts trace a series of stages characterizing social housing schemes in most industrialized countries, reflecting the interplay between socioeconomic development, the housing sector, and the state. C. C. McGuire defines four main stages:[2]

- Rapid industrialization and urbanization lead to a massive need for basic housing units, with those built generally of low quality with little, if any, public control.
- As demand for higher-quality and larger units grows, public authorities become involved in planning and regulating housing.
- Those efforts roughly satisfy demand for housing, but a combination of uneven living conditions and state subsidies prevails.
- Finally, the state withdraws from the housing sector while focusing on assisting marginalized groups.

Such models do not fully account for European or Asian history, with two caveats being central. First, development along such stages often does not follow a linear path. For example, in Europe, state intervention expanded after the first oil shock in 1974–76 provoked a crisis in the private housing sector. Housing stages are also likely to overlap in East Asia in that overall development took more than a century in Europe but East Asian countries face rapid new demands.

Second, two main patterns appear in the development of European housing policies: the "residual model" and the "mass model."[3] The residual model is characterized by small-scale housing programs targeted at the poor and marginalized. The mass model, in contrast, includes large-scale, subsidized housing targeted not at the poor but at the organized working class.[4] (In practice, the mass housing model often leaves room for residual social housing.) The two housing models reflect different socioeconomic, political, and cultural traditions, influenced by the relative importance of families, associations, and local authorities. Those factors also apply to the East Asian context.

This chapter summarizes key issues and lessons from Europe in the context of evolving East Asian economies. It emphasizes the Scandinavian experience, with no implication that this is representative of Europe or of best practices across the continent.

European Social Housing

Housing is a sensitive political issue, and Europe's history underscores the key role of political factors in designing social housing policies. Philanthropic groups and the labor movement and affiliated interest groups, especially tenants' associations, promoted early housing initiatives. Demographic changes also drove social housing policies, as growth in urban employment and decline in agriculture and traditional manufacturing created the basis for urban mass housing.

The state built early industrial multistory buildings to satisfy immediate needs, paying scant attention to the quality of these buildings and the security and health of their occupants. This resulted in significant problems. Beginning in the late 1960s, governments therefore directed much effort to urban renewal, with a combination of public health needs and commercial interests driving demolition of multistory buildings and whole urban areas. Political battles and street demonstrations sometimes followed in cities such as Berlin, Copenhagen, and Paris. Governments also sometimes upgraded older, large-scale housing estates into cooperative housing.

Local governments—backed by legislative changes—have located growing proportions of clients within residual housing schemes rather than mass housing schemes. However, social segregation—the development of enclaves of poor or marginalized people[5]— tends to be widespread even in countries with mass housing programs. Social segregation tends to reduce possibilities of exit both from the housing estate and from the housing unit itself. Although the voice of interest groups driving housing may remain strong, the voice of actual residents may be less articulate, often expressed through protests, vandalism, and violence.

Ironically, government support for owner-occupied housing through tax deductions has increased social segregation, because it has helped some households move from social housing to the private sector, where people tend to self-segregate. Political opposition to more public investment in social housing has led to lower-quality designs and structures than in the private housing sector, again motivating tenants with an economic alternative to live elsewhere.

Despite this marginalization, a new concept of social citizenship that includes housing rights has begun to emerge, especially in Scandinavia. There social citizenship conveys a general right to services, including housing, which are financed by public—mainly local—taxes. Local governments also take responsibility for providing such services, with public participation, especially from strong trade unions and social housing corporations, institutionalized at that level. Local responsibilities include planning and building new estates through social housing corporations, planning cooperative housing units, and approving sheltered housing for the elderly and special housing for young people attending school. Local governments also provide rent subsidies, housing deposits, heating subsidies, and emergency assistance and counseling to households facing housing problems.

In Denmark rent subsidies can take the form of payments that are based on the size of a unit or household and are awarded to households with low incomes or specific needs such as responsibility for many children or children with disabilities. The government also subsidizes the construction of low-rent apartments reserved for households with members who are elderly or who have disabilities, supports urban renewal projects, and helps relocate households from unsuitable environments to subsidized new or renovated social housing estates. The government may also regulate rents in the private market, establish local housing facilities ("council housing"), and involve either profit-making or non-profit groups in such efforts.

East Asian Experience with Social Housing

Much as the social responsibilities of key public and private players drove the development of social housing in Europe during the 19th and 20th centuries, East Asian countries today face similar pressures. However, they are developing at a much faster rate. The region's urban population has expanded some 5 percent annually, in contrast to around 2 percent for the total population. While the number of people in towns and cities of 20,000 and more in East Asia and the Pacific was estimated at 41 million in 1960, this figure was about 233 million in 2000. Bangkok, Jakarta, and Seoul have seen the number of inhabitants increase 10-fold since the 1950s. The public planning and management capacities to cope with this growth are not yet in place.

The recent economic crisis in East Asia, as well as changes in traditional family patterns (including growing numbers of women in the labor force), has put added strains on urban environments and has fed demands for clean housing at affordable prices.[6] As Bae-Gyoon Park has argued, "Housing is one of the most important aspects of social development; it is not just a matter of shelter and space, but it also affects access to other material and social resources."[7]

However, the political context in East Asia is quite different from that in northern Europe, in the sense that family ties and obligations and Confucian moral, religious, and political traditions have created welfare regimes much closer to those in Greece, Italy, Spain, and, to a lesser extent, France. One possible exception is Singapore, where welfare services include health, education, and housing but not the wide range of other social services of the Scandinavian systems.

Government intervention in social housing differs considerably from country to country in East Asia. For example, Korean traditions initially left little room to develop a comprehensive welfare system. The collapse of the Japanese empire and the Korean War resulted in massive migration to cities, especially Seoul. Shortly after the Korean War, the Republic of Korea's economy took off and grew at more than 10 percent per year. New population flows accompanying this growth led to massive housing problems.[8] At first, successive Korean governments resorted to demolishing areas that did not meet official health standards and also tried to divert migration to cities and support higher-quality housing. However, those efforts had no apparent effect on those excluded from housing.

In the late 1980s a study of urban problems in Korea concluded that "the public sector completed 44 percent of the housing units in the early 1980s."[9] However, in general, public intervention has been low, and real estate speculation, the existence of a renter class, and a severe shortage of housing have led to deterioration in housing conditions for people with relatively low incomes. This situation will worsen, as urbanization was expected to reach 86 percent in 2001.[10]

Singapore, in contrast, has maintained public control over land and housing, and prices have remained stable. Upon gaining independence in 1959, Singapore had one of Southeast Asia's largest slum and squatter populations.[11] Successive governments have since taken resolute steps to improve the situation, ensuring that enough housing units are available at a generally high standard. By the 1960s and 1970s the overwhelming majority of Singaporeans lived in housing financed and constructed by the government's Housing Development Board. However, a great number of public housing units have since become owner occupied.[12]

Hong Kong, China, has one of the most remarkable social housing programs of the region. As one analyst put it, "As everybody knows, with the possible exception of Mr. Milton Friedman, the free-market paradise of Hong Kong operates the second-largest public housing system of the capitalist world in terms of percentage of the population living in housing units developed, built, and managed by the government: about 45 percent in 1986."[13]

Public expenditure on housing for the elderly varies greatly across East Asia, and again Singapore is much more active than other countries in the region. This situation owes much to both cultural values and cultural changes. For instance, a

1988 survey suggested that whereas 65 percent of elderly Singaporeans preferred to live with or close to their children, only 36 percent of the younger generation supported the idea of remaining with their parents after marriage.[14]

Analysts regard Thailand as one of the countries with the poorest land and housing regulation. Constraints include the complex and segmented system of public management of land and development, as well as relatively weak local authorities in a system that is moving gradually toward local provision of social services.[15] A study showed that the rapid expansion of unregulated slum housing in Bangkok has proved difficult for the National Housing Association to navigate, a typical problem in countries experiencing rapid growth and urbanization. Still, the Thai government initiated an ambitious program to upgrade slum areas in the mid-1980s.

Rising land prices have made formal, private housing inaccessible to a large part of the Thai population. Some 45 percent of the population of Bangkok could not afford formal sector housing in 1986, and the situation was expected to deteriorate because of rising land prices.[16] The gap between low incomes and high housing costs is one of the major impediments to improving access to shelter for poor households across East Asia. Renting substandard houses in squatter areas and building low-cost huts remain the only alternatives for the majority of the region's poor.[17]

Cross-Regional Dilemmas in Social Housing

Social housing faces several challenges today, and the ways in which European countries address those problems may well be of wider interest. Even when overall social benefits are taken into account, rents in social housing units may be too high for the poorest residents. Poor tenants are very often effectively locked into their housing units, unable to improve their situation even when their households expand.[18]

Policymakers need to find ways to address the housing needs of specific groups, including the elderly, immigrants, and people with disabilities, without accentuating segregation. Yet the need to develop low-cost solutions often works against attempts to attract households with above-average incomes to guarantee a "social mix."

The choice between centralizing and decentralizing social housing efforts is also a key issue—one that entails new roles in managing and controlling housing for central governments, local authorities, and residents. Controversy over social justice and rights, added to competing views of the role of tenants in housing corporations, local planning, and managing housing estates, underlies these debates.[19]

The Scandinavian welfare states offer some tentative lessons regarding these challenges:

- *Mass housing schemes versus residual housing.* The transition from mass social housing to residual housing schemes may result in social ghettos.
- *Exit, voice, and loyalty.* Social stigma as well as financial constraints typically curtails the options of residents in social housing. Because the "exit" option is often unavailable, marginalized tenants may sometimes voice their dissatisfaction in destructive ways. This leads to further physical degradation and higher maintenance costs, and it discourages potential new residents.
- *Social citizenship and social housing.* A legal definition of social citizenship that includes the right to public sector housing may be too ambitious today. The financial implications of such a policy, especially for local taxes, are considerable, and local authorities may find it difficult to track residents who migrate in and out of social housing. Other social and planning measures must accompany a public guarantee to shelter and housing, including an assessment of the financial and management capacity of local administrations.
- *Popular participation and management.* The value of strengthening local planning through resident participation is one key lesson from the Scandinavian experience, because a participatory system can improve an otherwise weak sense of ownership by tenants of social housing. Experiments in tenant management of social housing estates have proven successful, with most transforming the estates into semiautonomous corporations with their own board, committees, and joint maintenance schemes.
- *Social protection.* Economic and social crises may trigger immediate housing initiatives, but housing policies alone cannot resolve economic and social issues. Policymakers must coordinate housing policies with local urban planning and employment policies.
- *Urban renewal and cooperative housing estates.* Few positive results have stemmed from urban renewal programs involving demolition and little if any public participation. However, the resulting protests have paved the way for a more participatory approach that entails complex, selective urban planning. This approach seems to have borne fruit, producing cooperative housing, for example. The danger is that the poorest tenants might not buy

into cooperative housing because of higher rents and deposits or a changed environment.

- *Council housing*. The European experience with council housing is mixed. In Scandinavia council housing exists on a large scale only in big cities, where it provides inexpensive shelter to those on waiting lists or to the clients of local social service agencies.[20] However, in the United Kingdom, council housing has proved to be a key solution to working-class and middle-class needs in local areas controlled by the Labour Party.[21]

Locally owned social housing requires considerable local administrative capacity. In most East Asian countries, local governments are not yet in a position to manage the registration, social services, and counseling—in addition to actual building management—that large numbers of social housing units entail. Any such arrangement should thus carefully consider local administrative capacity. In East Asian countries, direct financial support to poor families may often be a cheaper and more efficient solution than construction of special housing units.

Notes

1. After an initial philanthropic period, this Scandinavian approach to social housing was closely interlinked with the trade unions and social democratic movements of the Scandinavian countries.
2. Chester C. McGuire, *International Housing Policies: A Comparative Analysis* (Lexington, Mass.: Lexington Books, 1981).
3. See Michael Harloe, *The People's Home?: Social Rented Housing in Europe and America* (Oxford, England: Basil Blackwell, 1995).
4. Ibid., p. 524.
5. See, for example, S. Villadsen, ed., *Big City Politics, Problems and Strategies* (Roskilde, Denmark: University of Roskilde, FSØP, 1990) for a theoretical discussion of social segregation illustrated with examples from European cities. The volume includes thorough discussions of the early, prominent Chicago School and of Louis Wirth, as well as more recent research in this field.
6. Seong-Kyu Ha, ed., *Housing Policy and Practice in Asia* (London: Croom Helm, 1987).
7. Bae-Gyoon Park, *Where Do Tigers Sleep at Night? The State's Role in Housing Policy in South Korea and Singapore* (Economic Geography, 1995).
8. Ha (1987), op. cit.
9. Manuel Castells, Lee Goh, and R. Yin-Wang Kwok, *The Shek Kip Mei Syndrome: Economic Development and Public Housing in Hong Kong and Singapore* (London: Pion, 1990).
10. Seong-Kyu Ha, "Housing Problems and New-Town Policy in the Seoul Metropolitan Region," *Third World Planning Review* 20 (1998).
11. See Kwame Addae-Dapaah, "Formal Housing Finance and the Elderly in Singapore," in Kavita Datta and Gareth A. Jones, eds., *Housing and Finance in Developing Countries* (London: Routledge, 1999).

12. Castells et al., op. cit.

13. Ibid.

14. Addae-Dapaah, op. cit.

15. See the overview in Ministry of Environment and Energy (Denmark and Nordic Consulting Group, *Phase III of the Training for Urban Environmental Planning and Management Programme, Thailand* (1999).

16. Robert-Jan Baken and Jan van der Linden, *Land Delivery for Low Income Groups in Third World Cities* (Aldershot, United Kingdom: Avebury, 1992).

17. Ha, *Housing Policy* (1987), op. cit.

18. See Albert O. Hirschmann, *Exit, Voice, and Loyalty: Responses to Decline in Firms, Organizations, and States* (Cambridge, Mass.: Harvard University Press, 1970).

19. Participation and democratic management have been key features of recent development in social housing associations and their local branches. The strategy is to involve the tenants in the day-to-day management of their own housing estates and in this way engage the tenants in maintenance of the buildings and in social development.

20. It should be noted that in the Scandinavian context citizens have rights to social services, including rights to housing. This implies that the local council is obliged to secure some sort of housing within its jurisdiction—or try to find housing through other local authorities. A review of a major council housing area in Copenhagen was carried out by the author some years ago pointing to the participatory and social policy implications of urban renewal. See S. Villadsen and S. Haraszuk, *Byfornyelse I bebygglsen Mønten,* (Copenhagen: Ministry of Housing, 1992).

21. See Anne Power, *Property before People: The Management of Twentieth-Century Council Housing* (London: Allen & Unwin, 1987).

CHAPTER 10

Public Policies toward the Urban Poor: Recent European Experience

by Vincent Delbos

ABSTRACT: This chapter traces the evolution of Europe's approach over the past 20 years at both the national and regional levels to addressing the needs of poor urban areas. Some 75 percent of the European population now lives in cities, where unemployment, poverty, and other social ills concentrate. Contributing factors include migration patterns that present novel challenges to social inclusion, including new forms of poverty, high crime rates, and low participation in civic affairs. A comprehensive program of the European Union designed to target urban areas shows particular promise in combating these ills.

Over the past two decades, cities have emerged as major economic and political factors in the European agenda, as well as sources of problems and recipients of substantial public assistance. Some 75 percent of Europe's 350 million inhabitants live in urban areas, although governments have some difficulty distinguishing clearly between urban and nonurban populations.[1] Most social problems in the postwar era have concentrated in cities. This is true for unemployment: there is a sense throughout Europe, confirmed by empirical evidence, that urban areas have been hardest hit by the transition from manufacturing to service-based economies that began in the late 1970s. The observation also applies to poverty: some 50 million urban Europeans—5 percent of the urban population—fall below the poverty line. It also applies to homelessness: some 5 million European urban citizens are homeless, while 30 million are considered "poorly housed." European governments have thus faced the rise of a new social group, the "urban poor," which has required new instruments and policies.

Since it began the European welfare state has included programs and policies aimed at responding to urban challenges. This is especially true of social housing instruments, used from the late 19th century to address the housing needs of rural inhabitants migrating to cities to work in manufacturing enterprises. Slum eradication was often one of the first tasks of welfare states. And in the late 1940s and 1950s social housing instruments played a key role in rebuilding cities devastated by war and became central to urban planning. However, those instruments have proved of limited usefulness in the face of the new urban problems that arose in the 1970s and 1980s.

National governments, local authorities, and the European Union (EU) have thus spent hundreds of billions of dollars during this period to find innovative ways to prevent the spread of urban poverty and to create what they termed livable and sustainable cities. In the early 1980s, for example, the French and U.K. governments launched nationwide policies to tackle urban poverty, and in the 1990s the EU launched a similar initiative. The new EU framework recognizes the importance of incorporating the urban dimension into EU policies, especially mobilizing assistance through the structural funds that the European Commission provides to underdeveloped areas. The EU's regional development programs now include an explicit urban component, and they promise to make a vital contribution to balanced regional development over the next decade. An annual meeting of countries' urban affairs ministers helps coordinate this policy and provides a forum for linking urban institutions.[2]

The EU also conducted an "urban audit" from 1998 to 2000 with the aim of measuring the quality of life in towns and cities.[3] The audit has become an important tool for designing common European strategies. The pilot phase of this audit, which is the source of the data in this chapter, examined a small sample of 58 urban centers, so the results need to be interpreted with care. Nonetheless, they give some idea of the current urban situation in Europe.

This chapter focuses on how Europe has coped with poor urban areas over the past 20 years at both the national and regional levels. The first section offers a profile of urban poverty in Europe. The second section examines policies and strategies implemented to address this problem, and the roles various actors play and how they interact. The conclusion highlights lessons from these experiences.

Social Exclusion in Western European Cities

Today's urban question[4] encompasses several key phenomena: the "new migration" and its consequences for cities, new trends in crime, growing poverty linked to deindustrialization, and a push for greater democratic participation.

New Migration Patterns and Diversity

Countries throughout Europe are struggling to unprecedented degrees with racial diversity in politics and society. Driven by emigration from former colonies and demand for cheap labor (in some cases both), this new diversity has spawned a grimly familiar litany of problems: racism; discrimination in housing, education, and employment; political powerlessness; and even racial violence. Britons, for example, rarely pick up their newspapers without finding stories about racially charged encounters between London's police force and the city's black residents.[5]

For Europeans, problems surrounding racial diversity are relatively new. Although European countries ruled for centuries over multiracial colonial empires while struggling with national integration at home, only since those empires collapsed after World War II have they confronted significant challenges of racial diversity within their own borders.[6]

Although city planning in Europe has long subscribed to the ideal of promoting integrated and balanced communities, the foundations of modern urban development lie in the segregation of land use, density, and lot size, which in practice separate people by income, occupation, and class. This divergence between ideals and practice stems partly from different views of segregation and integration. For example, does homogeneity in income, class, race, ethnicity, lifestyle, or sexual orientation constitute segregation? At what geographic scale, block, subdivision, or district is integration to be realized?

The globalization process, the accompanying migratory flows across national and continental borders, and the emergence of an ethos of human rights are transforming attitudes of policymakers regarding urban planning. European and American perspectives on segregation are in many respects converging, as the ideology of multiculturalism grows along with recent large-scale immigration. This new view calls for a redefinition of the meaning of integration. Toward that end, the French Parliament adopted antidiscrimination measures in 2000 that were based on income rather than race and that aim to expand social housing in wealthy municipalities.

New Trends in Crime

European cities have seen crime rise sharply in recent decades. Three-fifths of cities covered by the EU urban audit reported increased crime rates beginning in the 1980s, although rates stabilized somewhat in the 1990s. These cities recorded an average of 110 crimes per year per 1,000 population, with crime rates markedly higher in northern and capital cities.[7] Although the ways that cities record crime statistics vary widely, almost all cities in which comparisons are possible report crime rates greater than national averages.

Policymakers' responses to rising crime have drawn inspiration from U.S. experience, as they have adopted "zero tolerance policies" and variations on "three strikes and you're out" laws.[8] European cities have also seen the emergence of private urban arrangements such as gated communities, which exacerbate violence by curtailing the free use of public space.

New Forms of Urban Poverty

The EU urban audit revealed three significant aspects of urban poverty. First, one-quarter of urban households received less than half the national average household income. Second, one-fifth of households relied on social assistance in the 24 cities in which it was available. And third, fewer than half of households owned a car in the 29 cities for which data were available.

Unemployment in EU urban areas averaged 10.1 percent in 1999, slightly above the EU average of 9.2 percent. Long-term and youth unemployment are also higher in cities than in rural areas, though urban unemployment rates vary considerably among EU member states.

Around three-fifths of working-age populations in the cities are actually working, with lower proportions in southern and peripheral cities. The proportion has declined in more cities than it has risen, although average levels rose between 1981 and 1996. Few general conclusions can be drawn from these numbers because the data are limited and cross-country comparisons are problematic, but the figures nonetheless indicate the dimensions and pattern of unemployment problems.

Two-thirds of the EU's most prosperous regions—those with a gross domestic product (GDP) per head that is 50 percent or more above the EU average—are urban. However, those urban areas are characterized by significant internal disparities. For example, unemployment rates vary significantly among districts in Edinburgh, Genoa, Glasgow, Hamburg, Naples, and Toulouse, with rates 10 times higher in the worst-affected neighborhoods.[9] Many European cites also report serious problems of poverty in specific districts.

The new social and spatial segregation is most pronounced in larger cities, especially the "global cities" that have become strategic nodes for transnational business. For instance, in the western part of the Paris region, the ratio of the highest to the lowest wages was 4 to 1 (for every low-wage earner there were four high-wage earners) at the beginning of the 1980s, and 10 to 1 at the end of the same decade.[10] The high cost of living in the core areas of global city regions forces low-income people into unaffordable housing at the center or pushes them, along with industries not associated with the global economy, to the periphery. Global cities whose fortunes are particularly tied to financial markets are highly sensitive to swings in those markets, with consequent serious instability in the livelihoods of their residents.

Urban deterioration follows a classic vicious circle. The process of social and economic segregation starts with outflows of better-off households toward other neighborhoods. Lower-income households, whose members have less education and lower skill levels and are prone to unemployment, replace those households. Real estate prices fall, thus locking small-property owners into their neighborhoods. As neighborhood income declines, business turnover also declines. Firms cannot find employees with appropriate skills and see their profits fall. This process produces a spiral of decline.

Some urban neighborhoods are now totally disconnected from the "official" national economy. The 25-year-old urban crisis not only has worsened living conditions for major parts of the urban population but also has made obsolete local solidarity institutions that had ensured minimal levels of social cohesion. Thus policymakers face a dual challenge: addressing uneven economic development and social fragmentation.

Civic Involvement and Local Democracy

Voter participation in the EU's urban audit cities is relatively low and declining. The average proportion of registered electors voting in the 1994 European parliamentary elections was 57 percent. For two-thirds of cities, these proportions are lower than national rates. The average proportion of the registered urban electorate voting in the last national election was 75 percent; for three-quarters of cities, these proportions are lower than national levels. The average proportion of the registered electorate voting in the last city elections was 61 percent, although this figure ranged widely, from 21 percent to 94 percent. The proportion of the registered electorate participating in city elections has dropped in two-thirds of the cities.

Political representation reflects the vivacity of local democracy, and migrants in these cities clearly lack representation. Even if migrants represent the largest population in some parts of cities, they rarely have representatives on municipal councils. A trend in most Western European cities, such as cities in the Netherlands, is to organize consultative councils for migrants, or to extend special provisions to allow voting in local elections. But are such efforts sufficient? Citizens and other residents need a voice in the future of their neighborhoods and to participate in other aspects of local affairs. Despite much experience in this field, no clear trends are yet apparent on how best to rebuild local democracy. The question has particular sensitivity in a globalized world, where people feel they exert no influence on either local or global decisions.

New Urban and Social Agendas

How can governments better distribute the fruits of economic growth within and across cities? Spatially targeted strategies concentrate action and programs in a specific area, mixing social housing policies with economic regeneration. People-based strategies focus on the specific problems of population segments, such as lack of training, education, and social assistance. "Trickle-down" strategies similarly assume that public investment will encourage private investment to return to deprived areas, while bottom-up strategies hold that better education and training and more confident human resources can solve urban employment problems. A comparison of networks of local policymakers in France and the United Kingdom shows that top-down strategies seem to have less effect, because strong frameworks for local actors are essential.[11] Bottom-up strategies yield better results in terms of creating jobs and rebuilding communities, but the effect is too limited to produce real change.

In pursuing these strategies, policymakers have long—and mistakenly—believed that even a limited response to social and economic fragmentation would facilitate the coming of large firms, which would create jobs. This cautious approach might have worked in times of fast economic growth, but it is poorly suited to current conditions. Policymakers need to pursue bolder and more comprehensive strategies to foster sustainable urban renewal and social cohesion at the local level. All Western European countries introduced public investment programs in the 1970s and 1980s that sometimes aimed to sustain local initiatives, but these were rarely successful. More recent policies aim to forge a common strategy among various actors in an area.

Most prominently, the EU's Urban Initiative has devoted massive funds—supplemented by national and local public funds—to a comprehensive effort to attract public investment to hard-hit urban areas. The initiative combines rehabilitation of obsolete infrastructure with economic and labor-market activities, complemented by measures to combat social exclusion and upgrade the environment. From 1994 to 1999 the initiative targeted 3.2 million people in 118 urban areas throughout Europe with a combined investment of 1.8 billion euros—an average of 560 euros per capita. Five years after their initial launch in 1994, programs funded under this initiative are beginning to deliver visible improvements in quality of life, revealing the value of integrated approaches in tackling the high concentration of social, environmental, and economic problems in urban areas.

In France, for example, the initiative has funded numerous projects in the Paris region, supplemented by local and national resources. In the town of Les Mureaux, the initiative supports measures designed to reintegrate isolated neighborhoods into mainstream urban life, establish business service centers to regenerate the local economy, and boost employment by creating a drop-in center for job seekers. Since 1996 local organizations have also collaborated to help unemployed women. For example, the local municipal authority is employing large numbers of women on the technical teams implementing the initiative. A literacy campaign also combines fast-track reception and registration with language courses designed to prepare enrollees for vocational training, while a day-care center helps women seeking work.

Aulnay-sous-Bois, another town in the Île-de-France region, is focusing on improving employment opportunities and quality of life through neighborhood services and a garbage-recycling scheme. Home to 5,000 units of local authority housing with acute problems, the town launched a major urban renewal program (*le Grand Projet*) in 1996 as a public-private partnership. One scheme provides round-the-clock security services to residents, together with a roving response team and offices for local associations. A job-creation scheme pays young unemployed people to visit local residents, teach them the purpose of recycling, and explain what they can do to help.

A clear trend at the national level—seen in France, the Netherlands, and the United Kingdom—is to establish contracts between central and local authorities to pursue urban renewal programs. This reflects the fact that most European countries have significantly decentralized policymaking over the past two decades, transferring fiscal and operational responsibility from the national to local levels. In France local authorities operating under "city contracts" (*contrats de ville*) agree on a diagnosis for their problems, create a long-term strategy for addressing them, and launch 5-year action programs supported by funds from national agencies such as employment, housing, and social and home affairs. In the United Kingdom, a city challenge program similarly concentrates public money, but it involves businesses rather than local elected authorities. Although these contractual strategies cannot alone address urban social exclusion, they help partners from both the public and private sectors work together on local aims. However, it is important to ask who is benefiting from new subsidies, because local corruption remains a risk.

One of the most interesting aspects of these policies is the growing involvement of the business community: public-private partnerships have become fashionable. A central question concerns the effects of this engagement. The share of private funds devoted to urban revitalization programs—either directly or indirectly—remains less than 5 percent. However, the private sector can often accomplish what the public sector cannot. For instance, in France the Vivendi Foundation has funneled more than US$15 million a year toward projects designed to create local jobs.

Such initiatives need a solid fiscal foundation to work well, and in that regard they still fall far short of those of U.S. foundations, which have long supported urban programs. In 1995, for example, the Ford Foundation's urban funds equaled the French public budget devoted to involving nongovernmental organizations in social housing. A cooperative of private foundations located near the European Commission now aims to foster common views on urban objectives and new funding approaches among its members.

Learning from the EU Experience

The urban crisis is not a collection of specific questions but a new global problem that calls for more holistic and efficient public policies. Until now European cities have not accepted a model of two-tier development. To do so would be to renounce a long tradition of support for social cohesion. Respecting this tradition calls for new models of development and of urban governance.

Unfortunately, devaluation-linked price increases, rising domestic and foreign debt service, and lower revenues have compelled governments to cut social expenditures, including health and education budgets. Nongovernmental organization (NGO) networks have expressed concern that these budget cuts will reduce the access of poor households to basic social services, while cutbacks in government and private sector donations limit the capacity of NGOs to pick up the slack.

Many urban residents are already angry that they have not fairly benefited from the years of growth and that they must pay the price for national and municipal debts accumulated by those who did. If policymakers pay insufficient attention to the growing urban divide, it could well provoke political crises, especially in countries that depend on immigration.

The market alone cannot confront the challenge of divided cities or weak urban governance. Public authorities (including central governments, local authorities, and regional organizations), joined by companies, clearly must maintain an active urban policy at the center of the social agenda.

Notes

1. Two criteria are generally used to distinguish urban from nonurban settlements: the concentration of nonagricultural production and a concentration of people high enough to warrant different kinds of infrastructure and services.
2. The forum includes the European Commission, the Council of Ministers, the Committee for Regions (representatives from regional and local authorities), and (to a lesser degree) the European Parliament.
3. The first version of the urban audit was published in September 2000 by the European Commission (Brussels: Office des Publications de l'Union Européenne, 2000).
4. Manuel Castells, in *La Question Urbaine* (Paris: F. Maspero, 1974), outlined how conflicts between labor and capital that largely set the public agenda during the 19th and 20th centuries were transformed into spatial issues in recent years. *La Question Urbaine* was published in English as *The Urban Question: A Marxist Approach*, trans. Alan Sheridan (Cambridge, Mass.: MIT Press, 1979).
5. See Robert C. Lieberman, *Constructing Race Policy in the United States and Great Britain: History and Politics in the Development of Employment Discrimination Policy* (New York: Columbia University and the Russell Sage Foundation, 1999).
6. On the historical construction of British national and racial identity, see Linda Colley, *Britons: Forging the Nation, 1707–1837* (New Haven, Conn.: Yale University Press, 1992) and Philip D. Curtin, *The Image of Africa: British Ideas and Action, 1780–1850* (Madison, Wis.: University of Wisconsin Press, 1964).
7. EU urban audit, op. cit.
8. See, for instance, Franklin Zimring, Gordon Hawkins, and Sam Kamin, *Punishment and Democracy: Three Strikes and You're Out in California* (Oxford, England: Oxford University Press, 2001). California's "three strikes and you're out" law, enacted by the state legislature in 1994 and subsequently adopted through a ballot initiative, is one of many such laws enacted by various U.S. states and the federal government during the 1990s.
9. EU urban audit, op. cit.
10. *Annales de la Recherche Urbaine,* Décembre 1991, La Région Île de France, Paris.
11. Peter John and Alistair Cole, "Local Policy Networks and Intergovernmental Coordination in Britain and France," a study pursued between February 1994 and February 1996.

CHAPTER 11

Europe and East Asia Confront Growing Migration

by Dieter Oberndörfer and Uwe Berndt

ABSTRACT: Immigration has recently emerged as one of the most important long-term issues in European domestic and foreign politics, whereas East Asia is just starting to experience large-scale labor migration in a pattern similar to that of Western Europe 50 years ago. Until now, East Asian countries have relied on ad hoc, short-term policies toward migrants, but the 1997–98 financial crisis highlighted the shortcomings of such policies. Future challenges for East Asian immigration policies include regional coordination, sharper attention to labor market demand, protection for female migrants, concern for returnees, and better evaluation of policies toward migrants. In all those areas European experience offers useful pointers.

After World War II, Europe experienced an unprecedented migration of workers to its traditional industrial heartlands, in particular those in the Benelux countries, France, Germany, Scandinavia, and the United Kingdom. This migration was generated by strong demand for labor. Most migrants came from southern Europe, including Greece, Portugal, Italy, and Spain, as well as from—in the case of Germany—Soviet-dominated Eastern Europe. France, the Netherlands, and the United Kingdom also experienced a large influx of migrants from former colonies in Africa, Asia, and the Caribbean.

In the 1980s, the former emigration countries of southern Europe—Greece, Italy, and Spain—became immigration countries, mirroring the rapid growth of their economies. In a manner similar to that in the traditional industrial and economic growth centers of Europe, migrants to Southern European countries found employment mainly in semiskilled or unskilled jobs, and the majority of the immigrants have been illegal or irregular (that is, not regularly registered by their host country and thus without formal authorization to remain there).

A large share of the labor migration in the 1960s was organized within the so-called guest-worker framework—through bilateral agreements between companies and governments. As a result, specific national groups came to dominate the foreign population of host countries: the Turks and Yugoslavs in Germany, the Algerians and Portuguese in France, and the Moroccans and Turks in the Netherlands. However, with rapid automation of manufacturing, mining, and agriculture, plus slower economic growth and even recession, contractual mass immigration ended abruptly in the early 1970s.

Despite measures aimed at stopping or curtailing the influx of foreigners, immigration continued. New arrivals soon outnumbered the modest level of "remigrants"—former immigrants returning to their countries of origin. Family reunification and, since the 1980s, mounting asylum requests also militated against a decline in the number of migrants. The outbreak of war in the former Yugoslavia, in particular, prompted asylum applications to soar in the 1990s. Though only a small minority of applicants has received asylum, many rejected applicants remain illegally. And owing to the protection of families and refugees under the constitutional and legal systems of Western Europe, the inflow of family members of resident aliens has come to dominate "regular" immigration, reinforced by migration of prospective spouses.

Many observers thought that immigration would be limited in scope and would cease once national economies no longer needed migrants. However, these assumptions have been proven wrong. Population pressures, growing mobility stemming from modernization and better education, and poverty and political instability around the globe have made Europe a haven for migrants seeking economic betterment and protection from political suppression. By blocking "front-door" migration, the European Union (EU) was bound to see "back-door" routes expand. Whereas Germany deals with immigration mainly from Central, Southeastern, and Eastern Europe, the southern rim of the EU—namely France, Italy, and Spain—is the destination of migrants from North Africa. These illegal immigrants partly fill demand at the lowest levels of the labor market previously met by immigrants from southern Europe.

In many European countries foreigners and naturalized foreigners now compose 8 percent to 10 percent of the population. In Switzerland the proportion of foreign nationals has reached 19 percent, while in Greece, Italy, and Spain, the proportion of foreigners is rising rapidly from its low level of 2 percent to 3 percent. Fostered by employers' interest in cheap labor, illegal immigration, with its attendant ills of exploitation and crime, has thus become one of the most important long-term issues in European domestic and foreign politics.

Migrants have enriched Europe economically and culturally, but immigration also brings severe conflicts. Native nationals must compete in the labor market with foreigners from all over the world—a constant source of xenophobia—and cultural antagonisms and entrepreneurs of religious fundamentalism have fanned the conflicts engendered by economic competition. As the naturalizations and urban agglomerations of migrants grow in number, migrants' votes will become important in local and national elections, changing the political arena.

Scientific and technological innovations will continue to drive global competition for highly skilled labor. This evolution can be seen in the German government's recent proposal to grant 20,000 five-year work permits (with a good chance of extension) to computer specialists from non-EU countries. The "green card" bill and subsequent "blue cards" for various groups of highly skilled workers have reopened debate on immigration regulations and integration in Germany, as politicians and industrial associations increasingly view immigration as a vital national interest.

In the long run all European states will need massive immigration to cushion the economic and social consequences of their shrinking and aging populations. European birthrates are far below the 2.1 children per woman needed to sustain the present population. The rapid decline in birthrates began in Germany in the early 1970s, and that country will feel the effect of this decline first. Stabilizing Germany's population at its present level will require net immigration of some 300,000–500,000 people annually; Germany can finance its welfare and pension system only through immigration.

Drops in the birthrate are particularly dramatic in countries such as Italy and Spain, where fertility rates are now significantly below those in Germany. One study suggests that Europe will need net immigration of 40 million to 50 million people in the coming decades. Birthrates and life expectancies in some Eastern European countries, particularly Russia, are already lower than those in Western Europe, so it is improbable that Eastern Europe can supply the needed immigrants.

The shrinking and aging of populations in highly industrialized countries may well result in strong global competition for skilled immigrants. Emigration may become an important issue in emerging Asian markets from which most of the migrants will come, because shortages of skilled labor and falling birthrates exert consequences there, too. Meanwhile East Asian countries are already confronting complex challenges in dealing with growing levels of both in-migration and out-migration.

The Social and Legal Status of Migrants in Europe

Despite guarantees of freedom of movement and policies that encourage migration within the European Union, as well as income differentials of as much as 5 to 1 (such as between Germany and Portugal), intra-EU migration of unskilled and semiskilled workers almost ceased in the 1990s. This occurred when the economies of sending countries such as Greece, Italy, Portugal, and Spain, starting growing rapidly, and people saw a chance to improve their status at home. In general, intra-EU migration now generally entails movement of highly skilled professionals in commerce, science, and information technology.

Admission policies for migrants have always varied from country to country, often in accordance with economic and political developments. Today the logic and dynamics of European integration—the free movement of goods, services, capital, *and people*—place enormous pressure on EU member states to cooperate in policing the alliance's external borders, especially those with the Czech Republic, Hungary, and Poland.

EU institutions have thus adopted a number of initiatives to harmonize immigration and asylum policies, but harmonization is far from complete. Under the Amsterdam Treaty, adopted in 1997, member states have agreed in principle on a common access policy, but the policy's actual content will reflect the complex EU decisionmaking process. The Schengen Agreement, adopted in 1995, distinguishes between EU citizens and noncitizens and is a step toward controlling every person who enters the EU.

Despite a ban on recruiting labor from outside the EU, guest-worker-style policies have reemerged, owing to migration pressures and labor needs in areas such as the service sector. Germany, in particular, grants temporary work permits to construction workers, seasonal farmhands, and trainees from Eastern Europe, despite the immigration of more than 2 million ethnic Germans from the states of the former Soviet Union since 1992, the migration of almost 1 million residents of the former German Democratic Republic to western Germany, and the movement of 500,000 commuters from eastern Germany across the former internal east-west border.

A large number of migrants have settled in their host countries, and their numbers will continue to grow strongly. In the Federal Republic of Germany alone, 35 million to 40 million migrants entered the country from the 1960s onward on short-term work permits. Some 7 million of them and their offspring have stayed more or less permanently. The presence and growth of new ethnic minorities have led to difficult debates over assimilation and multiculturalism, such as how to incorporate minorities into the larger society while protecting their cultural rights. Intermarriage between natives and people with an immigrant background is rising; in Berlin, such unions now account for 25 percent of all marriages. However, cultural assimilation will occur much more slowly than in the past, as satellite television and other modern media, as well as cheap transport, enable migrants to keep closer social and cultural contact with their home societies.

Non-Christians are adding religious diversity to formerly homogeneous societies and are challenging national identities. In France Muslim immigrants now constitute the second-largest denomination. These trends will continue. To minimize ethnic and cultural conflicts, European countries will have to create new identities that recognize residents' full and equal citizenship regardless of racial and cultural origin.

Under pressure from trade unions, civic organizations, and churches, all European countries have granted legal migrants equality under their labor and social security laws. The major area of dispute within and between European states concerns naturalization and security of residence versus enforced repatriation. Millions of permanent residents in the states of Western Europe still have not received citizenship or the right to vote. France and the United Kingdom have a long tradition of liberal rules on naturalizing immigrants, whereas Germany has considered migrant workers as guests who must leave after a limited period of time and hence makes no provision for naturalizing migrants. Still, various laws protect large groups of migrants, such as political refugees and long-time residents with good civic records, against enforced repatriation, even though they are not nationals. And reflecting a European trend in favor of liberalizing naturalization, a new law gives German-born children of foreigners the right to opt for German citizenship. Foreigners now qualify for German citizenship after 8 instead of 12 years of residence.

The East Asian Migration Experience

East Asia is just beginning to experience large-scale labor migration, raising it to the top of the sociopolitical agenda. The process through which Asia opened its doors to foreign workers was similar to that in Western Europe. Asian countries with a large supply of unskilled and semiskilled workers such as the Philippines became labor exporters, relying on migrants' remittances to finance the people's immediate needs as well as the country's economic development. (This pattern reflected that in southern Europe in the early stages of labor migration.) Later, when countries such as the Republic of Korea exhausted their supply of flexible and cheap labor in specific sectors, they permitted or tolerated recruitment of foreign workers. Hence, labor migration can be seen as a normal part of economic development.

So far, no more than 1 percent of the population and 2 percent of the labor force of East Asian receiving countries are foreigners, on average, but that will change. Among the factors that will boost labor migration in East Asia are uneven population and economic growth, labor shortages coexisting with labor surpluses, labor smuggling, and policies that first tolerate and then crack down on illegal workers.

Receiving and Sending Countries

The Republic of Korea, Malaysia, and Thailand have become labor-receiving countries in the course of rapid economic development. In Korea, and to some extent even in Thailand, declining fertility rates also play a role. Recent estimates put the number of documented migrant workers at more than 300,000 in Korea, 1.14 million in Malaysia, and 316,000 in Thailand. The number of undocumented workers may be larger than the documented population in Korea (by 123,299), Malaysia (by 560,000), and Thailand (by 943,000).

Some 2 million Korean nationals have worked overseas since the early 1960s, mainly on construction projects in the Middle East, and Korea still is a major labor exporter to Japan, where many of its emigrants work illegally. However, demographic changes and government policies aimed at rapid industrialization gradually turned Korea into an immigration country by the late 1980s. The official government position is that Korea does not need unskilled foreign workers, but irregular immigration developed quickly, and two-thirds of foreign workers are still undocumented. The government of the Republic of Korea could not stop migration flows because its so-called trainee system underestimated demand for labor in a growing economy. The trainee system, set up to train foreign nationals in Korean companies, became a source of cheap foreign labor, which is vital to the survival of Korea's small and medium-sized enterprises. The largest group of immigrants is Chinese (mostly Chinese-Koreans), followed by migrants from Thailand and the Philippines.

Malaysia is the major receiving country in the region, hosting more than 2 million migrant workers—one of Asia's largest pools of foreign labor. This large inflow reflects demand for low-cost labor by plantations and the construction, manufacturing, and service sectors. For geographic, historical, and cultural reasons, less-skilled workers from rural Indonesia are the main source of Malaysia's immigrant labor, most of which is illegal. Despite the large number of immigrants, the government and the media ignored the issue during the boom years of the early 1990s as economic needs predominated. However, by 1995, when ever-larger numbers of foreign workers began to make their presence felt, the real and perceived social costs of immigration became a major public issue. At the same time, an exodus has occurred of well-trained Malaysians, mainly of Chinese descent, seeking semiskilled white-collar jobs in Japan, Singapore, and Taiwan (China).

The Thai immigration pattern is similar to that of other Southeast Asian countries. Thailand initially focused its labor exports on the Middle East, but after a diplomatic incident with Saudi Arabia in the late 1980s, Thai labor shifted increasingly to Asia. The largest numbers of migrants work close to home, in Brunei Darussalam, Malaysia, Singapore, and Taiwan (China), where Thai workers form the largest major immigrant group. But owing to labor shortages and changing attitudes toward menial and low-paid work among Thais, Thailand became a country of immigration in the 1990s, as authorities started accepting low-skilled labor from neighboring countries, particularly Myanmar and the southern provinces of China. In 1997 more than 1 million migrants resided in Thailand, over 85 percent from Myanmar, most with irregular status.

Indonesia and the Philippines have remained labor-exporting countries. Given its large surplus of unskilled workers, Indonesia seems to have more potential for labor exports than other East Asian countries. Political uncertainties and their effect on the economy have strengthened emigration pressures, with preferred destinations increasingly other Asian countries. Migration from Indonesia to East Asian countries will be a critical issue for Indonesian economic development in the 21st century. The vast majority of Indonesian migrants are unskilled, and female migration is growing. Huge migration within Indonesia itself reflects a search for economic advancement and, in many cases, represents a first step toward going abroad.

Demand for temporary migrant workers in Arab states led the Philippines to become the world's leading source of migrants. In the 1980s the Philippine government began marketing Filipino labor aggressively. Migration gained further momentum in the 1990s, when President Fidel Ramos praised Filipino migrant workers as the country's "new heroes." In 1997 Filipino employment in Asia exceeded that in the Middle East. Yearly Filipino migration, including seamen, now exceeds 700,000, with women, most often employed in domestic work or the entertainment industry, accounting for 60 percent of the flow. More and more Filipinas move as independent economic migrants rather than as dependents of male migrants, with their movement often a family survival strategy.

Characteristics of East Asian Migration Flows

Until the early 1990s East Asia was a source of labor mainly for industrialized countries, but remarkable economic growth in newly industrializing countries triggered a dramatic increase in intraregional migration. The desire to sustain economic growth transformed Korea, Malaysia, and Thailand into labor-importing countries as they approached full employment and as their own populations moved into better-paying jobs, creating a shortage of local labor for the so-called 3D jobs—those that are dirty, dangerous, and difficult. Those receiving countries turned to foreign workers, some reluctantly, some more openly, to fill unskilled jobs in manufacturing, plantation work, agriculture and fisheries, and domestic service. The volume and complexity of migration flows within the region have since grown enormously, and migrants range from professionals to unskilled workers, filling positions from manager to maid. On the one hand, migration within East Asia still largely entails flows of unskilled or semiskilled workers. Migration from Asia to the postindustrial Pacific Rim countries, on the other hand—primarily Australia, Canada, and the United States—favors Asians trained in technical fields and professions in engineering, the sciences, information technology, and health care.

A growing proportion of Asian migrants are women employed in manufacturing, agriculture, entertainment, and domestic work. Physical abuse and other labor offenses are the most apparent and appalling costs of this migration.

The prevalence of clandestine migration is often overlooked in East Asia, but more than half of the 3 million East Asian migrants work abroad illegally. With many Asian nations refusing or restricting the number of unskilled foreign workers, many migrants rely on an often shadowy network of labor brokers, contractors, and transporters to help them enter and work in higher-wage countries. Private recruitment agencies, ranging from one-person operations to organized crime syndicates, are responsible for 9 out of 10 placements in Asia. Such intermediaries have facilitated the rise in the number of illegal migrants, because labor smuggling is a lucrative business. The proliferation of illegal channels can be attributed partly to the high costs and bureaucratic procedures of legal migration.

Effect of the 1997–98 Crisis on East Asian Migration Policies

Intra-Asian labor migration has played a vital role in the region's economic development, because migrant workers send home millions of dollars annually in much-needed foreign exchange. However, the region's financial and economic crisis has changed the context of migration in that migrant workers have often become a burden for governments, forming a particularly vulnerable group of workers and unemployed. Although no massive repatriation has occurred, host countries have not always treated migrant workers well. The crisis exerted hidden consequences in the form of pay cuts, longer working hours, and degraded working conditions, and migrant workers have often faced a hostile local population that perceives them as taking away jobs.

The latter sentiment is not quite consistent with reality. Migrant labor in Asia has mainly filled unskilled, low-paying jobs shunned by nationals except the very poor, as evidenced by shortages of low-skilled workers even in the midst of the crisis. Still, the popular media and vote-seeking politicians found it easy to make migrants the scapegoats for the economic downturn. Meanwhile, cutbacks in social welfare programs meant that governments in migrants' home countries could not support displaced returnees, and these governments did not want to antagonize destination countries by pressing for better treatment of their nationals, because out-migration eased pressure on domestic employment. Labor-sending and labor-receiving states alike in East Asia often subordinate the rights and interests of migrant workers.

Korea

Korea maintains the strongest measures to protect immigrants' human rights. In response to protests by undocumented workers and support from Korean civil groups, the Korean government announced in 1994 that it would uphold fundamental human rights by investigating labor abuses and industrial accidents and requiring companies to pay overdue wages. The country also extended equal protection to illegal foreign workers under the Labor Standards Act, and it repatriated perhaps one-third of irregular migrants under an amnesty program after the crisis. However, irregular migration is again on the rise as the economy recovers.

Malaysia

When the economic crisis struck in 1997–98, Malaysia perceived a dramatic increase in the number of undocumented Indonesian migrants as a threat to national security. The government drew up a plan to send home in batches foreign workers whose work permits had expired and began a nationwide crackdown on undocumented migrants, culminating in widely publicized clashes. In the following months, to address labor shortages in the plantation and manufacturing sectors, both hit less severely by the crisis than the construction sector, the government changed its stance, allowing recruitment of new migrants or redeployment despite fears of rising unemployment. This seemingly contradictory approach illustrates the persistence of migration flows and the fact that the state may not be the sole or dominant force controlling migration in many societies.

Thailand

Thailand repatriated 300,000 migrants in response to the 1997–98 crisis, 200,000 of them to Myanmar. But despite the fact that many Thai workers returned to rural areas from the cities, the agricultural sector soon began experiencing a severe labor shortage. Employers also had vested interests in sustaining irregular migration, and political and economic conditions in Myanmar also supported the flow of illegal migrants. In 1997 the Thai government announced that it would establish labor agreements with neighboring countries to stop the flow of migrant workers and protect their rights. The crisis also prompted Thais to consider working overseas in countries such as Israel, Japan, Korea, Singapore, and Taiwan (China).

Indonesia

Owing to enormous emigration pressures and an interest in good relations with its neighbors, Indonesia has adopted a passive approach to those countries' strong policies deterring migration. The Indonesian government has no reintegration program for returning workers, because generating domestic employment receives top priority.

The Philippines

Migration has become a major industry through the state's Philippine Overseas Employment Administration as well as hundreds of private recruitment and placement agencies. Although the economic crisis did not hit the Philippines as severely as other countries, mass repatriation did not occur. Because Filipino migrants are dispersed around the world, only a minority of Filipino migrants worked in countries severely hit by the crisis, and relatively few were employed in critical sectors such as construction. During the crisis the Philippine government explored new emigration markets previously avoided as potentially dangerous, such as Algeria. The government also encouraged migrants to save their jobs by scaling back their demands, even though the Philippines—with 2 million to 4 million nationals working abroad—has taken the lead in international forums in pushing for migrants' rights.

Lessons from the European and Asian Migration Experiences

East Asia is experiencing growing intraregional labor flows, and steps toward economic integration will generate a wave of new migration, as happened when southern Europeans sought jobs in northwestern Europe during the 1960s. The regional crisis has widened income disparities within and between countries, increasing emigration pressures, and geographic and cultural proximity will also encourage migration and settlement. As intraregional labor migration becomes more institutionalized, governments will face major challenges in planning, monitoring, and regulating overseas employment; protecting migrant workers; and strengthening regional cooperation (see Box 3.2). In Western Europe, the perceived failure of national migration policies has led governments, especially Germany, to look for a Europe-wide solution that includes cooperation with neighboring Central and Eastern European states. The East Asian socioeconomic crisis of 1997–98 similarly calls for a regional response to immigration control.

The crisis has exposed the shortcomings of a strictly temporary approach to labor migration. To prevent unskilled migrants from settling, East Asian countries strictly limit foreign workers to temporary stays, with no possibility for long-term integration. However, the most important lesson from Europe is that modern international migration acquires its own dynamics that surpass the laws of supply and demand. Once migrant networks are established, they tend to perpetuate migration, and guest-worker programs are easier to start than to stop. There is nothing more permanent than temporary workers. As they settle, migrants become less and less flexible buffers in the host country's labor market. Asian policies that rotate foreign workers may slow this settlement process but will not stop it. North American and European observers studying the evolution of labor migration in East Asia are often struck by familiar signs that workers are becoming settlers, and integrating foreigners may thus emerge as a major issue in East Asia.

In the long run, if economic growth in Indonesia and the Philippines offers hope to nationals who have migrated overseas for lack of opportunity, emigration may subside, as has occurred in Greece, Italy, Portugal, and Spain. A growing scarcity of labor in East Asia may then create an opening for the vast emigration potential of China, which—owing to a legacy of political and cultural antagonism with its East Asian neighbors—has remained largely untapped.

BOX 3.2

Challenges for East Asian Migration Policy
by Dieter Oberndörfer and Uwe Berndt

Potential steps that East Asia could take at the national and regional levels to deal fairly and effectively with the growing number of migrants include:

- *Regional coordination.* East Asian countries could help stem trafficking in migrants by easing labor restrictions to make clandestine channels less attractive; an effective long-term strategy depends on regional coordination and bilateral agreements, such as the agreement between Indonesia and Malaysia. In Europe an influx of asylum seekers and fear of a huge wave of migrants from the former Warsaw bloc countries gave new urgency to cooperative prevention of unwanted immigration. Many illegal migrants, in both Europe and Asia, have effectively settled in the receiving countries, and regularizing their stay seems more humane and possibly more effective than deportation.
- *Attention to labor market demand.* Most indicators point to more rather than fewer migrants in the 21st century. An appropriate policy regime in East Asia would facilitate rather than block migration by responding effectively to demand. Short-term policies in both sending and receiving countries that ignore labor market demand are likely simply to encourage illegal migration. A sensible policy would minimize the social costs and maximize the social benefits of international migration while promoting development.
- *Assessment.* Better empirical analysis of migration policies is needed, and adequate information to monitor labor inflows and outflows (migrants' skill levels, employment status, and gender) is essential. Countries also need to anticipate new patterns of demand for migrant workers and monitor related economic and structural changes, including the aging of the population. Much as Europe's population is declining and aging, population growth rates in East Asian countries are falling (birthrates have declined most sharply

continued on next page

---

in Thailand). It is in the common interest of demographers and policymakers in Europe and East Asia to link immigration to future labor requirements.

- *Protecting female migrants.* The predicament of migrant women should be a major public policy issue. Adequate legal protection of migrant women is already of growing concern to many individuals and groups in this region, both governmental and nongovernmental, and international and regional forums are beginning to adopt a gender-sensitive approach to migration issues.

- *Oversight of the recruitment industry.* The need to better regulate and control the activities of the "immigration industry" is urgent. This is difficult: private labor brokering is quite efficient in generating demand for labor, and sending states have an interest in allowing private recruitment agencies to operate at will. Government regulations should concentrate on licensing recruitment agencies, levying sanctions for unacceptable practices, and providing tax or other incentives for agencies that meet standards. Government-sponsored counseling and preparation for workers intending to go abroad can help; the Philippines offers "best practice" experience in this field. Countries could also make fuller and more effective use of nongovernmental organizations (NGOs); the Philippines and Sri Lanka entrust NGOs to provide information for potential migrants.

- *Legislative and other protective measures.* Concerted action is required at both national and international levels to combat the exploitation and physical, sexual, and other abuse of migrant workers, especially women. Establishing a legal foundation for the protection of nationals overseas is an important measure. One example is the Migrant Workers and Overseas Filipinos Act, passed by the Philippines in 1995. Adopting and respecting international labor standards protecting the rights of migrant workers are important steps for both labor-sending and labor-receiving countries. Governments can encourage migrant workers to build support structures and networks and improve relationships with local people and groups in the host country, and they can develop

BOX 3.2, continued

social centers for nationals abroad. For example, cultural facilities serve as focal points for communities of migrant workers in Europe.

- *Concern for returnees.* Remigration deserves special attention. Programs for reintegrating migrants are difficult to sell to the public because migrants are often perceived as privileged workers, but countries can mobilize the acquired skills and savings of returning migrants for economic development. In the Philippines, a welfare fund established with employer and migrant contributions has proven successful. Governments might also provide incentives to redirect a larger portion of remittance inflows from consumption to investment, especially to foster small enterprises and self-employment schemes. European experience suggests that such measures work best at the local level.

CHAPTER 12

Gender Equality and Social Policy in Europe and East Asia

by Ann-Charlotte Ståhlberg

ABSTRACT: Different social insurance and social security schemes affect men and women differently. This chapter analyzes the gender impact of various social insurance schemes in Europe, notably the family and individual models. This is significant because economic incentives significantly affect family labor supply; when regulations change, women change behavior more than men. The chapter reviews briefly labor force participation of East Asian women and explores lessons from the experience of European women.

Differences in traditions and cultures significantly affect women's level of activity in the labor market, but so do economic incentives. Specifically, the design of the social security system can influence the will to work, the division of labor within a family, and the distribution of income between women and men.

Even when regulations require social security systems to be gender neutral, they can still contain gender differences. In such cases the key issue becomes the result for women compared with men when gender-neutral regulations are applied to a reality that is systematically structured by sex. This chapter examines the mechanisms through which social systems and economic incentives produce different economic outcomes for women and men.

The first section presents two models for social security systems that influence women's decisions to enter the paid work force: the family model and the individual model. The second section explores how solutions to the problem of

I am grateful for comments on an earlier version of this chapter by Alia Ahmad, Anders Danielsson, Ramon Falcon, Marei John, Walter Korpi, and Noho Park.

income security redistribute income between women and men, and the third section summarizes lessons from Europe. The fourth section briefly describes the participation of women in several East Asian economies, and the final section suggests lessons from Europe for East Asia.

The Family versus the Individual in the Welfare State

Social policy and tax policy can encourage women to remain in the home or to participate in paid work. In the *family or single-earner model*, marriage enjoys a premium along with a clear division of labor between husband and wife. The man is the head of the family, which it is his duty to support by full-time work, whereas the woman bears primary responsibility for care and reproductive labor within the family, only occasionally functioning as a secondary breadwinner.[1]

Economic policy supports such division of labor through special allowances for spouses and children in the social insurance system and tax relief for men with wives and children at home, or through joint taxation, which penalizes a homemaker who enters the labor market by applying a higher marginal tax rate to her income (assuming that taxation is progressive). Joint taxation with income division, which allows a married couple to divide their income into two equal parts for tax purposes, also favors families with a single earner, especially those with higher incomes. If the head of the household makes social insurance payments for the family, a wife's employment has a direct impact on her husband's take-home pay. Such rules provide little incentive for women to engage in paid work and become economically independent.

In the family model, a wife's social insurance benefits are generally based on her husband's entitlements. If widowed, she receives a widow's pension, because the system assumes that her pursuit of wifely duties in the home has made it more difficult for her to reenter the labor market. Divorced women do not fare well under a social insurance model where the family constitutes the basic unit for benefits and contributions.

In the *individual or dual-earner model*, economic policy encourages women to participate continuously in the labor market, enables both men and women to reconcile parenthood with professional life, and attempts to redistribute unpaid care work within the family. Here both the social insurance and the tax systems are based on the individual and offer neither tax relief nor special allowances for a spouse working in the home. Income-related social insurance benefits make paid work an attractive option, and the system provides no widows' or widowers' pensions. The system also avoids income- and means-tested benefits, because their reduction against rising income raises the problem that composite marginal tax rates can be rather high and makes it more difficult to achieve the goal that as many people as possible should support themselves through market work.

Empirical research has shown that economic incentives—taxes and subsidies—significantly affect the family labor supply and that, when regulations change, women change their behavior more than men do.[2] Especially for women, income-tested benefits tend to lead into the poverty trap.

The Netherlands in the 1960s approximated the family model.[3] The family was the unit for benefits and contributions, and the tax system put married men at an advantage in relation both to married women and single people. Married women who were not earning more than their husbands lacked individual entitlement to social insurance benefits, and legislation did not prohibit employers from firing a woman for pregnancy, childbirth, or marriage until the 1970s. The incentives for married women to accept paid work were small, and only 5 percent of married Dutch women worked outside the family in the mid-1960s.

Sweden, in contrast, closely approximated the individual model in the 1960s. Single parents received the same tax advantages as married couples, all women with children received a child allowance, and married women enjoyed individual entitlement to benefits as a right of citizenship. Still, the family model influenced the tax system until 1971, when separate taxation of spouses gave families financial incentives to send more women into the paid labor force and distribute market work more evenly between spouses. Expansion of publicly subsidized daycare services also provided economic incentives and practical opportunities for mothers of preschool children to accept gainful employment. Parental insurance enabled women to keep their jobs and links to the labor market after the birth of their children, and provided strong economic incentives for women to hold paid jobs to build up their entitlement to the allowances.[4]

Around 1990 the individual model dominated in Denmark, Finland, Norway, and Sweden, while the family model was supreme in Austria, Belgium, France, Germany, Ireland, Italy, and the Netherlands.[5] Australia, Canada, Japan, New Zealand, Switzerland, the United Kingdom, and the United States recorded the lowest values for both the family and the individual models; these countries could be described as having a gender-neutral policy model. Not surprisingly, the smallest gender differences in labor force participation occurred in countries with a dual-earner model, and those countries also report more positive attitudes toward women's employment (see Table 12.1).

The individual model encourages women to work: in 1999 more than 70 percent of women in Denmark, Finland, Norway, and Sweden participated in the

**Table 12.1 Gender Policy Models and Gender Differences
in Labor Force Participation**

		Gender differences (%)			
Country	Gender policy model	Women/men outside labor force[a]	Married women/men outside labor force[b]	Mothers/men outside labor force[c]	Marginal job attachment[d]
Ireland	Family	55	57	60	2
Italy	Family	46	47	43	1
Netherlands	Family	43	42	58	8
Belgium	Family	36	34	28	4
Germany	Family	32	36	53	4
Austria	Family	(30)[e]	34	42	3
France	Family	26	29	33	3
Japan	Neutral	36	—	—	3
Australia	Neutral	34	34	47	4
Switzerland	Neutral	(30)[e]	—	—	—
United Kingdom	Neutral	25	24	47	11
New Zealand	Neutral	24	—	55	—
United States	Neutral	23	25	34	2
Canada	Neutral	23	19	28	2
Norway	Individual	17	15	16	10
Denmark	Individual	9	7	8	2
Finland	Individual	7	9	13	1
Sweden	Individual	6	5	7	3

a. Average difference between women and men, age 25–54 years in 1983 and 1990.

b. People about age 25–49 years, circa 1990.

c. People about age 25–39 and mothers with at least one preschool child, circa 1990.

d. People working short hours (no more than 20 hours/week) as percent of population age 16–64 years, average 1985 and 1994.

e. Denotes uncertain number.

Source: Walter Korpi, "Faces of Inequality: Gender, Class, and Patterns of Inequalities in Different Types of Welfare States," *Social Politics* 7, no. 1 (2000): 127–91.

labor force, whereas women's participation ranged from 45 percent to 64 percent in countries with strong support for the family model (see Table 12.2).

By creating an obvious link between reported incomes and future benefits, employment-based social insurance schemes also encourage people to participate in the formal economy.

Table 12.2 Labor Force Participation by Women in 1999 (%)

	Total[a]	Part-time women	Part-time men
Austria	62.7	24.4	14.3
Belgium	56.0	36.6	7.3
France	61.3	24.7	5.8
Germany	62.3	33.1	4.8
Ireland[b]	54.3	31.9	7.9
Italy	45.6	23.2	5.3
Netherlands	64.4	55.4	11.9
Denmark	76.1	22.7	8.9
Finland	71.2	13.5	6.6
Norway	76.1	35.0	8.2
Sweden	76.0	22.3	7.3

a. Proportion of women age 15–64 or 16–64.
b. The 1999 figures refer to 1998.

Source: Based on data from the Organization for Economic Cooperation and Development.

How Social Insurance Systems Affect Women

Benefits based on income perpetuate existing wage differentials between women and men. In addition, women may have lower chances of entitlement than men, and certain rules reinforce the unequal outcomes between women and men. Furthermore, there are differences in what women and men pay for the same insurance protection.

Minimum income and minimum working-hours requirements discriminate against part-time employees and disadvantage women. Disqualification because of stopping work and vesting rules that require several years of employment by one and the same employer put women at a disadvantage because they are often forced to change jobs after interruptions in their gainful employment during the period when they are raising young children. Unemployment insurance systems also usually incorporate requirements that conform poorly to women's employment patterns.

The right to social insurance can also accrue to a person based on citizenship or residence in a country. In the Netherlands, for example, as in the Nordic countries, there is a basic pension that everyone is guaranteed irrespective of income, and in Sweden, labor market allowances have been introduced to protect persons not covered by unemployment insurance. This has been especially valuable for women.

While flat rate benefits produce gender equality in distributional outcomes, earnings-related benefits lead to unequal outcomes by reproducing the differentials in women's and men's paid work, ultimately favoring men. A ceiling on benefits, however, would somewhat mitigate this inequity because more men than women would have incomes above the ceiling.

Income-related pensions are calculated either on the basis of life-cycle income or by using selected years (such as highest income years or final salaries). Pensions strictly proportional to earnings over the entire working life largely replicate the discrepancies between men and women in the labor market. For the same level of final earnings, the replacement rates are significantly lower for women than for men because women on average spend fewer years in paid work than do men. If the pension is determined by the best or final years, a higher pension is yielded than if it is calculated on the basis of life-cycle wages for those whose best or final annual salaries are higher than their average annual salary over their entire working life. For those who are paid low wages throughout their working lives, there is no difference. The differences in pensions between those whose salaries have followed a career growth pattern and those who have weak or no real wage growth over their working lives can, in other words, be greater when benefits are calculated on the basis of the best years or final salaries than if compensation is based on life-cycle incomes. Salaries with career growth patterns are more common among men than among women. Thus the best and final years rules are particularly advantageous to men as a group. However, women who alternate between part-time work and no paid work at all on the one hand, and full-time paid work on the other, also benefit from these rules.

A comparison of the benefit levels for women and men respectively conveys an impression of the distributional effects, but it does not give us the whole picture. Indeed, it can scarcely be said to give us the most essential part of the picture. To be able to determine who wins and who loses by different sets of rules, we need to compare individuals' expected benefits with their costs in the different programs.

For most people, insurance—whether commercial or social and occupational—entails a redistribution of income over time between different periods in their lives. We pay into the insurance system when we are healthy and have work, for example, and receive compensation from the system when we are sick or unemployed.[6] In addition, social insurance systems redistribute income, primarily between individuals who run different risks of being affected by sickness, occupational injury, invalidity, unemployment, and the like, but also, through the way the rules are designed, between different income groups. The social insurance system consciously redistributes income from persons at low risk to those at high risk. This is achieved partly by making it mandatory to join the system and partly by setting premiums (contributions) at the same level for all people, regardless of risk. Individuals who run a greater risk of being affected by sickness or unemployment pay the same contribution as individuals who are at less risk. In Sweden, for example, women have higher rates of absence from work because of sickness than men, but they pay the same social insurance contribution (percentage of their wages) as men. Thus, women gain from the nonactuarial premiums in a social insurance system based on the principle of solidarity.[7]

The old-age pension, whose purpose is largely to even out consumption opportunities between different phases of the same person's life, incorporates a smaller element of risk spreading or insurance and a larger element of saving than sickness and unemployment insurance.

Income-related pensions with defined benefits are often calculated on the basis of a selected number of years (for example, a number of best income years or final wages).[8] Contributions are in general proportional to income in all years, but the number of years required to qualify for a full pension is often set lower than the number of potential years of contributions. In terms of income redistribution, it is those who work most of their adult lives and have weak wage-growth profiles who are at a disadvantage, whereas those who work fewer years and have salaries that advance with their careers or are unevenly distributed over their life cycle benefit. If there is a ceiling on benefits but not on contributions, higher earners are at a disadvantage.

Certain rules can favor some women while putting other women at a disadvantage. Public pensions are favorable to women in that they do not take into account gendered life expectancies. The rule that the number of years required to qualify for a full pension is less than the number of potential years of contributions favors women who take a break from gainful employment while they have young children. Another rule that favors the group of women who alternate between no work, part-time work, and full-time work is one that stipulates that the pension is determined by a number of best years. Women who always work part time or have low wages throughout their working lives, on the other hand, are at a disadvantage under these rules.

Although few empirical studies have examined how pension systems with income-related benefits and contributions systematically redistribute income between women and men, one study of the Swedish public pension as it was prior to the 1999 pension reform found that the average benefit-cost ratio was higher for men than for women. Female unskilled blue-collar workers had the lowest benefit-cost ratio of all because this group includes women who both work for many years and have a weak wage progression over time. Female low-wage earners therefore get the least benefit out of their contributions to the earnings-related scheme.[9]

In a purely actuarial income-related pension system, the benefits to an individual depend linearly on his or her earlier contributions, and the system is redistributionally neutral. From that point of view, this type of system may appeal more to women as a group than a system where the pension is determined by the best or final years of income, under which women as a group may have to pay more than men for a pension of equal size.

All European countries subsidize parents' costs for children, but family policies differ in design and function. Child allowances are motivated by two main factors. The first is the need for children to grow up to be well-adjusted members of society. This is important not just for the children's parents but for all those who depend on the production and tax revenues that the younger generation is expected to contribute. The second argument links child allowances to income redistribution, because such allowances help compensate for differences among families. The administrative costs of child allowances are lower than the costs of means-tested allowances, and the risk of cheating is small. In many countries, income tax deductions supplement or substitute for child allowances, but this tax benefit is of value only if parents have taxable incomes, whereas the child allowance is payable irrespective of income.

Means-tested allowances redistribute income more accurately than flat-rate child allowances, and public expenses are fairly low. However, means-tested benefits lead to a poverty trap for women because cuts in payments as income increases may undercut the will to work and the supply of labor. To encourage gender equality, family allowances should restrict the yield of paid work as little as possible.[10]

Lessons from Europe

Overall, if countries want to stimulate both women and men to engage in paid work and enjoy economic independence, they will tie insurance rights to the extent that an individual participates in gainful employment. However, if such an insurance system is to yield equal economic outcomes for women and men, countries must also take serious measures to abolish the gender discrimination that prevents women from attaining and aspiring to higher-paid jobs. Pending such a situation, the insurance system should provide economic incentives for women to gain education and paid work—that is, avoid income-tested benefits and encourage income-related ones.

A key lesson from Europe is that, despite large differences in public spending on pensions and benefits and in the principles linking compensation to previous income, the average disposable income for elderly people varies little from country to country.[11] The mix of social, occupational, and personal systems varies rather than total protection as a whole. However, the proportion of elderly people with low income is lower in countries with guaranteed pensions, particularly Norway and Sweden. Since women as a group have lower pensionable incomes than men, this type of support means more to women than to men.

In a purely actuarial income-related pension system, the benefits to an individual depend linearly on contributions, and the system is redistributionally neutral. That type of system may appeal more to women as a group than one in which the best or final years of income determine the pension. In the latter system, contributions are proportional to wages, and women as a group pay more than men for a pension of equal size.

Since the illness rate is much higher for European women than for men, women gain from nonactuarial premiums in a public insurance system. When sickness benefits are company based, employers are reluctant to hire people with a higher probability of poor health. A private solution would also put women at a disadvantage, as higher probability of poor health pushes up their premiums.

Women in Indonesia, Malaysia, the Philippines, and Thailand

In East Asia, women generally occupy more vulnerable positions than men. In Indonesia, women's economic role is often viewed as secondary to their reproductive role, although women play an important decisionmaking role in many households. The Marriage Law identifies the husband as the head of household and income earner, whereas the wife carries the domestic responsibilities, including childcare. Women's participation in formal the labor force is low compared with men's, but rural women participate more widely than urban women. More women than men work in the informal sector—either self-employed or as unpaid family workers. Discrimination against women workers includes wage differentials between men and women and disproportionate representation of women among the temporary work force, which is likely to be vulnerable to poor working conditions, low wages, insecure employment, and a lack of nonwage benefits. A disproportionate number of female-headed households are poor.

Rapid economic growth since the 1970s, driven by export-oriented industrialization, has provided women (as well as men) in Malaysia more employment opportunities and better access to social services. But despite women's material gains, many factors perpetuate their disadvantaged position. These include discriminatory laws, poor working conditions in factories, the invisibility of rural women (especially unpaid female family workers), and patriarchal values cutting across diverse ethnic groups that define women's roles primarily in relation to reproduction. Women's participation rates in the labor force have risen over the years but are still significantly lower than those of men, and employment rates differ among the three ethnic groups: Chinese, Indian, and Malay. Women are mainly in unskilled or semiskilled jobs, or in support work such as clerical and other services. Substantial differences in wages for men and women are common.

Like their counterparts in many other countries, women in the Philippines bear the double burden of significant responsibility for domestic as well as productive work. Although their labor force participation rate is low compared with that of men, women predominate among professional and technical, clerical, sales, and service workers, and they are also extensively involved in low-wage and informal sector activities. Unemployment rates are higher for women than for men both in urban and rural areas. Despite the higher education of women than men at all levels, women face gender inequality in the labor market.

Women in Thailand, on the other hand, have equal rights, legal protection, and relative freedom and have traditionally played significant social and economic roles, garnering substantial respect as mothers and managers of households. Women have also always participated side by side with men in farm production (mainly rice) as well as in marketing. The rapid globalization of the Thai economy and expanded job opportunities for women in export-oriented industries that require a low-wage, disciplined work force have pulled them into productive work without reducing their domestic reproductive responsibilities.

Modernization and urbanization have brought tremendous changes to the traditional rural extended-family structure, which used to serve as a support system for childcare and household chores. Thailand's export-oriented industrialization has also expanded the informal sector of small, individually owned enterprises, homeworkers, and street vendors in both urban and rural areas. Many homeworkers and women in textile, electrical, electronic, and food factories face poor working conditions, long working hours, and low pay, and they also lack social security, medical care, and holidays. Women are more vulnerable and earn consistently less than men in all sectors.

What Might East Asia Learn from Europe?

Overall, in East Asia labor force participation rates are significantly lower among women than among men, women earn consistently less than men, and they work disproportionately in the temporary work force. Therefore, they do not qualify for occupational insurance to the same extent as men.

Income- and means-tested benefits are redistributionally effective and less costly than universal benefits, but European experience shows that they restrict the ability of individuals—especially women—to support themselves through paid work.

Nonactuarial public insurance systems based on the principle of solidarity aim to achieve a just solution but tend to be ineffective. They risk overuse because individuals' contributions do not reflect their use of the system, and they often subsidize both women and men who work less, diminishing the labor supply and driving up costs. However, social insurance can adopt an insurance-type design through actuarially fair financing and savings funds.

Savings funds balance variations in demographic trends and business cycles—particularly important in the case of old-age pensions—since a large time gap occurs between payments into the system and compensations paid out. However, pension rights do not need to be based entirely on savings. Under 1999 reforms to the Swedish pension system, the account set up for each insured individual consists only in part of premiums invested in shares. The remainder entails an officially recorded political promise that future taxpayers will finance pension payments.[12]

A mandatory, income-related, and actuarial pension, combined with a minimum pension that is pension tested against the income-related pension, could encourage women in East Asia to support themselves through market work while providing adequate protection. Combined with a flat rate labor market allowance to protect people not covered by unemployment insurance and a national child allowance, such provisions would decrease the need for means-tested assistance and constitute a great step toward gender equality in East Asia.

Notes

1. Diane Sainsbury, *Gender Equality and Welfare States* (Cambridge, England: Cambridge University Press, 1996).
2. Richard Blundell and Thomas MaCurdy, "Labor Supply: A Review of Alternative Approaches," in *Handbook of Labor Economics*, Vol. 3A, ed. Orley C. Ashenfelter and David Card (Amsterdam:

North Holland, 1999); and Tim Callan, Shirley Dex, Nina Smith, and Jan Dirk Vasblom, "Taxation of Spouses: A Cross-Country Study of the Effects on Married Women's Labour Supply," CLS working paper 99-02, Århus, Denmark, available at <http://www.cls.dk>.

3. Sainsbury, op cit.

4. Inga Persson, "The Third Dimension—Equal Status between Swedish Women and Men" in *Generating Equality in the Welfare State: The Swedish Experience,* ed. Inga Persson, (Oslo: Norwegian University Press, 1990).

5. Walter Korpi, "Faces of Inequality: Gender, Class, and Patterns of Inequalities in Different Types of Welfare States," *Social Politics* 7, no. 1 (Summer 2000): 127–91.

6. Whether contributions are paid in by the employer or personally by those insured is, however, of no real significance. It is still the employees who bear the cost in that their cash wages become lower in the long run than they would have been without the social insurance system. See, for example, Lawrence Thompson, *Older and Wiser: The Economics of Public Pensions* (Washington, D.C.: Urban Institute Press, 1998).

7. Per Johansson and Mårten Palme, "Do Economic Incentives Affect Work Absence? Empirical Evidence Using Swedish Micro Data," *Journal of Public Economics* 59 (1996): 195–218; Jan Selén and Ann-Charlotte Ståhlberg, "The Importance of Sickness Benefit Rights for a Comparison of Wages," Working Paper 1/2002, Swedish Institute for Social Research, Stockholm, available at <http://www.sofi.su.se>.

8. Pension experts usually distinguish between two pension plan types: the defined-benefit (DB) and the defined-contribution (DC) pensions. In a DB plan, a formula for retirement income based on the worker's wage and service is specified. In a DC plan, benefits at retirement depend on the total contribution the worker has accumulated into the plan by retirement age.

9. Ann-Charlotte Ståhlberg, "Life Cycle Income Redistribution of the Public Sector: Inter- and Intragenerational Effects," in *Generating Equality in the Welfare State: The Swedish Experience,* ed. Inga Persson (Oslo: Norwegian University Press, 1990) and Ann-Charlotte Ståhlberg, "Women's Pensions in Sweden," *Scandinavian Journal of Social Welfare* 4 (1995): 19–27.

10. However, a family policy cannot solve the problems caused by the division of the labor force into low-wage female work and better-paid male work.

11. Åsa Forssell, Magnus Medelberg, and Ann-Charlotte Ståhlberg, "Unequal Public Transfers to the Elderly in Different Countries—Equal Disposable Incomes," *European Journal of Social Security* 1, no. 1 (1999): 63–89. Similar results can be found in OECD, "Maintaining Prosperity in an Ageing Society: The OECD Study on the Policy Implications of Ageing," Working paper AWP 4.3 (1998).

12. Ann-Charlotte Ståhlberg, "Pension Reform in Sweden," *Scandinavian Journal of Social Welfare* 4 (1995): 267–73.

CHAPTER 13

Gender, Demography, and Welfare State Restructuring in Japan

by Ito Peng

ABSTRACT: Gender equality was at the core of several fundamental social policy reforms undertaken by successive Japanese governments in the 1990s. The reforms expanded childcare and long-term care for the elderly. The reforms reflect a profound shift in policymakers' attitudes toward gender, breaking with their traditional emphasis on the model of male breadwinner and female housewife. The shift occurred because women mobilized politically during the 1970s and 1980s, and because of demographic changes partly provoked by working women's reluctance to embrace married life. Japan now has the unenviable role of leading the way into uncharted waters of population aging and decline.

Changing gender relations and demographic patterns are challenging the model of the male breadwinner–female housewife family, which shaped Japan's postwar welfare regime. Growing employment of married women has put a sharp focus on elder care and childcare and highlighted the difficulties women face in balancing work and care obligations. The steadily declining fertility rates that so concern Japanese policymakers today are tightly linked to a gender structure that makes it impossible for people to reconcile work and family responsibilities. Many young people, particularly women, are deferring and even forgoing marriage and childbirth to pursue work and career, or because they fear marriage will constrain them to traditional gender roles and limit their freedom. The state worries that the impact of declining fertility on aging will lead to declining economic growth, rising dependency ratios, growing care burdens for families and local governments, and eventual population decline.

The author thanks John Campbell and Andre Sorensen for comments on an earlier draft.

Responding to these issues, the Japanese government dramatically changed its social policies during the 1990s. Acknowledging the reality of shifting gender relations, the state also took an active role in trying to reshape them. A vision of women as a central part of the productive labor force is replacing earlier expectations of women as dependent homemakers, primary caregivers, and peripheral members of the labor force, fostered by reforms in employment policies and the gradual expansion of care services. The state's aim is to free women and men from traditional gender roles and allow them to reconcile family and work responsibilities, thus encouraging higher birthrates.

Japan's welfare state restructuring in the 1990s reflects the collapse of old-style conservative politics dominated by the Liberal Democratic Party (LDP) and the reconfiguration of Japan's political economy.[1] The restructuring also reflects weakening bureaucratic control over the policymaking process stemming from growing politicization of social policy issues and the entry of participants such as women's groups into the policy debate. Ordinary Japanese now commonly use the term "low-birth and aging society" (shoshi-koreika shakai), which did not exist before 1994, and the idea of low fertility and rapid demographic aging infuses nearly every social policy debate. Social care policies now reflect a complex interdepartmental effort to address the social and economic challenges stemming from Japan's low-birth and aging society.

The Japanese Welfare State: Factors Driving the Care Crisis

Despite its expansion in the 1970s, the Japanese welfare state is still one of the leanest among the Organization for Economic Cooperation and Development (OECD) countries, ranking just below the U.S. welfare state in total expenditures as a share of gross domestic product (GDP)—at 12.4 percent in 1980 and at 14.5 percent currently.[2] Pension and health care insurance accounted for 90 percent of these expenditures in 1999.[3] Japan's low social security costs reflect the limited public role in providing social services.

Through the 1980s tight fiscal controls imposed under the state's new conservative regime (which introduced the "Japanese-style welfare society")[4] managed to curb growth in social security expenditures, which rose by only about 1 percentage point between 1980 and 1990 (from 12.4 to 13.6 percent of national income). This relatively modest increase, despite tremendous expansionary pressures from pensions and health care,[5] reflected a shift in care responsibilities back to the family, rolling back many policy reforms initiated in the 1970s. The state abolished free medical care for the elderly introduced in 1973, for example, and instituted user fees. The state also "rationalized" the income assistance program (seikatsu hogo)—which had expanded modestly during the 1970s—by imposing tighter means tests. Tougher income tests similarly retrenched the child allowance program introduced in 1971, which had expanded rapidly in the first half of the decade. A special child-rearing allowance and other financial assistance to single mothers faced similar cutbacks throughout the 1980s.

The welfare state retrenchment and policy emphasis on the family in the 1980s were not unique to Japan. Most European welfare states experienced similar policy shifts during that decade. What distinguishes the Japanese welfare state from many others is Japan's much greater institutional reliance on the family. The welfare retrenchment of the 1980s clearly illustrates the state's assumption that the family was the appropriate place to sustain welfare cuts. The results are evident in Japan's high level of co-residency and care dependency among elderly people and their children, the weakness of public and market care provision, and high dependency rates among unmarried adult children.

Co-residency between elderly people and their adult children in Japan is high compared to that of European welfare states. In 1980 nearly 70 percent of elderly people lived with their adult children. To encourage and maintain co-residency, the government in the 1980s introduced policies to support three-generation households and family-based care, including tax credits for three-generation households and allowances for family members caring for their elderly relatives. Though co-residency rates have been declining since the 1980s despite these policy efforts, more than half of the elderly continue to live with their children.[6] In 1997, 41.7 percent of people over age 60 in Japan were living with married children, compared with 4.7 percent in Germany and 3.6 percent in the United States. Furthermore, 17.2 percent of Japanese elders lived with unmarried children, compared with 8.2 percent in Germany and 12.5 percent in the United States.[7]

Levels of family care are extremely high in Japan. In 1998 only 3.6 percent of elderly people lived or were cared for in institutions, even though some 13 percent needed such care.[8] And in 1996 less than 1 percent of elderly people received community care, compared with 17 percent in Denmark and Sweden, 13 percent in the Netherlands, 8 percent in the United Kingdom, and about 8 percent in the United States.[9] The National Basic Survey (Kokumin Seikatsu Kiso Chosa) in 1995 found that co-residing family members were caring for 86.5 percent of bedridden people, whereas families who were not living with their bedridden relatives looked after another 6.3 percent. People who were not family members cared for only 7.2 percent of all bedridden elderly people.[10] Interestingly, a recent study based on the National Household Survey (Zenkoku Setai Chosa) shows an inverse relationship between postretirement income and the co-residency rate, and a positive relationship between the level of disability and co-residency rate, highlighting elderly people's economic and care needs as important variables in postretirement co-residency decisions.[11] Not only are families caring for a large proportion of elderly people in Japan, but also such care is partly preconditioned by a lack of public and institutional support.

Public provisions for childcare services, in contrast, show better coverage. In Japan publicly funded centers care for about 22 percent of all preschool-age children.[12] (Though employment rates for married mothers with small children are higher in the United States than in Japan, only 1 percent of U.S. children age 0–2 years and 14 percent of U.S. children age 3–5 years are in publicly funded childcare.) Japan also compares well with continental European welfare states such as Germany and the Netherlands, where 2 percent of children 0–2 years of age are in public childcare. The Japanese figure, however, is significantly lower than the figures in Denmark (where about half of children age 0–2 and four-fifths of children age 3–5 receive publicly financed care) and Sweden (where one-third of children age 0–2 and 72 percent of children age 3–5 receive publicly financed care).[13]

Public childcare in Japan faces significant problems. Childcare spaces still fall far short of needs. The number of children on official waiting lists rose from 26,114 in 1994 to 40,523 in 1997, as more mothers entered the labor market.[14] Public childcare also largely serves older preschool children. Whereas 31.8 percent of 3-year-olds and 26.7 percent of 4-, 5-, and 6-year-olds are cared for in public childcare, the figures drop to 17.1 percent and 4.7 percent for 2-year-olds and children under 2, respectively. Economic expediency and institutional legacies reinforce this pattern; care for children under 2 is more expensive than care for older children because of greater care needs, higher worker–child ratios, and special care and dietary requirements.

Many Japanese still subscribe to the "3-year-old myth," which admonishes mothers to stay home to care for their children during the first 3 years of their lives. Because most working women can take only up to a year of childcare leave, the lack of public childcare seriously affects anyone hoping to continue working. Private sector childcare services are inadequate in Japan, as they tend to be unlicensed, uncertified, and expensive. They are also considered unsafe and are frequently rocked by scandals of accidental death and abuse leading to death.[15] Most parents avoid private sector childcare unless absolutely necessary and rely instead on family, particularly grandparents, to care for their children. The employment rate for mothers living in three-generation households with the youngest child age 0–3 is 41.4 percent, compared with 25.2 percent for mothers living in two-generation households.[16]

Finally, the co-residency rate of young unmarried adult children and their parents is very high and has risen steadily. In 1996 approximately 80 percent of unmarried working adults age 20–29 lived with their parents (compared with 70 percent in 1975), whereas the proportion of those age 30–34 was about 70 percent (up from 50 percent in 1975). Nearly half of unmarried adults living with their parents received financial assistance from them, and most also enjoyed personal services such as cooking, cleaning, and laundry provided by their mothers.[17] Widening income disparities between young and older workers (and young adults' inability to achieve economic self-sufficiency),[18] high housing costs, and lack of adequate income support and housing subsidies for young people explain cohabitation between adult children and their parents.[19]

Those dependency patterns show how the family assumes a huge share of social security and personal welfare responsibilities in Japan and underscore how families' care burdens have increased rather than decreased over time. The family's capacity to care for its members reflects women's unpaid labor. In Japan social policies and employment practices that discourage adult women's economic independence and marital dissolution reinforce women's family care role. The married women's tax exemption, which allows housewives to earn up to 1.3 million yen (some 20 percent of the average male annual wage) without tax liability, encourages women to work only part time, whereas tax credits for three-generation households reinforce elderly co-residency and married women's care responsibilities. The lack of income assistance for divorced and unmarried single mothers, as well as punitive measures such as disqualification of divorced single mothers from income support for the first 6 months after divorce, discourage women from divorcing their husbands, particularly when their children are young. A lack of social support and of effective equal employment legislation limits opportunities for women to achieve economic independence.

For most of the postwar era, this welfare regime drew fairly wide public support. Until the mid-1970s, feminists supported "housewife feminism" (shufu feminism) and actively pushed for social policies to strengthen full-time homemakers' positions rather than demanding gender equality.[20] This stance reflected growing economic prosperity, except during the post–oil crisis years of 1974–75, as male wages that had expanded since 1955 relieved wives of having to work. The postwar Japanese welfare regime also opened opportunities for middle-class women to raise their social status as housewives,[21] as women's political and social mobilization focused on improving women's social and economic status as housewives.

However, as married women reentered the labor market after 1975 as the real value of the male wage began to decline, the issue of care for the elderly and children began to surface. By the 1980s the number of elderly people in need of care was considerable, and the lack of institutional and public home-care services had become glaringly obvious.

Imperatives for Change

Changing gender relations in Japan were most apparent in the erosion of the male breadwinner–female housewife family, as more than half of married women were working by 1986. Families' need for a second wage earner ran counter to policymakers' expectations that the family would care for the young and the old. State assumptions about the family's social welfare role reflected the LDP government's fixation on fiscal concerns and its clear underestimation of families' care burden.

In 1981 the Second Provisional Commission on Administrative Reform (Second Rincho) sought to achieve fiscal restructuring by cutting expenditures, and social welfare was one of the first targets. Those welfare reforms provoked two different responses. One came from housewives—mostly middle-class women in their fifties—who faced the growing burden of holding a job while caring for aged parents and parents-in-law and often dependent children as well. Those women responded to welfare retrenchments by directly challenging the government's family policy. The younger cohort reacted to the neoconservative politics of the 1980s not only by dissociating themselves from political activities but also by consciously or unconsciously controlling their marriage and fertility patterns in ways that contributed to the later fertility crisis.

Fearing that the new welfare reforms would push family care burdens to the limit, in 1981 women's groups began to mobilize at the grassroots level to protest the government's top-down policymaking process. Groups such as the Women's Committee for the Improvement of the Aging Society (WCIAS) (Koreika Shakai wo Yokusuru Josei no Kai) called attention to the problem of women's double burden,[22] and public support for these efforts proved surprisingly large. The WCIAS, which began as a gathering of 298 women in 1983, doubled its membership to 600 within a year, and by 1989 had become a nationwide network, with regular appearances on national media. The WCIAS undertook its own research and disseminated information on family care burdens.

This information highlighted the contradictions between the state's family policies and family realities. The evidence also highlighted the gender dimensions of family care. Although women accounted for an overwhelming majority of caregivers (85 percent), they were more likely to be institutionalized when their turn came to be cared for, as evidenced by their high representation (80 percent) in public institutions.[23] Men were either unwilling to assume their share of family care or were unable to do so because working conditions left them little time for family. The lack of political representation for women also underlined the need for women to engage in political action to push for their interests.[24]

The WCIAS brought together housewives and academics, social activists and social workers, and volunteers working with elderly people and people with disabilities on a common platform of care. Local chapters formed study groups and went on study tours to learn about long-term care policies and the condition of elderly people in other countries.[25] Not since the 1960s had women's groups been so politically active. Their social and political impact was considerable: these groups helped change public debate and redefine women's interests regarding social welfare policies, particularly care for the elderly. Rising public and media interest in social care for the elderly helped the WCIAS gain credibility as a public voice for women and the family. As women's mobilization gathered momentum, academics, the media, and politicians joined to lobby for extension of social care.

Despite this movement, in 1982 the government enacted the Health Care for the Aged law, which replaced free medical care for those over age 70 with a co-payment system. The law also introduced a cross-subsidization scheme among three public health insurance programs to cover the cost of medical care for the elderly and reduce the need to use general tax revenues to subsidize national health insurance.[26]

Notwithstanding these efforts, health care costs continued to rise. To raise revenue, the government introduced a 3 percent consumption tax in 1989 on the grounds that it was necessary for an aging society. Although women's groups had already severely criticized the LDP's family policy, the government chose to ignore their concerns, inviting an even larger political backlash. Voter revolt gave the LDP a humiliating loss in the Upper House election that year and gave a huge gain to the Japan Socialist Party (JSP), which ran on a platform of opposition to the consumption tax. To redress the situation, the LDP government introduced the Gold Plan (the Ten-Year Strategy on Health and Welfare for the Elderly) to justify the consumption tax and to show that it had heard public demand for more social care.[27] This helped quash public anger, and in 1992 the LDP recaptured most of the seats it had lost to the JSP.

Political fragmentation within the LDP in the early 1990s—which resulted in the formation of splinter groups, including the Democratic Party of Japan—

offered another opportunity for women's and other interest groups to enter public debate and push for social care.[28] Amid the economic transformation following the collapse of the bubble economy and a string of corruption scandals, the LDP gave way to a series of coalition governments.[29] The first such government, headed by the reformist Prime Minister Morihiro Hosokawa of the Japan New Party, opened the policy window for the idea of long-term care insurance that had been circulating among community groups and social bureaucrats within the Ministry of Health and Welfare.

Indeed, social bureaucrats had pursued long-term care insurance since the mid-1980s, closely studying Germany's debate over such insurance and forming a study group to examine the possibility of a comprehensive homecare program funded through social insurance.[30] This bureaucratic interest resulted partly from pressure from the Federation of National Health Insurance Associations and major business organizations such as Keidanren (National Association of the Employers) to ease the financial burdens imposed by the cross-subsidization scheme imposed by the Health Care for the Aged Law. The Ministry of Health and Welfare was also keen to support a social insurance scheme because, unlike tax revenue, funds would go directly into its own coffers rather than to the Ministry of Finance.[31]

Throughout this period, women's groups continued to call for the right to social care and proposed a social insurance scheme to ensure that right.[32] Thus, when the Hosokawa government expressed interest in a long-term care insurance scheme in 1994, social bureaucrats were prepared to seize the opportunity, and the window opened for women's groups to enter the policy debate. The WCIAS lost no time in linking its campaign for social care to the new policy proposal. The policymaking process for long-term care insurance became even more permeable when the head of the WCIAS, Higuchi Keiko, was invited to join the Ministry of Health and Welfare's Council on Health and Welfare for the Elderly (CHWE), which approves proposals before they go to parliament.

This kind of policy process is not new. Japanese policy bureaucrats have often been remarkably successful in co-opting powerful interest groups by using councils, or Shingikai, to reach consensus. However, people invited to join these councils tended to be well-known university professors and representatives of Keidanren or other economic and industrial leaders. The fact that bureaucrats invited the head of the WCIAS to join the CHWE attested to the group's legitimacy and the bureaucracy's sensitivity to public opinion. The bureaucracy clearly stood to benefit from public support from women's groups.

Cooperation between social bureaucrats and women's groups was most evident when long-term care insurance met unexpected opposition from conservative LDP members of a new coalition government in 1995. Realizing that the proposal for long-term care insurance was going nowhere, the WCIAS launched a campaign called the Ten Thousand Citizens' Committee to Realize Social Care (Kaigo no Shakaika wo Motomeru Ichiman'nin Shimin Iinkai) to galvanize public support. Drawing in support from the Liberal Democratic Party, the newly formed Democratic Party of Japan (DPJ), and other opposition parties, the committee took its proposal to socialize care to the parliamentary floor. In 1997, when the LDP coalition government realized that it needed DPJ support to pass a health care insurance reform bill, it agreed to accept the long-term care insurance bill.[33] Although this legislation did not include all the demands presented by the Ten Thousand Citizens' Committee to Realize Social Care, the WCIAS had significantly altered the course of welfare reform in Japan.

Changing Gender Relations among Young People

While housewives were taking on the state in fighting for social care, their younger cohorts pursued the route of political disengagement. Political participation among men and women under age 40 dropped steadily throughout the 1980s. Rather than challenge structural blocks through social and political mobilization, younger Japanese women focused on fulfilling their personal and career aspirations, refusing to subscribe to the traditional life course. The opportunities for young Japanese women in the 1980s were significantly different from those of the older cohort: expectations that women would marry and assume the role of full-time housewives had markedly declined. The Equal Employment Opportunity Law, which was introduced in 1986, did not guarantee women labor market equality; nevertheless, it gave them more employment opportunities and greater career prospects.

Even so, labor market structures remained hostile to career women with family and care obligations. Japan introduced parental leave and care leave legislation only in the 1990s, and companies did not integrate women into their career tracks in the 1980s despite the Equal Employment Opportunity Law. Meanwhile, women who wanted to marry found few ideal partners. Surveys show that although women look for men who will be good earners and accept more egalitarian relationships at home, most men prefer women who will assume more traditional gender roles.[34] Given such a lack of opportunity, women who wanted a career chose to postpone and even avoid marriage and childbirth, and those who wanted to marry found it difficult to find an ideal partner. The non-marriage rate for women between the ages of 25 and 29 rose from 20 percent to 50 percent between 1975 and 1995, whereas the average length of steady employment for women grew from 6.1 years in 1980 to 8.2 years in 1996.[35]

The aggregate effect of individual decisions to postpone or forgo marriage was significant. In 1989 the total national fertility rate dropped to 1.57 per 1,000—a critical psychological point for Japanese.[36] The "1.57 shock" set off a flurry of activity within the government as policymakers rushed to find solutions to the "quiet crisis." Social bureaucrats pushed researchers and academics to identify the causes of fertility decline and to come up with solutions to reverse or at least halt it.[37] Research pointed to existing gender relations as the causes of fertility decline,[38] specifically the high opportunity cost of having a child in the form of lost income[39] and women's inability to reconcile family and work obligations. Gender relations were forcing young women to choose either marriage or a career, and many young women postponed the choice or chose the latter option.

Social bureaucrats had assessed the European experience and were convinced that a family–work harmonization policy would be useful. The interests of the Ministry of Health and Welfare's Child and Family Bureau, which had tried in vain to raise the profile of child welfare from another angle, intersected with those of the ministry's Population Bureau, paving the way for interbureau consensus. European experience shows that throughout the 1980s women-friendly welfare states such as Sweden were successful in raising or maintaining the fertility rate, whereas family-centered welfare states like Italy were experiencing fertility declines even faster than Japan's. The policy implications were obvious: unlike the situation in the 1960s, child rearing and women's paid work in the 1990s were complementary rather than contradictory,[40] and countries that supported women's work and family harmonization had a better chance of preventing fertility declines.

In 1994 the Japanese government introduced the Angel Plan (the Emergency Five-Year Plan in Response to the Declining Fertility). Supported by five different ministries, the plan aimed to expand childcare services and introduce employment legislation to help women harmonize work and family responsibilities. Thus, in an entirely different way, young women had managed to reset the state's social policy agenda in the 1990s. In this case changes in individual behavior had become a powerful stimulus prompting the government to act.

The combination of women's political mobilization and the fertility crisis significantly reshaped political discourse and reconfigured political and institutional interests in Japan in the 1990s. From a focus on strengthening the family's traditional role, policy debate had shifted to how to save the family (that is, women) from collapse, and how to provide incentives for young people to get married and have children. By the beginning of the 1990s, even the most conservative LDP politicians were shying away from advocating the Japanese-style welfare society. The government had also abandoned its attempt to promote three-generation households, and instead began to consider married women's employment as a norm rather than an anomaly.

The fertility decline also redefined the long-term economic and social implications of the aging society. Current projections estimate that the proportion of people over 65 will double from 15.6 percent to 32.3 percent by 2050. At this rate, even with higher employment rates among women and elderly people, some analysts suggest that Japan will face serious labor shortages after 2005. Analysts also expect a sharp rise in dependency ratios—from 1 elderly person to 4.41 workers today to 1 elderly person to 1.7 workers by 2050.[41] The government estimates that the social security burden will rise from 18.9 percent of national income in 1998 to 29.5–35.5 percent by 2050.[42] This social insurance burden will siphon off more than 50 percent of national tax income—a figure that puts fear in the mind of many Japanese politicians, business leaders, and economists.[43]

Demographic changes will gradually undermine economic growth rates because labor productivity will decline and total capital assets will erode as more retired people begin to use up their savings. Forecasts indicate that average economic growth rates will drop to about 1.8 percent in 2010 and to about 0.8 percent by 2025.[44] High longevity and low fertility rates will worsen economic conditions over the next 50 years because Japan's purist (non) immigration policy seriously limits the government's options.

The decline in the fertility rate and rise in one-child families will bring sharp increases in households composed of elderly couples or elderly people living alone. The social impacts of these demographic changes are already apparent in rural areas, where migration of young people to large cities has aggravated population aging. By 2025 nearly 60 percent of all communities in Japan are expected to have over a third of their population over age 65, compared with 10 percent today, with obvious implications for care burdens for the family and for local governments.[45]

Finally, demographic projections suggest that, given current fertility rates, Japan's population will reach a peak around 2007 and thereafter decline steadily to about half the current level by the end of the 21st century.[46] This will have serious cultural and psychological impacts, undermining Japan's status as a major economic power as well as its influence in international politics.[47]

Social Policy Reforms since 1990

Japan's social welfare policies in response to gender and demographic imperatives in the 1990s shifted responsibility for personal care services noticeably, as the state took on a larger share and the market became an important player in the social care market. The two major social welfare reforms—long-term care for the elderly and family–work harmonization (or kazoku to shigoto no ryoritsu)—illustrate these changes well.

Social Care for the Elderly

The Gold Plan, introduced in 1989, was the first comprehensive policy framework for institutional and community-based care for the elderly. The plan not only expanded services but also shifted responsibility from central to local governments. Even though local governments were overwhelmed by demand for services almost from the start, the New Gold Plan, introduced in 1994, significantly expanded 5-year targets (see Table 13.1). The unexpected demand provoked much public criticism of the fact that almost all services were means tested and thus excluded most elderly people and that they were inadequate for low-income elderly people living alone or without family support.

The lack of public social care resulted in high personal costs and sacrifices. In 1995 some 90,000 women left the work force to care for aging relatives, and many others tried to manage care for aging parents and elderly relatives while continuing to work.[48] Despite the Gold Plans, female relatives still cared for 85 percent of elderly people.[49]

Problems with the Gold Plans help explain why women's groups supported the long-term care insurance scheme. That insurance, implemented in April 2000, transformed care for the elderly from a needs-based system to a universal rights-based scheme. Long-term insurance covers care for people over age 65 who are deemed to require it, as well as care for people age 40–64 who have aging-related disabilities such as Alzheimer's disease. The insurance covers both community-based and institutional care, with coverage based on the level of disability. Insurance contributions are compulsory for people over 40. In principle, with the introduction of this insurance, all elderly people requiring care will have the right to receive it.

Table 13.1   Summary of Gold and New Gold Plan Targets

Target activities or services	1989 figures	Gold Plan target (1994)	New Gold Plan target (1999)
Number of home helpers	31,405	100,000	170,000
Number of spaces for day services	4,274	10,000	17,000
Number of beds in short-stay centers	1,080	50,000	60,000
Number of community care support centers	n.a.	10,000	10,000
Number of visiting nurse stations	n.a.	n.a.	5,000
Number of spaces in special chronic care homes	162,019	240,000	290,000
Number of elderly health care institutions	27,811	280,000	280,000
Number of spaces in care houses	200	100,000	100,000
Number of elderly welfare centers	n.a.	400	400
Number of new community careworkers	n.a.	n.a.	200,000
Number of new nurses and nursing careworkers	n.a.	n.a.	100,000
Number of new occupational and physical therapists	n.a.	n.a.	150,000

n.a. = not available.

Source: Ministry of Health and Welfare, Elderly Welfare Bureau.

Family–Work Harmonization Policy

In tandem with policy reforms in long-term care, the family–work harmonization policy proceeded rapidly in the 1990s. Like the Gold Plans, the Angel Plans aimed to broaden public support for families with young children by expanding childcare and other services, and by overhauling the public childcare system (see Table 13.2).

In addition to expanding childcare services, the Angel Plan broadened the child allowance from 3 to 6 years and raised the income cutoff so that some 80 percent of families with small children qualify.[50] New employment laws implemented since 1994 also help working mothers. Paid parental leave introduced in 1994 allows parents to take up to 1 year of unpaid childcare leave with job guarantees. In 1998 legislation added an income replacement equivalent to 25 percent of salary and the costs of social insurance, and in spring 2000 the income replacement was further raised to 40 percent. Family care leave introduced in 1996 allows workers to take up to 3 months of unpaid care leave, and in 2000 an income replacement of 25 percent was added.

Together these reforms have significantly expanded social care and support for families with small children and reflect efforts to encourage women's labor market participation. They also reflect public recognition of the enormous care

Table 13.2   The 1994 Angel Plan and 1999 New Angel Plan

Target activities or services	1994	1999	2004 target
Number of childcare spaces for children age 0–2 years	470,000	580,000	680,000
Number of extended-hour childcare centers	2,530	7,000	10,000
Number of childcare centers operating during weekends and holidays	n.a.	100	300
Number of temporary childcare centers	n.a.	In 450 local communities	In 500 local communities
Multifunctional childcare centers	200	1,600	2,000
Childcare support centers for stay-at-home mothers	354	1,500	3,000
Temporary childcare support for stay-at-home mothers	600	1,500	3,000
After-school programs for children in elementary school	5,220	9,000	11,500
Treatment and counseling centers for infertile couples	n.a.	24	47

n.a. = not available.

Source: Ministry of Health and Welfare, *Heisei 12-nendo Kosei Hakusho* (1999).

burdens on women imposed by existing gender relations. The result was that social welfare expenditures nearly doubled between 1990 and 1998—from 4,799 billion yen to 8,323 billion yen, compared with an increase from 3,999 billion yen to 4,799 billion yen between 1981 and 1990.[51]

Expanding Social Care through Devolution and Deregulation

The expansion of social care occurred along with devolution of state welfare responsibilities and deregulation of social services.[52] Administrative responsibility for the Gold Plans, the long-term insurance scheme, and the Angel Plans all devolved to local governments, while the central government redefined itself as the coordinator and planning body within the new institutional arrangement. Although local governments now theoretically have more autonomy to respond to local social welfare needs, they are also subject to tremendous fiscal pressures because they cannot raise local taxes without central government approval. The expansion of social care responsibilities without the ability to raise their own revenues has pushed many local governments to near bankruptcy.[53] For local governments in rural areas, where economic growth is negative and demographic aging is more advanced than in urban centers, devolution comes as a harsh measure.

Deregulation of welfare services has also put pressure on public sector service providers. The 1996 child welfare reform replaced the system (sochi seido) that gave the state total control over placing children in public childcare centers with an individual contract system. This allowed parents to choose among childcare centers and services, and forced public childcare providers into market competition. Outcomes have been mixed. Although more childcare centers are providing longer hours of service, many state-run childcare centers have been forced to close and others to use part-time and contract workers to cut personnel costs, raising concerns about the quality of care.[54]

Long-term care insurance operates in a similar manner. Although local governments are responsible for administering insurance, private, voluntary, and other tertiary agents provide care services on a competitive basis. Since its implementation in 2000, market competition has not worked well, and elderly people and families do not necessarily receive more or better care. Criticisms focus on computerized methods of measuring disability that are inaccurate and screen out many people who need care, huge regional variations in services that contradict the principle of a universal right to care, and a 10 percent surcharge on services blamed for "care-shy" behavior among users.[55]

The valuation of care services under the long-term care insurance scheme is also seriously flawed. Because the government presets the costs of all services provided under the insurance, care providers set their rates accordingly. However, because the price of home-help services (including cleaning, cooking, shopping, and laundry) is about half that of physical care services, users tend to rely on home helpers to provide physical care while they clean the house. As a result of deregulation and changes in government roles, most careworkers have been laid off from local government jobs and often work for lower pay in the private sector.[56]

In sum, although decentralization and deregulation of social care can allow a better mix of services that meet individual needs more efficiently, such reforms raise questions regarding the capacity of local government to provide care and the wisdom of shifting public and private boundaries.

Lessons from the Japanese Experience

Japan's policy reforms of the 1990s suggest some interesting lessons. First, experience clearly shows the critical role of gender relations and demographic changes in shaping social policy today. Before 1990 policymakers focused on industrialization and urbanization as the cause of disintegrating families and communities, and policy responses aimed to reduce such fragmentation by reinforcing traditional gender roles. The new perspective, embodied by a recent Ministry of Health and Welfare white paper,[57] puts the blame for family and community disintegration squarely on traditional gender relations and seeks to redress them by reforming social and labor market policies. This suggests an important shift in the state's position in relation to women and the family.

Second, the political and demographic imperatives facing the Japanese welfare state illustrate what happens when traditional care and welfare responsibilities overburden families. The policy response suggests a dynamic relationship between the Japanese welfare state and its people, and calls attention to the importance of examining the interaction of social, economic, and political factors in policy change.

This experience is not Japan's alone. Similar shifts in gender relations and demography are occurring in other welfare states in the East and West. As the postindustrial economy draws more women into paid employment, the state will have to pay critical attention to tensions between changing gender relations and institutional arrangements that reflect the postwar male breadwinner–female housewife family model. Such tensions are particularly apparent in a family-centered welfare regime such as Japan's, but other conservative welfare states, including Germany, Italy, Portugal, and Spain, share similar concerns. Fertility rates in those countries are among the lowest in the European Union, suggesting that young people in those countries may also be realizing that they cannot afford to have children. Throughout its development, the Japanese welfare state has learned and adapted ideas from western welfare states. Japan is now in the unenviable position of leading the way into uncharted waters regarding population aging and decline.

The actions of the Japanese welfare state in the face of gender and demographic pressures, although clearly significant, have yet to show the desired results in reversing or even slowing fertility decline. Policy reforms have largely focused on relieving women of undue care burdens, but evidence suggests that the basic structure of gender relations remains unchanged and that women have not altered their fertility decisions. The state continues to define the problem in terms of adverse effects on fertility rather than in terms of gender inequality. More positive efforts to facilitate changes in gender relations are still needed.

Efforts to combine expansion and devolution of the welfare state, while certainly not unique to Japan (consider, for example, welfare reform in the United States, which expands services at the state and local level), merit more research and debate. In Japan researchers often discuss the two issues separately. But together they increase the complexity of the challenge, and the two processes have interacted both positively and negatively. For example, although expansion and devolution produce more services that respond better to community needs, those trends can also lower the quality of care and exacerbate regional disparities. And ironically, devolution and deregulation under Japan's expanded system of social care, which seeks to encourage women to work by relieving them of care burdens, appear to have produced a new system that employs women as low-wage, part-time, and contract workers.

Notes

1. T. J. Pempel, *Regime Shift: Comparative Dynamics of the Japanese Political Economy* (Ithaca, N.Y.: Cornell University Press, 1998).

2. Between 1970 and 1980, social security expenditure rose sevenfold, from 3,524 billion yen to 24,763 billion yen, or from 5.7 percent to 12.4 percent of national income.

3. National Institute of Population and Social Security Research (2000). <http://www.ipss.go.jp/English/Jasos/contents.html>.

4. The conservative welfare regime of the 1980s is often referred to as the "Japanese-style welfare regime" (*Nihongata Fukushi Shakai Regime*), a term first coined by the ruling conservative Liberal Democratic Party in 1979 in its policy paper calling for welfare policy review. In the 1970s it became the LDP's platform to steer the Japanese welfare state toward retrenchment and attack (Western-style) welfare state expansion. Redefining Japan as a welfare society, not a welfare state, the policy called for a new regime based on "individual self help and mutual aid between families, neighbors, and local community, and on the selective provision of public welfare by efficient state in accordance with the principle of the liberal economic society." See Economic Planning Agency, *Shin-Keizaishakai 7-kanen Keikaku (New Economic Society 7-Year Plan)* (Tokyo: Economic Planning Agency, 1979), p. 10.

5. Pressure on pension and health care spending stemmed from the maturing of pension schemes and population aging. The proportion of people over age 65 rose from 9.1 percent in 1980 to 12.1 percent in 1990. See Ministry of Health and Welfare, *Heisei 10-nendo Kosei Hakusho (1998 White Paper on Health and Welfare)* (Tokyo: Gyosei, 1998).

6. Ministry of Health and Welfare, *Heisei 12-nendo Kosei Hakusho (2000 White Paper on Health and Welfare)* (Tokyo: Gyosei, 2000).

7. Office of the Prime Minister, *Annual Report on the Family Income and Expenditure Survey* (Tokyo: Statistics Bureau, Management and Coordination Agency, 1997).

8. Campbell and Ikegami argue that if we account for "social hospitalization," the level of institutionalization for elderly people would come closer to 6 percent. This underscores the limited options for institutional care for the elderly. Because public institutional care is scarce and means tested, and because private institutional care facilities are lacking and expensive, elderly people in Japan must rely on their families much more than those in other countries. Social hospitalization is therefore a logical option for middle-class elderly people who cannot rely on their families for care. See John C. Campbell and M. Ikegami, "Long-Term Care Insurance Comes to Japan," *Health Affairs* 19, no. 3 (2000): 26–39. A survey by the Association of Women and Youth indicates that a majority of people claimed that they hospitalized family members at some point to meet their care needs. See Fujin Shoseinen Kyokai, *Shigoto to Kaigo to no Ryoritsu ni Kansuru Chosa*

(Survey on Work and Care Harmonization) (Tokyo: Fujin Shoseinen Kyokai, 1996). The national survey also found that about 41 percent of people have used private hospitals and that 37 percent of people have used public hospitals to meet family care needs, whereas about 11 percent of people have used home helpers and 3.6 percent have used public institutions for the aged. See Ministry of Labor, *Hataraku Josei no Jitsujo (The Condition of Working Women)* (Tokyo: 21-seiki Shokugyo Zaidan, 1998).

9. Diane Gibson, *Aged Care: Old Policies, New Problems* (Singapore; Cambridge, U.K.: Cambridge University Press, 1998).

10. Ministry of Labor (1998), op. cit.

11. Fumio Funaoka and Mitsuaki Ayusawa, "Koreisha no Dokyo no Ketteiyoin no Bunseki: kazoku no seikatsujokyo to hosho kino" ("Analysis of the Deciding Factors for Co-residency for the Elderly People"), in *Kazoku-Setai no Henyo to Seikatsu Hosho Kino (Family and Household Changes and the Social Security Function),* ed. National Institute of Population and Social Security Research (Tokyo: University of Tokyo, 2000).

12. Ministry of Health and Welfare (1998), op. cit.

13. Marcia K. Meyers, Janet C. Gornick, and Katherin E. Ross, "Public Childcare, Parental Leave, and Employment," in *Gender and Welfare State Regimes,* ed. Diane Sainsbury (Oxford, England: Oxford University Press, 1999), pp. 117–46.

14. Ministry of Health and Welfare (1998), op. cit. Unofficially, some 150,000 children are waiting for childcare space, according to Prime Minister Jun'ichiro Koizumi's campaign speech on July 14, 2001, *NHK National News.*

15. For example, see the *Japan Times,* "'Baby Hotel' Foibles Vex Working Mums: Shortage of Trustworthy Day Care Leads Some to Abandon Plans to Have Kids," June 7, 2001, p. 3.

16. Ministry of Labor (1998), op. cit., and Nobuhiko Maeda, *Shigoto to Kateiseikatsu no Chowa: Nihon, Oranda, America no Kokusai Hikaku (Work and Family Life Harmonization: A Japan, Netherlands, and U.S. Comparison)* (Tokyo: Nihon Rodo Kenkyu Kiko, 2000). Other studies note similar patterns.

17. Ministry of Health and Welfare (1998), op. cit.

18. Kazuo Seiyama, "Shotoku Kakusa wo Do Mondai ni Suruka: Nenreisonai Fubyodo no Bunsekikara" ("How to Problematize Income Disparity: From the Analysis on Interage Group Inequality"), *Kikan Kakei Keizai Kenkyu (Journal of Family Economic Research)* 51 (Summer 2001): 17–23.

19. Mami Iwakami, "Shoshi-Koreika Shakai no Oyako Kankei: 30dai wo shoten ni shite kangaeru" ("Parent–Child Relationship in the Low Fertility and Aging Society: With a Focus on People in Their Thirties"), *Seikatsu Kyodo Kumiai Kenkyu* 2 (2000): 19–26, and Michiko Miyamoto, "Ban-kon, Hikon Sedai no Chokumen suru mono: Parasite Single no Airo" ("The Issues Faced by the Late Marrying or Nonmarriage Generation: The Path of the Parasite Single," *Kikan Kakei Keizai Kenkyu* 47 (Summer 2000): 28–35.

20. Sakiko Shiota "Gendai Feminism to Nihon no Shakai Seisaku, 1970–1990" ("The Contemporary Feminism and Japan's Social Policy, 1970–1990"), in *Joseigaku to Seiji Jissen (Political Implications of Women's Studies),* ed. Society for Women's Studies Japan (Tokyo: Keiso Shobo, 1992), pp. 53–70.

21. Before the mid-1950s employment rates for married women in Japan were high; most worked on farms or in family businesses. Throughout the era of high economic growth, many women still had to work for a living. Single mothers, women in low-income households, and women with family businesses continued to work; poor women bore a heavy burden from the lack of welfare provisions, even though the popular image of married women was that of full-time housewives.

22. Keiko Higuchi, "Kaigo no Shakai-ka wo Koshite Susumeta" ("How We Promoted Socialization of Care"), in *Chiiki de Miru, Minna de Mitoru: Joseiga Susumeru Kaigo no Shakaika (Everyone in the Community Takes Care of the Elderly: Women Promoting Socialization of Care)*, ed. Keiko Higuchi (Kyoto: Minerva Shobo, 1997), pp. 136–70.

23. Ibid.

24. Koreika Shakai wo Yokusuru Josei no Kai, ed., *Tomodaore ka Tomodachi Shakai he (Together We All Collapse or Together We Support Together)* (Tokyo: Akashi Shoten, 1998).

25. Ibid.

26. Health insurance in Japan consists of three main programs: employee insurance for workers and their dependent family members through large, medium, and small firms; schemes organized by mutual aid societies for employees in public service, private schools, seamen, and dependent family members; and national health care insurance for the self-employed, retired, and those who do not fall into the first two categories. Not surprisingly, since employee health insurance does not cover most retired workers, they automatically switch to national health care insurance upon retirement. Although the government subsidizes about half the cost of national health care insurance from general tax revenues, the high proportion of elderly people in this insurance scheme has produced a serious financial crisis.

27. Campbell, for example, argues that it was crucial for the government to introduce a welfare reform policy for the aging society, as only then would voters support any new tax measure. See John C. Campbell, *How Policies Change: The Japanese Government and the Aging Society* (Princeton, N.J.: Princeton University Press, 1992).

28. Murase Mikiko Eto, "The Establishment of Long-Term Care Insurance," in *Power Shuffles and Policy Processes: Coalition Government in Japan in the 1990s*, ed. Hideo Otake (Tokyo: Japan Centre for International Exchange, 2000), pp. 21–50.

29. Pempel (1998), op. cit.

30. Eto (2000), op. cit.

31. Campbell (1992), op. cit.

32. Murase Mikiko Eto, "Public Involvement in Social Policy Reform: Seen from the Perspective of Japan's Elderly-Care Insurance Scheme," *Journal of Social Policy* 30, no. 1 (2001): 17–36.

33. For a more detailed discussion, see Eto (2001), op. cit., and Kunihiko Ushiyama "Shakaiundo no Atarashii Tenkai to Seisakukatei: kaigohoken no seidoka to Kaigo no Shakaika wo Motomeru Ichiman'ninshimin Iinkai" ("New Development in Social Movement and Social Policy: Long-Term Care Insurance and the Ten Thousand Citizens' Committee to Realize Social Care Campaign") in *Shakai Undo Kenkyu no Shindoko (New Developments in Social Movement Research)*, ed. Shakai Undoron Kenkyukai (Tokyo: Seibundo, 1999).

34. Ministry of Health and Welfare (1998), op. cit.

35. Ministry of Labor (1998), op. cit.

36. The figure 1.57 is critical because it marks the historical low. Fertility rates had previously dipped sharply and temporarily to 1.58 per 1,000 women (total fertility rate) in 1968 because that year was considered a particularly ominous year for childbirth, symbolized by the fire-breathing horse of the Chinese astrological calendar.

37. I was a member of the Ministry of Health and Welfare's Special Research Commission on Issues of Family and Low Birth (*Katei-Shussan Mondai Sogo Chosa Kenkyu*), which looked into this problem in 1992.

38. Eiko Nakano and Yoshikazu Watanabe, "Mikon Danjo no Kekkonkan" ("The Views of Marriage among Unmarried Youths in Contemporary Japan"), *Jinko Mondai Kenkyu (Journal of Population Problems)* 50, no. 3 (1994): 18–32, and Makoto Atoh, Shigesato Takahashi, Eiko

Nakano, Yoshikazu Watanabe, Hiroshi Kojima, Ryuichi Kaneko, and Fusami Mito, "Dokushin Seinenso no Kekkonkan to Kodomokan" ("Attitudes toward Marriage and Fertility among the Unmarried Japanese Youth"), *Jinko Mondai Kenkyu (Journal of Population Problems)* 50, no. 1 (1994): 29–49.

39. Katsura Maruyama, "The Cost Sharing of Child and Family Care Leave," *Review of Population and Social Policy* 8 (1999): 49–74.

40. OECD, *Caring World: The New Social Policy Agenda* (Paris: OECD, 1999).

41. Ministry of Health and Welfare (1998), op. cit.

42. Ibid., and National Institute of Population and Social Security Research (2000), op. cit.

43. Interestingly, national polls indicate that Japanese people appear to prefer increases in special insurance and fiscal contributions if they are assured that social welfare benefits will continue.

44. Ministry of Health and Welfare (1998), op. cit.

45. Ibid.

46. Ibid.

47. Noriyuki Takayama, *The Morning After in Japan: Its Declining Population, Too Generous Pensions and a Weakened Economy* (Tokyo: Maruzen, 2000).

48. Statistics Bureau, Management and Coordination Agency, *Employment Status Survey* (Tokyo: MCA, 1997).

49. Ministry of Health and Welfare (1998), op. cit.

50. The previous child allowance had a fairly low income cutoff, and as a result only about 60 percent of all families with children under the age of 3 qualified.

51. National Institute of Population and Social Security Research (2000), op. cit. Social security expenditure in Japan is broadly divided into pension, health, and social welfare; this amount only accounts for the social welfare portion of the total social security expenditure. Although social welfare accounted for just 11.5 percent of total social security expenditures in 1998—with pensions and health care insurance accounting for the other 88.5 percent—social welfare expenditures rose faster.

52. Currently the cost burden ratio between the central and local governments for most social care services is 50:50.

53. In 1999 total local government debt was estimated at 176 trillion yen, or 35.4 percent of the gross domestic product. A growing social movement during the 1990s, led by social policy experts, economists, and community activists, called for greater local autonomy.

54. Ito Peng, "A Recent Childcare Reform in Japan," in *Family Policy and Childcare*, eds. Thomas Boje and Arnlaug Leira (London: Routledge, 2000), pp. 175–205.

55. Long-term care insurance allows individuals to "purchase" a designated amount of care services each month, depending on their level of disability. Insurance (government) presets the cost of each service. However, users must pay 10 percent of this cost, the logic being that this makes services more transparent. The 10 percent surcharge has forced people with low incomes to limit the use of care services. The government's own survey has shown that demand for care services was much lower than initially expected because people shied away from using them because of the financial burden.

56. Before long-term care insurance, local governments employed most careworkers in Japan. Interviews with local governments and social welfare associations in Yokohama City and in Iwate and Hyogo prefectures, and with careworkers in the Yokohama chapter of the local government employees' union, May–December 2000.

57. Ministry of Health and Welfare, *Heisei 11-nendo Kosei Hakusho (1999 White Paper on Health and Welfare)* (Tokyo: Gyosei, 1999).

BOX 3.3

Social Exclusion Unit of the United Kingdom Government
by Tara Karacan

Remedies to issues of social exclusion are as varied as its definitions. Continental European welfare states have long wedded economic policies to social policies, whereas Anglo-Saxon countries traditionally conceived of poverty primarily as a social problem to be addressed outside the market. For example, the United Kingdom has a Social Exclusion Unit (SEU) incorporated in the Cabinet Office under the deputy prime minister. It was set up by the prime minister in December 1997 to help improve government action to reduce social exclusion by producing "joined up solutions to joined up problems."[1] It works mainly on specific projects, chosen by the prime minister following consultation with other ministers and suggestions from interested groups.

The SEU is staffed by a mixture of civil servants from a number of government departments and external secondees from organizations with experience in tackling social exclusion. The SEU works on issues that affect a range of government departments, though it does not duplicate work being done elsewhere. It also participates in work that has a close bearing on social exclusion elsewhere in government.

The SEU works on specific projects and has reported on five main areas:

- Youth 16–18 years old who are not in education or employment
- Teenage pregnancy
- People who sleep in public places
- Truancy and school exclusion
- The National Strategy for Neighborhood Renewal

The unit is currently working on four projects:

- Reducing reoffending rates among former prisoners
- Working with young runaways
- Raising the educational attainment of children in care
- Addressing transport and social exclusion

continued on next page

BOX 3.3, continued

What is defined as social exclusion in one country may be defined simply as poverty in another country, and so on. For example, ethnic exclusion is a major issue in many countries, but it is not on the agenda of the UK Social Exclusion Unit. Because of the varied character of social exclusion, policies to deal with social exclusion clearly cannot be generalized.

1. See <http://www.cabinet-office.gov.uk/seu/index/whats_it_all_about.htm> for an introduction.

BOX 3.4

The French Health System: Where It Stands and Where It Is Heading
by Louis-Charles Viossat

Rated number one worldwide in the 2000 *World Health Organization Report*,[1] the French health system would appear to offer excellent cause for patient—and government—satisfaction.

Indeed, the French population enjoys one of the longest life expectancies worldwide and has excellent access to medical services and pharmaceuticals, both in ambulatory care and hospitals. This is because of universal health insurance coverage, more than 100,000 medical practitioners and specialists, and an extensive and well-developed network of private and public local and university hospitals. Also of great importance are the high quality of medical training, the education system overall, and interesting innovations in evaluation practices.

The truth, however, is that French health system reform has been a headache for every government since the end of the 1970s. It is worth recalling that conservative governments repeatedly lost general elections—in 1981, 1988, and 1997—after implementing health reform plans that caused doctor and nurse strikes and demonstrations in the streets of Paris.

The government that was elected in May and June 2002 is, once again, faced with the underlying difficulties of health system reform. To deal with this challenge, the new health minister, Jean-François Mattei, a professor of medicine, has adopted a multipronged approach that is based on the following:

- Reinforcing the importance of public health. The French system is rich on curative care but poor on preventive care. This movement will be put into effect through a 5-year health program and priority legislation to be voted on in 2003.
- Decentralizing health care providers and programs. The government plans to pass a law that will create 22 regional health agencies, to be in charge of hospital and ambulatory care planning, financing, and supervision.

continued on next page

BOX 3.4, continued

- Improving the governance of health insurance funds that are, as in Germany, managed by representatives of employers and employees.
- Pushing for quality and excellence everywhere in the health system by accreditation, evaluation, and training programs.
- Reforming hospital management by streamlining hospital organization and procedures and unifying financing techniques.

1. World Health Organization, *World Health Report 2000* (Geneva: World Health Organization, 2000), available at <http://www.who.int/whr/2000/en/report.htm>, last accessed October 10, 2002.

BOX 3.5

Seminar on Social Capital, Social Exclusion, and the East Asian Crisis, Manila, November 5–7, 2001

This seminar was held in Manila at the headquarters of the Asian Development Bank (ADB), not long after September 11, 2001. This colored discussions of social exclusion, inequality, and poverty. The proceedings were among the most thought provoking and engaged among the project seminars, and a central conclusion was that such topics have urgent national, regional, and global dimensions.

Ambassador Howard Q. Dee (of the Philippines) and Colin Moynihan (of the United Kingdom) focused on exclusion as a phenomenon that could affect majorities of societies, with the critical barometer being youth and their sense of inclusion, commitment, and hope. Social exclusion is a specific problem for specific groups but can also apply much more broadly to the tenor of a society and to one country or society relative to others.

An introduction by Akira Seki of the ADB highlighted the importance of socially inclusive development, combining effective macroeconomic governance with pro-poor, sustainable economic growth. Economic growth, he said, can reduce poverty only when it forms part of a comprehensive national strategy that includes the development of human capital, provision of basic social services, removal of gender-based obstacles to inclusion, and expansion of social protection. Anita Kelles-Viitanen of the ADB highlighted the importance of Europe's social policy experience in addressing social capital and social exclusion.

The seminar was organized around seven topics. Jan Breman (University of Amsterdam) focused on two villages in rural Java, Indonesia. When the urban economy crashes, many workers become much poorer than the "myth of the peasant society" would lead us to believe, because there is no longer any land to go back to and no agricultural work to compensate for the loss of urban jobs. Gareth Api Richards (see Box 3.1) focused on the relevance of social capital in the field of development assistance, and participants agreed that proper conceptualization and measurement of social exclusion and social capital can

continued on next page

BOX 3.5, continued

add to understanding of poverty and enhance the effectiveness of social policy.

The second theme, regional strategies to fight social exclusion, drew on a presentation by Gabriella Battaini (see Chapter 27). European welfare states face serious challenges: aging, declining interest in collective action, and a trend toward fragmentation—all feeding the fear of a two-tier economic system. To address these challenges, public authorities could promote social partnerships, facilitate access to basic social rights, and fight exclusion on the basis of gender and race. Discussion focused on how to implement rights. Participants underlined the constructive role of the European Commission in peer-reviewing social policies at the European level.

The third topic focused on the urban poor through the work of Vincent Delbos on urban policies in Europe (see Chapter 10) and of Søren Villadsen on the role of the state in providing housing for the poor (see Chapter 9). The case of Hong Kong figured prominently: although self-reliance is at the heart of its welfare programs, 50 percent of its people live in public housing, and the government offers "interim housing arrangements" for the elderly and devotes 15 percent of public expenditures to social housing.

The fourth topic was the rural poor, grounded in Luis Frota's paper on social assistance for aging rural households (see Chapter 17). Discussion focused on whether the universal, pay-as-you-go pension system in Europe is suitable for East Asia. The politics of pension reform, especially in Scandinavian countries, where farmers' parties have actively participated in the policymaking process, was highlighted.

The fifth topic, social exclusion and gender, was based on a paper by Ann-Charlotte Ståhlberg on the gender impact of the welfare state (see Chapter 12). Discussion turned on the role of women in societies in change. In the transition from public to private sector–dominated economies in East Asia, women and low-skilled workers are the first to be laid off and the last to be hired. Pensions and social security schemes can play a critical role in preventing serious gender inequality. Women still benefit less from such schemes, even though in Europe they represent 70 percent of retirees.

BOX 3.5, continued

The sixth topic, the informal sector, was based on a paper by Jacques Charmes (see Chapter 18). Discussion highlighted the elusiveness of the notion of the informal sector, accentuated by the urban bias of policy-makers and the formal sector bias of economists and statisticians.

The seventh topic compared social exclusion in Europe and East Asia, with presentations by Isabel Ortiz of ADB on East Asia and Colin Moynihan on Europe. A broad conclusion was that many social protection instruments today are not effective, owing to their limited coverage and generally low levels of public expenditure. Discussion focused on the need for greater coordination among government policies and a larger role for the private sector.

PART IV

Facing Aging and
Providing Social Security

Introduction

This section addresses European and East Asian experiences in designing and revamping social security systems in the face of rapid social change. Pension reform is a particularly critical issue because rising life expectancy poses a fundamental challenge to the basic design of modern welfare states. Although industrialized economies face the most immediate challenges, the Republic of Korea and Taiwan, China, are already well into the demographic transition, and the challenge looms on the East Asian agenda.

In Chapter 14 Frank A. G. den Butter and Udo Kock analyze experiences with two types of social security systems in Europe—social insurance and redistribution—as well as the complex trade-offs among social security, equity, and economic growth. Although social security systems help overcome income inequality, for example, they can also hamper economic growth. However, social security systems can also foster economic growth if they enable unemployed workers to search for jobs that better match their skills. Hence designers of social security systems need to seek to balance equity and efficiency, with policymakers in developing countries especially avoiding too-generous systems that create a "social security trap." Box 4.1 is a thumbnail sketch of the history of social security in Europe.

In Chapter 15 Meesook Kim recounts the Republic of Korea's relatively fast development of a comprehensive social security system in the face of a bewildering array of social changes. Today the Korean system includes work injury compensation, health insurance, public pensions, and unemployment insurance, and the country also ensures a minimum income to all its citizens. Although many of those provisions are nearly universal, the author contends that the Republic of

Korea must further extend those protections to address high unemployment, continued rapid aging amid dissolving family networks, and possible reunification with the impoverished Democratic People's Republic of Korea.

In Chapter 16 Mauro Mare and Giuseppe Pennisi recount efforts to advance critically needed pension reform in Italy. After inconclusive debate in the 1980s, a foreign exchange and financial emergency in 1992 prompted major changes that continued under pressure from the impending European monetary union. Such experiences show that advocates of challenging reforms must act decisively given a window of opportunity, the authors say, and that pension reforms quickly reach a standstill if they do not form part of broader efforts to reform labor markets and the welfare state.

In Chapter 17 Luis Frota shows how countries have confronted the challenge of providing social insurance to agricultural households given rural aging. He recounts how European nations with large agricultural sectors have provided incentives to lure new generations to remain on farms, extended agricultural pensions to farmers who also hold jobs in other sectors, and boosted agricultural pensions up to those of other workers. He also examines East Asia's recent experience in extending social protection to rural communities experiencing out-migration, and he holds that fostering democratic participation in decision-making can help ensure that no farmers are left behind.

In Chapter 18 Jacques Charmes charts the changing views of public authorities toward the informal economy. In the early 1970s many analysts considered that sector a relic, destined to quickly disappear as countries embraced market and monetary economics. However, economic shocks in the 1980s prompted significant growth in the informal sector, which absorbed the resulting labor surpluses. Jacques Charmes shows that East Asian countries experienced an anomalous effect during the recent crisis. Because informal sectors in those countries are tightly linked to export markets, they could not absorb displaced workers (many of them women), who instead returned to the countryside. The significant share of subcontracting work in the informal sector makes it an important engine for growth; yet countries will have to confront major questions regarding how to design social security systems to cover families who work in it.

Finally Box 4.2 recounts the highlights of the February 2002 seminar in Rome/Caserta, which focused on the linked challenges of policymaking for the social sectors and managing reforms in social security regimes.

A Brief History of Social Security in Europe
by Frank A. G. den Butter and Udo Kock

We can distinguish three stages in the evolution of European social security systems.

In the *first stage,* charity was the main source of social protection for the poor.

In the *second stage,* in the aftermath of the Industrial Revolution, countries introduced social insurance schemes to cover the social risk of old age, occupational disability, and illness of workers in particular industries. Halfway through the 20th century, most such schemes were expanded to cover unemployment risk and all workers.

In the *third stage,* after World War II, prevention of social risks became important, and countries expanded social protection to cover almost all aspects of occupational and private life. In the 1970s many countries also introduced or extended early-retirement schemes in response to rising unemployment. Influenced by Keynesian ideas, social security policy had become a tool of macroeconomic policy.

Western European countries differ with respect to the speed of this historic process, depending on the degree and types of industrialization, the level of economic development, and changing social conditions. However, by the end of the 1960s all countries had developed a comprehensive system of social security.

CHAPTER 14

Social Security, Economic Growth, and Poverty

by Frank A. G. den Butter and Udo Kock

ABSTRACT: This chapter reviews both the literature and experience concerning social security systems in Europe. The focus is on two distinct but closely related approaches to social security—social insurance and redistribution—and their implications for economic welfare and economic growth. The chapter highlights the need for social security systems to balance equity and efficiency by making complex tradeoffs.

In modern industrial countries, social security arrangements purport to protect workers and their families from extreme income losses, and should, therefore, enhance economic welfare for risk-averse individuals. Solidarity is central to the philosophy of social security: it addresses the reality that private companies cannot insure against some risks, such as cyclical unemployment.

This chapter reviews both the economic literature on social security systems and practical experience in building them. The focus is on the complicated relationship among social security, economic welfare, and economic growth. The chapter makes special reference to the European experience because social security systems in Europe are much more elaborate and diverse than those in Japan and the United States. The aim is to draw policy lessons that might help developing countries build and reform social security schemes, especially East Asian countries, which are experiencing relatively fast catch-up with the industrial world. The caveat is that we do not address risk management tailored to social structures in developing countries.[1]

Discussions of social security hinge on three major attributes: efficiency, equity, and administrative feasibility. We focus mainly on efficiency, but policy-makers and analysts in Europe also heavily debate equity issues such as inequality and social integration.[2] We do not treat administrative feasibility because it is a rather technical issue with many legal and administrative implications. Pension schemes are also an important component of social security systems, but that topic deserves separate treatment (see Chapters 16 and 17).

The next section describes the main characteristics of two concepts of social security in use in Europe: the Beveridge concept and the Bismarck concept. Then we apply aspects of economic welfare theory to social security arrangements. Later we address experience with actual social security arrangements in Europe and the problems policymakers encounter when designing and implementing them. We conclude with lessons about the design and implementation of social security schemes.

Beveridge versus Bismarck

Two social security concepts emerged in Europe during the 20th century: the insurance concept and the redistribution concept (see Box 4.1 for a brief history of the development of social security in Europe). Bismarck introduced the insurance concept in Germany in the second half of the 19th century when he designed the first social protection schemes for workers. British reformer Lord Beveridge developed the redistribution concept during World War II.

The insurance concept focuses on insuring workers against income loss in the event of unemployment, disability, or retirement—the system smoothes lifetime income. Both contributions and benefits depend on earnings, and most programs are financed out of premiums and managed jointly by unions and employers.

Redistribution programs, by contrast, cover all citizens. Benefits are meant to be the last resort for workers without enough unemployment insurance, for households with no source of income, and for the working poor. The key focus is on poverty relief: benefits are means tested and provide only a minimum income guarantee. There is no link between contributions and benefits because they are financed through general taxes. Public administrative bodies usually administer the programs, which have few eligibility rules, although the means test is typically less strict for unemployed workers than for persons without employment history.

The difference between the two types of programs can be characterized as solidarity among insured workers and solidarity among citizens (see Table 14.1).

Table 14.1   Characteristics of Social Security Concepts in Europe

	Pure insurance (Bismarck)	Pure redistribution (Beveridge)
Main goal	To guarantee socioeconomic status	To guarantee income at subsistence level
Eligibility	Depends on contributions	Is independent of contributions
Expected benefits	Match contributions (contributions are income tested)	Are means tested
Type of benefits	Depends on previous wage and contributions	Is means tested and at a flat rate
Financing	Is through premiums	Is through general tax revenues
Administration	Is private	Is public
Focus	Is labor market	Is citizen's rights
Examples	Germany	United Kingdom

The savings concept represents a third alternative.[3] Compulsory savings provide social protection for individuals, not only for retirement pensions but also for contingencies such as unemployment, disability, and ill health. Benefits depend on the accumulation of an individual's compulsory savings. The typical case is the scheme in Singapore.

All European social security systems also provide some universal benefits: tax-financed benefits for specific contingencies that do not require either a contribution or a means test. They can include child benefits and the flat-rate retirement pensions in countries such as the Netherlands and Sweden, the National Health Service in the United Kingdom, and family support and child benefits in many other European countries.

We expect countries in which the redistribution concept dominates to spend a relatively large portion of revenues on social assistance and family allowances, and a relatively small portion on social insurance. The reverse pattern applies in countries in which the insurance concept dominates. Thus we can conclude that the insurance principle dominates in Germany and to a lesser extent in the Netherlands, whereas the redistribution principle dominates social security in the United Kingdom and to a lesser extent in Denmark and Sweden (see Table 14.2). Interestingly, although the insurance system provides relatively high benefits to a limited group, while the assistance concept grants relatively low benefits for a large group, overall spending as a percentage of gross domestic product does not differ much between the two systems.

In practice, of course, many European social security programs combine elements of both systems, and all countries have faced trade-offs. The concepts and

Table 14.2 Characteristics of Social Security Systems: Sources of Revenue and Type of Benefits

Country	Sources of revenue[a] (%)			Spending by type of benefit[c] (%)		
	Insured persons	Employers	State[b]	Social insurance[d]	Social assistance	Family allowance
Denmark:						
1960	n.a.	n.a.	n.a.	n.a.	n.a.	n.a.
1970	14.1	8.9	75.8	69.4	18.5	6.6
1980	1.8	5.9	90.2	68.3	24.2	3.0
1985	3.1	7.8	86.1	68.2	25.7	1.8
1990	4.6	5.1	87.8	62.6	28.6	3.3
1995[e]	10.8	9.5	73.7	n.a.	n.a.	n.a.
France:						
1960	18.9	68.9	11.1	n.a.	n.a.	n.a.
1970	18.9	68.4	10.3	n.a.	n.a.	n.a.
1980	21.0	53.4	24.1	62.6	15.8	10.6
1985	23.0	50.3	23.7	65.7	13.2	11.2
1990[e]	n.a.	n.a.	n.a.	71.9	4.6	11.9
Germany:						
1960	25.9	44.4	25.0	66.7	6.6	2.0
1970	28.9	42.3	25.1	70.8	4.7	2.6
1980	34.0	34.2	28.9	75.4	4.1	5.0
1985	36.3	34.7	26.4	78.3	4.9	3.3
1993	36.8	32.3	27.6	81.7	6.4	2.6
1995[e]	29.8	38.1	29.8	n.a.	n.a.	n.a.
Netherlands:						
1960	40.9	40.3	12.2	64.4	4.8	13.0
1970	38.5	42.9	12.3	69.4	4.8	10.3
1980	33.2	33.3	24.6	73.7	6.2	7.5
1985	39.5	31.8	16.3	76.5	3.5	7.2
1990	43.0	17.7	24.4	77.4	2.7	5.1
1993	46.0	18.0	21.4	77.5	2.2	4.8

Country	Sources of revenue[a] (%)			Spending by type of benefit[c] (%)		
	Insured persons	Employers	State[b]	Social insurance[d]	Social assistance	Family allowance
Sweden:						
1960	20.5	11.0	66.9	71.3	12.2	10.7
1970	11.4	27.7	54.6	80.2	14.7	5.1
1980	1.0	45.9	45.3	77.9	16.8	5.2
1985	1.3	36.4	52.2	84.5	0.3	15.3
1991	1.7	39.7	49.4	84.2	0.6	12.9
1993	1.0	43.0	56.1	83.8	1.5	12.8
United Kingdom:[f]						
1959–60	20.0	17.9	58.7	71.0	10.8	5.4
1969–70	19.9	24.9	53.0	70.5	15.0	5.4
1979–80	15.6	26.2	55.0	67.3	15.6	7.8
1984–85	18.3	23.5	55.5	58.8	24.5	7.0
1991–92	15.6	25.5	49.8	61.1	22.8	5.7
1993–94	14.0	22.8	54.7	57.8	26.2	5.6

n.a. = not available.

a. Includes medical care, sickness benefits, unemployment insurance, retirement pensions, employment injury benefits, family benefits, maternity benefits, invalidity benefits, and survivors' benefits. Totals do not add up to 100 percent because revenues from capital income and other sources have been omitted.

b. Includes special taxes allocated to social security and participation of other public authorities.

c. Total spending does not add up to 100 percent because benefits for pubic employees and war victims have been omitted.

d. Includes public health services.

e. The definition changed, so no consistent data were available.

f. Reference period is April–March.

Source: International Labor Office (1992), available at <http://www.ilo.org/public/english/protection/socsec>; Nicholas Barr, "Economic Theory and the Welfare State: A Survey and Interpretation," *Journal of Economic Literature* 30, no. 2 (1992): 741–803; and authors' calculations.

content of particular social security schemes have also changed according to the political and economic context, and because policymakers continue to fine-tune programs to suit economic and labor market conditions. Nevertheless, the classification of social security systems turns out to be remarkably stable over time. In fact, many countries have recently sharpened their profiles.[4] The United Kingdom has moved even further away from the insurance principle: unemployment insurance contributions have related to earnings since 1992, although the program pays a flat-rate benefit. France, Germany, and Spain, meanwhile, have strengthened the link between benefits and previous employment and contributions.

Considering Efficiency and Equity

Economists do not agree on whether a comprehensive system of social security and cuts in inequality from redistribution are an impediment or a spur to economic performance.[5] According to one argument, social security expenditures are thrown into a leaky bucket because the welfare loss of those who pay the social security premiums is larger than the welfare gain of those who benefit.[6] Others hold that inequality is harmful to economic growth[7] and that the metaphor of the leaky bucket wrongly assumes that we live in a perfect world with complete information and well-functioning markets. Those analysts advance the irrigation function as an alternative to the leaky bucket. According to that theory, workers with some economic security will be more eager to search for new jobs, and job destruction and creation can proceed at a good pace at the macro level, enhancing productivity and economic welfare.

The irrigation function underscores the desirability of social security systems in newly developing countries that, owing to technological catch-up with the industrial world, are witnessing fast economic growth. It is especially important for workers in those countries to spend time searching for good jobs and establishing good matches rather than earning a subsistence living in the informal sector.

How Can Social Security Enhance Welfare?

Formal modeling exercises show that the limited U.S. social security provisions give the United States lower unemployment than in Europe, but that European social security systems are more beneficial to economic welfare.[8]

Skill-biased technology shocks are the most important source of the difference between these two regions. These shocks imply that educational differences become more prominent as the labor market demands more capabilities and skills.[9] The effects of skill-biased technology shocks differ according to whether countries have extensive or limited social security systems. A generous social security system makes both employers and employees more choosy in establishing a good match. This mechanism gains importance when the demand for skills grows more heterogeneous, and leads to longer unemployment spells when social security is good. This explains why unemployment is higher in Europe than in the United States. But the quality of the matches increases and productivity is higher in the European situation because companies better exploit workers' skills.[10]

The trade-off reflects the equilibrium search theory of the labor market. The same models indicate that social security enhances the welfare of low-paid workers as well as the unemployed. The models do not reckon with risk-averse behavior, but a good social security system can enhance welfare by negating such behavior. (The models also do not allow for job mobility, in that they assume that only unemployed and not employed workers search for new jobs.) Although the models analyze the effects of differences among social security systems in the industrial world, the arguments about why a good social security system may enhance productivity and welfare also apply to developing countries undergoing fast economic development and extensive structural change.

Analyzing Reforms

The traditional aims of social security are to protect people from the financial consequences of unemployment, disability, retirement, and other social risks, and to reintegrate workers into the labor market. Analysts should use those two main goals to assess proposals to reform or implement social security programs.[11]

The first key question relates to the coverage and scope of a social security program or reform: who is entitled to benefits? Analysts often pose this question as a trade-off between general and targeted policies. The advantage of targeted policies is that they directly address the social risk of a narrowly defined group. A disadvantage is that people outside the target group have an incentive to adjust their behavior to become entitled to the benefit. The earned-income tax credit is an example of a targeted tax policy aimed at increasing the supply of low-wage workers. The disincentive of this policy is that high marginal tax rates in phase-out range give workers disincentives to invest in human capital. The policy also distorts the relative prices of labor.

General social security policies do not face these problems because their wider scope reduces people's incentives to change their behavior to become entitled to a benefit. However, general policies suffer from a large deadweight loss: a large number of recipients who are entitled to the benefit do not need it. A good example is the general income tax credit for workers, which was introduced under the Dutch tax reform and became effective in 2001. The credit aims to boost labor supply and cut unemployment. The deadweight loss arises because current workers are also entitled to the tax credit, without creating additional labor supply. Government budget constraints will limit the tax credit, further restricting its impact on labor supply and unemployment. On the positive side, the policy measure does not distort the labor market.

Once policymakers have determined a social security program's coverage and entitlement criteria, they have to enforce those criteria. Applications have to be evaluated and entitlement decisions made. This gatekeeper function determines who will receive a particular benefit and what its level and duration will be. The gatekeeper function is usually more important for targeted policies because those programs give people incentives to change their behavior and apply for a benefit, although their personal characteristics have not changed.

The gatekeeper function always involves social costs. A strict application of the rules implies that the chance that the system will admit someone who is not entitled to benefits is small. This is analogous to the error of the second kind in statistical testing. On the other hand, the error of the first kind—the probability that the system will not admit someone who is entitled—is rather large. The opposite holds for a generous application of admission rules. Policymakers can try to enhance the discriminatory power of the gatekeeper function by reducing the asymmetric information between the gatekeeper and the individual who seeks entitlement, but doing so will seriously enlarge the costs of gatekeeping.

Those first two criteria in analyzing social security reform—the trade-off between general and targeted policies, and the gatekeeping function—determine the number of people entering the system. The third criterion—incentives—determines outflow from the system. That is, social security programs for workers who are unemployed, have disabilities, or are ill should contribute to rapid reintegration in the labor market. The system can accomplish this in many ways, such as by integrating active labor market policies into the social security program.

Designing Incentives

If properly designed, social security programs can minimize their adverse effects on the labor supply. However, many social security programs in Europe cause severe incentive problems in the labor market. The magnitude and form of these problems depend on the scheme's institutional characteristics. For unemployment compensation programs, these characteristics include the following:

- Benefit level
- Benefit duration
- Contributions (in the form of taxes or premiums)
- Entitlement conditions (such as through layoffs rather than voluntary quits and other employment history)
- Job search conditions
- Job acceptance conditions (people may reject some unsuitable job offers)
- Means test (including other household income and housing property)
- Household circumstances (such as number of children)

The traditional negative incentive effect is that higher benefit levels and longer benefit duration may mean that workers are less willing to search for jobs or accept job offers. An increase in benefit levels will also increase the value of leisure, and the worker will reduce his or her search intensity, cutting the outflow rate from unemployment.[12]

High benefit levels certainly undercut workers' incentives to accept low-paid jobs, because their net gain in income will be small. In many European countries, supplementary means-tested benefits increase this problem. In Germany, the Netherlands, and the United Kingdom, unemployed workers receiving unemployment assistance are exempt from local taxes and are entitled to discounts for some educational and health services. In some countries rent allowances are linked to unemployment assistance. If unemployed workers accept a job, they will lose most of these additional benefits. This creates the "unemployment trap," by which workers remain unemployed voluntarily.

On the other hand, unemployed workers who are not entitled to unemployment insurance benefits will raise their search intensity when unemployment benefits become more generous, to find employment and hence qualify for unemployment benefits. The magnitude of this entitlement effect depends on the entitlement conditions.

Whether a country's social security system is mainly insurance based or redistribution based determines the incentive effects of unemployment compensation.[13] Insurance-based social security systems, such as in Germany, tend to exclude long-term unemployed workers from insurance. Because these unemployed workers usually receive means-tested unemployment assistance or a family allowance, the unemployment trap applies in particular to them.

In countries such as France, Germany, and the Netherlands, unemployed workers who reach the end of the maximum period of unemployment insurance benefits join the stock of unemployment assistance beneficiaries and face a sharp decline in benefit levels. This induces them to lower their "reservation" wage—the wage at which they will accept a new job—and increase their job search activities, raising the outflow from unemployment. Empirical studies have found a large rise in the outflow rate of unemployed workers toward the end of the benefit period.[14]

However, higher benefits extend the duration of unemployment only slightly,[15] because other policies counteract them. For example, Sweden introduced active labor market policies in the late 1960s and early 1970s while extending unemployment compensation.[16]

Practical Experience: The Spiral of the Wedge and the Supply Effect

Social security influences tax and premium rates, the development and pattern of labor force participation, and labor productivity.[17] The interaction of those macroeconomic variables can cause a negative spiral. High average and marginal tax and premium rates create a wedge between the gross and net wages of workers, inducing a decline in labor force participation and the number of hours worked, especially for women earning a second family income. Low labor force participation, in turn, provides a small base through which to finance benefits. A downturn of the business cycle will require a relatively large rise in premiums and taxes, inducing unions to demand higher wages. This reduces labor demand, shrinking the premium and tax base even further and increasing demand for social security benefits. High wage costs reinforce this mechanism—sometimes referred to as the "social security trap"—because employers have an incentive to increase productivity by investing in labor-saving technology and other innovations.

A major engine behind this negative spiral is that supply, as well as demand, determines the impacts of social security. The supply effect reflects the fact that people become more aware of their legal right to demand social security benefits, so more eligible people actually receive them. One investigation of such a supply effect in the Netherlands showed a sharp rise in the number of people who received benefits from 1970 to 1990,[18] even though the system did not add major new provisions.[19] Strengthening eligibility standards and applying stronger gate-keeping can decrease this effect, as can admonishing people not to abuse the system and providing training and work experience rather than just financial compensation (workfare instead of welfare). Because the indirect effects of the supply effect on labor participation are much higher than the direct effects, such institutional changes are essential to reducing the negative spiral and curbing it, especially in developing countries that are building a social security system.

To our knowledge, no comprehensive studies have examined the supply effect. However, a general comparison among countries can shed light on these relationships. If we take the United States as a benchmark, for example, Japan has high labor participation and low social security expenses and tax and premium rates, combined with low productivity. In France and the Netherlands, and to a lesser extent in Germany and the United Kingdom, labor participation is low, whereas social security expenditures and income and productivity levels are high (see Table 14.3).

Other Influences on the Economic Impact of Social Security

The impact of a social security system depends on circumstances in other parts of the economy and society. Economic growth, low unemployment, and high labor force participation may accompany a generous social security system, but if the macroeconomic, social, or technological environment changes, the same system could seriously frustrate economic development.

Many analysts maintain that economic turbulence caused by technological change and global competition underlies high and persistent unemployment in Europe, given a generous system of social security that reduces work and job search incentives. The developers of the social security systems in the 1950s and 1960s, a time when structural change and labor market dynamics were more modest, did not foresee those problems. Today workers lose skills when displaced and while unemployed, owing to the transition from a manufacturing to a service economy, economic globalization, and new information and communication technologies. This causes long-term unemployment because reservation wages are high relative to productivity.

Table 14.3 The Supply Effect of Social Security (1993): Labor Participation, Social Security Expenditures, and Productivity and Wage Cost Elasticities

| | Participation rate (labor years) | Social security expenditure (as a percentage of GDP) | Taxes and premiums (as a percentage of GDP) | GDP per worker (index, United States = 100) | GDP per hour worked (index, United States = 100) | Wage cost elasticities with respect to social security contributions | |
						Employer's contributions	Income taxes and worker's contributions
Netherlands	51	27	55	90	106		
France	56	24	47	94	97	0.40	0.40
United Kingdom	60	16	46	75	80	0.25	0.25
Germany	62	15	37	82	84	1.00	1.00
United States	65	13	32	100	100	0.00	1.00
Japan	67	12	33	75	63		

Source: Organization for Economic Cooperation and Development (OECD), The OECD Job Study (Paris: OECD, 1995); OECD, Labor Force Statistics (Paris: OECD, 1995); and K. van Paridon, "The Crucial Importance of High Labor Force Participation: The Dutch Case and Lessons for Europe," in Unemployment in Europe, ed. Michael A. Landesmann and K. Pichelmann, (London: Macmillan, 2000), 188–204.

However, economic turbulence can also be seen as a permanent shock that increases the value of the right match between jobs and workers.[20] Generous benefits allow workers to search longer for better matches, which increases the equilibrium unemployment rate. Mismatch declines, but at the expense of an inefficient level of investment in search.

Changing social and demographic patterns also influence the long-run impact of social security programs. Individualization and the growing number of divorced couples put more pressure on noncontributory programs such as family allowances and social assistance. In the United Kingdom policymakers considered social assistance a temporary provision in 1948, because they expected that eventually everyone would be self-supporting through work or unemployment insurance.[21] A social security system where benefits are highly dependent on labor market status, such as the German system, has trouble coping with changing social patterns outside the labor market. Structural changes in the employment pattern of workers, such as the sharp rise in the share of part-time workers in the Netherlands, also put pressure on existing social security programs, because unemployment and occupational disability programs often exclude workers with intermittent incomes.

Despite those changes, the number of disability beneficiaries in the Netherlands has exploded since the 1970s and now exceeds 900,000—far beyond expectations when Parliament unanimously passed the disability act in 1967. One study concludes that up to 50 percent of workers receiving disability benefits are in fact unemployed.[22] Because disability benefits are more generous than unemployment benefits, a high share of workers with disabilities raises wage costs and increases the government's budget deficit. If employment outflow is skewed toward disability benefits, it also makes the unemployment level artificially low. This generates biased and unintended labor market signals that could raise wages beyond economically sustainable levels. Yet for obvious political reasons, curbing this "curse of a good act" is extremely difficult.

This problem is not unique to the Netherlands. One study suggested that the unemployment rate in Norway also significantly affects the disability program.[23]

Conclusion: Providing a Trampoline Instead of a Hammock

The lesson for newly developing economies is that there is no such thing as a "natural next step," uniform blueprint, or optimal system in developing formal social security programs. Social security systems should be tailor made, adapted to the social structure and labor market in each country.

Social security systems may combine elements of the insurance concept and the redistribution concept. The system will always have to be based partly on solidarity, especially with respect to the poor, who should receive an above-subsistence income guarantee. On the other hand, the system should contain enough incentives to avoid moral hazard and free rider behavior. It is essential that incentives in the system encourage, not discourage, labor participation.

The redistribution inherent in social security systems is bound to diminish income inequality. Because of the trade-off between equity and efficiency, this may hamper economic growth. On the other hand, social security, owing to its irrigation function, can also foster economic growth because it allows the unemployed to search for good and productive job matches. Hence the design of a social security system should seek a balance between the negative equity-efficiency trade-off and social security's irrigation function.

A major lesson, especially suggested by the Netherlands experience, is that policymakers should not overdirect the initial design of the social security system toward provision of benefits. The mere availability of these benefits can evoke a supply effect strengthened by the negative wedge spiral: individuals' entitlement to social security benefits causes a negative externality for the employed, because they must pay higher social security premiums. Newly developing countries should avoid setting up too generous and passive systems: they should provide a trampoline instead of a hammock.

Notes

1. For more discussion see, for example, World Bank, *World Development Report 2000/2001: Attacking Poverty*, (Oxford, England: Oxford University Press, 2000).
2. See Nicholas Barr, "Economic Theory and the Welfare State: A Survey and Interpretation," *Journal of Economic Literature* 30, no. 2 (1992): 741–803, section 5, for a brief assessment of the distributional effects of social security in a number of Organization for Economic Cooperation and Development (OECD) countries.
3. Sara Connolly and Alistair Munro, *Economics of the Public Sector* (London: Pearson Education, 1999).
4. Günther Schmid and Bernd Reissert, "Unemployment Compensation and Labor Market Transitions," in *International Handbook of Labor Market Policy and Evaluation*, ed. Günther Schmid and Bernd Reissert (London: Edward Elgar, 1996), pp. 235–76.
5. See, for example, H. Borstlap, "Labour Market, Social Protection and Economic Performance," in *Economic Science: Art or Asset? The Case of the Netherlands*, ed. Peter A. G. van Bergeijk, A. G. van Bergeijk, A. L. Bovenberg, E. E. C. van Damme, and J. van Sinderen (Rotterdam, Netherlands: OCFEB, 1996).
6. Arthur M. Okun, *Equality and Efficiency: The Big Trade-off* (Washington, D.C.: Brookings Institution, 1975).

7. T. Persson and G. Tabellini, "Is Inequality Harmful for Growth?" *American Economic Review* 84 (1994): 600–21.

8. D. T. Mortensen and C. A. Pissarides, "Unemployment Responses to Skill Biased Technology Shocks: The Role of Labour Market Policy," *Economic Journal* 109 (1999): 242–65, and R. Marimon and F. Zilibotti, "Unemployment versus Mismatch of Talent: Reconsidering Unemployment Benefits," *Economic Journal* 109 (1999): 266–91.

9. See, for example, S. Machin and J. Van Reenen, "Technology and Changes in Skill Structure: Evidence from Seven OECD Countries," *Quarterly Journal of Economics* 113, no. 4 (1998): 1215–44, and E. Berman, J. Bound, and S. Machin, "Implications of Skill-Biased Technological Changes: International Evidence," *Quarterly Journal of Economics* 113, no. 4 (1998): 1245–79, for empirical investigations of the importance of these shocks.

10. R. Marimon and F. Zilibotti, op. cit.

11. See also *Scientific Council for Government Policy, Continued Growth of Labor Force Participation* (in Dutch), Report to the Government no. 57 (The Hague, Netherlands: Sdu, 2000), and F. A.G. den Butter and U. Kock, "More Labor Participation with Individual S.avings Accounts?" (in Dutch), *Openbare Uitgave* 32 (2000): 200–12.

12. See E. Karni, "Optimal Unemployment Insurance: A Guide to the Literature," World Bank mimeo (January 1999), for an overview of the theoretical literature on optimal unemployment insurance.

13. See also Schmid and Reissert, op. cit.

14. G. J. Van den Berg, "Nonstationarity in Job Search Theory," *Review of Economic Studies* 57 (1990): 255–77.

15. R. Layard, S. Nickell, and R. Jackman, *Unemployment: Macro-Economic Performance and the Labour Market* (Oxford, England: Oxford University Press, 1991).

16. A. Björklund and B. Holmlund, "Effects of Extended Unemployment Compensation in Sweden," in *The Political Economy of Social Security*, ed. B. A. Gustafsson and N. Anders Klevmarken (Amsterdam: North Holland, 1989), 165–83.

17. See K. van Paridon, "The Crucial Importance of High Labor Force Participation: The Dutch Case and Lessons for Europe," in *Unemployment in Europe*, ed. M. A. Landesmann and K. Pichelmann, (London: Macmillan, 2000), 188–204.

18. F. A. G. den Butter, "Supply of Social Security as a Cause of Low Labour Participation in the Netherlands: A Cliometric Analysis," (Free University Research Memorandum, Amsterdam, 1993), p. 56.

19. R. F. M. Lubbers, "De economische politiek in Nederland vanaf de jaren '60" (Economic policy in the Netherlands from the 1960s), in *Het sociaal-economisch beleid in de tweede helft van de twintigste eeuw*, ed. J. van Sinderen (Wolters-Noordhof, Netherlands: Groningen, 1990), pp. 14–19.

20. See the model by Marimon and Zilibotti, op. cit.

21. Nicholas Barr, *The Economics of the Welfare State*, 3d ed. (Oxford, England: Oxford University Press, 1998), p. 242.

22. L. J. M. Aarts and Ph. R. de Jong, *Economic Aspects of Disability Behavior* (Amsterdam: North Holland, 1992).

23. E. Bowitz, "Disability Benefits, Replacement Ratios and the Labor Market: A Time Series Approach," *Applied Economics* 29 (1997): 913–23.

CHAPTER 15

Social Security and the Social Safety Net in the Republic of Korea

by Meesook Kim

ABSTRACT: Social security in the Republic of Korea has developed rapidly in all three fields: social insurance, public assistance, and social services. Public expenditures have risen while coverage has gradually expanded to become almost universal in some areas. However, public expenditures are still below those of other Organization for Economic Cooperation and Development (OECD) countries, and the Korean social security system faces tough challenges ahead.

Although the Republic of Korea has developed an ever more elaborate social security system, successive governments have left major responsibility for protecting against risks to individuals, households, and the market. Until recently, social security and welfare goals were subordinate to economic growth. Social security became an important policy issue during the 1997–98 crisis, as unemployment soared. With unemployment came other social problems: rising poverty, family dissolution, homelessness, and child neglect. As a result, Korea acted to confront the urgent and overriding challenge of strengthening the social security system by earmarking higher budgets for the welfare system and reorganizing administrative structures.

This chapter introduces the overall Korean social security system—which includes social insurance, public assistance, and social services—and its limitations. The chapter compares Korea's social welfare expenditures and programs with those of other OECD countries, and it concludes with a summary of the future social security challenges facing Korea.

Social Insurance Components of Korea's Social Security System

Social security in Korea includes four social insurance components: work injury compensation, health insurance, public pensions, and unemployment insurance (see Table 15.1). The country laid the groundwork for its social insurance system over a short period of time. Work injury compensation insurance, introduced in 1964, is the oldest main component. Health insurance has expanded since 1977, and the country established a public pension program in 1988. Unemployment insurance, the newest social insurance element, was adopted in 1993.

Work Injury Compensation Insurance

Work injury insurance is financed exclusively by contributions from employers; employees are not required to make contributions.[1] The government covers the administrative costs of the system.

Beneficiaries and Benefits

The range of beneficiaries of work injury insurance has expanded. In 1964, one year after the workplace insurance law was enacted, it covered only miners, assembly workers, and workers at firms with more than 500 employees. Amendments to the law in 1972 extended insurance to workplaces with 30 or more employees. The government further extended insurance in 1992 to cover workplaces with five or more employees, and after the financial crisis, it extended

Table 15.1 Types of Social Insurance in Korea, 2001

Types	Recipients	Number of participants	Ministry, year established
Work injury compensation insurance	All workplaces	9.50 million workers[a]	Ministry of Labor, 1964
Health insurance	All people	Over 96% of population	Ministry of Health and Welfare, 1977
National pension	All people	16 million	Ministry of Health and Welfare, 1988
Unemployment insurance	Almost all workplaces	9.27 million workers	Ministry of Labor, 1995

a. Figure is from 2000.

Source: Ministry of Labor, *Report on Work Injury Compensation Insurance in 2000* (Seoul: Ministry of Labor, 2001); Ministry of Labor, *White Paper on Labor* (Seoul: Ministry of Labor, 2001); and Ministry of Health and Welfare, *White Paper on Health and Welfare* (Seoul: Ministry of Health and Welfare, 2001).

coverage to all workplaces. As of 2000, beneficiaries totaled 9.50 million workers at 706,231 workplaces nationwide.[2] Benefits include sick leave, a sickness compensation pension, and a disability benefit.[3] The insurance covers treatment of work-caused diseases and injuries, compensates for income losses, and helps prevent work-related injuries. The insurance also covers occupation-related diseases that develop over time.[4]

Future Tasks

Korea's work injury insurance is widely criticized for its stringent eligibility criteria and narrow range of coverage. Moreover, its benefit level is too low to protect the economic stability of injured workers. Because the prevention of work injury is even more important than its treatment, raising benefit levels alone is not sufficient: the country needs to pursue full-scale prevention strategies to reduce the possibility of injury and foster employers' and employees' awareness of workplace security.

Health Insurance

Health insurance is generally designed to reduce the financial onus imposed by accident, disease, delivery, and death. When Korea enacted its health insurance law in 1963, coverage was too narrow to function as a social security scheme. Only in the 1970s, when the country was in the throes of economic development, did health insurance become a social issue. Witnessing the need, President Chung Hee Park turned his attention to developing a social welfare program that included health insurance.[5] Against this backdrop Korea adopted a national health insurance system in 1977 that encompassed firms with more than 500 employees as well as medical assistance for the poor. In 1989, 12 years after its inception, the system was extended to cover everyone, including rural residents and the urban self-employed.[6]

Benefits and Types

Health insurance benefits consist of cash payments and in-kind benefits. The latter include medical consultations, drugs and other therapeutic materials, medical and surgical treatments, hospitalization, operations, and other services such as nursing care and transportation.[7] To prevent the unnecessary use of health care services and resources and save on public health care costs, the insured make co-payments when receiving medical services. For example, patients pay 20 percent of hospitalization fees. Cash benefits reimburse insured people and their dependents for medical care and delivery costs, and also provide a fixed amount for funeral expenses.[8]

Three health insurance schemes used to correspond to different target groups: government employees, private school employees, military service employees and their dependents, rural and urban self-employed individuals, and employees of industrial and commercial companies. In 1998 the country merged the first and third schemes, and in 1999 it incorporated all three into a single system under the National Health Insurance Act. Contributions from insured individuals, employers, and the government finance the system.

In 2000 Korea separated prescription services from dispensation services for the first time, to prevent the overuse and misuse of drugs and drug-related accidents.[9] Eight months later the National Health Insurance Corporation confronted a serious financial imbalance owing to growing fees required by medical service centers. The Korean government had to devise a coping mechanism to reduce the financial burden on medical insurance. The government took a loan from the banks, raised health insurance fees, drew tobacco tax money, raised drug prices and medication examination fees, and limited the services covered by the insurance to 365 per year.

Challenges Ahead

Korea has achieved near-universal health insurance within a short time frame. The country must now focus on the quality as well as the quantity of health care. Three issues should receive priority. First, people should pay insurance fees in proportion to their income to intensify the income redistribution role of the health insurance system.[10] Second, because existing schemes do not cover numerous services, future tasks include extending health services to examination of, treatment of, and rehabilitation from chronic disease. Health insurance should cover not only curative treatment of disease and disability but also prevention. Finally, the government needs to secure the health insurance system's finances by minimizing the provision of unnecessary health services by health centers. In the long run Korea must develop avenues for delivering cost-effective health services by connecting them to health centers and by connecting personal services to social welfare centers.[11]

National Pension Insurance Schemes

Korea first adopted a national pension system in 1988 by amending the unworkable, ineffective 1973 pension law. Before 1973 the pension system covered only government employees, military personnel, and private schoolteachers. The national pension scheme (NPS)—the centerpiece of public pensions in Korea—now covers everyone, including farmers, fishers, and the self-employed. The system provides the insured with financial security against aging, disability, and death.

National Pension Beneficiaries

National pension participants fall into two groups: workplace-based participants and residential area–based participants. Since 1991 the scheme has included employees in businesses with five or more workers, and rural dwellers have been able to participate since 1994. As of 1998 the scheme included 5.06 million workplace-based participants and 2.11 million regional participants.[12] In 1999 the country extended the scheme to the urban self-employed, employees at workplaces with fewer than five workers, and part-time workers. The scheme does not automatically cover full-time housewives and people under 23 years of age without an occupation, but they can participate voluntarily. The average income replacement ratio used to be 70 percent for those with 40 or more years of participation, but amendments reduced the benefit to 60 percent, although people now qualify for benefits after 10 years rather than 15.[13] Recipients receive pension benefits for life. So that the scheme can achieve financial stability, the minimum age for receiving pension benefits will rise from 60 to 65 in 2033.

Challenges Ahead

Challenges include the level of benefits, fund security, coverage, and links to other pension plans. The pension fund is on the verge of exhaustion because its benefit levels have been too generous compared with low contribution rates. This imbalance needs to be redressed so future generations do not carry the burden of financing the present generation's pension fund. The current pension fund is likely to be depleted by 2030 owing to accelerating population aging. Although the government recently took countermeasures to secure the fund by lowering benefits and raising the entitlement age, it still needs to find ways to manage the fund to make it secure and profitable. And even though coverage has expanded to include rural residents, self-employed people, and part-time workers, the system needs to expand further to include housewives and spouses working with their self-employed partners. Finally, because the present pension scheme is not linked to public pension schemes for government employees, military personnel, and private schoolteachers, insured people who move across schemes are likely to lose their entitlement if they do not fulfill the minimum contribution period for either scheme. Combining contribution periods would increase the portability of pensions.

Unemployment Insurance

Of the four types of social insurance, unemployment insurance is the newest; it was started in 1995, 2 years after the enactment of the Unemployment Insurance Act, when unemployment was fairly low. Unemployment insurance was designed not only to secure income for workers during unemployment but also to promote employment through job training and human development. The insurance now covers all full-time workers—9.27 million employees from 1,208,000 workplaces as of 2001. Unemployment benefits provide 50 percent of average income before unemployment, with a minimum of 250,000 won and a maximum of 900,000 won per month.[14] The insured must have worked at an insured company for at least 6 months to be eligible for benefits, and may receive benefits for 2 to 7 months.[15]

Public Assistance Schemes

Korea officially established its public assistance system in 1961, when the livelihood protection law took effect. Benefit recipients were initially to include two types: home and institutional care recipients, and self-support care recipients. Home and institutional care recipients were those unable to work, including the elderly, children, people with disabilities, and those cared for at welfare institutions. Self-support care recipients were those able to work but lacking enough resources to live. The scheme provided livelihood aid, maternity aid, and burial aid only to home care and institutional care recipients,[16] but the rest of the benefits were provided to both recipient groups.

The livelihood protection system was widely criticized because of its low benefit levels, unreasonably narrow selection criteria, and other structural problems. In 1999 the Basic Guarantee Law replaced the Livelihood Protection Act within a context of rising demand for public assistance after the economic crisis. The unemployment rate rose sharply during the crisis, from 2.6 percent in 1997 to 6.8 percent in 1998 and to 6.3 percent in 1999, and the poverty rate doubled. Korea's social safety net was clearly too weak to respond effectively: the livelihood protection system covered only 60.4 percent of the absolute poor. Because it also did not cover self-support care recipients and the low-income unemployed, they suffered most. The Basic Guarantee Law was the first legal mechanism to guarantee a "national minimum" and self-sufficiency for the poor.

Those eligible for benefits fall into three categories. The first includes elderly persons who are unable to support themselves, children under 18, expectant women, and people unable to work owing to disease or mental or physical disability. The second category includes those who have no one to support them. The third group includes people whose family per capita income and household property fall below a certain level. (In 2000, to be eligible, a recipient had to report family income of 930,000 won or less, and household property valued at 32 million won or less for a family of four).

The system includes seven types of protection: livelihood aid, housing aid (newly added), medical aid, educational aid, self-support aid, maternity aid, and burial aid. The new law has lifted demographic eligibility criteria, and anyone who fits the family income and property criteria is entitled to aid. Because the new law now includes housing aid for the first time, the Korean welfare system protects every aspect of basic living.

The new law clearly strengthens the Korean social safety net. The system provided over 1.5 million people in poverty with livelihood aid in 2000, against only 0.5 million people in 1999, when the income guarantee was not yet in effect (see Table 15.2). Moreover, the overall benefit level per beneficiary has risen. The number of homecare recipients has grown by only 9.0 percent, but the number of self-support care recipients, who were not eligible for livelihood aid under the old law, has risen by as much as 40.9 percent. The Korean government has markedly expanded the budget for basic livelihood aid. In 1997 the per capita basic livelihood aid budget was 639,000 won, but in 2001 it was 1.98 million won—an increase of as much as 210 percent.[17]

Although the effects of the basic livelihood guarantee have yet to be evaluated, several areas for improvement can be identified. First, since the poverty line is based on living costs in small and medium-size cities, the system excludes people from larger cities where living standards are higher.[18] The system also excludes some unprotected poor, elderly, people with disabilities, and children whose family income is above the poverty line but who live a very poor life. The

Table 15.2 Livelihood Aid Beneficiaries

	1997	*1998*	*1999*	*2000*
Total beneficiaries of public assistance (A)	1,410,000	1,470,000	1,920,000	1,510,000
Number of persons covered by livelihood aid (B)	370,000	440,000	540,000	1,510,000
B/A (percent)	26.2	29.9	28.1	100

Source: Mee-Gon Kim, "Basic Livelihood Guarantee System as a Social Safety Net" (paper presented at a workshop on Securing Social Safety Nets, Korea Institute for Health and Social Affairs, Seoul, 2001), p. 77.

government needs to readjust the minimum cost of living according to region, household size, and type of household. For instance, the cost of living for a family with a member with disabilities must be higher to reflect its medical fees.

The welfare administration system also needs improvement. Local government offices now lack enough personnel to satisfy all the need; as of 2001, one public employee dealt with 150 households in Korea, whereas in developed countries one public employee deals with 100 households.[19] This work overload means that the poor cannot get enough support or social services adapted to their type of household.

Medical Assistance

Those who are eligible for public assistance also receive medical assistance. This system was first adopted in 1961, when the livelihood protection law was enacted, but has since been managed separately for financial reasons. The system is more closely linked to the health insurance system, unlike in other countries, where medical assistance programs are typically part and parcel of public assistance.

To be eligible for benefits, individuals must demonstrate that they live below the poverty line. Beneficiaries may receive one of two kinds of medical assistance, depending on the degree of their poverty. First-class assistance, for those in the lowest-income class, provides various medical services, including hospitalization and outpatient services, free of charge. Second-class medical assistance, provided to people from the second lowest-income class, offers medical services for a small charge. For example, recipients pay 20 percent of hospitalization fees and 1,500 won per visit for outpatient services.[20]

Most recipients of medical assistance are those who have chronic diseases and those who are very poor and receive no family support. In particular, first-class medical assistance recipients tend mostly to be the severely sick or elderly people without a family. Those recipients need to consult with someone who can link them to other welfare services.

Social Services

Social services were devised to protect the socially disadvantaged, including the elderly, children, those with disabilities, single parents, and the homeless. Unlike social insurance and public assistance, social services provide clients with professional social work. Although this gives the socially disadvantaged added protection, benefit levels are so limited that the system covers only people with the lowest income, leaving out most socially disadvantaged persons.

Welfare Expenditures

Before the crisis, social welfare expenditures in Korea were low compared with those of other OECD countries. In 1990 the country spent 8 trillion won—only 4.52 percent of its gross domestic product (GDP)—on social security, according to OECD estimates (see Table 15.3). But in 1997 social security expenditures rose to 6.65 percent of GDP (30 trillion won),[21] and in 1998 they grew dramatically to 11.09 percent of GDP.[22] Those increases reflected growth in budgets devoted to social assistance and unemployment insurance.

Spending on health, which includes health insurance and medical assistance, constituted the largest share (37.0 percent) of total social security expenditures, followed by unemployment (34.9 percent), pensions (18.0 percent), compensation for work injuries (3.7 percent), social services (3.7 percent), and public assistance (2.7 percent). Korea's social expenditures were lower than those of some OECD countries in every category except work injury. However, expenditures on health and pensions are projected to reach those of developed countries in the near future.[23]

Table 15.3   Relationship between Social Security Expenditures and GDP, 1990–98

Year	Rate (%)
1990	4.52
1991	4.28
1992	4.63
1993	4.71
1995	5.23
1996	5.47
1997	6.65
1998	11.09

Note: This information is based on OECD estimates.

Source: Korea Institute for Health and Social Affairs, *Health and Welfare Indicators in Korea* (Seoul: Korea Institute for Health and Social Affairs, 2000), pp. 436–37.

Social security expenditures in Korea will inevitably rise, owing to the accelerating process of population aging and growing demand for social welfare. The underprivileged and the elderly will call for more government protection as the economy grows. In addition, already plunged into the morass of family dissolution and divorce fueled by the growing labor force participation of women, the elderly and children are bearing the brunt of the changing social mores that weaken the sense of familial responsibility. Those factors will make welfare for children, the elderly, and family even more important in the years to come. Growing demand for social welfare will require the Korean government to raise social security expenditures. Social welfare areas in urgent need of expansion include public assistance and health. A reasonable estimate of the proper ratio of gross expenditures on social security to GDP is 15 percent.[24] The Korean government will need to draw on the financial resources of both the public and the voluntary sectors to achieve that level.

Future Challenges for the Korean Social Security System

The Republic of Korea has recently faced a bewildering array of social changes: population aging, the adverse effects of the 1997–98 economic crisis, and the high expectation of unification with the Democratic People's Republic of Korea. All this has called attention to the necessity of strengthening social security and the social safety net.

The Republic of Korea will have to meet the welfare and health needs of its rapidly aging population. Over 90 percent of its elderly suffer from chronic diseases, and their financial situation is much worse than that of the younger generation.[25] Because of the diminishing role of the family as an informal care mechanism, the buck of protecting the elderly has passed to society as a whole.

The economic crisis brought an unemployment rate that is still lower than the OECD average but much higher than the precrisis level. Before the crisis the Republic of Korea was approaching full employment, with an unemployment rate of 2.0 percent, but its advancing economy is likely to face higher unemployment rates. Social protection for the unemployed will thus become an ever more important issue, and the country will need to establish a broad social safety net to protect its population.

The country also needs to prepare to raise the living standards of people in the Democratic People's Republic of Korea before taking further steps toward unification, because the poverty level is much higher and the gross national product is much lower there than in the Republic of Korea. A unified Korea would require a welfare system buttressed by higher expenditures and an appropriate combination of social safety measures to protect needy people in the Democratic People's Republic of Korea.

Existing welfare expenditures need to grow, and public sector participation in financing welfare funds needs to be strengthened. The current private sector contribution rate in Korea—26.5 percent in 1996—is much higher than that in other OECD countries (1993 rates: Germany—4.6 percent, Sweden—4.5 percent, the United States—3.0 percent, and the United Kingdom—1.0 percent).[26] Meanwhile, the private sector should continue to help strengthen the social welfare system through volunteer activities and donations.

In sum, in the midst of globalization and torrential social change, the Korean social security system needs to adopt new strategies and raise budget allocations to enhance programs, benefit levels, and coverage.

Notes

1. Yong-Ha Kim, J. Suk, and S. Yoon, *Efficient Management of Social Insurance* (Seoul: Korea Institute for Health and Social Affairs, 1996); Kyung-Suk In, *The Korea Welfare State: Ideals and Realities* (Seoul: Nanam Publishing, 1998).

2. All data in this paragraph are from the Ministry of Labor, *Report on Work Injury Compensation Insurance in 2000* (Seoul: Ministry of Labor, 2001).

3. In, op. cit.

4. Ibid.

5. Eunyoung Choi, J. Kim, and W. Lee, *Health Care System in Korea* (Seoul: Korea Institute for Health and Social Affairs, 1998).

6. In Hyop Chang, Hye Kung Lee, and Jungsoo Oh, *Social Welfare* (Seoul: Seoul National University Press, 1999).

7. Editing Committee of the White Paper on Welfare Reform, *Welfare Reform in Korea toward the 21st Century: To Enhance the Quality of Life in the Globalization Era* (Seoul: Ministry of Health and Welfare, 1998).

8. Choi et al., op. cit.

9. Editing Committee of the White Paper on Welfare Reform, op. cit.

10. Mandoo Kim and H. Han, *Modern Social Welfare* (Seoul: Hong-Ik Jae, 2000).

11. Ibid.

12. Suk-Myung Yoon, "National Pension," in *Goal Setup for Social Security Development and Current Issues* (Seoul: Korea Institute for Health and Social Affairs, 1998).

13. All data are from Chang et al., op. cit.

14. Ibid.

15. National Social Welfare Education Committee, *Introduction to Social Welfare* (Seoul: National Social Welfare Education Committee, 2001).

16. Ministry of Health and Welfare, *The Analysis of Livelihood Protection Recipients* (Seoul: Ministry of Health and Welfare, 1997).

17. Data are cited in Mee-Gon Kim, "Basic Livelihood Guarantee System as a Social Safety Net" (paper presented at a workshop on Securing Social Safety Nets, Korea Institute for Health and Social Affairs, Seoul, 2001).

18. Neng Hoo Park, "Productive Welfare." *Health and Welfare Forum* 60: 15–25.

19. Mee-Gon Kim, op. cit.

20. Ministry of Health and Welfare, *White Paper on Health and Welfare* (Seoul: Ministry of Health and Welfare, 2000).

21. Byug-Ho Choi and K. Ko, "Social Security Expenditure in Korea and Ways to Improve Its Level," *Health and Welfare Forum* 49: 48–58.

22. Korea Institute for Health and Social Affairs, *Health and Welfare Indicators in Korea* (Seoul: Korea Institute for Health and Social Affairs, 2000).

23. Choi and Ko, op. cit.

24. Ibid.

25. Kyung-Hee Chung, Y. Cho, Y. Oh, J. Byun, Y. Byun, and H. Moon, *A National Survey on the Elderly Life and Their Welfare Need* (Seoul: Korea Institute for Health and Social Affairs, 1998).

26. W. Ademan and M. Einerhand, "The Growing Role of Private Social Benefits," *Occasional Papers on Labour Market and Social Policy,* no. 32 (Seoul: Korea Institute for Health and Social Affairs, 1998).

CHAPTER 16

Italy's Pension Reform Process: Where Financial and Political Realities Meet

by Mauro Mare and Giuseppe Pennisi

ABSTRACT: In Italy, various attempts at pension reform, necessitated by dramatic demographic change, were unsuccessful until 1992, when an external crisis forced action. Political factors also played a vital role in successive reform measures, but their influence means that the process is far from complete. Despite significant differences in socioeconomic development, Italy's pension reform experience offers useful indications for East Asian countries that face the complex challenge of designing and developing their own pension systems. Few policy areas present such complex political challenges. The interplay of events during economic crises presents important opportunities.

The Italian pension system of the late 1980s was a highly fragmented, pay-as-you-go scheme financed by payroll taxes and employers' and workers' contributions. The system linked benefits largely to earnings in the latest or best years of working life.[1] The 25 percent of the gross domestic product (GDP) that Italy devoted to public welfare expenditures was broadly in harmony with the European average. However, the over 100 different public pension schemes that absorbed 60 percent of welfare expenditures and approximately 13 percent of GDP were way out of line.

The ratio of payroll taxes and contributions to wages and salaries was twice that in France and Germany and four times that in the United Kingdom, exerting a major effect on Italian labor costs and the competitiveness of Italy's companies. Transfers from the active population to pensioners—the resources that active workers funded above those that pensioners had paid in—totaled about 2,500 trillion lire. Such intergenerational inequity was socially unacceptable.

Organization for Economic Cooperation and Development (OECD) and International Monetary Fund (IMF) estimates indicated that without major reforms annual public expenditures on pensions would reach 21 percent of GDP by 2030 and that public pension-related debt would reach six times GDP by 2050, jeopardizing public and private spending on other social and economic activities. Econometric studies showed that such an imbalanced pension system would have severe implications for labor and capital markets and that this burden was a major cause of the Italian economy's sluggish growth.

The successive and often tortuous measures that Italy undertook to reform its pension system[2] can shed light on the complex political and economic realities that countries in East Asia and other regions will face as they pursue their own pension systems and create a wider social safety net.

Creating the Monster

The grave problems confronting Italy's pension system had evolved over less than a century, as Italy moved from an agrarian to a postindustrial, high value-added, service-oriented economy. Each stage of economic growth and transformation saw the introduction of a different pension system, and cumulative errors had created the severe financial and economic problems of the late 1980s.

Italy's pension system developed hand in hand with interwar industrialization. As people moved from rural areas to towns and from agriculture to manufacturing, the aged could no longer rely on the extended family for support. The solution was compulsory savings schemes that would provide an income when workers were no longer employed. Employers were required to contribute to these schemes because the consensus was that they should help support former employees after relying on the employees' human capital and skills during their working lives.

The pension system developed into a fully funded occupational scheme similar to those evolving around the same period in France and Germany.[3] In parallel, labor legislation and practices provided—first de facto and later de jure—lifetime employment in the growing Italian manufacturing sector.[4] Pension mechanisms gradually extended to employment outside manufacturing and the civil service (the first sector to adapt the idea to its own needs), as commerce, banking, and self-employed workers and professionals, plus, naturally, farmers developed their own fully funded occupational pension schemes. Those schemes worked relatively well before World War II, sometimes even providing a surplus to the general budget because of greater-than-expected financial yields.[5]

However, World War II and its aftermath brought high inflation, turmoil in financial markets, and extremely low yields for occupational pension funds invested in real estate and government bonds. To avoid sudden impoverishment of those already on pensions, the scheme gradually became a mixed system with both fully funded and pay-as-you-go features. The system was still structured along occupational lines and mostly financed by payroll taxes and by employer and employee contributions. However, the system made growing claims on general taxation to help offset the financial and economic effects of the war.

Haphazard changes—plus each occupational category's scramble to obtain a better pension and the shortsighted view that current payroll taxes and contributions could always be manipulated to meet the pension bill—helped create a serious "pension maze" from 1965 to 1969.[6] This maze entailed serious inequities between workers of the same generation but belonging to different occupational segments and even more severe disparities between workers of different generations.

Despite these problems, in the final years of its "economic miracle" in the late 1960s Italy had a young and expanding labor force, high multifactor productivity, a low unemployment rate (around 3 percent), and sustained GDP growth of about 5 percent per year. Political parties and trade unions thought that a general overhaul of the system would help "ensure that, after 40 years of work and contributions, workers would be entitled to a pension based on 80 percent of the average wage of their last three years in employment."[7] Thus, legislation introduced in March 1968 aimed to establish "the most advanced pension system in the world,"[8] and a bill filed in April 1969 introduced a general old-age pension for all Italians over 65 with no other income. In the case of the general old-age pension, benefits were indexed to wage increases rather than to the cost of living so that pensioners would profit from rising productivity. The scheme allowed early retirement after 35 years of service—even sooner for working mothers. Because the system based benefits on earnings in the last or best years of working life and not on payroll taxes and contributions, the system was termed a pay-as-you-go, earnings-related system.

Although it retained an occupationally based system, the legislation was designed to compensate for inequities within the same generation and thus temper political tensions and allow older workers to reap the benefits of the "economic miracle."[9] However, the system could meet these objectives only through a series of technical corrections to the combination fully funded, pay-as-you-go scheme, and the changes took on a highly political cast. Workers' and employers' contributions were no longer seen as a means of financing the system but as a levy on employers, often viewed as "exploiters" of the working class. Benefits were no longer linked to financial yields but to the broader aim of maintaining a standard of living that would favor workers with less successful working careers.

Within a few years of the pension system overhaul, changes in demography and the labor market meant that the new system was not financially sustainable: the ratio between the active and nonactive population dropped from 4.6 to 1 in the 1950s to 1.2 to 1 in the 1990s. The system also included built-in incentives that would create new inequities and encourage evasion of payroll taxes and contributions: employers and workers would tend to avoid payments except during the years used to compute benefits. Those inefficiencies and inequities worsened as Italy's economic and social structure changed from large manufacturing groups to burgeoning small enterprises in both industry and services and as the labor market evolved from reliance on lifetime employment to mobility from firm to firm, sector to sector, and location to location.

Why Reform Attempts Failed

Reform from 1978 to 1992, which aimed at remedying the most unsustainable, distorting, and inequitable features of the 1965–69 system, offered a sobering object lesson. Ministries of labor and social security, which were motivated by far-sighted visions, rather than finance ministers, who tended to be preoccupied with shorter-term financial issues, generally took the lead, and the larger unions also played constructive roles. However, the negative outcomes of these efforts prove a basic theorem of neoinstitutional economics: faced with abrupt and far-reaching changes, "old institutions" become more rigid and "path dependent"[10] until a drastic exogenous determinant breaks them up.[11]

During the years 1978–80, after a major study of the pension system by an independent committee that included representatives of trade unions and employers, Labor Minister Vincenzo Scotti attempted to raise the retirement age gradually to 65 years for men and 60 for women and to harmonize the nearly 120 "social security regimes." He also tried to modify the mechanisms allowing retirees to accumulate pensions and wages, to define new rules for self-employed workers, and to introduce incentives for private pension funds and other individual retirement systems. After 2 years of negotiations, however, the small and fiscally sensitive Republican Party blocked this "rationalization," arguing that transition costs would be too high because the program improved benefits for retirees at the lowest income levels—a concession that Scotti had made to win support from unions and the left-wing opposition.

In 1980 Labor Minister Italo Foschi raised the pension ceiling, streamlined payments, and established new procedures for computing supplementary pensions, but did not address the key issues of financial, economic, and social sustainability. In 1982 Labor Minister Michele Di Giesi again tried to harmonize the 100-plus regimes and increase the pensionable age to 60 years for women and 65 for men. A bill drafted after consultation with unions and employers' associations sailed through the Council of Ministers, but Parliament debated the discrimination that the measures would produce between different categories and generations of workers and dissolved before voting on critical sections of the bill.

During the years 1983–87 dynamic and energetic Labor Minister Gianni De Michelis charted a great and general pension reform by drafting four successive bills that would raise the pensionable age and pension ceiling, establish new procedures for calculating benefits, and create fiscal incentives to promote private pension funds; however, Parliament acted only to increase the pension ceiling and lengthen the period for computing average wages to 10 years. Labor Minister David Donat Cattin attempted similar reforms again in 1990, as did his successor Franco Marini, a former trade union leader.

The failure to approve similar proposals year after year cannot be laid solely at the door of resistance to change. In the 1980s Italy's central policy focus was developing a noninflationary growth path after the inflationary no-growth path of the 1970s.[12] This was not only a requisite for participation in European exchange rate agreements but also had high priority because of growing unemployment. Policymakers thus focused mostly on indexing of wages and salaries to inflation, and benign neglect of pension matters was often a means to forging agreement on those issues.

The 1992 Financial Crisis and Pension Reform

A financial and foreign exchange crisis in 1992 proved to be a turning point in Italian development, abruptly shifting priorities to controlling public expenditures and reforming factor and product markets, including pension systems.[13]

The Italian crisis had important similarities to the East Asian crisis of 1997–98. In Italy a pegged European exchange rate had not brought convergence of monetary and economic policies, creeping overvaluation of the exchange rate had undermined export competitiveness, and the economy relied on a high level of short-term financing in the international market. A series of judicial investigations and trials among the Italian ruling class only reinforced market skepticism of the capacity of Italy's often inexperienced leadership to come to grips with the requirements for European monetary union. When Italy asked for a suspension from the exchange rate mechanism and let its currency float, the Italian lira depreciated by nearly 30 percent.

Against this background the Italian government enacted a supplementary budget in 1992 designed to boost revenues and reduce expenditures to stem the looming crisis. Those measures prepared the ground for major pension reform, and Parliament gave the government authority to change the system without negotiating with employers and trade unions. Pension reform went hand in hand with reforms in other key elements of the social safety net, such as public health services and the labor market. However, the crisis-driven new policies lacked the long-term vision required for a sustainable, effective, and efficient new system.

Thus, the 1992–93 "Amato reform" did not change the basic design of the pay-as-you-go system but revised benefits downward by raising the pensionable age to 65 for men and 60 for women and extending the minimum number of contributory years from 15 to 20. The new system also based benefits on participants' entire working life rather than on the last 10 years and harmonized the yield on contributions to 2 percent a year, with a few notable exceptions for powerful occupational groups. Pensions were indexed to the cost of living rather than real earnings, with the possibility of future adjustments if higher productivity yielded great differentials between real earnings and inflation. Contributions were set at 26.5 percent of earnings for employees and 15 percent for the self-employed (and two-thirds for employers).

The new indexing measure proved to be the most effective in reducing future pension expenditures.[14] However, the Amato reform also drastically heightened intergenerational inequities by sharply differentiating between participants contributing for fewer than 15 years and other workers. More significantly, the reform did not tackle the basic conceptual flaws of the pay-as-you-go scheme. Although it was saluted as the definitive pension reform—a standard for all European and non-European countries[15]—the new government had to introduce a temporary freeze on implementation the very next year. The government again made pension reform a central item on its political agenda after the 1994 election, but the governing coalition dissolved around the proposal to abolish seniority pensions and drastically revise the benefit computation. Meanwhile, a new financial crisis was looming, caused by downward pressures on the exchange rate and upward pressures on interest rates.[16] Those market pressures finally convinced policymakers to overhaul the system.

The 1995–97 Reform and Other Options

The 1992 reform was intended to improve the financial sustainability of the pension system by abolishing indexation to real wages and extending the period of earnings on which pensions were computed. In contrast, the 1995–97 reform was aimed at stabilizing the impact of pension expenditures on GDP, boosting the efficiency of labor markets by reducing distortions and the "tax on labor," and enhancing the fairness of the overall pension system.

The 1995–97 reform significantly changed the basic functioning of the pension system. The government now strictly ties benefits to contributions paid during the working career (although the new rules apply only to contributions made after 1995). The reform thus shifted the system from a defined-benefit to a defined-contribution scheme. The pension is established by multiplying the balance in each individual's account by an age-related conversion coefficient to create an annuity. This coefficient can be modified every 10 years to reflect changes in life expectancy, rates of GDP growth, and earnings assessed for social security contributions. Workers may elect to begin receiving pensions between 57 and 65 years of age.

Although the reforms of the last 5 years have introduced important changes in the Italian pension system, they will fully affect only people who began working after 1995. The system still needs major structural reform that fully accounts for changing demographics and labor market conditions, stabilizing the ratio of expenditures to GDP. For example, the system could index benefits to increases in GDP rather than the retail price index. To equalize the rates of return for different individuals, new rules could apply benefit computation to everyone, even those who are now exempted. Those measures would leave the basic design of the 1995–97 reform largely unchanged.

Another possibility is to move to a mixed-pension system by allowing people to shift some contributions to private and occupational pension plans. Those options would strengthen property rights and sharply limit political interference in the system. A two- or three-pillar system would also diversify the economic, demographic, and financial risks of accumulated pensions and increase workers' commitment to the rules of the game. Fiscal and monetary incentives could encourage people of retirement age to continue working and thus curb the irregular economy, boosting employment and national income.

Another possibility is a fully funded government-run pension system patterned after a compulsory provident fund. But that option has major flaws because it would require a 70-year transition period and initially higher overall contributions. A more significant flaw is that, at the eventual steady state, such a system would pose enormous corporate governance issues, because the new fund would become a major stockholder in all Italian large and medium-size firms.

All these reform options are based on moving from a one-pillar, pay-as-you-go-system to a two- or three-pillar system with a greater role for fully funded mechanisms. East Asian countries are now attempting to develop pension systems anchored on fully funded mechanisms. However, the conventional wisdom concerning the advantages and costs of such systems seems to be flawed.

Can a fully funded system guarantee higher real returns? The most frequently cited advantage of a fully funded system is that it offers a return on investment in the capital market. Between 1960 and 1990, most pay-as-you-go systems offered much higher returns to the first generation because they had not reached maturity and benefited from high GDP growth rates and rising contributions. Recent studies show that pension funds invested in financial markets are more likely to provide high real rates of return over the long term.[17] However, the advantage tends to fade if we also consider the taxes that the generation in transition to the new system will have to bear.[18]

Will a fully funded system improve economic welfare for society as a whole? Some analysts have built models that generate efficiency gains from a transition to a funded system,[19] whereas others maintain that a welfare-improving transition to a funded system is impossible.[20] Generally, the latter is more plausible. Advantages for future generations tend to be somewhat offset by costs to present generations. A more interesting question is whether full funding can increase national savings, the stock of capital, and growth in financial markets, and thus boost national income. If the pie becomes bigger through growth of financial markets and the national income, this could relieve distributional conflict between generations.

Does full funding insulate the system against demographic shocks? An aging population means that pension funds will have to sell their assets to a smaller active population, undercutting the price of the assets and the resources available for pensioners.[21]

Lessons for Reform

The Italian experience shows how pension reforms quickly reach a standstill if they are not part of a broader reform of the welfare state and labor markets. Attention to pension reform in Italy was essential, but it diverted focus from tax and transfer mechanisms, which target poverty and people of working age. Since

1995 modest attempts to remedy this situation have been unsuccessful, and little has been learned because a well-functioning monitoring and evaluation system did not exist.

"Less pension, more welfare" is a call for a broad and deep revamping of social policies[22] that must include labor market reform to enhance flexibility, decentralized wage bargaining, and a breaching of barriers between the formal and informal employment sector.[23] Only such broader adjustments in social policy can prevent pension reforms from coming to a halt, given other elements of the welfare state. The recent white paper from the Italian government on labor policies augurs well.[24] If the Italian pension system moves gradually from an essentially one-pillar, pay-as-you-go system to a two- or three-pillar system with a growing fully funded leg, individual savings accounts should integrate the fully funded element with unemployment insurance—an approach that might also prove useful in Asia.[25]

Pension and welfare systems result from a delicate balance of economic, social, and political power. Shocks may forestall reforms, but they can also accelerate them. Students of market-supporting institutions know that several large shocks are sometimes needed to bring change.[26] Crises sometimes provide policymakers and politicians with opportunities to undertake bolder institutional reforms. Timor Kuran shows how crises can break through "public lies" in economic and social policies, especially in sensitive sectors such as pension and welfare systems.[27] Dani Rodrik shows how crises forestall conservative attempts by "political losers" to avoid change in obsolete institutions and can be a lever to create high-quality institutions.[28]

In Italy, as in other European countries, the 1992 foreign exchange and financial crisis and the path toward European monetary union gradually changed unions' outlook, which was often a stumbling block in pension, welfare, and labor market reform. This change entailed a move from a corporatist and conservative posture favoring "old institutions" of the "old economy" to broader, more socially responsible attitudes geared toward easing the transformation to a flexible, high value-added economy.[29]

Despite these changes, "nurturing" reform remains a difficult process. Momentum for definitive, longer-term pension reform in Italy has gradually waned. Policymakers took no substantive action after the 2001 checkup, and none of the possible models, nor any combination, is truly on the table. However, advocates of reform could seize the recent world economic slowdown and fear of a new crisis as an opportunity. For East Asian countries in particular, the recent crisis offers opportunities for reform advocates to establish an efficient, effective, sustainable, and equitable social safety net.

Notes

1. M. Ferrera, *Il welfare state in Italia* (Bologna, Italy: Il Mulino, 1984), and M. Ferrera, *Le trappole del welfare* (Bologna, Italy: Il Mulino, 1998).

2. For an exception, see G. Cazzola, *La fabbrica delle pensioni* (Rome: Ediesse, 1992).

3. P. Flora and A. J. Heidenheimer, eds., *Lo sviluppo del welfare state in Europa e in America* (Bologna, Italy: Il Mulino, 1983).

4. Giuseppe Pennisi, *La guerra dei trentenni: Italia e nuove generazioni* (Rome: Ideazione Editrice, 1997).

5. M. A. Coppini, *Le ragioni dello stato sociale* (Rome: Hediese, 1994).

6. O. Castellino, *Il labirinto delle pensioni* (Bologna, Italy: Il Mulino, 1975).

7. Maurizio Ferrera, *Modelli di Solidarieta* (Bologna, Il Mulino, 1993).

8. Act 238, March 18, 1968.

9. Ferrera, *Il welfare state in Italia*, op. cit.

10. Douglass C. North, *Institutions, Institutional Change, and Economic Performance* (Cambridge, England: Cambridge University Press, 1990).

11. Albert O. Hirschman, *Come far passare le riforme* (Bologna, Italy: Il Mulino, 1990), and Albert O. Hirschman, *Retoriche dell'intransigenza* (Bologna, Italy: Il Mulino, 1991).

12. A. Graziani, *Lo sviluppo dell'economia italiana: dalla ricostruzione alla moneta unica* (Torino, Italy: Bollati Boringhieri, 1998).

13. A. Monorchio, ed., *La finanza pubblica dopo la svolta del 1992* (Bologna, Italy: Il Mulino, 1996).

14. Ministero del Lavoro e delle Politiche Sociali, *Verifica del sistema previdenziale ai sensi della legge 335/1995 e successivi provvedimenti nell'ottica della competitività, dello sviluppo e dell'equità* (Rome: Commissione Brambilla, 2001).

15. Instituto Nazionale della Previdenza Sociale, *Le pensioni domani* (Bologna, Italy: Il Mulino, 1993).

16. M. Tivegna and G. Chiofi, *News e dinamica dei tassi di cambio* (Bologna, Italy: Il Mulino, 2001).

17. J. Siegel, "The Shrinking Equity Premium: Historical Facts and Future Forecasts" (mimeograph, 1999); P. Jorion and W. Goetzman, "Global Stock Markets in the Twentieth Century," working paper no. 7565, National Bureau of Economic Research, Cambridge, Mass., 2000; and W. Goetzman and P. Jorion, "A Century of Global Stock Market," working paper no. 5901, National Bureau of Economic Research, Cambridge, Mass., 1997.

18. The same story applies if we finance the payment of existing pension rights by issuing public debt. Someone has to pay the interest related to this debt, and this is the same as new taxes.

19. M. Feldstein, *Privatizing Social Security* (Chicago: University of Chicago Press, 1998).

20. P. Diamond, "Towards an Optimal Social Security Design," working paper no. 4, Cerp, Torino, Italy, 2001.

21. Or if elderly people demand more goods than are currently produced by active people—pensioners' desired consumption exceeds desired savings by workers—this will cause price inflation, reducing the purchasing power of pensioners' annuities.

22. Tito Boeri and Roberto Perotti, "Less Pensions, More Welfare," (paper presented at the Innocenzo Gosparini Institute of Economic Research conference "Pensioni: davvero una verifica?," Rome, September 28, 2001).

23. Pennisi (1997), op. cit.

24. Ministero del Lavoro e delle Politiche Sociali, Libro bianco sul mercato del lavoro in Italia, "Proposte per una società attiva ed un lavoro di qualità," Rome, 2001.

25. Joseph Stiglitz and J. Yun, "Integrating of Unemployment Insurance with Pension through Individual Savings Accounts" (mimeograph, 2001).

26. Raghuram Rajan and Luigi Zingales, "Financial Development and Growth," *American Economic Review* 88, no. 3 (1998).

27. Timor Kuran, *Private Truths, Public Lies: The Social Consequences of Preference Falsification* (Cambridge, England: Cambridge University Press, 1995).

28. Dani Rodrik, "Institutions for High Quality Growth: What They Are and How to Acquire Them," working paper no. 7540, National Bureau of Economic Research, Cambridge, Mass., 2000.

29. G. Bertola, T. Boeri, and G. Nicoletti, *Welfare and Employment in a United Europe* (Cambridge, Mass.: MIT Press, 2001), and T. Boeri, A. Brugiavini, and L. Calmfors, *The Role of the Unions in the 21st Century* (London: Oxford University Press, 2001).

CHAPTER 17

Social Insurance for Aging Rural Households: A Comparative Perspective

by Luis Frota

ABSTRACT: This chapter reviews the development of old-age social insurance schemes for farmers in six European countries. Declining numbers of agricultural workers have obliged European governments to provide special incentives to renew farming communities and to expand pensions for elderly agricultural households. These efforts have met considerable success, although pensions are still lower in rural areas than elsewhere. East Asian countries face similar challenges as they expand social insurance in agricultural communities.

Europe's agricultural landscape has experienced dramatic changes during the last 40 years, as the rural population, the number of farms, and farm employment have dropped significantly. Agricultural employment declined by 30 percent over the past 12 years, and only 10 percent of the total population is rural today compared with 40 percent in the 1950s. East Asian countries, too, have experienced rapid dislocation of agricultural populations. Consequences are particularly severe for older farmers.

This chapter examines the evolution of social insurance schemes for the rural elderly in six European countries—Austria, Finland, France, Germany, Greece, and Poland—and contrasts their experience with that of seven East Asian countries—China, Indonesia, Republic of Korea, Malaysia, the Philippines, Thailand, and Vietnam. The chapter suggests ideas for future research and action based on the European experience.

Changes in Europe's Rural Economy

Europe's Common Agricultural Policy, established by article 39 of the Treaty of Rome in 1957, aims to stabilize incomes and provide equitable living standards for the agricultural population. Productivity increases are the main achievement: in 1998 one German farmer could feed 124 consumers—about seven times as many as in 1960. Rising productivity has meant that average incomes of farming households are now comparable to national household averages. However, disparities in farm incomes have grown. Studies show that persistent low agricultural incomes are related to farm size; smaller farms run by the elderly tend to have low incomes.[1] Farmers with low income tend to seek new income sources, so part-time farming, multiple jobs, and occasional work are on the rise in Europe. These new work patterns are emerging as profitable new uses of land bring new wealth to rural settings.

European countries with civil law traditions—including the six that are the focus of this chapter—have sought to increase the average size of family farms as well as to raise productivity (see Table 17.1). As a result, the average size of German farms increased from 9.3 hectares in 1960 to 33.4 hectares in 1998, and the average Finnish farm size grew to 23.7 hectares in 1997. Greece and Poland are exceptions, with more than 50 percent of their farms still below 5 hectares. These countries made family farming, land planning, and spatial planning policy priorities, along with agricultural modernization, during the postwar period.[2]

Countries with common law traditions, such as Denmark, the Netherlands, and the United Kingdom, subject land use and its transfer to market rules and less regulation, which has discouraged traditional family farming. Civil law countries, in contrast, provide substantial guarantees to farmholders, allowing them to pass on leased property to heirs, for example, encouraging long-term investments.[3] Ownership and direct management—the norm in 1950s Europe—still constitute the bulk of agricultural activity, but leasing represented 65 percent of cultivated area in France in 1997, compared with 50 percent in 1970.

France, Germany, and other countries have introduced special provisions to facilitate family continuity on farms and smooth transitions in rural areas. The French civil code, modified in 1980, allows family members 18 years of age or older to claim accumulated revenues as an inheritance share, on the basis of their participation in farm work if that work was not previously remunerated.[4] Finland and France have provisions favoring new young entrants to farming and granting them loans and assistance, thus minimizing the financial sacrifice that young entrants must make to gain access to land.

Table 17.1 Number and Area of Holdings in 1997

Farm size	Percentage of holdings					
	Austria	Finland	France	Germany	Greece	Poland
0–5 hectares (%)	37.2	8.3	26.3	31.2	76.2	55.3
5–10 hectares (%)	18.9	15.9	9.2	14.6	14.2	25.5
10–20 hectares (%)	22.4	30.0	11.1	17.0	6.6	15.1
20–50 hectares (%)	17.2	36.8	23.5	23.0	2.6	3.7
> 50 hectares (%)	4.1	8.8	29.9	14.2	0.4	0.4
Total hectares	100.0	100.0	100.0	100.0	100.0	100.0
Average size (hectares)	16.3	23.7	41.7	32.1	4.3	8.0

Source: Statistical Office of the European Communities, "Agriculture in the Union, Economic and Statistical Information" (Luxembourg: Eurostat, 2000); data for Poland from "Agricultural Census of 1996" (Warszawa: 1998), 15–16.

Despite these efforts, rural aging problems loom even larger when family ownership is high because a significant proportion of agricultural households are elderly and the average number of family members per household has dropped, both reflecting the urban exodus of the younger generation. A particularly acute problem is elderly households with a single head of household, often female.

European demographic figures show that aging has progressed more rapidly in rural than in urban areas and that pension demands are likely to become more acute in light of sharply dropping birthrates. A declining active rural labor force and rising numbers of elderly farmers over the past five decades pose special challenges for social protection of the elderly population.

Until the mid-1990s, dependency ratios rose because of growing numbers of pensioners, a shrinking active labor force, and early retirement schemes. Although farmers' retirement has since stabilized and began to drop in the mid-1990s, the active labor force continues to decline (see Table 17.2).

Table 17.2 Old-Age Dependency Ratios in Selected European Countries

	Austria (1991) (%)	Finland (1996) (%)	France (1990) (%)	Greece (1991) (%)	Poland (1996) (%)
Urban (%)	33.4	29.0	30.4	27.9	23.2
Rural (%)	29.6	34.4	39.6	40.6	30.4

Source: United Nations Department of Economic and Social Affairs, Statistical Office, *United Nations 1997 Demographic Yearbook* (New York: United Nations, 1999).

In most European countries, farmers have remained a powerful social and political force even as agricultural employment has dropped. Farmers have long worked cooperatively to insure themselves against risks, exemplified by accident mutual funds in both civil law and common law countries. In contrast to common law countries, European countries with civil law traditions instituted distinct social security systems for farmers after World War II, reflecting relatively strong political representation of farmers.

How Agricultural Insurance Evolved in Europe

Over the last 40 years, rural social security systems have focused on two complementary tasks: to ensure a steady rise in agricultural households' living standards and to protect the older farmers during the reforms designed to bring this about. Over this period Europe has seen complex reforms in rural insurance schemes; the achievements of those reforms need to be read against the schemes' objectives and their degree of maturity. Figure 17.1 summarizes the evolution of rural pension schemes.

Most European countries have harmonized rules for these systems with those of other professional groups; this convergence allows countries to take into account new social risks, such as atypical working careers. Workers typically benefit from individualization of rights and greater possibilities to transfer them.

Agricultural insurance schemes reflect differing philosophies as well as varying circumstances and historical paths. For example, France has focused more explicitly on the problems of poor older people in rural areas, whereas in Germany the modernization of agriculture was the principal policy priority.

After unsuccessful efforts to introduce a voluntary pension scheme before World War II, French farmers after 1945 resisted government attempts to implement a nationwide farm pension system because they were powerful and would also be net contributors to the scheme.[5] Nevertheless, the French government moved to introduce a basic agricultural pension scheme in 1952, reinforced by a contribution-based system in 1955. In 1990 the farm pension scheme underwent a major overhaul, with contributions now paid on the basis of reported income instead of imputed income based on region and type of crop, making the system more comparable to other professional schemes. Family-based coverage of farmers is meanwhile diminishing as working women demand individual rights.

These successive reforms have brought minimum agricultural pension levels to national levels and good returns on investment, especially for lower-end

Figure 17.1 Development of Agricultural Pensions in Selected Countries in Europe

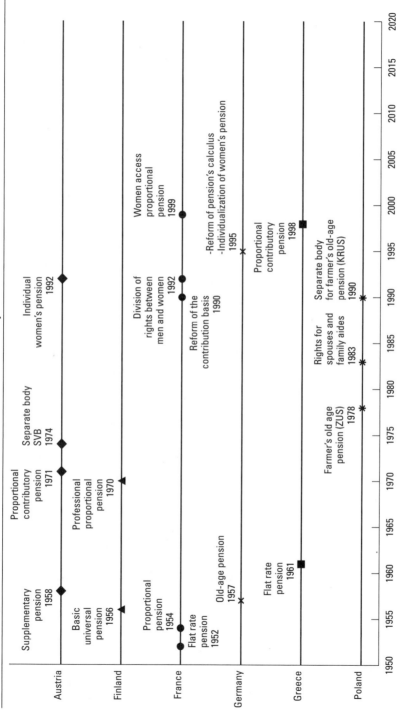

contributors. Agricultural pensions are nonetheless still below the national average. Equity between contributors is also a concern because the current system is not fully proportional to incomes. Larger-income earners criticize the system for its complexity and the possibility of political manipulation.

In postwar Germany rapid demographic changes called for swift policy intervention in rural areas. Policymakers opted for an unfunded pension scheme, seeking to shorten the time lag between contributions and entitlements. Early attempts to extend coverage through private voluntary insurance proved insufficient because only large farmers applied for the scheme. The Old Age Pension Law went into force in 1957, and in 1972 older farmers became formally eligible for a full pension. Those reforms have reduced the average duration of farmholders' contributions and produced gender equity. However, the scheme has accentuated inequalities between high-performing large farmholders and average-performing smaller farmholders because it provides relatively low, basic, flat rate benefits. Farmers can seek private insurance and supplementary coverage upon transmission of the farm.

The Finnish welfare state introduced a flat rate universal pension in 1956 that benefited farmers—especially small farmers, who were well represented in the Central Party (Keskustapuole-Kesk), an old agrarian party. A scheme for farmers established in the 1970s has achieved full individualization of rights, high levels of equality (higher contributions for higher incomes), rights equivalent to those of other professional groups, and stability and simplicity of rules.

In Austria in the 1950s, as family succession on farms began to change, a pension scheme was seen as a way to complement farm owners' obligation to take care of retired farm people and to meet appropriate retirement standards. A 1958 law instituted supplementary old-age insurance for farmers, Austria introduced a contributions-based social insurance scheme in 1971, and women gained full pension rights in 1992.

Greece introduced its Agricultural Social Insurance Organization system in 1961, which included old-age health care and insurance against diseases and bad weather. However, this system was marked by low coverage, noncompliance, and low pensions (although it did provide important supplementary income for very low end income earners). A major overhaul in 1998 integrated two separate schemes: a flat rate pension and a contributions-related fund created in 1987.

Finally, Poland first introduced agricultural social insurance in 1978 under the ZUS (main statutory social insurance scheme) general scheme, and a 1983 amendment extended coverage to spouses and family aides. Only in 1990 was a separate scheme for farmers introduced. The Polish scheme is said to provide fairly generous coverage; its benefits are rather low but are above poverty levels.

However, the scheme is administratively heavy, and its financial sustainability is in question (compliance is an important issue).

Characteristics of Old-Age Agricultural Social Insurance

By the early 1970s, after the creation of the Finnish professional pension in 1970, Europe's agricultural old-age pensions were fully elaborated. Still, debate about the adequacy of old-age benefits for farmers gained momentum from the mid-1980s. In 1986 the European Parliament called on the European Commission (EC) to examine specific agricultural social security schemes.[6] The EC lacked a juridical basis for action, but 6 years later an EC regulation sought to provide additional resources to enable older farmers to leave their farms. These early-retirement schemes have helped accelerate reform and change all over Europe.

European old-age agricultural schemes have many similarities and have confronted common problems.

Coverage and Requirements

Family coverage is the general rule. Spouses are automatically covered even if they do not work on the farm, but other family members must work on the farm from age 18 (16 in Poland). Children are normally covered.

Gender Issues

To a significant extent, agricultural social security was designed for a male bread-winner family model that no longer holds. Since women's life expectancy is higher than men's, the social risks facing rural women are great and growing. In Germany the pension scheme covered less than half of female-headed farms because the farms were smaller and women's labor, though significant, generally was not visible.

In traditional social security settings, women depended on (usually male) farmholders' capacity to pay their contributions. A complete transition to individual rights thus needs to ensure that whoever pays women's contributions does not have the power to decide whether it is appropriate to do so. Finland has achieved this by introducing a mandatory split of rights, unless both members of a couple decide otherwise. That is, women are automatically considered cohold-ers of farms. In contrast, Polish female farm workers' situations have deteriorated in the past 10 years. Women have reportedly withdrawn from labor markets both voluntarily and involuntarily, which may increase their vulnerability to poverty. Retired women receive only 74 percent of men's benefits.

Austria sought to address gender bias in agriculture in the 1990s by giving women equal rights to a contributions-related pension.[7] In 1999 France granted spouses the rights already granted to family aides. Today women in France can divide retirement rights, contribute to a proportional pension on the basis of the minimum income scale, or cohold with their husbands.

Minimum Farming Area

A minimum farming area is usually part of the benefits eligibility formula. France and Germany establish a minimum area deemed sufficient to allow subsistence, and the social security scheme automatically covers farms above half the minimum area. The minimum social threshold is around 25 hectares in France and around 4–5 hectares in Finland and Germany. Poland specifies a minimum of 1 hectare. Austria and Greece do not specify minimum farming areas. Instead, those countries' schemes automatically cover all farm households whose main activity is agriculture. Greece defines *main activity* as time spent or main income source and covers people living in areas with fewer than 5,000 inhabitants regardless of the origin of their income, except for salaried workers already covered by the main regime.[8] Austria defines a threshold of 1,526 euros in annual farm worth for social security purposes.

All contribution formulas today are based on proven income, except in Germany and Poland. Germany's contributions are flat rate, with a contribution allowance for incomes below 30,000 deutsche marks (15,339 euros) per year. Around 50 percent of the insured benefit from this allowance. Before 1995 the system estimated agricultural income based on land size and other regional factors, but it has used fiscal income since 1995. Poland at first implemented an income-related contribution based on farm size or income from certain products. However, this scheme generated opposition from farmers because their benefits did not relate directly to their contributions. Today contributions are flat rate but are considered very low, seen as an "eligibility criterion" rather than as a true contribution.

Compliance Issues

Compliance issues have arisen in collecting contributions. For example, Greece tried to set up a pension system in which farmers would contribute up to one-third of the costs. However, sluggish progress in collecting contributions and disproportionate administrative costs led to failure. Compliance problems in more-developed agricultural schemes are usually associated with underreporting of income, a common feature with other self-employed activities, which results in mistrust from other professional groups. In Germany less than 10 percent of contributors experience payment difficulties, most stemming from exceptional diseases or other risks as well as chronic losses characteristic of some crops and farm sizes. The government may exempt farmers from contributing if they experience exceptional, large income downturns.

In France, Finland, Germany, and Greece farmers are eligible for old-age benefits at age 60. In Austria and Poland men are eligible at age 65, whereas women can claim a pension from age 60. The schemes usually have a vesting period of 15 years or more. France grants the basic flat rate pension after 15 years of contributions but requires 37.5 years for a full income-related pension, whereas Poland requires 25 years for full entitlement. Most countries, except Finland and Greece, require farmers to leave the farm on retirement.

Minimum Guarantees

Countries vary in their minimum guarantees. Germany and Poland offer flat rate pensions, while Austria, Finland, and France offer income-related pensions with a guaranteed minimum. Austrian and Finnish pensions are easy to compute, with each year of income yielding a percentage of future pensions, but the French system is more complex and less proportional because it awards points for different income scales. This system improves low-end pensions at the cost of high-end earners, who are demanding a second pillar to top up the mandatory scheme.

The German system does not guarantee a minimum benefit if the contribution record is incomplete. Austria and France both offer a compensatory allowance that covers the difference between a national minimum and actual benefits. In France, old pensioners with short contribution histories and those who contributed when the scheme was less generous used to be overrepresented in this national minimum scheme. Polish benefits are aligned with minimum pensions for other workers, but farming pensions may fall below poverty thresholds as average workers' wages and benefits grow, and farmers are left behind.[9] Finnish farmers tend to be overrepresented in the universal basic pension because they have lower incomes and shorter contribution periods than people in other professions.

These characteristics of old-age agricultural insurance schemes inevitably challenge interprofessional equity. For example, German farmers pay 80 percent of the contributions of other workers for an equivalent pension. Almost 50 percent of farm pensions are subject to contribution allowances that raise benefit-contribution ratios. On average, French farmers will have benefit-contribution ratios equivalent to those of other workers as new regulations reach maturity in 2028, but low-income earners will be relatively better off. The contribution-income ratio for Finnish farmers seems comparable to that of other self-employed groups and categories of workers. Because farmers now rely mostly on basic pensions, they tend to have better benefits than other groups, but this difference will become marginal as farmers' incomes and years of contribution grow.

Financing

Governments pay a substantial share of agricultural social security budgets: about 70 percent in Austria and Germany, about 75 percent in Finland, and over 90 percent in Greece and Poland. France is an exception: direct state financing represents only 30 percent of the agricultural social security budget; 58 percent comes from "demographic compensation" by other professional schemes. State support compensates for differences in income per capita among different sectors.

Agricultural social insurance schemes display different demographics from those of general schemes. The number of pensioners has begun to decrease, and there is no "baby boom" effect on the horizon, so dependency ratios have stabilized. However, a significant generation gap still demands provisions for intergenerational equity that also recognize that elderly people today contributed to the system during a time of inadequate income levels and insufficient coverage. The sustainability of farmers' pensions remains under debate, notably in Germany.

Thus the systems will have to address the needs of a "new breed of farmers" while continuing to care for elderly farmers.

Governance of Pension Systems

Farmers' associations have generally been deeply involved in designing and running old-age insurance schemes. Farmers elect representatives to these associations, except in Greece and Poland where governments nominate candidates. In Austria the powerful chambers of agriculture, which farmers elect at the provincial level, until recently appointed the representatives. In Germany farmers elect regional representatives to a general assembly every seventh year, and those regional representatives elect the presidents of the administrative boards of 20 regional social unions. France maintains a similarly decentralized system, in which 76,000 elected peers (one for every nine insured people) participate in decisionmaking at both the local and national levels.

These farmer social security associations enjoy some genuine autonomy at regional or provincial levels in Austria, France, and Germany. In Finland the national professional institution has a lighter structure and is composed of the central agency. Though power rests at the central level, elected peers play an important role at the local level, as they are scattered throughout the country. Poland sees the strengthening of worker involvement in managing pension institutions as a prerequisite for further sustainable development of the scheme. Most schemes are still organized around the national structure, which plays an important operational and strategic role, pooling funds, guaranteeing uniformity and concerted action, and helping spread best practice (see Table 17.3).

Old-Age Social Insurance for Farmers in East Asia

Demographic trends in East Asia are less stark than in Europe, but East Asian countries face similar aging and a changing balance between rural and urban areas (see Table 17.4). The old-age dependency ratio is likely to double within the next 30 years.[10] In 1985 East Asia represented 28 percent of the world's population aged over 60; by 2025 this figure will be 58 percent. In China, aging in regions with low economic growth is three times the national rate.[11]

East Asian farmers are predominantly nonwage workers. Only around one-quarter of registered holdings belong to those who engage fully in agriculture; family members living on the other three-quarters of registered holdings, which are small, rely on a combination of income sources or live in great distress.[12] The shift toward export agricultural production, capitalistic land holdings, and higher internal mobility is integrating East Asia's agriculture into the global market. Notwithstanding potential benefits, the growing market character and globalization of agriculture are likely to increase economic vulnerability. Economic insecurity will particularly affect older farmers who use their plots of land as old-age security, because their plots are often too small and unproductive to remain internationally competitive.

The 1997–98 Asian crisis highlighted these issues. The crisis reversed rural–urban migration patterns: urban workers returned to their villages and plots of land, thus increasing the number of informal farmers. A more lasting

Table 17.3 Administration, Governance, and Risk Coordination of Selected National Agricultural Social Insurance Agencies

	Mutual fund[a]	Representatives from the profession	Elected administrators	Decentralization	Role of the central or national level	Risk integration	
						One-stop shopping	Agriculture insurance
Austria (SVB)	Yes	Yes	Administration elected indirectly by chambers of agriculture	Unified system	Strategic, pool of funds	Yes	No
Finland (MELA)	Yes	Yes	Administrators elected	National body	Operational role	Yes	No
France (MSA)	Yes	Yes	Peers elected at regional level	Significant operating autonomy at the department level	Strategic, pool of funds	Extended	No (until 1996)
Germany (GLA)	Yes	Yes	Peers elected at regional level	Significant regional operating autonomy	Strategic, pool of funds	Yes	No
Greece (OGA)	No	Yes	No elected administration	Network of local agencies (agriculture credit bank, rural cooperatives, and others)	High level of centralization (state agency)	No (many different delivery channels)	Yes
Poland (KRUS)	No	Yes	No, representatives chosen by the government	National body with own regional network	Centralized activity	Yes	No

a. Policyholders' contributions pay for the administration of mutual organizations, which are nonprofits managed by farming peers.

Note: SVB = Sozialvericherunganstalt der Bauern (Austria), MELA = Maatalonsyrittäjien Eläkelaitos (Finland), MSA = Mutualité Sociale Agricole (France), GLA = Gesamtverband der Ladwirtschaftlichen Alterskassen (Germany), OGA = Office Général d'Assurance des Agriculteurs (Greece), KRUS = Kasa Rolniczego Ubezpiezenia Spolecznego (Poland).

Table 17.4   Old-Age Dependency Ratios in Rural and Urban Areas in Selected East Asian Countries

	China (1990)	Indonesia (1995)	Korea (1995)	Malaysia (1991)	Philippines (1990)	Thailand (1990)	Vietnam (1992)
Rural (%)	14.1	13.0	29.0	12.1	10.5	11.3	14.5
Urban (%)	11.7	9.1	10.0	8.7	8.7	9.0	14.0

Source: Ronald Skeldon, *Ageing of Rural Populations in South-East and East Asia* (Rome: FAO, 1999).

consequence came with pressures for financial stabilization that led to general budget cuts. This shifted the burden of social security—particularly in countries without comprehensive social security coverage—to private and professional organizations.

Available evidence on land size and the extent of subsistence agriculture in most East Asian countries tends to underscore that the potential for capital accumulation for a large part of the farming population is very limited. Without such accumulation many older farmers will likely have to continue to work to make ends meet. For example, 44.5 percent of rural male Thais over age 60 worked in 1997, while only 29.4 percent of their urban counterparts remained active.[13]

Private landownership is now widespread in East Asia after successful land reforms, though inequality in access to land persists in some regions. Tenancy has been declining in favor of salaried work, though diverse tenure forms remain. Land lease increasingly tends to take the form of stable and long-term contracts.

Aging of the rural population has a gender dimension in East Asia, because women tend to outlive men—further increasing their vulnerability to poverty. For example, in Thailand in 1993 women averaged smaller agricultural holdings, except in the 20–24 age category.[14] Thailand, the exception, is interesting because it illustrates a paradoxical characteristic of Thai society. In keeping with matrilineal transmission of property, the elder daughter receives part of her parents' property when she marries, but women may be "ashamed of taking and managing their husbands' due."[15] Another reason for women's greater poverty is that they are less likely to remarry after separation or the death of their spouses. The percentage of widowed-divorced-separated persons is higher for rural women than rural men in Thailand.[16]

In East Asia community cohesion tends to be stronger in rural than in urban areas. Farmers' organizations play important roles in many settings. Korea's diverse and specialized farmers' organizations, for example, have helped bring modern techniques to farmers. Malaysia presents a similar pattern of diverse farmers' cooperatives and associations, with the addition of a central farmers' organization that covers around 80 percent of farmers.[17] Mutual fund arrangements have helped build local solidarity in Indonesia, though these grassroots farmers' organizations provide weak protection for local populations.[18] The proliferation of voluntary farmers' organizations in the Philippines highlights a lack of organizational capacity beyond local boundaries. In China collective farming included all farmers for many years. As independent agricultural activities grew from the mid-1980s, provision of welfare became more problematic. The new rural welfare system, still state organized, is decentralized and participatory, in keeping with the tradition of local participation in rural provinces. Vietnam's once highly centralized farming system appears to be decentralizing rapidly.

Traditional family support remains a primary source of social security in rural areas. In China, for instance, 1987 data show that children supported around 61 percent of people age 60–74 in rural counties, compared with 21 percent and 16 percent in towns and cities. However, with rapid demographic change, such informal protection mechanisms are eroding. Table 17.5 shows sharp differences between Korea and France in living patterns of the elderly, reflecting a lack of means for subsistence other than family support in Korea. High levels of co-residence and material support from the younger generation remain the norm in the Philippines, Thailand, and Vietnam (see Table 17.6).[19]

Korea and the Philippines maintain mandatory schemes for farmers covering retirement and survival risks, whereas China and Vietnam have developed voluntary schemes. Malaysia allows voluntary participation in its Provident Fund but is studying the possibility of extending mandatory coverage under a special fund for farmers. Indonesia has no equivalent formal social security provision (see Table 17.7).

Table 17.5   Living Arrangements of the Elderly (Over 65 Years)

	Living in institutions (%)	Lone elderly (%)[a]	Elderly couple (%)[a]	Living with children, relatives, or others (%)[a]
France	5.00	32.2	54.3	13.4
Korea	0.29	9.6	13.3	77.1

a. Elderly people living in domestic households.

Source: Didier Jacobs, *Social Welfare Systems in East Asia: A Comparative Analysis Including Private Welfare* (London: Centre for Analysis of Social Exclusion, London School of Economics, 1998); data are from 1995.

Table 17.6 Prevalence of Family Support for the Elderly (Age 60 or Older), percent

			Vietnam	
Support parameters	Philippines (%)	Thailand (%)	Red River Delta (%)	Ho Chi Minh City (%)
Co-residence[a]	70.6	72.5	74.0	85.9
Quasi-residence[b]	53.2	64.7	—	—
Monetary support:				
Any amount	86.6	88.1	—	—
Substantial amount	46.6	69.1	—	—
Material support	88.7	89.2	83.9	72.2
Social contact:				
Monthly or more	57.8	75.6	—	—
Weekly or more	72.3	88.3	—	—

a. Among respondents with 1+ adult.

b. Among respondents with 1+ non-co-resident child.

Source: Robert Holzmann, op cit. See also Association Internationale de la Sécurité Sociale, *Urban-Rural Differences in China* (Geneva: Association Internationale de la Sécurité Sociale, 2000), p. 50.

Ideas for Further Work and Analysis

Despite significantly different circumstances in East Asia and Europe, the European experience suggests priorities for East Asian countries in confronting the challenges of aging rural populations.[20]

First, effective social security schemes need to rest on formalized farming practices. Such schemes require strong and clear property rights, simplified administrative procedures, recognition of existing informal rights, and nationwide databases on rural populations and their income.

Second, a sound, effective, and equitable contribution base is essential, with the foregoing characteristics crucial for establishing such a base.

Third, a priority for reform is to help low-income earners gain access to social insurance. This effort needs to include support for individuals' contributions; progressive schemes based on income, especially for countries with large income disparities; and provision of in-kind benefits for elderly people to complement cash transfers, such as affordable housing for retired elderly farmers. Women's needs require particular attention.

Fourth, empowering farmers' organizations and thus improving farmers' participation in decisionmaking is essential for timely reform. Such democratic processes can help ensure that no elderly farmers are left behind.

Table 17.7 Main Features of Rural Social Protection in East Asia

	Safety nets (social assistance type)	Formal social insurance coverage		
		Retirement	Survival	Invalidity
China	Emergency social relief, emerging local rural assistance	Voluntary farmers' funds cover around 83 million rural residents.	—	—
Indonesia	Emergency assistance (disaster relief, social unrest)	None.	—	—
Korea	Public assistance programs: low flat rate benefits for needy elderly and other in-kind assistance	Yes. Farmers, fishers, and the rural self-employed pay 3% of their earnings (scheduled to rise to 9% by 2005). The government pays for administrative costs and subsidizes premiums for low-income farmers and fishers.	Coverage includes survival, risk.	Yes
Malaysia	Minimal provisions from the Ministry of National Unity and Community Development	The Provident Fund is voluntary for the self-employed. Extension of the scheme to different self-employed groups, including farmers, is under study. Such a scheme would be set up through partnerships with farmers' organizations.	—	—
Philippines	In-kind assistance (Social Welfare Department)	Yes, the general statutory scheme covers all self-employed.	Yes	Yes
Thailand	Subsistence allowances to indigent elderly in rural areas; low coverage, restricted access	None.	—	—
Vietnam	In 1993 land distributed to elderly for subsistence farming	Voluntary scheme is managed by the Vietnam Farmers' Union. Annual contributions with a value of 80 kg of rice are paid over 20 years, which yields a pension entitlement of about 6 kg of rice per month.	—	—

Sources: Association Internationale de la Sécurité Sociale, *Urban-Rural Differences in China* (Geneva: Association Internationale de la Sécurité Sociale, 2000); Didier Jacobs, *Social Welfare Systems in East Asia: A Comparative Analysis Including Private Welfare* (London: Centre for Analysis of Social Exclusion, London School of Economics, 1998); International Labor Organization (2000); Robert Holzmann, "The World Bank Approach to Pension Reform," *International Social Security Review* 53, no. 1 (2000): 11–34.

Finally, national organizations will need to pool funds from regional organizations and ensure regional compensation, with contributory flexibility at the local level. Countries need to develop a clear rationale for those measures. The challenge is to preserve a high degree of regional autonomy while ensuring national coordination so the whole effort reaps economies of scale, shares know-how, and attains geographical equity. These goals will require a sound, integrated information system and clear rules assigning responsibility to different levels of government.

Notes

1. John Bryden, *Structural Changes in Rural Europe* (Aberdeen, Scotland: Arkleton Centre for Rural Development Research, University of Aberdeen, 2000).

2. Neil Ravenscroft and research team members, *Private Sector Agricultural Tenancy Arrangements in Europe: Themes and Dimensions—A Critical Review of Current Literature* (Madison, Wis.: Land Tenure Center, University of Wisconsin–Madison, 1999).

3. A market for "usufruct rights," created with transmission of production quotas under the European Common Agriculture Policy, has become a complementary, informal source of capital.

4. The same right has been extended to spouses under the 1999 Agriculture Guidance Law (*Loi d'orientation agricole*). If the family member does not take over the farm, the law allows purchase of rights to a pension.

5. Peter Baldwin, *The Politics of Social Solidarity: Class Bases of the European Welfare State, 1875–1975.* (Cambridge, U.K.: Cambridge University Press, 1992).

6. European Parliament, *Documents de Séance, 1983–1984, Rapport sur la nécessité d'instaurer un nouveau régime de retraite agricole* (Commission des affaires sociales et de l'emploi du parlement européen).

7. E. Talos and C. Badelt, The Welfare State Between New Stimuli and New Pressures: Austrian Social Policy and the EU," *Journal of European Social Policy* 9, no. 4 (1999): 351–61.

8. With expansion of off-farm work, agricultural activities escape traditional definition. To what extent should nonagricultural activities be included under agricultural social security coverage? The boundaries of coverage for nonfarm work in rural settings will have a substantial effect on the number of insured people. In France the informal definition of agricultural activity is more comprehensive than the legal and fiscal one. Yet general legal rulings tend to be more restrictive than specific social security schemes would wish. In 1999 France simplified the rules for entitlement, establishing that nonfarm workers may draw a pension from the scheme under which they have worked longer. Their full income, including nonagricultural activities, would count toward the agriculture entitlement. However, the farmer can be exempted from social security contribution in agriculture if it is not his or her main activity. The same holds true for Greece, though for residents in very small towns social security coverage is compulsory. Given widespread part-time work, Germany needs to ensure that part-time agriculture work is covered if nonagriculture work is not sufficiently rewarding. Under current legislation, if total income exceeds 640 deutsche marks, the farmer may be exempted from social security coverage. In Austria insurance for part-time workers became compulsory in January 2000.

9. Agnieszka Chlon, Marek Góra, and Michal Rutkowski, "Shaping Pension Reform in Poland: Security through Diversity," Social Protection Discussion Paper No. 9923 (Washington, D.C.: World Bank, 1999).

10. Jill Armstrong, with Louis-Charles Viossat, *Towards an East Asian Social Protection Strategy* (Washington, D.C.: World Bank, East Asia Human Development Unit, 1999).

11. Association Internationale de la Sécurité Sociale, *Urban-Rural Differences in China* (Geneva: Association Internationale de la Sécurité Sociale, 2000), p. 50.

12. Frithjof Kuhnen, *Synthesis of Current State of and Trends in Land Tenure and Land Policy in Asia* (Deutsche Gesellschaft fur Technische Zusammenarbeit, 1996).

13. Sutthichai Jitapunkul and Srichitra Bunna, *Aging in Thailand* (Bangkok, Thailand: Thai Society of Gerontology and Geriatric Medicine, 1998).

14. Libor Stloukal, "Rural Population Aging in Poorer Countries: Possible Implications for Rural Development," *SD Dimensions* (May 2001).

15. Kuhnen, op. cit.

16. Sutthichai Jitapunkul, op cit.

17. Association Internationale de la Sécurité Sociale, op. cit.

18. John Ingleson, "Mutual Benefit Societies in Indonesia," *International Social Security Review* 46, no. 3 (1993): 69–77.

19. Robert Holzmann, "The World Bank Approach to Pension Reform," *International Social Security Review* 53, no. 1 (2000): 11–34.

20. For a discussion of limitations on cross-country transfers of experience and what can be learned from policy experiences in different national settings, see Ehtisham Ahmad, Jean Dreze, John Hills, and Amartya Sen, *Social Security in Developing Countries* (Oxford, England: Clarendon Press, 1991).

CHAPTER 18

Social Policy
and the Informal Sector

by Jacques Charmes

ABSTRACT: The informal sector, often underestimated in assessing national economies, plays a particularly important role during periods of crisis. This chapter reviews the historical evolution of the links between the informal sector and social security systems. The chapter also highlights significant differences in the East Asian sector's response to economic crisis compared with that of other regions.

Although informal activities account for a significant share of gross domestic product (GDP) in many countries, knowledge of the informal sector's size, dynamics, and links with formal sectors of the economy tends to be partial and patchy.[1] The informal sector is still widely—and wrongly—interpreted as synonymous with illegal or underground activities. Yet in reality more and more industrial wage employment has become informal and thus precarious, temporary, and often home based, especially for female workers.

Global economic turbulence has added a new dimension to this growth, as countries expect informal sectors to absorb labor and support people during tough times. The East Asian 1997–98 crisis put a new spotlight on this phenomenon. This chapter builds on empirical evidence about the dynamics of self-employment and the informal sector in creating jobs and generating income.

Views of the Informal Sector

The views of public authorities regarding the informal sector—or the "traditional sector," as it was formerly known—have changed dramatically. In the early

1970s, when belief in Western models of modernization and industrialization was widespread, many policymakers and analysts considered the informal sector a relic, destined to quickly disappear as countries embraced market and monetary economies. Although most economic activities, including agriculture, were traditionally informal, rapid progress in building states and judicial systems was supposed to encourage people to shift rapidly to more formal means of earning livings and running businesses.

The international oil shocks and debt crises of the 1980s, however, prompted significant and lasting growth in the informal sector, which absorbed labor surpluses in countries with no unemployment benefits. The informal sector allowed formal workers to survive when real wages dropped dramatically. Economists and policymakers thus changed their views of the sector, seeing it now as providing temporary positions for rural migrants whose ambition was to seek jobs in the formal sector;[2] they regarded underemployment in the informal sector more favorably than open unemployment.

After these crises, national and international institutions began to explore two types of policies toward the informal sector. Policies of the first type aimed to encourage income-generating activities, especially survival activities by the poor, to alleviate poverty and vulnerability. Policies of the second type were designed to support microenterprises, which employ permanent wage workers, to sustain job creation and investment.

Those policy initiatives posed significant questions for economic development theory and policy: Why should the state and international institutions support activities that are growing naturally? Would such intervention disturb subtle mechanisms? Would government do better to address unemployment among retrenched workers of the formal sector, as well as young unemployed graduates, more directly? Policymakers concluded that direct support for the informal sector was necessary because its growth related closely to the market distortions targeted by structural adjustment policies.[3]

East Asian countries rarely participated in these debates as they focused on industrialization policies. However, the role of subcontracting in the region has influenced thinking about the informal sector. Economists have long seen small subcontracting firms—often in industrial districts or clusters—as fueling industrial growth by providing export-oriented firms with labor-intensive raw materials.[4] For example, industrial districts in northern Italy provided an effective response to prolonged economic crisis because they continued to create jobs and improve productivity even when Italian unemployment rates reached high levels.[5] Informal family- and ethnic-based networks in the Philippines and Indonesia resemble such industrial clusters and help keep small firms alive. In fact, many analysts see the role of subcontracting in fostering links between the informal and the formal sectors as the key to East Asia's successful industrialization.

Extending Social Protection to the Informal Sector: The European Experience

In Europe, "out-work" intensified during the 19th-century Industrial Revolution, especially in rural areas. European countries expanded their social security systems, and especially the right to employment benefits, only gradually, as informal workers became part of the formal wage sector.[6] At the beginning of the 20th century, a legal framework emerged to control the sweatshop system that employed women working at home. More than 40 years intervened between the first laws forbidding any wage differential between homeworkers and industrial workers and contemporary laws stipulating that homeworkers have the same legal and regulatory rights as wage employees.

When countries adopt and enforce such new laws, the number of out-workers drops dramatically, as recently observed in Ireland. Thus out-work declined continuously until recently, when the number of employees equipped with computers began to grow. The extension of social security systems to self-employed workers remains a challenge.

European governments, long convinced of the major role of micro- and small enterprises (termed the "MSE sector")[7] in creating employment and building social capital and networks, have designed specific policies to support it, such as temporarily exempting the sector from fiscal and social regulations. Microcredit policies have also helped the unemployed create their own jobs, underscoring the importance of the informal sector in alleviating poverty.

Analysts have focused on two major roles of the informal sector in social protection: the role of informal firms in absorbing labor and the role of households in meeting basic needs. The former focuses on the informal sector's countercyclical role. The share of the informal nonagricultural labor force rises rapidly in most regions and countries during economic downturns, although it does not drop as quickly during economic upturns because of its labor-absorbing role.

When crises occur and inflation rises sharply, households of the self-employed in the informal sector, as well as in agriculture, who do not consume imports and can adjust prices to reflect cost and demand, are supposed to support family and community members who have lost jobs or face straitened circumstances. When that occurs, overall living standards drop and the number of households living under the poverty line rises, because many households have lost their main source of income even while they must support more members. In some developing countries the share of private household transfers of income has reached 10 percent to 25 percent of GDP[8]—a share comparable to that of public transfers in European countries.[9]

Thus households seem to come to the rescue when the state is unable to provide social benefits. But the reverse is also true: if the state establishes a universal system of social protection, households can restrict their private transfers to the optimum required to maintain social relationships and social capital.

This raises the question of whether and when the state should provide social protection for all its citizens. The 1991 International Labor Conference debated the dilemma posed by the informal sector: "whether to promote the informal sector as a provider of employment and incomes; or to seek to extend regulation and social protection to it and thereby possibly reduce its capacity to provide jobs and incomes for an ever expanding labor force."[10] The World Trade Organization is debating the same issues, largely in the context of unfair competition.

In many developing countries, social protection systems cover self-employed as well as wage employees. However, many self-employed workers remain unregistered, and the informal sector remains outside the social security system. Because formal social protection is often limited to health services and family allowances, and because benefits are uncertain, with retirement pensions appearing especially distant, many wage employees in the informal sector are reluctant to accept deductions from their earnings for these ephemeral benefits. Strict enforcement of social security laws can therefore mean retrenchment for employees in the informal sector who work for wages.

The Informal Sector in East Asia

In contrast to Europe, industrialization in East Asia and other developing regions appears to rely heavily on the informal sector because it allows low pay, child labor, and flexibility. The contribution of the informal sector to GDP in East Asian countries is actually much smaller than employment figures would suggest (see Table 18.1).

This probably reflects the fact that most labor force statistics do not document the importance of home work well, and production statistics do an even poorer job.[11] In 1999 Thailand found that homeworkers (80 percent women, and 90 percent in manufacturing) constituted only 2 percent of nonagricultural employment. In contrast, a 1993–95 Philippine survey showed that homeworkers (80 percent women) accounted for 14 percent of manufacturing output because the survey included the secondary activities of women farmers.

Table 18.1   Percentage of Informal Sector in Sectoral GDP in East Asia

	Indonesia (%)		Korea (%)		Philippines (%)		
Sector	1997	1998	1990	1995	1996	1997	1998
Agriculture	78.0	79.2	95.4	95.2	64.3	65.3	63.6
Industries	15.2	16.7	12.6	8.9	33.4	32.3	35.2
Trade	74.9	77.2	48.8	42.4	50.6	51.0	51.4
Services	28.6	30.5	26.8	23.4	22.6	22.1	22.3
Total nonagriculture	30.2	31.6	22.8	16.6	31.7	30.8	31.9
Total GDP	25.4	25.5	21.0	15.5	25.2	25.1	26.5

Sources: Calculations based on Statistics Indonesia (BPS/SDN), *Gross Domestic Product Indonesia 1997 and 1998*; Philippine National Statistical Coordination Board (NSCB), Economic and Social Statistics Office, *National Accounts of the Philippines, 1990–98*.

Those workers offer enterprises flexibility during periods of growth as well as decline, but the drawbacks for households can be severe, since social protection systems do not cover them. They have obtained benefits only through mutual social insurance schemes and grassroots organizations, such as those that promoted recent International Labor Organization (ILO) resolutions on homeworkers like the Declaration on the Fundamental Principles and Rights at Work and its follow-up, adopted in 1998.

Despite their reliance on the informal sector, East Asian countries have generally ignored its counter- and pro-cyclical contributions. However, when unemployment rates rose during the 1997–98 crisis, these countries expected the informal sector to function as a safety net by preventing many retrenched workers from falling into poverty (see Table 18.2).

East Asia thus turned out to be a special case; the "survivalist" component of the informal sector was already saturated and could not absorb retrenched workers

Table 18.2   Trends in Labor Force Indicators

	Indonesia (%)			Philippines (%)			Thailand (%)		
Indicators	1997	1998	1999	1997	1998	1999	1997	1998	1999
Participation rate	66.3	66.9	67.2	65.5	66.0	n.a.	71.7	70.6	n.a.
Unemployment rate	4.7	5.5	6.3	7.9	9.6	n.a.	0.9	3.4	n.a.
Underemployment rate	12.0	9.3	12.6	20.8	23.7	n.a.	n.a.	n.a.	n.a.
Share of agriculture	40.7	45.0	43.2	40.4	39.9	41.0	50.3	51.3	48.5
Share of informal sector	45.8	42.8	n.a.	40.3	n.a.	n.a.	25.2	24.6	26.5

n.a. = not available.

Source: Author's calculations based on countries' national surveys and records.

during the crisis, especially when purchasing power in urban areas fell suddenly and dramatically. Subcontracted by formal firms through intermediaries and then laid off, many workers returned to their previous status in the countryside as farmers, family workers, and housewives. These workers are mostly female and undertake a high share of home work as a secondary activity, with agriculture as the main activity (in this case the return to farming did not imply any return migration). In Indonesia, for example, although the informal sector did not respond significantly, the share of agriculture in total employment grew from 40.7 percent to 45.0 percent between 1997 and 1998. The Philippines is an exception: a late 1997 drought stemming from El Niño and excessive rainfall from La Niña in late 1998 and 1999 prevented such an absorption and aggravated the effects of the crisis.

Such behavior is probably specific to the region, because the informal sector was so tightly linked to the formal sector. Because the agricultural sector was both export oriented and subsistent—safeguarding purchasing power in rural areas without consuming significant imported goods—it played the role that the informal sector usually filled. These results show that it is important to distinguish the part of the informal sector linked to the formal sector from independent microenterprises and the "survivalist" countercyclical component of the informal sector.

The significant share of subcontracting work in the informal sector, particularly the female share, makes it an important engine for growth. The World Bank recently assessed the role of homeworkers in the Philippines and Indonesia during the crisis, and the ILO is doing the same in Thailand.

Overall, the significance of the informal sector raises the following important questions for global development policies:

- How and how far can the informal sector be an engine for growth in developing economies?
- Can it play an efficient role in providing social insurance for the poor and victims of economic turbulence?
- Can social insurance policies directed at workers in the informal sector help promote gender equality in labor relations?
- Can public intervention support private household social insurance, and can governments design social security systems to cover families in the informal sector?

The World Bank and ILO studies show promise in launching a debate and further analysis to offer answers to these questions.

Notes

1. Clearer international definitions and harmonized methods for measuring the informal sector would be very helpful.

2. Examples include the models of Lewis, Harris, and Todaro, which are based on unemployment as a factor of equilibrium on the urban labor market. Such models recognized the role played by the informal sector.

3. Jacques Charmes, "Le développement du secteur informel: Entre le laisser-faire et la promotion dans la formalisation, quelle voie pour les politiques publiques et les agences d'aide?" (communication at a seminar of OECD's Centre de Développement et du Comité d'Aide au Développement on "le secteur informel dans les pays en développement," Paris, December 13–14, 1990).

4. As stylized by Hubert Schmitz, "Trust and Inter-firm Relations in Developing and Transition Economies," *Journal of Development Studies* 34 (April 1998): 32–61.

5. M. Maruani, B. Reynaud, and C. Romani, eds., *La flexibilité en Italie: Débats sur l'emploi* (Paris: Syros Alternatives, 1989), p. 317.

6. R. Salais, N. Baverez, and B. Reynaud, *L'invention du chômage. Histoire et transformations d'une catégorie en France des années 1890 aux années 1980* (Paris: Presse Universitaires de France, Economie en liberté, 1986), p. 267.

7. European economic history and policy commonly use the term "MSE sector" rather than "informal sector" to refer to economic activities that are not officially or statistically registered.

8. Jacques Charmes, "Informal Sector and Social Capital: Resilience of African Economies during Crisis and Adjustment" (Programme CODESRIA of the MacArthur Foundation on Real Economies in Africa, Zanzibar, July 5–10, 1999), p. 26.

9. Institut National de la Statistique et des Études, *Données Sociales* (Paris: Institut National de la Statistique et des Études, 1999), p. 350.

10. International Labor Organization, *The Dilemma of the Informal Sector, Report of the Director General,* International Labor Conference, 78th session (Geneva, 1999), p. 65.

11. Jacques Charmes, "The Contribution of Informal Sector to GDP in Developing Countries: Assessment, Estimates, Methods, Orientations for the Future" (OECD-EUROSTAT-State Statistical Committee of the Russian Federation, Nonobserved Economy Workshop, Sochi, Russia, October 16–20, 2000), p. 14.

BOX 4.2

Conference on Social Policymaking in Europe and East Asia, Roma/Caserta, February 21–23, 2002

This final project seminar, jointly sponsored with the Italian Higher Institute of Public Administration and the Ministry of Finance, focused on how social policy is formulated in terms of issues and institutional arrangements. The seminar covered six topics, with pension reform, particularly Italy's recent experience, a focal point.

The seminar first explored social security systems broadly, introduced by Meesook Kim's paper on the Republic of Korea's social security system (see Chapter 15). Discussion focused on the role of active labor policies in Korea compared with some European countries, especially Ireland and the United Kingdom, which share a common experience in their move from passive to active labor policies. The notion of an optimal level of social spending sparked particular interest; participants noted wide variation across Europe in social spending (from 35 percent of gross domestic product in Sweden to 15 percent in Iceland) and in the composition of social policies. Political and institutional factors play a central role in how countries balance social spending and economic growth, whereas welfare policies reflect different value systems built over long periods.

Second the seminar addressed Italy's experience with pension reform, with a presentation by Giuseppe Pennisi and Mauro Mare (see Chapter 16). Discussion ranged widely over common and different pension system challenges in Europe and East Asia, which include acute financial imbalance in many European public pension schemes, as well as the relative advantages and disadvantages of pay-as-you-go and funded systems.

The third topic focused on labor market policies, with presentations by Jonas Gahr Støre on the Norwegian experience (see Chapter 7) and Dzung Nguyen Huu (Vietnam) on Vietnam's labor policy reforms. Jonas Støre's fascinating case study underscored how a comprehensive labor policy could fight unemployment while avoiding serious macroeconomic

continued on next page

BOX 4.2, continued

imbalances. However, Norway's Solidarity Alternative now faces serious challenges, including the need to maintain macroeconomic stability, balance rights and obligations of social partners, and contend with strong labor unions. Growing absenteeism and use of sick leave are symptoms of a system in crisis.

Mr. Huu noted that active labor policies in Vietnam are still at a nascent stage, even though unemployment is a central social concern. Recent measures to curb unemployment include the National Program on Employment (1992), designed to encourage demand for labor through public investment in social infrastructure. Despite such efforts, many vulnerable groups—especially demobilized military personnel, redundant workers from state enterprises, and female workers—remain outside the social protection system. Links between labor policy and pension systems, balancing work and family for working women, and family care for children and the elderly alike are topics of almost universal concern. The solidarity formula was of particular interest to the group.

The fourth topic focused on health insurance policies, focusing on Thailand (presentation by Juree Vichit-Vadakan) and Italy. Participants noted striking parallels between challenges facing the two health systems, particularly in measurement, equity, and the role of public versus private services. Participants discussed the complexities of forging consensus on priorities for health spending and the implications of decentralization (a particularly sensitive issue in both Thailand and Italy), seeing efficiency in spending as a vital barometer.

The fifth topic was the role of information in social policymaking, with Giuseppe de Filippi (Mediaset, Italy) in the chair, and a presentation by Colin Moynihan, who emphasized how new information technologies shape policymaking. Pitfalls include a premium on public relations as opposed to policy discussion, and cynicism about statistics and a disdain for projections—which foster short-term approaches and yawning knowledge gaps. Possible solutions include publication of efficiency and effectiveness indicators for social policy. Discussion emphasized the crucial role of education in raising public awareness of social policy issues and thus overcoming short-termism.

BOX 4.2, continued

The final session looked to new ventures in social policy, based on presentations by Jean Wolas (intergovernmental delegation for social innovation, France) and Luc Tholoniat (see Box 6.2). Jean Wolas spoke of "social economy" as a new venture for social policy in France. Globalization has changed relationships between the global and local economy, raising challenges to democratic governance, benefit sharing, and protection of local stakeholders. In contending with those challenges, the French government has rediscovered the value of the third sector—civil society. Luc Tholoniat outlined the open method of coordination that has emerged within the European Commission in response to criticism that the European Union lacked coherent social policy. More use of benchmarking is an important new policy direction.

Labor and the Welfare State

Introduction

Part V addresses a critical set of social policy issues: the need for countries to boost employment and maintain an active and viable work force. The world of work is changing dramatically in virtually every part of the world, including both Europe and East Asia, owing to globalization and the advent of the knowledge-driven economy. Countries face complex choices in deciding how best to prepare for such challenges.

In Chapter 19 Stein Kuhnle, Aksel Hatland, and Sven Hort show how the supposedly hidebound Scandinavian countries have transformed universal social security benefits into provisions that promote work—thereby sparking strong economic growth. The authors argue that the vibrant records of Denmark, Finland, and Sweden show that strong welfare states are compatible with economic growth. These states are in fact the most family friendly in Europe, maintaining policies that encourage the participation of both women and men in the labor force. Scandinavian nations nonetheless appear to have coped successfully with these new challenges, showing that developed democratic welfare states are quite good at preserving the legitimacy of social systems while pursuing economic transformation and new vitality. The chapter concludes with a thoughtful discussion of the many noneconomic dimensions of social policy, including its reflection of social and political norms and values and the central goals of combatting poverty and maintaining social peace.

In Box 5.1 Gazier and Herrera trace parallels in the experiences of governments during the Great Depression and during the recent East Asian crisis in tackling large-scale unemployment. Although efforts to enhance employment can prove helpful in the short run, this experience highlights how extensive state involvement in creating jobs can prove counterproductive. Today countries can use public expenditures as a lever while ensuring that social partners take more responsibility for enhancing the mobility of workers and unemployed people.

In Chapter 20 Colin Moynihan and Jacqueline Butler tackle the daunting challenge of youth unemployment, which is twice as high as adult unemployment in both industrial and developing countries. Young people's transition from education to working life is critical, because early unemployment points squarely to joblessness later in life. However, European experience shows that broad labor market programs rarely improve job prospects for the young. The Nordic countries again offer the best model, integrating education, labor market, and welfare policies with local community agencies that provide the individualized services youth need. Most important, strong overall growth in employment is essential to ensuring jobs for youth. Box 5.2 focuses on the United Kingdom's efforts to address youth unemployment. The United Kingdom has systematically engineered new institutions to improve young people's transition to employment, including the creation of a "New Deal" for young people.

In Chapter 21 Jacques Rojot explores the many different forms of worker participation in play in Europe—all based on the notion that employees perform better when their work is useful, interesting, and meaningful, as well as when they hold well-designed jobs for which they are well qualified. The author argues that, as East Asian countries move to high-quality, high-tech manufacturing, enhancing worker initiative and involvement in firms' decisionmaking will become crucial, and he examines how East Asian countries might encourage such participation.

In Chapter 22 Ruud Dorenbos investigates the role of public employment services, which aim to match employees with jobs, promote equal opportunity, and enable labor markets to function more efficiently. The author provides information on how such services operate in both Europe and Asia. Globalization, technological development, and changing labor markets and state roles are bringing profound changes to these services as former bureaucratic organizations move toward customer-oriented services and collaborate with private employment agencies.

In Chapter 23 Bernard Gazier and Rémy Herrera recount the effects of the 1997–98 crisis on employment and incomes in the Republic of Korea and the country's response in the form of active labor market policies, including extended vocational training and public works jobs. Korea also relaxed regulations limiting firms' ability to lay off workers and allowed growth among agencies that provide temporary workers. As recent European experience shows, today's "transitional labor markets"—the global shift from long-term to short-term jobs and discontinuous careers—can accommodate older workers and enhance gender equality, but they also imply the need for a strong government role in retraining the work force.

In Chapter 24 Christine Erhel outlines European experience in monitoring and evaluating the effects of active labor market policies to determine whether the benefits of such programs are worth their cost. Such analysis is especially important because active labor market policies can hurt some groups. Evaluations can range from surveys and interviews with participants to scientifically based studies and macroeconomic analysis. European experience sheds light on how best to conduct such complex studies, as well as on which active labor market policies prove most effective (or ineffective).

In Chapter 25 Eduardo González-Biedma traces the evolution of European thinking on how to tackle structural unemployment, which the region has faced since the oil shocks of the 1970s and 1980s. Governments throughout Europe are moving toward more flexible labor markets, which can generate more jobs than rigid labor regulations in the long run. New approaches to tackling unemployment also include enhancing job seekers' mobility and fostering open relationships between management and unions, as well as careful government efforts to spark new industries. Overall, the author argues, crises can provide the crucible in which economies shed their inefficient industries and embrace more vibrant sources of growth and employment.

Boxes 5.3 and 5.4 provide highlights of two seminars that concentrated around the challenges for labor markets arising from the East Asia crisis. The first was a major conference in Seoul in December 2000, which weighed flexibility versus security and situated labor policy instruments within broader social policies. The Bangkok seminar in October 2000 was a joint venture with the International Labor Organization, which stretched boundaries of cross-discipline reflection. Among interesting facets was a discussion of media roles in policy formulation and a probing exploration of social standards.

CHAPTER 19

A Work-Friendly Welfare State: Lessons from Europe

by Stein Kuhnle, Aksel Hatland, and Sven Hort

ABSTRACT: This chapter focuses on issues for the welfare state, particularly in periods of recession and economic recovery. It reviews the experience of European welfare states in their multifunctional, challenged, and reforming dimensions. It argues that a strong and well-developed welfare state can be a strong asset, as illustrated by recent developments in the Nordic countries. It discusses the interaction between social security and labor markets, and it suggests some lessons from Scandinavian and European experience.

The Scandinavian countries have made a remarkable recent comeback as interesting cases of social, economic, and political development after many economists and commentators had essentially categorized them as hopelessly overloaded welfare states in which economic growth and dynamism were hampered. Scandinavian growth performance, trend growth of gross domestic product (GDP) per employed person, government employment, and social expenditures all suggest that comprehensive social security and welfare indeed need not represent barriers to economic growth, and they may even prove advantageous when countries are hit by economic turbulence. A combination of comprehensive welfare and social security programs with economic growth is possible and may offer a path that reduces poverty and opens possibilities for development with fewer inequalities of income distribution.

In this chapter we contend that European welfare states and social security programs have historically fulfilled, and still fulfill, several functions. Examples of interactions between social security and the labor market are outlined, with a special focus on what has happened in Scandinavian countries in recent decades. The Swedish old-age pension reform of the late 1990s is presented as a particularly interesting example of a "work-friendly" social security and welfare arrangement.

We argue that national unemployment insurance schemes are intrinsically work friendly. Finnish and Swedish developments during the 1990s show how an elaborate social security system functioned as an important shock absorber when the countries fell victim to sudden economic downturns, helping generate rapid recuperation and new economic growth at low social cost. In this era of economic globalization, there may be a still greater objective need for a consolidated national social security system than before. Changing characteristics of labor markets in the global economy may encourage changes in pension systems, like those in Sweden, that make them more transparent and more fair, in the sense that pensions reflect contributions during all working years. The Scandinavian welfare state emphasis on public social services for children, the elderly, and the sick suggests some lessons, perhaps controversial in other cultural contexts, about the evolution of both work-friendly and family-friendly social security and welfare state programs.

A comprehensive welfare state is not a necessary prerequisite for a good society, but neither are the two incompatible. In our view, the welfare state historically and at present serves multiple functions, and its achievements and success can be measured only against considerations of specific values and political and social goals (for example, fairness, justice, cohesion, stability, material and physical security, well-being, and economic growth). Economic growth is possible with or without an advanced welfare state and a strong government role for welfare responsibility. Developments over the last 20 years bear out the empirical possibility of alternative visions of a good society that are based on different value assumptions and political choices. It is perhaps time to recognize this fact more generally—not least when considering lessons to be drawn for other regions of the world whose political histories, traditions, and cultures differ from those that spearheaded industrial modernization and development of social security institutions.

Welfare States, Recession, and Economic Recovery

Many economists and commentators used to portray the Scandinavian or Nordic states as victims of a "welfare state sclerosis."[1] These countries, however, have made a remarkable image comeback and are now at the center stage of theory and practice of social and economic development.[2] When the 1997–98 crisis hit Asia, the Nordic countries (with the important exception of Norway) were still, like Japan, struggling to overcome the effects of the recession of the early 1990s. Their situation has changed dramatically since then. Finland, the hardest hit by the Nordic recession,[3] ranked number 1 among nations in the World Economic Forum's recent survey of the global business environment,[4] replacing the United States, which was ranked top the previous 2 years. Three other northern European countries made the top 20: Denmark, number 6 (up from number 7 in 1999 and number 8 in 1998); Sweden, number 7 (previously numbers 4 and 7); and Norway, number 20 (previously numbers 18 and 14). Among East and Southeast Asian countries, Singapore, number 9 (previously numbers 12 and 10), Japan, number 14 (previously numbers 14 and 18), and Hong Kong, China, number 16 (previously numbers 21 and 12) were among the top 20. Those results are quite consistent with similar rankings and evaluations for the same period.[5] Both investment banker Merrill Lynch and the U.S. Internet Council recently published reports that likewise single out the countries of northern Europe as business-friendly environments, in this case Sweden (number 1), as well as Finland (number 5) and Denmark (number 8).

In important respects the Nordic countries have defied expert advice from organizations such as the Organization for Economic Cooperation and Development (OECD)[6] and the International Monetary Fund (IMF). Witness a recent statement:

> Sweden should cut taxes and overhaul its unemployment benefit system if it wants its current economic upswing to continue. . . . The IMF said there was "considerable room" for tax cuts and urged the country not to use its current surplus to increase spending. It also supported lower long-term unemployment benefits to encourage recipients to seek jobs."[7]

A similar IMF statement about Norway included sweeping advice that the public sector must be made more efficient and reduced in size. The experience on the ground, however, suggests that the economy and the public sector (mostly the welfare state part of it) have grown in parallel,[8] and today even the IMF indirectly admits that a different tune has worked in Sweden, although it still claims the familiar old tune as an eternal favorite.

Tables 19.1 and 19.2 show indicators of economic growth since 1970 in the Nordic countries and the United States, as well as averages for the European Union (EU) and OECD countries. Tables 19.3 and 19.4 offer data on relative scope of government employment and social expenditure as a percentage of GDP for four different groups (and types) of European welfare states.

Table 19.1   Growth Performance, Selected Countries, 1970–99 (average annual rates of change in GDP)

	1970–1980 (%)	1980–1990 (%)	1990–1998 (%)	1999 (%)
Denmark	2.2	1.9	2.3	1.6
Finland	3.4	3.1	1.5	3.5
Norway[a]	4.2	1.5	3.1	0.8
Sweden	1.9	2.1	1.1	3.8
European Union	3.0	2.4	1.7	2.3
OECD[b]	3.4	3.0	2.3	2.7
United States	3.2	3.2	3.0	4.2

a. Data for Norway are for the mainland only: the oil and gas sector is not included.

b. Data for the OECD average excludes the Czech Republic, Hungary, and Poland.

Source: J. Elmeskov and S. Scarpetta, "New Sources of Economic Growth?" (paper presented at the 28th Economic Conference of Österreichische Nationalbank, Vienna, June 15–16, 2000).

Table 19.2   Trend Growth of GDP per Person Employed, 1980–90 (average annual rates of change)

	1980–90 (%)	1990–98 (%)
Denmark	1.5	2.4
Finland	2.4	2.9
Norway	2.1	2.5
Sweden	1.6	2.4
European Union	2.3	1.8
OECD	2.8	2.4
United States	1.1	1.7

Source: J. Elmeskov and S. Scarpetta, "New Sources of Economic Growth?" (paper presented at the 28th Economic Conference of Österreichische Nationalbank, Vienna, June 15–16, 2000).

Table 19.3   Government Employment as a Percentage of Total Employment 1974–95 in Different Types of European Welfare States (unweighted averages)

	1974 (%)	1985 (%)	1995 (%)
Continental Europe[a]	14.7	18.7	18.8
Scandinavia[b]	20.0	26.9	29.4
Southern Europe[c]	10.5	14.2	15.5
United Kingdom	19.6	21.5	14.4

a. Continental Europe includes Austria, Belgium, France, Germany, and the Netherlands.

b. Scandinavia is Denmark, Finland, Norway, and Sweden.

c. Southern Europe includes Greece, Italy, Portugal, and Spain.

Source: S. Kuhnle and M. Alestalo, "Introduction: Growth, Adjustments, and Survival of European Welfare States," in *Survival of the European Welfare State*, ed. S. Kuhnle (London and New York: Routledge, 2000).

Table 19.4   Social Expenditure as a Percentage of GDP in Different Types of European Welfare States, 1980–95 (unweighted averages)

	1980 (%)	1990 (%)	1995 (%)
Continental Europe[a]	28.1	29.6	30.1
Scandinavia[b]	25.6	28.1	32.1
Southern Europe[c]	15.0	18.0	22.2
United Kingdom	21.5	24.3	27.7

a. Continental Europe includes Austria, Belgium, France, Germany, and the Netherlands.
b. Scandinavia is Denmark, Finland, Norway, and Sweden.
c. Southern Europe includes Greece, Italy, Portugal, and Spain.

Source: S. Kuhnle and M. Alestalo, "Introduction: Growth, Adjustments, and Survival of European Welfare States," in *Survival of the European Welfare State,* ed. S. Kuhnle (London and New York: Routledge, 2000).

These data are not directly comparable. They nonetheless illustrate that economic growth, even if sometimes modest, has on the whole been quite steady;[9] that the Nordic countries had higher labor productivity, defined as GDP per person employed, in the 1990s than the average of EU countries[10] and the United States; that labor productivity rose over the last decade compared to the previous one; that European countries vary significantly in terms of scope of government employment and size of public sector; that growth in government employment has been quite compatible with expanding welfare states and economic growth in Scandinavia; that there is thus no clear-cut relationship between scope of the welfare state and economic performance; and that on average the share of GDP spent on social purposes increased all over Western Europe until the mid-1990s. These data clearly do not prove how and to what extent the type and size of the welfare state is conducive to economic growth, but the data indirectly do indicate that, at the macro level, welfare state growth and economic growth have occurred simultaneously during the last 20 years.

Sweden, like other Scandinavian countries, illustrates that a combination of high tax revenues, labor market security, declining unemployment, generous universal welfare services, and economic growth is possible. The IMF, interestingly, credits the renewed Swedish economic upswing in part to Sweden's creativity and entrepreneurship, and to the persistent Swedish government emphasis on core welfare state policies such as a broad tax basis, high tax revenues, security in the labor market, the world's most generous paid parental-leave schemes, increased child allowances, and extra resources for universal preschools and public care.

Finland is an even more elegant example of such a happy marriage between a generous universal welfare state and strong economic growth.[11] Finland's experience suggests that if low poverty levels and relatively high levels of income equality are the objective, then it pays to have a well-developed, universal welfare state in place when a sudden economic shock or crisis hits, as it did Finland, partly as a result of the breakup of the Soviet Union, in the early 1990s. Finland's advanced welfare state not only served those goals but also was conducive to rapid economic recovery thereafter, with steady, solid economic growth since 1994 (see Table 19.5). Though social security and welfare reforms (such as cuts in benefit levels) were undertaken in the1990s, they were handled in a politically consensual way that avoided both new poverty and increased income inequality.[12] Finland was the only OECD member country in which the recession of the 1980s or 1990s was deeper than the Great Depression of the 1930s,[13] but with the fundamental difference that an advanced welfare state was in place when the later crisis hit. The dramatic social and political repercussions of the 1930s were avoided (repercussions which were moderate in Scandinavia compared with the rest of Europe, thanks to other factors such as crucial social-political pacts between agrarian and industrial interests as well as labor and employers). The Finnish example demonstrates the positive potential of a strong welfare state in a time of crisis, with advantages both during the crisis period and thereafter.

Recent and historical European and Scandinavian developments underscore the ways in which the character and direction of social policy and the quality of links between the state and major economic groups in society at critical junctures

Table 19.5   Economic Recession and Recovery in Finland

Year	Real growth of GDP (%)	Real growth of social expenditures (%)	Social expenditures (as a % of GDP)	Unemployment rate (%)
1989	5.7	2.9	23.8	3.1
1990	0.0	6.9	25.2	3.2
1991	−5.9	8.8	29.9	6.6
1992	−3.2	7.1	33.6	11.7
1993	−0.6	2.0	34.6	16.3
1994	3.7	2.5	33.9	16.6
1995	3.9	0.7	32.0	15.4
1996	4.1	2.6	31.5	14.6
1997	5.6	−0.8	29.4	12.7
1998	5.6	−0.5	27.4	11.4

Source: Hannu Uusitalo, "Social Policy in Deep Economic Recession and After: The Case of Finland," Paper presented at ISSA Conference on Social Security, Helsinki, September 25–27, 2000 (<http://www.issa.int/pdf/helsinki2000/topic4/2uusitalo.pdf> accessed October 28, 2002).

of economic, social, or political crisis have importance for the way out of the crisis. The Finnish and Swedish experience of the last decade also illustrates how democratic systems and institutions *can* adapt to new or unexpected challenges. What institutions are in place matters when a sudden, unexpected crisis in society occurs.

Contemporary European welfare states, some argue, face challenges of an entirely new character: "rapid transition to post-industrialism, increasing globalization, sweeping changes in demography and social relations, trends towards supranational integration and a new, post–cold war politics."[14] These states nonetheless appear to have coped quite successfully with the significant new challenges in the 1990s.[15] This supports the hypothesis that developed democratic welfare states are quite good at making adjustments in public policies in such a way that the legitimacy of the system can be preserved at the same time that new vitality and economic transformation are achieved.

European countries have worked to create work-friendly welfare states (that is, welfare states that promote high labor force participation conducive to productivity). All of the Nordic countries (which are among Europe's most comprehensive welfare states because they provide income transfers and services on a more universal basis) showed increasing labor productivity in the 1990s compared with the previous decade, at levels everywhere higher than for the United States and for the EU average (see Table 19.2). Among European welfare states, the Nordic countries were also the most family friendly, in that they have developed policies conducive to labor force participation of both women and men in families with children or other care responsibilities (this also relates to work friendliness) (see Table 19.6). The Nordic countries have long had the most

Table 19.6 Female Labor Force as a Percentage of Total Female Population Aged 15–64 in Different Types of European Welfare States, 1960–95 (unweighted averages)

	1960 (%)	1974 (%)	1995 (%)
Continental Europe[a]	42.1	44.9	59.2
Scandinavia[b]	48.9	60.9	72.5
Southern Europe[c]	31.6	37.6	49.0
United Kingdom	46.1	54.3	66.0

a. Continental Europe includes Austria, Belgium, France, Germany, and the Netherlands.
b. Scandinavia is Denmark, Finland, Norway, and Sweden.
c. Southern Europe includes Greece, Italy, Portugal, and Spain.

Source: S. Kuhnle and M. Alestalo, "Introduction: Growth, Adjustments, and Survival of European Welfare States," in *Survival of the European Welfare State*, ed. S. Kuhnle (London and New York: Routledge, 2000).

extensive provision of local government welfare and care services for children and the elderly among American or European welfare states.[16]

Work friendliness is also related to issues of a "business-friendly environment." We argue that social security and business are not incompatible phenomena like fire and water: whether they are in harmony or conflict depends on the concrete construction of the system of social security and its interplay with the society in which it works, as well as the cultural and political characteristics of that society.

European Welfare States: Multifunctional, Challenged, and Reforming

The welfare state is a European political invention[17] developed, expanded, adjusted, refined, and modified over a period of more than 100 years since Bismarck launched a comprehensive compulsory social insurance program in Germany in the 1880s. That action spurred Europe-wide legislative initiatives on *Arbeiterfrage* (the social question). European nation-states have developed welfare state institutions and programs of varying characteristics, but whatever the brand of the welfare state, in its post–World War II shapes it must be seen as a significant institution conducive to the consolidation of democratic development.

A basic principle for economic transfers forms part of this history and is still crucial to social security; it was first elaborated in the British 1834 Poor Law report. The "principle of less eligibility" means that income of those people who receive benefits should always be lower than the lowest-paid members of the labor force; the underlying assumption—that it will never pay for individual citizens or households to prefer social security benefits to work or gainful employment—still applies. This principle is defended partly with economic arguments (incentives) and partly with arguments of justice or fairness. There are two important exceptions. The first and most important is the basic pension (and other basic benefits), because its main goal is to prevent and relieve poverty (though if income from paid work is lower or similar, these benefits may create a disincentive to work). The second exception is sickness benefits. Quite often in Europe, especially in Scandinavia, employees in collective agreements, and sometimes in legislated schemes, receive full pay, or close to full pay or income compensation, during periods of sickness. How different compensation levels of health-related benefits affect labor participation and duration of absence is a major theme in political debates in many European countries.

Interaction between Social Security and the Labor Market

In Europe compulsory social security systems have coexisted with modern labor markets since the end of the 19th century. The Bismarckian national legislation in Germany set the stage for the development of social insurance and simultaneously forced the collective actors on the labor market—employer associations as well as trade unions—to become social partners involved in the daily business of providing pecuniary supplements to the working population. Institutions of social insurance became tripartite organizations that were jointly supervised and sometimes also administered by the central or local state and the social partners on the labor market. As an unintended consequence, labor market participation in due course became partly regulated by agreements and regulations addressing not only wages—the wage-labor contract between the organized actors on the labor market—but also wage or earnings-related cash and in-kind benefits, so called benefit tide-overs. Over the years such benefits have become part of a mixed incentive system of sticks and carrots to get people into gainful employment.

Scandinavian experience over the last century illustrates the interactions between high and increasing labor market participation and expansion of social security systems. From the 1960s onward "high and sustainable" full employment (expanded from male to include also female breadwinners) became the public policy norm of Keynesian demand management. Unemployment was no longer viewed as a private matter, but rather as a central public concern. Expansion of social security, meanwhile, involved upgrading, in terms of pecuniary generosity and population coverage, all or most branches of social insurance. At the macro level, unemployment insurance is expansionary also, despite some theories that suggest unemployment insurance offers incentives for individuals to withdraw from the labor market (implicitly an opposite effect). Thus, the labor market has developed into a key aspect of the monetized economy, whereas social security systems have become core institutions of the modern welfare state. Macroeconomic steering became part of societal governance.

Much more is at stake. In Scandinavia, systemic integration has gone hand in hand with social integration. At the micro level the implication and risk for the individual of being out of work is marginalization and social exclusion. At the macro level, the government responsibility to create conditions under which enterprises can flourish has become linked to the general duty of every able-bodied person to work or achieve an education, schooling, or practice in order to enter into gainful employment. In sum, values other than those implicit in the rationality of the pure economic man have long been in force.

Notwithstanding the existence of an elaborate system of social security providing transfer payments of different types, from child benefits to sick pay to old-age pensions, the dominant norm in Western societies, including Scandinavia, has been that young and middle-age adults—in recent decades to an increasing degree also including women—should be active in the labor market to gain an income. Persons with severe disabilities (the "deserving poor") are the exception to this norm. Acceptance of this norm has been sustained and reinforced by the fact that not only money income, but also such social characteristics as power, prestige, and status in the community are affected by whether an individual works and by the type of work he or she performs. Following social control mechanisms in fairly coherent communities such as Scandinavia, where the distinction between state and society to a great extent has been blurred, "disobedience" can lead to a loss of reputation or even exclusion from the dominant social group, even if disobedience is to the pure pecuniary advantage of the individual. This is an important aspect of the moral logic of the modern welfare state.

In Scandinavia, labor force participation rates in the "modern sectors" of the economy (thus excluding agriculture and unpaid household work) have increased throughout the 20th century, with the exception of parts of the 1930s and parts of the 1990s (decades of economic downswings or crisis in northern Europe). In the post–World War II period, with the exception of Denmark, men's participation rates increased until the late 1970s, whereas women were still entering the labor market until the early 1990s, and in Norway throughout the 1990s. In Scandinavia, "housewives" have more or less disappeared as a social category. The impact of the development of the education system and the increasing emphasis on higher competence and skills has meant that the definition of working-age adults has been adjusted upward because most of those in the age group 16–24 are now students. The age and gender composition of the labor force in Scandinavia has been drastically transformed during the last century.

Low mobility, both within and across nations, has been a long-standing and serious problem for Europe's economic development. Workers often find it too risky to leave their job or local community to look for a job elsewhere. When workers carry the economic risks connected with loss of jobs, they are likely to fight for strong employment protection, making labor markets less flexible. Nationwide schemes, which cover employees and workers independently of specific employment conditions or characteristics of place and type of firms or employers, may thus be advantageous to labor mobility, structural economic change, and economic growth, because national social security systems can be constructed and administered in ways that encourage higher mobility or at least reduce the risk or cost for the individual worker who wants to look for a better job. Unlike under many employers' pension plans, employees do not lose pension rights under national (public) schemes if they move from one company to another. There are also advantages to systems that coordinate across unemployment benefits and employment services (such systems date back as early as 1909–11 in England). In sum, an adequate social security system can offer a health-bringing medicine for labor market "sclerosis."

The development of a free labor market in the EU and the European Economic Area, with the concomitant coordination of national social security systems so that social rights are to a great extent transportable *across* countries, represents an additional incentive to labor mobility and labor productivity in Europe and can form part of a response to economic globalization and increased international competition. The fact that intra-European labor mobility has been very limited can partly be explained by Europe-wide problems of unemployment, but perhaps more by the variations in languages and cultural habits.

Many European countries have developed alternative strategies of job creation that differ from the liberal market approach that emphasizes deregulation and minimal welfare. Such alternatives have typically involved combined packages of social security reforms—that is, stricter conditions for receiving benefits, better training programs, job-search training, and so forth. The Netherlands is an interesting case, where the "Dutch disease" was apparently (or allegedly) cured and transformed into the "Dutch miracle" through a host of policy reforms during the 1990s.[18] This example and others indicate that European welfare states have the ability to reform their societies toward what is generally considered "better" through piecemeal, democratic political processes and channels, involving civil society or organized actors in the labor market.

The changing role of women in the labor force has particular importance; witness the Scandinavian countries. Because they face significant employment problems associated with taxation, social security contributions, and unemployment benefits,[19] a distinctive feature of Nordic welfare states since World War II has been the goal of full employment. Until the mid-1960s, this meant primarily full male employment, but women's opportunities for paid employment gradually increased, especially in the public ("welfare") sector. In Finland that entailed predominantly full-time jobs, whereas part-time work has been more common in the other Scandinavian countries. Female employment in Scandinavia has reached the highest level among West European OECD countries (see Table 19.6), though female labor force participation rates have increased in all parts of Western Europe since the 1960s and 1970s (also an element of the Dutch miracle).

The increasingly generous maternity and paternity benefits and parental-leave schemes during the 1980s and 1990s have been conducive to high female labor force participation in Scandinavia, as well as gradual development of childcare services (though this is not peculiar to Scandinavia). One factor explaining the development of these generous schemes, making Scandinavian countries at once more work friendly, women friendly, and, in a sense, family friendly, is very likely the rapid political mobilization of women in political parties; trade unions; and decision-making arenas like the parliament, government, and public bureaucracy.

Welfare State Reforms: Some Scandinavian Examples

Since the late 1950s and 1960s, Scandinavian countries have moved to transform universal and flat rate or means-tested social security benefits into more work- or income-related mechanisms. This has happened in pension systems (Denmark being a slightly deviant case with generous universal basic pensions and supplements linked to employment period), sickness benefits, and unemployment benefits. Social security systems have come to be based more on the loss-of-income principle, or "status-maintenance" principle of the Bismarckian system, thus introducing a stronger work incentive yet at the same time sustaining universal pensions for all citizens—irrespective of labor market participation—in order to prevent poverty.[20] Early retirement schemes, made more generous in recent years, could, on the contrary, be looked upon as promoting work disincentives, thus transmitting the notion that exit from work (among those who have worked for a long time) is a welfare gain.

The Nordic economic and welfare systems experienced a decisive reorientation in the late 1980s and early 1990s.[21] Scandinavian welfare states have in significant respects been work oriented at least since World War II (some might argue since the Reformation in the 1500s), but increasing levels of unemployment, which have remained relatively high for longer periods in Denmark (since the mid-1970s) and Finland and Sweden (since the early 1990s), gave rise to debates about labor market rigidities, and taxation systems and generosity of social security benefits came under scrutiny as possible work (or employment) disincentive factors. Taxation does not appear to explain unemployment problems, because unemployment was low (except in Denmark) in the 1980s at a time when marginal tax rates were high.[22] Similarly, it is not clear that the tax reduction reforms in the late 1980s and early 1990s had any major effect on work effort, measured by labor force participation and hours of work.[23] Lower taxes may have induced employers to hire new workers and employees, but we have no data to

Table 19.7   Unemployment Rates (Commonly Used Definitions), Selected Years 1988–98

	1988 (%)	1990 (%)	1992 (%)	1994 (%)	1996 (%)	1998[a] (%)
Denmark	8.6	9.6	11.3	12.2	8.8	7.4
Finland	4.5	3.5	13.1	18.4	16.3	13.7
Norway	3.2	5.2	5.9	5.9	4.9	4.2
Sweden	1.7	1.6	5.3	8.0	8.0	7.5
European Union	9.4	7.9	9.6	11.6	11.3	10.8

a. Figures for 1998 are projections. Compare with the lower figures for Finland 1996–98 in Table 19.5.

Source: P. Kosonen, "Activation, Incentives, and Workfare in Four Nordic Countries," in MIRE, *Comparing Social Welfare Systems in Nordic Europe and France* (Nantes, France: Maison des sciences de l'Homme Ange-Guépin, 1998).

corroborate this. The connection between economic work incentives and employment is far from clear.[24] On the other hand, social security benefits, which largely depend on previous earnings, create incentives to be employed (but to be efficient, require that the characteristics of the benefit systems are known to the unemployed, not at all an obvious assumption!). If there is a lesson to be learned, it must be that direct links do not necessarily exist between taxation levels, unemployment and employment, and generosity of social security benefits. Tables 19.7 and 19.8 give an overview of development of unemployment and employment rates in the Nordic countries.

The early 1990s saw a declining trend in employment levels and an increase in unemployment levels, whereas in the latter half of the 1990s, the opposite trend was apparent (at the same time as increasing numbers of young working-age people were engaged in higher education, perhaps affecting unemployment statistics). Although employment rates on average declined in the EU in the 1990s, the rates increased in Ireland and the Netherlands.[25] Labor utilization is

Table 19.8   Employment Rates (Employed Persons/Persons of Work Age, %), Selected Years 1983–96

	1983 (%)	1990 (%)	1994 (%)	1996 (%)
Denmark	71.7	77.1	72.8	74.7
Finland	73.2	74.1	60.1	62.2
Norway	73.9	73.9	72.7	76.8
Sweden	78.5	80.9	70.2	72.7

Source: P. Kosonen, "Activation, Incentives, and Workfare in Four Nordic Countries," in MIRE, *Comparing Social Welfare Systems in Nordic Europe and France* (Nantes, France: Maison des sciences de l'Homme Ange-Guépin, 1998).

Table 19.9   Average Annual Working Hours for Total Economy, 1980, 1990, 1998

	1980	1990	1998
Denmark	—	1,492	1,527
Finland	1,755	1,677	1,674
Norway	1,512	1,432	1,401
Sweden	1,439	1,480	1,551
European Union	1,755	1,659	1,620
United States	1,831	1,819	1,833

Source: J. Elmeskov and S. Scarpetta, "New Sources of Economic Growth?" (paper presented at 28th Economics Conference of Österreichische Nationalbank, Vienna, June 15–16, 2000).

lower in the EU than in the United States. The Nordic countries have higher employment rates than the United States, but this is offset by lower hours worked and results in lower labor utilization (see Table 19.9).

Various evaluations of the effects of active labor market policies (training, education, protected work, and so forth) in the Nordic countries indicate that the effect seems to be positive, seen from the perspective of both the unemployed and the employers. Incentives to be employed have become stronger rather than weaker (given income-related social security benefits and pensions) in Scandinavia in recent years, but policies have also changed to greater use of the stick: more elements of control and discipline are imposed on the unemployed.

Pension Reforms and Welfare State Issues

The role of pension systems in overall social security systems and in labor incentives has particular importance. European old-age pension systems are often extremely complicated, developed through long historical processes. Benefit schemes often include elements that were perhaps justifiable when they were introduced but have survived long beyond their initial rationale. Those benefits create their own interest groups that fight for their privileges. A good example is the retirement age for police and army officers. Their low pension age was justified at a time when they had to engage in physical fights and had to be fit until they retired. Today such officers usually have paperwork jobs after age 50, and there is no longer any good reason why they should retire earlier than other groups of white-collar workers.

European pension systems have faced two important and related problems: first, a complexity that makes the systems difficult to understand at the most basic level, and second, internal contradictions and complex features, arising from their historical development, which may go in opposite directions from both original intent and contemporary policy. Public conceptions, and widespread misconceptions, about how the system works cause adaptations that are counterproductive to work-friendly welfare states (for example, a system may offer higher earnings if one retires early from a full-time job than if one gradually reduces hours worked and retires later). A major recent study of social security, published by the International Labor Organization, comments on aspects of this problem:

> There is often a lack of transparency in the administration of social security provisions. This weakness applies to the failure to explain adequately the broad concepts and objectives of the scheme, and to the failure to advise the insured persons how their pension records are progressing or what is happening to the contributions they have paid. Many schemes do not issue regular pension or contribution statements. Often the legislation is complex and difficult to understand for insured persons, employers and even administrators. The problem applies across the whole spectrum of social security provisions, but is particularly acute in the case of pensions since, first, the contribution rates are highest and, second, benefits may not be payable for 30 years—on retirement. People inevitably wonder what is happening to their contributions.[26]

The modern Scandinavian pension system reforms are an interesting case, notably the Swedish pension reform of the late 1990s. A central aim was to make the pension system more work friendly by making it more transparent, at the same time retaining the element of universal income guarantee for all elderly persons.

The lack of clear and understandable links between contributions and benefits is a main reason Sweden introduced a new pension system during the latter half of the 1990s. It was launched in 1999 and will be phased in gradually. Since 1960 Sweden has had an obligatory two-tier pension system, with a universal flat rate basic pension for all inhabitants and an earnings-related supplementary pension. This pension scheme met rising criticism during the 1980s and 1990s, and a political consensus gradually evolved on the system's main weaknesses: expenditures were not linked to economic growth (or change), and supplementary pensions presupposed a growth of approximately 2 percent annually, so if the growth rate was slower (as it had been in the 1975–95 period), contributions had to be increased. Longer life expectancy and growing numbers of pensioners added to the bill. But an important problem was a fundamental unfairness in the lack of a link between contributions and benefits:

> The national supplementary pension favors those with erratic earning trends or those who work for a short time, while being unfair to those whose income develops consistently and who work for a long time. This is due to the benefit formula determining pension rights on the basis of the 15 years of highest income and a minimum qualifying period of 30 years. Two people with the same lifelong earnings may receive very different pensions, although they have both paid in the same amount in contributions. It is not fair that those who work all their lives and have a steady earnings profile should receive less from the system than those who enjoy a short career.[27]

The new scheme is based on the principle of lifelong earnings. Each year employers and employees pay contributions amounting to 18.5 percent of the income of all economic active residents in Sweden. Pensions will be equivalent to the value of all paid-in contributions at the time of retirement. For many years the retirement age in Sweden has been 65, but in the new system there is no fixed retirement age. Pensions can be claimed from the age of 61, and there is no upper age limit. Annual benefits are calculated on the basis of the person's remaining life expectancy at the time of retirement. The later a person retires, the higher the annual pension. It is also possible to take out reduced pensions and combine these with part-time work. Individuals who have earned little or no pension are guaranteed a minimum pension, financed by general taxes, paid after age 65. Persons who have earned pensions through contributions that are below the guarantee level will always receive a higher pension than the minimum. Income is supplemented (financed by taxes) for parents who care for small children, for national service, and for recipients of certain disability and early retirement pensions. These additions are financed by taxes.

This new Swedish pension system gives a simple and clear message to all residents in Sweden: it always pays to work. All income from work will increase pension rights. The system is work friendly and transparent. Everyone can see the principle of justice that it is based on: proportionality between work and pension rights.

Concluding Comments

Social security and welfare state arrangements serve many purposes. Social security policies are about political and social preferences, shaped by culture, traditions, economic and technological developments, social structure, and social relations. We should be particularly cautious about claiming any "correct path" for social policies because values and preferences affect perceptions about fairness, social justice, social cohesion, stability, and equalization of life chances. There is, nonetheless, a core aspect of social security systems, which is how to organize support in ways that also offer incentives to work, an important goal of most governments. There are many rather unexplored linkages. Unemployment insurance systems can facilitate the process of restructuring in industry and business. Economic security may reduce workers' and employees' resistance to change. Compulsory government schemes, which cover employees and workers independently of specific employment conditions or characteristics of place and time of firms or employers, may favor labor mobility, structural economic change, and economic growth. National schemes for unemployment insurance are in very important respects work friendly.

Recent European experience indicates that there are no obvious links between size of the welfare state, taxation levels, employment rates, labor productivity, and economic growth. The examples of Sweden and, especially, Finland during the 1990s show that comprehensive, democratic welfare states are fully capable of making policy adjustments to stimulate new economic growth when hit by serious economic recession. Social security represents a shock absorber, while democratic institutions are responsive to economic and social challenges. We can expect, in this world, more rapid changes in labor markets, more mobility, more flexible work, and more career shifts during the period of labor market participation. Those new patterns will demand changes in pension systems to make them more transparent and less dependent on "best years" and "last years" of earnings, and thus more fair, in the sense that the pension reflects contributions during all working years. The Swedish pension reform of 1999 offers other European as well as East Asian countries a lesson because it combines the manifest work-friendly aspect with a universal guarantee of income security in old age. Status maintenance is combined with poverty prevention.

Another aspect of Scandinavian welfare states, their emphasis on public social services for children, the old, and the sick, is less universally accepted. Such government schemes may be considered both work friendly and family friendly. If families are relieved of some of their burden (itself a contested concept) as caregivers (for their young, old, and sick family members), labor market activity and labor mobility can increase, and thus also can economic productivity and growth. Government social policies can provide the basis for flexible solutions for families, for workers and employees, and for firms. Social policies can make it possible, if desired, for both husband and wife to combine family obligations with full-time (or part-time) gainful employment. If globalization also has a cultural dimension, such as spreading the idea, demand, and expectations of greater gender equality in all spheres of society, it may well be that welfare states with social policies that are relatively more gender sensitive will be the most successful in terms of both economic development and social peace and harmony. Family friendliness of social policies can also affect fertility rates (lack of such policies in parts of Europe such as Italy and Spain may have contributed to sharp drops in fertility rates, whereas strong policies may have spurred relatively higher rates in the Nordic countries).

Whether the welfare state—with its programs for retirement and disability pensions, sickness insurance, occupational injury insurance, maternity insurance and paid parental leave, child and family benefits, unemployment insurance and labor activity programs, health and personal social services, kindergartens, and so forth—is a blessing or not for economic growth and efficiency is a topic for much research and debate.[28] At least seen at the macro level and over longer time spans, the welfare state and economic growth have gone hand in hand. Economic growth is possible with a number of welfare state constructions of varying scope and generosity.

Economic growth and efficiency are, however, clearly not the only goals of European national welfare policies. Politics and welfare state construction are also about equalization of life chances, social justice, social security, social cohesion, and stability, all in various ways related not only to economic growth and dynamics of economic development, investment climate, and so forth, but also to political preferences, ideologies, interests, and values. Thus, what kinds of welfare state policies are possible is also at all times a question of what is considered desirable by governments and voters, and what is considered desirable—what the state can and *ought to* do[29]—is a question of political and cultural context (norms, expectations, value structures) as much as a question of level of economic development and theories and knowledge of prerequisites for economic growth and efficiency.

An important lesson from the European experience is a simple one: the welfare state does and may serve many functions. Debates on what are proper lessons to be learned and what are proper welfare policy solutions in other, non-European, contexts can thus be framed in many ways. Social protection and welfare are often discussed in terms of poverty relief and meeting minimum needs for income and services. Poverty reduction was historically a central reason that governments put social legislation on the agenda. But the establishment of European welfare states is about much more, especially in their Nordic and continental European variants. Originally, considerations of social harmony and regime support were important. Over time, many programs were developed to insure against events and risks that cause income loss, to allow reallocation of income over the life-cycle and redistribution across social groups, and to provide a sense of security for all citizens.[30] Europe's welfare states appear to have been a societal stabilizer, preventing serious social rebellion, strong revolutionary movements (except for right-wing extremism in the pre–World War II period when the welfare state and parliamentary democracy were still weak and underdeveloped institutions in many parts of Europe), and extensive poverty. The combination of structures of democratic governance, regulated capitalist market economies, and relatively comprehensive welfare institutions has rather successfully accommodated changing social needs. Social and political challenges have continuously filled government agendas, but empirically dramatic crisis theories since the mid-1970s have fared rather poorly in the European context.[31]

Notes

1. F. W. Scharpf, "The Viability of Advanced Welfare States in the International Economy. Vulnerabilities and Options," *European Review* 8, no.3 (2000): 399–426; Maurizio Ferrera and Martin Rhodes, eds., *Recasting European Welfare States* (London: Frank Cass Publishers, 2000), and Stein Kuhnle, ed., *Survival of the European Welfare State* (London and New York: Routledge, 2000). See, for example, Assar Lindbeck et al., *Turning Sweden Around* (Cambridge, Mass., and London: MIT Press, 1994), for a penetrating analysis not only of how the Swedish welfare state is (or was) perceived to be in a severe crisis, but also of Sweden's economic and political institutions.

2. Kuhnle, op. cit.

3. *Financial Times*, August 9, 2000.

4. The World Economic Forum's list, compiled in cooperation with the Center for International Development at Harvard University, available at <http://www.cid.harvard.edu/cidglobal/compet.htm>.

5. For instance, the 2001 survey of the International Institute for Management Development in Lausanne, Switzerland.

6. OECD, *The Welfare State in Crisis* (Paris: OECD, 1981).

7. *Financial Times*, September 2000, pp. 9–10.

8. Stein Kuhnle and Matti Alestalo, "Introduction: Growth, Adjustments, and Survival of European Welfare States," in *Survival of the European Welfare State*, ed. S. Kuhnle (London and New York: Routledge, 2000).

9. Labor productivity also increased in Germany and Portugal in the 1990s.

10. M. Heikkilä and H. Uusitalo, eds., *The Cost of the Cuts: Studies in Cutbacks in Social Security and Their Effects in the Finland of the 1990s* (Helsinki: STAKES, 1997); H. Uusitalo, "Social Policy in

Deep Economic Recession and After: The Case of Finland," paper presented at ISSA Conference on Social Security, Helsinki, September 25–27, 2000. <http://www.issa.int/pdf/helsinki2000/topic4/2uusitalo.pdf>.

11. P. Eitrheim and S. Kuhnle, "Nordic Welfare States in 1990s: Institutional Stability, Signs of Divergence," in *Survival of the European Welfare State*, ed. S. Kuhnle (London and New York: Routledge, 2000).

12. Uusitalo, op. cit.

13. Ferrera and Rhodes, op. cit.

14. Ferrera and Rhodes, op. cit., p. 1

15. J. Kohl, "Trends and Problems in Postwar Public Expenditure Developments in Western Europe and North America," in *The Development of Welfare States in Europe and America*, eds. A. J. Heidenheimer and P. Flora, (New Brunswick, N.J., and London: Transaction Books, 1981); Mikko Kautto, Matti Heikkilä, Björn Hvinden, Staffen Marklund, and Niels Ploug, eds., *Nordic Social Policy: Changing Welfare States* (London and New York: Routledge, 1999).

16. Anthony B. Atkinson, *The Economic Consequences of Rolling Back the Welfare State* (Cambridge, England: Cambridge University Press, 1999); A. Sandmo, "Social Security and Economic Growth," in *European Institute of Social Security Yearbook 1994* (Leuven, Belgium: Acco, 1995).

17. Stein Kuhnle, "European lessons of the 1990s," in *Survival of the European Welfare State*, ed. S. Kuhnle (London and New York: Routledge, 2000).

18. J. Visser and A. Hemerijck, *A Dutch Miracle: Job Growth, Welfare Reform, and Corporatism in the Netherlands* (Amsterdam: Amsterdam University Press, 1997).

19. This is underlined in many OECD publications, in particular in the *OECD Jobs Study* (Paris: OECD, May 1994), as well as in EU reports. See also P. Kosonen, "Activation, Incentives, and Workfare in Four Nordic Countries," in MIRE, *Comparing Social Welfare Systems in Nordic Europe and France* (Nantes, France: Maison des Sciences de l'Homme Ange-Guépin, 1998).

20. The main source of information is *The Pension Reform—Final Report* (June 1998) <http://www.pension.gov.se>.

21. According to P. Kosonen, op. cit.

22. Comparing tax reforms and unemployment patterns, Kosonen (op. cit.) comes to this conclusion.

23. N. A. Klevmarken, I. Andersson, P. Brose, E. Gronqvist, P. Olovsson, and M. Stotlenberg-Hansen, *Labor Supply Responses to Swedish Tax Reforms, 1985–1992* (Stockholm: National Institute of Economic Research, Economic Council, 1995); R. Aaberge and J. Dagsvik, "Labor Supply Responses and Welfare Effects of Tax Reforms," *Scandinavian Journal of Economics* 97, no. 4 (1995): 635–59.

24. Kosonen, op. cit.

25. Jorgen Elmeskov and S. Scarpetta, "New Sources of Economic Growth" (paper presented at the 28th Economic Conference of Österreichische Nationalbank, Vienna, June 15–16, 2000).

26. C. Gilion, J. Turner, C. Bailey, and D. Latulippe, eds., *Social Security Pensions: Development and Reform* (Geneva: International Labor Organization, 2000), pp. 244–45.

27. *The Pension Reform—Final Report*, op. cit., p. 9.

28. Atkinson, op. cit.; Sandmo, op. cit.

29. Kees Van Kersbergen, "The Declining Resistance of Welfare States to Change" in *Survival of the European Welfare State*, ed. S. Kuhnle (London and New York: Routledge, 2000).

30. Atkinson, op cit., 5–6.

31. Van Kersbergen, op. cit.

BOX 5.1

Social Protection and Experience from the Great Depression
by Bernard Gazier and Rémy Herrera

The Great Depression was a laboratory for social protection measures, and the successes and failures of the wide range of programs introduced in its wake have relevance today. Three countries took quite different approaches in responding to social needs during the crisis and saw different results in both the short and long term.

France's[1] situation was dire from 1929 to 1939, as it confronted 10 percent losses in gross domestic product during the first 4 years, followed by lingering stagnation. What is striking, however, is that the unemployment rate reached only 6 percent. The explanation lies not in the French economy's strength nor in any "active" labor market policy but in two self-reinforcing factors. First, official figures counted only people who lost jobs, excluding newcomers to the labor market. Second, France was still largely a rural country with close family ties, so many people returned to the countryside to participate in harvesting and other rural activities when they lost jobs. They found shelter and relied on family solidarity, both more or less sufficient. Thus, although many people faced sharply curtailed incomes, alternatives worked reasonably well.

The New Deal initiatives that the Roosevelt administration pursued in the United States are still impressive today. The Civil Works Administration (CWA) hired 4 million unemployed in January 1934, and the Federal Emergency Relief Administration (FERA) reported 20 million beneficiaries during winter 1934. The Social Security Act, passed in 1935, created retirement, health protection, and family assistance programs.

Public works programs were perhaps the most controversial and complex of those initiatives. In the face of criticism that it paid too-high wages and disrupted labor markets, CWA was abolished in 1934. It was quickly replaced by the Works Progress Administration (WPA), which paid wages that varied with local conditions. The WPA's coverage steadily became more restrictive: it funded 2.9 million jobs in 1936, 1.5 million in 1937,

continued on next page

BOX 5.1, continued

and 3 million for a very short period during the 1938 slump, compared with a maximum of 11 million to 12 million unemployed in the 1930s. FERA programs also excluded many "real" unemployed, referring them to employment agencies. After providing emergency help in 1934, the U.S. government essentially chose to rely on private employment to assist most unemployed, despite very low economic activity. Social distress in the 1930s was relieved only by World War II, which reemployed most of the unemployed, and the peace that followed, which provided jobs for both veterans and civilians.

For its part, the United Kingdom developed a deliberately counter-cyclical policy in tandem with important social developments after 1935, and the country recorded strong growth from 1935 to 1940. The United Kingdom created social protections progressively, introducing unemployment benefits and pensions without spectacular breaks or reforms. Laws and other incentives encouraged construction of individual and standardized dwellings, prompting a housing boom: newly built houses doubled in the 1930s compared with the 1920s. After 1937 paid holidays stimulated mass leisure. Together those factors boosted popular consumption.

The policies that the Republic of Korea and other East Asian countries pursued in the wake of the 1997–98 economic crisis present parallels with the French, U.K., and U.S. experience. The East Asian approaches included traditional solidarity, mass emergency public works and attendant problems when they halted, and countercyclical macroeconomic policies as the backdrop.

Family solidarity worked quite well in East Asia during the crisis. Even in urbanized Korea, rural and traditional solidarity still operates. Strong saving behavior indicates a community that can act as a buffer and accumulate private income protection and assets without relying on state help. Some East Asian initiatives resemble those of the United Kingdom, with macroeconomic policies complementing public works programs, enhancing the economy's ability to absorb laid-off workers and helping reconcile mobility and solidarity.

Some elements of the CWA-WPA process in the United States highlight the limits and potential conflicts of public policies designed to

BOX 5.1, continued

address crisis conditions. State-managed mobility is always difficult in times of tight budget constraints. It begins with volunteers and can end in authoritarian decisions that either suppress programs or, more likely, reorient them in restrictive ways. This applies especially to relatively "small" or "lean" welfare states, which experience both implementation and legitimacy problems when they expand their social protection programs rapidly. In response, governments often develop less attractive forms of "workfare" and direct—quickly and bluntly—those with poor reemployment prospects to private labor markets. This process can aggravate segmentation of the labor market.

Can countries escape this vicious circle? Maintaining extensive state involvement in jobs and labor market mobility over an extended period is neither possible nor desirable. Transitional labor markets encourage more decentralized control of labor market policies and expenditures by municipalities and nonprofit organizations. The French experience during the 1930s resembles an informal transitional labor market, strongly unequal and heterogeneous.

Today governments must actively respond to social needs while making their social protection policies fairer and more efficient. To meet that challenge, they must fulfill two closely linked conditions. First, they need to develop alternatives to the stark dichotomy between public and private management. Second, they must ensure that social partners assume some responsibility for enhancing the mobility of workers and unemployed. Overall, the state should not bear the entire social protection burden. Public expenditures can and should be used as a lever, together with active mobilization of social networks and activities in the third sector. Some networks and activities can be informal (through associations, cooperatives, and mutual benefit societies), supported by the traditional solidarity links that remain particularly strong in parts of East Asia.

1. Bernard Gazier, *La crise de 1929* (Paris: Presses Universitaires de France, 1989).

CHAPTER 20

Youth Unemployment: Challenges and Ideas

by Colin Moynihan with Jacqueline Butler

ABSTRACT: This chapter sets youth unemployment in the context of globalization trends, which threaten to worsen social exclusion among young people. The chapter highlights experience with programs designed to foster youth employment in Europe and some of the risks and pitfalls demonstrated in recent experience. It highlights the importance of a sharp focus on the transition period from education to employment and the vicious circle that can trap young people who do not make the transition smoothly. The most successful programs have a sharply targeted and tailored character and are part of sound national strategies and effective public-private partnerships.

New industries, cross-border trade, and a diverse global labor market offer the possibility of providing decent work for people in all societies. But we also risk a more divisive scenario: a recent report by the U.K. Industrial Society, *Wherever Next? Work in a Mobile World*, contrasted a "supermobile elite" with an "immobile poor" and spelled out the potentially damaging consequences.[1]

Many contemporary economic changes, including technological innovation and liberalization of international trade and finance, have far-ranging repercussions for those who lack access to transport and face local exclusion from work opportunities, shops, banking, and other services. Many new jobs require skills in information and communication technologies and the ability to operate in new forms of work. Yet only 1 in 250 Africans has access to a telephone.

The digital divide is more acute in developing countries but is by no means restricted to them. More than 100 million people in industrial societies live below the poverty line, defined as half the median income, and 37 million are jobless.[2]

In Europe higher levels of growth offer great potential for reducing social exclusion, but the very globalizing trends and communications revolution that contribute to Europe's healthy balance sheet have adversely affected the employment prospects of those in the weakest position in the labor market.

In seeking solutions to these problems, policymakers must focus on youth employment. Most young people are better educated, are wealthier, are physically healthier, and live longer than their elders, but changes in the labor market, family relations, and social structures present them with new sets of risks and challenges. Opportunities for those without skills are fewer, traditional sources of employment are disappearing, and people are far less likely to hold a job for life. Young people today face the prospect of periodic successive job change and the need to acquire new skills throughout their working lives to remain employable.

This chapter addresses European efforts to help ensure that all young people acquire such skills and can move successfully from learning to work.

Social Exclusion, Social Capital, and Youth Unemployment

Social exclusion has become a catchall phrase for some of society's most entrenched problems: sharp income inequality, unemployment, poor access to services, child poverty, homelessness, and drug and alcohol abuse. Solutions to social exclusion and youth unemployment are inextricably linked because social exclusion is both a cause and effect of youth unemployment.

Social exclusion results from a paucity of social capital and also tends to erode it. Social capital is an asset embedded in relationships—among individuals, communities, networks, and societies. Social networks have always been an important resource for recruiting people into a range of economic activities. Those networks work less well in areas with entrenched long-term unemployment.

In Europe a lack of access to support networks that help people land an education, homes, jobs, services, and benefits is contributing to what the U.K. think-tank Demos calls "network poverty."[3] Those who lack appropriate skills, are in difficult social or economic situations, have disabilities, face personal and institutional prejudice, or lacking learning opportunities, may find themselves caught in a vicious cycle. Poor and unemployed people are less likely to live in communities where others might be able to put them in touch with a job, and role models are limited or negative.

This pattern has a particularly detrimental impact on young people because risk factors for social exclusion cross generations. In the United Kingdom, 34 percent of sons and 37 percent of daughters of men who fall in the lowest quartile of earnings also end up in the lowest quartile. Only 13 percent of such sons and 12 percent of such daughters end up in the top quartile. The daughter of a teenage mother is 1.5 times more likely to become one herself than is the daughter of an older mother. And during the 1980s, young men age 23–33 were twice as likely to be unemployed for at least 1 year if their father had been unemployed at age 16.[4]

Young people are most vulnerable to social exclusion when leaving home, leaving care, and leaving education, times at which wider changes have weakened or removed some of the support systems on which people, particularly adolescents, have traditionally depended. For many young people, family ties have become fluid and more fragile. More young people have grown up in single-parent households, which are disproportionately likely to be low income, and they may be less well equipped to cope with other difficulties.

Weaknesses in government policies can compound the resulting problems. Homelessness, teenage pregnancy, and unemployment cross boundaries between services and departments, which can lead to "orphan" issues, underenrollment in services, and duplication of effort. Policy coherence, among government departments and between local and national levels, is key to addressing both social exclusion and youth unemployment.

Increasingly, the issue of social exclusion is assuming center stage. The European Union states that "the fight against social exclusion is of the utmost importance for the Union,"[5] reflecting the view that social exclusion carries high costs in the form of reduced social cohesion, higher crime and fear of crime, a less-skilled work force, and a drain on public finances. If social exclusion is reduced, then society as a whole will benefit.

Businesses are also realizing that corporate success depends on both social *and* economic outcomes, and that investing in young people is a business imperative. This is reflected in corporate-backed ventures that aim to improve young people's lives and their workplace experiences and opportunities. One such initiative is the International Youth Foundation's[6] Global Alliance for Workers and Communities, whose members include Nike, Gap, the World Bank, the John D. and Catherine T. MacArthur Foundation, Penn State University, and St. John's University. Kevin Quigley, executive director of the Global Alliance, observed recently that because the average age of employees in factories in developing countries is 23, and 80 percent to 85 percent are female, "we see the workplace as a venue for human development and an opportunity to help people develop skills that will enable them to build better lives for themselves and their families."[7]

The Dimensions of Youth Unemployment

The best defense against social exclusion is a job, and the best way to get a job is to have a good education with the right training and experience. However, the International Labor Organization (ILO) reports that unemployment rates are twice as high among the 15–24 and 25+ age groups than among adults across both industrial and developing countries. ILO research also shows that youth unemployment rates were significantly higher in the 1990s than in the 1980s in a number of countries. The young do not choose to be unemployed: as ILO notes, "the army of the unemployed is a conscript rather than volunteer army,"[8] and it considers the large and growing number of unemployed youth "one of the most daunting problems faced by developed and developing countries alike."[9]

Early unemployment can permanently impair people's future productive capacity; the longer an unemployment spell lasts, the more difficult it is to find work. Unemployment can prevent young people from making the passage from adolescence to adulthood that entails establishing a household and a family. Evidence also suggests that unemployed young people suffer more health problems than those who are employed, including lower rates of general health, more anxiety and depression, high rates of smoking, and higher suicide rates. Young people are clearly at high risk of social exclusion if they fall into a downward spiral of worsening health and unemployment.

Young people's transitions have always been difficult, but recent research underscores that the transition to adulthood is more complicated today. Distinctions between childhood and adulthood have blurred, with many young people remaining dependent on their parents into their twenties and beyond, even while they experience more autonomy earlier in their teenage years.

At the extreme end of the spectrum, high levels of youth unemployment can lead to alienation from society and from the political process, which may in turn give rise to social unrest. This is the soil in which the seeds of terrorism can find root. Poverty breeds resentment, resentment breeds hatred, and hatred breeds terrorism. It is no accident that terrorism has found adherents in the Palestinian territories, where standards of living have fallen by some 40 percent since the signing of the Oslo accords, and unemployment rates range from 20 percent to 30 percent.

In seeking solutions to youth unemployment, we must clearly identify its causes. Social exclusion is both a cause and effect of unemployment, but social exclusion alone does not explain the high and persistent patterns of youth unemployment. Indeed, a superficial examination would suggest that the economic situation of youths should have improved, thanks to declining cohort size,[10] longer education, and higher skills. So why has the economic position of young people deteriorated? The ILO has ruled out a number of causes, including high youth wages (they have been falling) and minimum wages (they are low). The evidence does not suggest that youths are being priced out of the market in any major way. Indeed, the relative pay of youths has dropped throughout the countries of the Organization for Economic Cooperation and Development (OECD).[11]

Changes in aggregate demand, the growing demand for skilled workers, and the rising participation of women who compete with the young for jobs appear to explain in large measure the rise in youth unemployment.[12] Another explanatory factor in OECD countries is the role of higher home ownership, which impairs people's mobility—critical in economies that depend on flexibility and adaptability. If the biggest cause of youth unemployment is the level of aggregate demand, solutions to youth unemployment are inextricably linked to reducing overall unemployment, even if the youth share of the population continues to fall. Unfortunately, unemployment in general, and youth unemployment in particular, fluctuate in large irregular cycles, and we are a long way from understanding why aggregate employment has trended upward over the last couple of decades.

Knowledge about how to enhance employment-intensive economic growth is also rather scant. Despite conventional wisdom, high unemployment does not primarily seem to result from job protection, labor taxes, the power of trade unions, or wage inflexibility. Recent research suggests a number of alternative explanations. Above all, changes in commodity prices, especially oil prices, seem to predict cyclical movements in unemployment in Europe and the United States reasonably well.[13] Those findings suggest that the most important factor in unemployment is the macroeconomic environment. Economic stability and growth drive employment; a strong economy generates jobs.

But although a strong economy may create employment, it will not create employability. Thus our educational system, our processes for enabling youth to make the transition from education to employment, and our safety nets for catching those who slip through the cracks assume central importance.

European Solutions to Youth Unemployment

Skills and education are at the very heart of the problem. Firms no longer simply recruit from the pool of available unemployed if those in that pool do not possess the necessary skills. The search for talent is global, and enlarging the pool of talent is critical. As requirements for knowledge, qualifications, and skills rise and populations age, young people cannot afford to enter the labor force unequipped for changing career patterns.

The good news is that young people in OECD countries seem to be recognizing the new realities of the labor market and are responding by postponing their entry and undertaking more education.[14] In virtually all OECD countries, enrollments in higher education rose from the 1980s to the 1990s. Research in the United Kingdom has shown that higher education brings earnings that are 20 percent higher on average, and a chance of unemployment that is 50 percent lower.[15] A few decades ago in the United Kingdom, only a minority stayed in education until age 18 or 21. This new trend toward higher education is partly a response to poor labor market conditions and partly a response to the demand for higher skills.

An extraordinary meeting of the European Council in November 1997 produced the European Employment Strategy, whose full employment goal[16] entails disseminating best practices to reflect the interdependence among national labor markets. The strategy recommended that member countries adopt early intervention programs to combat youth unemployment typified by the Nordic approach, given that youth unemployment is lowest in Denmark, Norway, and Sweden.[17]

The United Kingdom has responded with the New Deal for Young People, a welfare-to-work program that links income assistance to a requirement that recipients participate in work programs or education and training (see Box 5.1). France has established Emplois Jeunes (Young Jobs), backed by an employment counseling service, and Germany has created the Immediate Action Program for the young unemployed.

In general, the burden of joblessness among the young falls on the least educated and the least skilled. For example, some 40 percent of young people participating in the United Kingdom's New Deal cannot read "the basic instructions on a medicine bottle."[18] Education systems across Europe are facing new challenges that affect all participants. For generations, teachers have been the gatekeepers of knowledge, but technology is challenging that role. More information is now available to the connected student than any individual teacher could know, and education needs to draw on a new and wider range of resources. But the United Kingdom is now demanding higher standards and more ambitious targets from an increasingly outdated infrastructure—the schools and universities retain basic structures that are centuries old.

The Lisbon European summit in March 2000 set a goal to halve the number of 18- to 24-year-olds with only lower-secondary-level education by 2010. Toward that end the summit called for developing schools and training centers into multipurpose local learning centers, linked to the Internet and accessible to all, and for establishing learning partnerships among schools, training centers, firms, and research facilities.

Advances in secondary schooling in France, the Netherlands, and Sweden appear to have more impact than labor market programs and work experience and training for unemployed youth.[19] High-quality early childhood intervention also appears to exert lasting effects. The Perry Pre-School Program in the United States is a well-known example: disadvantaged, low-IQ children given intensive support from age 4 to 5 report higher adult earnings and lower levels of criminal behavior. In fact, research on the program suggests that for every US$1 invested in a preschool child, the taxpayer saves US$7 over time. The benefits of more education cross generational boundaries. Research from the United Kingdom's Social Exclusion Unit shows that by age 22 months, children whose parents stayed in school beyond the minimum leaving age develop significantly faster than those whose parents left school at the minimum age.[20]

The challenge for Europe is to develop coherence among education, employment, and income-support policies, because the transition from initial education to working life for young people is so critical and prone to pitfalls and traps. The United Kingdom's Social Exclusion Unit has shown that a lack of participation in education, training, or employment for 6 months or more between ages 16 and 18 is the single most powerful predictor of later unemployment. This pattern is also associated with high levels of depression and poor health as well as with teenage parenthood (for women) and a criminal record serious enough to be a barrier to employment (for men).[21] The goals are therefore to keep the numbers of young people who are not in education, employment, or training to a minimum and to ensure that the small numbers who do fall through the cracks rapidly reenter education and training.

Some countries are making more progress than others at finding pathways into work for the young, as demonstrated by OECD studies. Although debates continue about education versus training, it is well understood that young people need solid qualifications and expertise in broad occupational fields as well as reasoning, problem-solving, and communication skills. Countries that emphasize apprenticeship and quasi-apprenticeship have more effective transition outcomes,[22] but a broad mix of apprenticeship, school-based vocational training, and general education is what is most needed.

What is called for are coherent national packages that draw from a definable number of key ingredients:

- A healthy economy and labor market
- Well-organized pathways from initial education to work and further study
- Opportunities to combine study and workplace experience

- Safety nets for those at risk
- Effective information and guidance systems
- Policy processes that involve governments and other stakeholders

Countries can achieve good transition outcomes with different combinations of the key pieces, but sadly the general pattern among OECD countries is a lack of policy coherence and insufficient commitment and resources in most countries.

Several OECD countries have set up labor market programs designed to help youths in the job market. On the supply side are programs that link schooling to work and second-chance programs that boost the skills of youths who encounter trouble in the job market. On the demand side are programs that raise youth wages through a minimum wage and that target specific employment opportunities at youths.

However, large untargeted youth employment and training programs generally do not improve either employment prospects or earnings for the young, especially the disadvantaged.[23] Indeed, such programs are often a sign of a country's failure to develop more effective pathways for young people. One study found that large-scale programs designed to move young people from unemployment to work, such as the United Kingdom's Youth Opportunities Program and Youth Training Scheme in the 1990s, actually lowered the probability of employment.[24]

Narrowly targeted and carefully evaluated programs can assist specific youth categories, but far more important are local partnerships between educational institutions, employers, and communities in easing the school-to-work transition. This explains the success of apprenticeships such as those in Germany and Japan, whose Jisseki-Kankei system achieves good transition outcomes for young people.[25]

If active labor market programs do not help unemployed youth into jobs, then what approach does work when transitions from education to work have failed? The OECD was particularly impressed by the Nordic countries, which developed a "youth guarantee" during the 1980s, after many programs developed earlier yielded disappointing results.[26] The new programs integrated education, labor market, and welfare policies and local delivery mechanisms. Most important, this safety net is not standardized: it deals with each young person on a case-by-case basis. Local providers track early school leavers and work closely with a wide range of community agencies to provide the services youth need.

What Might European Experience Offer East Asia?

Some 60 percent of the world's youth live in the developing countries of Asia, and the East Asian economic crisis in 1997–98 showed that here also younger people are more vulnerable to external shocks because they are the first to be retrenched. Although any policy designed to address such challenges must take into account national labor market conditions, educational institutions, and traditions, European experience can offer both positive and negative lessons in this effort:

- The right macroeconomic policies—sustainable job-enhancing economic growth—remain an indispensable component of any strategy to redress youth unemployment.
- Education and training systems must be geared toward the demands of the labor market to expand the pool of talent.
- Prevention is always better than cure.
- Investment in better, earlier, and longer education helps prevent social exclusion, but it must develop the attitudes, competencies, and skills required for the world of work.
- Countries should consider preschool programs that intervene early in the lives of children and their parents.
- Effective transition from education to work is vital, and safety nets and universal access to high-quality career information are two key features of effective transition systems.
- Labor market programs rarely improve overall job prospects for the young, but narrowly targeted and carefully monitored and evaluated programs can be effective for some young people.

Because of its vital social and political importance, the search for remedies to youth unemployment is akin to a worldwide quest for the Holy Grail. Solving the enigma is a matter of finding and assembling the right elements. No country has yet cracked the code and found a total solution, although some have made better progress than others. At the heart of all solutions is the need to establish a clear transition and strong connections between general education and continuing study at higher levels, and between education and work.

Notes

1. Judith Doyle and Max Nathan, "Wherever Next? Work in a Mobile World," Industrial Society Futures, April 26, 2001.

2. Demos, *The Wealth and Poverty of Networks: Tackling Social Exclusion,* Demos collection 12, (London: Demos, 1997/1998).

3. Ibid.

4. Social Exclusion Unit, U.K. Government, *Preventing Social Exclusion* (London: March 2001).

5. Presidency conclusions, Stockholm European Council, March 23–24, 2001.

6. The International Youth Foundation was set up 12 years ago to improve young people's prospects and now operates in more than 60 countries. See Web site <http://www.iyfnet.org>. The Global Alliance for Workers and Communities Web site is <http://www.theglobalalliance.org>.

7. United States–Indonesia Society (USINDO), "Economic Briefing," available at <http://www.usindo.org/brief_26.htm>.

8. ILO, *Employing Youth: Promoting Employment-Intensive Growth* (report for the ILO Interregional Symposium on Strategies to Combat Youth Unemployment and Marginalization, December 13–14, 1999, published in 2000).

9. Ibid.

10. The percentage of the world's population represented by youths age 15–24 is declining. From 1980 to 1995 it dropped slightly, from 19 percent to 18 percent. This decline occurred in all regions except Africa, where the number of youths as a percentage of total population continues to rise.

11. David G. Blanchflower and Richard B. Freeman, "Cohort Crowding and Youth Labor Markets: A Cross-National Analysis," in *Youth Unemployment and Joblessness in Advanced Countries,* ed. David G. Blanchflower and Richard B. Freeman (Chicago: University of Chicago Press and NBER, 1999).

12. ILO, op. cit.

13. Ibid.

14. Ibid.

15. *Ambitions for Britain,* the Labour Party's manifesto, 2001.

16. "The European Unit and the member states are fully committed to the goal of full employment and see it as an important way of meeting the challenge of an aging population." Presidency conclusions, Stockholm European Council, March 23–24, 2001.

17. OECD, *From Initial Education to Working Life: Making Transitions Work* (Paris: OECD, 2000).

18. Tessa Jowell, minister for employment, welfare-to-work, and equal opportunities, Minutes of Evidence to House of Commons Education and Employment Committee, May 17, 2000.

19. OCED, op. cit.

20. Social Exclusion Unit, U.K. Government (2001), op. cit.

21. Social Exclusion Unit, U.K. Government, *Bridging the Gap: New Opportunities for 16–18-Year-Olds Not in Education, Employment, or Training,* report for the Cabinet Office, Deputy Prime Minister, London, July 1999.

22. Greece, Hungary, Italy, Portugal, and the United Kingdom have the least successful outcomes, according to the OECD, op. cit.

23. Ibid.

24. ILO, op. cit.

25. Jisseki-Kankei is a system of semiformal contact that exists within the strong institutional linkage between schools and employers in Japan.

26. OECD, op. cit.

BOX 5.2

How the United Kingdom Has Addressed Youth Unemployment

by Colin Moynihan

Most young people in the United Kingdom enjoy a fairly smooth transition from school to work. Full-time study leads to higher education or to reasonably skilled and secure employment at around age 18, which can include an apprenticeship at age 16. However, a large minority lacks guidance and a clear path to a good job and career opportunity. At any one time, 9 percent of the 16–18 age group does not participate in education, training, or work for long periods after leaving school at age 16.

The United Kingdom has systematically engineered new institutions to improve young people's transition to employment. Local Training and Enterprise Councils act as brokers between training providers, employers, and young people, and as facilitators of large public programs, including the New Deal for Young People (NDYP) and Modern Apprenticeships.[1] Numerous other local, regional, and national agencies also offer education and training. Critics, however, question the cost and effectiveness of so many intermediaries and of reforms designed by central administrations and implemented by bodies that owe their existence to the program. The government is thus trying to reform its approach by providing clear incentives for young people to stay in education through age 18, by providing education maintenance allowances, and through youth cards that would offer access to leisure, sports, and transport.

The United Kingdom's NDYP targets youths age 18 to 24 who have been unemployed for at least 6 months. The mandatory program includes a 4-month "gateway" period of advice and support followed by one of four options: subsidized employment, full-time education and training, voluntary work, and environmental work. Participants receive an allowance that is to cover exceptional expenses.

Each participant is assigned a personal adviser, who provides assistance with job search, career advice and guidance, and preparation for

continued on next page

BOX 5.2, continued

the four options, which are designed to help enrollees progress toward finding and remaining in employment:

- The employment option provides a subsidized, waged job with an employer.
- The environmental task force option provides a job with a wage or, more often, a "benefits-plus" package.
- The voluntary sector option provides work with a nonprofit organization on either a benefits-plus or a wage basis.
- The full-time education and training option can last up to a year.

If a participant leaves an option early without good reason, he or she may lose 2 weeks of benefits, with subsequent violations resulting in a loss of benefits for 4 weeks and then 6 months. However, some 60 percent of those entering NDYP find employment before they reach the end of the gateway period. The program provides further assistance if participants return to the unemployment register.

Tables have turned since the privatizations of the 1980s under the Conservative Party. The Labour government now favors some private sector involvement in solving both youth unemployment and education challenges, though the issue remains controversial.

Community involvement by the private sector can ensure that young people, especially those living in areas of high unemployment, can make contact with the world of work. Such contact can occur through mentoring, work experience, school–business partnerships, or direct business involvement in community projects. Partnerships between local governments and employers especially can improve the transition between school and work.[2]

The United Kingdom has created Employment Zones where public–private partnerships pursue efforts similar to the NDYP for the long-term unemployed (these are not aimed specifically at youth). These initiatives are appreciably more flexible than the New Deal. Personal advisers may combine benefit and training money into packages that enable people to obtain the help they need to return to work. Working Links, the company that runs most Employment Zones, receives most

BOX 5.2, continued

of its payment only when a client has remained employed for 13 weeks. This approach has not only moved people into employment but also has helped create small businesses, which in turn have hired more participants in the program. Not only do Working Links advisers find jobs for about half of enrollees—about twice the number for most welfare-to-work programs—but also most participants keep their jobs longer.

1. The numbers in apprenticeship programs declined steadily in the United Kingdom between 1960 and 1990. The number of apprentices in manufacturing fell from 240,000 in 1964 to 54,000 in 1990. The Modern Apprenticeships programs was launched as a national initiative in 1995 to provide young people age 16–25 with training leading to NVQ/SVQ (National Vocational Qualification/Scottish Vocational Qualification) skills at Level 3 or more. In February 1998 there were 117,000 modern apprentices. They are regulated by training frameworks designed for each sector by employers in conjunction with the relevant National Training Organisation and the Department for Education and Skills. For more information see <http://www.lgnto.gov.uk> on National Occupational Standards.

2. Organization for Economic Cooperation and Development, *From Initial Education to Working Life: Making Transitions Work* (Paris: Organization for Economic Cooperation and Development, 2000).

CHAPTER 21

Worker Participation in Europe and East Asia

by Jacques Rojot

ABSTRACT: Worker participation encompasses a diverse array of techniques designed to enhance employees' stake in the success of their firms and ultimately in their national economies. This chapter outlines different strategies in use in Europe, an experience that could prove useful as East Asian countries move from low-wage industrialization to high-tech manufacturing, which requires a high degree of worker efficiency and initiative.

This chapter focuses on participatory schemes at the enterprise level—elements of social policy that indirectly affect countries' economic and social outcomes. The chapter's guiding framework is management theory rather than economics or political science.

Both in theory and in practice, worker participation is difficult to define. The dictionary lists several meanings for "participation," including to take part in something, to share something, to partake of some quality, and to belong to a larger entity. All those meanings apply to worker participation. We can distinguish two further aspects of participation: cooperative participation, in which all join together to work toward the same goal, and deliberative participation, in which debate and possible disagreement occur before a decision is made.

Followers of many different ideologies have advocated worker participation under various guises. For anarchists it might mean free individuals operating in perpetually changing relationships; for revolutionary socialists it might mean that every worker has an equal voice in managing an undertaking. For social democrats participation might take the shape of nationalization, through which ownership of the main means of production and exchange passes to the people; under Christian social doctrine participation implies collaboration between labor and capital toward a greater goal. Finally, managers might see participation as a tool to foster a more harmonious working relationship with workers to yield a more efficient and effective enterprise.

As might be expected, this chapter focuses on the final point of view. Even then another misunderstanding occurs in that worker participation unavoidably addresses power but is often confused with full and unquestioning cooperation by employees with the goals of management. As with all industrial relations, participation involves a mix of conflict and cooperation and enables parties to manage temporarily an opposition of interests.

Forms of Worker Participation in Europe

Worker participation includes at least six possible strategies for a firm:

- Job and organizational redesign and improvements in the quality of life at work
- Involvement of employees in managerial decisionmaking
- Employee sharing in profits or cost reductions
- Employee ownership
- Employee identification with the company
- Promotion of corporate citizenship

Job and Organizational Redesign and Improvement of Quality of Life at Work

The working hypothesis behind this strategy is dual. First, employees will perform better when their work is useful, interesting, and meaningful, and when they hold well-designed jobs for which they are well qualified. Further, when they understand the meaning and usefulness of their work, workers will develop self-esteem and a feeling of achievement and thus will fulfill their potential in performing their work. The organization of work should allow workers to apply all their competence to the tasks at hand, and thus to achieve a degree of self-realization. Examples include new ways of organizing work and developing organizations, job enlargement and enrichment, ergonomics and health and safety, semi-autonomous work teams, and quality circles (when they include efforts to improve working conditions).

Quality circles are an interesting example of a double cultural twist. Designed initially by a U.S. academic expert (Deming) for managing production and later extended to the whole organization by another expert (Juran), quality circles were used extensively in post–World War II Japan and are widely credited with Japan's rapid and dramatic improvement in production and quality. The concept then recrossed the Pacific and was implemented in the United States, and it subsequently crossed the Atlantic to Western Europe. The social and lifestyle conditions prevalent in Japanese enterprises favored the growth of quality circles, but they required specific training and a change in scope in U.S. and European settings, where they have proved less successful.[1]

The conditions under which quality circles were implemented made the difference. Work groups were already common in Japanese enterprise, and Japanese managers also allowed rank-and-file employees to express new ideas more easily. The absence of sharp distinctions between negotiation, consultation, and cooperation in Japan further facilitated employee involvement.[2]

The basic techniques of a quality circle are simple. It consists of 3 to 15 employees, usually ones from the same work group or ones holding similar jobs, who meet at least monthly to share work experiences and identify and solve problems. The team is composed of volunteers who sometimes meet on their own time (formerly in Japan) or on company time (in the United States and often also in Japan nowadays). A supervisor (most often in Japan) or an emerging leader within the group (often in the United States) guides the group, and meetings occur outside the hierarchical context. Members learn basic statistical methods and receive all quality control information.

The team focuses on continuously improving the management of the work site to boost quality and achieve individual and mutual self-realization. Objectives are thus not limited to corporate goals but also include creating a workplace worthy of members of the enterprise, one that respects its human resources and contributes to limitless progress in the competence of each member. At each meeting, the group selects issues that may cause problems down the line, whose cause cannot be attributed to other work groups and whose solution can better the working environment and make work easier.

Facilitators may train members, guide the initial meetings, solve problems within the group, and serve as a liaison between the group and the staff members controlling the resources to which the group needs access. Expected results include not only better quality, more efficient and practical procedures, and reductions in waste, but also better teamwork and interpersonal relationships as well as higher wages for members.

Examples of quality circles include health and safety committees, employees' referendums, German-style *Mitbestimmung*, information and consultation schemes, and works councils (at the plant, company group, and European levels).

The quality circle concept may also encompass employee membership on the board of directors, user involvement, and, in the narrowest definition, groups exclusively geared toward improving the quality of a firm's services or products.

Employee Involvement in Managerial Decisionmaking

The hypothesis here is that employees are motivated to perform their best if they have significant input into decisions concerning their work and their fate. They can better implement decisions they help make. Moreover, nobody knows jobs better than the people who hold them, and thus they have the potential—equal to if not vastly superior to management's—to make the enterprise more efficient.

Employee involvement in managerial decisionmaking can entail variations in

- Scope: from routine work performance to overall strategy
- Extent: from basic information to an equal voice in decisionmaking
- Nature: direct or indirect, through representatives elected or appointed, union or not
- Type: from informal to highly formalized
- Level: from job-site workers to boards of directors
- Time span: from execution of decisions to their design
- Domain: from the social to the financial operations of a firm

The German system of codetermination (*Mitbestimmung*) is one significant example of this type of participation. The German system complements rather than substitutes for collective bargaining. Collective agreements establish minimum wages and conditions at a regional level, and two worker-participation channels complement this at the enterprise or plant level.

Boards of Directors

Worker representation on boards of directors is the best known but probably not the most important form of German codetermination. In Germany, unlike in the United States and most of Europe, company boards are split into two different bodies: the managing board (*Vorstand*) and the supervisory board (*Aufsichsrat*), which appoints and controls the managing board and can request detailed information but does not perform any direct management function. Three forms of worker representation on the board of directors coexist. The first is limited to enterprises with more than 1,000 employees in the mining, coal, and steel industries. Here the supervisory board generally includes 11 members (in some cases 15 or 21). Five members represent shareholders, and five represent employees;

together they elect one neutral member. Two of the employee representatives must belong to the enterprise, but the remaining three can, and often do, come from outside bodies such as union federations. In this specific model alone, workers also have a representative on the managing board.

The second model applies to certain types of enterprises such as joint stock companies that employ at least 500 employees. One-third of the members of the supervisory board, whose number depends on company size, must be workers' representatives. If worker representation exceeds two, the additional members can be outsiders chosen by the workers.

The third model applies to all enterprises with more than 2,000 employees, whatever legal form the enterprise takes. In this case the supervisory board consists of an equal number of shareholders' and workers' representatives, with the board's size depending on the number of employees working at the enterprise. Since this board has no neutral chair, the shareholders have the final word in case of deadlock because a shareholder representative chairs the board.

Works Councils

The most important feature of the German codetermination system, works councils, are compulsory in every plant with more than five employees. By law these councils represent all workers in a plant, whether or not they are union members. However, in practice the councils and the unions maintain close ties because a large majority of council members are union members. Unlike in many other countries, where works councils include management representatives, in Germany the councils are composed exclusively of workers' representatives and act as counterparts to managers. Workers elect council members for 4 years by secret ballot and may reelect the members. The size of the council depends on the number of employees. When a council exceeds 100 members, it may appoint a committee dealing with economic affairs. Multiplant (or multioffice) enterprises establish a general works council.

The purview of works councils ranges from a mere right to information and consultation to a veto over decisionmaking, to the most important: codetermination of enterprise decisions. Codetermination means that management cannot legally make any decision without the consent of the works council. Codetermination also gives both sides the right to take initiatives and to involve a conflict-resolving body in case of disagreement.

Works councils apply their participation rights in three arenas: personnel, economic, and social. Personnel matters include planning for staffing and vocational training as well as hiring, transferring, and dismissing employees. Economic matters include all aspects of the economic management of the enterprise, including investment, production, and marketing. Social matters focus on the social consequences of economic decisions. Full codetermination applies to an impressive list of social matters, including work rules, work time, pay systems, and health and safety. Works councils maintain veto power in personnel matters, but in economic matters they hold only the right to information and consultation, except where decisions might cause substantial disadvantages to the work force, such as partial or total closure of a work site or a merger of the company. In those cases management must reach a compromise with the works council. This wide range of participative powers makes the the works council central to both daily life and exceptional circumstances at a work site.

Employee Sharing in Profits and Cost Reductions

The working hypothesis is that employees will be motivated to perform their best if they feel they will benefit financially from their efforts. Examples of this form of participation include piece rates and wage individualization; suggestion boxes; profit-sharing formulas (based on profits, income, or other indexes, calculated for individual employees or for teams); and gain sharing.

France is probably the birthplace of profit sharing. The country officially recorded the first example in 1842, and it is the only European nation to require profit sharing by law. A complex web of procedures governs this multipronged system, which can include employee ownership.

Gain Sharing
This wide-ranging process applies to enterprises ranging from private sector firms to public services with an industrial or commercial purpose, without restriction on enterprise size or profit making. Gain sharing can be applied at the level of individual enterprises, components of an enterprise, or groups of enterprises. By law gain sharing must have a collective nature, but it does not have to apply to every employee.

Gain sharing must be established by one of four methods of agreement between management and employees. It may be part of a traditional collective agreement with a union, a specific agreement with representatives of a plant union, a special agreement between an employer and a works council (which may or may not be union), and a proposition by the employer ratified by two-thirds of employees (provided that at least one union agrees, if any unions exist at the plant). Specific criteria used to measure gains and compute bonuses are selected from three broad categories—profit or performance under any definition, an increase in productivity, and any mode of collective payment allowing an effective association of the employees to the enterprise—or from any mix of the three. Within that broad definition, the only real mandatory conditions are that gain sharing must be linked to a collective effort to improve the performance of the enterprise, and it must not substitute for any part of an existing wage. Gain sharing may not exceed 20 percent of an enterprise's wage bill and an individual maximum. Important tax advantages accrue to both enterprises and employees on their gain shares, particularly if employees freeze their bonuses for 5 years in an enterprise savings plan (described briefly later).

Profit Sharing

Profit sharing is compulsory by law but much more restricted in scope, applying to enterprises earning a taxable profit and employing more than 100 workers. The amount and computation of profit sharing follows a complex legal formula that now includes a fallback version. Profit sharing applies to all employees, and important tax advantages accrue to the company and employees, whose profit share is frozen for at least 5 years. A firm must introduce profit sharing through modes similar to those of gain sharing, or fiscal penalties apply. A profit-sharing firm decides how to manage the frozen bonuses. Shares may accrue in the form of company shares to employees, insured loans by employees to the enterprise for investment, investments outside the enterprise, and investments in enterprise savings plans.

Enterprise Savings Plans

All enterprises may establish enterprise savings plans, which manage voluntary contributions from employees and possible matching contributions from employers within legally established ceilings, as well as employees' profit-sharing and gain-sharing bonuses. Firms may establish enterprise savings plans through the same methods as gain-sharing plans or may do so outside any agreement. Payments into the plan are frozen for 5 years and invested in either company shares or in the stock market. Tax advantages apply to matching contributions from the enterprise and to profits reinvested for employees.

Impact of Gain Sharing and Profit Sharing

Profit sharing, which is mandatory, is more cumbersome and has had a limited impact except in large enterprises, where it is prevalent. Such schemes cover some 5 million wage earners, of whom 60 percent received a bonus recently. Interestingly, gain sharing, which is voluntary, has grown annually since a new form was established in 1986, and it is prevalent in small and medium-size businesses. Some 3 million wage earners received a voluntary bonus in recent years.

Employee Ownership

The working hypothesis is that employees will give their best performance if they feel they are investing in businesses of which they own a part. Examples include individual shareholding plans (employee stock option plan type, generally used in the United Kingdom), matching savings plans, collective shareholding plans, and deferred stock options (the last two usually only for managers or very senior managers). Scandinavian employee ownership also includes wage funds, which are countrywide or voted on by unions.

Employee Identification with the Company

The working hypothesis is that employees will identify with and remain committed to their company if they feel it has their interests and welfare at heart, or if they feel they belong to a working community that shares common values. Examples of types of participation that foster employee identification include cultural engineering, survey feedback, organizational development, enterprise projects, and perhaps total quality management, although the latter borrows features from several other types of participation.

Promotion of Corporate Citizenship

The working hypothesis is that labor is not a commodity like any other. If treated as a responsible citizen of the organization, an employee will behave like a citizen. Here the employee is considered as more than a seller of skills in a labor market or an individual in a hierarchy; he or she is also and foremost a participant in a civic order. Thus superiors must treat the employee with dignity, he or she must have a say in his or her life at work, and he or she must benefit from guarantees in the exercise of hierarchical power. Some ways to promote corporate citizenship include implementing industrial democracy in the Scandinavian meaning, establishing nonunion grievance procedures and open-door policies, appointing ombudsmen or employee delegates, and allowing appraisals of management by subordinates.

Success of European Worker Participation Strategies

None of these working hypotheses have been proven, but the abundant literature tends to indicate that such programs are often effective when sensible and applied by believers. Evidence also underlines the relative efficiency of well-implemented programs. However, the results are difficult to generalize across organizations because careful implementation is crucial. Critical success factors seem to include full organizational commitment, reliable implementation, and a clear and fair strategy.

Worker Participation in East Asia

Indonesia, the Republic of Korea, Malaysia, the Philippines, and Thailand have each adopted a strategy for industrial development that holds significance for worker participation: they have emphasized, to different degrees, export-oriented industrialization as opposed to import substitution.[3] The foremost need was formerly to structure industrial relations to dampen conflict and encourage economic development, or to attract foreign direct investment to low-wage production areas. Government—the main actor in industrial relations in these countries—therefore restricted the formation of unions, prohibited strikes in essential or export sectors, and regulated overtime.

Strategic industrialization, however, has brought these countries within the orbit of globalization. The result is growing pressure to remain competitive in a liberalized product market. Instead of focusing on low-cost production of light manufacturing goods for export, these countries are moving to higher-value products and innovation in the manufacturing process. At this stage these countries cannot remain competitive simply by controlling labor costs: they also must now rely, to an ever-larger extent, on employees able to operate complex high-tech machinery. These countries must thus pursue a strategy aimed at both boosting skills and creating a more flexible labor market.[4] The strong emphasis on education and the high level of literacy[5] in East Asia makes such a strategy possible.

Flexibility, however, entails complex tradeoffs. Flexibility can be categorized under five main headings:[6]

- *External quantitative flexibility,* which includes temporary work, short-term contracts, part-time work, call contracts, zero-hour contracts, long trial periods before definite hiring, job sharing, and massive use of government-sponsored schemes for integrating young people into the labor force
- *Externalization,* which includes buying instead of making components, using self-employed labor, contracting out work, and using independent contractors or employees "on loan" from other firms
- *Internal numerical flexibility,* which includes the use of variable and flexible working hours, night work, overtime, weekend shifts, and annualized duration of work to better modulate the volume of labor according to demand while keeping labor costs constant

- *Functional flexibility,* which includes encouraging employees to perform multiple tasks, hiring consultants, abolishing craft barriers, providing on-the-job and formal training, planning for human resource management, and improving employees' adaptability to change
- *Wage flexibility,* which links the rate of pay to a firm's financial constraints, either indirectly through mechanisms from the simple (piecework rates) to the complex (dual wage scales) or directly through unpaid overtime or pay cuts in bad times

Firms need the flexibility to manage the size and wages of their labor force, which implies the use of traditional authoritarian, Taylorist tools. Yet efficiency and high-quality production require individual initiative and a positive attitude on the part of employees because many jobs in technology-intensive environments are too complex for managers to clearly outline in advance. Management cannot simply demand or even simply pay for cooperation and initiative—they must be voluntary.[7] Firms will have to find ways to manage this contradiction, and some worker participation options may help.

Social protection in the five East Asian countries will also affect the outcome. Unemployment insurance exists and to a limited extent, only in Korea.[8] Despite an aging population and relatively early retirement age, many countries lack effective pension plans, and postcrisis plans to stimulate self-employment and create small and medium-size enterprises face significant challenges. Here again some participative tools might be useful.

Three of the six models of participation seem ill adapted to transfer to East Asia, although some features might be of interest. Promoting corporate citizenship is linked to industrial development in Western Europe and the high levels of individualism that prevail there. Fostering employee identification with the company similarly aims to introduce features already seen as more prevalent in Asia, such as widespread community spirit. Employee ownership assumes a well-developed stock market, so the approach will be less relevant in countries with numerous small enterprises and a significant informal sector. However, several forms of participation could prove particularly useful.

Participation in Decisionmaking

Worker participation can improve the quality of decisionmaking because it brings together different strands of information and enables participants to anticipate consequences. Employees also implement joint decisions faster and better because they understand them. Participatory techniques may be especially helpful when used to establish sensible criteria for unavoidable layoffs and priorities for rehiring, shorter work hours, transfers, and early retirement. The benefits of participatory methods are more obvious still in gaining meaningful and informed cooperation from employees facing complex tasks. The involvement of differing points of view also satisfies procedural justice, because those who may stand to suffer will have been heard.

Wide-ranging possibilities for such participation encompass the level (from job-site councils to national tripartite economic and social councils), extent (from simple information to codetermination), field (from personnel matters to strategic financial choices), and channels (from union to elected to appointed representatives). The German model is often credited with fostering smoother and more efficient industrial relations. Its features are closely linked to German history and social features and need considerable adaptation elsewhere, but the ideas can apply beyond Germany.

Job and Organization Redesign and Improvement of Quality of Life at Work

Employees react in a variety of negative ways to a working life that is tedious and set within an oppressive authoritarian hierarchy. Those reactions range from uncooperative attitudes to low-quality work even when the labor market prevents more active responses such as absenteeism and turnover. This is particularly true if employees' education and training create a gap between their expectations and the realities of the job. Individuals have many and varied talents; the managerial system and organizational structure can encourage them to use those talents to benefit the enterprise. Employees at the bottom of the hierarchy also have intimate knowledge of daily work unequaled anywhere else in the organization.

At the company level, options include restructuring work methods, adapting technology to the needs of employees, and redesigning the organization's social structure. Work restructuring can range from simply introducing buffer zones on assembly lines to replacing assembly lines with moving platforms, culminating in decentralized autonomous work teams. A much cited example of work redesign is the creation in Japan and the spread in Europe and North America of the "lean production model" in the automotive industry.

Employee Sharing in Profits and Cost Reductions

A clear system of profit sharing reinforces cooperation between employees and management, and appears to boost productivity.[9] Such systems do not necessarily exclude a union role, which can be instrumental in creating them and ensuring their fairness and clarity. However, profit sharing also builds expectations and puts pressure on management to improve efficiency.

Of particular interest is a combination of profit sharing with tax exemptions. Employers can deduct profit- and gain-sharing contributions from taxable income and wage taxes, so those mechanisms stimulate employment. Employees, too, can usually exclude the benefits from income tax if several years elapse before they receive them in cash. During that time the funds are invested and accrue interest, so they act as forced savings that can help mitigate the lack of retirement pensions and unemployment compensation and work to stimulate entrepreneurship.

A further possibility is to contribute frozen profit shares to enterprise savings plans. Held in the name of employees, the shares remain at the disposal of the enterprise for investment and development. Such a system, designed to build complementary pensions, has created a powerful tool for expanding enterprise capital in West Germany and could help develop young enterprises in East Asia. The contributions need to go into a general fund that protects the shares of employees if an enterprise fails.

Conclusion: Introduce Elements of Participation Carefully

It is beyond the scope of this discussion to propose a model for implementing participation schemes, but several factors can prove crucial. First, a national regulatory framework is essential. European experience shows that the more freedom to experiment these frameworks allow, the better.

Cultural features need careful consideration. References to "Confucian traditions" and other East Asian features are often too sweeping to be useful. Still, participation programs should take careful account of national characteristics, especially when they are favorable. For instance, Korea has already partially implemented labor–management councils at the enterprise level,[10] as well as a tripartite consultation procedure at the national level.[11] Malaysia could tie profit-sharing schemes to its Provident Fund.

Each country must determine the degree to which unions should be involved in any system of participation. Data on the five East Asian crisis countries indicate a low rate of unionization on average, generally around 10 percent, although this information varies with the source and reference year.[12] Plural unionism tends to be the norm, and fragmentation into multiple small bodies, as in Malaysia,[13] may make coordinated activities difficult. A large informal sector further complicates the involvement of organized labor, as does the participation of some labor movements in separatist and class struggles. Still, unions are an irreplaceable tool for collective bargaining, which in turn is essential to participation. Above all, any participation strategy needs to be multipronged, because employee participation in decisionmaking, for example, is likely to create expectations for profit sharing, organizational redesign, and a higher quality of life at work, and vice versa.

Notes

1. R. Wood, F. Hull, and K. Azumi, "Evaluating Quality Circles: The American Application," *California Management Review* 26, no. 1 (1983): 37–53.

2. T. Hanami, *Managing Japanese Workers* (Tokyo: Japan Institute of Labor, 1991).

3. S. Kuruvilla, "Linkages between Industrialization Strategies and Industrial Relations/Human Resource Policies: Singapore, Malaysia, the Philippines, and India," *Industrial and Labor Relations Review* 49, no. 4 (1996).

4. S. Kuruvilla and C. Erickson, "The Impact of Globalization on Industrial Relations in Asia: A Comparative Review and Analysis" (paper presented to the 12th World Congress of the International Industrial Relations Association, Tokyo, May 29–June 2, 2000).

5. I. Gough, "Welfare Regimes in East Asia and Europe" (paper presented at the parallel Asia-Europe Meeting (ASEM) session to the Annual World Bank Conference on Development Economics Europe 2000, Paris, June 27, 2000). (See Chapter 1.)

6. J. Rojot, "National Experiences in Labour Market Flexibility," in *Labour Market Flexibility, Trends in Enterprises,* ed. Organization for Economic Cooperation and Development (OECD) (Paris: OECD, 1989).

7. Ibid.

8. G. Bechterman, "Labor Market Impacts of the East Asian Economic Crisis" (paper presented to the 52nd Annual Conference of the Industrial Relations Research Association, January 6–10, 2000, Boston, Joint Seminar with the North American Economics and Finance Association on International Perspectives on Unemployment); Gough, op. cit.

9. A. Le Roux, "L'Intéréssement des salariés: contribution à l'identification des conditions de succès," (doctoral thesis, Université de Paris 1, 1999).

10. Chi Sun Kim, "South Korea," monograph in the *International Encyclopedia for Labor Law and Industrial Relations* (Deventer, Netherlands, and Boston, Mass.: Kluwer, 1995).

11. D. Campbell, "Recovery from the Crisis: The Prospects for Social Dialogue in East Asia" (paper presented to the 12th World Congress of the International Industrial Relations Association, Tokyo, May 29–June 2, 2000. For example, compare G. Bechterman, op. cit., with P. Arudsothy, "Malaysia," monograph in the *International Encyclopedia for Labor Law and Industrial Relations* (Deventer, Netherlands and Boston, Mass.: Kluwer, 1995).

12. Compare G. Bechterman, op. cit., with S. Kuruvilla and C. S. Venkataratnam, "Economic Development and Industrial Relations: The Case of South and South East Asia," *Industrial Relations Journal* 27, no. 1 (March 1996), for instance.

13. P. Arudsothy, op. cit.

CHAPTER 22

Public Employment Services in Europe and Asia

by Ruud Dorenbos

ABSTRACT: In Europe, public employment services play a key role in fighting unemployment. This chapter explores programs and institutions across the continent that help job seekers find work. The chapter also examines public employment services in East Asia and highlights future needs and options in both regions.

This chapter reviews European experience with public employment services (PES), which help people prepare for and find decent work. PES activities cover a wide variety of tasks, including identifying job openings, helping job seekers assess employment opportunities, and matching job seekers with employers. All Western European countries pursue PES activities, and they are becoming more important in transition and developing countries, including East Asia.[1]

Rationale for Public Employment Services

Unemployment and unfilled labor demand often occur side by side, even in relatively homogeneous segments of the labor market such as submarkets for a specific profession in a specific region. Thus, unemployment—in this situation called "equilibrium" or "frictional unemployment"—prevails. Surplus labor supply or high excess demand may also persist, with many countries facing persistently high unemployment known as "structural unemployment." Employment services are a key instrument for addressing such structural problems in the labor market.

Government does not always have to provide such services; in many countries private placement and training agencies step in. However, PES constitute a large share of the employment services market in many countries, and most analysts recognize that PES can solve problems that the market cannot:[2]

- Private agencies cannot provide the collective good of improving transparency in the labor market because they view information on job seekers and vacancies as a proprietary asset.
- Private agencies serve only some employers and the few job seekers who can afford them.
- Long-term unemployed need sheltered jobs[3] and government aid.
- Placement services may benefit from economies of scale that only the government can provide.
- Private services may exploit weak and inexperienced participants in the labor market.
- In European Union (EU) countries, many job seekers receive unemployment benefits, and the government must review eligibility criteria such as availability for work and job search intensity.

These arguments suggest that governments play an important role in the employment services market, though the important contributions of private employment agencies to the functioning of labor markets have gained growing recognition.

Scope of PES Responsibilities

Public employment services usually focus on two main objectives: to make the labor market function more efficiently, and to promote equal opportunities for different groups of job seekers. PES originally linked job seekers and vacancies by providing information and brokering matches. However, with the rise in unemployment in Europe, fewer vacancies are available to serve the unemployed. When full employment is unattainable, countries can at least try to avoid a situation where unemployment hurts some groups more than others, so PES now promote equal opportunities and try to prevent long spells of unemployment.

PES typically include the following:[4]

- Providing information on both the current and future labor market
- Offering information on occupational and educational choices

- Brokering jobs
- Implementing active labor market policies, which can include training, placement, and job subsidies
- Managing the selection of participants in such services and administering unemployment benefits

PES may also play a central role in promoting coherence among labor market policies, though the Ministry of Labor often performs this task. In some countries PES also include responsibilities in immigration and job protection.

Each European country handles these tasks differently. For example, in Greece PES rather than employers nominate half the candidates for subsidized hirings. In Ireland PES post job descriptions, job seekers ask for more details, and job officers select suitable candidates—an approach that may better meet the needs of both job seekers and employers. In Portugal PES use computer programs, self-service techniques, and the Internet to quickly match job seekers with jobs.[5]

Institutional Structure

In most European countries PES is a department of the central government, usually the Ministry of Labor (see Table 22.1).[6] Only in Australia has a private corporation replaced PES, which contracts with private, community, and public sector agencies to place unemployed people in jobs.[7] Public services may operate as a fully integrated part of the Ministry of Labor or as a separate executive agency.

The PES head is normally accountable to the minister regarding objectives, resources, and performance. The minister maintains direct control over PES if they are fully integrated into the department.[8] However, services for job seekers and employers have become more important, and government organizations are rarely known for being client friendly. PES may also suffer from arbitrary political intervention, leading to unsound business decisions. Structuring PES as an executive agency within a government department solves most of those problems, but success depends on a good working relationship between the minister and the head of PES.

In most EU countries, the government and social partners such as unions and employers jointly administer PES. This allows PES to gain the partners' trust and inclines them to include target job seekers in their collective agreements. However, this presupposes a well-developed system of industrial relations, and even then individual employers may not offer jobs to targeted groups. The success of this popular model depends on mutual understanding among ministers,

Table 22.1 Employment Services in Europe

	Administrative structure	Concentration/ deintegration	Centralization/ decentralization	Financing	Unemployment benefits	Private employment services
Belgium (ONEM)[a]	ONEM implements measures drafted by three directorates of the Employment Administration.	Three regions are responsible for placing workers in three subdivisions of ONEM and for vocational training. The federal government is responsible for social security.	A central office regulates and monitors regional and community offices.	Financing is partly public and partly from unemployment insurance funds.	Under federal law, ONEM is responsible for distributing unemployment benefits.	Private employment services are allowed (state monopoly was abolished in the 1990s). Like in the Netherlands, temporary work agencies are the most important private organizations in the recruiting process.
Denmark (AF)[b]	Ministry of Labor manages PES indirectly through National Labor Market Authority. Tripartite commissions participate in management at national and regional level.	Labor market policies and services are usually separated, but regional offices can decide on their own structure.	Councils at regional level have considerable influence. Some conflicts with the national goals of the Ministry of Labor and National Labor Market Authority have emerged.	Direct expenses are financed by general taxation through the Ministry of Labor. Part of the costs of services can be charged to employers. Unemployment insurance is financed through general taxation and compulsory employee contributions.	Ministry of Labor administers unemployment benefits, with tight supervision by PES and ministry of benefits and sanctions for refusing suitable work. PES implement "activation" obligations after people have received insurance benefits for 2 years.	PES monopoly was abolished in 1990. No restrictions exist for private employment services.

Finland (VTML)[c]	Ministry of Labor manages PES at regional and local levels. Tripartite council for labor affairs advises the ministry.	Concentration of services is high. PES aim to provide employers and job seekers with one contact person or division.	Decisions concerning placement into subsidized jobs and other selective employment measures have been delegated to regional and local offices.	State finances the flat rate unemployment allowance. Unemployment insurance benefits are cofinanced by the state, employers, and employees, and the state finances active labor market policies.	A different ministry pays insurance benefits, but PES offices retain the power to determine recipients' availability for work and thus eligibility for benefits. PES have little influence over municipalities' decisions concerning social assistance benefits.	Private agencies may not charge fees to workers for services aimed at employment.
Germany (BA)[d]	Ministry of Labor and Social Affairs provides legal supervision. Tripartite system directly influences the BA's purpose and the way it operates	PES are responsible for job brokering, vocational guidance, unemployment compensation, and active labor market policies, but these divisions are rather separated.	Local PES offices are tightly supervised by headquarters but also have growing responsibility. The self-governing principle is systematically applied at all administrative levels.	Financing is partly public and partly from unemployment insurance funds. Budgets are prepared mainly by the agencies and approved by the federal government.	Unemployment insurance is managed within the PES administrations. Recipients must register at PES and be available for work. Social assistance is administered by different Lander.	Private employment services are allowed but only employers pay fees.

continued on next page

Table 22.1, continued

	Administrative structure	Concentration/ deintegration	Centralization/ decentralization	Financing	Unemployment benefits	Private employment services
Greece (OAED)[e]	An independent agency manages PES. The impact of social partners is relatively limited owing to conflicts between employers and trade unions.	Despite formal integration, PES functions are largely separated.	Regional offices have administrative autonomy, and decentralization is increasing.	Largest part comes from employer and employee contributions, with substantial support from ESF. Some financial support comes from the general taxation through the Ministry of Labor.	Unemployment benefits are administered by PES, but people entitled to benefits can maintain their claims through the local benefit office and sign on with no obligation to visit employment offices regularly.	PES enjoys a quasi-monopoly. Since 1931 private employment services operating on a commercial basis (not nonprofit organizations) have been banned.
Ireland (LES)[f]	PES is an independent agency. The impact of social partners is relatively high owing to consensus between employers and trade unions.	PES focus mainly on vocational training, but different managers oversee each PES function. Local offices have a higher concentration of functions.	LES is decentralized by design, but basic reporting requirements are centralized. Within the main PES agencies, decisionmaking authority at the lower level is limited.	Unemployment benefits are financed through a global social insurance fund (employers, employees, and self-employment contributions). The state may add extra funds. Active labor market policies are mainly financed by FAS. Unemployment assistance is financed by the general taxation.	Unemployment benefits are administered by a separate office network. Registration with FAS or LES is not a condition for benefit receipt.	Temporary employment agencies and private placement agencies are allowed to operate under license. FAS and private agencies cooperate by advertising vacancies in local offices.

Italy (SCI)[g]	Ministry of Labor manages PES offices at all levels. Tripartite commissions play an important role at all levels.	PES services are rather separated.	Legislation establishes the duties of regional and local offices, but each level has some autonomy.	Social security payments are handled by INPS. Employers pay most unemployment benefits. Employment subsidy and grant programs are financed through the general budget. Training is financed by the regional government and European Social Fund (ESF).	INPS directly handles payment of special benefits, such as in case of effective dismissal, but SCIs handle ordinary unemployment benefits.	Private agencies are not allowed in Italy, with the exception of some headhunting offices.
The Netherlands (Arbeidsvoorziening)	Arbeidsvoorziening is supervised by the Ministry of Employment and Social Affairs. Some parts of Arbeidsvoorziening are independent.	Although divisions perform different tasks, they cooperate closely and often reside in the same building.	Although divisions perform different tasks, they cooperate closely and often reside in the same building.	Financing is partly public and partly from unemployment insurance funds.	Unemployment benefits are regulated by several separate divisions that will become one-stop centers.	Private employment services are allowed, and some divisions of Arbeidsvoorziening are also being privatized.

continued on next page

Table 22.1, continued

	Administrative structure	Concentration/ deintegration	Centralization/ decentralization	Financing	Unemployment benefits	Private employment services
Portugal (IEFP)[h]	Ministry of Labor and Solidarity has overall responsibility for PES. A permanent council for social cooperation that includes the government, trade unions, and employer associations has an advisory role.	PES deconcentrated into 6 divisions, although they overlap.	IEFP has been given national targets for direct job creation. The targets are distributed across regions and offices.	Labor market policy is financed out of the global social insurance fund: contributions from employers, employees, and the self-employed. A small percentage of value added tax also goes to the fund. IEFP receives 4.7% of the fund's annual income. ESF and the European Regional Development Fund are also principal sources of income.	Unemployment benefits are administered by a separate office network with local offices. Integration of benefit and placement functions is extensive.	Temporary work agencies and private placement agencies operate under license and supervision and must notify PES of vacancies filled on a biannual basis.

Sweden (Af)[i]	National Labor Market Board (AMS), which falls under the Ministry of Labor, is responsible for employment services.	Sweden has a one-stop entry service, which means that all measures are available through the same organization.	AMS lays down general guidelines for employment services, but employment services decide how to implement them.	Financing is partly public and partly from unemployment insurance funds. ESF pays a small part of active labor market policies.	Unemployment insurance funds or trade unions administer unemployment benefits.	Private employment services for assisting and hiring out labor are prohibited from requiring payment from employed or unemployed job seekers.

a. ONEM = Office National de l'Emploi

b. AF = Arbejdsformidlingen

c. VTML = Valtion Työmarkkinalaitos

d. BA = Bundesanstalt für Arbeit

e. OAED = Labor Force Employment Organization

f. LES = Local Employment Service

g. SCI = Sezione Circoscrizionale per l'Impiego

h. IEFP = Instituto do Empreso e Formaçao Profissional

i. Af = Arbetsförmedlingen

Sources: OECD, *The Public Employment Service—Denmark, Finland, Italy* (Paris: 1996), and OECD, *The Public Employment Service—Greece, Ireland, Portugal* (Paris: 1998).

EXHIBIT 22.1
Tripartism in Italy and Ireland

A high degree of tripartism, such as in Italy, can contribute to relative neglect of the weakest unemployed. In Italy tripartite influences have worked to focus both unemployment benefits and active placement efforts on victims of collective layoffs, rather than on people from small firms who have lost work or those who have been unable to find a first job.

In Ireland area-based partnerships in disadvantaged regions address economic disintegration and offer a new framework for creating jobs and fighting persistent unemployment. A partnership run by an 18-member board includes public employment services, social partners, and community groups.

---

social partners, and PES leadership. In Greece, for example, the impact of social partners is limited by conflicts between employers and trade unions. In Ireland, in contrast, partners' impact is strong because of a high degree of consensus between employers and trade unions (see Exhibit 22.1).

Countries have often had to adjust PES organizations to accommodate new employment and labor market policies, decentralized government activities, integration of social services, and competition in delivering them.

Integrating Public Employment Services

Integrating job counseling, unemployment benefits, and active labor market programs is desirable,[9] but the same institution need not deliver them (see Exhibit 22.2 and Table 22.1). Sweden, for example, combines job counseling, training, and labor market measures but leaves unemployment insurance to trade unions.[10] In Germany and the Netherlands municipalities play a key role in implementing job-creation schemes for the long-term unemployed, because such individuals often rely on social assistance handled by municipalities. However, since municipalities lack the expertise to place unemployed persons in unsubsidized jobs, cooperation between municipalities and PES is essential.[11]

Two new approaches help in organizing service integration:[12] customer-focused integration, also known as one-stop centers, and tiered service delivery. One-stop centers can integrate aid and quickly resolve problems for unemployed people. The U.S. government has been a pioneer of this approach, and France, the Netherlands, Sweden, and the United Kingdom, have recently set

---

EXHIBIT 22.2

Integration of Public Employment Services in Greece and Ireland

In Greece public employment services (PES) formally integrate placement, benefit administration, and referrals into active labor market programs. However, people can sign up for and maintain their benefits through the local benefit office with no obligation to visit employment offices regularly. So despite formal integration, PES functions retain a degree of separation.

In Ireland, the social benefit network administers some types of subsidies for hiring and the employment office network administers others. Differences in culture and attitude between the two administrations have complicated strategic planning and made it difficult for staff to provide clients with information and advice on the full range of programs.

---

up one-stop centers. The tiered delivery approach tailors PES services to the needs of job seekers and employers,[13] which means that those in greatest need can receive the most assistance.

Centralized versus Decentralized Structure

Most European countries have decentralized PES, often by giving regional PES boards autonomy (see Table 22.1). Decentralization makes services more accessible and targets them to specific regional needs, but central management provides less detailed oversight. Sound policy guidelines and trust in local judgment are therefore essential prerequisites. Too much decentralization can lead to uncertainty among job seekers and employers about what they can expect from PES, and practical problems may occur when regional PES organizations use different information systems. A highly decentralized structure introduced in the Netherlands in 1991 faced such problems. As a result, the government reduced the autonomy of the regional PES boards after 4 years, though they still have considerable freedom in choosing the mix of policies and determining how to implement them (see Exhibit 22.3).

Managing Unemployment Benefits

Administering unemployment benefits through PES, as in Austria, Germany, Japan, and Norway, can enable the system to identify highly motivated or unmotivated job searchers and to adjust regulations to motivate people to accept jobs

---

EXHIBIT 22.3

Decentralization in Finland, Denmark, and the United Kingdom

In Finland and Denmark decentralization combined with monitoring of procedures and rewards for performance has encouraged regional managers to follow national strategies and have perhaps motivated staff. Most important, decentralization has helped managers adapt labor market strategies to local needs.

In the United Kingdom locally administered job-search programs have allowed staff to maintain close contact with both clients and employers. This cooperation helps in tracking labor market trends. So for example, as part-time jobs have grown, they have been pushed as an attractive option for young people.

---

and employers to hire them. Such a structure may also encourage administrative efficiency and improve monitoring. However, disadvantaged groups normally rely on social assistance rather than on unemployment benefits, which municipalities usually provide, so PES may pay less attention to people who need help the most (see Exhibit 22.4 and Table 22.1).

Some analysts favor close administrative relationships between unemployment benefits, PES, and local one-stop functions.[14] In the Netherlands, one-stop offices register newly unemployed persons and use the information to determine enrollees' benefits and their "distance" to the labor market, which determines the assistance they receive for reintegrating into the market.

Integrating unemployment benefits with PES is particularly important in countries facing mass unemployment. However, such integration can produce unexpected and dramatic results. For example, the initial version of Poland's unemployment compensation system caused an "added-worker effect": all registered unemployed people were eligible for unemployment benefits, they need not have been previously employed, and the entitlement period was open ended. This encouraged many "secondary workers"—household members not included in the labor force under the centrally planned government—to enter the labor market. The number of unemployed people registering in the labor offices was thus greater than the number who were laid off. To avoid paying unemployment benefits to people who were actually outside the labor market, Poland quickly modified the eligibility criteria.

EXHIBIT 22.4

Combining Unemployment Benefits with Public Employment Services in Portugal, Ireland, and Finland

The Organization for Economic Cooperation and Development reports that in countries where people must register with public employment services (PES) to receive unemployment benefits, more unemployed participate in PES. In Portugal, this has helped raise the proportion of the unemployed who register with PES to high levels. In Ireland, where such an obligation does not exist, only about half of the unemployed register for PES, making it difficult for job counselors to quickly match job seekers with vacancies.

In Finland unemployed workers often refuse to enter training or accept short-term jobs because doing so resets their unemployment duration at zero. Because PES staff members allocate subsidized jobs according to how long people have been unemployed, this greatly reduces their chances of receiving a subsidized job. This interaction between benefit administration and the allocation of subsidized jobs does not promote efficiency in labor market services.

Financing

Most EU countries finance active labor market policies and unemployment insurance benefits through both general revenues and employer and employee contributions. The European Union also finances a significant portion of active labor market policies (Table 22.1).

In Germany, employees' and employers' contributions largely finance the PES, Bundesanstalt für Arbeit (BA). The BA has its own budget, which requires the approval of the federal government. The BA transfers any budget surplus to the reserve fund and draws on the fund to cover budget deficits. The federal government provides the liquidity needed to balance the accounts in the form of an interest-free loan. The BA uses its funds mainly to provide unemployment benefits and active labor market services such as vocational training, vocational rehabilitation of persons with disabilities, and promotion of job creation.

In Greece and Portugal, employer and employee social security contributions similarly finance unemployment benefits and a large portion of active labor market policies, although the European Social Fund and the European Regional Development Fund (Portugal) also finance employment subsidies and vocational training. The PES agency in Greece (OAED) operates its own budget, though ministerial decrees specify spending targets for active labor market policies in consultation with the OAED board of directors. EU funds are channeled to OAED through the labor ministry.

PES in Portugal (Instituto do Empreso e Formação Profissional—IEFP) prepare the annual budget based on projected social security contributions, the ministry's spending targets, and budget submissions by regional directorates. After assessments from the governing board and the supervisory commission, the central office decides how much will go to regional directorates in detailed program categories. Each region then manages its own budget (see Exhibit 22.5).

In Ireland, unemployment insurance benefits are financed through the social insurance fund, which collects contributions from employers, employees, and the self-employed. The state may add a small subsidy from the general budget. The proportion of the fund allocated to paying unemployment insurance varies according to need. Assistance for job seekers entitled to no or reduced insurance benefits accounts for over three-quarters of spending on unemployment benefits, entirely financed—like other social assistance programs—through general taxation.

In Denmark, Finland, and Italy, insurance contributions partly fund employment services but do not cover labor market policies. General taxation covers direct expenses such as staff wages through the Ministry of Labor. In the Scandinavian countries PES now can ask for fees from employers.

Measuring Market Shares and Output

Placing job seekers is usually seen as the core business of PES. However, employers advertize and fill vacancies, and job seekers look for and find jobs, through avenues other than PES, so the role of PES in this placement market is of interest. PES may execute the brokering function through various means.[15] Active brokering entails a large role for the job officer, who when notified of an opening contacts suitable candidates and selects some for an interview. This method quickly connects job seekers with jobs, but it requires heavy staff input.

Under semi-open advertising, job seekers can ask for more details regarding an advertised vacancy and job description at PES, and a job officer selects suitable candidates. This method may be more successful in meeting the preferences of both job seekers and employers.

Under fully open advertising, PES make public all details regarding vacancies, but job seekers must take all further action. This can occur through self-service job shops where job seekers can find information through billboards and computers. Job seekers can contact a PES officer for more information or address

EXHIBIT 22.5
Budget Allocations to Regional and Local Offices in Portugal

In Portugal indicators such as working-age population and number of registered and long-term unemployed are used to determine regional budgets for public employment services. Each region then manages its own budget. The national budget is usually revised twice a year. In the course of the year, requests for adjustment usually come from the regional directorates after feedback from their local offices. The headquarters agency may authorize transfers of funds between regional budgets, and regional directorates themselves can shift funds. However, any funding shifts between training centers and employment services must be decided at the national level. This process of budgetary adjustment in consultation with various bureaucratic layers allows a flexible response to local needs and program take-up.

the company directly. A disadvantage is that it is difficult for PES to determine the status of vacancies and whether information provided by PES helped a company fill a vacancy or a job seeker find a job.

Data from the Organization for Economic Cooperation and Development (OECD) show that PES market shares vary from less than 5 percent of all hires in the United States and Switzerland to around 30 percent in the United Kingdom and Italy. The average market share is 16.4 percent, which means that almost 85 percent of placements occur through other search and recruitment channels. Those channels include newspaper advertisements and informal channels as well as private placement agencies.

Measuring Impact

Countries commonly use market shares, registration rates, and filling rates to measure the impact of PES, though not all are meaningful. Job matching is only one type of PES activity and may thus not convey the actual impact of services. PES are most important as a search channel for individual job seekers, especially the unemployed. Indicators of the net output or net impact of PES—the degree to which PES activities make a difference in the functioning of labor markets—are still needed. The answers to two questions can shed light on net impact:

- Do PES activities increase the total number of filled vacancies?
- Do PES activities lead to more equality in employment opportunities?

Recent analysis indicates that PES activities exert a limited impact on the functioning of the labor market.[16] The evidence suggests that they help improve the labor market situation of disadvantaged groups such as the long-term unemployed, but deadweight, substitution, and displacement effects are high even among those groups.

To maximize net output, PES often give high priority to people who have difficulty finding a job. Placement activities are often insufficient, so PES usually offer training and placement subsidies. PES may outsource some of these activities to external agencies. People trained with a PES subsidy or who receive other PES services may find jobs through search channels other than PES. However, those cases do not count as PES placements, so the placement concept may not prove useful.

PES should not concentrate entirely on disadvantaged groups for two reasons. Some labor market shortcomings such as lack of information and underinvestment apply to most participants. And concentrating entirely on disadvantaged groups might discourage employers from registering their vacancies with PES.

Evaluating Public Employment Services

Evaluations of public employment services are indispensable in justifying and improving them. The three evaluation phases include ex-ante evaluation, evaluation during implementation (performance evaluation), and ex-post evaluation (impact evaluation).[17] Most studies have focused on the impact of active labor market policies on the employment and earnings of unemployed job seekers. Studies of PES in Canada, Hungary, Poland, the United Kingdom, and the United States can shed light on the effectiveness of these services.[18]

In Hungary and Poland an evaluation of the impact of specialized employment services (ES) on employment and earnings suggested that the ES did not exert a significant impact.[19] However, if the economy is improving, some subgroups who chose to use ES assistance—particularly women—fared significantly better than those who did not. The results underscored that ES consisted of more than job referral.[20] In Hungary ES acted as a one-stop shopping center for all forms of reemployment services as well as income support for the unemployed; administrative costs per person were relatively small.

In the United Kingdom an evaluation of state employment services indicated that most job seekers used more than one method of job search[21] and that use of PES is countercyclical, with greater reliance on PES during recessions. It indicated that job centers exert the most beneficial impact on groups who tend to make more use of them—the less skilled and the long-term unemployed. The evaluation further showed that the use of job centers raised the probability that people would move from unemployment to employment. Another study showed that job seekers who turn to PES over other job-search methods had shorter unemployment spells than those who did not.[22]

An examination of 18 evaluations of job-search assistance/employment services concluded that job-search assistance is one of the most successful active labor market programs.[23] In general, such assistance costs little. Not surprisingly, however, the results depended significantly on whether the economy was growing and on the availability of public funds.[24]

All studies indicate that PES activities lead to private payoffs—that is, PES help integrate the unemployed back into work, especially the long-term unemployed. However, the studies did not examine whether PES are meeting their goal in the most efficient way and, therefore, whether they should be the main actors in employment services. Nor did evaluations assess program design and implementation, staffing, and intensity and quality of services—all of which help determine whether employment services will succeed.

Most Western European countries have reached social consensus on the desirability of employment services: their right to exist does not depend on their effects, and measurement of success or failure is designed to improve their efficiency. However, the questions surrounding PES can be broader in transition and developing countries because immature institutions can produce unsuccessful outcomes. Nonetheless, overall, the administrative costs of PES per unemployed person are relatively small, whereas the social value of PES services is large.

Role of Private Employment Services

Until the 1990s regulations were so tight in most European countries that few private job placement agencies existed because they were restricted to specific segments of the labor market. However, Australia, Switzerland, the United Kingdom, and the United States, have a long history of private job placement services, while other countries such as the Netherlands have allowed commercial temporary work agencies.[25] In the 1990s many European countries abolished the state monopoly in job brokerage. In most cases PES continued to exist as a government-funded organization, but job-placement activities and efforts to reintegrate target groups were privatized (see Table 22.1).

This partial privatization of PES activities stemmed from several factors. Dissatisfaction with PES pushed employers toward other channels of placement, constraints on public spending hurt PES, and people became convinced that private companies can produce higher-quality products and services more efficiently.

The "carrier-wave theory" holds that PES help the disadvantaged only when the services retain a high market share because only then will employers register their vacancies with PES. If PES concentrate their activities on the disadvantaged, companies will be reluctant to list their vacancies. If this theory holds, it would not make sense to allow PES to compete with private placement services. However, private employment services do not necessarily reduce the market share of PES,[26] because many unemployed persons have to register with PES to receive unemployment benefits. This gives PES a clear advantage over private competitors. Furthermore, PES can offer services for free, whereas employers have to pay for private employment services. PES may therefore continue to play their traditional role even when the state monopoly in job brokerage is abolished. The roles of public and private employment services may become more complementary, with PES concentrating more on the disadvantaged. This is a third model between state monopoly and maximum private sector involvement (see Exhibit 22.6).

Data on private placement services are scarce, particularly in transition and developing countries. However, the expectation is that the role of private job placement agencies will grow. Transition and developing countries should devote extra attention to the legal and regulatory framework governing private employment agencies.

Although the market for job placement on a purely commercial basis may be limited in many countries, governments can enhance the role of the private sector. In the extreme case, a job network of private, community, and governmental organizations can replace PES, as occurred in Australia. Because agencies receive a fee for each unemployed person they place in a job and win extra fees for placing long-term unemployed, the system is strongly driven by outcomes. The Australian government took considerable risks in introducing this far-reaching reform in a short time span,[27] and employment ministers all over the world will follow the pioneering step closely.[28]

The Netherlands has pursued a more cautious approach, with reintegration activities still publicly financed but implementation outsourced to private companies. In this model the government still plays an important role because it finances employment services, prioritizes labor market reintegration measures, chooses among competing bids, and regulates the employment services sector.

EXHIBIT 22.6

Collaboration between Private and Public Employment Services in Sweden, Switzerland, and the Netherlands

In Sweden public employment services (PES) accept advertisements for their vacancy lists from private agencies if the advertisements include information on employers or if PES are familiar with the listing firms. This allows PES to offer services to a broader public, because private agencies have established themselves in areas that PES have been unable to supply or that would be inappropriate for PES intervention.

In Switzerland private employment agencies predate PES, and the law expressly calls for collaboration between public and private placement agencies. Facing growing unemployment, the government encouraged regional placement offices and private employment agencies to exchange information on vacancies and job seekers and provided common training to both partners. The regional offices also have the option of contracting with private agencies to provide services.

Representatives of both public and private placement agencies initially expressed fears and reservations. Local governments were especially concerned that private agencies would confine their efforts to the most easily placed workers, leaving the regional placement offices to contend with the most difficult-to-place job seekers and discouraging employers from contacting them. The private placement agencies, for their part, feared that the regional placement offices represented unfair competition, since they were subsidized by the state. Thanks to a working group that brings the parties together regularly to discuss problems and determine how best to collaborate, those reservations have practically disappeared.

In the Netherlands a public–private partnership begun in 1995 resulted in a joint venture between PES and two private organizations to deliver services to employers in the area of temporary work.

In all these cases cooperation has broadened the expertise of both public and private employment agencies and enhanced the ability of job seekers to obtain the information they seek on vacancies and training.

With the rapid growth of private employment agencies, public and private operators have had to cooperate. Such cooperation can take many forms, including detailed contractual arrangements, more general contracts with close monitoring of financial results, informal arrangements organized at the local level, or some combination of the three. Complementary arrangements between the public and private sectors are most appropriate for specific labor market segments and services.

Future Directions

Globalization, enhanced competition, technological development, and changing state roles are bringing profound changes to PES as former bureaucratic organizations move toward customer-oriented services. Changing labor markets are also forcing PES to rethink their institutional role, working methods, and goals.

Setting Priorities for Concerted Action

The new EU employment policy focuses on PES, and the 1998 employment guidelines define four major pillars (see Exhibit 22.7).[29]

EXHIBIT 22.7
EU Employment Guidelines 1998

Public employment services (PES) are a key institutional component of the 1998 European employment guidelines and are based on four pillars:

- *Improving employability.* The 1998 guidelines assign a high priority to improving the employability of the unemployed. PES are directly and indirectly responsible for assisting job seekers by providing counseling in job-search techniques, establishing work and training incentives, and improving access to training and work experience.
- *Developing entrepreneurship.* The employment guidelines call for encouraging self-employment and job creation in social services and other activities that serve needs that the market does not yet recognize.
- *Encouraging the adaptability of businesses and their employees.* Aside from helping the unemployed, PES need to manage structural change within enterprises and economic sectors by helping workers and employers minimize the risks of unemployment and find alternative jobs. Cooperation with social partners can help relieve potential tensions.
- *Strengthening equal opportunities between women and men.* PES should promote female participation in the labor market and more equal gender representation in occupational sectors with a traditional gender bias. PES can play important roles in improving the employment prospects of handicapped workers and fighting unequal access to jobs among racial and ethnic minorities, as well as among older and younger workers.

Promoting Access to Vacancies

PES are expected to provide ever more help to employers seeking new employees. PES in various EU countries have already introduced technological innovations and developed new ways of bringing employers and job seekers together. The Internet will potentially have the most profound implications. An interesting example is the Internet-based self-service system in Sweden, which allows applicants to search vacancies by occupation or regional municipality as well as find career information. In the Netherlands the *kansmeter* assesses the "distance" of job seekers from the labor market to help tailor employment services to their needs.

Ensuring Systematic Case Management

The European employment strategy encourages PES to focus on the individual needs of problem groups, such as youth and the long-term unemployed, through careful diagnosis. Interviews and tailor-made action plans have proven effective in preventing long-term unemployment.[30]

Coordinating Delivery of Services to Job Seekers

PES can offer a full range of labor market services such as income replacement, information, counseling, brokerage, and training. PES themselves need not perform all these tasks, but they should coordinate them.

Exploiting Synergies between PES and Other Actors

PES must not only coordinate different employment services but also interact with other participants in the labor market, such as regional and local authorities, trade unions, educational institutions, and private employment agencies.

Using PES to Facilitate International Labor Mobility

PES heads in the European Union and European Economic Area (EU/EEA) have agreed to strengthen their cooperation, with the principal aim of facilitating international labor mobility within the EU/EEA.

Employment Services in East Asia

Indonesia, the Republic of Korea, Malaysia, the Philippines, and Thailand all maintain public employment services, though they are at quite different stages.

In Korea PES are responsible for job-search assistance, vacancy tracking, and placement. They also administer unemployment benefits and offer counseling and career information. In 1998 the Korean government introduced comprehensive measures such as job retention, job creation, vocational training, job placement, and social protection to address growing unemployment. It has expanded the number of government-managed PES agencies from 52 in February 1997 to 134 in March 1999 (Table 22.2); local governments run 281 employment services.

Korea has relaxed regulations on private placement agencies, and that measure plus rising Internet use in Korea has boosted the number of private agencies. PES, too, have made use of the Internet by adapting the Canadian WorkInfoNet, an electronic labor exchange system known in Korea as Work-Net. The system aims to provide information on vacancies, training, career information, and employment policies, though in practice it gives limited information compared with the Canadian system. The Korean government is now developing databases of registered unemployed and has introduced a worker-profiling system that can be used to identify long-term unemployed early. Despite these changes, PES agencies are still considered less than efficient; counselors are inexperienced and they provide limited information.

Malaysia PES handle registration and placement, counseling services, occupational guidance, promotion of occupational mobility, and regulation of private employment agencies. Public employment agencies focus only on domestic labor, whereas private agencies include foreign labor. Private employment agencies must register under the Private Employment Agencies Licensing Unit and report regularly to PES (before the crisis quarterly, now monthly) on the number of registrations and placements. The crisis increased the need for clear labor

Table 22.2 Number of Public and Private Employment Agencies in Korea

Date	Private	Public, managed by central government	Public, managed by local government
February 1997	1,432	52	285
March 1999	1,756	134	281

Source: Korea Labor Institute, "Policy Options for Income Support and Active Labor Market Programs: A Synthesis of the Korean Experience," paper prepared for the conference "Labor Market Policy: Its Implications for East and Southeast Asia," Manila, March 1–2, 2001.

market information, as retrenchment of workers was common. PES reacted by registering those workers and making special efforts to help them find jobs. The system successfully placed many workers in 1998.

In the Philippines the economic crisis hastened the establishment of employment services. The main PES tasks are to register the unemployed, establish a national registry of labor skills, provide job placement information, and mediate employment programs and services. Under the Public Employment Service Offices Act 1998, the government aims to establish a PES office in every province, key city, and highly urbanized municipality. Those local offices are supposed to detect firms that may lay off workers and try to take measures to help both workers and firms. The government improved the labor market information system and created the Phil-Jobnet, an Internet-accessible job-matching system, in November 1998. Those who do not have direct Internet access can use public workstations in 43 regional offices. The number of PES agencies and private job agencies has grown. The latter offer paid services to job seekers and employers, locally and abroad, monitored and regulated by the government. A radio station broadcasts job openings and is collaborating with public employment services to provide other job-related information.

Thai PES offer assistance to job seekers and employers through 85 branches, 9 located in Bangkok. The branches register and place unemployed, provide job counseling and career guidance, and organize job fairs to enable employers and job seekers to meet and to provide job orientation and career guidance. PES offers a free skills test to help match job seekers to vacancies. The public employment office encourages Thais to work abroad by providing information on foreign jobs. The government supervises private agencies to protect workers from dishonest agencies. Private agencies are quite popular, especially among unskilled workers.

PES in Indonesia are responsible for registering unemployed people and for providing information to job seekers and matching them with employers. PES provide services for domestic placement only, whereas private agencies also provide placements abroad. The government strictly regulates private agencies.

Cross-Regional Experience

Much European PES experience has relevance for East Asia, though not in any mechanistic way, because institutional structures, labor market characteristics, and economic restructuring differ markedly even within countries.

(a) Improving the labor-market information system: Information technology can make labor market demand and supply more transparent and enhance the impact of PES. In the 1980s the International Labor Organization (ILO) identified four major obstacles to building labor market information capacity in developing countries: inadequate relationships between customers and producers, underuse of existing resources, an information gap in the informal sector, and inadequate understanding of methodology.[31] European PES are developing a full-fledged self-service system called EURES that will offer first-line counseling and job-brokerage services. The system, which uses the Internet and other media, makes services accessible anytime and anyplace and covers the entire European labor market. The system will be linked to easily accessible personal employment services. East Asian countries, with numerous foreign workers, might benefit from a regional approach to labor market information systems. A job database would enable employers to advertise vacancies outside their national borders, greatly enlarging the labor pool and helping PES fill vacancies.

(b) Training personnel: Labor offices in Eastern Europe have been unable to provide high-quality employment services,[32] and similar problems have arisen in East Asian countries when the number of registered unemployed rises sharply and quickly. Besides a bigger workload, labor office employees confront a relatively new problem: placing job seekers in a shrinking labor market. Counselors need more information and training. European PES prefer to hire people with backgrounds in public administration, but even they need additional training.[33] Developing and using a regional database would also require training. Determining how best to allocate funding for training staff members is critical. On-site training as well as study visits to other regions could prove beneficial.

(c) Improving services and information for job seekers and employers: Europe has substantial experience in this area, both positive and negative. Employers often consider PES clients low skilled, not very productive, and lacking the right attitude toward work. The very existence of PES can raise expectations: jobless people who otherwise might have left the market remain registered because information and counseling give them new hope of finding a job. Results, however, are the key objective, and that means producing a high job-placement rate because both job seekers and employers must see PES as responsive.

(d) Involving social partners (tripartism): PES systems in Europe that are jointly administered by the government and social partners are the most popular and successful. This structure depends on mutual understanding among ministers, social partners, and PES leadership. Such an approach, especially if it includes employers' organizations, makes PES more effective: it is difficult to provide high-quality job training without fine-tuning curricula to employers' needs. The specific role of the social partners depends on the national context, but their involvement seems especially advisable in countries with a well-developed industrial relations system.

(e) Establishing active labor market programs: Although active labor market programs appear to have limited direct impact on workers' employability and earnings, they serve important social goals. Europe has won clear consensus on the need to pursue such policies, and PES are likely to play an important role in further developing such policies in East Asia, and in targeting vulnerable groups. Programs that promote self-employment in rural and informal sectors seem especially important in East Asia, and efforts to foster entrepreneurship and micro, small, and medium-size enterprises deserve priority.

(f) Private and public employment services: Strengthening the PES system— particularly setting up an efficient labor market information system—rather than further deregulating the placement system appears to be a sensible first priority in East Asia. Governments can develop and run such information systems. The aim should be to diffuse information widely, although the government may decide to charge private placement agencies for the information they use. Government regulation of private placement services deserves careful design. European experience shows that collaboration between PES and private employment agencies can enable job seekers to obtain the information they need on vacancies and training.

(g) Flexibility: Flexibility and responsiveness in PES organizations are key, given the changing labor market.

(h) Assessing training needs: PES can play several important roles in designing and implementing training and education policies. They can monitor labor markets and observe where matching problems occur, and they can make labor

market forecasts to detect and prevent future skill shortages. PES can also provide information on the labor market to parents, children, the training and education sector, and the private sector. PES can fund occupational education and training to address mismatches in the labor market.

Conclusion

Overall, an approach aimed at counteracting unemployment and boosting employment must rest on three interlocking subsystems:

- A macroeconomic policy conducive to creating new jobs
- An active labor market policy that includes efforts to improve labor market efficiency and flexibility
- Effective coordination of programs to combat unemployment

Combining a range of policies into a cohesive program requires rigorous adaptation of the institutional framework and the willingness of policymakers from different arenas to build a strong coalition.

Notes

1. The chapter focuses on the five East Asian countries most affected by the 1997–98 crisis: Indonesia, the Republic of Korea, the Philippines, Malaysia, and Thailand.
2. H. Mosley and S. Speckesser, "Market Share and Market Segment of Public Employment Services" (discussion paper, WZB, Berlin, 1997).
3. Sheltered jobs allow the unemployed to obtain some work experience and thus improve their position in the labor market.
4. The range of PES activities varies from country to country.
5. OECD, *The Public Employment Office in Greece, Ireland, and Portugal* (Paris: OEDC, 1998).
6. P. Thuy, E. Hansen, and D. Price, *The Public Employment Service in a Changing Labour Market* (Geneva: International Labor Office, 2001).
7. Ibid.
8. Ibid.
9. *The OECD Jobs Study: Evidence and Explanations* (Paris: OECD, 1994).
10. Thuy et al., op. cit.
11. Alternatively, municipalities can hire private companies to place their clients in jobs.
12. Thuy et al., op. cit.

13. Ibid.

14. Ibid.

15. OECD, *The Public Employment Office in Denmark, Finland and Italy* (Paris: OECD, 1996).

16. J. De Koning, "Aggregate Models for Aggregate Impact Analysis," in *Labour Market Policy and Unemployment: Impact and Process Evaluations in Selected European Countries*, ed. J. De Koning and H. Mosley (Cheltenham, England: Edward Elgar, 2001).

17. J. De Koning, "Evaluation of Employment Policies: The Dutch Experience" (paper presented at the Danish Presidency Conference on the effect and Measuring of Effects in Labor Market Policy Initiatives, Kolding, Denmark, May 24–26, 1993).

18. These evaluation summaries are based on H. W. Risher and C. Fay, eds., *New Strategies for Public Pay: Rethinking Government Compensation Programs* (San Francisco: Jossey-Bass, 1997).

19. Christopher T. O'Leary, "Evaluating the Effectiveness of Active Labor Programs in Poland," Upjohn Institute Technical Report No. 98-012 (1998), and Christopher T. O'Leary, "Evaluating the Effectiveness of Active Labor Programs in Hungary," Upjohn Institute Technical Report No. 98-012 (1998).

20. O'Leary 1998, op. cit., p. 97.

21. P. Gregg and J. Wadsworth, "How Effective Are State Employment Agencies?: Job Center Use and Job Matching in Britain," *Oxford Bulletin of Economics and Statistics* 58, no. 3 (1996).

22. J. M. Thomas, "Public Employment Agencies and Unemployment Spells: Reconciling the Experimental and Non-Experimental Evidence," *Industrial and Labor Relations Review* 50, no. 4 (July 1997).

23. Amit Dar and Zafiris Tzannatos, *Active Labor Market Programs: A Review of the Evidence from Evaluations* (Washington, D.C.: Social Protection Department, Human Development Network, World Bank, 1999).

24. Ibid.

25. Firms use temporary work not only to cope with fluctuations in output but also as a recruitment device. When labor demand is rising, firms are often uncertain whether their increased need for labor is permanent. Temporary labor allows them to buy time. Firms may also be uncertain about the productivity of newly recruited workers. Firms can monitor temporary workers for some time and then decide to offer a permanent contract. Thus, even with an official state monopoly in job brokerage, private agencies can fill a considerable share of vacancies. In the Netherlands, the share of temporary work agencies was almost as high as that of the PES. In most countries, however, the market share of the private agencies was much smaller.

26. F. Buttler and U. Walwei, "Different Situational Arrangements for Job Placement," in *Institutional Frameworks and Labor Market Performance, Comparative Views on the U.S. and German Economies*, ed. F. Buttler, W. Franz, R. Schettkat, and D. Soskice (London and New York: Routledge, 1995).

27. Thuy, et al., op. cit., p. 129.

28. Thuy, et al., op. cit.

29. European Commission, *The Modernization of Public Employment Services in Europe—Three Key Documents* (Brussels: Employment and Social Affairs, Employment and European Social Fund, European Commission, 1999).

30. Ibid.

31. L. Richter, *Upgrading Labour Market Information in Developing Countries: Problems, Progress, and Prospects* (Geneva: ILO, 1989).

32. R. J. Dorenbos, "Labour Market Adjustments in Hungary and Poland" (Thesis, University of Groningen, Netherlands, 1999).

33. In several countries PES may themselves hire long-term unemployed as part of a work experience project. However, this system is not always very effective. Witness Finland, where subsidized hires lasted for only 6 months, imposing a heavy burden on experienced staff members. See OECD (1996), op. cit.

CHAPTER 23

Active Labor Market Policies in the Republic of Korea and Europe

by Bernard Gazier and Rémy Herrera

ABSTRACT: This chapter examines the effects of the 1997–98 crisis on employment in the Republic of Korea, and the safety net and active labor market policies the government pursued in response. The chapter explores "transitional labor market" policies—schemes tailored to respond to non-traditional working situations—which have recently emerged in Europe as a possible model for countries facing economic transformation.

The Republic of Korea is often cited as a capitalist success story for its part in the "Asian miracle."[1] Before the economic crisis, Korea experienced the fastest real growth in gross domestic product (an average of 8.7 percent a year from 1985 to 1995) and the lowest unemployment rate (2.0 percent in 1996) among all Organization for Economic Cooperation and Development (OECD) countries.[2] But the picture changed dramatically during the 1997–98 economic crisis, as Korea's per capita gross national product dropped from US$10,550 in 1997 to US$7,970 in 1998,[3] while its rank in purchasing power parity per capita fell from 24 to 55.

The government responded by introducing or expanding a wide range of labor market interventions and social protection programs. For example, the government broadened unemployment insurance and vocational training, wage subsidies, and job placement efforts. It also launched a public "workfare" scheme, expanded a temporary noncontributory livelihood protection program, and created a social pension scheme. The wage-subsidy program was massive, paying up to two-thirds of a worker's wage and covering 800,000 workers in 1998. But despite these extraordinary efforts, significant gaps remained.

Despite its recent high degree of government activism, Korea continues to face tight economic constraints because it belongs to a weakly integrated region, it is highly dependent on business cycles, and it has limited stabilization tools. Korea also faces classic "European problems" such as a rapidly aging work force, concerns about work incentives, and demands for flexible labor markets.[4] Europe's beginning embrace of the new concept of "transitional labor market" policies to fight unemployment may offer new possibilities for Korea and other East Asian nations.

The Impact of the Crisis on Korea's Labor Market

Open unemployment more than quadrupled in Korea between October 1997 and February 1999. This dramatic tightening of the labor market resulted from massive bankruptcies,[5] large-scale corporate restructuring, and dwindling employment in all sectors. In February 1999 unemployment peaked at 8.7 percent of the work force, with more than 1.8 million workers officially registered as unemployed.[6] Rising unemployment was accompanied by a significant fall in labor force participation rates,[7] a shift from formal jobs to informal activities, and an increase in agricultural and unpaid family employment (implying growing underemployment). Joblessness affected mostly the young and the less educated, with production workers in the industrial sector accounting for 53 percent of the newly unemployed.

The crisis also brought marked change to the composition of employment, as many workers shifted from higher-wage, indeterminate-term jobs to lower-wage, determinate-term jobs. The OECD estimated that permanent workers declined by 0.9 million people by 2000, a phenomenon "unprecedented in Korea, where legislation had limited the ability of firms to dismiss workers prior to early 1998."[8] By mid-1998, 6.5 million workers—half of the 13 million–person work force—were part-time and contingent employees.

Also, real wages fell in Korea by 12.5 percent from mid-1997 to the end of 1998, as the share of salaries in national aggregate income declined sharply from 55.0 percent in 1997 to 50.8 percent in 1998, whereas profits rose from 9.2 percent to 9.4 percent. Despite unions' relative weakness (the number of unionists fell from 1.667 to 1.402 million between 1993 and 1998), this trend led to growing labor disputes throughout the country.[9]

The Social Impact of the Crisis

Massive unemployment and sharply declining incomes caused a rapid increase in inequality. The income of the four lower quintiles of urban households declined in the first half of 1998, whereas the income of the top quintile rose steadily, thanks to higher real interest rates and favorable tax systems.[10]

Both the International Labor Organization and the United Nations Development Programme reported a rise in national poverty to more than 12 percent, corresponding to 5.5 million persons. The number of ultrapoor—households with per capita consumption less than 80 percent of the poverty line—skyrocketed from 1.1 million in 1997 to 3.0 million in 1998, and the number of marginal poor (per capita consumption of 80 percent to 100 percent of the poverty line) rose from 1.7 million in 1997 to 3.3 million in 1998.[11] The number of poor (around US$8 per capita per day) also rose from 2.8 million to 6.2 million, and the number of near poor (per capita consumption at 100 percent to 120 percent of the poverty line) expanded from 2.7 million to 4.1 million.

Korea experienced a sharp increase in the proportion of urban poor,[12] from 7.5 percent in the first quarter of 1997 to 22.9 percent in the third quarter of 1998. This rate dropped in the last quarter of 1998 but was still more than twice the rate of the precrisis period. Homelessness was widespread in Korea's largest cities, a phenomenon almost unknown before the crisis.[13]

Because public schools charge fees, at least 10 percent of unemployed low-income households withdrew their children from school from 1997 to 1998,[14] and dropouts were significant even among the upper classes.[15] These changes went in tandem with a decline in public spending on education[16] and are particularly worrying given the significant role of education and human capital in long-run economic growth.

Family transfers of funds to the poorest attenuated some of these effects; some 50 percent of unemployed relied on family support. However, the crisis damaged the traditional family structure itself, as indicated by marked increases in domestic violence, divorce, child abandonment, and abuse. Suicides climbed from a monthly average of 620 in 1996 to more than 900 in 1998. The crisis exerted other socially destabilizing impacts: crime rose by 17.2 percent and violent offenses by 14.5 between 1997 and 1998, and property crimes committed by youth under age 18 rose by 17.5 percent. Those indicators show the dire plight of many Koreans and widespread social unrest.

Korea's Social Assistance and Labor Market Policies

The Korean government pursued an austerity program that included slowing inflation and controlling the money supply (by tightening credit, raising interest rates, increasing savings, and removing indexation); reducing budget deficits (by raising taxes and cutting expenditures and subsidies for the public sector); and balancing foreign payments (by devaluing the exchange rate). Encouraged by international financial institutions, Korea integrated this austerity program into efforts to liberalize financial, public, and labor markets through privatization, deregulation, and openness to foreign capital.

Despite continuing doubts about the necessity of a welfare state in Korea, the government also decided to implement a series of programs to assist low-income unemployed households with few assets. One such program was Support for Living Costs, Temporary Livelihood Protection, which included loans for housing and new businesses, as well as assistance with tuition and school lunches.

The Livelihood Protection Program, designed to assist people "unable to work, such as the handicapped, the elderly, and children," strictly excludes unemployed people and those whose income exceeds about 20 percent of the average nonfarm wage or who have family members capable of helping them. Although this program cost 1.45 billion won in 1999—compared with 1.50 billion won devoted to unemployment benefits—the average allowance remained well below the national poverty line. In 1999, for example, benefits ranged from US$44 to US$124 per person per month.[17] Many analysts stress this program's inefficiency: "the incremental budget of the Korean Livelihood Protection Program only reached 7 percent of the new poor while total coverage (such as for the former and new poor) dropped from 32 percent prior to the crisis to just over 17 percent in 1998."[18]

Even though Korea already had a high degree of wage flexibility, the government's core labor market goal was to further expand flexibility by allowing firms to freely lay off workers and offer determinate-term jobs. The Basic Employment Act, adopted in February 1998, gave firms the right to lay off workers in case of "urgent managerial needs," including deteriorating business conditions that could force the firm into bankruptcy, reorganizations undertaken to improve labor productivity, and the introduction of new technology. Court decisions also recognized business transfers, mergers, and acquisitions as other "managerial reasons" for laying off workers. Firms that want to use layoffs to reduce costs must give 60-day advance notice to worker representatives on steps to avoid layoffs and standards for dismissing workers and must sometimes notify the ministry of labor.[19] Abuse of the newly legalized layoff system was widespread: firms registered only 10 percent of the 120,000 employees reportedly laid off in 1998.

To help create new jobs, the government subsidized the wage costs of firms that hired workers dismissed for "adjustment need," paying two-thirds of such wages for small workplaces and one-third for large workplaces or firms. The government also awarded wage subsidies to employers who tried to retain redundant employees by reducing wages and bonus payments, suspending recruitment, cutting working and extra hours, closing temporarily, dispatching workers to affiliated firms, and promoting early retirement. In 1998 almost 4,200 firms received such subsidies, involving more than 780,000 workers. The government temporarily extended these subsidies from 6 to 8 months in the first half of 1999, funding the program through a payroll tax of 0.3 percent on employers.

Although the Public Employment Service tried to improve job placement, the placement ratio remained below 10 percent of job seekers and lower still for low-wage, "3-D" (dirty, dangerous, and difficult) workers in 1998. This poor efficiency reflects acute staff shortages; public agencies retained only one staff member for every 8,000 unemployed persons. Meanwhile the government progressively eliminated curbs on the job categories private employment agencies could address, and in 1998 more than 1,650 fee-charging offices had established files on 1,435,000 job seekers.

The Manpower Leasing Act of February 1998 also relaxed the rules governing private agencies that dispatch temporary workers, whose numbers reached 42,000 by the end of 1998, employed by some 800 such agencies. Unlike in most other OECD countries, in Korea regulations do not limit the employment periods of temporary workers.

The government strongly encouraged early retirement, and more than 260,000 workers retired "at the recommendation of the employer" in 1998, although 15 percent of all firms gave children of people who retired early preference in hiring. The result was that the 50–59-year-old age group saw a large drop in employment in from 1998 to 1999.

To respond to rapid economic restructuring, the government systematically expanded vocational training. Funded by both a tax on employers (0.1 percent to 0.7 percent of payroll, depending on the size of the workplace) and general tax revenues, this program absorbed about 15 percent of the budget for labor market policies in 1998, and more than 10 percent of the 68.4 percent rise in labor market spending in 1999. People covered by unemployment insurance are eligible for a three-stage reemployment training program lasting from 1 month to 1 year.[20] Stipends paid to participants not receiving unemployment benefits vary from 60 percent to 90 percent of the minimum wage, and the stipends fall during training.

Nevertheless, only about a quarter of all unemployed received vocational training in 1998. And just 134,000 of 340,000 persons who participated in the program finished their courses, while fewer than 27,000 succeeded in finding a new job. The government developed a voucher program (in 1998) and a tailor-made training system (in 1999) to raise the proportion of hired trainees, fulfill the needs of business, and develop competition among training centers, which included colleges and universities as well as traditional educational institutions.

In 1998 central and local government also created more than 437,000 public works jobs lasting 4 to 5 months, whose holders repaired public buildings and improved the environment, among other tasks. Wages ranged from 50 percent of the minimum wage for unskilled labor (former industrial daily workers) to 60 percent of average nonfarm earnings for skilled labor (unemployed university graduates). This program was designed to give priority to low-income unemployed people with dependents and with few assets.

Despite criticisms that public works jobs went to ineligible candidates, the government decided to intensify employment creation in early 1999, when the problem of joblessness was most acute. That policy produced positive outcomes, even though the jobs created were only short term, and reflects the preference of Korean authorities for creating jobs rather than assisting unemployed workers. For example, the state-owned Korea Telecom and Korea Electric Power Corp. used massive investments in new infrastructure projects to create additional short-term jobs.[21]

Improving Unemployment Insurance

Until very recently, Korea had no social security system or social safety net for the unemployed, testifying to the government's laissez-faire approach to social issues. The only significant welfare scheme available to Korean employees was Industrial Accidents Insurance.[22] The first priority in the government's welfare policy was consistently job creation,[23] and numerous firm-level welfare provisions also enhanced the key role of employment in welfare.[24] Thus Korea ranked among the lowest in the world in social spending as a share of central government expenditure (8.1 percent in 1985) in the 1980s.[25]

The expansion after March 1998 of employment insurance and other counter-measures against unemployment was closely tied to unions' acceptance of the relaxation of job security. The latter measure responded partly to pressure from Korean employers' organizations since the end of 1996 for a flexible work-hour system (introduced in 1997) and free layoff procedures. Government action to establish and to some extent improve the social insurance system was also designed to moderate social unrest, which had been rising since the late 1980s.[26]

Korea's unemployment benefit scheme, launched in July 1995 under the Employment Insurance Act, was the direct result of a wave of strikes and labor protests from 1987 onward.[27] When the financial crisis struck in 1997, Korea was thus one of four Southeast and Pacific Asian countries (with China, Japan, and Mongolia) with an unemployment benefit program. However, the explosion of unemployment and its duration completely overtook that scheme because only 7 percent of the unemployed received an allowance. The worsening crisis stimulated a rapid expansion of the scheme in March 1998 under the Wage Bond Guarantee Fund Act and the Labor Welfare Fund for Small and Medium Enterprises Act.

The state-managed compensation fund is financed by contributions shared equally between employers and employees. Contribution rates vary with company size, amounting to 0.9 percent of payroll for small firms, 1.1 percent for medium-size firms, and 1.3 percent for large firms. The unemployment benefit (job search allowance) is half of a worker's salary during the month before the dismissal. In March 1998 the minimum amount was raised from 50 percent to 70 percent of the minimum wage. Because the minimum wage is about 25 percent of national average manufacturing earnings, the minimum unemployment benefit is extremely low. The maximum is 80 percent of the average manufacturing wage. Average benefit levels are thus lower than in other OECD countries.[28]

The duration of unemployment benefits remains relatively short, reflecting the view that the scheme should be an incentive to employment rather than long-term income support.[29] Benefits last from 3 to 6 months for workers age 30 to 50, and from 4 to 7 months for workers over age 50. Unemployed workers whose benefits expired between July 1998 and June 1999 were eligible for a special 2-month extension, prolonged until the end of 1999.[30] In June 1999 the minimum contribution period required to qualify for unemployment benefits was shortened from 1 year to 6 months. To encourage job search, the state pays those who find a new job within less than half the period for which they are entitled to benefits—a lump sum equal to one-third of the remaining benefit.

Unemployment insurance was initially limited to workers in companies with 30 or more employees, but the scheme was expanded in January 1998 to firms with at least 10 workers, in March 1998 (after legislative changes to enhance labor flexibility) to firms with 5 or more workers, and in October 1998 to enterprises with fewer than 5 workers. Beginning in July 1999, the scheme covered temporary workers (who were employed at least 1 month a year), part-time workers (who work more than 18 hours a week), and daily employees (who work less than 30.8 hours a week). The system excludes public officials (who enjoy exceptional employment security), teachers at private schools, postal workers, new workers over age 60, and workers over age 65. When unemployment benefits expire, the unemployed are eligible for public works jobs and vocational training. Thus they can potentially qualify for assistance for a total of 18 months, though in practice few employees receive such extended help.[31]

Despite the program's rapid expansion, just under 15 percent of the unemployed (up from 1.9 percent initially) received benefits in January 1999, the worst period of the crisis.[32] Unemployment allowances totaled US$1 billion from June 1996 to June 1999 for some 700,000 persons, an average of US$1,500 per beneficiary, underscoring the extreme modesty of the system.

Recent Trends: Encouraging or Worrying?

Korea's unemployment rates declined sharply and rapidly, and wages grew from early 1999, as economic growth recovered. However, the government cannot afford to be complacent, and further large-scale job losses may result with restructuring of *Chaebôl* conglomerates.[33] Youth unemployment remains high, standing at 12 percent in February 2000 in the 15- to 24-year age group, compared with around 7 percent before the crisis.[34] The government is offering funds to encourage large companies to offer internship programs to young people, but the program is still quite limited. A serious unresolved problem is the scarcity of secure long-term jobs; the Korean Labor Institute (KLI) forecasted that firms would create some 823,000 new jobs in 2000, most of them short-term.

Long-term unemployment is becoming a structural problem. The KLI indicates that people out of work for more than 6 months accounted for almost 20 percent of total unemployment in November 1999—considerably more than before the crisis. According to the OECD data the over-6-month unemployment rate rose from 16.8 percent to 21.3 percent for men and from 10.3 percent to 13.1

percent for women between 1998 and 1999. The OECD projected unemployment rates of 4.5 percent for 2000 and 4.1 percent for 2001. This jobless total is far higher than Korea has been used to, and the country's days of unemployment in the 2 percent or 3 percent range are over. Thus the need for an enhanced social security system and labor market policies remains undiminished.

The Emerging Concept of Transitional Labor Markets

In Europe a single authority now wields tools such as determining interest rate and currency devaluations, and member states can use budgetary weapons only within the strong constraints of the Maastricht criteria. This means that if a demand or supply shock hits a sector, a country essentially cannot react with classic macroeconomic tools. This reality is not yet fully apparent because the euro is new and the European zone has not faced major shocks so far, but the question will inevitably arise of how to respond to such events. Local and regional efforts to encourage worker mobility, offer wage adjustments, and address continued changes in the labor market will therefore assume growing importance.

As in other regions, the center of gravity in European labor markets is shifting from large firms offering long-term jobs to networks offering shorter employment contracts but richer reemployment prospects. This new career profile links to the expansion of the service economy, the feminization of the work force, and the need for periodic retraining. Other trends include greater worker autonomy and responsibility, the growth of a results-sensitive component of wages, reduction in hierarchical levels, and intensified competition between firms and shareholder pressures. Worker preferences are also shifting toward more discontinuous careers that include personal or family leaves. Such departures from classic full-time employment and the negotiated processes that create and allocate new arrangements are known as "transitional labor markets" (TLMs).

The German economist Günther Schmid articulated this perspective and inspired a host of studies during the 1990s, many financed by the European Community.[35] According to this analysis, two main solutions are possible for managing "transitions." In the luxury version, a highly qualified new entrant to the work force first travels around the world to gain some knowledge of a firm's multiple activities and then takes a relatively safe first job. The employee then accepts a position with more responsibility and tries to diversify his or her experience before moving on to higher-level challenges. That pattern can accommodate some personal leaves to acquire missing skills or raise children, and firms can adapt compensation to include premiums, stock options, and pension funds to each situation. The problem is that this luxury version is relevant for only a few large firms and high-level employees. Most workers can choose among only a few ill-paid and even stigmatizing transitions.

TLMs offer a second solution. Transitions can occur in five areas: within a job (from full-time to part-time, from salaried to self-employment); between training institutions and employment (either initial transition, such as apprenticeship, or retraining); between unpaid socially useful activities and employment (childcare, but also voluntary or political activist work); between unemployment and employment (job search); and between retirement and employment. The idea is to "make transitions pay" by periodically reexamining each worker's situation. TLM measures fall between two controversial social policy tools: providing a universal basic income that delinks work and income, and offering employment subsidies that tie full-time work and income closely.[36] The midway position may foster more equilibrium between paid work and useful but unpaid social activities.

The TLM approach can open alternatives to older workers. For example, early retirement is a costly arrangement often involving no flexibility. Fragmentary French evidence shows that early retirement can be a positive deal for low-skilled and vulnerable older workers, because they receive state payments for a social "resting" policy. Some highly qualified workers can also benefit from retiring early, even if they would prefer to continue working, because they have higher purchasing power and the freedom to look for pleasant unpaid activities such as traveling. However, traditional skilled workers appear to suffer negative outcomes, because they are often strongly attached to their professional life and their enterprise and can be condemned to inactivity and social reclusion. The overall impact appears to be neutral in the short term and negative in the long term.

The TLM approach can enable older workers to opt for part-time early retirement while they pursue complementary part-time work with, for example, nonprofit institutions. Although such arrangements are more complicated than full-time early retirement, the participation of municipalities and nonprofit institutions can lower the costs to the state, and higher productivity and better social integration can compensate firms for their extra costs.

With its more systematic use of negotiated mobility, TLM could also help rebalance opportunities between men and women in both the workplace and the home. In Denmark, for example, women take most leaves, which almost always widen gaps between male and female career prospects. Throughout their careers women face fewer job choices, practical constraints (complex schedules and lack of promotions), and unfair competition with men.

Danish labor market policies now include job rotation, which helps ensure that no one stays unemployed without obtaining training or work experience. Workers may take voluntary, paid, 6-month, or 1-year leaves for training and childcare, in which they are replaced by an unemployed person. After the leave period, the previously employed person returns to work, while the person who replaced him or her has gained 6 months to a year of work experience and an employment network, and thus can more easily find work. This rather costly and sophisticated device can help some stigmatized and discouraged persons.

The concept of employability encompasses some of these provisions. Employability-enhancing policies are interventions on the supply side of the labor market (the worker) that are designed to improve recruitment and ease employment decisions.[37] They are based on tailor-made and future-oriented interventions, including personal evaluations of competencies and retraining trajectories performed by specialized staff of employment agencies. The beneficiary agrees to these elements.

In its 1998 employment guidelines, the European Commission promoted both an "activating" and an "employability-enhancing" approach. The guidelines require each member state to propose a personalized route back to employment for every adult unemployed for more than 1 year and youth unemployed for more than 6 months. The goal was to engage a minimum of 20 percent of the unemployed in training or retraining programs. Each member state submits an annual report on its labor market policies showing how it has reached the goals or giving reasons for noncompliance.

This approach depends on decentralization because local governments must manage such transitions. Germany illustrates the initiative power of local *Länder*, whereas France has explored global budgets for local agencies. The main risk is inequality among regions, with richer ones fostering effective transitions while poorer regions offer more limited menus. Transfers of some public funds can help adjust for local variations in unemployment and poverty levels.[38] Privatization could emerge as a mean of fostering competition and innovation in a field often criticized for bureaucratic bias, but it can also foster competition among local agencies, and experience underlines the need to avoid "skimming," in which agencies place the easiest to place and train the easiest to train.

Though elaborated in nations with fully developed social protection systems, TLM approaches may also be relevant for Korea and other East Asian countries, as they, like European nations, face constraints in defining and implementing macroeconomic policies. TLM options enable communities and regions to combine state intervention with for-profit and nonprofit initiatives in both formal and informal sectors. The new challenge is for communities to negotiate novel arrangements that limit the costs and rigidities in labor markets while also addressing rising inequality and social exclusion.

Notes

1. World Bank, *The East Asian Miracle: Economic Growth and Public Policy* (New York: Oxford University Press, 1993).
2. The Republic of Korea entered the Organization for Economic Cooperation and Development (OECD) as a permanent member in December 1996.
3. The data are taken from Tamar Manuelyan Atinc, "From Economic Crisis to Social Crisis," in *East Asia: Recovery and Beyond* (Washington, D.C.: World Bank, 2000), pp. 123–51.
4. Ibid, p. 144.
5. Because Korean unemployment figures do not include self-employed people whose businesses have gone bankrupt, unemployment rates would have been 0.3 or 0.4 percentage points higher if measured by OECD standards. Many small, healthy enterprises closed down because of the "credit crunch."
6. Numbers from the National Statistical Office of the Republic of Korea.
7. The participation rate (the labor force as a percentage of the total working-age population) declined from 62.2 percent to 60.7 percent between 1997 and 1998, whereas the inactive population increased by 1.2 million people.
8. OECD, *Republic of Korea*, Economic Studies (Paris: OECD, 2000).
9. In 1998 there were 129 disputes involving 146,065 workers and 1,452,096 lost working days, compared with 78 disputes involving 43,991 workers and 444,720 lost working days in 1997. See National Statistical Office, *Korea Statistical Yearbook 1999* (Seoul: National Statistical Office, 2000), pp. 178–79.
10. Ibid.
11. Nicholas Prescott and Nanak Kakwani (1999). "Impact of Economic Crisis on Poverty and Inequality in Korea." Processed. World Bank, Washington, D.C.
12. This poverty incidence is derived from national poverty lines, on the basis of consumption expenditures, and is calculated for urban households only.
13. For example, François Godement reports that the number of homeless living at the Seoul central railway station was counted at 3,000 in August 1998. See François Godement, "Models and Politics for Asian Social Policies," paper prepared for the Asia-Europe Meeting (ASEM) Social Lessons Project, May 2000, p. 10, available at <http://www.worldbank.org/eapsocial/library/godement.pdf>.
14. Students enrolled in middle school declined by 6 percent, from 2,012,000 in 1997 to 1,897,000 in 1998.
15. This rate was as high as 36 percent in some sections of the upper school.
16. The *Korean Statistical Yearbook 1999* (National Statistical Office, op. cit.) shows a declining share of education in government expenditure from 1996 to 1998.

17. According to personal communications with the Ministry of Health and Welfare.

18. Atinc, op. cit.

19. Firms must notify the ministry if layoffs exceed 10 employees in firms with fewer than 99 employees, 10 percent of employees in firms with between 100 and 999 employees, and 100 employees in firms with more than 1,000 employees.

20. These benefits are halved during the second period of courses and canceled during the third.

21. Intelligence Economic Unit, *South Korea*, second quarter 1999, p. 22.

22. Industrial Accidents Insurance revealed difficult working conditions in Korea.

23. J. Dreze and A. Sen, *Hunger and Public Action* (Oxford: Clarendon Press, 1989).

24. Active promotion of firm-centered welfare schemes includes provision of secondary education on company premises, dormitories, and medical facilities.

25. You Jong-il, "Labor Institutions and Economic Development in the Republic of Korea," in *Workers, Institutions and Economic Growth in Asia*, ed. G. Rodgers (Geneva: International Institute for Labor Studies, 1994).

26. A national pension scheme was established in 1988, but few Koreans were initially covered. The scope of Industrial Accidents Insurance (created in 1964) and the patchy Medical Care System (implemented in 1977) were also extended.

27. This replaced a former small-scale scheme, the Severance Allowance System, which served as both a pension fund and an unemployment allowance designed to help young people enter the labor market.

28. As the International Labor Organization (ILO) notes, this scheme allows for some vertical redistribution of income by having a maximum benefit but no maximum contribution (see ILO, "List of ILO Activities in the Asian Region," annex in *Decent Work in Asia: ILO Activities in the Region*, Thirteenth Asian Regional Meeting, Bangkok [August 2001]).

29. The minimum benefit period was doubled to 60 days in 1998. Before the crisis, it was between 30 and 210 days.

30. For example, a person 30–50 years old who had been in the Employment Insurance Scheme from its inception in July 1995 would receive benefits for 4 months, plus the 2-month extension, for a total of 6 months.

31. OECD, op. cit., p. 162.

32. Atinc, op. cit.

33. Proposed foreign ownership (potential bidders being General Motors, Ford, Daimler-Chrysler, and Fiat) aroused strong union opposition urging nationalization. To back this demand, workers at all Korea's main auto plants went on strike for a week in April 2000.

34. Personal communication with the Ministry of Labor.

35. For initial formulations, see Günther Schmid, "Is Full Employment Still Possible? Transitional Labor Market as a New Strategy of Labour Market Policy," *Economic and Industrial Democracy* 16 (August 1995): 429–56. Also see G. Schmid and B. Gazier, eds., *The Dynamics of Full Employment: Social Integration by Transitional Labor Markets* (Cheltenham: Edward Elgar, 2000).

36. P. Van Parijs, *Real Freedom for All* (Oxford: Oxford University Press, 1995), and E. S. Phelps, *Rewarding Work: How to Restore Participation and Self-Support to Free Enterprise* (Cambridge, Mass.: Harvard University Press, 1997).

37. For a comprehensive analysis, see B. Gazier, ed., *Employability: Concepts and Policies* (Berlin: Institute for Applied Socio-Economics, 1999), p. 329.

38. This opens the thorny issue of relevant indicators, discussed in B. Gazier, "L'articulation justice locale/justice globale: Le cas des "marchés transitionnels du travail," *Revue Economique* (May 2000).

CHAPTER 24

Evaluation and Monitoring of Active Labor Market Policies

by Christine Erhel

ABSTRACT: The cost and effectiveness of programs designed to help people find jobs vary widely, so monitoring and evaluating such programs is essential. Europe's experience in pursuing different types of evaluation sheds light on their strengths and weaknesses, and lessons from this experience could save time and effort elsewhere.

Active labor market policies are a key element of employment strategies in Europe. Such policies fall into three broad types:

- Measures to reduce mismatch and enhance job search (public employment as well as placement and counseling activities)
- Measures to improve the skills of job seekers (training)
- Measures to subsidize employment opportunities for target groups

Each category encompasses many different types of programs, which can range from short-term to 5-year efforts (such as Swedish relief work and French youth employment contracts). Target groups also vary, although in Europe the main targets are youth and the long-term unemployed.

Because governments can choose among different measures to reach a given policy goal, they need to assess the relative efficiency of such measures to understand what works best.[1] Public finance is another argument for monitoring and evaluation. Average expenditures on active labor market policy are quite low—in 1997 the typical Organization for Economic Cooperation and Development country spent about 0.8 percent of gross domestic product (GDP)[2]—(ranging from 0.1 percent of GDP in Japan to 2 percent in Sweden. However, participants in and expenditures on active labor policies have grown over the last 20 years in most European countries, and some programs are very expensive in unit costs. Governments have clear incentives to obtain information about the impact of programs to optimize their budgetary choices.

From a macroeconomic perspective, the effects of active labor market policies are unclear: some countries treat these programs as a tool for moderating wage increases, whereas others use them to boost wages. The impact on unemployment depends crucially on this wage effect. This complexity calls for systematic evaluation. It also explains why methodological debates are important in this field: good methodologies are a prerequisite to reliable results.

Countries need to tailor their policies to their national labor markets, another important argument for effective evaluation as a basis for policymaking. Countries differ in their implementation and funding of active labor market policies. Some public employment services are directly responsible for programs, whereas others receive only referrals. Some countries administer their programs at the national level, whereas others rely on regional or local levels. Funding may be governed centrally or regionally. These differences lead evaluators to focus particular attention on the institutional context of active labor market policies.

Most European countries have made monitoring and evaluation schemes an integral part of their active labor market policies. Europe's heterogeneity of experience and relatively low expenditures on evaluation have favored cheaper and practical methodologies, with comparative research assuming growing importance.

The chapter is organized around the main approaches to evaluating labor market policies. These include monitoring, a prerequisite to basic knowledge about labor market policies; microeconomic studies, which have spawned classic debates on the use of experimental and nonexperimental methods and cost-benefit analysis; and aggregate impact and macroeconomic evaluation. Each section highlights good practice.

Monitoring Active Labor Market Policies

Efforts to monitor active labor market policies should ideally include the following:

- Goals specified by political and administrative authorities at the national, regional, and local levels
- Defined indicators that allow goals to be measured

- The actual monitoring process, based on goals and definitions plus the information-gathering framework
- Feedback loops to ensure that policymakers take observed patterns into account[3]

A successful monitoring system depends on planning at the early stages of policy formation, simplicity of indicators, and links to reliable labor market statistics. Monitoring begins at the policy definition stage: the choice and design of programs should include definitions of clear goals and corresponding indicators. Practically, this means that laws and regulations creating new policies should explicitly include monitoring.[4] Basic indicators for a monitoring process are financial data (budget allocated versus budget used), information on participants (total numbers and target groups or sectors), and costs per unit (people served per hour expended). Monthly or at least quarterly data are crucial. The overall system should be simple enough to apply to all administrative levels—local, regional, and national.

Agencies responsible for administering labor market policy (and political authorities) need reliable and comprehensive information about numbers of participants, program costs, their targeting, and all types of implementation problems. Monitoring facilitates evaluation, since the availability of detailed firsthand data can relieve the need to gather information later, saving time and money. A good monitoring system should rely on a two-level information system that provides both simple and synthetic indicators to help the implementation and decisionmaking process.

Monitoring also encompasses two "feedback loops." First is feedback between monitoring and implementation: any indicator turning "red" should lead to remedial action. Second, the results of monitoring should inform decisions on the design of new programs. But in Europe, especially, other incentives also have emerged for active labor market policy monitoring, such as the following:

- *Fiscal Constraints and Public Sector Reform.* All European countries have faced tight fiscal constraints over the last 10 years owing to the Maastricht criteria, the economic downturn of the early 1990s, and high levels of public debt, just as they sought to reform public services. Modernization of public services has taken several forms, including decentralization, introduction of private sector management methods (for instance, management by objectives), and market-oriented goals. In France, Germany, and Sweden, decentralization entails giving local employment offices full responsibility for an overall budget that they allocate among programs for the unemployed. This process promotes the introduction of monitoring systems, because local providers, central agencies, and local branches of central agencies all need information on the programs.

- *Role for the European Commission in Activating Labor Market Policies and Sharing Information among Countries.* Since the 1994 Essen summit, the European Council has consistently stressed monitoring of employment trends and policies of member states, and the commission has worked to establish employment indicators.[5] The November 1997 Luxembourg summit underscored the need for member states to exchange information and good practice, and European labor market initiatives include clear incentives to develop monitoring systems. For example, the European Union (EU) employment policy guidelines include a series of indicators of results, and the European Social Fund, which cofinances many active labor market programs, requires effective monitoring.

European Experience with Monitoring

Of course, the reality of monitoring in Europe differs from the ideal. Most countries are now setting up monitoring schemes, but, with the exception of Sweden, they do not systematically pursue quantitative indicators. Identifying the difficulties that have hindered development of monitoring despite significant incentives is useful, and several effective efforts to develop comparative monitoring are also illuminating.

Problems that have hindered monitoring include the following:

- Lack of data.
- Lack of financial and human resources. Budgets and means devoted to administering labor market policies are scarce in most countries, and monitoring rarely brings extra resources.
- Coordination problems. Institutions matter—if there are split responsibilities for implementing active labor market policies, monitoring becomes difficult. This is the case in France, where monitoring of active labor market policy falls to two different directorates in the Ministry of Labor, the center for adult vocational training (Association Nationale pour la Formation Professionelle des Adultes), and, in some cases, UNEDIC (unemployment insurance, run by social partners). All these institutions also have regional, departmental, and local agencies. Some progress toward better coordination,

especially in collecting data and making it accessible, has occurred, but the complex institutional structure is an obstacle to a comprehensive monitoring system.

- Absence of clear program goals. Weak monitoring systems and a lack of relevant indicators for a given employment measure impede policymaking.

Although there are no ready solutions for fragmented institutional structures and weak overall labor market statistics, policymakers can at least identify gaps and problems as they develop monitoring systems.

The Swedish Experience:
Toward a Comprehensive Monitoring System

Information and statistics on labor markets and programs have been part of the Swedish model since the early 1950s.[6] The sharp rise in unemployment in the early 1990s reinforced information needs and prompted debates on labor market policy. Sweden has thus developed a comprehensive monitoring system that includes the following elements:

- Budget and expense tracking. For each labor market office, data are projected and collected on planned and actual expenditures and planned and actual participants for all labor market programs.
- Ongoing follow-up and feedback. At the national level, continuous budget checks, monthly follow-up of results, annual surveys of firms and participants, and staff surveys every 2 years are all part of the information system (AIS) run by the Labor Market Administration.
- An auditing system. The regional office spends 2 days a year auditing each local office, and the central office spends 3 days every 2 years overseeing the activities of each regional branch.

All labor market and AIS data are available online.

This comprehensive monitoring system not only provides a good basis for evaluation but also is closely related to the decentralization that occurred during the 1990s. The monitoring system allows each placement officer to check budgets and calculate expenditures for a given unemployed person, and thus helps agencies allocate budgets and make decisions. Local offices, in turn, provide regular information and feedback to central offices, thereby improving the reactivity of labor market policies and budgets.

Comparative Monitoring at the European Level

Comparative monitoring of labor market policies has developed following the recommendations of the European Commission. The goals are to identify Europe's best performers, overall as well as on a given employment goal, and facilitate information exchange on successful experience.

The EU labor market information system, known as the European Employment Observatory,[7] dates from 1982. This system began as an informal network of national correspondents in national ministries, but it has evolved toward more formal activities. Since 1996 the observatory has consisted of two networks (MISEP and SYSDEM) and an advisory group (RESEARCH). MISEP (Mutual Information System on Employment Policies) collects, summarizes, translates, and publishes information on labor market measures to support employment services and policymaking. A group of national correspondents, nominated by national ministries, and a secretariat meet twice a year. SYSDEM (System of Documentation, Evaluation, and Monitoring of Employment Policies) was initially designed to provide information on labor markets and employment policies in member states, but it now reports on labor market topics from a comparative perspective and provides information to the European Commission. It consists of a network of correspondents from leading independent research institutions. All information gathered through the European Employment Observatory will soon be available on the Internet.

This system provides good information on country performance and allows some comparative evaluations.[8] However, it is still far from ideal because it offers little feedback on policy decisions and design and is far from the goal, advanced at the Luxembourg summit, of coordinating national employment policies. Nevertheless, the system enhances member states' awareness of the need for good follow-up of labor market policies.

Microeconomic Evaluations

The broadest goal of evaluation in labor market policy is to determine what is working and what is not. Micro evaluation addresses this question at the agency or individual level. Such evaluation requires two key pieces of information:

- *What effects does a given program have on the future prospects of program participants?* Variables include earnings and job status (employment versus unemployment) and type of job (short-term or regular contract, full time or part time).

- *Does the program affect nonparticipants?* Some programs may have adverse side effects. For instance, if a policy subsidizes firms that hire long-term unemployed, some firms will reduce their hiring of short-term unemployed.

A program is efficient if it has a positive impact on participants' situations and if potential negative effects on nonparticipants (and more generally on the labor market) are minimal. Some negative effects may be acceptable: in the example above, labor market authorities may prefer to help the long-term unemployed obtain jobs even if doing so implies more short-term unemployment. Efficiency indicators thus need to link to a policy's goals.

Governments developed microeconomic evaluations to measure efficiency and thus to choose among different programs (such as temporary public jobs versus subsidies to private sector jobs) and different schemes (for example, between classroom and on-the-job training). Follow-up indicators cannot provide a good measure of efficiency, but microevaluations such as cost-benefit analyses can link outcomes to costs, facilitating comparison of various programs.

Microeconomic evaluations have been the subject of continuing debates regarding experimental procedures. Understanding these debates is crucial to governments' choices despite their technical character because only evaluations grounded in reliable methodology can produce robust results.

Methodologies used to evaluate active labor market policies fall into four main categories:

- *Interviews.* Because microeconomic evaluation focuses on the impact of labor market policy on program participants or the firms hiring them, interviews can provide useful information. However, answers may be biased if employers or participants believe that results will be used to make policy decisions.
- *Postprogram Surveys.* Surveys follow the labor market status of participants after a program concludes at various points in time to evaluate differences in individuals' situations before and after participation. Evaluators cannot measure program impact on a simple before-and-after comparison basis: differences might result from factors that have nothing to do with the labor market policy, such as changes in the general labor market situation. Data on nonparticipants with comparable characteristics are therefore needed to measure program impact.
- *Random Assignment Experiments ("Experimental" Evaluation).* These techniques resemble those used to evaluate a new medical treatment or drug. Individuals who would like to participate in a program (and who fulfill the

eligibility criteria) are randomly allocated to either a treatment/experimental group or to a control group. The individuals in the treatment/experimental group benefit from the program, whereas those in the control group do not. Evaluators collect outcome variables for the two groups at various points in time, with the difference in outcomes interpreted as the program's impact. Theoretically, the estimated impact is free of selection bias because selection occurred on a purely random basis.

* *Quasi-experiments.* Rather than relying on random assignment, here evaluators use general labor market information to construct a control group, matching its characteristics as closely as possible to those of program participants. The evaluator then gathers data on participants (such as from postprogram surveys) and nonparticipants. The program's estimated impact is the difference between the outcomes for participants and members of the control group. Evaluation frameworks using a constructed control group are termed "quasi-experimental."

Analysts have traditionally considered random assignment experiments the most reliable in evaluating the impact of labor market policy programs because experimental designs are typically free of selection bias and provide easy-to-understand results. This type of evaluation has been implemented mainly in the United States, which has performed some well-known studies of active labor market policies such as the Job Training Partnership Act.[9] Quasi-experimental approaches were developed as an alternative to random assignment experiments. The main problem lies in correcting for selection bias because this involves econometric analysis, which is based on implicit assumptions about the bias.[10]

Cost-Benefit Analysis:
Estimating Effects on Employment and Nonparticipants

To develop a comprehensive picture of the effects of active labor market policies, governments must know more than simply the effect on participants. If policymakers target policies at specific groups such as young people and long-term unemployed, they will exert negative effects on the labor market. The most important of these is termed "substitution displacement." For schemes that entail transfers of public funds to private firms (such as job subsidies), if job creation might have occurred in any event, public funds do not contribute to any labor market goal: there is no employment effect. Windfall and substitution could explain 90 percent of the apparent employment effect for some wage subsidies.[11] When active labor market policies are implemented on a large scale, the potential effects on nonparticipants cannot be neglected, though standard impact evaluation cannot identify those effects[12] because microeconomic studies usually focus on a small sample.

Cost-benefit analysis uses both microeconomic evaluation and financing data to relate the outcomes of employment programs to their costs. Studies show very different costs for the same efficiency level: for instance, in France, among public temporary employment programs targeted at young people, the cost of a public temporary employment program was half the cost of a comprehensive employment program, despite comparable effects on employment rates at the end of the 1980s. This type of information is very helpful to policymakers, although they must also take social considerations into account.

The most basic cost-benefit evaluations relate microeconomic results (effects on employment and wages) to unit costs. The main difficulty lies in the concept of unit cost, which can be understood as either the cost of the program over its whole duration or its average annual cost. On the one hand, the latter allows evaluators to compare different labor market policy measures directly and is also consistent with annual financial data. On the other hand, average annual costs do not account for heterogeneity of expenditures within a given program.

At a more rigorous level, cost-benefit analysis requires evaluators to estimate many different gains and losses. An ideal cost-benefit analysis should estimate monetary gains and losses for participants (compared with nonparticipants), gains in relation to wages, losses in relation to forgone social benefits, gains in relation to reduced social expenditures, and higher tax revenues versus the costs of the program. To be comprehensive, such an analysis should also include direct and indirect effects on nonparticipants, because some individuals might have lost jobs because of the program, representing a cost to society. These effects are very difficult to estimate and integrate into the cost-benefit framework: most studies, therefore, remain partial and must be interpreted with caution.

Given these difficulties European countries have produced very few examples of cost-benefit analysis. This does not mean that knowledge of relative cost-benefit ratios is lacking: labor market agencies calculate annual unit costs, which they can relate to outcome indicators or the results of microevaluations. But the absence of standard cost-benefit ratios is more problematic in making international comparisons and identifying best practices.[13]

The methodological challenges can be summarized as follows: To quantify the impact of an active labor market program on participants, evaluators need a differential measure (comparing participants' outcomes with those of a control group, either experimental or quasi-experimental). The simplest way to perform such a comparative evaluation is to use random assignment experiments, but evaluators need to consider experimental design and ethical questions carefully. Quasi-experimental evaluations have become reliable. Since technical aspects are crucial to the robustness of results, specialists should conduct such evaluations. Evaluations of impacts on participants should be complemented by studies estimating the impact on nonparticipants, as well as windfall effects. Econometric studies provide the most robust estimates, but interviews can also provide interesting information and are easier to conduct. Good microeconomic evaluation requires explicit attention to context as much as technical debate among experts.

European Experience with Microeconomic Evaluations

Most microeconomic evaluations in Europe do not meet the foregoing standards. Ethical considerations exclude most random assignment experiments,[14] and proper quasi-experiments are not widely used, although their number is growing. Many studies compare the situation of participants before and after the program, or compare participants and nonparticipants with similar characteristics, but without constructing a control group.[15]

Several factors have curtailed the development of microeconomic evaluation. These include

- A lack of monitoring results in a lack of data.
- An evaluation culture is absent in political and academic fields.
- In some countries (especially the Nordic countries and Germany), active labor market policies were part of a political and social consensus, so discussion of their efficiency and costs was limited until financial constraints and rising unemployment launched new debates.
- Compared with those in the United States, evaluation programs are smaller, although they are numerous.
- In some countries, such as France, employment schemes have varied widely, making it difficult to conduct evaluations.

In a 1998 survey I found four examples of random assignment experiments. Three evaluated the effects of job-search assistance for the unemployed, and one evaluated the impact of a training program. I summarize two here.[16] The first exemplifies good acceptance by program administrators, whereas the second illustrates hostility toward random assignment. In both cases, biases affected the experimental outcomes:

- *Job-search assistance in Elskistuna, Sweden.*[17] The evaluated program was a new experimental scheme offering intensified job-search assistance to the unemployed. The sample was composed of 400 participants unemployed for a minimum of 3 months and enrolled in a local employment service. Individuals were randomly assigned to an experimental group receiving intensified service (216 unemployed) and a control group (194 unemployed). The experimental group received on average 7.5 hours of assistance for 3 months (consisting of interviews with placement officers), compared with an average of 1.5 hours for the control group. Data collected included individuals' labor market status (short-term contracts versus regular jobs or unemployment) and average monthly income gains at the end of the 3-month period. Results showed a clear positive effect from intensified job-search assistance: 48 percent of the experimental group members were employed after 3 months versus 34 percent of the control group. The difference was also significant for employment type: 92 percent of the employed in the experimental group had obtained regular employment versus 68 percent for the control group. The data also showed a positive program impact on average monthly earnings.

- *Training program in Norway.*[18] Unlike the previous example, the evaluated program was an existing training program. Random assignment was restricted to 18 employment offices facing excess demand for services. Employment offices selected candidates on the basis of criteria normally used and then randomly assigned them to an experimental or a control group. One year after the program's end, evaluators asked experimental and control group members about their labor market situation (employment or unemployment). The training program had no significant impact on the employment rate. However, strong resistance among administrators resulted in selection bias at the eligibility-control step.[19] In one employment office, 10 training places were available, and the administrators found only 10 unemployed among 80 eligible for the program. The random assignment procedure thus did not work. Most employment offices also provided the control group with comparable services, which caused a substitution bias.

Despite their weaknesses, these examples suggest interesting methodological lessons. First, they differ from U.S. examples in size: the samples are small, and the number of observation periods is limited. Consequently, costs are also relatively low. Second, they confirm the importance of cooperation from program administrators. In two of the four European experiments, the administration showed some hostility to random assignment. Experimental design seems more readily accepted in a new program that will be developed on a larger scale if outcomes are good, as in the Swedish experiment.

Another study, evaluating personnel increases in the Swedish Public Employment Service, offers an interesting European example of cost-benefit analysis.[20] In 1987 the Swedish government gave the National Labor Market Board extra funds to add 250 placement officers and counselors to the Public Employment Service, boosting their numbers by about 5 percent. The first step in assessing the efficiency of this staff increase was an impact evaluation. Estimates of impact were based on before-and-after comparisons of three employment offices where the staff grew by 15 percent to 25 percent (program offices), and three offices where the number of staff either remained unchanged or expanded only slightly (comparison offices). The three program offices were matched with comparison offices serving a labor market with similar characteristics. Negotiations between the National Labor Market Board, the Ministry of Labor, and evaluators were used to assign offices to the two groups.

The study focused on two types of impact: the duration of unemployment for job-seeking clients and the duration of job vacancies. The results showed no effect from expanded staff on the average length of unemployment but revealed significant effects on the duration of vacancies, which dropped by an average of about 1 day. Evaluators also estimated the real costs of resources such as wages, training, computers, and incidental material associated with the rise in personnel. Evaluators then compared those costs with the market value of the output (MVO) arising from the accelerated vacancy filling. That value was measured by firms' willingness to pay for more goods and services, estimated on the basis of average wage costs. The difference between benefits (MVO) and costs was found to be negative. With no effect on the average duration of unemployment, the staff increase also failed to produce effects on public finance (if duration of unemployment falls, then costs for public assistance also drop, and tax payments rise).

The staff increase clearly failed the cost-benefit test because it did not cover its costs to the government. The study suffered from important methodological weaknesses, however, because the sample size was small and the process of selecting program offices and comparison offices was likely biased. This test was also performed in a period of economic expansion, when employment services seem to have less influence on labor markets.

The most interesting European microeconomic evaluations are based on panel data, which France systematically developed in the 1980s and used during the 1990s. Panels provide information about participants' backgrounds before they begin a labor market program and rely on a quasi-experimental design to evaluate the program's net effect on employment rate and wages. The labor market exhibits some duration and path-dependence (hysteresis) effects: the probability of getting a job usually decreases with the length of unemployment. Whatever the interpretation of this phenomenon (depreciation of human capital, signaling, stigmatization), longitudinal data provide some information about the impact of programs on this path-dependency effect.

Panel data generally contribute to a better understanding of how employment policies affect labor market dynamics. For example, the French CEREQ (Research Center on Employment and Qualifications) panel studied the integration of young people into the labor market in relation to their educational level and qualifications. The French Ministry of Labor also developed other panels to evaluate labor market policies or drew them from more general labor market surveys.

French experience, however, highlights some drawbacks. First, the reliability of results depends crucially on the period of observation, which can be quite short for a standard impact evaluation but must be longer when the aim is to identify trajectories. Evaluators also need to consider attrition rates, which usually rise with length of observation. Second, results can be difficult to interpret. Impact evaluations using longitudinal data take human capital and job-search models as a theoretical background, but they do not interpret results in accordance with those frameworks. Nevertheless, longitudinal data and the debates surrounding interpretation of results contribute to a better understanding of labor markets and policies.

The French experience with youth programs illustrates the need for systematic evaluation of active labor market policies. Until the end of the 1980s the only available information was based on interviews and postprogram survey data. Most studies calculated the employment rate of participants 3 months after the program. With that approach, the most efficient scheme (*contrat d'adaptation*, which provides on-the-job training) achieved an 80 percent employment rate, while the less-efficient scheme (the TUC—public temporary employment scheme) had a 30 percent employment rate.

During the 1990s evaluators developed rigorous quasi-experimental designs using panel data. The results differ markedly from prior conclusions. If the impact on employment rates is the difference between participants and a matched control group, the only efficient program is the one showing a positive net impact. Some youth programs had a negative impact—participants had lower employment rates 3 months after the program than comparable young people.

This result may stem from the impact of program participation on job-search intensity (participants reduced their job search) and stigma effects (employers are reluctant to hire young people who participate in an employment program because they might have problems).

The efficiency of a program should not be judged solely on the basis of interviews and survey results. In this example, a program's efficiency ranking changes if evaluators use rigorous methods. The evaluators were well aware that their previous results were fragile, but the new results strongly influenced the government's assessment of youth programs. They also clarified the need for regular rigorous evaluation.

What Do the European Evaluations Show?

Empirical micro studies often provide ambivalent and even contradictory results. Nonetheless, recent surveys and analysis highlight converging outcomes.[21]

Empirical results from training and retraining are disappointing, despite their good reputation. Many studies find either very small positive effects or no effect at all, and some evaluations even point to a negative impact. Training is also very expensive. These results could reflect the fact that any positive effects of training on productivity and earnings occur only after a long delay. Studies cannot measure such long-term effects because evaluators generally do not collect data over a long period (except in the case of some panel data), and long-term impacts are difficult to estimate because they require controlling for many variables.

Temporary public jobs may exert some positive effects. In Germany, especially over the past decade in the territory of the former German Democratic Republic, public job creation is clearly effective in raising participants' probability of future employment. The impact is higher if temporary public jobs are combined with training. These programs seem to give better results for hard-to-place people. For the most qualified groups of unemployed, temporary public jobs may have a stigmatizing effect, which can reduce future earnings. A French study that compared wages for participants in a temporary public job program with those of a matched control group found a negative impact on wages, at least for young people with some education.

Job-search assistance through placement services and intensive counseling are the least-contested active labor market policy. The impact of job-search assistance on the probability of finding a job is always positive. Evaluators found one of the most impressive effects under the British Work Trials Initiative, which combined traditional job-search assistance with incentives for employers to take on people who had been unemployed for more than 6 months. During a 3-week trial period, participants continued to receive benefits plus compensation for work expenses. An evaluation showed increases in employment rates of 34–40 percent 6 months after the program ended.[22]

Several European countries have developed programs to encourage the unemployed to become self-employed, using benefits as a subsidy. Evaluations report good results where implementation is careful and enterprise projects are preassessed. Recent studies suggest that "activation" of unemployment benefits—making them more work-oriented—yields positive results.

Evaluation contributes to institutional reform. Several European countries have at least partially privatized public employment services. Such reforms appear to increase reemployment probability, even for hard-to-place unemployed. In Germany, a quasi-experimental evaluation compared long-term unemployed and very hard-to-place people (elderly, disabled, ex-addicts) reintegrated through commercial or semipublic temporary work agencies versus public employment services (control group). The reintegration rate of the experimental group was significantly higher (27.4 percent versus 14.2 percent).

Aggregate Impact and Macroeconomic Evaluations

Aggregate impact studies aim to integrate all the direct and indirect effects of labor market policies on unemployment levels, employment, and wage bargaining. Such evaluations, which are a distinct part of the European approach, do not require specific surveys or data collection because they generally use administrative information (financial data, number of participants) and general labor market statistics (employment, unemployment, wages).

Despite some methodological limitations, European aggregate impact studies have produced interesting results, examples of which follow.[23]

Active labor market policies moderate wages. Active labor market programs tend to boost the employability of the unemployed, thus increasing competition in the labor market. This has a wage moderation effect. Only in Sweden did a study find a positive effect on wages (wage pressure effect).[24] Traditional Swedish labor market policy differs from that of other European countries in that expenditures are higher and programs are more job oriented (involving training and retraining and mobility allowances), with little hard-to-place targeting.[25] In this context, active labor market policies will not lead to a competition effect and may well encourage workers to ask for wage increases.

Active labor market policies support labor market transitions. Most empirical studies based on a matching model find that active labor market policies have a positive impact on outflows from unemployment and improve the labor market's overall functioning. Nevertheless, such policies can produce negative effects. For example, several studies suggest that although targeted measures boost outflow from unemployment for the targeted group, outflow among other groups tends to decline. Policymakers should consider targeting cautiously and conduct comprehensive evaluation studies to understand its effects.

Most studies find that active labor market policies reduce unemployment, but the effects of specific programs vary. For example, subsidies create high displacement, substitution, and deadweight as well as exert a minor impact on aggregate employment levels. Such policies can nonetheless be efficient if they are targeted to the very long-term unemployed or to depressed areas such as the former German Democratic Republic. Temporary public jobs also risk displacement and substitution, but those effects are lower than for job subsidies if the temporary jobs are limited to nonmarket activities. Most studies find better results for training, especially if it is short, targeted, and market oriented.

Long-term impact may differ from short-term impact. Long-term effects will reflect the impact of wage bargaining, external competitiveness (including exchange rate effects), and budgets. Active labor market financing (through taxes, reductions in other public expenditures, and deficits) also influences macroeconomic performance.

Overall, macroeconomic evaluations of labor market policies have two main advantages. First, data requirements are manageable because they rely on administrative data (expenditures, number of participants) and general labor market statistics (unemployment, employment, wages). More sophisticated evaluation methods require information on outflow from unemployment toward employment and inactivity. Second, although such studies might at first seem complicated to nonspecialists, estimation techniques are far simpler than those required for microeconomic quasi-experimental studies, and methodological problems are well known.

The main drawbacks relate to the level of evaluation. First, aggregate impact evaluation does not reflect whether a country has very low employment expenditures and very few program participants. Furthermore, an evaluation of the overall effects of reduced unemployment may mask negative outcomes for some individuals, who may suffer from lower wages or bad working conditions, for instance. That is why macro and micro approaches are complementary, especially when micro evaluations are nonscientific. In that case, aggregate impact analysis will give some indication of the direct and indirect effects that are reducing the net impact of active labor market policies (windfall, substitution, deadweight). Simple surveys or interviews will help evaluators understand the consequences of program participation for individuals.

Policy Recommendations

Diversity is an important feature of European experience in monitoring and evaluating active labor market policies: there is no single model. European countries are still developing approaches to monitoring and evaluation, scientific as well as nonscientific. This experience has relevance for East Asian countries, which might benefit from the following lessons learned in Europe:

- *Monitoring should be developed at a very early stage, when new policies are being implemented.* This calls, first, for collecting basic data on programs and, second, for giving program administrators basic training in the importance and methods of using data to improve program implementation.
- *Evaluation is necessary if governments want to make good use of public funds.* Policymakers can use many techniques to evaluate active labor market policies. It is naturally better to use scientific methods, but surveys or interviews can provide interesting and useful information as long as they are not misinterpreted. At the microeconomic level, it is impossible to measure the net impact of a program without a control group.
- *To measure net efficiency, evaluators must use random assignment or quasi-experimental methodologies to estimate individual impact.* Random assignment is easier, but this procedure works best for small samples or the cost of evaluation may be very high. Using random assignment to evaluate new programs lowers resistance among administrators and participants, and it helps policymakers decide if a program is worth continuing and how to improve the program. For ongoing schemes, it is better to use quasi-experimental evaluation, although these methodologies are more technically complex and thus require expert assistance. The main limitations are likely to be data problems, underscoring the importance of data collection, especially some longitudinal (panel) data for future evaluation. This requires regular surveys of a sample of participants and unemployed people.

- *Macroeconomic and aggregate impact evaluations are a useful complement to other forms of evaluation.* Macroeconomic evaluations are easy to perform with relatively minimal levels of expertise and basic data. Such evaluations can also allow international comparisons, especially when countries have similar economic and labor market characteristics. East Asian nations might find such comparisons particularly useful.

Notes

1. See Peter Robinson, "Active Labour Market Policies: A Case of Evidence-Based Policy Making?" *Oxford Review of Economic Policy* 16, no. 1 (2000): 13–26, for more on this aspect.

2. I use a classic definition of "active labor market policies" based on Organization for Economic Cooperation and Development categories. Active measures aim directly to return people to work (job-creation schemes, hiring subsidies, job-search assistance) or maintain their employability (training).

3. P. Auer and T. Kruppe, "Monitoring of Labor Market Policy in EU Member States," in *International Handbook of Labor Market Policy and Evaluation,* ed. G. Schmid, J. O'Reilley, and K. Schomann (Cambridge, England: Edward Elgar, 1998), pp. 899–922.

4. See, for instance, the French 5-year-employment law of 1994.

5. MISEP (Mutual Information Systems on Employment Policies), see section on Comparative Monitoring at the European level.

6. The high degree of reactivity of Swedish active labor market policy has been studied in depth by Ohlsson. He shows that the number of participants in temporary jobs in the public and nonmarket sector is closely related to economic cycles, following a countercyclical trend. Countercyclical responsiveness is made possible by good follow-up indicators of business cycles and labor market policies. See H. Ohlsson, "Job Creation Measures as Activist Fiscal Policy: An Empirical Analysis of Policy Reaction Behavior," *European Journal of Political Economy* 8 (1992): 269–80, and H. Ohlsson, "Lags in the Effects of Labor Market Policy: An Empirical Analysis of Job Creation Measures," *Applied Economics* 25 (1993): 343–48.

7. Data from the European Employment Observatory, available at <http://www.eu-employment-observatory.net>.

8. See, for instance, a German study of policies to integrate youth into the labor market: L. Tronti, *Benchmarking Employment Performance and Labor Market Policies* (European Commission, Employment Observatory, RESEARCH network, April 1998), pp. 63–68, and Auer and Kruppe, op. cit., on labor market training comparative monitoring.

9. For details on the U.S. experiments, see A. Bjorklund and H. Regner, "Experimental Evaluation of European Labor Market Policy," in Schmid et al., op. cit., pp. 89–111; H. Regner, "Choosing Among Alternative Non-Experimental Methods for Estimating the Impact of Training: New Swedish Guidance," Working Paper No. 8 (Swedish Institute for Social Research, Stockholm University, 1995). U.S. Department of Labor, "What's Working (and What's Not)" (draft, 1995).

10. Good methodological surveys can be found in R. Fay, "Enhancing the Effectiveness of Active Labor Market Policies: Evidence from Program Evaluation in OECD Countries," *Labor and Market Social Policy Occasional Papers* 18 (1996); Schmid et al., op. cit.; and J. Martin, "What Works among Active Labor Market Policies: Evidence from OECD Countries' Experiences," *OECD Economic Studies* 30 (1999): 79–113.

11. J. Gautié, "Les evaluations d'ordre micro-economique: impact sur les bènéficiaires et effets directs sur l'emploi," in *Les politiques de l'emploi en Europe et aux Etats-Unis*, ed. J. C. Barbier, J. Gautié (Cahiers du CEE: Presses Universitaires de France, 1998).

12. They are also an important source of bias (the hypothesis that the control group is not affected by the program is not true). Many European authors discuss these problems. See Gautié, op. cit.; L. Bellmann and R. Jackman, "Aggregate Impact Analysis," in Schmid et al., op. cit., pp. 143–60; and L. Calmfors, "Does Active Labor Market Policy Increase Employment?: Theoretical Considerations and Some Empirical Evidence from Sweden," seminar paper for the University of Stockholm, Institute for International Economic Studies, March 1995.

13. The European Commission is encouraging development of cost-benefit analysis to support labor market policy analysis and coordination.

14. I found four in the European Union. See C. Erhel, "L'Evaluation Macroeconomique des politiques de l'emploi," in *Les politiques de l'emploi en Europe et aux Etats-Unis* (Cahiers du CEE: Presses Universitaires de France, 1998), pp. 257–76.

15. In a survey of 95 evaluations undertaken in the Netherlands, De Koning found only 4 that used a control group. See J. De Koning, "Training for the Unemployed: The Dutch Experience," paper for the TRANSLAM Project, Netherlands Economic Institute, Rotterdam, October 1997, p. 27.

16. The two other experiments are described in C. Gorter and G. Kalb, "Estimating the Effect of Counselling and Monitoring the Unemployed Using a Job Search Model," *Journal of Human Resources* 31, no. 3 (1996): 590–610, and M. White and J. Lakey, *The Restart Effect: Does Active Labor Market Policy Reduce Unemployment?* (London: Policy Studies Institute, 1992).

17. L. Delander, "Studier kring den arbetsförmedlande verksamheten," *Statens Offentliga Utredningar* 60 (1978): 183–248.

18. O. Raaum and H. Tort, *Evaluering av AMO-kurs: Sysselsättningseffekter og seleksjon till kurs*, report 72 (Oslo: SNF, 1993).

19. The estimated impact of training was not significant or very weak.

20. This paragraph is based on L. Delander and H. Niklasson, "Cost Benefit Analysis," in Schmid et al., op. cit., pp. 183–87. The original reference is L. Behrenz, *Effekt- och effektivitetsanalys av 1987 års personalförstärkning till arbetsförmedlingen* (Lund, Sweden: Department of Economics, 1993).

21. For recent surveys, see G. Schmid, "Activating Labor Market Policy: 'Flexicurity' through Transitional Labour Markets," paper prepared for the Foundation Saint Gobain Conference in Paris, November 8–9, 2000, and Robinson (2000).

22. M. White, S. Lissenburgh, and A. Bryson, *The Impact of Public Job Placing Programmes* (London: Policy Studies Institute, 1997).

23. For surveys, see L. Bellmann and R. Jackman, "Aggregate Impact Analysis," in Schmid et al., op. cit., pp. 143–60; L. Bellmann and R. Jackman, "The Impact of Labor Market Policy on Wages, Employment, and Labor Market Mismatch," in Schmid et al., op. cit., pp. 725–43; and Erhel, op. cit.

24. Such a positive impact is not systematically found in the Swedish studies: country results are contradictory.

25. This description of the Swedish model holds for the 1970s and the first half of the 1980s, but the sharp rise in unemployment at the end of the 1980s weakened these Swedish trends.

CHAPTER 25

Employment Policies: The Case of Spain

by Eduardo González Biedma

ABSTRACT: Europe has faced decades of stubborn structural unemployment since the oil crisis of 1973, and the European Union as well as every member state has proclaimed efforts to create jobs a policy priority. This chapter describes European efforts to combat unemployment, using Spain as a case study, and also traces unemployment in East Asia in the wake of the economic crisis. The chapter argues that crises can stimulate economies to shed inefficient industries and overly rigid labor regulations while creating more viable businesses and jobs in the long run.

The oil shock of 1973 and the Asian financial crisis of 1997–98, although very different in many respects, both spawned unusually high levels of unemployment accompanied by inflation and stagnation. The 1973 shock led to an unfamiliar phenomenon in Europe—lasting structural unemployment—whereas in East Asia traditionally low unemployment rates rose significantly with the crisis, although they were somewhat disguised by underemployment.

The European Union (EU)—as well as every member country—has proclaimed the struggle against unemployment its foremost policy goal. The best way to create employment, analysts now maintain, is to establish the right macroeconomic environment, deregulate the economy, and foster flexibility by relaxing labor regulations. Governments have also turned to active labor market policies to bolster human capital and adjust labor to the needs of business, thereby unleashing the working potential of society and minimizing pockets of structural unemployment. This broad approach harks back to the Treaty of Rome, the EU's founding charter, but what is most significant is that Europe's employment goals depend on the efficient functioning of the common market.

This chapter examines remedies to unemployment pursued in Europe since the oil shock, highlighting the evolution of such policies in Spain and underscoring those that have proved most successful. The chapter also examines recent unemployment in East Asia. The chapter argues that crises can create the conditions for renewed economic growth and employment if governments pursue flexible labor laws and careful investment rather than over-regulation and direct public subsidies.

Unemployment in Europe: A Pervasive New Phenomenon

During the 1960s unemployment rates in Western Europe were insignificant. The United Kingdom, the Federal Republic of Germany, France, and Switzerland welcomed large waves of immigrant labor, some from former European colonies and others from southern Europe. Policymakers maintained confidence in the "healing effects" of the European market and its freedom of movement for capital, services, and workers.

This full-employment dream lasted until the 1973 oil shock, which brought an abrupt halt to the era of smooth and stable economic growth. Concerted action by members of the Organization of Petroleum Exporting Countries, triggered by the Palestinian–Israeli conflict, produced sudden shortages in oil supplies and a fourfold increase in the price of crude oil.[1] Because energy was an essential resource for both work and capital, less energy meant lower productivity.[2] Europe had no mechanisms for addressing this disruption. Workers preferred massive dismissals and plant closures to lower salaries, whereas capitalists did not accept the need to boost productivity, hoping instead that investments in productive capacity would magically restore prosperity.[3]

The crisis led to a rapid transformation in international trade and financial markets, exacerbated by growing international competition, provoking further crises in business cycles. These shocks helped expose long-term inefficiencies that European economies could no longer bear.

Employment and Social Policy in Europe after 1973

The 1973 crisis and a second crisis triggered by another oil shock in 1980–81 dramatically altered views of full employment. Policymakers no longer viewed it as a self-adjusting phenomenon but as a major social issue that called for an explicit policy response. Public authorities described unemployment as the most glaring problem facing the European Community, which issued formal declarations, bills, projects, and blueprints designed to address it.

The Social Action Program of 1974 represented the first formal step toward "the realization of full and better employment" in the European Community. The program included the following major goals:

- Improving hiring services
- Providing professional training, including creating a European center for professional training
- Fostering equal opportunities for men and women
- Promoting free international movement of workers
- Establishing fair policies for dealing with workers from developing countries
- Aiding people who have special difficulty obtaining employment, including youth, older people, and people with disabilities
- Humanizing work and living conditions
- Improving social security, including for those ineligible for regular programs
- Promoting worker participation in company decisions
- Protecting workers during company mergers and takeovers
- Reducing work time by establishing a maximum workweek of 40 hours and mandating 4 weeks of paid vacation
- Coordinating domestic regulation of layoffs

The program sought to avoid or contain layoffs provoked by the crisis and suggested social protection for dismissed workers or those employed by companies facing economic difficulty. Despite these provisions, the document ignored the core problem: a lack of jobs.

The Second Social Action Program, triggered by the 1980–81 oil shock, followed a similar path, as did ensuing documents. For example, the 1989 European Community Charter of Workers' Fundamental Social Rights established an employment "observatory," funded a program to create jobs for specific groups, and improved information exchange on job demand and supply. Those policies did not prove effective; unemployment remained stuck in the 9–10 percent range throughout the European Community.

The 1994 Jacques Delors white paper constituted a turning point in employment policy, stating categorically that employment was the absolute policy priority. The paper focused on two main remedies: active employment policies—specifically professional education and special training for youth as well as enhanced hiring services—and efforts to foster economic growth to generate employment. This document underscored the need to stimulate small and medium-size businesses, which would in turn create jobs.[4]

Earlier programs and papers had assumed that employment policy was somehow unrelated to economic policy, and that social measures and labor legislation would achieve employment goals. The white paper stressed the importance of maintaining social rights and creating high-quality jobs, but it also recognized that achieving full employment might well require restricting funding for social policies and weakening some labor standards.

The Essen European Council of 1994 underscored the goal of "good" employment as well as full employment, implying that this might require providing unemployed people with social benefits rather than simply creating poor-quality jobs. To expand employment, the council called for reducing indirect labor costs—namely, social security taxes.[5] The European Council of 1997 advanced the important idea of mobilizing new technologies and the European network to create new industries and small and medium-size businesses, and thus long-term jobs, with US$10 billion in funding from the European Investment Bank over 3 years.

Interestingly, before European Council authorities had reached these conclusions, European trade unions and employers' associations had signed agreements in 1986 and 1992 that contained clear policy prescriptions for creating employment. These documents called for creating jobs by rapidly reducing interest rates, which would follow from appropriate macroeconomic policies.

The Case of Spain

Spain exemplifies the move toward macroeconomic stability and flexible labor laws as the cornerstone for economic growth and job creation. In Spain the 1973 oil shock coincided with a change in political regime: dictator General Francisco Franco died in 1975, and the country passed a new constitution in 1978, which in turn brought political troubles, legal reforms, and economic transformation. Spain was emerging from the economic and political isolation of the 1960s, although it did not yet belong to the European Community.

Spanish unemployment rates have traditionally been higher than the European Community average, but after the oil crisis Spain began to experience unprecedented unemployment stemming from sudden inflation, trade imbalances, and an obsolete industrial fabric based mostly on state-owned enterprise. Spain's legal and economic framework, encumbered with governmental controls, proved unprepared for open economic competition. Economic indicators fell even more rapidly than in other European economies: inflation peaked at 24 percent in 1978 and unemployment rose as high as 22 percent. These problems have persisted, although unemployment rates have since dropped significantly.

The government responded to the crisis by softening regulations affecting dismissals, worker mobility, payroll taxes, and compensation. These reforms paralleled "emergency labor laws" throughout Europe. Unions sought to tighten employment regulations, including unemployment benefits, to minimize the impact of the crisis on workers. However, the Social Democratic Party, which ruled from 1982 to 1996, seldom met those demands, instead deregulating some aspects of employment law and stressing the role of collective bargaining. For example, the Estatuto de los Trabajadores, the main employment statute, allowed employment contracts to become more flexible.

The government faced two general strikes and a falling out with its traditional partner, the General Worker's Union (UGT), which was particularly angry about statutes that allowed the creation of companies that provide temporary workers, as well as apprenticeship contracts that offer low-paid jobs. Ironically, unions sought to keep regulations enacted during the dictatorship while adding collective bargaining and the right to strike, which Franco had forbidden as too demanding for an aging and inefficient economic fabric.

The newly revamped policies coincided with a new focus on active market policies, as the government spent considerable funds on professional education and subsidized full-time employment and new jobs. These measures enjoyed only modest success. Economic policy, meanwhile, focused on opening the economy to international financial markets and trade, made easier as well as necessary after Spain joined the European Community.

Most specialists agreed that fundamental changes in employment regulations were essential to improve labor market participation rates and fight unemployment. However, pressure from unions and many progressive politicians had sapped the will to pursue deeper reforms. The result was that inflation, the colossal and inefficient public sector, budget deficits, high interest rates and taxes, an outdated and inadequate infrastructure, and weak entrepreneurship continued to present major hurdles to investment and the creation of new jobs. Thus, despite economic growth from 1986 to 1992, unemployment was surprisingly persistent, topping out at 22 percent in 1991.

Increasing the Dynamism of the Economy

Beginning in 1996, the conservative Popular Party government focused on further opening markets to competition and reducing the government role in the economy through privatization.[6] Those measures, plus restrictive fiscal policies entailing "zero deficits" in public accounts, generated annual economic growth of 3.5 percent to 4 percent as well as sharp declines in unemployment.

The legislature's Employment Program 2000 now aims to improve the business environment by easing taxes and interest rates, especially for service industries (tourism is Spain's largest source of income) and information technology firms. The plan also endeavors to bolster research and development in information technology. Employment Program 2000 has further eased regulations on part-time jobs and calls for retraining workers to fill companies' needs. Other aspects of the plan are designed to enable the country to assimilate immigrants and to reconcile family life and work by easing pressure on women's jobs.

This program represents the state of the art in employment policy: ensuring a healthy economy through balanced public accounts, low interest rates, public investment oriented to economic growth, reduced direct public intervention in the economy, and changes in employment regulations that pose hurdles to investment. However, the program has yet to fully address Spain's still thin safety net and pension system.

East Asian Experience with Unemployment

Employment challenges in East Asia are complex, given the region's diverse labor markets. Some 70 percent of Indonesians work in the informal sector, while 40 percent to 50 percent of the Thai labor force works in agriculture. Meanwhile 80 percent of the Republic of Korea's labor force is urban, segregated among firms of different size. Malaysia counts 1.7 million foreign workers in a labor force of 8.7 million.[7]

The East Asian crisis of 1997–98 stemmed mainly from a weakly regulated financial sector and an economy largely financed by short-term debt. Yet the crisis bore a striking similarity to that in Europe in 1973, in that external factors sharply interrupted a period of economic growth and prosperity and created unexpected and unfamiliar social problems, particularly unemployment. For the five most affected East Asian countries, the crisis led to a sharp fall in demand, accompanied by price changes and dampened public spending.[8] The result was a stunning decline in output: 15 percent in Indonesia, 7 percent in Thailand and

Korea, 5 percent in Malaysia, and 0.5 percent in the Philippines. The more industrialized the country, the tougher the consequences of the crisis.

The impacts on employment and wages were dramatic. Indonesia was the most affected country; some 5 million workers shifted from the formal to the informal sector, and salaries declined by 34 percent. In Thailand, unemployment rose from 2.3 percent to 5.4 percent, and salaries fell by 6 percent, which economic recovery did not entirely redress. In Korea, unemployment reached a peak of 8.7 percent from 2.5 percent, and many people stopped looking for work. However, recovery was equally dramatic, and by October 1999 unemployment had declined to 4.6 percent.

Malaysia and the Philippines were the least affected, Malaysia because it shifted job losses to immigrants, who accounted for as much as 20 percent of the work force. Salaries declined by 12.5 percent, then partly recovered during the first half of 1999. In the Philippines, the unemployment rate of 8 percent to 9 percent changed little.

Meanwhile work force participation rates changed little in Thailand and in the Philippines; in Malaysia and Korea they fell; and in Indonesia they grew because underemployed women entered the labor market to offset the loss of household income. Reduced employment opportunities obliged people to accept part-time and low-paid jobs,[9] a phenomenon most pronounced in rural areas, which had the flexibility to absorb new workers.

New Approaches to Unemployment

The three classic approaches to unemployment include boosting demand through public investment in infrastructure and community works, supporting unemployed people through unemployment benefits, and pursuing active labor market policies. Europe's Employment Plan 2000 focuses on encouraging a more flexible work force through employment legislation, stimulating the economy by investing in information technology, and fostering the economic and political conditions for growth. These approaches, pursued by member countries, have generally proved successful.

Analysts have discredited public works as a way to cut unemployment, because that approach entails serious public debt and usually causes a rise in interest rates, taxes, or both, whereas the ratio of jobs created to public expenditures is relatively low. Analysts view excessive public intervention in the economy as ineffective and unsustainable; it fails to create durable jobs and makes employment overly dependent on public sector initiative and management. Furthermore, although urban and rural public works programs offering low salaries may be helpful to very poor people, they do not attract blue-collar workers laid off during a crisis.[10]

This means that governments should rely on public works only when necessary and should apply strict measures of efficiency. However, Europe has succumbed to the temptation to create artificial jobs. Such programs, which tend to require little capital and use many workers, have limited multiplier effects and foster continuous dependence on public funds, creating expensive pockets of inefficiency that are very hard to remove. Indonesia, the Philippines, and Thailand have experience along these lines.

Assistance to the Unemployed

Assisting the unemployed may seem essential, but avoiding fraud and mismanagement are difficult. Unemployment insurance tends to exclude people most in need: those in the informal sector and agriculture, as well as the self-employed and youth. To be eligible for benefits, people usually must have contributed to social security, but the people most acutely affected by a crisis tend to be those in the informal sector and those who have never held a job. Some people will opt to combine unemployment benefits with participation in the informal sector, so unemployment benefits could actually subsidize, and even promote and perpetuate, a form of labor relations that assumes a worker has other funds. To address these problems, unemployment benefits need to be geared to groups that truly need assistance, and special care must be taken to avoid fraud. Flexible unemployment benefit programs can make more sense than systems based on rigid rules.

In East Asia, Korea alone now maintains a reliable unemployment insurance system. For other countries, this appears to be a good moment to establish flexible assistance schemes rather than formal insurance programs.

Active Labor Market Policies

Policies such as wage subsidies, professional training, job placement services, encouragement of jobs for youth and aged people, and support for self-employment, can be viewed as complements to other policies.[11] In Europe, they are essentially considered social measures to help disadvantaged people and a vehicle for creating human capital. However, they are not effective in times of crisis when jobs are simply unavailable. The experience of Eastern European countries shows that a well-educated population does not automatically bring low unemployment rates; overqualified workers who do not meet the needs of domestic businesses may have to emigrate in search of work. Organization for Economic Cooperation and Development (OECD) experience suggests that active labor market programs "tend to be small (on average their expenditures come to half of those spent for income support to the unemployed), and they entail high deadweight loss. For example, for every five wage subsidies paid to employers, only one fills in a genuine vacancy—the rest are used by employers for jobs that they were already willing to fund."[12] The same comments apply to job placement agencies: they can do very little when the problem is a lack of jobs. Active labor market policies thus work best in meeting real and routine needs to enhance the quality of the work force rather than in responding to crisis.

The classic approaches to unemployment are necessary and effective but insufficient. Recent European experience underscores the importance of flexible employment systems, active efforts to attract new technologies, and efforts to enlarge markets and involve labor and employers in creating employment.

Deregulating Aspects of Employment Regulations

Deregulating aspects of employment regulations has proved successful in addressing unemployment, particularly during crises. European countries have sought to protect employee compensation and provide generous unemployment benefits while allowing layoffs, flexible forms of contracting, mergers, and negotiations on new working conditions. Without such measures, crises could have been far worse. Governments essentially aimed at minimizing bankruptcies rather than blindly protecting worker expectations that proved unaffordable. Labor often demands stricter employment regulations to defend workers against layoffs. However, making employment regulations more rigid can create more unemployment and force many workers to shift to the informal sector. Concessions on working conditions, lower payroll taxes, and easing the hiring of part-time or temporary workers may be efficient short-run solutions in fighting unemployment.[13]

The former ideal of a full-time, lifetime job for everyone seems to be fading. The requirements of open economies, the characteristics of new kinds of business, and the explosion of the service economy all point to higher worker turnover and more temporary and part-time jobs. These should not be considered underemployment. The new jobs will ensure higher salaries and some stability in family income, even though they do not involve a permanent job for life. Employment regulations need to ease the growth of this new economy and meet its requirements insofar as they point in generally positive directions.

Functional and Geographical Mobility

Mobile workers can take advantage of employment opportunities. Government investments in education and training are essential in creating functional mobility.

Open Relationships among Management, Unions, and Government

Efforts to repress unions undermine basic human rights, are incompatible with modern democratic societies, and create unnecessary social tension and unrest. However, overregulation of labor markets can make the situation worse. Governments should focus on bringing workers and employers together and balancing the interests of labor and management in specific industries.[14]

Market Specialization and Enlargement

Crises often produce at least one positive result: they can clean up an economy. Extinction of inefficient industries can exert an effect similar to that of a fire in an old forest: the scene is nasty the next day, but in the long run the crisis allows stronger, greener, and more fruitful industries to grow. Crises can also help countries discover their areas of comparative advantage with the help of pressures and opportunities in the global economy, re-creating more stable and efficient employment.

In Spain the oil shock prevented the government from further subsidizing coal and steel industries, which had experienced growing losses. The shutdown of several mines and factories forced their communities to live a tragedy. A few years later, however, most of those communities have shifted to the tertiary sector or other types of manufacturing at no cost to the public budget, and they are now making much more money than before. The crisis clearly proved beneficial in the long run, although this was hard for people caught in the throes of turmoil to realize.

New Technologies and the Information Society

The European Union has focused its latest employment plans on developing jobs in the information and services sectors. The role of government here is delicate: it must continue to provide essential assistance to people in need while pursuing active labor market policies that help spawn new businesses. Crises in Europe helped the economy shift strategically away from old industries that were no longer viable toward more up-to-date activities.[15]

Conclusion: Crises Can Foster Economic Renewal

An unexpected conclusion is that crises are not entirely detrimental to employment and economic growth. European experience highlights how crises can help economic systems mature. Governments that allow economic forces to generate new ideas and resources can deal with crises and the resulting unemployment better and reasonably quickly. The best option is always to create the macroeconomic conditions for growth. Above all, governments should avoid overprotective measures such as nationalization of companies and unnecessary or costly public subsidies whose sole purpose is to create new jobs; those actions can cause long-term misbehavior in the economy.

Governments must alleviate the plight of unemployed people, basing benefits not solely on former contributions to social security but on real needs. Systems should not discourage job search or subsidize the informal sector or under-employment. Ironically, flexible labor legislation is frequently effective in maintaining employment and protecting existing workers because it helps create new jobs and heal companies in trouble. Active labor market policies are useful in maintaining an economy's competitiveness, a key condition for growth and development. However, in the short run they are unlikely to relieve unemployment. Overall, union involvement, social dialogue, and social peace are essential ingredients for boosting employment.

Notes

1. See Geoffrey Heal and Graciela Chichilisky, *Oil and the International Economy* (Oxford, England: Clarendon, 1991), p. 74; Raymond Vernon, ed., *The Oil Crisis* (New York: W. W. Norton, 1976); and Romano Prodi and Alberto Clo, "Europe," and Robert S. Pyndyck and Julio Rotemberg, "Energy Shocks and the Macroeconomy," in *Oil Shock: Policy, Response, and Implementation*, ed. Alvin L. Alm and Robert J. Einer (Cambridge, Mass.: Ballinger, 1984).

2. R. A. Gonzalez and R. Nils Folsom, "Responding to the Oil Shock: The U.S. Economy since 1973," *The Freeman*, The Foundation for Economic Education (February 1989).

3. See Pyndyck and Rotemberg, p. 110–11.

4. Jacques Delors, *European Social Policy, Way Forward for the Union, A White Paper*, COM (94) 333, July 1994.

5. European Commission, *Employment Rates Report 1998, Employment Performance in the Member States*, p. 16. This report underscored that "taxation has important effects on the functioning of the labor market," since "taxes on labor are often highlighted as one of the main culprits of high unemployment in Europe, as they increase labor costs and may also affect the composition of labor supply and demand." Yet "over the last 15 years the development of taxation systems (taxes and social security contributions) shows a fiscal bias unfavorable to employment-creation in most Member States." On average in the European Union between 1980 and 1996 the burden of taxes

and charges on labor has increased steadily (from 35 percent to almost 43 percent), whereas it has decreased for other factors of production, mainly capital (from 42 percent to 36 percent) and has remained stable for consumption (close to 14 percent). Taxation has important effects on the functioning of the labor market. Taxes on labor are often highlighted as one of the main culprits of high unemployment in Europe, because they increase labor costs and may also affect the composition of labor supply and demand. The incidence of taxes can be magnified if the degree of competition is also low in product markets (since taxes can be easily shifted forward on product prices) and may also depend on the kind of wage-negotiating mechanisms prevailing in labor markets.

6. See J. I. Perez Infante, "Reformas laborales y creación de empleo en la economía española en el contexto de la unión monetaria," in *Euro y empleo,* ed. J. Aragon Medina (Madrid, 1998), p. 150.

7. As reported in World Bank, "A Way Forward," prepared for the Bangkok Social Meeting, 1999. <http://www.worldbank.org/eapsocial>.

8. World Bank, *Social Issues Arising from the East Asia Economic Crisis: A Work in Progress,* draft, 1999, p. 6.

9. A. Cox Edwards and C. Manning, *The Economics of Employment Protection, and Unemployment Insurance Schemes: Reflections on Policy Options for Thailand, Malaysia, the Philippines, and Indonesia,* World Bank report, October 5, 1999, p. 2.

10. Other active policies, such as wage subsidies, loans for small business start-up, youth training, and in-service retraining for workers whose skills no longer fit their employers' requirements, may be relevant.

11. For a discussion of the impact of such policies, see Gordon Betcherman, Amit Dar, Amy Luinstra, and Makoto Ogawa, "Active Labor Market Policies: Policy Issues for East Asia," World Bank, Social Protection Unit, December 1999. The authors question such approaches on the basis of OECD country experience. They conclude that, "Ultimately ALMPs [active labor market policies] are judged by their performance in improving the employability and earnings of workers and the evaluations indicate that the investments made often have little or no impact on these outcomes." However, they also recognize other helpful outcomes of those policies, such as their social impact and integration of economically marginalized and at-risk groups.

12. See Cox and Manning, op. cit., p. 3, who also refer to two major recent research products: OECD, "The Adjustment Potential of the Labor Market," part II of the *OECD Jobs Study: Evidence and Explanations* (Paris: OECD, 1994), and G. Saint-Paul, "The Political Economy of Employment Protection," Economics Working Paper No. 355, Universitat Pompeu Fabra, National Center for Research Science, 1999.

13. See the research by Duncan Campbell, *Globalization and Change: Social Dialogue and Labor Market Adjustment in the Crisis-Affected Countries of East Asia* (Washington, D.C.: World Bank, 1999), p. 36, who concludes that "social dialogue and positive economic outcomes move together—they are positively related. Examples have been shown where this is the case. Or, at the very least, the various examples do not disprove the point. Of course, neither the evidence presented nor the concepts argued have been so compelling as to foreclose all debate. For example, the most extensive and influential example of tripartite crisis management has clearly occurred in the Republic of Korea, and it is the Korean economy that has shown the strongest recovery."

14. European Commission, *Employment Opportunities in the Information Society: Exploding the Potential of Information Revolution,* Report to the European Council, 1998, available at <http://www.europa.eu.int/comm/dg05/soc-dial/info_soc/jobopps/joboppes.pdf>.

15. World Bank, *A Way Forward,* op. cit., p. 2.

BOX 5.3

Seminar on Flexibility vs. Security: Social Policy and the Labor Market in Europe and East Asia, Seoul, December 2000

The most ambitious single event under the Asia-Europe Meeting (ASEM) project was a major conference held in Seoul, Korea, in December 2000. It was jointly organized with the Korean Social Security Association, the Korea Labor Institute, the Korea Institute for Public Finance, and the Korea Institute for Health and Social Affairs. The overarching theme was labor market policies, with the objective to focus on implications of more flexible labor market policies for future employment in the Republic of Korea and elsewhere. More than 100 people attended and there was active newspaper coverage. Korea's Minister of Labor opened the conference.

The conference focused on four major topics. The first was the role of employment within social policy more generally. Discussion was based on papers presented by Stein Kuhnle (Bergen University, Norway) on the "Work-Friendly Welfare State" and Chul-In Lee (Korea Institute for Public Finance) on "Globalization, Employment, and Productive Welfare." The second topic focused on the role of trade unions, with presentations by Johannes Schmidt (Research Center on Development and International Relations, University of Åalborg, Denmark) on "Restructuring Social Welfare in East and Southeast Asia: Corporatism with or without Labor?" and Joohee Lee (Korea Labor Institute) on "Protecting Worker Welfare in the Age of Flexibility: Employment Adjustment and the Trade Union Movement in Korea." The third topic examined the issue of trade-offs between security and flexibility, with presentations by Eduardo González-Biedma (Seville University, Spain) on "Unemployment in East Asia: Lessons from Spain and Europe" and Kyung-Soo Choi (Korea Development Institute) on "Job Security and Flexibility in Korea." The final topic addressed postcrisis adjustment and social policies in Korea and revolved around presentations by Rémy

continued on next page

BOX 5.3, continued

Herrera (University of Paris I, France) on "Escaping from Crisis and Activating Labor Market Policies in Korea" and Soonman Kwon (Seoul National University) on "Security in the Korean Health Care System." Last, the topic of human capital and social policy was discussed in a roundtable format.

The conference highlighted Korea's active focus on labor market policies in the wake of the 1997–98 crisis, as well as the practical issues of concern to academic and policy leaders there. Experience around labor market trends and practices lent itself particularly well to interregional and cross-country exchange.

BOX 5.4

Seminar on Governance and Social Policy, Bangkok, October 26–27, 2000

The seminar in Bangkok was jointly organized with the regional office of the International Labor Organization (ILO) and focused on five key issues surrounding governance and social policy.

The first topic was macroeconomic and social linkages, with a provocative presentation by Robert Wade of the London School of Economics (Box 2.2). He acknowledged the macroeconomic constraints on social welfare policies but countered arguments that globalization is prompting a "race to the bottom," maintaining that no substantial evidence supports the thesis of a convergence toward a "low-tax, low-spending, minimum welfare state." Social welfare is one of the main factors sustaining demand, which in turn is one of the main spurs to economic growth. Growth in developing countries has lagged behind that of Organization for Economic Cooperation and Development (OECD) countries in part because developing economies have been more dependent on exports, and world supply exceeds world demand.

Discussion turned on how social policies can redress the inequalities sometimes created by economic growth. The role of the minimum wage entered the debate: instead of being seen as a disincentive to production, the minimum wage was described as a prime mechanism to ensure political stability both in times of rapid growth and in times of crisis. An OECD report shows that if market incomes become more unequal during periods of fast growth, fiscal mechanisms can prevent household incomes from becoming just as unequal. Participants often underscored social dialogue as an essential tool in implementing socially sensitive macroeconomic policies, for example, through negotiation between employers and employees.

The second topic concerned the links between social policy and social standards, and was based on a presentation by Markus Zöeckler (see Chapter 26). He maintained that social rights are crucial because they

continued on next page

BOX 5.4, continued

obligate states to pursue international cooperation to achieve them. Given other treaties and conventions, notably the 182 ILO conventions, much legal and intellectual fodder for a rights-based approach now exists. Participants rejected arguments that rights are culturally biased but raised many questions about how to implement those rights and balance them with responsibilities.

The third topic focused on the role of the media, with a presentation by Chris Greene (BBC World Service Trust) on the trust's experience in supporting social policy in various countries. The trust establishes schools of journalism; finances production of documentary films, soap operas, and radio shows; publishes books; and produces a Web site on health choice and rights, especially in Eastern Europe. The assumption is that the media can raise awareness and spark debates on dormant social issues. Discussion highlighted the importance of the media in expanding public knowledge of social issues and promoting social policy. Participants underscored the media's role in diffusing misconceptions, with some concern about unchecked investigative reporting.

The fourth topic focused on papers by Peter Scherer on family obligations in Europe and East Asia (see Chapter 2), and Mr. Cuong (Ministry of War Invalids and Social Affairs, Vietnam) on international efforts to deal with the growing welfare divide between developing and industrial countries. Mr. Cuong focused on the "20:20 initiative" in Vietnam, launched at the World Summit on Social Development in Copenhagen in 1999, which committed developing countries to allocate 20 percent of their budget to social development and industrial countries to devote 20 percent of their aid to social development programs. In Vietnam, the 20:20 initiative took the form of a broad hunger eradication and poverty reduction program. A second program within the 20:20 initiative identified the 2,000 most remote communes in Vietnam and focused food and health assistance there.

Discussion focused on the role of the family in social development and the ambiguities entailed in social assistance. For example, using legal requirements to formalize family obligations can lead families to think that they must look after themselves. Formal arrangements can also crowd out informal ones.

BOX 5.4, continued

The fifth topic, worker participation, was based on a paper by Jacques Rojot (see Chapter 21). Participants explored union roles compared with other forms of worker participation, as well as the complexity and potential pitfalls of various participation schemes. Such systems were seen as more relevant for Europe than for East Asia because trade unions are particularly weak in the latter region.

Moves toward Global Standards

Introduction

This book has explored the social needs and social policies of individual countries in both East Asia and Europe while also highlighting the expanding role of the European Union (EU) in setting and influencing social policy. Part VI extends this discussion by examining how regional and international organizations and statutes do—and might—influence social standards and hence social policy.

Box 6.1 highlights the evolving social agenda for the EU, with the employment challenge as its key starting point. Further delineating the role of regional institutions, in Box 6.2 Luc Tholoniat examines the EU's "open method of coordination"—a recent set of mechanisms aimed at establishing specific regional benchmarks in significant areas of social policy such as employment and pension reform.

In Chapter 26, Bruno Simma and Markus Zöeckler discuss the role of international agreements on human rights in setting and enforcing social standards. They hold that viewing economic and social rights as fundamental human rights can provide a clear compass that could help turn vague humanitarian aspirations into clear-cut obligations. They highlight the United Nations and the International Labor Organization covenants, which undergird those rights. They maintain that economic and social rights should be an essential element of development, countering notions such as cultural relativity used to oppose such an approach. This chapter does not address two important developments that have taken on central roles since it was prepared—the increasing use of Poverty Reduction Strategy Papers (PRSPs) to sharpen the focus on poverty reduction and strengthening consensus on tangible Millennium Development Goals. Both point in the same direction, seeking tougher standards and clearer benchmarks in the fight against poverty and for greater social justice.

In Chapter 27, Gabriella Battaini-Dragoni explores the unique experience of the Council of Europe in establishing core rights and social standards for 44 member countries. Some of the statutes guaranteeing such rights include legal remedies, but enforcing them ultimately requires the cooperation of member states. She holds that regional standards are essential in ensuring social cohesion during both periods of strong economic growth and periods of economic crisis, and that Europe and East Asia can learn from each other in determining how best to establish and apply social standards.

Box 6.3 focuses on the particular issues surrounding "social dumping." In Box 6.4, Bob Deacon maintains that strong regional trading blocks can counter the effects of neoliberal globalization by setting social standards, and he calls for the Association of Southeast Asian Nations to take a more active role while also appealing to the European Union to put social development in the south ahead of its regional trade interests. Box 6.5 gives a summary account of the Brussels seminar, which focused on social policies to cope with economic instability.

Social Agenda for the European Union
by Willem van der Geest

Over the period 1973 to 1997, the unemployment rate in the European Union (EU) jumped from 3 percent to nearly 11 percent, involving some 15 million persons. High unemployment, particularly among low-skilled workers, is almost a structural feature in many European countries, although there are significant regional and gender imbalances. While the average employment rate stands at 63 percent of persons of working age, some regions in fact have a rate of only 40 percent. Even more significant is that 80 percent of men age 25–55 have a job, but only 50 percent of the women.

In analyzing this problem, traditional trade theories tend to blame globalization, in particular the fact of increased competition with low-wage countries (North–South trade). Yet, recent reviews[1] conclude there is no strong evidence to show that trade with nonmember countries of the Organization for Economic Cooperation and Development has been the fundamental factor causing declining employment opportunities for unskilled workers and rising wage inequalities. Rather, competition among similarly endowed economies and the volatility of global financial flows are the main driving force behind these trends. More specifically, uneven technical change and internal trade *within* the EU are the primary causes.

For this reason, the policy debate in Europe has moved away from trade protectionism and toward reform of Europe's social policies. Thus it is not surprising that the political commitment at the EU Lisbon Council of 2000 included an integrated social component: "Full employment is the aim of economic and social policy." Further priority areas of policy reform included changing tax and benefit systems to raise employment instead of discouraging it; modernizing work organization,

Based on the introduction by Willem van der Geest, Director, European Institute for Asian Studies (EIAS), at the Brussels Asia-Europe Meeting (ASEM) conference, December 2001.

continued on next page

BOX 6.1, continued

in particular life-long learning; making social security systems employment friendly; and making regulatory approaches entrepreneur friendly.

The European Council first and foremost underscored that Europe is not ready to abandon its unique approach of seeking to combine progressive social values with successful economic growth. However, it acknowledged without hesitation that the present design, structure, and application of economic and social policies are not up to the challenge of rapid and continuous technological change that characterizes globalization.

A key policy research issue for programs like the Asia-Europe Meeting (ASEM) Trust Fund is to ensure that reform of Europe's own social policies—seeking to enhance social welfare in a long-term, sustainable way—will be compatible with improving social welfare elsewhere.

1. Paul Brenton and Jacques Pelkmans, *Global Trade and European Workers* (New York: St. Martin's Press in association with the European Institute for Asian Studies, 1999), and Ludo Cuyvers, ed., *Globalization and Social Development: European and Southeast Asian Evidence* (Cheltenham, England: Edward Elgar, 2001).

The Open Method of Coordination: A New Venture for European Social Policy

by Luc Tholoniat

The open method of coordination is a new approach to making and coordinating policy at the European Union (EU) level. It entails

- Setting common goals and guidelines for all member states, together with specific timetables and targets to achieve those goals
- Translating the common objectives and guidelines into national policies through "national action plans" and strategies
- Establishing indicators and benchmarks as a means of comparing best practices
- Pursuing periodic monitoring, evaluation, and peer review

The approach was conceived as a complement to more traditional instruments of EU social policy: European legislation, European social funds, and "social dialogue." The method advocates a fully decentralized approach, in that national, regional, and local authorities translate EU guidelines into concrete policies. Systematic monitoring, evaluation, and peer review are designed to boost the effectiveness of EU policies and stimulate innovation among member states.

Inspired by economic convergence programs of the 1990s, the EU first applied the approach to the European Employment Strategy in 1997 and expanded it to other policy fields following the European Council of Lisbon of 2000, especially to social exclusion and poverty (since 2000) and pensions (since 2001). The following tables summarize EU actions to implement this new approach.

Based on a presentation at the Asia-Europe Meeting (ASEM) seminar, Rome, February 2002.

continued on next page

BOX 6.2, continued

Common Objectives/Guidelines

	Employment	*Social inclusion*	*Pensions*
Source of objectives	Guidelines (4 pillars)	Common objectives	Common objectives
Timeline	(Nov. 1997, annual)	(Dec. 2000–end 2002)	(June 2001–end 2004)
Objectives	1. Increase employability	1. Ensure employment and access to rights	1. Ensure the adequacy of pensions
	2. Foster entrepreneurship	2. Prevent exclusion	2. Ensure their financial sustainability
	3. Increase adaptability	3. Help the most vulnerable	3. Modernize pension systems
	4. Foster equal opportunities	4. Mobilize actors	

Targets

	Employment	*Social inclusion*	*Pensions*
EU-quantified targets for 2010 (Lisbon and Stockholm)	EU employment rate = 70% Employment of women = 60% Employment of workers age 55–65 = 50%	No targets proposed by the commission	No targets
Recommendations to states	57 in 2001, 58 in 2000	No targets	No targets

National Action Plans

	Employment	*Social inclusion*	*Pensions*
Type of plans	National action plans for employment	National action plans against social exclusion and poverty	National strategy reports on pensions
Issue date	Annual since May 1998	Every 2 years since June 2001	September 2003

BOX 6.2, continued

Monitoring and Peer Review at EU Level

	Employment	Social inclusion	Pensions
Type of report	Joint report on employment (annual since September 1998)	Joint report on social inclusion (every 2 years since December 2001)	Joint report on pensions (December 2002)
Type of indicators	Structural and performance indicators	List of 18 common indicators (December 2001)	Existing indicators (work in progress)
Type of exchange program	Exchange program to promote local initiatives	Exchange program to combat social exclusion	Not applicable

CHAPTER 26

Global Social Standards

by Bruno Simma and Markus Zöeckler

ABSTRACT: The notion of global standards for core human rights is gaining ground among key international institutions, and it was accentuated by the effects of the East Asian crisis. This chapter argues that social and economic rights should be central in thought and action about economic development.

The Chinese characters for "crisis" combine the two meanings "danger" and "opportunity," reminding us that living through dangerous times can also open new horizons. The East Asian crisis was a catalyst for social policy reform in the affected countries and a spur for the international community to act more boldly and humanely on social dimensions of economic policy. Caught by surprise, national governments and the international community confronted problems born of the region's weak social protection systems.

The experience reinforced a growing international consensus on the need for meaningful policies that address social needs head on. The East Asian crisis thus fueled broader discussion about the need for more focus in global financial and economic architecture on mechanisms to ensure greater equity and social justice. Participants in international forums have long proclaimed respect for human dignity, freedom, equality, solidarity, and basic principles of social justice.[1] Especially significant is the growing recognition that practical application of rather abstract values requires principles and standards to guide the design and implementation of social policies.

This chapter highlights human rights—particularly economic and social rights—as core norms underpinning national and international development agendas. The chapter explores the relationships between social and economic rights and development concepts, and obstacles to implementing those rights and concepts at both national and international levels.

Human Rights as Social Standards

Although most national constitutions define explicit standards for social policy, international norms are needed to orient development aid and international finance institutions. The United Nations (UN) system and agencies such as the International Labor Organization (ILO)[2] have special roles in developing such global social standards.

Those institutions have undertaken substantial standard-setting work. The nucleus of social standards for development is the Universal Declaration of Human Rights, which the UN General Assembly adopted more than 50 years ago: "Everyone is entitled to a social and international order in which the rights and freedoms set forth in this Declaration can be fully realized."[3] Besides guaranteeing classic civil and political rights, this resolution encompassed fundamental economic, social, and cultural rights, and it became the starting point for intensive standard-setting activity in the UN organization.

Human rights treaties later made more concrete the declaration's fairly general provisions, turning pronouncements into legal obligations for all signatory states. The International Covenant on Economic, Social and Cultural Rights (ICESCR) provides the most comprehensive coverage of these rights and outlines a holistic approach to social and economic development. The ICESCR obliges states to cooperate and provide international assistance to fulfill human rights, thus offering guidance for a socially just international order.

Special treaties that prohibit racial and gender discrimination and protect the rights of children supplement the ICESCR,[4] and the 182 conventions adopted by the ILO develop labor and social security rights in more detail. The ILO has identified eight core conventions establishing freedom of association and abolishing forced labor, child labor, and job discrimination as fundamental human rights at work, and these conventions constitute a global consensus on minimum labor standards.[5] UN and ILO mechanisms have ensured dialogue on implementing these rights. The Committee on Economic, Social and Cultural Rights, which monitors the ICESCR implementation, has worked to clarify the obligations of states, the content of specific rights, and the obligations incurred by third states and international organizations.

International conferences consistently confirmed the UN human rights treaties and core ILO conventions during the 1990s. Potential further refinements provide ample scope for debate, but these statutes proclaim a broad core set of objectives for political, administrative, and judicial institutions. Those provisions qualify as the most authoritative and comprehensive principles to guide the design and implementation of national economic and social policies and a framework for international development policy.

Development and Human Rights

Until recently, human rights seldom entered international discourse on development. The phrase "human rights" appeared only rarely in publications of the United Nations Development Programme (UNDP) and the World Bank before the 1990s, and the UN strategies for the recent "development decade" mentioned human rights only in passing. In the early 1990s, then-Secretary-General Boutros-Ghali's Agenda for Development—the product of intensive consultation and negotiation among UN agencies—addressed the social justice and democracy dimensions of development and focused on improving human well-being, but included no explicit reference to human rights.[6]

However, as human rights emerged from the ideological constraints of the East–West conflict, international financial institutions began to acknowledge their relevance more formally. Many international institutions now maintain that a broad spectrum of development work is largely directed toward promoting human rights.[7]

Using the language of human rights is not the same as a rights-oriented approach to development. Development policies are often only marginally influenced by economic and social rights, which can be regarded as at best a positive side effect. Development discourse has produced a variety of concepts such as human development, human well-being, human security, basic needs, good governance, participatory approaches, and good social practices. Proponents increasingly integrate these concepts with human rights issues,[8] but the concepts remain rather fuzzy and fall well short of what could be termed a human rights approach to development. For example, everyone agrees on the urgent need to implement policies that alleviate the plight of the poor. Unfortunately, and not surprisingly, there is no consensual definition of poverty and its dimensions, and hence little agreement on how to identify the poor and formulate and target policies that reduce poverty.[9]

Many new development concepts confine policymaking to a minimalist or underinclusive approach. For example, discussions of "social protection" and "social safety nets" in no way point toward anything that approaches even a modest welfare state. These ideas focus instead on a minimum baseline for cushioning social and potentially political side effects of cyclical downturns and economic transitions.[10] Proponents of "good governance" often limit the idea to laws and institutions that guarantee the smooth functioning of markets.[11]

Perhaps most important, none of these concepts address the question of accountability. Who is responsible for implementing social development policy, and what role should international organizations play? The responsibility question is crucial if a global financial and economic architecture is to support socioeconomic development.

Development discourse in the 1990s gradually included more human rights issues but still fell far short of integrating concepts of rights fully into the formulation and implementation of socioeconomic policies. A human rights approach to economic and social policy entails more than new labels. Poverty reduction and participatory governance goals would change significantly if they included explicit human rights standards.

A rights approach to development is sometimes belittled as impractical,[12] or it is regarded as politically unwise because it may become entangled in disputes about cultural relativity.[13] Nevertheless, countries, international organizations, and civil society are showing a growing willingness to recognize the fulfillment of human rights as the central task of socioeconomic development and to explore how specific policies and programs can implement those rights.[14]

Rights and Obligations versus Appeals and Charity

Approaching economic, social, and development policies from a human rights perspective can turn vague humanitarian aspirations and advisable policies into clear-cut obligations.[15] As long as we regard lack of food, health care, housing, and basic education as a deplorable tragedy calling for our sympathy and do not treat this disrespect for human dignity as a violation of an individual's rights, we are not taking these needs seriously enough. All human rights presuppose an institutional setting that assigns specific actors responsibility for ensuring their realization. The law can recognize and enforce rights to food, housing, and social security as long as institutions can clearly identify an obligee.[16]

Primary responsibility for human rights lies with the state, and those rights include freedom from state interference as well as the state's obligation to intervene. States may provide an enabling environment so individuals can fulfill their rights on their own, or they may protect them against interference from private actors. Only if all other positive actions fail will the state be obliged to provide the goods or services that are essential for individuals to realize their rights.[17] These obligations apply to all countries: high per capita income does not absolve them from addressing problems of homelessness and other forms of social exclusion.

Growth in gross domestic product (GDP) and improvements in overall economic indicators do not fulfill human rights as long as economic development excludes some people; not every pro-growth policy is also pro-poor.[18] A rights approach entails policies that address the demands and needs of vulnerable and disadvantaged groups, often through supplementary programs. This bottom-up perspective implies the need to intensify microeconomic analysis at the household and intrahousehold level, and to integrate such information into policymaking to target society's most needy.

A rights approach points to both direct and indirect action. Governments confront a multitude of tasks, but the complexity of the interplay between financial and economic policies, human development, and governmental institutions becomes ever more apparent. Given a maze of difficult choices and constrained resources, a rights approach would oblige governments to make protecting the most vulnerable social groups a clear priority.

Progressive Realization versus Minimum Standards

The sharpest difference between today's development framework and a human rights approach is that the latter obliges governments to realize rights progressively and commit to continuous improvement.[19]

The first step is thorough analysis of a country's socioeconomic situation. Policymakers can then develop specific benchmarks to measure progress. Higher spending does not automatically further the right to education or health care among disadvantaged groups: a government needs to design and implement programs specifically tailored to provide basic health care and primary education for all, and it should promise to reach those goals within, say, 5 years.

A rights approach to socioeconomic development requires transparent accountability mechanisms, beginning with monitoring and including policy design, implementation, and evaluation. Individuals and groups whose rights have not yet been realized must be enabled and encouraged to bring that fact to the attention of public authorities. Judicial remedies are sometimes the most effective, but other administrative and even legislative procedures can enable individuals and groups to help formulate and evaluate socioeconomic policies.

Rights do not provide a specific blueprint. What is required is a dedicated and principled approach to results-oriented policies. A rights approach will not always provide a clear answer when governments must make hard choices in times of limited resources, but it should provide a compass to help orient social policies and weigh competing interests.

Human Rights and the International Community

The International Covenant on Economic, Social and Cultural Rights implies that third states and the international community have positive obligations to assist other states in realizing economic and social rights. The ICESCR has stressed that "the realms of trade, finance and investment are in no way exempt from these general principles and that the international organizations with specific responsibilities in those areas should play a positive and constructive role in relation to human rights."[20]

The ICESCR framework calls on the International Monetary Fund (IMF) and the World Bank to encourage states to recognize economic, social, and cultural rights; help countries identify specific benchmarks; and facilitate development of policies that fulfill those rights.[21] This mandate includes an obligation on the part of donor countries and agencies to provide financial and technical assistance to countries that lack the resources to fulfill economic and social rights and to design programs that support countries' efforts to realize those rights progressively.[22]

Addressing Arguments against a Human Rights Approach

Several arguments are advanced as to why it is difficult to more fully incorporate human rights into national and international economic and development policies.

The Cultural Relativity of Human Rights

Ideological preconceptions and political and economic interests have dominated disputes about the universality of human rights. Many inquiries into the conceptual foundations of human rights find them embedded in all cultures.[23]

The universality of human rights is not about uniformity. Rights demand respect for different cultural identities that may be crucial to sensibly implementing economic and social rights. A human rights approach demands that governments and international organizations respect cultural conditions in each country and community. Foreign assistance must recognize the primary responsibility of the recipient country and respect its discretion to implement the most appropriate social policies.[24]

Liberal Economic Paradigm

With the end of the ideological East–West conflict, economic growth, free markets, and economic efficiency have become almost uncontested values among economists. A utilitarian approach combined with liberal economic theory asserts that growth promulgated through efficient markets is the essential prerequisite for improving human well-being. Adherents of this view subject other global values to the test of whether they conform to the overarching goal of a free market economy.

Proponents of the market approach tend to view ILO occupational safety and health standards through the lens of raising productivity and reducing economic losses.[25] Rights of girls and women to equal access to education and training are taken more seriously with statistical evidence that such policies support overall economic growth. Countries and other players may promote the reproductive rights of women because the use of contraceptives reduces population growth and furthers economic growth.[26] Providing primary education for all children is recognized as a promising investment in human capital conducive to economic growth. Freedom of association and collective bargaining, meanwhile, will find their way into the new international economy if the exercise of these rights exerts a positive economic effect.[27] Economic and social rights of the elderly, people with disabilities, the unskilled, and many others may not pass the test of economic efficiency.

A perspective that measures human rights in terms of their costs and benefits for an efficient market economy may help persuade decisionmakers of the advantages of some policies that advance such rights. However, this approach runs counter to core human rights obligations of states and the international community.

The real world challenges economists' trust in the allocative efficiency of market equilibrium. With imperfect information and market failures, a clear separation of growth- and redistribution-oriented programs is difficult to maintain.[28] The real world shows that efficiency and equity need not imply a trade-off:

equity-oriented social policy may well enhance sustainable economic performance. National and international policies have never followed a purely economic impulse. Efforts to guarantee minimum social order, if only to secure popular support for a government, are a common motivator for state and international action. Neglect of social concerns will jeopardize the fruits of economic growth.

Governments and international organizations should not address human rights because it is economically or politically opportune to do so, but because they have an obligation to do so. The international economic order will become meaningful only with a principled approach that stresses that economic development, market mechanisms, and economic efficiency are not intrinsic values but must first and foremost improve the well-being of all people.

Legal Constraints and Fragmentation of the International Order

Legal roadblocks are sometimes cited as obstacles to human rights. The World Bank advocates good governance, public participation and inclusion, and local empowerment despite the prohibition against "interfering in the political affairs" of member states.[29] Its operational directives now address issues such as forced labor, equal opportunity, and child labor. The fundamental principles outlined in the Comprehensive Development Strategy focus on poverty reduction[30] and are strongly in line with human rights principles. International financial organizations have an important role in implementing economic and social rights as global social standards. The strong member states of the IMF, the World Bank, and the World Trade Organization (WTO)—and particularly the European Union—have the responsibility to steer these big ships on a human rights course.

Lack of Knowledge and Commitment

A major obstacle to wholehearted recognition of economic and social rights is a lack of knowledge of these rights and the corresponding obligations of states and organizations, but these deficiencies can be easily remedied. The real obstacle seems to be not lack of knowledge but rather lack of will. However, practical resistance to economic and social rights may be dwindling. The UNDP works closely with the UN High Commissioner of Human Rights to integrate sustainable human development into its activities. World Bank partnerships with the ILO have been greatly enhanced. What is weakest is active exchange and cooperation with the UN Committee on Economic, Social and Human Rights. The committee's two main tasks are to constructively and cooperatively monitor the implementation of the ICESCR and to develop a jurisprudence that clarifies its substantive provisions. The covenant envisaged an implementation mechanism that allows intensive exchange between the committee and states and organizations that influence the implementation of human rights. Failure to create this institutional relationship has deprived the committee of the chance to build on the expertise of organizations such as UNDP and the World Bank, and it has impoverished those organizations in their search for social standards.

Mainstreaming human rights in all areas of development policy would profoundly affect institutional structures and the distribution of economic and political power. Only committed implementation of such rights will be a meaningful response to the quest for fundamental social values in a globalized economy.

Notes

1. UN General Assembly, Millennium Declaration, September 8, 2000, UN Document A/55/2, para. 5 f.; G8 Summit Okinawa, *Poverty Reduction and Economic Development: Report from G7 Finance Ministers to the Heads of State and Government*, July 21, 2000, para. 3; IMF, OECD, UN, and World Bank Group, *A Better World for All* (Washington, D.C., June 2000); UN General Assembly, *World Summit for Social Development and Beyond: Achieving Social Development for All in a Globalizing World*, Proposals for Further Initiatives for Social Development, Political Declaration, unedited final document, July 1, 2000.

2. The ILO charter charges nations to promote "higher standards of living, full employment, and conditions of economic and social progress and development" (Art. 55 [a]), and "universal respect for, and observance of, human rights and fundamental freedoms for all without distinction as to race, sex, language, or religion" (Art. 55 [c]). ILO, Philadelphia Declaration Concerning the Aims and Purposes of the International Labour Organisation, May 10, 1944, section III.

3. Article 28 of the Universal Declaration of Human Rights (UDHR), December 10, 1948, UN General Assembly Res. 217 A (III). See also Article 22 of the UDHR: "Everyone, as a member of society, has the right to social security and is entitled to realization, through national effort and international co-operation and in accordance with the organization and resources of each State, of the economic, social and cultural rights indispensable for his dignity and the free development of his personality."

4. International Convention on the Elimination of All Forms of Racial Discrimination, March 7, 1966 (660 UNTS 195); Convention on the Elimination of All Forms of Discrimination against Women, December 18, 1979 (1249 UNTS 13); Convention on the Rights of the Child, November 20, 1989, General Assembly, 44th Sess., Resolutions, p. 166.

5. ILO declaration on fundamental principles and rights at work, International Labour Conference, 86th Sess., June 1998. The core ILO conventions are no. 87, "freedom of association"; no. 98, "right to organise and collective bargaining"; nos. 29 and 105, "abolition of forced labour"; no. 100, "equal remuneration"; no. 111, "discrimination"; no. 138, "minimum age"; and no. 182, "worst forms of child labour."

6. Report of the Secretary-General pursuant to the statement adopted by the Summit Meeting of the Security Council on January 31, 1992, "An Agenda for Peace: Preventive Diplomacy, Peacemaking and Peace-keeping," June 17, 1992.

7. World Bank, *Development and Human Rights: The Role of the World Bank* (Washington D.C.: World Bank, 1998).

8. See the concordance of human rights and development policy goals outlined in Clare Ferguson, *Global Social Policy Principles: Human Rights and Social Justice,* April 1999.

9. See the evaluation of poverty concepts presented in OECD Development Assistance Committee, *Scoping Study of Donor Poverty Reduction Policies and Practices* (London: Overseas Development Institute, 1999): 5 ff.

10. See, for example, Peter S. Heller, "Social Policy Concerns for the New Architecture in Asia," remarks prepared for the Manila Social Forum, sponsored by the Asian Development Bank and World Bank, November 1999, p. 2: "[T]hese ongoing reforms should be complemented by a social policy framework, both to ensure the capacity to address the social consequences of inevitable cyclical downturns and to foster a flexible labor market and achieve the investment in human capital *necessary for growth*" [emphasis added].

11. See the critique of Philip Alston, "The Myopia of the Handmaidens: International Lawyers and Globalization," *European Journal of International Law* 8, no. 3 (1997): 435.

12. OECD Development Assistance Committee (DAC): "The practical implications of considering the poor not just as 'poor people' but as 'rights-holding citizens' are thus unclear." See OECD DAC, op. cit., p. 22. The report suggests that clarifying how a rights-based approach can be operationalized is "urgently required, drawing on lessons learned from the considerable work by lawyers on this issue."

13. Bob Deacon, *Globalization and Social Policy: The Threat to Equitable Welfare,* UNRISD, occasional paper 5, March 2000, p. 15: "Moralizing about rights is counterproductive."

14. Today UNDP approaches development from a fairly clear human rights perspective; see UNDP, *Human Development Report 2000,* Chapter 1. See also the Report of the UN High Commissioner for Human Rights (UN Document A/53/36) and India's approval of a rights approach to development (<http://www.un.int/india/ind240.htm>). Several European countries, including the Nordic countries and recently the United Kingdom, opt for orienting development policies along the lines of economic and social rights. See, for example, UK Department for International Development, *Human Rights for Poor People: Strategies for Achieving the International Development Targets,* February 2000. Among nongovernmental organizations, see especially Human Rights Council of Australia, *The Rights Way to Development: A Human Rights Approach to Development Assistance, Policy and Practice,* 1998.

15. UN Secretary General, *Report on the Work of the Organisation,* 1998, para. 174: "The rights-based approach to development describes situations not simply in terms of human needs, or of developmental requirements, but in terms of society's obligation to respond to the inalienable rights of individuals. It empowers people to demand justice as a right, not as charity, and gives communities a moral basis from which to claim international assistance where needed."

16. Martin Scheinin, "Economic and Social Rights as Legal Rights," in *Economic, Social and Cultural Rights,* ed. A. Eide, C. Krause, and A. Rosas (Boston, The Hague, and Norwell, Mass.: Dordrecht and Martinus Nijhoff, 1995), pp. 41–62; Asbjørn Eide, "Economic, Social and Cultural Rights as Human Rights," in A. Eide, C. Krause, and A. Rosas, op. cit., pp. 21–40; and Veli-Pekka Viljanen, "Abstention or Involvement? The Nature of State Obligations under Different Categories of Rights," in *Social Rights as Human Rights: A European Challenge,* ed. K. Drzewicki, C. Krause, and A. Rosas (Turku, 1994), pp. 43–66.

17. Cf. Human Rights Committee, general comment no. 6, "The Right to Life" (Art. 6), July 30, 1982, para. 5: "[T]he Committee has noted that the right to life has been too often narrowly interpreted. The expression 'inherent right to life' cannot properly be understood in a restrictive manner, and the protection of this right requires that States adopt positive measures. In this connection, the Committee considers that it would be desirable for States parties to take all possible measures to reduce infant mortality and to increase life expectancy, especially in adopting measures to eliminate malnutrition and epidemics."

18. David Dollar and Aart Kraay, *Growth Is Good for the Poor,* Development Research Group, Macroeconomics and Growth, World Bank, Policy Research Working Paper 2587 (Washington, D.C., 2001).

19. UNICESCR, general comment 3: "The nature of States parties obligations," Article 2, Fifth Sess., December 14, 1990, para. 2: "Thus while the full realization of the relevant rights may be achieved progressively, steps towards that goal must be taken within a reasonably short time after the Covenant's entry into force for the States concerned. Such steps should be deliberate, concrete and targeted as clearly as possible towards meeting the obligations recognized in the Covenant." Para. 9 states: "[T]he phrase [achieving progressively the full realization] must be read in the light of the overall objective, indeed the raison d'être, of the Covenant which is to establish clear obligations for States parties in respect of the full realization of the rights in question. It thus imposes an obligation to move as expeditiously and effectively as possible towards that goal." See also "Limburg Principles on the Implementation of the International Covenant on Economic, Social and Cultural Rights," reprinted in *Human Rights Quarterly* 9 (1987): 122 ff.

20. ICESCR, *Statement on Globalization and Economic, Social and Cultural Rights,* May 1998, para. 5.

21. Ibid., para. 7.

22. See the case of the Philippines, *Concluding Observations of the Committee on Economic, Social and Cultural Rights,* Philippines, June 7, 1995, UN Document E/C.12/1995/7, para. 24: "The Committee also recommends that greater emphasis should be placed within the framework of official development assistance (ODA) provided by donor countries to support social adjustment programmes for purposes such as the financing of low interest credit to the poorest farmers, slum upgrading and other programmes for housing the poor. The Committee recalls that every effort must be made in times of structural adjustment to ensure that the basic economic, social and cultural rights of the poorest and most disadvantaged sectors of the population are protected to the greatest extent possible."

23. See Amartya Sen, "Human Rights and Asian Values," *New Republic,* July 14–21, 1997; and "East and West: The Reach of Reason," *New York Review of Books,* July 20, 2000: 33–38.

24. In case of dispute over a government's social policy course, the final decision over its concordance with economic and social rights should be left to the ILO and treaty-based organs of the United Nations.

25. For discussion, see Geert van der Linden, "The Role of Safety, Health, and Productivity in Improving Labor Standards," *ADB Review* 32, no. 2 (2000): 12–14.

26. World Bank, *World Development Report 2000* (Washington, D.C.: World Bank, 2000): 49 (Box 3.1).

27. See remarks by Robert Holzmann, World Bank, at "Seminar: A Role for Labor Standards in the New International Economy?" September 29, 1999, Washington, D.C.

28. Andres Solimano, Eduardo Aninat, and Nancy Birdsall, eds., *Distributive Justice and Economic Development: The Case of Chile and Developing Countries* (Ann Arbor, Mich.: University of Michigan Press, 2000); Vito Tanzi, Ke-Young Chu, and Sanjeev Gupta, eds., *Economic Policy and Equity* (Washington, D.C.: IMF, 1999). See also the survey of the economic literature in a draft paper of Ravi Kanbur and Nora Lustig, "Why Is Inequality Back on the Agenda?" April 1999.

29. Articles of Agreement of the World Bank, Article IV, sec. 10.

30. The new strategy emphasizes domestic ownership of reform programs and stresses that "In formulating and implementing reform, the country must be in the driver's seat, with civil society and the private sector involved, or reform cannot be sustained." World Bank Operations Evaluation Department, *Toward a Comprehensive Development Strategy,* précis no. 197, autumn 1999, p. 2.

Social Dumping versus Wage Competition
by Frank Westermann

The issue of social dumping arises when unequal regions engage in trade and firms compete on prices in a common market. Cutting social spending and standards is one way to allow domestic firms to undercut the prices of foreign competitors, attract mobile factors of production in the international capital market, and deter an influx of recipients of social welfare. As every country faces this problem, competition can lead to lower overall social spending, suggesting that international harmonization of social policy is desirable to prevent the erosion of the welfare state.

The economic analysis of social dumping, however, is often misunderstood.[1] It is important to distinguish social benefits that redistribute income within a country—from rich to poor, or from young to old—from benefits that are implicitly part of the wage rate. Government policies that simply lead to a more flexible labor market and lower implicit wages should not be subject to the criticism of social dumping. Such policies lead to lower labor costs and higher employment and are consistent with the principles of a market economy.

Most popular discussion of social dumping focuses on the latter phenomenon, and many debates refer to the wage level itself, which is the sum of net wages and wage side costs. Eastern countries are often said to undercut average European Union (EU) wage levels by reducing social security at all levels, thus gaining an advantage in sales of manufactured goods. Similarly, countries in East Asia, which export to both the EU and the United States, are seen to constitute a threat to employment in the older manufacturing industries of advanced economies. This is a discussion about losing market share to a more competitive country with lower wages.

In itself, trade based on lower wages is not unfair, because both trading partners gain from trade—in the long run, market forces will lead to an equalization of wages in the absence of trade barriers. Trying to harmonize wage rates more quickly, however, can have severe consequences

continued on next page

BOX 6.3, continued

for economic performance. Europe provides recent examples of mistaken attempts to coordinate wages across regions. The rapid equalization of wages in the former German Democratic Republic (GDR) and the former Federal Republic of Germany after unification has led to high unemployment in the former GDR and a dramatic decline in manufacturing output because many of its firms cannot operate profitably at western wages. In Italy common wage and social schemes across all regions, introduced in the 1960s, have prevented southern Italy from developing and catching up with the economically prosperous northern regions.[2]

In contrast, social transfers, which are financed by taxes and redistribute income among different groups within a society, are at the core of the social dumping problem. Here the small open economies of East Asia as well as Europe risk eroding welfare services supplied by the state. A harmonization of social polices among countries facing this predicament can prevent that process and lead to sustainable welfare systems. However, countries need to introduce coordinated policies cautiously, carefully differentiating among different types of social benefits.

1. See, for example Hans-Werner Sinn, *The New Systems Competition*, Yrjö-Jahnsson lectures, (Oxford, England: Basil Blackwell, 2001), and *Social Dumping in the Transformation Process*, CESifo working paper no. 508 (Munich, Germany, 2001).

2. See Hans-Werner Sinn and Frank Westermann, *Two Mezzogiornos*, CESifo working paper no. 378 (Munich, Germany, 2000), for a comparison.

CHAPTER 27

Global Standards:
The European Experience

by Gabriella Battaini-Dragoni

ABSTRACT: This chapter outlines the role of international and regional institutions in defining and applying social standards, using the Council of Europe as a case study. The chapter compares the challenges facing Asia and Europe and highlights what they might learn from each other in creating formal frameworks to ensure social protection.

Social cohesion encompasses two main elements: (1) an adequate standard of living and social well-being, and (2) democratic participation for all. The relationship of the individual to the state, the market (especially the labor market), and family and personal resources—in other words, political liberty, economic opportunity, and civil society—are key to ensuring democratic participation. Core rights and minimum standards, meanwhile, are an important part of any strategy to promote social cohesion. Like the United Nations (UN) and the International Labor Organization (ILO), the Council of Europe, an intergovernmental organization with 44 members, aims to facilitate economic progress while guaranteeing social cohesion by establishing core rights and minimum standards.[1] This chapter addresses the statutory basis for such efforts, as well as the importance of regional standards in ensuring social cohesion and social rights.

What Are Social Rights?

Claiming a right is very different from asking for a favor; the former presupposes a relationship among equal human beings and implies that the state has a legal responsibility. A right is the very basis for human dignity, and European history has been marked by a fight for the inalienability of human rights.[2] The idea of rights as a basis for human dignity is an essential underpinning for the work of the Council of Europe. Under this notion, social benefits are not acts of charity but the fulfillment of a contract between the state and the individual.

Basic human rights include civil and political rights on the one hand and economic, social, and cultural rights on the other. Whereas Europe has a long tradition of accepting the importance of civil and political rights—most national constitutions incorporate them—many people have argued that social rights are not legally enforceable. However, after World War II both the United Nations and the Council of Europe accepted the idea of the indivisibility of social and political rights.

Social rights center on employment: the idea that all individuals should be able to earn a decent standard of living for themselves and their families. Those whom the working process cannot assimilate, either temporarily or permanently, should receive protection from poverty and social exclusion. The Council of Europe therefore focuses on the organization of employment and the special risks linked to the process of work as well as the life cycle.

Rights must be concrete enough to serve as a basis for action—especially the right to social security included in international legal documents. Thus setting standards is essential for fulfilling social rights. If the Council of Europe wants member states to act in a certain manner and pursue a common policy, it must define "social security" and establish standards that oblige countries to structure social security systems to fulfill those standards. The Council of Europe therefore both guarantees rights and sets standards.

Standards can propose optimal solutions, but they can also simply establish a minimum that all countries must uphold. Minimum standards are a basis on which to build more demanding standards.

How Far Do the Council of Europe's Binding Documents Go?

The path of elaborating standards at the international level has been long. In the age of industrialization, the loss of a job, whether temporarily or permanently, usually meant poverty. Because the risks of losing a job were foreseeable, governments could build up protective systems. But countries regarded the costs of these systems as a competitive disadvantage if all countries did not bear them. Thus the idea of internationalizing protective labor and social security laws accompanied the first national protective laws.[3]

The need for an internationalized approach has become greater still in the age of globalization. Global trade, capital flows, technological change, and conflicts often determine the economic risks that exert a dramatic impact on the lives of the most disadvantaged people. An international perspective is therefore crucial in complementing country-specific actions to set social standards.

After World War II, European countries adhered to the standards of the UN and the ILO but wanted to define their own standards as well, drawing on their specific experience and taking into account their own needs. Thus the Council of Europe established the European Social Charter in 1961, as well as the revised European Code of Social Security in 1996.[4] Together the two codes[5] guarantee a minimum level of protection in nine traditional branches of social security: medical care, sickness benefits, unemployment benefits, old-age benefits, employment injury benefits, family benefits, maternity benefits, invalidity benefits, and survivors' benefits.[6]

The charter protects labor rights such as the right to work and to just conditions of work, as well as social security rights such as the right to social and medical assistance and the right to benefit from social services.[7] The charter also protects certain disadvantaged groups. The revised social code reinforces these elements and introduces several new rights, including the right to protection against poverty and social exclusion and the right to protection against discrimination on the grounds of sex.

All 44 member countries of the Council of Europe have either signed or ratified the European Social Charter or the revised European Social Charter. This means that poorer countries as well as relatively prosperous countries accept these common standards.

The charter's supervisory machinery plays a decisive role in implementing these rights, allowing regular and systematic legal appraisal of national reports to determine whether states are fulfilling these rights.[8] Although the council does not hear individual complaints, a protocol introduced in 1995 does allow groups to bring collective complaints. This system has already produced tangible effects, such as introducing and raising standards in the field of child labor.

The European Convention on Human Rights of 1950, the best-known instrument of the Council of Europe, focuses on civil and political rights and establishes judicial control of violations by member states.[9] This means that other contracting states as well as individuals can file complaints. The European Court of Human Rights has interpreted all the rights in this convention, a jurisprudence that can be compared to that of national constitutional courts. The jurisprudence of the court also affects interpretation of the social rights, such as when certain social security benefits are understood as property.

The European Convention on Social Security of 1972 modifies two preliminary instruments dating from the 1950s addressing the social security rights of migrant workers.[10] The basic principles concern equality of treatment, maintenance of acquired rights, and the payment of benefits abroad. The European Convention on the Legal Status of Migrant Workers of 1977 addresses recruitment, occupational tests, residence permits, and work permits, as well as social security and social and medical assistance.[11]

Unlike national legislation, international law can rarely respond immediately to new challenges. What is more, among resolutions, declarations, recommendations, guidelines, and conventions, only the latter are legally binding. That is why both the European Social Charter and the European Code of Social Security maintain special importance, even though other Council of Europe documents in the social sphere also have legal relevance.

Nonetheless, even conventions fixing legal obligations can exert only limited influence on member states, because legislatures must approve programs to fulfill the obligations. This means that actual practice often does not mirror ideal models but rather what is feasible at a certain point in time within each country.

The absence of coercive means also limits the role these provisions play. If member states do not comply, the Council of Europe can rely only on continuing dialogue and persuasion; it cannot force countries to change their legislation or their practice. Therefore the cooperation of both governments and national social actors is crucial.

The Impact of Standards and Rights during Economic Growth and Crisis

Social standards serve both as a springboard to promote economic growth and as a safety net to lessen the impacts of economic downturns.

The Role of Standards and Rights during Economic Growth

Market economies are able to produce great wealth for their populations but also often create highly stratified and fragmented societies. This risk is real in both Europe and Asia. Even countries with similar levels of economic growth and productivity exhibit wide variations in their levels of socioeconomic equality.

The European experience suggests that minimum social and labor standards have positive consequences during periods of economic growth. *Politically*, minimum standards guarantee a degree of social cohesion, reducing conflicts within enterprises as well as society as a whole. Thus they allow for more stable economic development.

Economically, minimum standards help foster labor market flexibility, labor productivity, business confidence, and economic investment. Providing a minimum level of social protection helps limit the negative impacts of macroeconomic trends such as rapid changes in labor markets. And *socially*, minimum social and labor standards help build a more inclusive, pluralistic society with a higher standard of living.[12]

The Role of Standards and Rights during Economic Crisis

Economic and financial crises cause great instability for states and populations, raising levels of social vulnerability and poverty. All social segments suffer from these shocks, but the most vulnerable, including women and young workers, suffer the most, because they are often forced to take precarious and low-quality jobs in the informal sector. Most social indicators, such as rates of malnutrition, infant mortality, and school attendance, deteriorate during periods of economic crisis.

Mechanisms for managing crisis can be informal, based on human and social capital, and formal, based on legal rights and standards. *Informal mechanisms*—networks that people build to resolve shared difficulties, obtain collective advantage, and exercise some control over their surroundings—are very helpful during crises. Social capital enables individuals, groups, and communities to gain access to information, educational opportunities, employment, and social mobility. However, reliance on human and social capital is not sufficient: *formal mechanisms* such as international minimum standards can help identify social priorities and enable vulnerable groups to manage or mitigate social risks derived from economic instability. A dialogue between states and the Council of Europe helps countries make decisions on social priorities during crises.

Similarities and Differences between Europe and Asia

Regional and global standards have not influenced social policymaking in Asia to the same degree as in Europe. Although a majority of states worldwide ratified the UN Covenant on Economic, Social and Cultural Rights, no Asian country other than Japan has ratified the ILO conventions on social security (nos. 102, 121, 128, 130), and no legal instrument in Asia compares to the European Code of Social Security.

The two regions also differ in the level of diversity among countries, the structure of their labor markets, the amount of human and social capital, demographic trends, and the level of social stratification:[13]

- *Relative homogeneity versus diversity.* Whereas Western Europe is relatively homogeneous, Asian-Pacific countries are highly diverse in the size of their territories, populations, and economies. Asia includes powerful economies, such as China and Japan, and very poor economies, such as the Lao People's Democratic Republic and Cambodia, and encompasses a variety of political, ethnic, cultural, and religious profiles. Social development has been uneven between and within countries, social sectors, ethnic groups, and genders. Asian countries reveal varying levels of human development determined by their level of economic growth, degree of political order, and quality of governance.
- *Structure of the labor market.* More than 60 percent of Asian populations still live in rural communities, and agriculture is still the main productive sector. Most poverty in the region is also rural based. The limited industrialized sector operates within informal market structures, which affect the quality of the job market and the employment of millions of people.[14]
- *Human and social capital.*[15] Asia's system of kinship groups and extended families—a form of indigenous social capital—was a major factor moderating the social and economic impact of the financial crisis, because families provided food and housing to factory workers. But urbanization, industrialization, and globalization seem to be eroding this form of social capital and replacing it with ties based on formal work, as in the majority of European countries.
- *Demographic trends.* Asian societies have recently witnessed a demographic boom, and the pressure of young generations on the labor market is a major challenge. The aging of the population and the decline in birthrates, considered key challenges for European countries, are not yet as acute in Asia, although longevity in Japan is the highest in the world, and China experiences the effects of its one-child policy. (See Figure 27.1)
- *Social stratification.* Social stratification is much more pronounced in Asia than in Europe, with huge income inequality along ethnic, caste, and racial cleavages. Illiteracy, especially female illiteracy, is still widespread. One explanation is the percentage of national budgets allocated to social security (see Table 27.1).

Figure 27.1 Average Annual Growth Rates of Population Groups

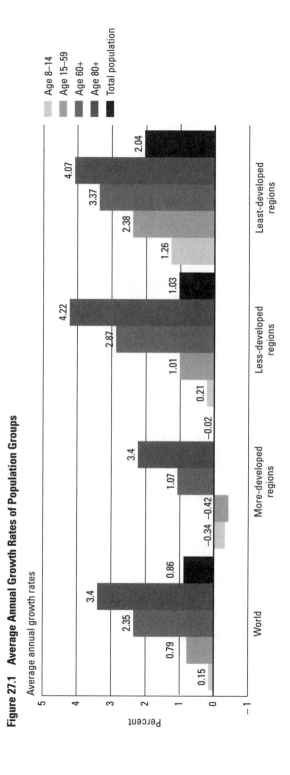

Table 27.1   Social Security Expenditures

Country	Total social security expenditure (% of GDP)	Pensions (% of GDP)	Health care (% of GDP)
All countries	14.5	6.6	4.9
Africa	4.3	1.4	1.7
Asia	6.4	3.0	2.7
Europe	24.8	12.1	6.3
Latin America and Caribbean	8.8	2.1	2.8
North America	16.6	7.1	7.5
Oceania	16.1	4.9	5.6

GDP = gross domestic product

Source: International Labor Organization, *World Labor Report 2000,* Geneva, Table 14.

Despite these differences, European and Asian countries also face common challenges. Economic globalization is producing repercussions in the form of long-term unemployment, changes in family structure, and gender inequality, as well as growing disparities in economic growth among regions and communities. The persistence of long-term unemployment puts particular pressure on social systems in both Europe and Asia.

Major structural changes stemming from the advent of a knowledge-based society and the spread of information and communication technologies are leading to new risks of poverty and social exclusion for vulnerable groups in both regions. Growing ethnic, cultural, and religious diversity stemming from accelerating international migration is also posing new challenges to social cohesion, and thus to policymakers.

What Europe and Asia Can Learn from Each Other

Treaties that define basic social rights and minimum standards cannot solve all social problems. However, they can stabilize common values, help countries avoid ruinous competition, encourage dialogue on adequate remedies, and provide international norms on which to base national policies.

National policies can change whenever governments change, and countries can abandon the goals of social cohesion whenever economic or financial crises occur. International norms can serve as a corrective mechanism and a brake, preventing the poor from becoming poorer during crises while enabling them to obtain a just share during times of economic growth.

Europe's recent history shows the value of a solid and effective framework of regional cooperation built on joint charters, research, and policy development. The European Social Charter and the European Code of Social Security cannot and should not be exported to Asia, but they might serve as examples of good practice as Asian countries consider whether and how to establish similar instruments.

The European Code of Social Security, however, assumes that labor relations must be formalized.[16] Financing social protections by taxes and contributions is possible only if agencies register employers and employees, and labor inspectors enforce the norms.

Some parts of Europe today face rapid growth of the informal sector. This places millions of workers, especially in southern European countries such as Bulgaria, Croatia, and Romania, beyond the reach of social security collection agencies and thus excludes them from benefits. Ensuring a sound financial basis for social security systems, and wider coverage, requires an innovative method of collecting contributions. Such a system might link to employers' ability to obtain equipment and other material essential for business activity. Europe has no experience in this field, and the Asian record might prove helpful.

Despite disparities between Asia and Europe, the need for a dialogue on setting and implementing social standards between the two regions is urgent. In the age of globalization, social problems as well as the exchange of goods are universal. Why should experience in one part of the world not prove helpful in another?

Notes

1. Council of Europe, European Committee for Social Cohesion, *Strategy for Social Cohesion* (Strasbourg, France: Council of Europe Publishing, 2000); Council of Europe, *Opportunity and Risk: Trends of Social Exclusion in Europe* (Strasbourg, France: Council of Europe Publishing, April 1998); International Labor Organization, *Social Security: Issues, Challenges and Prospects*, International Labor Conference, 89th session, Geneva, 2001.

2. Paul Hunt, *Reclaiming Social Rights: International and Comparative Perspectives* (Dartmouth Publishing, 1996).

3. Bernd Baron von Maydell, and Angelika Nussberger, eds., *Social Protection by Ways of International Law* (Berlin: Duncker and Humblot, 1996); Angelika Nussberger, *Social Standards in Voelkerrecht* (forthcoming, Council of Europe); Nicolas Valticos, *International Labour Law* (Boston and Deventer, Netherlands: Kluwer, 1995); Pierre-Yves Greber, "Les principes fondamentaux du droit international et du droit suisse de la securite sociale" (Ph.D. dissertation, 1984).

4. Angelica Nussberger, *European Standards in the Field of Social Security: A Critical Analysis,* Council of Europe working paper, Directorate General Social Cohesion (Strasbourg, France: Council of Europe Publishing, 2000).

5. Council of Europe, *European Code of Social Security* and *Protocol to the European Social Security,* 16.4.1964, European Treaty Series no. 48 (Strasbourg, France: Council of Europe Publishing, 2000).

6. Council of Europe, *European Code of Social Security: Short Guide* (Strasbourg, France: Council of Europe Publishing, 2002).

7. Council of Europe, *European Social Charter and Protocol* (Strasbourg, France: Council of Europe Publishing, 2000); cf. Council of Europe, *European Social Charter: Short Guide* (Strasbourg, France: Council of Europe Publishing, 2000).

8. Council of Europe, *European Social Charter: Short Guide,* p. 31 et seq.

9. Council of Europe, *European Convention on Human Rights: Collected Texts* (Strasbourg, France: Council of Europe Publishing, 1994).

10. Council of Europe, *European Convention on Social Security and Supplementary Agreement for the Application of the European Convention on Social Security,* 14.12.1972, European Treaty Series no. 78 (Strasbourg, France: Council of Europe Publishing, 1999).

11. Council of Europe, *Explanatory Report on the European Convention on the Legal Status of Migrant Workers,* no. 93 (Strasbourg, France: Council of Europe Publishing, 1985).

12. Mary Daly, *The Gender Division of Welfare: The Impact of the British and German Welfare States* (New York: Cambridge University Press, 2000); Floris Goyens, "The Impact of the European Code of Social Security on the National Level: Report for the Colloquy with Regard to the European Code of Social Security, Its Protocol and the Revised Code of Social Security" (Strasbourg, France, October 25–26, 1999).

13. Isabel Ortiz, "Social Policies in Asia and the Pacific into the 21st Century," and Lee Jong-Wha and Rhee Changyong, "Social Impacts of the Asian Crisis: Policy Challenges and Lessons," in UN Development Programme, *Globalization with a Human Face,* background papers, vol. 1, *Human Development Report 1999*; C. Hernandez, "Reflecting on Pathways to Social Development: The Asia-Pacific Region" (paper for the Expert Group Reflection on Pathways to Social Development, North–South Centre of the Council of Europe, Convento de Arrabida, Portugal, May 28–30, 2001).

14. Jacques Charmes, "The Informal Sector, an Engine for Growth or a Social Insurance for the Poor: Its Role in Economic Growth and during the Recent Financial Crisis in Asia, in the Light of Some European Views on the Informal Sector," paper presented at the World Bank/Asia-Europe Meeting/Asian Development Bank Conference on Social Exclusion, Social Capital, and the East Asian Crisis, Manila, November 5–7, 2001, available at <http://www.worldbank.org/eapsocial/asemsocial/files/837_The_Informal_Sector_-_Eng__for_Growth.pdf>, accessed October 11, 2002.

15. Organization for Economic Cooperation and Development (OECD), *The Well-Being of Nations: The Role of Human and Social Capital* (Paris: OECD, 2001).

16. Daly, op. cit.; G. Esping-Andersen, "Welfare States and the Economy," in *The Handbook of Economic Sociology,* eds. Neil J. Smelser and Richard Swedberg (Princeton, N.J.: Princeton University Press, 1994), pp. 711–32.

The Social Dimension of Regionalism: An Alternative Approach to Globalization?
by Bob Deacon

Strong regional trading blocks can offer an approach to the forces behind globalization by taking responsibility for their own social measures rather than adhering to global standards, where the questions of who sets them and who pays for them become insurmountable obstacles. The regional alternative carries further weight because neoliberal globalization has so far been associated with residual safety nets rather than more substantial forms of social protection. Current forms of globalization also tend to break down national social contracts in developing countries and to segment social policy, so the rich gain from access to private global welfare markets while the poor are provided only with safety nets.

Regional social policy could permit more substantial social protection along the lines that European Union (EU) member states provide for their citizens. Regional groupings also have a stronger voice in the international community and can help redistribute income between richer and poorer countries, promulgate social rights and set social standards, and facilitate exchange of best practices and regional cooperation on social dimensions. But do regional social policies exist anywhere outside of Europe?

MERCOSUR (Latin America Common Market) is the most developed regional bloc outside the EU, with significant labor and social declarations and joint health and safety inspections. SADC (Southern Africa Development Community) also has developed an important institutional framework and policy instruments, though less so in the social policy

Based on a presentation at the Asia-Europe Meeting (ASEM) in Brussels in December 2001. For an elaboration of the argument, see "The Social Dimension of Regionalism: A Constructive Alternative to Neoliberal Globalization," Globalism and Social Policy Programme, occasional paper no. 9 (Finland: STAKES, 2001), available at <http://www.gaspp.org>.

continued on next page

BOX 6.4, continued

area. ASEAN (Association of Southeast Asian Nations) is the least developed in terms of its regional social policy. Why? Partly because the alliance was predicated on noninterference in each nation's policymaking, which has slowed development in many areas. However, the ASEAN regional declaration on caring societies reveals the stirrings of a regional social policy. (See Table on next page.)

Can Europe, as a model of a socially regulated alliance with regional institutions, further the social dimension of regionalism in East Asia? ASEAN has not generally viewed Europe as a model and generally interprets European attempts to influence regional policy unfavorably because it regards the EU as a northern protectionist bloc. The Asian Development Bank tends to favor economic liberalism over regional social protection. However, the EU could potentially play a role in countering such perspectives within the Asian Development Bank. Furthermore, if the EU wishes to counter the negative light within which it is sometimes seen and help build socially responsible regional blocs that reflect its commitment to promote international human rights, it will also have to provide north–south resource transfers and put its social development policy before its trade interests.

Economic integration will not act as the sole engine of growth on the regional social dimension. In all likelihood, international articulation of social rights will converge with regional social movements to force the issue. However it is achieved, the regional vision of social protection is an alternative to "globalization plus," because regional blocs may deglobalize to a degree and follow the European road. They do have a choice.

BOX 6.4, continued

Aspects of Social Policy for SADC, MERCOSUR, and ASEAN

Aspect of regional social policy	SADC	MERCOSUR	ASEAN
Regional redistribution	Customs duties; no new initiatives.	Talk of a regional social fund. A few regionally funded projects in border areas.	Nothing significant. Some capacity building for new members.
Regional social and labor regulations	No, although Congress of South African Trade Unions is campaigning for them.	Important declaration on labor and social rights. Reciprocal social security entitlement. Joint health and safety inspection.	Recent declaration on caring societies. No legal force.
Regional health policy	Yes, and recently strengthened with equity concerns.	Little documented.	Yes, but depends on external funds. Recent trade and health initiative.
Regional education policy	Recent capacity review. Quality assurance and other measures.	Mutual recognition of qualifications.	ASEAN university scholarships and exchanges. Curricula design in schools.
De facto private regionalism	New initiatives by regional private health care companies.	Beginnings of cross-border private provision.	Major lobbying by international health insurance companies.
Cross-border learning from best practice	Yes, especially pensions and grants to school attenders.	Cuts both ways. World Bank promotes Chile as an example, but Uruguay is seen as alternative approach.	Recently through safety-net working party.
Human rights, including social rights.	SADC Gender Unit as model. Call for SADC court of rights.	Civil society lobby with regional focus. Possible new MERCOSUR working group.	Policy of strict noninterference. Little evidence of regional lobbies, but may be changing.

BOX 6.5

Seminar on Social Policies to Cope with Economic Instability: Lessons from Europe and East Asia, Brussels, December 6, 2001

This seminar was organized at the European Commission headquarters jointly with the European Institute for Asian Studies. A central aim was to facilitate discussion of the Asia-Europe Meeting (ASEM) project experience with officials of the European Commission. The focus was the core challenges highlighted through the project, especially social policy in times of economic instability. The seminar covered three major topics: links between macroeconomic and social policy, regional issues for social policy, and European lessons and international experience.

The first topic was grounded in presentations by Robert Wade and K. S. Jomo (see Boxes 2.1 and 2.2). Robert Wade challenged conventional thinking on openness and "globalization plus" (often referred to as the Washington consensus). Historically, Germany, the United States, and the countries of East Asia, Japan in particular, erected barriers to nurture local export industries. This approach produced such fast growth that the countries required only limited social protections. For developing countries, therefore, catch-up strategies need not always imply demanding social policies. Participants stressed the diversity of countries in East Asia, each of which experiences different levels of demand for social protection.

K. S. Jomo's presentation focused on two major themes: the opportunity for change in macroeconomic policy resulting from September 11, and the need to balance social and macroeconomic policies. He strongly advocated restoring social policy to its rightful place as more than an instrument focused on social safety nets. He maintained that countries should see social policy as an integral part of industrial policy and therefore macroeconomic policy, particularly the "second-tier" newly industrializing countries of Southeast Asia. Discussion focused on the use of regional social policy as a possible counter to primary reliance on international organizations to address economic crisis and set policy frameworks and standards.

continued on next page

BOX 6.5, continued

The second topic turned to interregional dimensions, with a presentation by Bob Deacon (Box 6.4). Bob Deacon argued that regional trading blocks can promote social policies to counter the tendency of globalization to undermine national social contracts. He maintains, however, that regional economic integration does not automatically produce regional social policies. Discussion highlighted the ASEM process as a potential framework for pursuing regional social policy, as well as the role of the World Trade Organization and other international organizations.

The third topic focused on possible European policy lessons for the rest of the world, with a presentation by Ian Gough (Box II). Discussion focused on dilemmas in pension reform. Participants voiced concern about privately funded pension schemes, which could spur further volatility in financial markets. They concentrated on the differences between Europe and East Asia more than on similarities.

Concluding Note: Where Next?

In the course of encounters, whether meetings, seminars, or dialogues, an image or phrase sometimes "sticks," taking on symbolic importance and guiding participants' thought process from that point on. Several such turning points occurred during this project—incidents that offered fresh images, insights, and new directions. That was, in fact, the project's central merit: its capacity to surmount conventional debates and offer new ways to approach what often appeared to be intractable problems.

Two moments of insight can offer an appropriate conclusion to the book and also point to future directions. The first was a comment by a senior European official, a specialist in social policy, that he was deeply troubled that he could not explain his grandmother's pension rights to her. Historical evolution and successive modifications had made the system so complex that no one could decipher the resulting maze. This vignette resurfaced again and again, along with its core message that social policy must be explainable if it is to be fair and equitable.

The "incident" highlighted three fundamental changes in the way social policy is perceived, both in East Asia and Europe. First, social policy is indeed becoming more complex to understand and to manage. This increased complexity follows from changes in economies, in societies, and in family and industrial structures alike. We do not live in a world where a sole, male breadwinner is guaranteed a secure job for life. Women have entered labor markets massively, from Norway to the Republic of Korea. Perhaps most important, the expectations and demands of individuals have changed, with greater participation, more attention to individual needs, more liberty, and more empowerment.

Second, social policy has also changed because the role of public policy has changed. Some decades ago, state retrenchment was seen as essential, with severe cuts in public spending in most countries, and trimming the public mission to the bone. For social policy, this brought in a wide range of new social partners (labor and business), local governments, nongovernmental organizations (NGOs), and others—a creative and positive development overall. In the 1990s, a "rebalancing" occurred, in part with a recognition that social dialogue needs a strong state that guarantees fair and constructive exchange and arbitrage. There are new roles ahead for public policy, some linked to social change, some to the new global environment and its risks.

A third message in the grandmother's difficulty in understanding even her own most basic entitlements is that despite this increased complexity, social policy needs to be conceived and explained more clearly. This underscores the vital importance of public information and communication as a central tenet of social policy action. All policymakers, social analysts, and social critics need to keep this basic challenge squarely in mind. Citizen understanding is essential not only because empowerment is one of the new goals of social policy, but also because people's participation is now understood as a key element in the success of any policy, and above all in the social arena.

A second moment of insight occurred during a somewhat heated exchange on philosophies and approaches to elder care in European and East Asian societies. Some East Asian representatives spoke with pride about the culture of care and respect for the elderly that prevailed in their society. Several women in the room exchanged knowing glances, and an East Asian woman spoke up. She argued that care and respect for the elderly in East Asian societies was important and valuable, but it could in effect become a sentence for women and especially daughters-in-law to devote years of their lives to elder care, often at a cost to their own children and to their personal and professional interests. The line that emerged was drawn less between cultures than between genders within each culture, and the story resonated with many if not all the women and many of the men.

In sum, social issues do not reflect abstract policies but rather the questions, conundrums, and problems that people face every day, wherever they live. The risks of life are universal, though far more severe for those with few resources in reserve to meet them. The social agenda is the fundamental human agenda, and policy analysts and practitioners need to tackle its challenges and complexities in that spirit.

The book and the project on which it is based represent a beginning, not an end. The fascinating material presented here scratches only the surface of potential networks, case studies, and questions for further investigation.

Welfare Regimes in East Asia

by Ian Gough

This appendix describes and classifies welfare regimes in the Republic of Korea, Malaysia, Thailand, the Philippines, and Indonesia and examines their outcomes.[1]

The State

State revenues and expenditures account for just under one-fifth of gross domestic product (GDP) in East Asia—not noticeably lower than in other middle-income countries (see Table A.1). However, state expenditures on social programs are very low, except on education. Total spending on education, health, and social security varies with level of development, ranging from 3 percent of GDP in Indonesia, to 6 percent in the Philippines and Thailand, to 8 percent in Malaysia, and to 11 percent in Korea. The share of total government spending devoted to social services ranges from around one-quarter in the Philippines to just over one-half in Korea. However, rapid economic growth means that real resources devoted to the social sector have expanded faster than in most countries. In general, East Asian nations evince hostility to Western ideals of the "welfare state," yet provide extensive and generous social benefits to state personnel such as civil servants, the military and police, and teachers.

Table A.1 Public Expenditures (percentage of GDP)

	Total government revenue in 1996 (%)	Total government expenditure in 1996 (%)	Education in 1990–96 (average %)	Health in 1990–97 (latest available %)	Social security in 1990–97 (latest available %)	Total education, health, social security (%)	Total social services in 1997 (% of total government expenditure)
Korea	25.2	21.2	3.9	1.9	5.2	11.0	51.9
Malaysia	22.9	22.0	5.4	1.4	1.4	8.2	42.5
Thailand	18.3	14.3	3.9	1.3	0.7	5.9	39.1
Philippines	18.7	18.5	2.5	0.7	2.8	6.0	26.5
Indonesia	14.8	14.8	1.3	0.7	1.1	3.1	36.2
Average	**19.98**	**18.16**	**3.41**	**1.19**	**2.24**	**6.84**	**39.24**

Sources: Asian Development Bank 1998, Figures 2.7, 2.8; World Bank, *World Development Indicators 1999*; except for social security: Korea, OECD 1996; Philippines, International Labor Organization, available at <http://www.ilo.org/public/english/protection/socsec/publ/css/phil93e.htm>.

Education

East Asian governments have consistently emphasized the central role of education in economic development, though they do not match this emphasis with higher-than-average expenditures. But real spending has climbed rapidly with fast economic growth (except in the Philippines), and these countries seem to target resources on basic education more rationally than other developing countries.[2]

All five countries have achieved near-universal primary education. Secondary-school enrollment is rising, but the countries are at different stages on this path: the Philippines and Korea enrolled over one-half of children in the 1970s, and Malaysia did so in the 1980s, whereas Thailand and Indonesia remain below this level today (see Table A.2). Higher education is expanding but remains remarkably undeveloped in Malaysia and Indonesia. Korea offers the greatest opportunities, with a tertiary enrollment rate of 50 percent, with the Philippines (27 percent) and Thailand (21 percent) some way behind. Malaysia offers the lowest access to tertiary education (10 percent). The average duration of studies has risen rapidly in East Asia, but in 1992 it was higher in Korea and the Philippines than in the other three countries.[3]

On all quantitative indicators the Philippines scores much higher than its per capita income would warrant—a reflection of the U.S. legacy. Overall, however, high standards of achievement in Korea contrast sharply with lower-than-average standards in Southeast Asia.

Table A.2 Education Indicators

Indicator	Korea (%)	Malaysia (%)	Thailand (%)	Philippines (%)	Indonesia (%)	Average (%)
Net enrollment ratio:						
Secondary 1994	96	61	49	80	45	66.2
Tertiary 1994	51	10	21	27	9	23.6
Average years of study, 1992	13.1	9.3	8.9	11.6	9.0	10.38
Achievement scores:[a]						
9–10 years	+0.7	n.a.	n.a.	−0.4	−1.0	
13–15 years	+0.9	n.a.	−0.2	−0.6	n.a.	

n.a. = not available.

a. Standardized deviation from the international mean.

Source: Alan Mingat, "The Strategy Used by High-Performing Asian Economies in Education," *World Development* 26, no. 4 (1998): 695–715, Tables 8, 5.

Health

Health expenditures are low in East Asia compared with those in other middle-income countries, and actually fell as a share of GDP in the 1990s in all countries except Thailand.[4] Because private spending accounts for about half of total expenditures on health, public expenditures are remarkable low: between 0.7 percent of GDP in Indonesia and 2.3 percent in Korea (though Korea's absolute spending dwarfs the rest). Not surprisingly, health inputs (doctors, nurses, hospital beds) are scarce on a world scale (see Table A.3), yet East Asian countries do provide reasonable access to basic and preventive health care.

Mortality, including infant mortality, has declined remarkably in the last three decades, with Korea and Malaysia the star performers. Those two countries also provide superior levels of sanitation, water, and preventive health care compared with the other countries. Less impressive are high levels of maternal mortality and child malnutrition, notably in Indonesia and the Philippines, reflecting a major failure to diminish inequalities in access to health-related services such as immunization, obstetric care, piped water, and sanitation. The region also faces new health threats stemming from aging, urbanization (such as traffic accidents), and lifestyle changes (such as more smoking).[5] Korea and Malaysia do better on all fronts, whereas the Philippines does worse than its income level would warrant, reflecting persistently high levels of poverty and inequality.

The dominant medical system in the region is "public provision, private finance" (see Table A.7), under which users pay from half to three-quarters of health care costs. All countries except Malaysia have explicit medical assistance

Table A.3   Health Indicators

Indicator	Korea	Malaysia	Thailand	Philippines	Indonesia	Average
Under-5 mortality rate (%), 1997	11.0	14.0	38.0	41.0	56.0	32.00
Life expectancy (years), 1997	72.0	72.0	69.0	68.0	65.0	69.20
Maternal mortality rate (%), 1990–97	30.0	34.0	200.0	210.0	390.0	172.80
Doctors/1,000 people	1.2	0.4	0.2	0.1	0.1	0.40
Nurses/1,000 people	2.3	1.6	1.0	0.4	0.7	1.20
Hospital beds/1,000 people	4.4	2.0	1.7	1.1	0.7	1.98

Source: World Bank, East Asia and Pacific Region, Human Development Sector Unit, *East Asia Health, Nutrition, and Population Strategy* (Washington, D.C.: World Bank, 1999).

Table A.4 Health Care Systems

Country	Public	Universal assistance	Social insurance	Provident fund
Korea	Public health services	Medical assistance (1977)	Medical insurance program (1977), universal Medical Insurance Plan (1989), National Health Insurance Act (1999)	
Malaysia	National health service, rural health service			Employee Provident Fund: Account III
Thailand	Public health services, medical benefits for civil servants	Free medical care for poor, aged, and children; community health card; public assistance	Social security system (1992)	
Philippines	Public hospitals	Free services for indigent	Medicare	
Indonesia	Public health centers	Means-tested free services	ASKES *(Asuransi Kesehatan Pegawai Negeri):* civil servants and military; JAMSOSTEK *(Jaminan Sosial Tenaga Kerja):* private sector	

Sources: Mishra Ramesh, with Mukul Asher, *Welfare Capitalism in Southeast Asia: Social Security, Health and Education Systems* (New York: St. Martin's Press, 2000), Table 4.3; Dong-Myeon Shin, "Financial Crisis and Social Security: The Paradox of the Republic of Korea," *International Security Review* 53, no. 3 (2000): 83–107.

programs for the indigent (see Table A.4), and state employees have superior systems of insurance and provision. Private provision of health services was rising in the region until the financial crisis, with all countries experimenting with efforts to decentralize or "corporatize" (transform public services from a government department into a separate legal entity) public hospitals and with contracting out key services. The rich have the further option of obtaining treatment abroad in regional centers such as Singapore, Hong Kong (China), and Australia.

Despite these commonalities, countries vary significantly in the institutional structures of their health care systems. The Philippines has a long-established health insurance system, but with low coverage and erratic provision of services. The country plans to provide universal health care by 2010 under the provisions of the 1995 National Health Insurance Act. Korea has moved to a full-fledged national health insurance system: universal, integrated, and redistributive (though with high co-payments). Thailand and Indonesia have introduced rudimentary health insurance for limited sections of the population, backed up by medical assistance schemes.

Pensions

East Asian countries exhibit a portfolio of different pension schemes (see Table A.5), but coverage under each major national program is growing rapidly. Civil servants and some other public sector employees have more generous pension systems than the rest of the population. For example, the Indonesian program for civil servants has a membership of 4 million and more than 1.5 million recipients, whereas another program covers 500,000 members of the military and the police force.[6] (It is difficult to know whether international data on pension expenditure and coverage include these schemes.) Second, large and multinational companies tend to provide a range of retirement schemes, some of which are regulated by national governments. Third, the official retirement age is the same for men and women and relatively low: 60 in Korea and the Philippines and 55 elsewhere.

National pension systems are of two main types (see Table A.6):

- *Defined-benefit social insurance.* In the Philippines this system is more than 40 years old and continues to expand its coverage, including voluntary membership even for Filipinos working overseas. The program nominally replaces 60 percent of retirees' salaries, but the employer compliance rate is low, with up to two-thirds of members not contributing at any one time.[7] In Korea the system started later, in 1988. The national pension scheme is extending coverage and building up a transitional fund over a 20-year period; full pensions will not begin until 2008. In January 1999 Thailand added an old-age pension element to the Social Security Act of 1990. This defined-benefit, pay-as-you-go scheme will not pay out full pensions until 2014.

Table A.5 Old-Age/Retirement Programs

	Social assistance programs	Social insurance programs	Provident fund	Mandated occupational programs	
				Defined-benefit	Defined-contribution
Korea	Public assistance program (1969)	National pension scheme (1988), universal coverage (1999)		Schemes for civil servants, military, and private schoolteachers	Company severance pay schemes
Malaysia	Social assistance program		Employee Provident Fund (1951)	Civil servant and company schemes (lump sums)	
Thailand		Social Security Act (1990, implemented 1998)		Government pensions and provident fund for state employees	Large corporations: voluntary Provident Fund Act (1987/96)
Philippines		Social security system (1957)	Pag-IBIG Fund 1998	Government service insurance system	Company pension schemes
Indonesia			JAMSOSTEK (1951/92)	TASPEN (*Tabungan dan Asuransi Pegawi Negeri*—Government Civilian Employees' Savings and Insurance Scheme): civil servants; ASABRI (Armed Forces Social Insurance Plan): military and police	Large-company schemes

Sources: David I. Stanton and Peter Whiteford, *Pension Systems and Policy in the APEC Economies* (Manila: Asian Development Bank, 1998), Tables 4.2, 4.3; World Bank, "Towards an East Asian Social Protection Strategy," East Asia and Pacific Region, draft, September 1999, p. 70; Mishra Ramesh, with Mulkul Asher, *Welfare Capitalism in Southwest Asia: Social Security, Health and Education Systems* (New York: St. Martin's Press, 2000), p. 65.

Table A.6   Design Features of Main Public Pension Schemes

	Type of scheme	Coverage (% of total labor force)	Retirement age	Total contributions (% of total labor costs)	Assets (% of GDP)
Korea	Social security (defined-benefit)	41+	60	9	6
Malaysia	Provident fund	61	55	23	45
Thailand	Social security (defined-benefit)	7	55	4.5	0.2 (3.6[a])
Philippines	Social security (defined-benefit)	28	60	8.4	6.7 (12.7[a])
Indonesia	Provident fund	16	55	7.7	0.9 (6.7[a])

a. Including assets of other funded schemes

Sources: Stanton and Whiteford (1998), Tables 4.2, 4.3; Mukul Asher, "The Future of Retirement Protection in Southeast Asia," *International Social Security Review* 51, no. 1 (1998): 3–30; World Bank, "Towards an East Asian Social Protection Strategy," East Asia and Pacific Region, draft, September 1999, p. 40; Shin, personal communication.

- *Provident funds.* In Malaysia the Employee Provident Fund, now in its 50th year, is a developed, expensive, and savings-effective fund. Since 1994 members have been able to opt for an annuity instead of a lump sum. Reforms have established separate accounts for education and health and have encouraged more flexible individual investment. In *Indonesia* the JAMSOSTEK fund, despite an equally long history, has small coverage, uneven record-keeping, and tiny reserves, but coverage climbed in the 1990s. The fund provides only a lump-sum payment on retirement.

Safety Nets

In East Asia formal safety nets—public programs targeted to the poor with the objective of raising living standards to a social minimum—are limited in scale, coverage, and cost, but they have expanded in response to the crisis. Safety nets can take the form of cash transfers, public works jobs, and subsidies for important needs such as food and housing. As a share of GDP they are most extensive and expensive in Korea (2 percent of GDP in 1999) and Indonesia (1.25 percent GDP—planned in 2000), and are smallest in Malaysia and Thailand.[8]

Labor Markets

Over the two decades preceding 1997, the East Asian labor force grew by 2 percent annually across the region. The work force participation rate is high, ranging from 89 percent in Thailand to 66 percent in Malaysia. The labor force is becoming feminized, but with the exception of Thailand, where it is higher, the overall share of women in the work force remains at about 40 percent—roughly the world average.

Unemployment rates escalated during the crisis of 1997–98 but are now declining. From the early 1980s to 1997, unemployment rates were consistently low in Thailand (below 1 percent), Korea (2–3 percent), and Indonesia (4–5 percent). Unemployment rates were consistently high in the Philippines (8–10 percent) and falling in Malaysia (from 8 percent in the mid-1980s to around 3 percent in 1997).

Only Korea maintains an unemployment insurance scheme, established in 1995 and expanded in 1998. All countries have enacted wide-ranging labor legislation covering minimum wages, hours of work, paid leave, employment security, protection against dismissal, redundancy pay, and occupational health and safety.[9] However, the other consistent finding is that enforcement of these laws and regulations is weak or nonexistent owing to weak government agencies and bribery of public officials. The World Bank concludes that East Asian labor markets have been relatively flexible, but that "working conditions are poor and often alarming."[10]

Private Provision of Social Services and Benefits

The role of the market in the social sector in East Asia is substantial and growing fast, with a temporary pause after 1997 (see Table A.7). One-half of all education spending and almost two-thirds of all health spending are privately financed. Much of this is reactive and unorganized, consisting of out-of-pocket expenditures, book purchases, and self-medication. In Korea, households spend high proportions of their income on education (10 percent) and health (5 percent), compared with 1.4 percent and 1.3 percent in the United Kingdom.[11]

Government regulation of private providers is typically weak but is becoming more proactive. Malaysia is a regional exception, and in 1999 it decided not to privatize or "corporatize" its public hospitals,[12] though it is now directing its provident fund to invest more in equities, indirectly encouraging privatized

Table A.7   Private Provision and Financing of Social Services

	Korea (%)	Malaysia (%)	Thailand (%)	Philippines (%)	Indonesia (%)	Average (%)
Private education, 1990:						
Secondary enrollment	61[a]	n.a.	10	36	50	32.0
Higher enrollment	81	8	6	83	58	47.2
Private financing in public institutions, end-1980s	60	15	26	85	48	46.8
Private health, 1990:						
Private expenditure	48	56	79	47	67	59.4
Hospital beds	95	25	25	50	31	45.2

n.a. = not available.

a. Senior secondary enrollment in 1993.

Sources: Mishra Ramesh, with Mulkul Asher, *Welfare Capitalism in Southwest Asia: Social Security, Health and Education Systems* (New York: St. Martin's Press, 2000), Tables 5.1 and 4.4; Alan Mingat, "The Strategy Used by High-Performing Asian Economies in Education," *World Development* 26, no. 4 (1998): 695–715, Tables 6 and 7.

provision of social services. The region has few cases of private insurance or pensions, with the exception of flourishing occupational pension schemes in Indonesia and those run by multinationals elsewhere. "Voluntary enterprise welfare" accounts for 7.5 percent of total labor costs in Korea, a figure unlikely to be matched elsewhere.[13]

Communities and Nongovernmental Organizations

Nonprofit and nongovernmental organizations (NGOs) active in the field of human development and welfare are a recent phenomenon in East Asia, where authoritarian regimes have discouraged them.[14] The one exception is the Philippines, where such groups have a longer history owing to the American legacy and the Catholic Church.

A certain tension persists between NGOs and governments in Malaysia and Singapore and has only recently diminished in Indonesia. However, following democratizing changes in the 1980s in Korea, the Philippines, and Thailand, NGOs have developed rapidly. The emergence of a middle class, new needs following rapid economic development and urbanization, and the decentralization of the public sector have provided further impetus.

All East Asian countries have seen the emergence of networks of NGOs and umbrella organizations. Community development is also burgeoning and includes innovations such as community health financing in Thailand. However, funds for such uses remain small relative to Thailand's total health expenditures.[15] Moreover, all NGOs remain heavily dependent on external sources for funds, notably official aid organizations, U.S. philanthropic funds, and Japanese corporate funds. (In Korea, the *chaebol* have generated philanthropic funding to an extent unknown in the other countries, mainly as a form of tax evasion.)

The Family and Household

Despite rapid economic development and urbanization, the extended family persists as a provider, saver, and income redistributor in East Asia. Private economic transfers add between 9 percent and 20 percent to average household incomes in Indonesia, Malaysia, and the Philippines (see Table A.8). The extent to which these transfers benefit the poorest households is uncertain, though evidence for Malaysia suggests that they are redistributive.

In the 1980s, a majority of people over 60 years of age in the Philippines and Thailand were receiving income from family members, and an even higher proportion lived with children or other family (75–90 percent). These remarkably

Table A.8 Household Transfers

	Households receiving private transfers (%)	Average percentage of income of receiving households	Persons over 60 years living with children or family (%)	Remittances from overseas (1990, % of GDP)
Korea (1990)		4.2	72	
Indonesia (1982)				
Rural	31	10	76	
Urban	44	20		0.3
Malaysia (1977–78)	19–30	11 (46)[a]	82	
Philippines				
1978	47	9	92	
1993	77	12		6.4

a. Proportion of households in lowest-income quintile.

Sources: World Bank, *Averting the Old Age Crisis* (Washington, D.C.: OUP, 1994), p. 63, available at <http://www.world-bank.org/poverty/safety/design/choosing2p28.htm>, Table 1; last column: International Labor Organization, "Migrant Worker Remittances, Micro-finance and the Informal Economy: Prospects and Issues," Social Finance Unit Working Paper 21 (2000): Table 2, converted to percentage of GDP, available at <http://www.ilo.org/public/english/employment/ent/papers/wpap21.htm>; Korea: Shin, personal communication.

high proportions are falling, but if Japan and Korea are models, they will decline only slowly in the face of rapid modernization.

The region's high level of savings, except for in the Philippines, should allow families to "self-insure": save in good times and spend in bad times.[16] Despite impressive development of microfinance and other credit schemes, however, the unequal distribution of incomes outside Korea undermines this effort.

The dominant international household strategy is labor migration and remittances of money from overseas. The Philippines is a big exporter of labor. By 1995 1.5 million Filipinos lived abroad as permanent immigrants, and a further 2 million worked temporarily abroad or at sea.[17] The remittances these workers send home total 6.4 percent of Philippine gross national product (GNP), according to the International Labor Organization (ILO). This figure rises to nearly 10 percent of GNP if it includes unrecorded cash and goods that workers bring home.[18] These flows, together with household flows within the country, constitute a significant element of the Philippine welfare regime. However, the country is an exception. Korea and Malaysia are both net importers of labor; Indonesia is a net exporter but remittances appear to be small; and Thailand is both an importer and exporter, recording a small net inflow of remittances.[19] The significance of worker remittances in the Philippines reflects the country's poor economic performance within a dynamic region.

International Aid for Social Spending

Official development assistance from Organization for Economic Cooperation and Development countries fell throughout the 1990s as a share of donors' and recipients' GNP as well as in dollars per capita. Before the Asian financial crisis, Korea and Malaysia received no overseas development assistance, but it remains significant—at 0.4–0.8 percent of GNP—in the other three countries. The Philippines relies on loans chiefly from Japan, the World Bank, and the Asian Development Bank. However, the country spent only one-tenth of those loans on human development, apparently reflecting the government's reluctance to use official loans for such purposes.[20] Following the 1997–98 financial crisis, International Monetary Fund loans to Malaysia and Korea resumed and were extended to all five countries. The World Bank, Asian Development Bank, and United Nations (UN) agencies have made substantial efforts to give greater priority to projects concerned with poverty alleviation, social safety nets, and human development.[21]

Human Development Outcomes

The Human Development Index (HDI), published by the United Nations Development Programme (UNDP), provides a synthetic measure of achievements in longevity, knowledge, and standard of living.[22] To account for the distribution of well-being, the UNDP also calculates a Gender-Related Development Index (GDI) and a Human Poverty Index (HPI).

Both the HDI and GDI reveal high levels of human development in East Asia compared with countries at similar levels of economic development. However, the HPI shows that about one-sixth of the population in Malaysia, the Philippines, and Thailand is capability-poor, as is over one-quarter of the population in Indonesia (see Table A.9).

More conventional measures constructed by each country reveal an impressive reduction in poverty rates for all countries except the Philippines: from above 40 percent in the 1970s to around 10 percent or less in the 1990s. In the Philippines, poverty rates remained almost unchanged at nearly 50 percent throughout this period. The simplest measure of all—the proportion of the population living on less than $2 per person per day—shows very high rates for the Philippines and Indonesia (63 percent and 50 percent) and lower rates for the other three countries.

Table A.9 Welfare Outcomes

	HDI, 1997 (rank)	HPI, 1997 (%)	Poverty, 1990s national measures (%)	Poverty rates: <US$2 a day, 1994–96 (%)	Poverty gap at US$2 a day (%)	Gini index (1990)
Korea	85	n.a.	n.a.	n.a.	n.a.	0.28
Malaysia	77	14	n.a.	22	7	48
Thailand	75	19	13	24	5	46
Philippines	74	16	38	63	27	43
Indonesia	68	28	35	50	15	37
Average	76	19.25	28.67	39.75	13.5	34.86

n.a. = not available.

Source: United Nations Development Programme, *Human Development Report* 1999 (Oxford, England: Oxford University Press, 1999); World Bank, *World Development Indicators* (Washington, D.C., World Bank, 1999).

Notes

1. Countries in this appendix are ordered in accordance with present income per capita.

2. World Bank, *The East Asian Miracle: Economic Growth and Public Policy* (Oxford: Oxford University Press, 1993), pp. 192–203.

3. Alan Mingat, "The Strategy Used by High-Performing Asian Economies in Education," *World Development* 26, no. 4 (1998): 695–715; Linda Low, "Human Resource Development in the Asia-Pacific," *Asian-Pacific Economic Literature* 12 no. 1 (1998): 27–40.

4. Mishra Ramesh, with Mukul Asher, *Welfare Capitalism in Southeast Asia: Social Security, Health and Education Systems* (New York: St. Martin's Press, 2000), Table 4.5.

5. World Bank, "East Asia Health, Nutrition and Population Strategy," East Asia and Pacific Region, Human Development Sector Unit, draft (October 1999).

6. Mukul Asher, "The Future of Retirement Protection in Southeast Asia," *International Social Security Review* 51, no. 1 (1998): 3–30.

7. Ramesh, op. cit., p. 71.

8. World Bank, "Towards an East Asian Social Protection Strategy," Human Development Unit, East Asia and Pacific Region, draft (September 1999), Table 3.

9. S. Deery and R. Mitchell, "Introduction," in *Labour Law and Industrial Relations in Asia*, ed. S. Deery and R. Mitchell (Melbourne, Australia: Longman Cheshire, 1993); Jonathan Rigg, *Southeast Asia: The Human Landscape of Modernization and Development* (London: Routledge, 1997), 223–27.

10. World Bank (1993) op. cit., pp. 261–73, and World Bank (September 1999), op. cit., p. 7.

11. Dong-Myeon Shin, "Economic Policy and Social Policy: Policy Linkages in an Era of Globalisation," *International Journal of Social Welfare* 9 (2000): 17–30.

12. Economist Intelligence Unit (EIU), *Healthcare Global Outlook, 2000,* ed. J. Haresnape (London: EIU, 1999).

13. Shin, op. cit.

14. T. Yamamoto, "Integrative Report," in *Emerging Civil Society in the Asia Pacific Community*, ed. T. Yamamoto (Singapore: Institute of Southeast Asian Studies and Tokyo: Japan Center for International Exchange, 1995).

15. Suwit Wibulpolprasert, "Community Financing: Thailand's Experience," *Health Policy and Planning* 6 (December 1991): 354–60.

16. World Bank, "World Development Report 2000/1: Attacking Poverty 2000," consultation draft (January 2000), Chapter 5.

17. A. Woodiwiss, *Globalisation, Human Rights and Labour Law in Pacific Asia* (Cambridge, England: Cambridge University Press, 1998), p. 101.

18. International Labor Organization, *Migration Worker Remittances, Micro-Finance and the Informal Economy: Prospects and Issues,* Social Finance Unit Working Paper 21 (2000), Tables 2 and 4.

19. See also Ronald Skeldon, *Emigration Pressures and Structural Change in Southeast and East Asia,* (Geneva: ILO, 1999).

20. Judith Randel and Tony German, eds., *The Reality of Aid 1998/1999* (London: Earthscan, 1998), pp. 200–05.

21. For example Isabel Ortiz and J. Abada, eds., *Social Protection in Asia and the Pacific* (Manila: Asian Development Bank, 2001).

22. United Nations Development Programme, *Human Development Report* 1999 (Oxford, England: Oxford University Press, 1999), pp. 159–60.

Social Policies in Europe

by Ian Gough

Education

European countries achieved universal provision of secondary education and are now extending access to further, higher, and continuing education to a majority of their populations. The quality of education is generally superior to that in East Asia, though on some measures Korea and other richer East Asian countries achieve better results. The costs of social protection have constrained educational resources in Europe, but demographics are more favorable than in East Asia (though they are changing there). In both regions the state plays the dominant role, and this is unlikely to change.

European educational systems exhibit great variation, although none follow the pattern of mass education and access to higher education found in the United States. German-speaking countries (Germany, Austria, and Switzerland) plus the Benelux countries (Belgium, the Netherlands, and Luxembourg) maintain selective secondary education, whereas other European countries provide comprehensive, nonselective secondary schooling. Postcompulsory education and training similarly varies between the German-speaking countries, where it is primarily work based, and elsewhere, where it is predominantly school based. France and the Mediterranean countries maintain central control of education, the German-speaking countries and Belgium allow regional control, and Nordic countries offer local control. In the United Kingdom, the central government retains substantial powers but has also devolved control to markets and providers.

Despite their differences, these systems have had to respond to common economic, demographic, and cultural changes, including greater competition from

East Asian economies. This has led to common policy developments. Access to postcompulsory education and training has expanded, more so in laggard countries such as the United Kingdom, leading participation rates to converge.[1] Countries have also begun to encourage "lifetime learning," and European Commission (EC) initiatives such as ERASMUS and SOCRATES have begun to internationalize the provision and consumption of higher education. Growth in other parts of the welfare state has constrained education budgets, meanwhile, and has thus forced countries to adopt cost-efficiency measures. Moves to promote diversity of providers and parental choice of school are playing out within institutional settings where actors hold differing amounts of power.

Health

European countries provide curative and palliative health care as a right of citizenship (in contrast with the United States, where some 40 million people lack health insurance, insured coverage for specific treatments is patchy, and co-payments can be high). Health care systems in Europe divide into two main types: tax-financed, publicly delivered national health services (in the United Kingdom, Nordic countries, and southern European countries), and health insurance schemes with public and private health care providers (such as in France and Germany). Italy and Spain, among other countries, have switched from national health insurance to national health services since the early 1970s.

All European nations face rising cost pressures from aging populations, technological advances, and growing public expectations. However, the responses to these common pressures differ between the two types of health care systems. National health services are generally able to control overall costs, unless political pressure dictates a rise, but usually at the cost of lower levels of service and longer waiting lists. The common solution has been to develop "internal markets" to encourage efficiency. National health insurance systems are less able to resist cost overruns, especially when coupled with a fee-for-service system for paying doctors and hospitals. The common solution has been to impose or negotiate expenditure ceilings (notably successful in the corporatist environment in Germany) and higher user charges and to encourage more competition among providers. The share of expenditures on private health provision has risen to an average of 0.5 percent of gross domestic product (GDP) in 1993, but it remains below East Asian levels (0.75 percent of a much lower GDP) and is remarkably lower than the U.S. level (5.3 percent of GDP).

Pensions

Throughout the European Union (EU) public pensions and supplements guarantee income security in old age, though at widely different levels across the 15 countries. All such systems entail publicly managed or mandated, pay-as-you-go, defined-benefit pensions. By the 1950s all countries had "Bismarck" earnings-related social insurance pensions (common in continental Europe), "Beveridge" (more accurately, "Nordic") flat rate citizenship pensions (Scandinavia and the United Kingdom), or hybrids of the two. Beginning in the late 1950s, the Bismarckian countries built minimum pensions into the social insurance framework, whereas the Beveridgian countries added second-tier earnings-related schemes to their universalist basic pensions.

Three changes began to erode the common basis of European pension systems in the 1980s: prospective population aging, a slowdown or reversal in employment growth and wage growth, and a decline in inflation. These changes have generated a wave of reforms, but no European country has introduced a privately managed, fully funded individual account tier. Rather, governments have preferred low-visibility reforms, including changing the index of pension benefits from gross to net earnings, degrading benefit formulas, raising the retirement age, introducing an incremental funded element, and, most interestingly, shifting to a "notional defined contribution." The latter relates pensions paid out to average life expectancy (Germany and Sweden) or to the projected number of pensioners (Italy), thus automatically restraining expenditures.[2] Those measures will retrench future pension levels and may make them more variable. Only the United Kingdom has experimented with fully individualized pension accounts. Indeed, some European countries continue to extend pension credits for time spent on education, childcare, and unemployment (Sweden), or have introduced new insurance benefits (Austria and Germany).

Safety Nets

Most countries in Europe now have social assistance programs that provide a national safety net. In 1992, within the then 12 countries of the European Community, 6.3 percent of the population received social assistance benefits costing 1.9 percent of European GDP. However, the EU shows great variability (see Table B.1). This variability corresponds to the four European welfare regimes (see Chapter 1), except for distinctive patterns in Austria, Norway, and Switzerland.

Table B.1   Social Assistance in Europe

Social assistance clusters	Country clusters
1. Centralized, extensive, inclusive, above-average benefits	Ireland, United Kingdom
2. Separate categorical schemes, below-average extent, average inclusion, average benefits	Belgium, France, Germany, Italy, Luxembourg, Spain
3. Mixed central-local, average extent, average inclusion, generous benefits	Denmark, Finland, Netherlands, Sweden
4. Local, low extent, exclusive, above-average benefits	Austria, Norway, Switzerland
5. Minimal extent, exclusive, very low benefits	Greece, Portugal

Since 1992 the European Community has fostered new proposals in Portugal and Spain, the former implementing a guaranteed minimum income in 1997. However, countries have also moved to cut benefit levels, especially for the unemployed, and to link welfare to work. These goals lie on a continuum between activation and workfare[3] that includes

- Activating workers rather than reducing benefits and wages
- Improving the skills and work experience of the unemployed rather than merely boosting their mobility and job-search efficiency
- Offering training and education rather than work-for-benefit
- Empowering recipients rather than controlling and punishing them
- Offering inclusive workfare programs rather than programs targeting only the unemployed

This may represent an area of convergence between the two regions: Europe is adding work force activation strategies to existing social assistance programs, whereas East Asia is using work programs along with consumption and, occasionally, income subsidies in early moves toward national safety nets.

Notes

1. Organization for Economic Cooperation and Development (OECD), *Life Long Learning for All* (Paris: OECD, 1996).

2. Giuliano Bonoli, Vic George, and Peter Taylor-Gooby, *European Welfare Futures: Towards a Theory of Retrenchment* (Bristol, England: Policy Press, 2000), chapter 2; Evelyne Huber and John Stephens, "The Political Economy of Pension Reform: Latin America in Comparative Perspective," United Nations Research Institute for Social Development, Occasional Paper no. 7 Geneva, 2000.

3. Jacob Torfing, "Workfare with Welfare: Recent Reforms of the Danish Welfare State," *Journal of European Social Policy* 9, no. 1 (1999).

Select Bibliography

Ahmad, Etisham, et al., eds. 1991. *Social Security in Developing Countries*. Oxford: Clarendon Press.

Ahn, C. Y. 2001. "Financial and Corporate Sector Restructuring in South Korea: Accomplishments and Unfinished Agenda." *Japanese Economic Review* 52, no. 4: 452–70.

Ahuja, Vinod, Benu Bidani, Francisco Ferreira, and Michael Walton. 1997. *Everyone's Miracle? Revisiting Poverty and Inequality in East Asia*. Washington, D.C.: World Bank.

Anand, Sudhir, and Ravi Kanbur. 1993. "Inequality and Development: A Critique." *Journal of Development Economics* 41: 19–43.

Ariff, Mohamed. 1991. *The Islamic Voluntary Sector in Southeast Asia*. Singapore: Institute of Southeast Asian Studies.

Ariff, Mohamed, and Ahmed M. Khalid. 2000. *Liberalization, Growth and the Asian Financial Crisis: Lessons for Developing and Transitional Economies in Asia*. Cheltenham, England: Edward Elgar.

Asia-Europe Meeting. <http://europa.eu.int/comm/external_relations/asem/intro>.

Asia Foundation and AKATIGA. 1999. *The Impact of Economic Crisis on Indonesian Small and Medium Enterprises*. Jakarta: Asia Foundation.

Asian Development Bank. 1997. *Emerging Asia: Changes and Challenges*. Manila.

Asian Development Bank and World Bank. 2000. *The New Social Policy Agenda in Asia: Proceedings of the Manila Social Forum*. Manila: Asian Development Bank (August).

Atkinson, Anthony Barnes. 1996. *Incomes and the Welfare State: Essays on Britain and Europe*. Cambridge, England: Cambridge University Press.

Baldwin, Peter. 1990. "Class Interests and the Post-War Welfare State in Europe: A Historical Perspective." *The International Social Security Review* 43, no. 3: 255–69.

Barr, Nicholas. 1994. *The Economics of the Welfare State*. Oxford, England: Oxford University Press.

Bean, Charles, Samuel Bentolila, Giuseppe Bertola, and Juan J. Dolado. 1998. *Social Europe: One for All?* London: Centre for Policy Research.

Bertola, Giuseppe, T. Boeri, and G. Nicoletti. 2000. *Welfare and Employment in a United Europe*. Cambridge, Mass.: MIT Press.

Betcherman, Gordon, and Rizwanul Islam, eds. 2000. *East Asian Labor Markets and the Economic Crisis: Impacts, Responses, and Lessons*. Washington, D.C.: World Bank.

Birdsall, Nancy. 2000. "The Social Fallout: Safety Nets and Recrafting the Social Contract." In Stephan Haggard, ed., *The Political Economy of the Asian Financial Crisis*. Washington, D.C.: Institute for International Economics.

Blundell, Richard, and Thomas MaCurdy. 1999. "Labor Supply: A Review of Alternative Approaches." In C. Orley Ashenfelter and David Card, eds., *Handbook of Labor Economics*, Vol. 3A. Amsterdam: Elsevier.

Boeri, Tito. 2000. *Uno stato asociale: perché è fallito il welfare in Italia*. Bari, Italy: Laterza.

Boeri, Tito, and R. Perotti. 2001. "Less Pensions, More Welfare." Paper presented at the Igier-RDB conference on *Pensioni: davvero una verifica?* September 28. Rome.

Boeri, Tito, Axel Borsch-Supan, and Guido Tabellini. 2002. "Pension Reform and the Opinions of European Citizens." *American Economic Review, Papers and Proceedings* (U.S.) 92, no. 2: 396–401.

Boeri, Tito, Agar Brugiavini, and Lars Calmfors, eds. 2001. *The Role of the Unions in the 21st Century*. London: Oxford University Press.

Bonoli, Giuliano, Vic George, and Peter Taylor-Gooby. 2000. *European Welfare Futures: Towards a Theory of Retrenchment*. London: Polity Press.

Bourdieu, Pierre. 1986. "The Forms of Capital." In J. Richardson, ed., *Handbook of Theory and Research for the Sociology of Education*. New York: Greenwood Press: 241–58.

Bradshaw, Jonathan. 2002. *Children and Social Security*. Burlington, VT: Ashgate.

Callan, Tim, and Brian Nolan. 2000. "Taxation and Social Welfare." In Brian Nolan, Philip J. O'Connell, and Christopher T. Whelan, eds., *Bust to Boom? The Irish Experience of Growth and Equality*. Dublin: Institute of Public Administration, Johnswood Press.

Callan, Tim, Shirley Dex, Nina Smith, and Jan Dirk Vlasblom. 2000. "Taxation of Spouses: A Cross-country Study of the Effects on Married Women's Labour Supply." *Oxford Economic Papers*.

Campos, Jose Edgardo. 1996. *The Key to the Asian Miracle: Making Shared Growth Credible*. Washington, D.C.: Brookings Institution.

Castellino, O. 1975. *Il labirinto delle pensioni*. Bologna, Italy: Il Mulino.

Castells, Manuel. 1974. *La Question Urbaine*. Paris: F. Maspero.

Cazzola, G. 1992. *La fabbrica delle pensioni*. Rome: Ediesse.

Chang, H. J., and H. J. Park. 2000. "An Alternative Perspective on Government Policy towards the Chaebol in Korea: Industrial Policy, Financial Regulations and Political Democracy." In S. H. Jwa and I. K. Lee, eds., *Korean Chaebol in Transition: Road Ahead and Agenda*. Seoul: Korea Economic Research Institute.

Chang, H. J., H. J. Park, and C. G. Yoo. 1998. "Interpreting the Korean Crisis: Financial Liberalisation, Industrial Policy and Corporate Governance." *Cambridge Journal of Economics* 22: 735–46.

Chang, In-Hyup, H. Lee, and J. Oh. 1999. *Social Welfare*. Seoul: Seoul National University.

Choi, Byug-Ho, and K. Ko. 2000. "Social Security Expenditure in Korea and Ways to Improve Its Level." *Health and Welfare Policy Forum* 49: 48–58.

Choi, Eunyoung, J. Kim, and W. Lee. 1998. *Health Care System in Korea*. Seoul: Korea Institute for Health and Social Affairs.

Chow, Peter, and Bates Gill, eds. 2000. *Weathering the Storm: Taiwan, Its Neighbors, and the Asian Financial Crisis*. Washington, D.C.: Brookings Institution Press.

Chung, Kyung-Hee, Y. Cho, Y. Oh, J. Byun, Y. Byun, and H. Moon. 1998. *A National Survey on the Elderly Life and Their Welfare Need*. Seoul: Korea Institute for Health and Social Affairs.

Coleman, James S. 1988. "Social Capital in the Creation of Human Capital." *American Journal of Sociology* (Supplement: *Organizations and Institutions: Sociological and Economic Approaches to the Analysis of Social Structure*) 94: 95–120.

Colley, Linda. 1992. *Britons: Forging the Nation, 1707–1837*. New Haven, Conn.: Yale University Press.

Collier, Paul. 1998. "Social Capital and Poverty." Social Capital Initiative Working Paper no. 4., World Bank, Social Development Department, Washington, D.C.

Coppini, M. A. 1994. *Le ragioni dello stato sociale*. Rome: Ediesse.

Corden, Max. 1999. *The Asian Crisis: Is There a Way Out?* Singapore: Institute of Southeast Asia Studies.

Corsetti, G. 1998. "Interpreting the Asian Financial Crisis: Open Issues in Theory and Policy." *Asian Development Review* 16, no. 2: 18–63.

Curtin, Philip D. 1964. *The Image of Africa: British Ideas and Action, 1780–1850*. Madison, Wis.: University of Wisconsin Press.

Danish Ministry of Economic Affairs. 2000. *The Law Model Microsimulation Models*. Copenhagen.

Deacon, Bob, Michelle Hulge, and Paul Stubbs. 1997. *Global Social Policy: International Organizations and the Future of Welfare*. London: Sage.

Demetriades, P. O., and B. A. Fattouh. 1999. "The South Korean Financial Crisis: Competing Explanations and Policy Lessons for Financial Liberalization." *International Affairs* 75, no. 4: 779–92.

De Soto, Hernando. 1989. *The Other Path: The Invisible Revolution in Third World*. New York: Harper and Row.

Doyal, Len, and Ian Gough. 1991. *A Theory of Human Need*. Basingstoke, England: MacMillan.

Easterly, William. 2001. *The Elusive Quest for Growth: Economists' Adventures and Misadventures in the Tropics*. Cambridge, Mass.: MIT Press.

Economist Intelligence Unit. 2001. *Ireland—Country Report*. London.

EDAP Joint Policy Studies. 1998. *Social Implications of the Asian Financial Crisis*. Seoul, Korea: Korea Development Institute.

Editing Committee of White Paper on Welfare Reform. 1998. *Welfare Reform in Korea toward the 21st Century: To Enhance the Quality of Life in the Globalization Era.* Seoul: Ministry of Health and Welfare.

Edwards, B., M. Foley, and M. Diani, eds. 2000. *Beyond Tocqueville: Civil Society and the Social Capital Debate in Comparative Perspective.* Dartmouth, Mass.: University Press of New England.

Esping-Anderson, Gosta, ed. 1996. *Welfare States in Transition: National Adaptations in Global Economies.* London: Sage.

European Commission. 2002. *An Introduction to the Asia-Europe Meeting—ASEM.* Brussels.

Feldstein, Martin. 1998. *Privatizing Social Security.* Chicago: Chicago University Press.

Ferrera, M. 1984. *Il welfare state in Italia.* Bologna, Italy: Il Mulino.

———. 1993. *Modelli di solidarietà: politica e riforme sociali nelle democrazie.* Bologna, Italy: Il Mulino.

———. 1998. *Le trappole del welfare.* Bologna, Italy: Il Mulino.

Fine, Ben. 2000. *Social Capital versus Social Theory.* London: Routledge.

Flora, P., and A. J. Heidenheimer, eds. 1983. *Lo sviluppo del welfare state in Europa e in America.* Bologna, Italy: Il Mulino.

Fondazione Ideazione. 2001. *Pensioni: guida ad una riforma.* Rome, Italy: Ideazione Editrice.

Fornero, E. 1999. *L'economia dei fondi pensione.* Bologna, Italy: Il Mulino.

Forssell, Åsa, Magnus Medelberg, and Ann-Charlotte Ståhlberg. 1999. "Unequal Public Transfers to the Elderly in Different Countries—Equal Disposable Incomes." *European Journal of Social Security* 1, no. 1: 63–89.

Franco, D. 2000. "Italy: A Never-Ending Pension Reform." Paper presented at the NBER-Kiel Institute conference on *Coping with the Pension Crisis: Where Does Europe Stand?* March. Berlin, 20–21.

Frankenberg, Elizabeth, Duncan Thomas, and Kathleen Beegle. 1999. "The Real Costs of Indonesia's Economic Crisis: Preliminary Findings from the Indonesia Family Life Surveys." Land and Population Working Paper Series, no. 99-04. Rand, Santa Monica, Calif.

Geanakopolos, J., O. Mitchell, and S. Zeldes. 1999. "Social Security Money's Worth." In O. Mitchell, R. Myers, and H. Young, eds., *Prospects for Social Security Reform.* Philadelphia: University of Pennsylvania Press.

Gertler, Paul, and Jacques van der Gaag. 1990. *The Willingness to Pay for Medical Care: Evidence from Two Developing Countries.* Baltimore, Md.: Johns Hopkins Press.

Goodin, Robert. 1992. "Towards a Minimally Presumptuous Welfare Policy." In Philippe van Parijs, ed., *Arguing for Basic Income.* London: Verso.

Goodin, Robert E., Bruce Headey, Ruud Muffels, and Henk-Jan Dirven. 1999. *The Real Worlds of Welfare Capitalism.* Cambridge, England: Cambridge University Press.

Goodman, Roger, Gordon White, and Huck-Ju Kwon, eds. 1998. *The East Asian Welfare Model: Welfare Orientalism and the State.* London: Routledge.

Gough, Ian. 2000. *Global Capital, Human Needs and Social Policies: Selected Essays 1994–99.* London: Palgrave Macmillan.

Gough, Ian, and Gunnar Olofsson, eds. 1999. *Capitalism and Social Cohesion: Essays on Exclusion and Integration.* London: Palgrave Macmillan.

Gray, Alan W., ed. 1997. *International Perspectives on the Irish Economy.* Dublin: Indecon Economic Consultants.

Graziani, A. 1998. *Lo sviluppo dell'economia italiana: dalla ricostruzione alla moneta unica.* Torino, Italy: Bollati Boringhieri.

Haggard, Stephan. 2000. *The Political Economy of the Asian Financial Crisis.* Washington, D.C.: International Institute of Economics.

Haggard, Stephan. 2000. "The Politics of the Asian Financial Crisis." *Journal of Democracy* 11, no. 2: 130–44.

Hart-Landsberg, M., and P. Burkett. 2001. "Economic Crisis and Restructuring in South Korea—Beyond the Free Market–Statist Debate." *Critical Asian Studies* 33, no. 3: 403–30.

Hirschman, Albert O. 1990. *Come far passare le riforme.* Bologna, Italy: Il Mulino.

———. 1991. *Retoriche dell'intransigenza.* Bologna, Italy: Il Mulino.

Holzmann, Robert, and Steen Lau Jorgensen. 1999. "Social Protection as Social Risk Management: Conceptual Understandings for the Social Protection Sector Strategy Paper." Social Protection Discussion Paper 9904. World Bank, Washington, D.C.

———. 2000. "Social Risk Management: A New Conceptual Framework for Social Protection and Beyond." Social Protection Discussion Paper 0006. World Bank, Human Development Network, Washington, D.C.

Honohan, Patrick, ed. 1997. *EU Structural Funds in Ireland; A Mid-Term Evaluation of the CSF 1994–99.* Luxembourg: Office for Official Publications of the European Communities.

International Labor Organization (ILO). 1996. *Social Exclusion and Anti-Poverty Strategies.* Geneva: ILO, International Institute for Labour Studies.

International Monetary Fund (IMF). 1999a. *Republic of Korea. Selected Issues.* IMF Staff Country Report no. 98/74. IMF, Washington, D.C.

———. 1999b. *IMF-Supported Programs in Indonesia, Korea and Thailand: A Preliminary Assessment.* Occasional Paper 178. IMF, Washington, D.C.

———. 2000a. *Korea's Crisis Resolution Strategy Aims to Restore Confidence and Promote Sustained Recovery.* IMF Survey. March. IMF, Washington, D.C.

———. 2000b. *Republic of Korea: Economic and Policy Development.* IMF Staff Country Report, no. 00/11. IMF, Washington, D.C.

Jackson, Karl D. ed. 1999. *Asian Contagion: The Causes and Consequences of a Financial Crisis.* Boulder, Colo.: Westview Press.

Jesse, Andy, and Wouter van Ginneken. 1998. *Social Security for the Informal Sector: Annotated Bibliography on Developing Countries, 1990–1997.* Geneva: ILO.

Johansson, Per, and Mårten Palme. 1996. "Do Economic Incentives Affect Work Absence? Empirical Evidence Using Swedish Micro Data." *Journal of Public Economics* 59: 195–218.

Jomo, K. S., ed. 1998. *Tigers in Trouble: Financial Governance, Liberalisation and Crises in East Asia.* London: Palgrave-Macmillan.

Jorion, P., and W. Goetzmann. 2000. "Global Stock Markets in the Twentieth Century." National Bureau of Economic Research (NBER) Working Paper no. 7565. NBER, Cambridge, Mass. (February).

Kawai, M., R. S. Newfarmer, and S. Schmukler. 2001. *Crisis and Contagion in East Asia: Nine Lessons.* Policy Research Working Paper 2610. World Bank, East Asia and Pacific Region, Office of the Regional Vice President and Macroeconomics and Growth, Washington, D.C.

Kim, D. 1999. "IMF Bailout and Financial and Corporate Restructuring in the Republic of Korea." *Developing Economies* 37, no. 4: 460–513.

Kim, H. R. 2000. "The Viability and Vulnerability of Korean Economic Governance." *Journal of Contemporary Asia* 30, no. 2: 199–220.

Kim, Mandoo, and H. Han. 2001. *Modern Social Welfare.* Seoul: Korea Institute for Health and Social Affairs.

Kim, Mee-Gon. 2001. "Basic Livelihood Guarantee System as a Social Safety Net." Paper presented at the Workshop on Securing Social Safety Nets. Korea Institute for Health and Social Affairs. Seoul.

Kim, Y. T. 1999: "Neoliberalism and the Decline of the Developmental State." *Journal of Contemporary Asia* 29, no. 4: 441–61.

Kim, Yong-Ha, J. Suk, and S. Yoon. 1996. *Efficient Management of Social Insurance.* Seoul: Korea Institute for Health and Social Affairs.

Knowles, James C., Ernesto M. Pernia, and Mary Racelis. *Social Consequences of the Financial Crisis in Asia.* Economic Staff Paper (International) 60, Asian Development Bank, Manila, 1–79.

Korea Institute for Health and Social Affairs. 2000. *Health and Welfare Indicators in Korea.*

Korpi, Walter. 2000. "Faces of Inequality: Gender, Class, and Patterns of Inequalities in Different KIHASA Types of Welfare States." *Social Politics* (Summer): 127–91.

Kotlikoff, Lawrence. 1998. "Simulating the Privatization of Social Security in General Equilibrium." In Martin Feldstein, ed., *Privatizing Social Security.* Chicago: Chicago University Press.

Krugman, Paul. 1994. "The Myth of Asia's Miracle." *Foreign Affairs* 75 (November–December): 62–78.

———. 1998. "Will Asia Bounce Back?" Speech for Credit Suisse First Boston, Hong Kong, China. <http://web.mit.edu/krugman>: 1–7.

———. 1999a. "Analytical Afterthoughts on the Asian Crisis." <http://web.mit.edu/krugman>: 1–8.

———. 1999b. "Balance Sheets, the Transfer Problem, and Financial Crises." <http://web.mit.edu/krugman>: 1–24.

Kuhnle, Stein, ed. 2000. *Survival of the European Welfare State.* London: Routledge.

Kuran, T. 1995. *Private Truths, Public Lies: The Social Consequences of Preference Falsification.* Cambridge, England: Cambridge University Press.

Kyung-Suk, Kim. 1998. *The Korea Welfare State: Ideals and Realities.* Seoul: Nanam Publishing.

Layte, Richard, B. Maitre, B. Nolan, D. Watson, C. T. Whelan, J. Williams, and B. Casey. 2001. *Monitoring Poverty Trends and Exploring Poverty Dynamics in Ireland.* The Economic and Social Research Institute. Policy Research Series Number 41. Dublin: Argus Press.

Lee, In-Jae. 1998. "Evaluation on Social Welfare Policies and Tasks." In *Reality of Social Welfare in Korea and Policy Issues.* Korea Social Science Research Council. Seoul: Human and Welfare Publishing.

Lee, J. J. 1989. *Ireland: 1912–1985. Politics and Society.* Cambridge, England: Cambridge University Press.

Lustig, Nora, ed. 2000. *Shielding the Poor: Social Protection in the Developing World.* Washington, D.C.: Brookings Institution.

Mathews, J. A. 1998. "Fashioning a New Korean Model out of the Crisis: The Rebuilding of Institutional Capabilities." *Cambridge Journal of Economics* 22: 747–59.

Matthews, A. 1994. *Managing the Structural Funds in Ireland.* Cork, Ireland: Cork University Press.

McAleese, Dermot. 1997. "Economic Policy and Performance: The Irish Experience." *Journal of the Statistical and Social Inquiry Society of Ireland* 37, no. 5: 1–31.

———. 2001. *Economics for Business, Competition, Macro-Stability, and Globalisation.* 2d ed. Dublin: Trinity College, Prentice Hall.

Ministero del Lavoro e delle Politiche Sociali. 2001a. *Verifica del sistema previdenziale ai sensi della legge 335/1995 e successivi provvedimenti nell'ottica della competitività, dello sviluppo e dell'equità.* Rome: Commissione Brambilla.

Monorchio, A., ed. 1996. *La finanza pubblica dopo la svolta del 1992.* Bologna, Italy: Il Mulino.

Moon, H., H. Lee, and G. Yoo. 1999. "Social Impact of the Financial Crisis in Korea: Economic Framework." Background paper for J. C. Knowles, E. M. Pernia, and M. Racelis, *Social Consequences of the Financial Crisis in Asia.* Economic Staff Paper 60. Asian Development Bank, Manila.

Muet, Pierre-Alain, and Joseph E. Stiglitz, eds. *Global Government Markets and Equity.* New York: Oxford University Press.

Noble, Gregory W., and Hohn Ravenhill, eds. 2001. *The Asian Financial Crisis and the Architecture of Global Finance.* Cambridge, U.K.: Cambridge University Press.

Nolan, Brian, Philip J. O'Connell, and Christopher T. Whelan. 2000. *Bust to Boom? The Irish Experience of Growth and Inequality.* Dublin: Institute of Public Administration, Johnswood Press.

North, D. C. 1990. *Institutions, Institutional Change, and Economic Performance.* New York: Cambridge University Press.

O'Connell, P., and D. Rottman. 1992. "The Irish Welfare State in Comparative Perspective." In J. Goldthorpe and C. Whelan, eds., *The Development of Industrial Society in Ireland.* London: British Academy and Oxford University Press.

O'Connell, Philip J. 2000. "Are They Working? Market Orientation and the Effectiveness of Active Labour Market Programmes in Ireland." Economic and Social Research Institute, *European Sociological Review.*

O'Donnell, Rory. 1998. *Ireland's Economic Transformation.* Working Paper no. 2. Center for West European Studies, European Union Center. University of Pittsburgh, Pittsburgh, Pa.

———. 2001. "Towards Post-corporatist Concertation in Europe?" In Wallace Hellen, ed., *Interlocking Dimensions of European Integration.* New York: Palgrave Macmillan.

O'Grada, Cormac. 2001. "From 'Frugal Comfort' to Ten Thousand a Year: Trade and Growth in the Irish Economy." University College Dublin. Processed.

O'Grada, Cormac, and Kevin O'Rourke. 1995. "Irish Economic Growth 1950–1988." In N. F. R. Crafts and G. Toniolo, eds., *Economic Growth in Europe since 1945.* Cambridge, England: Cambridge University Press.

Oh, J. K.-C. 2000. *Korean Politics.* Cornell, N.Y.: Cornell University Press.

O'Hearn, Denis. 1998. *Inside the Celtic Tiger: The Irish Economy and the Asian Model.* London: Pluto Press.

Organization for Economic Cooperation and Development (OECD). 1998. "Maintaining Prosperity in an Ageing Society: The OECD Study on the Policy Implications of Ageing." Working Paper AWP 4.3. OECD, Paris.

———. 1999. *OECD Economic Surveys 1998–1999 Ireland.* OECD, Paris.

O'Riain, Sean, and Philip J. O'Connell. 2000. "The Role of the State in Growth and Welfare." In Brian Nolan, Philip J. O'Connell, and Christopher T. Whelan, eds., *Bust to Boom? The Irish Experience of Growth and Equality.* Dublin: Institute of Public Administration, Johnswood Press.

Ortiz, Isabel, J. Abada, et al., eds. 2001. *Social Protection in Asia and the Pacific.* Manila: Asian Development Bank.

Pempel, T. J., ed. 1999. *The Politics of Asian Economic Crisis.* Ithaca, N.Y.: Cornell University Press.

Pennisi, Giuseppe. 1997. *La guerra dei trentenni: Italia e nuove generazioni.* Rome: Ideazione Editrice.

Persson, Inga. 1990. "The Third Dimension—Equal Status between Swedish Women and Men." In Inga Persson, ed., *Generating Equality in the Welfare State. The Swedish Experience.* Oslo: Norwegian University Press.

Radelet, Stephen, and Jeffrey Sachs. 1997. "Asia's Re-emergence." *Foreign Affairs* 76, no. 6: 44–59.

Rajan, Raghuram, and Luigi Zingales. 1998. "Financial Development and Growth." *American Economic Review* 88, no. 3.

Ramesh, Mishra, with Mukul Asher. 2000. *Welfare Capitalism in Southeast Asia: Social Security, Health and Education Policies.* New York: St. Martin's Press.

Rice, Gerry, and Irene Johnstone. 2000. *Scotland's Global Opportunity.* Glasgow: University of Glasgow Business School.

Rodrik, Dani. 1999. "The Asian Financial Crisis and the Virtues of Democracy." *Challenge* (U.S.) 42 (July–August): 44–59.

———. 2000. "Institutions for High Quality Growth: What They Are and How to Acquire Them." NBER Working Paper no. 7540. NBER, Cambridge, Mass.

Sabel, Charles F. 1996. *Local Development in Ireland. Partnership, Innovation, and Social Justice.* Paris: OECD.

Sainsbury, Diane. 1996. *Gender Equality and Welfare States.* Cambridge, U.K.: Cambridge University Press.

Selén, Jan, and Ann-Charlotte Ståhlberg. 2002. "The Importance of Sickness Benefit Rights for a Comparison of Wages." Working Paper 1/2002. Swedish Institute for Social Research, Stockholm.<http://www.sofi.su.se>.

Sen, Amartya. 1999. *Development as Freedom.* New York: Knopf.

Sinn, Hans-Werner. 2002. "The New Systems Competition." NBER Working Paper no. 8747, NBER, Cambridge, Mass. (January), 1–24.

———. 2001. "Social Dumping in the Transformation Process." NBER Working Paper no. 8364. NBER, Cambridge, Mass. (July), 1–36.

Sinn, Hans-Werner, and Frank Westermann. 2001. "Two Mezzogiornos." NBER Working Paper no. 8125. NBER, Cambridge, Mass. (February), 1–36.

Ståhlberg, Ann-Charlotte. 1990. "Life Cycle Income Redistribution of the Public Sector: Inter- and Intragenerational Effects." In Inga Persson, ed., *Generating Equality in the Welfare State. The Swedish Experience.* Oslo: Norwegian University Press.

———. 1995a. "Women's Pensions in Sweden." *Scandinavian Journal of Social Welfare* 4: 19–27.

———. 1995b. "Pension Reform in Sweden." *Scandinavian Journal of Social Welfare* 4: 267–73.

Statistics Denmark. 1998. "A CGE Analysis of the Danish 1993 Tax Reform." Economic Modelling Working Paper no. 6. Government Statistics Office, Copenhagen.

———. 2000. "A CGE Analysis of the Danish Ageing Problem." Copenhagen.

Stiglitz, Joseph, and J. Yun. 2002. "Integrating of Unemployment Insurance with Pension through Individual Savings Accounts." National Bureau of Economic Research Working Paper Series (U.S.) No. 9199. Cambridge, Mass.: NBER.

Stiglitz, Joseph, and Shahid Yusuf, eds. 2001. *Rethinking the East Asian Miracle.* New York: World Bank and Oxford University Press.

Sumarto, Sudarno, Asep Suryahadi, Lant Pritchett. 2000. "Safety Nets and Safety Ropes: Who Benefited from Two Indonesian Crisis Programs, the 'Poor' or the 'Shocked'?" Washington, D.C.: World Bank, East Asian and Pacific Region, Environment and Social Development Sector Unit.

Sweeney, Paul. 1998. *The Celtic Tiger: Ireland's Economic Miracle Explained.* Dublin: Oak Tree Press.

Thompson, Lawrence. 1998. *Older and Wiser: The Economics of Public Pensions.* Washington, D.C.: Urban Institute Press.

Tivegna, M., and G. Chiofi. 2001. *News e dinamica dei tassi di cambio.* Bologna, Italy: Il Mulino.

United Nations Development Programme. 1999. *Human Development Report.* New York and Oxford, England: Oxford University Press.

van der Gaag, Jacques. 1995. *Private and Public Initiatives Working Together for Health and Education.* Directions in Development Series. Washington, D.C.: World Bank.

Verneroso, F., and Robert Wade. 1998. "The Asian Crisis: The High Debt Model versus the Wall Street-Treasure-IMF Complex." *New Left Review* 228: 3–22.

Wade, Robert. 1999. "Gestalt Shift: From 'Miracle' to 'Cronyism' in the Asian Crisis." *IDS Bulletin,* University of Sussex, 30 (January): 134–50.

Watson, C. Maxwell, Bas B. Bakker, Jan Kees Martijn, and Ioannis Halikias. 1999. *The Netherlands: Transforming a Market Economy.* Occasional Paper 181. IMF, Washington, D.C.

World Bank. 1993. *The East Asian Miracle: Economic Growth and Public Policy.* Washington, D.C.: World Bank and Oxford University Press.

———. 1998. *East Asia: The Road to Recovery.* Washington, D.C.: World Bank.

———. 1999. *Republic of Korea. Establishing a New Foundation for Sustained Growth.* Washington, D.C.: World Bank.

———. 2001. *World Development Report 2000/2001: Attacking Poverty.* Washington, D.C.: World Bank and Oxford University Press.

———. 2002. *Lessons towards a New Social Policy Agenda: Beyond the East Asia Socio-Economic Crisis.* <http://www.worldbank.org/eapsocial/asemsocial>.

Yoon, Suk-Myung. 1999. *National Pension—Goal Set-up for Social Security Development and Current Issues.* Seoul: Korea Institute for Health and Social Affairs.

Zimring, Franklin, Gordon Hawkins, and Sam Kamin. 2001. *Punishment and Democracy: Three Strikes and You're out in California.* Oxford: Oxford University Press.

List of Contributors

Gabriella Battaini-Dragoni is the director general for social cohesion at the Council of Europe, Strasbourg. Her career at the Council of Europe has been largely with the Directorate of Social Affairs and Health, where she gained experience in dealing with the social dimension of development and human rights perspectives on social cohesion. Her work focuses mainly on Eastern European countries and human dignity dimensions of development. She has promoted pilot projects on integrated social policies, particularly in Southeast Europe.

Uwe Berndt is a political scientist and staff member of the Arnold Bergstraesser Institute for Socio-cultural Research in Freiburg and assistant professor of political science at the University of Freiburg im Breisgau, Germany. His research topics include local government integration strategies toward immigrant ethnic minorities in Germany and the Netherlands. He has authored several articles on migration in Europe.

Eduardo González Biedma, Ph.D., J.D., M.P.A., is a professor of labor law at the University of Sevilla, Spain. He is a practicing lawyer and consultant for the European Commission, and he worked for several years for the Constitutional Court in Spain. He is also a columnist for the local press and the author of five books and several articles.

Jacqueline Butler has worked as a speechwriter and political secretary to Lord Moynihan since 1997, specializing in foreign and constitutional affairs. She was a special assistant in the campaign division of the Democratic National Committee in Washington, D.C., and New Jersey during the 1996 presidential election. Before that, she worked for CMA Consultants in London and as a researcher in the House of Commons. She has written a number of policy papers with Lord Moynihan.

Olivier Butzbach worked with the World Bank from 1999 to 2002, and as project coordinator for the European Social Policy Lessons Project since 2000. An M.A. graduate of the Johns Hopkins University School of Advanced International Studies, he is now a Ph.D. candidate in political science at the European University Institute in Florence, Italy. His present research interests include comparative social policy, corporate governance, and the study of financial systems.

Thørkil Casse is an associate professor of environment and economics at the University of Roskilde, Department of Geography and International Development Studies, Denmark. He has done research on structural adjustment policies in Korea. He writes for a joint publication on globalization and economic growth in Asia.

Jacques Charmes is a professor of economics at the University of Versailles–St. Quentin en Yvelines. He is engaged in a United Nations Development Programme project on social statistics and on employment and human development in Haiti. He was formerly director of the Societies, Urbanization, and Development Department at ORSTOM (the French Scientific Research Institute for Development and Cooperation). His research interests include informal sector measurement as well as gender and the informal sector, and he has published several reports on these subjects.

Bob Deacon is a professor of international social policy at Sheffield University, United Kingdom. He is director of the Anglo–Finnish Globalism and Social Policy Programme (GASPP) (<http://www.gaspp.org>) and editor of the journal *Global Social Policy.* He has acted as adviser on aspects of globalization and social policy to the World Health Organization, International Labor Organization, United Nations Development Programme, European Union, and Council of Europe, as well as to national governments.

Vincent Delbos is vice president of the Court of Versailles, France. He is with the Justice Department of the government of France. His professional interests include crime prevention in urban areas and all forms of conflict resolution by alternative means.

Frank A. G. den Butter is a professor and head of the Economics Department at the Free University of Amsterdam and a member of the Dutch Scientific

Council for Government Policy. He is founder and director of Applied Labour Economics Research Team (ALERT) and a former director of the Tinbergen Institute. He is also chairman of the Royal Netherlands Economic Association and a member of the Central Statistical Committee. Publications include several books and about 150 articles in both international and Dutch journals.

Ruud Dorenbos is a senior researcher at ECORYS-NEI (the Netherlands Economic Institute) in the division of Labor and Social Policy. He has carried out several international projects such as the evaluation of active labor market policies in Bulgaria, public works and public employment services in Croatia, and youth employment programs in Asia and the Pacific. He has been seconded twice to the World Bank. He is the author of "Labour Market Adjustments in Hungary and Poland," published by University of Groningen in 1999.

Christine Erhel, Ph.D. in economics, is an assistant professor at the University of Paris 1 and a member of MATISSE, a French research unit. Her main research topics are labor market policy evaluation, working time policies, international comparisons in employment policies, and social protection.

Luis Frota is currently European affairs officer at the Caisse Centrale de la Mutualité Sociale Agricole, the French Statutory Social Insurance Fund for Agriculture Households. He is a practitioner of European social affairs. He has managed a number of European cooperation projects in social and local development for the European Commission with partners from the European Union and member countries.

Bernard Gazier is a professor of economics at the University of Paris 1. From 1993 to 2001, he was director of a research institute, METIS (the name changed from MATISSE, Modélisations Appliquées aux Trajectoires Institutionnelles et aux Stratégies Socio-Economiques), focused on labor economics and industrial economics. Professor Gazier is an expert on employment policies and has written reports for the French Ministry of Employment and Social Affairs, the European Community, and the International Labor Organization. Among his recent publications is *The Dynamics of Full Employment: Social Integration through Transitional Labour Markets*, published by Edward Elgar in 2002.

François Godement is chairman of the International Business Department at INALCO (French Institute of Oriental Languages and Civilization). He is a senior associate responsible for Asia Pacific Affairs at IFRI (French Institute of International Relations).

Ian Gough has been a professor of social policy at the University of Bath since 1995. He was previously professor of social policy and political economy at the University of Manchester. Professor Gough is the author of numerous articles and books, including *The Political Economy of the Welfare State*, which has been translated into six languages, and *A Theory of Human Need*, winner of both the Deutscher and the Myrdal prizes. His latest book—*Global Capital, Human Needs and Social Policies*—comprises selected essays from the past decade. He is editor of the *Journal of European Social Policy*.

Sandra Hackman is a developmental editor and writer of books, reports, and other publications focusing on public policy. She collaborates with researchers at many different institutions, including Harvard's Kennedy School of Government, and has worked on several books for the World Bank. She was formerly acting editor-in-chief and managing editor of MIT's *Technology Review*.

Aksel Hatland, Ph.D. from the University of Oslo, is director of the Welfare Research Programme for the Norwegian Research Council, based at the national research institute NOVA (Norwegian Social Research) in Oslo. He has published extensively on social security and welfare issues, including the book *Den norske velferdsstaten* (*The Norwegian Welfare State*, co-edited with Stein Kuhnle and Tor Inge Romøren, rev. ed., 2001).

Rémy Herrera is an economist. He is a researcher at the French National Scientific Research Council (CNRS) and teaches at the University of Paris 1. His main research topics include development economics, growth theories, public spending, and the role of the state. He has authored several articles on these topics.

Sven Hort is the founding chairperson and professor in sociology at the recently established Södertörn University College, Sweden. He directs a multidisciplinary research program focusing on urban policy, social exclusion, and regional welfare and is a member of the Research Council of the Swedish Association of Local Authorities. His main research topics are urban and regional welfare—social exclusion and integration—and social policy, as well as the macrohistorical development of the welfare state. He has authored several articles and books, including *Social Policy and Welfare State in Sweden*, *Scandinavia in a New Europe*, co-edited with Thomas P. Boje, and *Social Security in Sweden and Other European Countries—Three Essays*, jointly written with two colleagues.

K. S. Jomo (Kwame Sundaram) is a professor in economics and administration, University of Malaya. His teaching experience includes the Science University of Malaysia, Harvard, Yale College, National University of Malaysia (UKM), Wolfson College, Cambridge, and Cornell University. His most recent publications include *Rents, Rent-Seeking and Economic Development: Theory and the Asian Evidence* (edited with Mushtaq Khan, Cambridge University Press, 2000); *Malaysian Eclipse: Economic Crisis and Recovery* (Zed Books, London, 2001); *Globalization Versus Development: Heterodox Perspectives* (editor) and *Southeast Asia's Industrialization* (editor).

Tara Karacan works at the World Bank as a consultant and coordinator for the Asia-Europe Meeting (ASEM) Trust Fund "Social Policy Lessons" project and as a research analyst for the Library of Congress' Federal Research Division. She has an M.A. in international affairs and international economics from the School of Advanced International Studies at Johns Hopkins University.

Mats Karlsson is vice president for external and United Nations affairs at the World Bank, responsible for managing the World Bank's global communications programs, extending outreach to key constituencies, and overseeing relations with the United Nations. Before joining the World Bank in 1999, he was the state secretary for international development cooperation at the Swedish Ministry of Foreign Affairs. He joined the Swedish International Development Agency (SIDA) in 1983. Among many positions he held, he was Sweden's governor for the African, Asian, and Inter-American Development Banks from 1994 to 1999.

Meesook Kim is a research fellow at the Korea Institute for Health and Social Affairs. She received her Ph.D. in sociology from Purdue University. Her research interests include social welfare facilities, quality of life, and the status of social workers.

Udo Kock is an economist at the International Monetary Fund (IMF) in Washington, D.C. Before that, he worked as an assistant professor in economics at the Vrije Universiteit Amsterdam. In 1998–2000 he was a member of the Standing Committee for Economic Affairs, Social Policy, and Employment Policy of the Amsterdam City Council. He holds a Ph.D. from the Vrije Universiteit Amsterdam. He has published several articles on labor economics, social benefits, and other topics, both in the Netherlands and abroad. His publications can be found on the Internet at <http://www.udokock.com>.

Stein Kuhnle is a professor of comparative politics and head of the Department of Comparative Politics, University of Bergen. He is the author of *Velferdsstatens utvikling. Norge i et komparativt perspektiv* (*The Development of the Welfare State: Norway in a Comparative Perspective*) (1983), co-editor of *Government and Vol-*

untary Organizations: A Relational Perspective (1992), co-editor of *Party Systems and Voter Alignments Revisited* (2000), and editor of *Survival of the European Welfare State* (2000). He has been editor of *Tidsskrift for velferdsforskning* (*Journal of Welfare Research*) since 1998.

Tamar Manuelyan Atinc is sector manager for poverty reduction in the East Asia and Pacific Region of the World Bank. Her recent professional interests have focused on issues related to poverty, inequality, and labor markets in East Asian countries. She is currently managing analytical work on household level vulnerability arising from trade liberalization. She holds a master's degree in public policy from JFK School of Government at Harvard University.

Mauro Mare is a professor of public economics at Tuscia University, Viterbo. He has been adviser to the Italian Minister of Economy, the European Commission, and the Organization for Economic Cooperation and Development. He is author of several publications on pension reforms and tax coordination in the European Union.

Katherine Marshall works in the field of international development, with a focus on issues for the world's poorest countries, including social policies. She has worked as a senior officer at the World Bank since 1971 and is currently responsible for a broad range of issues revolving around ethics, values, rights, and faith in development work. She previously was director for World Bank programs in East Asia (focus on social policy and governance), Africa, and Latin America.

F. Desmond McCarthy is an international economist and consultant to the World Bank in Washington, D.C. He is the former World Bank economic adviser in the office of the senior vice president and chief economist, reporting to Messrs. Fischer, Summers, Bruno, and Stiglitz during their time. He has also held positions at the Center for International Studies at the Massachusetts Institute of Technology and International Institute for Applied Systems Analysis Austria and was a consultant to the Agency for International Development, U.S. Department of Transportation, Federal Aviation Administration, International Labor Organization, and the Food and Agriculture Organization.

Lord Moynihan (Colin) was the conservative foreign affairs spokesman in the House of Lords from 1997 to 2000. He was the member of parliament for Lewisham East from 1983 to 1992 and served in both the Thatcher and Major administrations, as parliamentary undersecretary of state at the Department of Environment in 1987–90, as minister of sport in 1987–90, and as minister for energy in 1990–92. He has undertaken consultancy work for the World Bank on a number of occasions. Currently, he is chairman of Consort Resources Limited.

Christian Oberländer, M.P.A., is currently a visiting scientist at the University of Tokyo Hospital and senior lecturer at the Department for Japanese Studies at the University of Bonn. He previously taught at the University of Halle. His recent publications include *Technology and Innovation in Japan,* co-edited with Martin Hemmert (London: Routledge, 1998) and "The Rise of Scientific Medicine in Japan" in *Building a Modern Nation* (London: Curzon, in press), edited by Morris Low.

Dieter Oberndörfer, now professor emeritus, has been holder of the Chair of Political Science at the University of Freiburg im Breisgau and was director of the Arnold Bergstraesser Institute for Socio-cultural Research. He has been visiting professor at Dartmouth College and at the Bologna Center of the Johns Hopkins University. He has written extensively on development issues (about 200 publications). Professor Oberndörfer is president of the German Council on Migration (Rat für Migration) and board member of the German Foundation for Peace and Development. He holds a Ph.D. from the University of Erlangen.

Ito Peng is an associate professor of social policy at the Department of Sociology, University of Toronto, Canada. She previously taught social policy and social security at the School of Policy Studies at Kwansei Gakuin University, Japan. Her research focuses on gender and welfare states; comparative welfare states, especially East–West comparisons; and comparative family policies. She has published several articles and chapters on the Japanese welfare state, and on gender and social policies in Japan. She is currently writing a book on lone-mother families in Japan and working on a research project comparing policies on families and women in Japan, the Republic of Korea, and Taiwan (China).

Giuseppe Pennisi is a professor of economics at Italy's National Public Administration Institute. He is also a member of Scientific Committee of the Italian Trade Institutes and sits on the board of several Italian foundations. He has held several positions in the World Bank from 1968 to 1986. He has worked for the Food and Agriculture Organization and International Labor Organization as well as in senior capacity in the Italian Public Administration. He has authored or co-authored 15 books and writes frequently for newspapers and periodicals.

Gareth Api Richards is a visiting associate professor at the Department of Political Science and research fellow at the Third World Studies Center, both at the University of the Philippines. He is co-editor of *Asia-Europe Interregionalism:*

Critical Perspectives, a special issue of the *Journal of the Asia-Pacific Economy* (1999), and has written numerous articles on Asia–Europe relations. His current research examines the political economy of development and, in particular, the responses of labor-based social movements to globalization.

Jacques Rojot is a professor of management at the University of Paris. He has been a visiting professor in universities in Asia, Europe, and North America and a consultant with the Organization for Economic Cooperation and Development, the European Union, and several private firms. He is the editor of the "Revue de la Gestion des Ressources Humaines" and sits on the editorial board of several journals of management and human resources. He is also a member of the Scientific Council of France's Institut de l'Entreprise and the French correspondent for the National Academy of Arbitrators. Professor Rojot has authored numerous books and articles on management and human resources.

Peter Scherer is counselor to the director for employment and social affairs for the Organization for Economic Cooperation and Development and coordinates the organization's work on health policy. An Australian, he studied at Monash University, the Australian National University, and Cornell University, where he obtained his Ph.D. After working as a university lecturer and researcher, he entered the Australian public service and eventually became deputy director of the Bureau of Labor Market Research. He joined the Organization for Economic Cooperation and Development in 1986.

Jean-Michel Severino is director general of the French Agency for Development. Previously, he was inspector general of finance in the Ministry of the Economy, Finance, and Industry, and associate professor at the Center for Studies and Research on International Development (CERDI), University of Auvergne. He was vice president of the East Asia and Pacific Region at the World Bank from 1997 to 2000 and director of the World Bank country department responsible, among other things, for Bosnia.

Bruno Simma has been a professor of international law and European Community law at the University of Munich since 1973. Formerly he was visiting professor at the University of Siena and the University of Michigan. From 1987 to 1996 he was a member of the United Nations Committee on Economic, Social and Cultural Rights. From 1995 to 1997 he served as dean of the Munich Faculty of Law. Since 1996 he has been a member of the United Nations International Law Commission. Professor Simma holds a doctorate of law from the University of Innsbruck, Austria.

Ann-Charlotte Ståhlberg is an associate professor of economics at the Swedish Institute for Social Research, Stockholm University, Sweden. She holds a Scientific Council Research appointment in *Research on Gender Equality in Economics.* Her main research interests are the economics of social insurance, nonwage benefits differentials, and income distribution. One of Sweden's leading pension experts, she has published many studies on the Swedish retirement system and its recent reform. She is on the editorial board of *European Journal of Social Security.*

Jonas Gahr Støre is chairman and partner of ECON, an Oslo-based center for research and analysis, engaged in particular in the fields of macroeconomic policies, energy, environment, industry, and development. He is a former state secretary at the office of the prime minister of Norway and has served as executive director of the World Health Organization (WHO). He continues to serve as a senior policy adviser to Director-General Gro Harlem Brundtland of WHO.

Luc Tholoniat works at the Directorate General for Employment and Social Affairs of the European Commission. He is a graduate of Sciences Po (Fondation Nationale des Sciences Politiques) in Paris and the London School of Economics.

Willem van der Geest is director of the European Institute for Asian Studies (EIAS) in Brussels. Previously he was a senior economist at the International Labor Organization; an adviser on Asia and Africa to the United Nations Conference on Trade and Development, the United Nations Development Programme, and the World Bank; and a lecturer at the University of Leiden, Netherlands. He has published several books and numerous articles in his area of expertise, including *Adjustment, Employment and Missing Institutions, Negotiating Structural Adjustment,* and *Trade Diversification in the Least Developed Countries.*

Søren Villadsen works with the Nordic Consulting Group, Denmark. Previously he was an associate professor in Denmark. He has more than 20 years of experience in teaching and research in local government, labor market studies, social policies, housing, and public administration. In addition, he has conducted comprehensive studies of urban renewal and local government projects.

Louis-Charles Viossat is chief of staff in the French Ministry of Health, Family, and Disabled Persons. He is also a professor of health and social policy at the Institut de Sciences Politiques, Paris. Previously he spent a year at a pharmaceutical firm, Eli Lilly and Company, as director of corporate affairs in France, following a 2-year secondment on social policy at the World Bank. He also worked in the French government in the areas of health and social policy from 1992 to 1998.

Robert Wade is a professor of political economy at the London School of Economics and Political Science. A New Zealand citizen, he earlier worked as a World Bank economist and taught at the University of California–San Diego, Princeton University, Massachusetts Institute of Technology, and Brown University. He is the author of *Governing the Market: Economic Theory and the Role of Government in East Asia's Industrialization* (Princeton, 1990), *Village Republics: Economic Conditions of Collective Action in South India* (Institute for Contemporary Studies, 1984), and "U.S. Hegemony and the World Bank: The Fight over People and Ideas," *Review of International Political Economy* 9, no. 2 (2002).

Frank Westermann is an assistant professor at CESifo, a joint initiative of the University of Munich and the ifo Institute. He has been visiting assistant professor at the University of California at Los Angeles and holds a Ph.D. in international economics from the University of California at Santa Cruz. His main research topics include boom–bust cycles in middle-income countries, the economic crisis in Japan, and the consequences of common policies for unequal regions. He has written several articles on these issues.

Markus Zöeckler has been a lecturer in the interdisciplinary research project at the University of Munich, Germany, since 1999. He studied law and philosophy at the Universities of Göttingen and Freiburg im Breisgau and at the University of Iowa law school. His research interests include economic and social rights, humanitarian law, European Community law, and international financial and economic integration.

Index